Alan Rogers

2006

GW00367878

Britain
& Ireland

Quality camping & caravanning parks

INSPECTED CAMPSITES & SELECTED

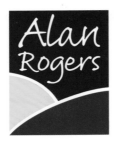

Compiled by: Alan Rogers Guides Ltd

Designed by: Paul Effenberg, Vine Design Ltd

Maps created by Customised Mapping (01769 560101) contain background data provided by GisDATA Ltd
Maps are © Alan Rogers Guides and Gis DATA Ltd 2005

Published by: Alan Rogers Guides Ltd,
Spelmonden Old Oast, Goudhurst, Kent TN17 1HE
www.alanrogers.com Tel: 01580 214000

British Library Cataloguing-in-Publication Data:
A catalogue record for this book is available from the British Library.

ISBN-13 978 0954 52717 4
ISBN-10 0 9545271 7 8

Printed in Great Britain by J H Haynes & Co Ltd

CONTENTS

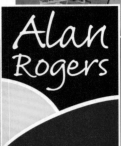

" ...the campsites included in this book have been chosen entirely on merit, and no payment of any sort is made by them for their inclusion."

Alan Rogers, 1968

the Alan Rogers
approach

IT IS NEARLY 40 YEARS SINCE ALAN ROGERS PUBLISHED THE FIRST CAMPSITE GUIDE THAT BORE HIS NAME. SINCE THEN THE RANGE HAS EXPANDED TO SIX TITLES. WHAT'S MORE, ALAN ROGERS GUIDES HAVE BECOME ESTABLISHED IN THE NETHERLANDS TOO: ALL SIX TITLES ARE ALSO PUBLISHED IN THE NETHERLANDS AND STOCKED BY WELL OVER 90% OF ALL DUTCH BOOKSHOPS.

THERE ARE OVER 5,000 CAMPING AND CARAVANNING PARKS IN BRITAIN AND IRELAND OF VARYING QUALITY: THIS GUIDE CONTAINS IMPARTIALLY WRITTEN REPORTS ON WELL OVER 500, INCLUDING SOME OF THE VERY FINEST, EACH BEING INDIVIDUALLY INSPECTED AND SELECTED. ALL THE USUAL MAPS AND INDEXES ARE ALSO INCLUDED, DESIGNED TO HELP YOU FIND THE CHOICE OF PARK THAT'S RIGHT FOR YOU. WE HOPE YOU ENJOY SOME HAPPY AND SAFE TRAVELS – AND SOME PLEASURABLE 'ARMCHAIR TOURING' IN THE MEANTIME!

A question of quality

The criteria we use when inspecting and selecting parks are numerous, but the most important by far is the question of good quality. People want different things from their choice of campsite so we try to include a range of campsite 'styles' to cater for a wide variety of preferences: from those seeking a small peaceful campsite in the heart of the countryside, to visitors looking for an 'all singing, all dancing' park in a popular seaside resort. Those with more specific interests, such as sporting facilities, cultural events or historical attractions, are also catered for.

The size of the park, whether it's part of a chain or privately owned, makes no difference in terms of it being required to meet our exacting standards in respect of its quality and it being 'fit for purpose'. In other words, irrespective of the size of the park, or the number of facilities it offers, we consider and evaluate the welcome, the pitches, the sanitary facilities, the cleanliness, the general maintenance and even the location.

Independent and honest

Whilst the content and scope of the Alan Rogers guides have expanded considerably since the early editions, our selection of campsites still employs exactly the same philosophy and criteria as defined by Alan Rogers in 1968.

'telling it how it is'

Firstly, and most importantly, our selection is based entirely on our own rigorous and independent inspection and selection process. Campsites cannot buy their way into our guides – indeed the extensive Report which is written by us, not by the site owner, is provided free of charge so we are free to say what we think and to provide an honest, 'warts and all' description. This is written in plain English and without the use of confusing icons or symbols.

Expert opinions

We rely on our dedicated team of Site Assessors, all of whom are experienced campers, caravanners or motorcaravanners, to visit and recommend parks. Each year they travel some 100,000 miles around Europe inspecting new campsites for the guide and re-inspecting the existing ones. Our thanks are due to them for their enthusiastic efforts, their diligence and integrity.

We also appreciate the feedback we receive from many of our readers and we always make a point of following up complaints, suggestions or recommendations for possible new parks. Of course we get a few grumbles too – but it really is a few, and those we do receive usually relate to overcrowding or to poor maintenance during the peak school holiday period.

Please bear in mind that, although we are interested to hear about any complaints, we have no contractual relationship with the campsites featured in our guides and are therefore not in a position to intervene in any dispute between a reader and a campsite.

Highly respected by site owners and readers alike, there is no better guide when it comes to forming an independent view of a campsite's quality. When you need to be confident in your choice of campsite, you need the Alan Rogers Guide.

- ✓ Parks only included on merit
- ✓ Parks cannot pay to be included
- ✓ Independently inspected, rigorously assessed
- ✓ Impartial reviews
- ✓ Nearly 40 years of expertise

WRITTEN IN PLAIN ENGLISH, OUR GUIDES ARE EXCEPTIONALLY EASY TO USE, ALTHOUGH A FEW WORDS OF EXPLANATION REGARDING THE LAYOUT AND CONTENT MAY BE HELPFUL. FOR ENGLAND WE HAVE USED OFFICIAL TOURIST BOARD REGIONS AND THE COUNTIES WITHIN THEM. FOR WALES, SCOTLAND AND IRELAND (NORTH AND SOUTH) WE USE THE COUNTIES.

Tourist Board area

The Reports – *Example of an entry*

Number **Park name**

Postal Address (including county)

A description of the park in which we try to give an idea of its general features – its size, its situation, its strengths and its weaknesses. This section should provide a picture of the park itself with reference to the facilities that are provided and if they impact on its appearance or character. We include details on pitch numbers, electricity (with amperage), hardstandings etc. in this section as pitch design, planning and terracing affects the park's overall appearance. Similarly we include reference to pitches used for caravan holiday homes, chalets, and the like. Importantly at the end of this column we indicate if there are any restrictions, e.g. no tents, no children, naturist sites.

Facilities

Lists more specific information on the park's facilities, as well as certain off site attractions and activities.

Open

Park opening dates.

At a glance

Welcome & Ambience	✓✓✓✓	Location	✓✓✓✓✓
Quality of Pitches	✓✓✓✓✓	Facilities	✓✓✓✓

Our inspectors grade each park out of five, giving a unique indication of certain key criteria that may be important when making your decision.

Directions

Separated from the main text in order that they may be read and assimilated more easily by a navigator en-route. Bear in mind that road improvement schemes can result in road numbers being altered.

O.S.GR: Ordnance Survey grid references are included for those using OS maps.

GPS: references are provided as we obtain them for satellite navigation systems (in degrees and minutes).

Charges 2006

Reservations

including contact details.

Indexes

Our three indexes allow you to find parks by their number and name, by region and park name, or by the town or village where the park is situated. See also the handy Quick Reference sections at the back.

Campsite Maps

The maps at the back relate to the geographical areas and will help you identify the approximate position of each campsite. The colour of the campsite name indicates whether it is open all year or not. You will certainly need more detailed maps for example the Ordnance Survey road atlas.

Facilities

Toilet blocks

We assume that toilet blocks will be equipped with WCs, washbasins with hot and cold water and hot showers with dividers or curtains, and will have all necessary shelves, hooks, plugs and mirrors. We also assume that there will be an identified chemical toilet disposal point, and that the campsite will provide water and waste water drainage points and bin areas. If not the case, we comment. We mention certain features that some readers find important: washbasins in cubicles, facilities for babies, facilities for those with disabilities and motorcaravan service points. Readers with disabilities are advised to contact the park of their choice to ensure that facilities are appropriate to their needs.

Shop

Basic or fully supplied, and opening dates.

Bars, restaurants, takeaway facilities and entertainment

We try hard to supply opening and closing dates (if other than the campsite opening dates) and to identify if there are discos or other entertainment.

Children's play areas

Fenced and with safety surface (e.g. sand, bark or pea-gravel).

Swimming pools

If particularly special, we cover in detail in our main campsite description but reference is always included under our Facilities listings. Opening dates, charges and levels of supervision are provided where we have been notified.

Leisure facilities

For example, playing fields, bicycle hire, organised activities and entertainment.

Dogs

If dogs are not accepted or restrictions apply, we state it here. Check the quick reference list at the back of the guide.

Off site

This briefly covers leisure facilities, tourist attractions, restaurants, etc. nearby.

At a glance

All Alan Rogers parks have been inspected and selected – they must meet stringent quality criteria. A campsite may have all the boxes ticked when it comes to listing facilities but if it's not inherently a 'good park' then it will not be in the guide.

These 'at a glance' ratings are a unique indication of certain key criteria that may be important when making your decision. Quite deliberately they are subjective and, modesty aside, are based on our inspectors' own expert opinions at the time of their inspection.

Charges

These are the latest provided to us by the parks. In those few cases where 2005 or 2006 prices are not given, we try to give a general guide.

Opening dates

These are advised to us during the early autumn of the previous year – parks can, and sometimes do, alter these dates before the start of the following season, often for good reasons. If you intend to visit shortly after a published opening date, or shortly before the closing date, it is wise to check that it will actually be open at the time required. Similarly some parks operate a restricted service during the low season, only opening some of their facilities (e.g. swimming pools) during the main season; where we know about this, and have the relevant dates, we indicate it – again if you are at all doubtful it is wise to check.

Special Pitches

We note an ever increasing number of 'special' pitches under a variety of fancy names (for example, Executive, Panorama, Super). These provide a range of extra facilities such as waste water disposal, TV and phone connections, hardstanding, patios, etc. and they are often booked up well in advance. Readers interested in such pitches should contact the park concerned to check exactly what is provided. People with disabilities are also advised to telephone before turning up to ensure that facilities are appropriate to their particular needs.

Whether you're an 'old hand' in terms of camping and caravanning or are contemplating your first trip, a regular reader of our Guides or a new 'convert', we wish you well in your travels and hope we have been able to help in some way. We are, of course, also out and about ourselves, visiting parks, talking to owners and readers, and generally checking on standards and new developments.

We wish all our readers thoroughly enjoyable Camping and Caravanning in 2006 – favoured by good weather of course!

THE ALAN ROGERS TEAM

have you visited
www.alanrogers.com
yet?

INSPECTED CAMPSITES & SELECTED

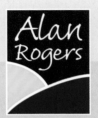

Thousands have already, researching their holiday and catching up with the latest news and special offers.

Launched in January 2004 it has fast become the first-stop for countless caravanners, motorhome owners and campers all wanting reliable, impartial and detailed information for their next trip.

It features a fully searchable database of the best campsites in the UK & Ireland, and the rest of Europe: over 2,000 campsites in 26 countries. All are Alan Rogers inspected and selected, allowing you to find the site that's perfect for you, with the reassurance of knowing we've been there first.

SCOTLAND

Northumbria

NORTHERN IRELAND

Cumbria

Yorkshire

North West England

Heart of England

REPUBLIC OF IRELAND

East of England

WALES

Southern England

London

South West England

South East England

Channel Islands

THE ALAN ROGERS AWARDS 2005

In 2004 we introduced the first ever Alan Rogers Campsite Awards.

BEFORE MAKING OUR AWARDS, WE CAREFULLY CONSIDER MORE THAN 2000 CAMPSITES FEATURED IN OUR GUIDES, TAKING INTO ACCOUNT COMMENTS FROM OUR SITE ASSESSORS, OUR HEAD OFFICE TEAM, AND, OF COURSE, OUR READERS.

OUR AWARD WINNERS COVER A MASSIVE GEOGRAPHICAL AREA FROM THE IBERIAN PENINSULA TO EASTERN SLOVENIA, AND, IN OUR FIRST YEAR, WE MADE AWARDS TO CAMPSITES IN 11 DIFFERENT COUNTRIES.

NEEDLESS TO SAY, IT'S AN EXTREMELY DIFFICULT TASK TO CHOOSE OUR EVENTUAL WINNERS, BUT WE BELIEVE THAT WE HAVE IDENTIFIED A NUMBER OF CAMPSITES WITH TRULY OUTSTANDING CHARACTERISTICS.

IN EACH CASE, WE HAVE SELECTED AN OUTRIGHT WINNER, ALONG WITH TWO HIGHLY COMMENDED RUNNERS-UP.

Listed below are full details of each of our award categories and our winners for 2005, followed on page 12 by our first ever winners from 2004.

Alan Rogers Progress Award 2005

This award reflects the hard work and commitment undertaken by particular site owners to improve and upgrade their site.

WINNER
Camping Idro Rio Vantone, Italy

RUNNERS-UP
Camping Le Moulin Fort, France
Camping Mas Nou, Spain

Alan Rogers Welcome Award 2005

This award takes account of sites offering a particularly friendly welcome and maintaining a friendly ambience throughout reader's holidays.

WINNER
Camping Coin Tranquille, France

RUNNERS-UP
Woodlands Park Touring Park, Ireland
Camping t'Strandheem, Netherlands

Alan Rogers Active Holiday Award 2005

This award reflects sites in outstanding locations which are ideally suited for active holidays, notably walking or cycling, but which could extend to include such activities as winter sports or water sports

WINNER
Camping Wulfener Hals, Germany

RUNNERS-UP
Camping Ty Naden, France
Ferienparadies Natterer See, Austria

Alan Rogers Motorhome Award 2005

Motor home sales are increasing and this award acknowledges sites which, in our opinion, have made outstanding efforts to welcome motorhome clients.

WINNER
Camping La Barbanne, France

RUNNERS-UP
Camping El Garrofer, Spain
Oxon Hall Touring Park, England

Alan Rogers 4 Seasons Award 2005

This award is made to outstanding sites with extended opening dates and which welcome clients to a uniformly high standard throughout the year.

WINNER
Caravan Park Sexten, Italy

RUNNERS-UP
Brighouse Bay Holiday Park, Scotland
Camping L'Escale, France

Alan Rogers Seaside Award 2005

This award is made for sites which we feel are outstandingly suitable for a really excellent seaside holiday.

WINNER
Camping Union Lido Vacanze, Italy

RUNNERS-UP
Lanternacamp, Croatia
Playa Montroig Camping, Spain

Alan Rogers Country Award 2005

This award contrasts with our former award and acknowledges sites which are attractively located in delightful, rural locations.

WINNER

Camping La Ribeyre, France

RUNNERS-UP

Camping Alte Sagemuhle, Germany

Ruthern Valley Holidays, England

Alan Rogers Rented Accommodation Award 2005

Given the increasing importance of rented accommodation on many campsites, and the inclusion in many Alan Rogers guides, of a rented accommodation section, we feel that it is important to acknowledge sites which have made a particular effort in creating a high quality 'rented accommodation' park.

WINNER

Yelloh! Village Le Club Farret, France

RUNNERS-UP

Centro Vacanze Pra' Delle Torri, Italy

Camping & Bungalow Park Sanguli, Spain

Alan Rogers Unique Site Award 2005

This award acknowledges sites with unique, out-standing features – something which simply cannot be found elsewhere and which is an important attraction of the site.

WINNER

Topcamp Feddet, Denmark

RUNNERS-UP

Camping Mazurski Eden, Poland

Skjerneset Camping, Norway

Alan Rogers Family Site Award 2005

Many sites claim to be child friendly but this award acknowledges the sites we feel to be the very best in this respect.

WINNER

Camping Les Medes, Spain

RUNNERS-UP

Trevornick Holiday Park, England

Camping Breebronne, Netherlands

Alan Rogers Readers' Award 2005

In 2005 we introduced a new award, which we believe to be the most important, our Readers' Award. We simply invited our readers (by means of an on-line poll at www.alanrogers.com) to nominate the site they enjoyed most. The outright winner is a well known and much loved Italian site celebrating its 50th anniversary in 2005:

WINNER

Camping Union Lido Vacanze, Italy

Alan Rogers Special Award 2005

A special award is made to acknowledge sites which we feel have overcome a very significant set-back, and have, not only returned to their former condition, but has added extra amenities and can therefore be fairly considered to be even better than before. In 2005 we acknowledge three sites, all of which have overcome major problems.

Yelloh! Village Le Serignan Plage, France

Camping Arinella Bianca, France

Slavoj Autocamp Litomerice, Czech Republic

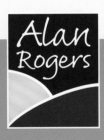

In 2004 we introduced the first ever Alan Rogers Campsite Awards.

BEFORE MAKING OUR AWARDS, WE CAREFULLY CONSIDER MORE THAN 2000 CAMPSITES FEATURED IN OUR GUIDES, TAKING INTO ACCOUNT COMMENTS FROM OUR SITE ASSESSORS, OUR HEAD OFFICE TEAM, AND, OF COURSE, OUR READERS.

OUR AWARD WINNERS COVER A MASSIVE GEOGRAPHICAL AREA FROM THE IBERIAN PENINSULA TO EASTERN SLOVENIA, AND, IN OUR FIRST YEAR, WE MADE AWARDS TO CAMPSITES IN 11 DIFFERENT COUNTRIES.

NEEDLESS TO SAY, IT'S AN EXTREMELY DIFFICULT TASK TO CHOOSE OUR EVENTUAL WINNERS, BUT WE BELIEVE THAT WE HAVE IDENTIFIED A NUMBER OF CAMPSITES WITH TRULY OUTSTANDING CHARACTERISTICS.

IN EACH CASE, WE HAVE SELECTED AN OUTRIGHT WINNER, ALONG WITH TWO HIGHLY COMMENDED RUNNERS-UP.

Listed below are full details of each of our award categories and our first ever winners from 2004.

Alan Rogers Progress Award 2004

This award reflects the hard work and commitment undertaken by particular site owners to improve and upgrade their site.

WINNER
Camping und Freizeitpark Lux Oase, Germany

RUNNERS-UP
Trethem Mill Touring Park, England
Camping Les Deux Vallées, France

Alan Rogers Welcome Award 2004

This award takes account of sites offering a particularly friendly welcome and maintaining a friendly ambience throughout reader's holidays.

WINNER
Camping Caravaning Les Pêcheurs, France

RUNNERS-UP
Balatontourist Diana Camping, Hungary
Camping des Abers, France

Alan Rogers Active Holiday Award 2004

This award reflects sites in outstanding locations which are ideally suited for active holidays, notably walking or cycling, but which could extend to include such activities as winter sports or water sports

WINNER
Castel Camping Le Ty Nadan, France

RUNNERS-UP
Camping Menina, Slovenia
River Dart Adventures, England

Alan Rogers Motorhome Award 2004

Motor home sales are increasing and this award acknowledges sites which, in our opinion, have made outstanding efforts to welcome motorhome clients.

WINNER
Camping El Garrofer, Spain

RUNNERS-UP
Castel Camping Sequoia Parc, France
Camping Jungfrau, Switzerland

Alan Rogers 4 Seasons Award 2004

This award is made to outstanding sites with extended opening dates and which welcome clients to a uniformly high standard throughout the year.

WINNER
Camping Caravaning L'Escale, France

RUNNERS-UP
Camping Vilanova Park, Spain
Ferienparadies Natterer See, Austria

Alan Rogers Seaside Award 2004

This award is made for sites which we feel are outstandingly suitable for a really excellent seaside holiday.

WINNER
Camping Union Lido Vacanze, Italy

RUNNERS-UP
Yelloh! Village Le Brasilia, France
Pentewan Sands Holiday Park, England

Alan Rogers Country Award 2004

This award contrasts with our former award and acknowledges sites which are attractively located in delightful, rural locations.

WINNER

Castel Camping Pyrénées Natura, France

RUNNERS-UP

Camping Il Collaccio, Italy

Camping Elbsee, Germany

Alan Rogers Rented Accommodation Award 2004

Given the increasing importance of rented accommodation on many campsites, and the inclusion in many Alan Rogers guides, of a rented accommodation section, we feel that it is important to acknowledge sites which have made a particular effort in creating a high quality 'rented accommodation' park.

WINNER

Camping and Bungalows Sanguli, Spain

RUNNERS-UP

Sunêlia Les Bois du Bardelet, France

Sandy Balls Holiday Centre, England

Alan Rogers Unique Site Award 2004

This award acknowledges sites with unique, out-standing features – something which simply cannot be found elsewhere and which is an important attraction of the site.

WINNER

Bøsøre Strand Ferie Park, Denmark

RUNNERS-UP

Skånes Djurparks Camping, Sweden

Camping De Vechtstreek, Netherlands

Alan Rogers Family Site Award 2004

Many sites claim to be child friendly but this award acknowledges the sites we feel to be the very best in this respect.

WINNER

Woodlands Leisure Park, England

RUNNERS-UP

Camping de Molenhof, Netherlands

Camping Cambrils Park, Spain

Alan Rogers Special Award 2004

A special award is made to acknowledge sites which we feel have overcome a very significant set-back, and have, not only returned to their former condition, but has added extra amenities and can therefore be fairly considered to be even better than before.

In 2004 we acknowledged 3 French campsites, all of which have undergone major problems and all of which have made highly impressive recoveries.

Domaine de la Rive, France

Domaine du Colombier, France

Domaine de Gaujac, France

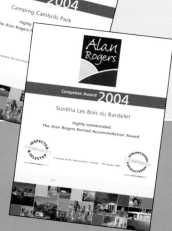

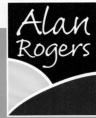

The West Country is a diverse region of beautiful sandy beaches, steep craggy cliffs, desolate moors and rolling green hills. Home of clotted cream teas, it also boasts a range of historical and modern attractions, including the celebrated Eden Project.

THE SOUTH WEST COMPRISES: CORNWALL, DEVON, SOMERSET, BATH, BRISTOL, SOUTH GLOUCESTERSHIRE, WILTSHIRE AND WEST DORSET.

With its dramatic cliffs, pounded by the Atlantic ocean, and beautiful coastline boasting warm waters, soft sandy beaches and small seaside towns, Cornwall is one of England's most popular holiday destinations. The coast is also a surfers' paradise, while inland the wild and rugged Bodmin Moors dominate the landscape. In Devon, the Dartmoor National Park has sweeping moorland and granite tors where wild ponies roam freely. Much of the countryside is gentle rolling green fields, dotted with pretty thatched cottages. The coastline around Torbay is known as the English Riviera which, due to its temperate climate, allows palm trees to grow. Stretching across East Devon and West Dorset is the fossil-ridden Jurassic Coast, a World Heritage Site. West Dorset is also home to Lyme Regis and Weymouth, which comes alive in summer when regular entertainment, including a carnival and fireworks, is held along the seafront. Famous for its cider and cheese, Somerset is good walking country, with the Exmoor National Park, which also straddles Devon. Wiltshire's natural attractions include the Marlborough Downs, Savernake Forest and the River Avon. It also boasts one of the most famous prehistoric sites in the world, the ancient stone circles of Stonehenge.

Places of interest

Bath: World Heritage Site full of Roman and Georgian architecture, elegant streets such as the Circle and Royal Crescent, Roman baths

Bristol: steeped in maritime history with the world's first great Ocean Liner; Brunel's Clifton Suspension bridge; range of museums and art galleries

Cornwall: seaside town of St Ives; Land's End; Eden Project; Penzance and St Michael's Mount

Devon: popular seaside resorts of Torquay, Paignton and Brixham; cities of Exeter and Plymouth

Somerset: Weston-Super-Mare; Wells Cathedral; Cheddar Gorge and Wookey Hole caves

West Dorset: Dorchester, home of Thomas Hardy; Isle of Portland; Abbotsbury village, with swannery

Wiltshire: Salisbury; Glastonbury; Longleat manor house and safari park

Did you know?

Chesil Beach is an 18 mile stretch of fortress-like walls of pebbles, formed 12,000 years ago

There are numerous white horses carved into the landscape across the South West

The Jurassic Coast is a Natural World Heritage Site stretching for 95 miles

The Black Death entered England through the port in Weymouth in 1348

Britain's oldest complete skeleton, Cheddar Man, was buried in Gough's Cave 9,000 years ago

At 404 feet Salisbury Cathedral has the tallest medieval spire in the world

UK0440 Dolbeare Caravan & Camping Park

St Ive Road, Landrake, Saltash PL12 5AF (Cornwall)

Mark and John are proud of their small, but well kept park. In a rural setting (but very easily accessible from the main A38) and consists of a large rectangular field of neat grass edged with trees and sloping slightly at the top, connected by a gravel road. Caravans and motorcaravans go mainly around the edge, with most of the terraced pitches having hardstanding. Tents tend to go in the central area where there is also play equipment. All 60 numbered pitches are of comfortable size, 53 with electricity (16A). An extra field doubles as a rally and games field and part is set aside for a dog exercise area. Leaflets provide suggestions for what to do. Kennels nearby can provide day care from £3.50, but the drawback is that there could be some noise depending on wind direction. This is a usefully situated park said to be 20 minutes from everywhere - Plymouth, beaches, Dartmoor and Bodmin Moor, etc.

Facilities
The bright, cheerful and well kept heated toilet block to one side of the field is fully equipped. Indoor dishwashing sinks. Laundry next to reception. Motorcaravan services. Reception doubles as a small shop for basics including gas (limited hours out of main season). Park has arranged discounts at the St Mellion Golf and Country Club for golf and leisure facilities. Site barrier (card system with £5 deposit). Off site: Fishing 3 miles. Golf 5.5 miles.

Open
All year.

At a glance
Welcome & Ambience ✓✓✓✓✓ Location ✓✓✓✓
Quality of Pitches ✓✓✓✓✓ Range of Facilities ✓✓✓

Directions
After crossing the Tamar Bridge into Cornwall, continue on A38 for a further 4 miles. In Landrake village turn right following signs and site is 0.75 miles on the right. O.S.GR: SX366616.

Charges 2005
Per unit incl. 2 adults and car	£ 9.00 - £ 15.50
extra adult	£ 2.75
child (5-16 yrs)	£ 1.75
awning	£ 1.00

Reservations
Made with £20 non-refundable deposit.
Tel: 01752 851332.
Email: dolbeare@btopenworld.com

UK0280 Powderham Castle Tourist Park

Lanlivery, Lostwithiel PL30 5BU (Cornwall)

This is a most pleasant, peaceful touring park with plenty of sheltered green space and a natural, uncommercialised atmosphere. This has been enhanced by careful planting of trees and shrubs to form a series of linked paddocks with a small unfenced stream running through. The nearest beach at Par is some 4 miles. The park has 38 private caravan holiday homes in a separate field and 72 numbered touring pitches spread round the perimeter of the paddocks, each with 10-15 pitches. All have electricity connections (5/10A) and 12 have hardstanding (awning groundsheets must be lifted alternate days). There is an 'adult only' section for tents and touring caravans. For children, a large, well equipped activity play area with a super range of adventure type equipment on grass is in one of the hedged paddocks with a fenced paddling pool. Indoor tennis courts (Bodmin) and a swimming pool are near. The village pub is within walking distance and there are several good local restaurants. The Eden Project is very close.

Facilities
The single central toilet block is good but is quite a walk from some pitches. Hot showers are free, with curtained cubicles in the ladies' and a family washroom with shower, basin, WC, etc. Separate dishwashing area with five sinks. Fully equipped laundry room. Motorcaravan service point. Gas supplies. Play area. Torch useful. Off site: Fresh water fishing 1.5 miles or sea fishing 3 miles. Bicycle hire 4 miles. Riding 2 miles. Golf 1.5 miles.

Open
Easter/1 April - 31 October.

At a glance
Welcome & Ambience ✓✓✓✓ Location ✓✓✓✓
Quality of Pitches ✓✓✓✓ Range of Facilities ✓✓✓

Directions
Park approach road leads off A390 road 1.5 miles southwest of Lostwithiel. Follow white or brown camping signs. No other approach is advised. O.S.GR: SX083592.

Charges 2005
Per unit incl. 2 persons and electricity	£ 10.00 - £ 14.00
extra person	£ 1.00 - £ 2.00

No single sex groups (excl. bona fide organisations). No credit cards.

Reservations
Made with £20 deposit. Tel: 01208 872277.
Email: powderhamcastletp@tiscali.co.uk

15

UK0400 Trelay Farmpark

Pelynt, Looe PL13 2JX (Cornwall)

Situated a little back from the coast, just over three miles from Looe and Polperro in a rural situation, this is a real gem of a park. Neat, tidy and quiet, despite the name, there is no farm. On your right as you drive in, and quite attractively arranged amongst herbaceous shrubs, are caravan holiday homes (some let by the park, 15 privately owned). The touring area is behind and slightly above, on level to gently sloping, neatly cut grass. An oval hard-core road connects the good sized, numbered pitches that border the site and back onto hedges, the majority with rural views. There are 43 pitches with electricity, with a further 12 pitches for tents, etc. Outside the main season the central area is kept free for ball games. You will receive a good welcome from the enthusiastic owners, Heather and Graham Veale and their family, who live in the chalet bungalow near the entrance where the small reception is located.

Facilities

Excellent, spacious chalet-type toilet block, purpose built, heated, well equipped and maintained, with large cubicles. Some semi-private washbasins. En-suite unit with ramp for disabled visitors (key from reception); it includes a baby bath. Two dishwashing sinks and a laundry sink. Washing machine and dryer. Gas supplies. Free use of fridge/freezer and ice pack service. Tourist information including map sales and loan. Off site: Village with pub, shops and bus service 0.5 miles. Looe and Polperro within 3 miles. Bus service from the village.

Open

1 April - end October.

At a glance

Welcome & Ambience	✓✓✓✓	Location	✓✓✓✓
Quality of Pitches	✓✓✓✓	Range of Facilities	✓✓✓

Directions

From A390 Lostwithiel road take B3359 south at Middle or East Taphouse towards Looe and Polperro. Site is signed 0.5 miles past Pelynt on the left. From Looe take A387 towards Polperro and after 2 miles turn right onto B3359 towards Pelynt. Site is signed 1 mile on right. O.S.GR: SX210545.
GPS: N50:21.735 W04:31.133

Charges 2005

Per unit incl. 2 persons	£ 7.50 - £ 11.00
extra person over 5 yrs	£ 2.50 - £ 3.50
child (under 5 yrs)	£ 1.50
electricity	£ 2.00
dog	£ 0.70

No credit cards.

Reservations

Advised for July/Aug. Tel: 01503 220900.
Email: stay@trelay.co.uk

UK0270 Mena Caravan & Camping Park

Lanivet, Bodmin PL30 5HW (Cornwall)

This peaceful Cornish site is a credit to its owners and their welcome and enthusiasm. Eight years ago it was a field for cows and with hard work and care it has been developed into a comfortable attractively landscaped site. Set in 15 acres of secluded countryside, it is spacious and never crowded offering only 25 level grass pitches. There are 12 electricity connections (10A). A large comfortable area with a veranda and facilities for making tea and coffee provides a focal point for an evening get together or singsong. A wonderful little fishing lake is well worth a visit even if you do not fish to have a picnic. Created from scratch, it is now a wildlife haven, quiet and peaceful, and is a down hill walk from the site. Mena means 'hilltop' in the Cornish language and the site is actually situated at the geographical centre of Cornwall, overlooked by Helman's Tor. It is also close to the Saints' Way, the pilgrim route from Ireland where they crossed by land from Padstow to Fowey on their way to France.

Facilities

Four toilet and washbasin cabins are in an older wooden building. Two new showers and two toilets are behind the veranda building. On the opposite side of the site is a new en-suite facility for disabled visitors, part of a building housing a large games room with three quarter size snooker table, TV and darts. Swings, etc. for children in the central grass area. Fishing lake (licence required). Two mobile homes for hire.

Open

1 May - 1 October.

At a glance

Welcome & Ambience	✓✓✓✓✓	Location	✓✓✓✓
Quality of Pitches	✓✓✓✓	Range of Facilities	✓✓✓

Directions

From Bodmin by-pass take A391 for St Austell. After 0.5 miles take first left (unsigned). In 0.75 miles turn right signed Lostwithiel. In 0.5 miles at top of hill turn right keeping the Celtic Cross on your left. Continue straight on for 0.5 miles (road narrows) and turn right into site lane. O.S.GR: SX041625.
GPS: N50:25.816 W004:45.43

Charges year

Per unit incl. 2 persons	£ 7.00 - £ 9.00
incl. electricity	£ 9.00 - £ 11.00
extra person	£ 3.00
child (4-6 yrs)	£ 1.00 - £ 1.50

Reservations

Made for high season (min. 2 nights); contact site.
Tel: 01208 831845.
Email: mena@campsitesincornwall.co.uk

UK0330 Killigarth Manor Caravan Park

Polperro, Looe PL13 2JQ (Cornwall)

A substantial part of Killigarth Estate is occupied by caravan holiday homes but a separate part is allocated to touring units and it is a good choice for those that like a range of facilities and entertainment. It provides 202 marked, level or gently sloping grass pitches, of which 75 are taken by seasonal units, and a tenting paddock. There are 73 electric hook-ups (16A) for tourers. Several bars and a large entertainment area with stage, mini-cinema, family room, amusements and games areas, a new restaurant, takeaway and bar snacks, a heated indoor pool (adult £2, child £1), fitness centre with gym, sauna and sun bed, and a sun terrace with beautiful views. Early evening 'young entertainment' is followed later by live shows, discos or groups and a programme of competitions, quizzes or family films in a big screen cinema. This park is popular with families with children of all ages and there is much to do in the area.

Facilities

One large, and fully equipped toilet block is supplemented by a small 'portacabin' unit with toilet facilities for peak season which receive heavy use. Dishwashing facilities under cover. Facilities for disabled visitors are in the main block. Well equipped laundry with sinks. Well stocked mini-market (all season). Bars and restaurant. Takeaway. Indoor pool with children's pool. Fitness centre. Indoor play area for under-fives and other play areas. Mini cinema. Amusement arcade. Tennis court. Skittle alley, croquet, draughts, badminton and crazy golf. Bus service in high season. Off site: Fishing 1 mile.

Directions

From Looe take A387 towards Polperro. After 3.5 miles, fork left immediately past a bus shelter and phone box at sign to Killigarth. Site is 0.25 miles. O.S.GR: SX213519. GPS: N50:20.291 W04:30.608

Charges guide

Contact site. Tel: 01271 866766.
Email: holiday@johnfowlerholidays.com

Open

1 March - 31 October.

At a glance

| Welcome & Ambience | ✓✓ | Location | ✓✓✓✓ |
| Quality of Pitches | ✓✓✓ | Range of Facilities | ✓✓✓✓ |

UK0320 Polborder House Caravan & Camping Park

Bucklawren Road, St Martins by Looe PL13 1QR (Cornwall)

Polborder House is a lovely site which may appeal to those who prefer a quiet, well kept little family site to the larger ones with many on-site activities. With good countryside views, up to 37 touring units can be accommodated on well tended grass. Pitches are marked with some hedging between pairs of pitches to give privacy and there are 28 electrical connections (10A). There are also several hardstandings and 10 serviced pitches. The owners live on the park and are most helpful. Polborder is well situated with Seaton only 2 miles, Looe 2.5 and the nearest beach a 20-25 minutes walk from a gate in the corner of the park. This is a good area for walking with links to the coastal path through Duchy woodland.

Facilities

The well kept, fully equipped sanitary block (key entry) includes a baby room, fully equipped laundry room, and three covered sinks outside for dishwashing. En-suite toilet unit for disabled visitors has a ramped approach. Shop (all season) for gas and basics, and some camping accessories. Toddler's play area. Off site: Fishing, golf and boat launching within 2 miles. Riding 8 miles. Restaurant 500 m.

Open

25 March - 4 November.

Directions

Park is less than half a mile south of the B3253. Turn off 2 miles east of Looe and follow signs to park at junctions; care is needed with narrow road. O.S.GR: SX283555. GPS: N50:22.633 W004:25.11

Charges 2005

Per unit incl. 2 persons	£ 8.60 - £ 12.00
extra person	£ 3.80 - £ 4.50
child (5-16 yrs)	£ 1.20 - £ 1.75
electricity	£ 2.00

Reservations

Any period, £25 deposit (non-refundable). Tel: 01503 240265. Email: reception@peaceful_polborder.co.uk

At a glance

| Welcome & Ambience | ✓✓✓✓ | Location | ✓✓✓✓ |
| Quality of Pitches | ✓✓✓✓ | Range of Facilities | ✓✓✓ |

17

UK0190 Polruan Holidays Camping & Caravanning

Polruan-by-Fowey PL23 1QH (Cornwall)

Polruan is a rural site in an elevated position not far from Fowey in an area of 'outstanding natural beauty', 200 metres from the Coastal path. With 47 touring pitches and 11 holiday homes to let, this is a very pleasant little site. The holiday homes are arranged in a neat circle, with a central area for some tourers, including 7 pitches with gravel hardstanding and electricity, one fully serviced. The remaining touring pitches are in an adjacent field with 8 electricity hook-ups, which is part level for motorcaravans and part on a gentle slope for tents. There are marvellous sea views, but it could be a little exposed when the wind blows off the sea. A raised picnic area gives more views across the estuary to Fowey. This is a nice little park in a popular tourist area, within walking distance (downhill all the way, and vice-versa!) of the village, where there are various hostelries and a passenger ferry to Fowey. A member of the Countryside Discovery group.

Facilities

The fully equipped sanitary block of older design has modern, controllable showers, large enough for an adult and child. New laundry room and dishwashing sinks. Motorcaravan service facilities. Range of recycling bins. Reception (with a small terrace) doubles as a small shop for basics and gas and also an off-licence. There is a drinks machine and a freezer for ice packs, tourist information and bus timetables (for Looe, etc). Sloping field area for children's play with swings. Off site: Fishing 0.5 miles. Riding or bicycle hire 3 miles. Golf 10 miles. Coastal path 200 m.

Open

Easter - 1 October.

At a glance

Welcome & Ambience	✓✓✓✓	Location	✓✓✓✓✓
Quality of Pitches	✓✓✓	Range of Facilities	✓✓✓

Directions

From main A390 at East Taphouse take B3359 towards Looe. After 5 miles fork right signed Bodinnick and ferry. Watch for signs for Polruan and site to left. Follow these carefully along narrow Cornish lanes to site on right just before village. O.S.GR: SX133509.

Charges 2005

Per unit incl. 1 or 2 persons and electricity	£ 9.00 - £ 13.00
extra person	£ 2.00
dog	£ 0.75

No credit cards.

Reservations

Advised for July/Aug. and made with £30 deposit. Tel: 01726 870263. Email: polholiday@aol.com

UK0195 Penmarlam Caravan & Camping Park

Bodinwick-by-Fowey, PL23 1LZ (Cornwall)

Penmarlam is situated high above the estuary opposite Fowey, close to the village of Bodinnick which is famous for being the home of Daphne du Maurier. Marcus Wallace took over this park in 2003 and has been busy developing it by adding a new camping field, new toilet facilties and a new reception and shop which also acts as the village shop for Bodinnick (this means it is well stocked). The original field is level and sheltered with a circular concrete access road and 37 electric pitches on grass. The new field has a slight slope, is divided with wild banks and enjoys good countryside views. There are 28 pitches with electricity here (in total over the two fields there are 65). The new building that houses reception, shop and the toilet facilities is well situated between the two fields. It is fitted with a loop system for deaf visitors, the owner can 'sign' as well as speaking French, Spanish and some German! Internet access is provided here, with wireless access possible from the pitches. Some of our readers will be attracted by easy access to a slipway (£6) and boat moorings near the park entrance, This also makes for a pleasant walk with picnic tables overlooking the river at the bottom.

Facilities

The modern, colourful and heated toilet block is fully equipped including a baby and toddler room in the ladies', a separate en-suite unit for disabled visitors which can double as a family room. Licensed shop with fresh fruit and vegetables, Video, DVD and book library open all year. Off site: Car or passenger ferry for Fowey. Annual Daphne du Maurier Festival of Arts and Literature is held in Fowey every May. Fowey Regatta held in August when some 2,500 visiting yachts boost the substantial resident yacht population.

Open

Easter - October.

At a glance

Welcome & Ambience	✓✓✓✓	Location	✓✓✓✓✓
Quality of Pitches	✓✓✓✓	Range of Facilities	✓✓✓

Directions

From the main A390 roadat East Taphouse take B3359 towards Looe. After 5 miles fork right, signed Bodinnick and ferry. Site is signed on the right 1 mile past village of Lanteglos Highway, just before Bodinnick village. O.S.GR: SK130527.

Charges 2005

Per unit incl. 2 persons	£ 8.00 - £ 13.50
incl. electricity	£ 10.00 - £ 15.50
extra person	£ 1.50 - £ 3.00
child (3-6 yrs)	£ 1.00 - £ 2.00

Reservations

Made with deposit (£20). Tel: 01726-870088. Email: info@penmarlampark.co.uk

UK0410 **Heligan Woods Holiday Park**

St Ewe, St Austell PL26 6EL (Cornwall)

A peaceful park in a mature garden setting, Heligan Woods complements its sister site, Pentewan Sands with its busy beach life and many activities. Part of this park's boundary actually edges The Lost Gardens of Heligan (although nothing can be seen), and at some time the land must have been part of the Gardens. One can enjoy the mature trees and flowering shrubs here which have been further landscaped to provide an attractive situation for a number of holiday homes (some for rent, 5 privately owned). These face out over a part of the 'Lost Valley' of Heligan fame and are interspersed with touring pitches, with some below on sloping grass and others in a more level situation amongst trees and shrubs. In all, there are 100 good sized touring pitches, 80 with 16A electricity connections. The many facilities of Pentewan Sands are open to visitors to Heligan Woods. There is access to the Pentewan Trail to ride or cycle into Mevagissey or Pentewan.

Facilities

Fully equipped and well kept, the modern, heated toilet block includes a unisex room with bath and small size bath. Dishwashing sinks under cover. Fully equipped laundry room. Small shop (peak season only). Adventure playground. Off site: Riding 4 miles, golf 5 miles. Lost Gardens of Heligan next door.

Open

19 March - 30 October.

At a glance

Welcome & Ambience	✓✓✓✓	Location	✓✓✓✓✓
Quality of Pitches	✓✓✓✓	Range of Facilities	✓✓✓

Directions

From St Austell ring road take B3273 for Mevagissey. After 3.5 miles, pass Pentewan Sands, continue up the hill and turn right following site signs. Park is on left just before reaching Heligan Gardens. O.S.GR: SW999464. GPS: N50:17.330 W04:48.725

Charges 2005

Per unit incl. 2 adults, electricity	£ 9.60 - £ 21.50
extra adult	£ 1.75 - £ 3.85
child (3-15 yrs)	£ 1.00 - £ 2.80

Reservations

Made with deposit (£40-£75, acc. to season), fee (£7) and compulsory cancellation insurance, for min. 1 week in high season. Contact park in writing or call booking line. Email: info@heliganwoods.co.uk

UK0255 **Sun Valley Holiday Park**

Pentewan Road, St Austell Bay, Mevagissey PL26 6DJ (Cornwall)

This very neat, tidy holiday park has been developed in the grounds of a country house which is now split into holiday apartments. Set in a sheltered situation on the road from St Austell to Pentewan, Sun Valley has the appearance of a park, helped by wonderful mature cedars. Over 75 caravan holiday homes have been carefully landscaped into the 20 acres, together with 25 level touring pitches. Hardstandings and 10A electricity are available. Excellent facilities include a restaurant, bar, indoor heated pool and tennis courts. Children are not forgotten either with a paddling pool, soft ball play area, a games room, an adventure play area, plus equipment for under 5s, not to mention resident donkeys. There is lots to do here, never mind the wonderful sandy beach down the road, and plenty of places to visit in the area.

Facilities

Heated en-suite family rooms offer home from home comfort with a baby changing station and ramped access for disabled people. Dishwashing undercover. Fully equipped laundry in the pool block. Washing lines provided. Shop (limited hours in low seasons). Clubhouse with bar, restaurant (also limited in low season). Indoor pool (all season). Off site: Beach 1 mile. Golf 1.5 miles. Riding 5 miles Bus stop at park entrance (hourly service).

At a glance

Welcome & Ambience	✓✓✓✓✓	Location	✓✓✓✓✓
Quality of Pitches	✓✓✓✓	Range of Facilities	✓✓✓✓✓

Directions

From St Austell ring road take B3273 for Mevagissey. After London Apprentice look for entrance in 1 mile). O.S.GR: SX006484. GPS: N50:18.030 W04:48.070

Charges 2006

Per unit incl. 2 persons, electricity	£ 12.50 - £ 28.00

Reservations

Made with £30 deposit, Sat. to Sat. periods 28/5-4/6 and 16/7-27/8. Tel: 01726 843266. Email: reception@sunvalleyholidays.co.uk

Open

Easter/1 April - October half term.

UK0290 Carlyon Bay Caravan & Camping Park

Bethesda, Carlyon Bay, St Austell PL25 3RE (Cornwall)

Tranquil open meadows edged by mature woodland, well cared for by the Taylor family, provide a beautiful holiday setting with the nearest beach five minutes walk from the top gate. The original farm buildings have been converted and added to, providing an attractive centre to the park, also home for the owners, with a certain individuality of design which is very pleasing, particularly in the impressively tiled toilet blocks which are of excellent quality and design. The 180 pitches in five areas are spacious and allow for a family meadow and a dog free meadow (high season only). All are on flat, terraced or gently sloping grass with flowers and flowering shrubs in some areas. The 115 pitches with electricity (10/16A) are marked and include 8 with full services, 6 with hardstanding. The attractive kidney shaped, heated swimming pool is walled and paved for sunbathing. This is part of the central, covered area used for entertainment in high season for families and children. There is also a pleasant family pub and Ben's Playworld for children within walking distance. The coastal footpath passes nearby.

Facilities

Three individually designed, modern toilet blocks (one heated) provide a full range of comfortable for all your needs - almost home from home! Dishwashing sinks. Fully equipped laundry room (hot water metered). Modern reception with little shop (limited hours out of season). Takeaway (May - mid-Sept). Swimming and paddling pools (Whitsun - Sept). TV lounge, crazy golf, table tennis and pool table. Two play areas. Eden Project tickets available. Off site: Golf course near the park entrance. Riding 3 miles. Bicycle hire 4 miles. Sailing 2 miles. Boat launching 5 miles.

Open

Easter/1 April - end-September.

At a glance

Welcome & Ambience	✓✓✓✓	Location	✓✓✓✓✓
Quality of Pitches	✓✓✓✓	Range of Facilities	✓✓✓✓

Directions

From Plymouth direction on A390, pass Lostwithiel and 1 mile after village of St Blazey, turn left at roundabout beside Britannia Inn. After 400 yds turn right on a concrete road and right again at site sign. O.S.GR: SX053526. GPS: N50:20.451 W04:44.233

Charges 2005

Per unit incl. 2 persons	£ 8.00 - £ 23.50
extra adult	£ 4.00
child (3-17 yrs)	£ 3.00
electricity	£ 2.50
awning or small tent	£ 1.50

Reservations

Made with £50 deposit and £2 fee (min. 7 nights 23/7-29/8). Tel: 01726 812735. Email: holidays@carlyonbay.net

UK0155 **Tregarton Park**

Gorran, Mevagissey, St Austell PL26 6NF (Cornwall)

Run by the welcoming Hicks family, Tregarton Park itself dates back to the 16th century. It is little wonder that the listed buildings have created some problems in providing modern facilities, although the Hicks have done well with their conversions to create a pleasing environment. The 12-acre caravan park is made up of four meadows, with wonderful rural views. The 125 pitches, all with electric hook ups (10A), are of generous size with most separated by either hedges or fencing. All have been terraced, although the park itself is quite hilly. Reception provides a well stocked shop, tourist information and a takeaway service. This offers freshly cooked food including a daily delivery of Cornish pasties. The large heated outdoor pool (the focal point of the park) is surrounded by decked terraces, with tables and chairs where one can relax and watch the children. An adventure playground is in one of the meadows along with goal posts and an impressive all-weather tennis court (free). Close to the small harbour town of Gorran and about 2.5 miles from Mevagissey, with several beaches close by, this is an ideal site for those not wanting lots of entertainment, but would enjoy the option of various activities available nearby.

Facilities

The tiled toilet block is fully equipped. Laundry room and enclosed dishwashing area. Well stocked shop with groceries and camping supplies. Takeaway. Gas supplies. Heated swimming pool. Tourist information. Dog exercise meadow. Playground. Facilities are open Whitsun - mid Sept. Off site: Eden project 9 miles. Heligan Gardens 2 miles. Mevagissey 2 miles. Beaches 2 miles. Fishing trips available from Mevagissey and Gorran Haven.

Open

1 April - 30 September.

At a glance

Welcome & Ambience	✓✓✓✓✓	Location	✓✓✓✓✓
Quality of Pitches	✓✓✓✓✓	Range of Facilities	✓✓✓✓

Directions

Leave St Austell travelling south on the B3273 and pass through London Apprentice and Pentewen. Follow Tregarton Park's brown tourist signs by turning right at the crossroads at the top of the hill towards the Lost Gardens of Heligan and Gorran Haven. Do not go into Mevagissey. O.S.GR: SW989435. GPS: N50:15.528 W04:49.765

Charges 2005

Per unit incl. 2 persons, electricity and awning	£ 4.95 - £ 19.50
extra person (over 4 yrs)	£ 2.00 - £ 3.00
dog (max. 2)	free - £ 2.00

Reservations

Made with deposit (£4 per night booked) and £1 fee. Tel: 0845 10 80 113. Email: reception@tregarton.co.uk

UK0415 **Trencreek Farm Country Holiday Park**

Hewas Water, St Austell PL26 7JG (Cornwall)

Trencreek Farm is a friendly well-equipped family owned park set in 56 acres of rolling Cornish countryside, close to a number of well known sights, notably The Eden Project and The Lost Gardens of Heligan. Although no longer a working farm, a number of animals roam freely within the park's farm area. Amenities here include a heated swimming pool, a tennis court and four small lakes, each of which is stocked with a different range of fish. Pitches are grassy and of a good size, most with electricity although a number of non-electric tent pitches are also available. The camping area has been attractively developed to encircle the central farm buildings which now house various amenities including the Farmer's Den bar, a restaurant, takeaway and a shop. In peak season a children's club is organised, along with a number of family events. Mobile homes, chalets and ready-erected tents are available for hire. A member of the Surf Bay Leisure group.

Facilities

The two sanitary blocks are well maintained. Laundrette. Shop. Bar, restaurant. Takeaway food. Heated swimming pool. Tennis court. Sports field. Fishing (small charge). Play area. Children's TV and games room. Children's farm. Off site: Nearest beach (Carlyon Bay) 8 miles. Golf (18 hole) 3 miles. Shipwreck rescue and heritage centre 5 miles. The Lost Gardens of Heligan 3 miles. Eden Project 3 miles.

Open

2 April - 29 October.

At a glance

Welcome & Ambience	✓✓✓✓	Location	✓✓✓✓
Quality of Pitches	✓✓✓✓	Range of Facilities	✓✓✓✓

Directions

Site is four miles west of St Austell. Take the A390 and then fork left to join the B3287 and the site is 1 mile further on the left. O.S.GR: SW965484.

Charges 2006

Per pitch incl. 2 adults	£ 7.00 - £ 13.50
with electricity	£ 8.95 - £ 15.50
extra person (over 3 yrs)	£ 1.50
dog	£ 0.75

Reservations

Made with deposit of £25 per pitch per week. Tel: 01726 882540. Email: reception@trencreek.co.uk

UK0250 Pentewan Sands Holiday Park

Pentewan, St Austell PL26 6BT (Cornwall)

Pentewan Sands is a popular, well managed family park with an ideal position right beside a wide sandy private beach. A busy, 32 acre holiday park with lots going on, there are 501 touring pitches, 401 with electricity, and 120 caravan holiday homes for hire. The good-sized pitches are on level grass with nothing between them, and are marked and numbered by frontage stones, mostly in rows adjoining access roads. A good sized free heated pool with a paddling pool is beside the Beach Club. This contains a restaurant, two bars upstairs and a further one downstairs opening on to the pool area, open all day and serving good value food in season. A full entertainment programme, beach activities, scuba diving, windsurfing courses and a club for children are organised, and a small watersports centre is on the beach. Jet-skis are not permitted and 4-wheel drive vehicles are not allowed on the beach. The Pentewan Valley Trail, a six mile route for cycling or walking follows the old carriageway to Mevagissey with its throngs of tourists (two miles by the main road). The park and the beach have been owned by the Tremayne family for over 60 years.

Facilities

Four main toilet blocks receive heavy use in peak season but are maintained by individual cleaners. Two bathrooms, a baby room and facilities for disabled people. Well equipped laundry room. Motorcaravan service point. Large, self-service shop with off licence, bistro and fast food (Whitsun - mid-Sept). Bars, bar meals (Easter - mid-Sept, limited hours early and late season). Entertainment programme. Swimming pools (supervised and open Whitsun - mid Sept). Playground. Games room with arcade games. Tennis courts (one full size, one compact). Bicycle hire. Slipway and boat launching (Whitsun - mid Sept). Freezer service for ice packs, battery charging. Gas. Caravan and boat storage. Dogs are not accepted. Off site: Riding or golf 2 miles. Bicycle hire in village 0.5 miles.

At a glance

Welcome & Ambience	✓✓✓✓	Location	✓✓✓✓✓
Quality of Pitches	✓✓✓✓	Range of Facilities	✓✓✓✓✓

Directions

From St Austell ring road take B3273 for Mevagissey. Park is 3.5 miles, where the road meets the sea.
O.S.GR: SX018468. GPS: N50:17.297 W04:47.145

Charges 2005

Per unit incl. 2 adults, electricity	£ 10.65 - £ 24.85
extra adult	£ 1.78 - £ 4.60
child (3-15 yrs)	£ 1.10 - £ 3.45

Sea front pitch plus 10-20%.
Camping Cheques accepted.

Reservations

Made Sat - Sat or Wed - Wed with deposit (£40-£80, acc. to season), £7 booking fee and compulsory cancellation insurance (£5-10). Tel: 01726 843485. Email: info@pentewan.co.uk

Open

18 March - 30 October.

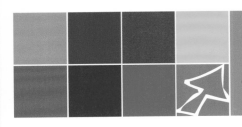

Planning your
next holiday?

don't forget to look at our directory
ON PAGE 314

UK0150 **Sea View International**

Boswinger, Gorran Haven, St Austell PL26 6LL (Cornwall)

Sea View is an impreesive, well cared for park, its quality reflected in the awards it has won. The enthusiastic owners Mr and Mrs Royden and their team are continually improving the park with the aim of providing quality camping. Although somewhat exposed, the park is colourful with flower beds and flowering shrubs and has well manicured grass of exceptional quality. The area around the swimming pool is particularly attractive, with sunbathing areas with free sun-beds on tiled terraces surrounded by flowers creating private little areas, all with magnificent views of the sea and the distant headland. A whole new area has been developed at the top of the park with uninterrupted views, 31 large, hedged, fully serviced grass pitches and a new toilet block providing excellent, en-suite family shower rooms. The remaining, established pitches (163, also with views) all have 16A electricity and 43 are fully serviced, including 12 hardstandings suitable for large motorhomes. There are 38 caravan holiday homes for hire in a separate area. A family barbecue area has been established in the large recreation field between the two areas. There is plenty to do and see in this area, from the Gardens of Heligan and Trelissick, to Lanhydroc House and the seal sanctuary, not forgetting the safe beaches, one of which is only a half mile walk from the park. A member of the Best of British group.

Facilities

Excellent toilet facilities are well maintained and heated providing for all needs, including en-suite facilities, bathrooms (on payment), baby baths and facilities for disabled visitors. Campers' kitchen. Dishwashing area. Well equipped laundry. Motorcaravan services. Shop and off-licence with gas (June-end Sept). Takeaway (Whit-mid Sept). Swimming pool (all season, heated end May-mid Sept). Large play field allowing room for activities including tennis, volleyball, badminton, football, putting green, table tennis, crazy golf, petanque. Fenced play area for under 7s. Adventure playground. Games room. Bicycle hire. Field for dog walks. Certain breeds of dog are not accepted. Off site: Fishing 0.5 miles. Boat launching 2 miles. Riding 1 mile. Golf 9 miles. Community bus picks up at the park.

Open

1 April - 31 October.

At a glance

Welcome & Ambience	✓✓✓✓✓	Location	✓✓✓✓✓
Quality of Pitches	✓✓✓✓✓	Range of Facilities	✓✓✓✓

Directions

From St Austell take B3273 towards Mevagissey; 1 mile before Mevagissey village turn right at Gorran and camp sign and continue towards Gorran for 5 miles. Fork right at camp sign and follow signs to park. O.S.GR: SW991412.
GPS: N50:14.214 W04:49.202

Charges 2005

Per unit incl. 2 persons, electricity	£ 11.00 - £ 26.00
incl. water and drainage	£ 13.00 - £ 28.00
extra person (over 4 yrs)	£ 3.50 - £ 5.00
pup tent	£ 2.00
dog (limited breeds and numbers)	£ 2.00
Special off-peak offers.	

Reservations

Min 7 nights, w/e - w/e, 19/7-30/8. other times, any length, with £50 deposit and £2 fee.
Tel: 01726 843425.
Email: holidays@seaviewinternational.com

UK0090 **Trethem Mill Touring Park**

St Just-in-Roseland, St Mawes, Truro TR2 5JF (Cornwall)

St Mawes is a very popular, pretty village on the Roseland peninsula, which is itself an 'area of outstanding natural beauty'. Only three miles away, Trethem Mill is well placed for either sailing, walking the coastal path around the peninsula, visiting the gardens of Trelissick or Heligan, or simply lazing on the nearby beaches. The Akeroyd family are proud of their park and work hard to keep it really well maintained. Trethem is a 'strictly touring' park with 84 pitches, of which 50 have 16A electricity and with several classified as all-weather. The pitches are large, most on slightly sloping ground, with the lower field more level and sheltered. All are individual or in bays, divided by hedging (some still growing) giving your own area. Generally there is a good spacious feel, with a tarmac circular access road and careful landscaping (it is a mass of colour in season). The area around reception is particularly pretty where a small watermill has been built amongst the flowers – the sound of gently flowing water is very relaxing. Trethem Mill aims to attract couples and families who seek peace and tranquillity, and can manage without a bar and on site entertainment.

Facilities

The central toilet block is of a very high standard and kept spotlessly clean. Heated in cooler weather, it is well equipped. A room for disabled visitors doubles as a family room. Laundry and dishwashing sinks. Reception/shop, only small but well stocked and licensed. Freezer for ice packs (free). Motorcaravan services. Games room. Well equipped, fenced adventure playground (closed at 9 pm). Large field alongside the park is used as a recreation and ball game area. Extra field for dog walking. Off site: Fishing 1.5 miles. Boat launching 2 miles. Bicycle hire 4 miles. Golf 6 miles. Riding 8 miles.

At a glance

Welcome & Ambience	✓✓✓✓✓	Location	✓✓✓✓✓
Quality of Pitches	✓✓✓✓✓	Range of Facilities	✓✓✓

Directions

From Tregony follow A3078 to St Mawes. Avout 2 miles after passing through Trewithian, watch for caravan and camping sign. O.S.GR: SW863264.

Charges 2005

Per unit incl. 2 persons	£ 10.00 - £ 14.00
with electricity	£ 2.00
extra person	£ 4.00
child (3-14 yrs)	£ 3.00
dog	£ 1.00

Reservations

Made with £30 deposit. Tel: 01872 580504. Email: reception@trethem.com

Open

1 April - mid October.

UK0180 Carnon Downs Caravan & Camping Park

Carnon Downs, Truro TR3 6JJ (Cornwall)

Carnon Downs is an excellent all year park run personally and enthusiastically by Simon Valence, a very forward thinking owner. It has been thoughtfully laid out so that all pitches back onto attractive hedging or areas of flowering shrubs and arranged to provide some pleasant bays or other, more open grass areas. Gravel roads connect the 140 pitches, most with electricity (10/16A) and over 70 with hardstanding. Of these 43 are fully serviced, with the new ones being exceptionally large and surrounded by young shrubs. On arrival you will receive a warm welcome, a neatly presented layout plan of the park and a touring information pack including comprehensive details on walks and cycle paths leading from the park. Some of the park's amenities are to be found in the round-house next to the TV and information room. The round-house used to house the donkeys that turned the mill which once operated on the site! Although one side of the park is next to the A39 road, it is well screened with a band of mature woodland so noise should be minimal. This quiet, quality family park is well situated to explore the tip of Cornwall. A member of the Best of British group.

Facilities

An excellent modern, light and airy, heated block provides 12 en-suite units and dishwashing. Two other well maintained toilet blocks, also heated, include some washbasins in cubicles and showers (unisex). Three good family bath/shower rooms, one suitable for use by disabled people or families. Mother and toddler room, two baby sinks and full sized bath. Two laundries with freezers. Motorcaravan service point (ask at reception). Gas, newspapers and caravan accessories. General room with TV, library, table tennis and tourist information. Recycling centre. Good dog walks. Caravan storage. Off site: Pub/restaurant 100 yds across the road. Fishing 3 miles. Riding or bicycle hire 2 miles. Golf 1 mile. Walks direct from site.

At a glance

Welcome & Ambience	✓✓✓✓✓	Location	✓✓✓✓
Quality of Pitches	✓✓✓✓✓	Range of Facilities	✓✓✓

Directions

From Truro take A39 Falmouth road. After 3 miles, park entrance is directly off the Carnon Downs roundabout. O.S.GR: SW805406.

Charges 2005

Per unit incl. 2 persons, electricity	£ 13.00 - £ 18.00
extra adult	£ 2.00
child (5-14 yrs)	£ 1.70
all service hardstanding	£ 2.00

Reservations

Made with £20 deposit p/week. Tel: 01872 862283. Email: info@carnon-downs-caravanpark.co.uk

Open

All year.

UK0450 Pennance Mill Farm Chalet & Camping Park

Maenporth, Falmouth TR11 5HJ (Cornwall)

Pennance Mill Farm has been in the hands of the Jewell family for three generations and is listed as a typical Cornish farmstead in an Area of Outstanding Natural Beauty (ANOB) and you can enjoy the woodland walk with 200 year old beech trees. In the high season skittles, country games and barbecue evenings are organised, all in keeping with the relaxed and friendly atmosphere generated by the owners. The camping area is situated in three sheltered south-facing and fairly level fields with views over the countryside and providing for 75 pitches, 40 of which have 16A electricity and 3 hardstanding. Caravans are accepted however this is not a site for those who like neat manicured lawns and flower beds. An old mill wheel reminds one of the site's origins and you book in at the farmhouse. Continuing on past the site for half a mile, you come to the sandy beach at Maenporth safe for bathing, windsurfing and diving.

Facilities

The two toilet blocks are fully equipped. The first near the entrance is the original one but it is well kept with good hot water, washing machine, dryer, laundry and dishwashing sinks. The block in the top meadow is more modern, heated and includes dishwashing sinks. Small farm shop including some basic provisions (open 9.00-10.30 and 5.30-6.30). Gas available. Small play meadow with new play equipment. Table tennis. Off site: New Maritime Museum. Tennis courts, golf course and pitch and putt within walking distance. Coastal footpath to the Helford River.

Open

Easter - November.

At a glance

Welcome & Ambience	✓✓✓✓	Location	✓✓✓✓
Quality of Pitches	✓✓✓	Range of Facilities	✓✓✓

Directions

From Truro, follow signs for Falmouth on A39. At first roundabout pass Asda then turn right at next roundabout signed Maenporth and industrial estates (on Bickland Water Road). Follow brown international camping signs for 1.5 miles and continue down the hill to site on your left as the road bends to the right. O.S.GR: SW789307.

Charges 2006

Per adult	£ 4.00 - £ 5.00
child (over 3 yrs)	£ 1.50 - £ 2.00
pitch	£ 3.00 - £ 4.00
awning	£ 1.50 - £ 2.00
electricity	£ 2.00
dog	£ 1.50

Reservations

Contact park. Tel: 01326 317431.

UK0070 Silver Sands Holiday Park

Gwendreath, Ruan Minor, Helston TR12 7LZ (Cornwall)

Under new ownership, Silver Sands is a small, peaceful 'away-from-it-all' park in a remote part of the Lizard peninsula, the most southerly part of mainland Britain and an 'area of outstanding natural beauty'. The park is only reached after passing Culdrose Naval Base and the Goonhilly Earth Station down a single track road. Silver Sands is tucked away behind two other holiday home parks (possible noise in season) . A half mile footpath leads down through a small valley to the twin beaches of Kennack Sands (one is dog-free) divided by a small headland. This is generally an unspoilt walking area with the coastal path passing through and under the care of English Nature. The park itself has 14 caravan holiday homes, along with 36 touring pitches of which 20 have 5A electrical hook-ups. The pitches are large, attractively situated and divided into individual bays by growing flowering shrubs and bushes. The adjoining tent field has similar pitches (4 with electricity) where the shrubs are growing (some pitches are slightly sloping). A member of the Countryside Discovery group.

Facilities

The toilet block has been completely refurbished to provide modern facilities. En-suite room for disabled visitors, doubling as a family room. Some play equipment. An undeveloped three-acre field can be used for walking, kite flying, etc. Off site: Restaurant 20 yards on the next park, pub within walking distance. Fishing 1 mile. Bicycle hire 5 miles. Boat launching 2 or 7 miles. Riding 5 miles. Golf 6 miles.

Open

Easter - mid September.

At a glance

Welcome & Ambience ✓✓✓✓✓ Location ✓✓✓✓
Quality of Pitches ✓✓✓✓ Range of Facilities ✓✓✓

Directions

From Helston take A3038 Lizard road. After Culdrose turn left on B3293 passing Goonhilly after 4 miles. At next crossroads turn right (Kennack Sands), continue for 1.5 miles then left to Gwendreath on single track road - site is 1 mile. O.S.GR: SW732170.

Charges 2005

Per unit incl. 2 adults, 2 children and electricity	£ 11.00 - £ 16.50
extra adult	£ 2.50 - £ 3.90
child (3-16 yrs)	£ 1.10 - £ 1.80
extra pup tent	£ 1.70
dog	£ 1.10 - £ 1.80

Reductions for some bookings.

Reservations

Made with 25% deposit, min. £30; balance on arrival. Tel: 01326 290631.
Email: enquiries@silversandsholidaypark.co.uk

UK0490 Mullion Holiday Park

Helston TR12 7LJ (Cornwall)

For those who enjoy plenty of entertainment, both social and active in a holiday environment, Mullion would be a good choice. This holiday park is situated on the Lizard peninsula with its sandy beaches and coves. It has all the trimmings - indoor and outdoor pools, super play areas, clubs, bars and a wide range of nightly entertainment. Recent developments include a new look 'Stargate Club' and a 'village square' with a bandstand. These amenities form the core of the park and are well organised and managed. The touring area past the holiday homes has a more relaxed atmosphere and is set on natural heathland with clumps of bramble and gorse which provide breaks and recesses making for a more informal layout. Linked by a circular gravel road, all 160 pitches are numbered, 10 with hardstanding and 105 with electricity connections (16A). Land drainage could be a problem if there is heavy continuous rain. A resident warden is now based at the entrance to the touring section. Eurotents for hire. There is much to see in the area including Goonhilly Satellite Station and Flambards Village, the theme park, Lizard Point and Lands End.

Facilities

A central modern toilet block is fully equipped and includes a baby unit and bath. It is supplemented with additional 'portacabin' style facilities for high season. Dishwashing sinks under cover, two laundry sinks and two washing machines. Large launderette in main complex. Freezer pack service. Large supermarket with off licence. Pub with family room, restaurant and takeaway (half board or breakfast options). Stargate Club with live shows and cabarets, big screen satellite TV. Excellent outdoor play areas (fenced). Toddlers' soft play area. Amusement arcade, bowling alley. Heated outdoor pool and paddling pool (26/5-8/9). Heated indoor fun pool with slide, both supervised. Sauna and solarium. Crazy golf, pitch and putt. Barbecue.

Open

20 May - 9 September.

At a glance

Welcome & Ambience ✓✓✓✓ Location ✓✓✓✓
Quality of Pitches ✓✓✓ Range of Facilities ✓✓✓✓✓

Directions

From Helston take A3083 for The Lizard and continue for 7 miles. Site on left immediately after the right turning for Mullion. O.S.GR: SW698185.
GPS: N50:01.267 W05:12.883

Charges 2005

Per pitch (incl. free club membership)	£ 12.50 - £ 25.50
electricity	£ 3.00
super hook-up incl. electricity, TV point, fresh water	£ 17.00 - £ 30.00
awning	£ 5.00
dog (one only)	£ 5.00

Half board or breakfast options available.

Reservations

Contact site. High season and Spr. B.H. bookings must be Sat. - Sat. Tel: 0870 4445344.
Email: touring@weststarholidays.co.uk

See advertisement on pg 104

BOSCREGE
CARAVAN & CAMPING PARK

★ Special out of season offers
★ Award winning quiet family park close to local beaches and attractions with no bar or clubs
★ Free showers ★ Microwave facilities
★ Games room ★ Child's play area
★ Laundry ★ Pets welcome

For Brochure Telephone:
01736 762231
www.caravanparkcornwall.com
enquiries@caravanparkcornwall.com
Ashton, Nr Helston, Cornwall TR13 9TG

UK0480 Boscrege Caravan Park

Ashton, Helston TR13 9TG (Cornwall)

A pretty little site covering 12 acres and hidden deep in the countryside in an area of outstanding natural beauty (ANOB), Boscrege will suit those who want a quiet peaceful base for their Cornish holiday. The main large touring field nestles at the foot of Tregonning Hill with its striking hill top cross, and has neatly cut grass with a gentle slope from the top. The pitches are generously spaced around the edge, backing on to hedging and leaving plenty of room in the centre for ball games. Three small, attractive paddock areas, two with caravan holiday homes (26 in total), the other for tourers, complete the total provision of 51 pitches, 28 with 10A electricity. A nature trail has been developed which will help you identify the birds which can be seen around the park. This is a welcome retreat for couples and families with young children.

Facilities	Directions
The traditional style toilet block is showing its age somewhat but is fully equipped including a smaller basin for children (M/F). Dishwashing sinks, laundry sink, washing machine and dryer and microwave. Reception keeps emergency supplies. Two play areas for smaller children and central ball area. Amusement machines, pool table and TV room. Off site: Godolphin House and garden. Whole of the tip of Cornwall easily accessible – the Lizard, Lands End. Nearest beach (Praa Sands) 2 miles. Fishing 1 mile. Golf and riding 2 miles. Bicycle hire and boat launching 5 miles.	From Helston take A394 for Penzance. At top of Sithney Common Hill turn right just before Jet garage onto B3302 (Hayle) road. Pass Sithney General Stores on left and take next left for Carleen and Godolphin Cross. Continue on this road to Godolphin Cross village and turn left at side of Godolphin Arms signed Ashton. Proceed up hill bearing left at top until you see camp signs where road turns sharply left and go straight over into lane leading to Boscrege. O.S.GR: 593305.

Open

Easter/1 April - 31 October.

Charges 2005

Per unit	£ 6.75 - £ 13.75
electricity	£ 2.50
extra small tent	£ 2.50
No charge for dogs (max. 3).	

At a glance

Welcome & Ambience	✓✓✓	Location	✓✓✓✓
Quality of Pitches	✓✓✓	Range of Facilities	✓✓✓

Reservations

Made with deposit of £35 per week or part week.
Tel: 01736 762231.
Email: enquiries@caravanparkcornwall.com

UK0065 Wayfarers Camping & Caravan Park

Relubbus Lane, St Hilary, Penzance TR20 9EF (Cornwall)

Wayfarers is a neat and tidy, garden like park reserved for adults only in rural Cornwall. Sheltered by perimeter trees and consisting of two finely mown fields interspersed by shrubs and palm-like trees, 42 places are available for caravans (up to 23 ft, single axle), motorcaravans (up to 22 ft) and tents, plus 4 holiday caravans to rent. There are 32 pitches with 16A electricity with hardstanding available on 22. The Lizard and Lands End with the Minnack Theatre wait to be explored and St Michael's Mount is only 2 miles away. Should you enjoy walking you can follow the River Hayle down to St Erth. There are many more suggestions with maps and leaflets in the information room, including a star chart. The owners Elaine and Steve live on site and make you very welcome maintaining the park to a high standard. Do look at the dolls house in the shop. Built by Elaine's father the detail is amazing.

Facilities	Directions
The modern toilet block is fully equipped. Ladies have a wash cubicle and there are two smart en-suite shower rooms (key system). Fully equipped laundry. Dishwashing sinks in own house. Recycling bins. Shop stocks basics. Off site: Two pubs with food in Goldsithney 1 mile. Fishing 1 mile. Golf 1.5 miles. Riding 1 mile. Bicycle hire 2 miles. Boat launching 5 miles. Beach 2 miles. Sailing 5 miles.	Following the A30 Penzance road take the A394 Helston road after the St Ives turning. Follow for approx 1 mile then turn left on the B3280 and pass through Goldsithney village and site is 1 mile further on left. O.S.GR: SW559314. GPS: N50:07.990 W05:25.010

Open

March - October.

Charges 2005

Per adult	£ 1.75 - £ 3.00
pitch	£ 4.00 - £ 5.00
incl. electricity	£ 6.00 - £ 7.00
dog	£ 1.50

At a glance

Welcome & Ambience	✓✓✓✓✓	Location	✓✓✓✓
Quality of Pitches	✓✓✓✓	Range of Facilities	✓✓✓

Reservations

Made with £20 deposit. Tel: 01736 763326.
Email: wayfarers@eurobell.co.uk

South West England

(27)

UK0060 River Valley Country Park

Relubbus, Penzance TR20 9ER (Cornwall)

River Valley is a quiet park in the natural environment of a pleasant river valley. Run by Brian and Eileen Milsom, it provides 150 large, well spaced touring pitches in small meadows or natural clearings. Most are clearly defined with shrubs, hedges or trees which have been planted to supplement where needed and in the more open areas to edge the pitch space thus giving your own individual area. Most pitches have electrical connections (15A) and hardstanding, with special sections for families, couples and tents. There are now 60 caravan holiday homes and lodges, some privately owned, in more or less separate areas, beside the river at the far end of the park or on the hillside at the back. There is no playground, but tame ducks on the river will entertain. A fence separates the park from the river and there is a pleasant walk for 2.5 miles alongside it, popular for dog walks. St Michael's Mount is only 3 miles and can be reached by footpath. Much of the valley is a protected nature reserve and the park encourages wildlife by not using weed killers and by leaving parts uncut - badgers, foxes, herons, kingfishers and glow-worms are regular visitors. A member of the Best of British group.

Facilities

Three good quality, carefully maintained toilet blocks are well placed for all pitches. Two male and two female family shower rooms are in the block at the far end. Some private cabins for ladies and make-up room with hair dryers. Separate laundry facilities and baby bath. Covered dishwashing sinks. Motorcaravan service point. Shop/reception. Off site: Bicycle hire 5 miles, riding or golf 3 miles.

Open

23 March - 31 October and Christmas.

At a glance

Welcome & Ambience	✓✓✓✓✓	Location	✓✓✓✓✓
Quality of Pitches	✓✓✓✓✓	Range of Facilities	✓✓✓✓

Directions

From A30 at St Michaels Mount roundabout, take A394 towards Helston. At next roundabout take B3280 to Relubbus. In approx. 3 miles in village turn left just over a small bridge. O.S.GR: SW566320.

Charges 2005

Per unit incl. 2 adults	£ 7.00 - £ 12.00
incl. electricity	£ 8.50 - £ 13.50
extra person	£ 1.50 - £ 3.25
dog	£ 1.50

Min. charge 2 adults per vehicle.

Reservations

Any period with deposit (£20). Tel: 01736 763398. Email: rivervally@surfbay.dircon.co.uk

Situated in one of the most picturesque Valleys in Cornwall

Located along the bank of a clear shallow stream, River Valley offers you a sense of utter peace and tranquillity.

Discover River Valley

- 150 Touring, Motorhome or Tent pitches
- 18 Acres of partly wooded countryside
- Luxury Caravan Holiday Homes available
- Shop and Launderette
- Wooden Lodges available

River Valley Country Park, Relubbus, Penzance, Cornwall, TR20 9ER
Tel 0845 60 12 516   Fax 01736 763398
www.rivervalley.co.uk   rivervalley@surfbay.dircon.co.uk

UK0040 Trevalgan Holiday Farm

Trevalgan Farm, St Ives TR26 3BJ (Cornwall)

Trevalgan is now owned by the same family that own Ayr Holiday Park (page 31). It is a quiet, traditional style of park, located on the cliffs 1.5 miles west of bustling St Ives. There are 120 clearly marked pitches (at least 43 with 16A electricity) in two level fields edged by Cornish stone walls – it could be a little exposed on a windy day. The park is very popular with walkers with direct access to the coastal path. It is a 45 minutes walk to St Ives. A member of the Countryside Discovery group.

Facilities

A purpose built toilet block has curtained washbasins, plus a baby room, laundry and washing up, and even a hot drinks machine. Small shop (1/6-15/9). Takeaway (July/Aug), popular for breakfast or suppers. Gas available. Games field, play area and crazy golf. Games room and a comfortable upstairs TV room. Off site: Fishing 3 miles, bicycle hire 8 miles, riding and golf 2 miles. In July/Aug. bus service from the park to St Ives (10 am. returning at 5 pm).

Open

Easter - 30 September.

At a glance

Welcome & Ambience	✓✓✓✓	Location	✓✓✓✓
Quality of Pitches	✓✓✓	Range of Facilities	✓✓✓

Directions

Approach site down a narrow Cornish lane from the B3306 St Ives - Lands End road, following sign. O.S.GR: SW490400.

Charges 2005

Per caravan or tent	£ 4.50 - £ 7.00
motorcaravan	£ 5.50 - £ 9.00
car	£ 1.00 - £ 2.00
adult	£ 2.50 - £ 4.00
child (5-16 yrs)	£ 1.25 - £ 2.00
serviced pitch met elektriciteit	£ 2.75

Reservations

Contact park. Tel: 01736 796433. Email: camping@trevalganholidayfarm.co.uk

UK0470 Little Trevarrack Tourist Park

Laity Lane, Carbis Bay, St Ives TR26 3HW (Cornwall)

Little Trevarrack is a traditional Cornish park covering 16 acres, with wonderful views from the top of the site across St Ives bay towards Hayle and the surrounding countryside. It is owned by Neil Osborne, son of the owners of Polmanter Park, and now has a smart, large, new reception and entrance. There are 233 pitches, in four open fields (the top ones with gentle slopes), 168 with 16A electricity. Bushes are now growing and beginning to form hedging to provide individual type pitches and give a continental appearance to the park. Further developments include a new play area and a games room in the reception building with pool tables, table football and table tennis. Carbis Bay is less than a mile and in high season a bus runs hourly into St Ives (10.00-23.30 hrs). This is a developing park which will provide a quiet, peaceful base from which to explore St Ives and the southern tip of Cornwall.

Facilities

The large, central toilet block is modern and well equipped. Dishwashing sinks under cover. Baby room and new facilities for disabled visitors in the reception building. Laundry. Games room. Play area and play field. Putting. No kites allowed. Early and late arrivals area.
Off site: Dogs are banned from the St Ives beaches in high season. Supermarket nearby, also fish and chips and pasta restaurants. Fishing 1 mile. Golf and riding 2 miles. Beach 1 mile.

Open

Easter - end-October.

At a glance

Welcome & Ambience	✓✓✓✓	Location	✓✓✓✓
Quality of Pitches	✓✓✓✓	Range of Facilities	✓✓✓

Directions

Follow signs for St Ives and take A3074 to Carbis Bay. Site is signed on left opposite junction to Carbis Bay beach. Follow road for 150 yds, cross small crossroads and site is 250 m. on right . O.S.GR: SW52737
GPS: N50:11.234 W05:28.250

Charges 2005

Per unit incl. 2 persons	£ 9.00 - £ 16.00
incl. electricity	£ 11.50 - £ 18.50
extra adult	£ 2.50 - £ 4.50
dog (max. 2)	£ 1.00 - £ 1.50
child (3-15 yrs)	£ 1.75 - £ 2.50

Reservations

Made with non-returnable deposit of £35 per week booked. Tel: 01736 797580.
Email: littletrevarrack@hotmail.com

UK0050 Polmanter Tourist Park

Halestown, St Ives TR26 3LX (Cornwall)

The Osborne family have worked hard to develop Polmanter and it is a good example of a sympathetic conversion of a farm from agricultural to leisure use. The park is attractively laid out with wonderful country and sea views. The converted farm buildings provide a cosy bar lounge overlooking the heated swimming pool, toddler's pool and sunbathing area and good value meals are served. There is a family area with high chairs and a conservatory between the bar and the pool provides extra space for families (open all day, with a hot drinks machine). Occasional entertainment is organised in season. The 260 touring pitches (no caravan holiday homes) are well spaced in several fields with growing, but established, shrubs and hedges giving large, level, individual pitches with connecting tarmac roads. There are 87 serviced pitches with electricity, water and waste water, 10 with hardstanding. The other 115 pitches all have 16A electricity. It is a busy park with a happy atmosphere within 1.5 miles of St Ives - a footpath leads from the park (20 minutes downhill) or there is a bus service from the park in high season (hourly, 10 am. - midnight). The park gates are closed midnight - 6.30 am. with outside parking. A member of the Best of British group.

Facilities

The toilet blocks vary - as the park has grown, so extra blocks have been added. All can be heated and one has been nicely refurbished with 4 family rooms and facilities for diabled visitors. Two extra family shower rooms and a baby room beside the fully equipped laundry. Dishwashing sinks. Motorcaravan service point. Well stocked shop, bar with food and family area (Whitsun - mid Sept). Takeaway. Swimming pool (Whitsun - mid Sept). Tennis courts. Minigolf. Play areas. Sports field. Games room with two pool tables, table tennis and games machines.
Off site: Golf 1 mile. Fishing, riding, bicycle hire and boat launching facilities within 2 miles. New indoor pool and leisure centre at St Ives. Note: dogs are banned from the St Ives beaches in high season.

At a glance

Welcome & Ambience	✓✓✓✓✓	Location	✓✓✓✓✓
Quality of Pitches	✓✓✓✓✓	Range of Facilities	✓✓✓✓✓

Directions

Take A3074 to St Ives from the A30 and then first left at a mini-roundabout taking 'Holiday Route' (B3311) to St Ives (Halestown). At T-junction turn right for Halestown, right again at the Halestown Inn then first left. O.S.GR: SW509392.
GPS: N50:11.771 W05:29.461

Charges 2005

Per unit incl. 2 persons, awning	£ 11.00 - £ 19.00
incl. mains services	£ 13.50 - £ 24.00
extra adult	£ 2.50 - £ 5.00
child (3-15 yrs)	£ 2.00 - £ 4.00
dog	free - £ 2.00

Camping Cheques accepted.

Reservations

Made with £30 non-refundable deposit. Contact site for details of min. stays. Tel: 01736 795640.
Email: reception@polmanter.com

Open

Easter - 31 October (full facilities to 10 Sept).

UK0030 **Ayr Holiday Park**

Higher Ayr, St Ives TR26 1EJ (Cornwall)

Ayr Holiday Park has an unparalleled position overlooking St Ives Bay and Porthmeor beach and is a popular well cared for site. On first arrival it may seem to be all caravan holiday homes, but behind them is a series of naturally sloping fields with marvellous views providing a total of 90 pitches, of which 40 are for touring caravans and motorcaravans. These pitches are on grass, all with 16A electricity and 15 fully serviced. An extra field for tents is open in July and August. A 'state of the art' toilet block provides excellent facilities in a colourful and modern design. St Ives centre with restaurants, bars and supermarkets is within easy walking distance, as is the new Tate Gallery. There is direct access to the coastal footpath.

Facilities

The super new toilet block includes two family shower rooms and facilities for baby changing and disabled people. Wetsuit showers. Fully equipped laundry room. Motorcaravan point. Games room with pool table and TV, hot drinks and snack machines. Adventure play area and football field. One dog per pitch, up to medium size, is permitted but contact the park as dogs are not allowed on St Ives beaches in high season. Off site: Spa shop nearby. Tate Gallery and beaches within walking distance. Leisure centre with indoor pool nearby. Golf 1 mile. Riding 2 miles. Sea and coarse fishing 2-3 miles.

Open

All year.

At a glance

Welcome & Ambience	✓✓✓✓	Location	✓✓✓✓✓
Quality of Pitches	✓✓✓✓	Range of Facilities	✓✓✓✓

Directions

Three hundred yards after leaving the A30 turn left at mini-roundabout following signs for St Ives for heavy vehicles and day visitors (not town centre direction). After approx. 2 miles this joins the B3311 and then the B3306 about 1 mile from St Ives (an octagonal building on your left). Still heading for St Ives turn left at a mini-roundabout following camping signs through residential areas. Park entrance is 600 yds at Ayr Terrace. O.S.GR: SW515388.

Charges 2005

Per adult	£ 2.75 - £ 4.50
child (5-16 yrs)	£ 1.30 - £ 2.25
pitch	£ 5.50 - £ 13.00
with services, plus	free - £ 3.00
awning	£ 2.50 - £ 5.00
dog	free - £ 1.50

Reservations

Made with £35 deposit. Tel: 01736 795855.
Email: recept@ayrholidaypark.co.uk

UK0015 **Rose Hill Touring Park**

Porthtowan, Truro TR4 8AR (Cornwall)

The road down to Porthtowan takes you past tall chimneys, stark on the skyline, evocative of the Cornwall mining era. Porthtowan itself is a super little Cornish holiday village offering one of the UK's premier surfing beaches (with 'Blue Flag' status). Cafés, bars, surf schools – it has it all, but the park itself, situated back from the village and hidden from it, is something else again. It has a sheltered situation in a quite steep, wooded valley of broad leaf trees edged with natural vegetation that encourages wild life. We understand, for example, that the garlic mustard plant attracts the orange tipped butterfly and a tawny owl nests every year overlooking the park. The 50 grass pitches, terraced where necessary, are neatly cut and just fit in, with car space allocated where necessary. All pitches have 10/16A electricity and 8 have hardstanding. The village and beach are within easy walking distance (4 minutes) and should meet all your needs. It is wiser to leave your car on site. If you want to go further, St Austell with the Eden Project, Falmouth with the Maritime Museum and St Ives with the Tate Gallery are all nearby. In fact, Lands End is only 28 miles. The site is family run, very comfortable and well maintained in a delightful environment – good for families or couples, not suitable for huge twin axle caravans.

Facilities

Modern heated toilet block with coded access, very well equipped with some en-suite units. Facilities for disabled people but some up and down walking. Wet suit wash, also useful to wash sand off! Covered dishwashing sinks. Fully equipped laundry, sink useful as baby bath. Telephone - mobile phones do not work on site or in the village. Small licensed shop (some camping equipment; limited hours out of season). Crusty bread, croissants and traditional cornish pasties baked to order. Dogs not accepted July/Aug (dogs are not allowed on the beach Easter Sunday - 1 Oct). Off site: Large play area in village.

Open

1 April - 26 September.

At a glance

Welcome & Ambience	✓✓✓✓✓	Location	✓✓✓✓✓
Quality of Pitches	✓✓✓✓	Range of Facilities	✓✓✓✓

Directions

From Chiverton Cross roundabout on A30 (near Redruth) take exit for St Agnes (B3277) and follow for about 1 mile. Turn left for Porthtowan, passing garage on right and Beach Road (which goes into the village), and continue up hill to site 100 yds on left. O.S.GR:SW693472

Charges 2005

Per unit incl. 2 persons and car	£ 12.00 - £ 18.00
extra person	£ 5.00
child (over 2 yrs)	£ 2.50
electricity	£ 2.50
dog (excl. July/Aug)	£ 1.80

Caravans not taken 16 July - 4 Sept. Discounts for couples and families (outside July/Aug).

Reservations

Made with non-refundable deposit (£5 per day). Tel: 01209 890802.
Email: reception@rosehillcamping.co.uk

UK0120 **Silverbow Park**

Goonhavern, Truro TR4 9NX (Cornwall)

Silverbow has been developed by the Taylor family over many years and they are justifiably proud of their efforts. It is a select and spacious park seeking to encourage couples and quiet families with young children (no over 12s). The Taylors believe Silverbow is a way of life and staying is an experience – they have certainly created a relaxed and tranquil atmosphere. Hard work, planting and landscaping has provided a beautiful environment set in 21 acres. There are 90 tourist pitches, all of good size and with 69 'super' pitches in a newly developed area, with electricity, water and drainaway, which are even larger. Many are on a slight slope with some attractive views. There are also 15 park-owned, high quality leisure homes. Much free space includes an excellent sports area with two all-weather tennis courts (free coaching in season), two outdoor badminton courts, as well as wild meadow and wooded areas ideal for walks. A natural area with ponds has been created to encourage wildlife (Silverbow was the first in Cornwall to gain the coveted '5-year Bellamy Gold' award). The park is 2.5 miles from the long sandy beach at Perranporth (30 minutes walk away from traffic) and 6 miles from Newquay.

Facilities	Directions
Three good toilet blocks include private cabins for each sex, four family shower/toilet rooms, two accessible for wheelchairs, and a bath on payment. Enclosed dishwashing sinks. Laundry room. Motorcaravan services. Recycling bins. Free freezer service. Shop (mid May-mid Sept). Attractive, kidney shaped, heated swimming pool and small paddling pool (mid-May - mid-Sept) sheltered by high surrounding garden walls. Games room with pool table, table tennis and tourist information. Adventure playground and general play field. Tennis and badminton courts. Short mat bowls. Mountain biking from the park (but no bikes on site). Off site: Riding and fishing nearby. Concessionary green fees at Perranporth golf club. Pub within walking distance.	Entrance is directly off the main A3075 road 0.5 miles south of Goonhavern. O.S.GR: SW781531. GPS: N50:20.194 W05:07.238

Charges 2005

Per unit incl. 2 adults	£ 8.00 - £ 17.00
extra adult under 50 yrs	£ 3.00 - £ 6.00
extra child (2-12 yrs) or adult over 50 yrs	£ 2.50 - £ 4.50
full service pitch incl. electricity	£ 4.00
Discounts available.	

Reservations

Made with £20 p/week deposit (Sat. - Sat. only 17/7-21/8). Tel: 01872 572347.

Open

4 May - 28 September.

At a glance

Welcome & Ambience	✓✓✓✓✓	Location	✓✓✓✓✓
Quality of Pitches	✓✓✓✓	Range of Facilities	✓✓✓✓

UK0012 **Killiwerris Camping & Caravan Park**

Penstraze, Chacewater, Truro TR4 8PF (Cornwall)

Tucked down a Cornish lane, Killiwerris is a rare find. Lin and Mike Hill have developed a small and delightful touring park which provides 20 good-sized pitches. Seventeen are semi-separated either by low fencing or hedging, nine with hardstanding in the front field which is more like a garden with flowering shrubs sheltered by Monteray pines and other indigenous trees. The birds love it, as do adult humans – the park is 'adult only' so it is very peaceful. Electricity (10/16A) is available for all the pitches with water points between two. This is an ideal base and you will be sure of a warm welcome.

Facilities	Directions
A small heated toilet block provides for all needs with ladies having one cubicle. Laundry room. Off site: Bus stop 8 minutes walk. Village (shop, pub, etc.) 1 mile. Beach 4.5 miles. Fishing 2 miles. Golf 2 miles. Bicycle hire 2-3 miles.	From the A30, exit at Chiverton Cross roundabout (28 miles west of Bodmin signed Truro/St Agnes). Take exit for Blackwater. Turn left into Kea Down Road to park in 1 mile. O.S.GR: SW753455.

Open

Easter - end October.

Charges 2005

Per unit incl. 2 persons, electricity	£ 10.00 - £ 12.00
extra adult	£ 3.00

Reservations

Made with deposit. Tel: 01872 561356.
Email: lin@killiwerristp.fsnet.co.uk

At a glance

Welcome & Ambience	✓✓✓✓✓	Location	✓✓✓✓
Quality of Pitches	✓✓✓✓✓	Range of Facilities	✓✓✓

UK0010 Chacewater Park

Cox Hill, Chacewater, Truro TR4 8LY (Cornwall)

For those who want to be away from the hectic coastal resorts and to take advantage of the peace and quiet of an 'adults only' park, this will be an excellent value-for-money choice. Chacewater has a pleasant rural situation and the site is run with care and attention by Richard Peterken and his daughters Debbie and Mandy. It provides 100 level touring pitches, all with electricity (10A) and 80 with hardstanding, in two large field areas (slight slope) edged with trees or in small bays formed by hedges. There are 29 serviced pitches (electricity, water, drainage and sewage) and an area for dog owners. The modern reception is not at the entrance but through the park to one side in a pleasant courtyard area. Truro is only 5 miles and there is a good choice of beaches north or south within 5-10 miles.

Facilities

The main toilet block provides well equipped showers and two en-suite units, along with dishwashing sinks under cover and a laundry room. Second fully equipped block near reception providing roomy showers open direct to outside. Gas supplies. Icepack service. Only adults are accepted (over 30 yrs). One dog only (by arrangement).
Off site: Golf, riding and bicycle hire, all within 3 miles. Cornish tramways/railway coast to coast trail to walk or cycle nearby.

Open

1 May - 30 September.

At a glance

Welcome & Ambience	✓✓✓✓	Location	✓✓✓✓
Quality of Pitches	✓✓✓✓✓	Range of Facilities	✓✓✓

Directions

From the A30 about 28 miles west of Bodmin take A3047 signed Scorrier and continue under bridge to roundabout and take left towards St Day. Continue for 500 yds turning right at the crossroads on B3298 (St Day) and continue for 1 mile. Turn left at crossroads and continue for 0.75 miles, then turn left at blue camping sign (by Truro Tractors). Chacewater Park is the next right. O.S.GR: SW742439.

Charges 2005

Per unit incl. 2 persons from   £ 11.00 - £ 14.50
Weekly rates for pre-booked pitches. Discounts for senior citizens. Weekly rates for pre-booked pitches.

Reservations

Made with a deposit of £15 (standard pitch) or £25 (serviced pitch) per week or part week, balance on arrival. Tel: 01209 820762.
Email: chacepark@aol.com

UK0510 Summer Valley Touring Park

Shortlanesend, Truro TR4 9DW (Cornwall)

Approached down a short single track road from the Truro - Perranporth road this is a quiet and mature, but very pleasant, small rural park suitable for visiting both the north and south coast of Cornwall. South facing, the park consists of a large well kept grass area with reception and facilities to one side. A tarmac road circles this and mature trees edge the whole site providing shelter but still allowing rural views. Caravans go on the central area which slopes gently and is divided down the centre with more mature trees and shrubs. The pitches around the perimeter area are semi-divided by shrubs and used more for tents. In total there is provision for 60 units of all types, 45 with electricity connections (10/16A). A pleasant little sitting room provides a small library and tourist information. The owners live on site and provide a warm welcome. A Countryside Discovery site.

Facilities

A good quality, solid toilet block is well maintained with ladies to the left and men to the right, plus unisex showers. Washbasins in cabins and one shower/toilet en-suite per sex. Dishwashing and laundry sinks are in the same building. Laundry facilities. Reception/licensed shop (basics) with freezer pack service (reduced hours out of main season). Gas supplies. Small play area hidden in a corner but part of the central area is left for ball games.
Off site: Village of Shortlanesend within walking distance with post office and pub. Fishing 2.5 miles. Golf 3 miles. Riding 5 miles. Bicycle hire 2.5 miles. Perranporth beach 6 miles (dogs are allowed away from the village end).

At a glance

Welcome & Ambience	✓✓✓✓	Location	✓✓✓✓✓
Quality of Pitches	✓✓✓✓	Range of Facilities	✓✓✓✓

Directions

From Truro take B3284 north, signed Perranporth. Follow for 2.5 miles and site is signed on left just through the village of Shortlanesend. O.S.GR: SW 800479.

Charges 2006

Per unit incl. 2 adults, electricity	£ 11.00 - £ 14.00
extra adult	£ 1.50
child (3-16 yrs)	£ 1.00
pup tent	£ 1.00
dog	£ 0.25

Reservations

Made with deposit (£25 per week); balance on arrival. Tel: 01872 277878.
Email: sv@summervalley.co.uk

Open

31 March - 31 October.

UK0160 Newperran Holiday Park

Rejerrah, Newquay TR8 5QJ (Cornwall)

This is a large, level park in rural Cornish countryside. Being on high ground, it is quite open but this also gives excellent views of the coast and surrounding district. The owners, Keith and Christine Brewer, have rebuilt the reception, shop and pub to a very high standard and in tradtional Cornish style. The Pub or Cottage Inn, as it is called, is now a very comfortable area with a log burner for low season and family entertainment such as quiz nights in high season. A separate café is operated on a franchise basis. The traditional layout of the park provides a number of flat, well drained and hedged meadows divided into over 235 individual pitches. Some fields have larger and reservable spaces with more free space in the middle. There are 175 electrical connections (10A) including 14 'all-service' pitches. Five caravan holiday homes are available for rent. Newperran is only 2.5 miles from Perranporth beach, but there is a free heated swimming pool with sunbathing area and paddling pool on the park. This is a well run park with plenty of space and activities for families.

Facilities

Toilet facilities comprise four clean blocks, two heated. One block has been completely refurbished, others will follow. Facilities include washbasins in cabins, family rooms, baby room, hairdressing room and a unit for disabled visitors. Dishwashing sinks. Refurbished, fully equipped laundry room. Good self-service licensed shop. Licensed bar (mid May - Oct). Café (mid May - Sept). Outdoor heated swimming pool with paddling pool (Whitsun - Sept). Adventure playground and separate toddlers' play area. Games room with TV, pool tables and games machines. TV room. Crazy golf. Off site: Riding or golf 2 miles. Fishing 1 mile. Goonhavern village within walking distance with pubs and post office. Beach 2.5 miles.

At a glance

Welcome & Ambience	✓✓✓✓	Location	✓✓✓✓
Quality of Pitches	✓✓✓✓	Range of Facilities	✓✓✓✓✓

Directions

Turn off A3075 to west at camping sign 7 miles south of Newquay and just north of Goonhavern village. O.S.GR: SW794546. GPS: N50:21.026 W05:06.109

Charges 2005

Per adult	£ 3.95 - £ 6.50
child (3-16 yrs)	£ 2.50 - £ 3.95
pitch incl. electricity	£ 2.75
serviced pitch plus	£ 6.25
car	£ 1.00
dog	£ 1.00 - £ 1.50

Reservations

Advised in high season; made with £25 p/w deposit and £2.50 fee. Tel: 0845 1668407. Email: holidays@newperran.co.uk

Open

Easter - October.

South West England

UK0165 Monkey Tree Holiday Park

Rejerrah, Newquay TR8 5QR (Cornwall)

Monkey Tree has almost doubled in size in recent years, now covering 56 acres and boasting an impressive entrance and smart new reception. There are now 500 pitches with 450 for touring units and 50 caravan holiday homes to rent in their own area. The pitches in the original part of the park benefit from mature hedging which offers a degree of privacy which the new ones lack, but all are of a good size and over 400 have electricity (13/16A). During the holiday season there is lots going on at Monkey Tree and all the family should find something to keep them amused. For the little ones there is a morning Kid's Club, for older children there is a super adventure playground, well fenced for safety, an amusement arcade and pool tables. For everyone there is an outdoor heated pool, paddling pool and a sauna. The club and restaurant are popular with entertainment for children in the early part of the evening and bingo, karaoke, disco and cabaret acts to follow. Themed weekends are organised early and late in the season, with Halloween being especially popular. Venturing off the park there are wonderful beaches, a range of watersports and places such as the Eden Project and Flambards.

Facilities

The original block (refurbished) supplements two new modern timber blocks providing for all needs including facilities for babies and disabled visitors. Laundry. Motorcaravan services. Gas supplies. Shop (mornings only in low season). Club with entertainment, bar, and restaurant (main season and BHs). Takeaway (high season). Outdoor pool and paddling pool (Whitsun - end Sept). Adventure play area. Amusement arcade. Pool tables. Caravan storage. Off site: Fishing 2 miles. Golf, riding, sailing 5 miles.

Open

Week before Easter - 31 October.

At a glance

Welcome & Ambience	✓✓✓✓	Location	✓✓✓✓
Quality of Pitches	✓✓✓✓	Range of Facilities	✓✓✓✓

Directions

Follow the A30 ignoring all signs for Newquay. At Carland Cross with windmills on the right, carry straight over for Perranporth. After 1 mile turn right at Boxheater on B3285 (Perranporth, Goonhavern). After 0.5 miles turn right into Scotland Road for 1 mile to park on the left. O.S.GR: SW801546.

Charges 2005

Per person	£ 3.00 - £ 5.95
child	£ 1.50 - £ 3.50
pitch incl. electricity	£ 3.00

Reservations

Made with deposit (25%) and booking fee (£4). Tel: 01872 572032. Email: enquiries@monkeytreeholidaypark.co.uk

AWARD WINNING TOURING FAMILY HOLIDAY PARK
Just minutes away from Perranporth and Newquay

Monkey Tree HOLIDAY PARK

FREE Heated Pool
FREE Family Entertainment
FREE Kiddies Club
Luxury Caravans available
Tel: 01872 572032
www.monkeytreeholidaypark.co.uk
Monkey Tree Holiday Park. Rejerrah, Newquay, Cornwall TR8 5QR. Ref: ARG1

UK0200 Newquay Holiday Park

Newquay TR8 4HS (Cornwall)

Part of the Parkdean Group, Newquay Holiday Park lies peacefully on a terraced hillside only just outside the town, 2 miles from the beaches and town centre. Its main feature is an attractively laid out group of three heated pools with a giant water slide and surrounding 'green' sunbathing areas over-looked by a terrace for cool drinks. With a large proportion of caravan holiday homes (for let), there are still 212 marked pitches for touring units in a series of hedged fields, some sloping. Some fields are just for caravans, others are for tents. Most pitches are individual ones marked out by lines on ground but with nothing between them. Electricity points (16A) are provided for caravans and tents, plus 10 special 'star' pitches with hardstanding, water and drainage. Family entertainment is provided each night with live music, discos etc. in the site's Fiesta Club which also has a bar, TV lounge and games room with pool and snooker tables. A bus service runs to Newquay from the main road at the site entrance.

Facilities

Two good-sized, modern toilet blocks include a unit for disabled visitors and baby bath. An extra block is opened for the main season when facilities may be under pressure. Covered dishwashing sinks. Launderette. Well stocked self-service shop (gas from reception). Bar/lounge with Sky TV. Café/restaurant with all day food (all season). Outdoor pool complex with slide (and lifeguards). Pitch and putt and crazy golf. Playground for little ones and adventure play area for older children. Children's club. Recreation field for football and volleyball. Amusement arcade. Pool tables. Dogs or other pets are not accepted.

At a glance

Welcome & Ambience	✓✓✓✓	Location	✓✓✓✓
Quality of Pitches	✓✓✓✓	Range of Facilities	✓✓✓✓✓

Directions

Park is east of Newquay on A3059 road 1 mile east of junction with A3058. O.S.GR: SW853626. GPS: N50:25.350 W05:01.470

Charges 2005

Per unit incl. 4 persons	£ 7.00 - £ 24.00
with services	£ 9.00 - £ 27.00
extra person	£ 2.00

Reservations

Advised for peak season and made with deposit; contact park for details. Tel: 01637 871111. Email: enquiries@parkdean.com

Open

Easter - October.   *see advert on pg 43*

Holiday Ideas in Cornwall...

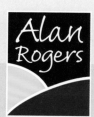

UK0170 **Trevella Caravan & Camping Park**

Crantock, Newquay TR8 5EW (Cornwall)

One of the best known and respected of Cornish parks with its colourful flower-beds and driveway (a regular winner of a 'Newquay in Bloom' award), Trevella is also one of the first to fill up and has a longer season than most. Well organised, the pitches are in a number of adjoining meadows, most of which are on a slight slope. Of the 250 pitches for touring units (any type), some 200 can be reserved and these are marked, individual ones. Over 200 pitches have electricity (10A), with 59 'premium' serviced pitches (with hardstanding, electricity and TV hook-ups, water, waste water, sewage). Trevella is essentially a quiet family touring park with the accent on orderliness and cleanliness; on-site evening activities are limited. Access is free to two fishing lakes, (permits from reception); with some fishing instruction and wildlife talks for youngsters in season. There is a pleasant walk around the lakes, a protected nature reserve, and it is also possible to walk to Crantock beach but check the tides first. A member of the Best of British group.

Facilities

Kept very clean, three blocks provide sufficient coverage with individual washbasins in private cabins for ladies, hair-dressing room and baby room. New Laundry. Well stocked supermarket and heated outdoor pool (both Easter - October). Freezer pack service. 'Nicky's Kitchen' offers hot dishes and snacks to take away or eat there, open late. Games room with pool tables and table tennis. Separate TV room. Crazy golf, large adventure playground, separate play and sports area and pets corner. Fishing. Off site: Shuttle bus service to Newquay in high season. Nearest beach is 0.5 miles on foot, 1 mile by car and Newquay is 2 miles. Pubs and restaurants at Crantock, 1 mile. Riding 1 mile. Golf 3 miles.

Open

Easter - 31 October.

At a glance

Welcome & Ambience ✓✓✓✓✓ Location ✓✓✓✓✓
Quality of Pitches ✓✓✓✓ Range of Facilities ✓✓✓✓

Directions

To avoid Newquay leave A30 or A392 at Indian Queens, straight over crossroads with A39 and A3058, left at A3075 junction and first right at camp sign. O.S.GR: SW802598.
GPS: N50:23.838 W05:05.768

Charges 2005

Per adult	£ 3.60 - £ 6.50
child (3-16 yrs)	£ 1.95 - £ 4.50
pitch incl. electricity	£ 3.00
with services	£ 6.50
dog	£ 1.00 - £ 1.50
Families and couples only.	

Reservations

Made with £30 deposit and £3 booking fee (16/7-27/8: Fri/Fri or Sat/Sat only) Tel: 01637 830308. Email: holidays@trevella.co.uk

See advertisement on pg 38

UK0210 **Hendra Holiday Park**

Newquay TR8 4NY (Cornwall)

Hendra is a long-established holiday park for the family that likes to be entertained, as the entertainment programme here is very comprehensive. There are comedians, show bands, cabaret, dancing, bingo, discos, plus entertainment and clubs for children. The 700 pitches are on various well mown, slightly sloping grass fields with country views and mature trees, some more sheltered than others. There are tarmac roads and lighting and 200 pitches have electricity (16A). Some landscaped hardstanding 'super' pitches have individual water, electricity, light, sewer drainage and satellite TV connections (dogs are not accepted on these pitches) and 12 new 'super' pitch type '2' have been added which are larger and have individual service bollards, purpose built car spaces and innovative awning pads. There are caravan holiday homes for hire, including 27 new luxury ones, but they are separate from the tourers. The entrance and reception are very attractive with a mass of well tended flower beds which, along with the other facilities, form an attractive, village-like centre to the park. The 'star of the show' at Hendra is the Oasis complex consisting of an indoor fun pool with flumes, river rapids and beach. It is open to the public – really a mini water-park. The outdoor heated pool with grass sunbathing area is free to campers and activities are well catered for with a range of amenities. The park is only 1.5 miles from Newquay and its fabulous surfing beaches. Hendra welcomes families and couples.

Facilities

Three modern toilet blocks are fully equipped and the park reports totally refurbished toilet and shower facilities, including some facilities for babies and disabled visitors. Large launderette. Motorcaravan services. Gas supplies. Well stocked shop. Various bars and restaurants, open all season (limited hours in early season), breakfast included. Pizzeria (main season only). Takeaway. Outdoor swimming pool. Indoor pool complex (cost £2.20 per family group, max. 4 persons, under 5s free; timed sessions are if very busy). Various play areas including one for soft play. Tennis. Minigolf. Bowling. Off site: Fishing or riding 1 mile. Bicycle hire or golf 2 miles. Beach 1.5 miles.

At a glance

Welcome & Ambience ✓✓✓✓ Location ✓✓✓✓
Quality of Pitches ✓✓✓✓ Range of Facilities ✓✓✓✓✓

Directions

Park is on left side of A392 Indian Queens - Newquay road at Newquay side of Quintrell Downs. O.S.GR: SW833601. GPS: N50:24.146 W05:02.949

Charges 2005

Per adult	£ 4.10 - £ 6.95
child (3-14 yrs)	£ 1.20 - £ 4.99
vehicle	£ 1.15 - £ 1.50
hardstanding pitch	£ 3.95
'super' pitch	£ 10.00 - £ 15.00
dog	£ 3.15

Reservations

Made with deposit (£ 30) and fee (£3). Tel: 01637 875778. Email: enquiries@hendra-holidays.com

Open

23 March - 31 October.

See advertisement on pg 39

UK0220 Trevornick Holiday Park

Holywell Bay, Newquay TR8 5PW (Cornwall)

Trevornick, once a working farm, is now a modern, busy and well run family touring park providing a very wide range of amenities close to one of Cornwall's finest beaches. A modern reception with welcoming staff sets the tone for your holiday. The park is well managed with facilities and standards constantly monitored. It has grown to provide caravanners and campers (no holiday caravans but 68 very well equipped 'Eurotents') with 450 large grass pitches (350 with 10A electricity and 55 fully serviced) on five level fields and two terraced areas. There are few trees, but some good views. Providing 'all singing, all dancing' facilities for fun packed family holidays, the farm buildings now provide the setting for the Farm Club. Furnished in keeping, it has a bar and food, children's rooms and a cafeteria 'De Caff' with terrace and takeaway, plus much entertainment from bingo, quizzes to shows, discos and cabaret. The rest of the development provides a pool complex, an 18 hole golf course, with a small, quiet club house offering bar meals and lovely views out to sea and three fishing lakes. Next door is the Holywell Bay 'fun' park (reduced rates) and the sandy beach is five minutes by car. An innovative idea is the 'Hire shop' where it is possible rent anything you might have forgotten from sheets, a fridge, travel cot, etc. to a camera or a wet suit to catch the famous Cornish surf!

Facilities

Five toilet blocks of a standard modern design provide coin-operated showers (20p), a family shower room, two bathrooms (50p), baby bath, dishwashing, laundry facilities, and provision for disabled visitors. Well stocked supermarket with bread made on site (both from late May). Hire shop. Bars (with TV), restaurant, cafe and takeaway. Entertainment (every night in season). Impressive new pool complex with outdoor pool, paddling pool, sunbathing decks, solarium, sauna and massage chair. Super Fort Knox style adventure playground, crazy golf, Kiddies Club and indoor adventure play area (supervised for 2-8 yr olds at a small charge). Amusement arcade and bowling alley. Teenage meeting room. 18-hole pitch and putt with golf pro shop. Bicycle hire. Coarse fishing with three lakes. Dogs are accepted in one field only. Off site: Boat launching 4 miles, riding within 1 mile.

At a glance

Welcome & Ambience	✓✓✓✓	Location	✓✓✓✓✓
Quality of Pitches	✓✓✓✓	Range of Facilities	✓✓✓✓✓

Directions

From A3075 approach to Newquay - Perranporth road, turn towards Cubert and Holywell Bay. Continue through Cubert to park on the right. O.S.GR: SW776586. GPS: N50:23.099 W05:07.736

Charges 2005

Per adult	£ 4.45 - £ 7.75
child (4-14 yrs)	£ 1.15 - £ 5.50
electricity	£ 3.75
'super' pitch incl. electricity	£ 7.75
dog	£ 3.00

Families and couples only. Many special discounts.

Reservations

Made with £ 30 deposit per week (Sat. to Sat. only July/Aug). Tel: 01637 830531. Email: bookings@trevornick.co.uk

Open

Easter - mid-September.

See advertisement on pg 39

UK0530 Trethiggey Touring Park

Quintrell Downs, Newquay TR8 4LG (Cornwall)

Trethiggey is a garden-like park with a ten month season, set some three miles back from the busy Newquay beaches and night life. The 157 pitches are in sharp contrast to some of the large, open fields of some of the bigger sites, broken up by trees, shrubs and plants to provide a pleasant 'green' atmosphere. With natural areas including a small wildlife pond and fishing lakes to enjoy, conservation is high on the agenda. There are 32 hardstandings and 94 numbered pitches have electricity (6/12A) with 12 caravan holiday homes interspersed amongst the touring pitches and a tent field open in main season. Some level pitches are formally arranged with others more informal on gently sloping grass. Facilities keep the informal touch with reception alongside the Trethiggey Trading Post which provides basic supplies, an off licence and a small library. A snack bar with covered eating area operates in the school holidays for breakfasts and simple evening meals, curries etc. with children catered for.

Facilities

The traditional style toilet block can be heated and is fully equipped, including an 'easy access' toilet/washbasin for disabled people, baby bath, wetsuit washing point, laundry and dishwashing sinks. New toilet block (virtually complete when we visited) near the tent area provides en-suite toilet/washbasins, showers, unit for disabled people and a laundry room to increase facilities for high season. Games room with TV, 2 amusement machines and a pool table. Shop. Snack bar/takeaway. Play area and recreation field. Coarse fishing. Gates locked at midnight. Off site: All the delights of Newquay within 3 miles with nightly minibus service (book in shop). Pub within walking distance.

At a glance

Welcome & Ambience	✓✓✓✓	Location	✓✓✓✓
Quality of Pitches	✓✓✓✓	Range of Facilities	✓✓✓✓

Directions

Site is a few hundred yards south of roundabout where A393 crosses the A3058 at Quintrell Downs (beside the A3058). O.S. GR:SW846596. GPS: N50:23.810 W05:01.698

Charges 2005

Per adult	£ 3.70 - £ 6.00
child (5-15 yrs)	free - £ 3.45
car	free - £ 1.00
pitch incl. electricity	£ 2.75
dog	£ 1.80 - £ 2.00

Min. stay 3 nights at B.Hs.

Reservations

Made with £15 deposit per pitch, per week. Tel: 01637 877672.

Open

2 March - 2 January.

CHOOSE YOUR BEST HOLIDAY EVER FROM ONE OF NEWQUAY'S FINEST PARKS...

Trevella Park
CARAVAN & CAMPING PARK

LUXURY ROSE AWARD CARAVANS, SPACIOUSLY SITUATED

Family run with families in mind, located in beautiful parkland surroundings with modern spotless facilities and friendly service.

Trevella Park is ideally situated only two and a half miles from Newquay.

Our park is renowned for its cleanliness and hygiene and we spare no effort to maintain this reputation.

There's plenty to do...

- Heated swimming & paddling pools
- Large adventure playground • Crazy Golf
- Television room showing FREE childrens videos
- Swings, see-saw, slide and playhouse • Pets corner
- Nature reserve and two FREE fishing lakes

Ideally situated to visit the 'EDEN PROJECT'

CRANTOCK • NEWQUAY • CORNWALL TR8 5EW
TEL: 01637 830308 (24 HRS) FAX: 01637 830155
EMAIL: holidays@trevella.co.uk
WEB: www.trevella.co.uk

...WHERE DREAMS ARE MADE

UK0315 **White Acres Holiday Park**

White Acres Country Park, White Cross, Newquay TR8 4LW (Cornwall)

White Acres is an impressive park in a rural setting, inland from Newquay, and is part of the Parkdean Group. The main emphasis here is on holiday homes and lodges which are well spaced around the park. A very popular and attractive feature, 15 coarse fishing lakes, complete with tackle shop, are in a woodland setting at the bottom of the site. This facility is also open to the public. There is provision for 40 touring units near the lakes, mostly on grass and level with 16A electricity, some hardstandings and including 25 with water and drainage. There are some sloping tent pitches. The extensive site facilities are arranged around the entrance with a leisure complex including indoor heated pool, sauna, jacuzzi, gym and an on-site beautician. A comprehensive entertainment programme caters for all the family with daytime clubs for under fives, 5-10 year olds and for teenagers. Ten pin bowling is an added attraction. This is a well organised park with lots going on to suit all ages. Should you tire of all that is on offer the popular resort of Newquay with its surfing beaches is 5 miles down the road and the Eden project is nearby.

Facilities

Two modern toilet blocks offer roomy shower cubicles which include washbasins, 2 baby rooms, unit for disabled visitors. Dishwashing sinks and launderette. Shop. Restaurant, pizzeria and takeaway. Range of bars. Coffee shop. Indoor swimming pool with lifeguards. Sauna, spa, gym, and sun beds. Beautician and hair stylist. Play areas, 'Fun factory' and inflatable jungle run. Amusement arcade. Crazy golf. Football pitch. Evening entertainment with bingo, cabaret, disco, quizzes and competitions.

At a glance

Welcome & Ambience	✓✓✓✓✓	Location	✓✓✓✓✓
Quality of Pitches	✓✓✓✓	Range of Facilities	✓✓✓✓✓

Directions

From A30 or A39 take A392 Newquay road and after about 1 mile park is on right. O.S.GR: SW889597.

Charges 2005

Per unit incl. 4 persons	£ 9.00 - £ 28.00
incl. electricity	£ 12.50 - £ 32.00
extra person	£ 3.50 - £ 5.00
serviced plus pitch	£ 2.00
dog	£ 3.00

Reservations

Made with £25 deposit or full amount if less.
Tel: 0845 4580065.
Email: enquiries@whiteacres.co.uk

Open

March - October.

UK0140 **Penrose Farm Touring Park**

Goonhavern, Truro TR4 9QF (Cornwall)

Penrose Farm is a quality, family park for tourers only, with a quiet comfortable atmosphere on the edge of the village of Goonhavern. The park is level and sheltered, with the pitches spread over five fields with flower beds and bushes set amongst them. These colourful flowers and those at the entrance give the park a neat and well cared for feel. The enthusiastic owners, Alan and Sharman, take pride in the pitches and facilities they provide and enjoy getting to know their customers, many of whom return each year. Children have a well kept adventure playground and an indoor animal centre with guinea pigs, rabbits, chickens, fish, terrapins and birds to admire. An area for larger animals with space for picnics is under construction. There are over 75 pitches with 16A electricity and 8 pitches with hard-standing (all with electricity), some seasonal places and 5 privately owned caravan holiday homes. Alan ensures that each unit has plenty of space and does not feel overcrowded. It is only a short walk to the village and its popular pub, and buses to Newquay stop in the village. The superb beach at Perranporth is only 2.5 miles. To retain the quiet family image, there are no plans for bars or entertainment and only couples and families are welcome.

Facilities

The fully equipped toilet block is well maintained and includes four excellent family rooms containing an adjustable shower, washbasin, WC and hairdryer. One of these rooms is also accessible for wheelchairs. Well equipped laundry. Dishwashing sinks. Small shop for gas and basics (Easter, then May - Sept). Adventure playground. Table tennis. Caravan storage. Off site: Fishing or riding 0.5 miles, golf 1 mile.

Open

1 April - 31 October.

At a glance

Welcome & Ambience	✓✓✓✓✓	Location	✓✓✓✓
Quality of Pitches	✓✓✓✓✓	Range of Facilities	✓✓✓

Directions

Take A30 from Exeter past Bodmin and Indian Queens. Just after wind farm take B3285 to Perranporth. Park is on the left as you enter Goonhavern village. O.S.GR: SW790535.
GPS: N50:20.408 W05:06.394

Charges 2005

Per unit incl. 2 persons	£ 9.00 - £ 14.00
incl. electricity	£ 12.00 - £ 17.50
extra person (5 yrs and over)	£ 3.00 - £ 3.50
dog	free - £ 2.00

Families and couples only.
Less 50p for over 60s if booked.

Reservations

Made with £30 deposit. Tel: 01872 573185.

UK0205 Treloy Touring Park

Newquay TR8 4JN (Cornwall)

Treloy is a surprisingly pretty park considering it was leased by the present owner's father to the RAF during wartime. Now the concrete bases from the Nissan huts provide hardstanding for caravans and are interspersed with shrubs which form a pleasant landscape feature. Elsewhere hydrangeas edge the roads around the more open pitches and more trees are being planted. All the 180 pitches are clearly marked, many are level but some are sloping. There are 145 pitches with 16A electricity and 10 are fully serviced. All are used for touring units and perhaps this helps towards the relaxed family atmosphere. Despite its proximity to St Mawgan, the RAF air sea rescue base and Newquay's airport there is little disturbance – just the odd amazing close-up view of a take off. There is an hourly bus service for Newquay from the entrance which means the beach can be enjoyed without parking problems. On return to Treloy there is the Park Chef and the Surfrider's Barn for meals and drinks. If you do not fancy the beach there is a pool on the park. Family owned and managed, this is a real family park providing for all ages.

Facilities

Two toilet blocks of similar design, one newer with toilets and washbasins only and one with showers as well. Baby room with two large sinks. En-suite facilities for disabled visitors (key). Laundry and dishwashing. Gas. Shop with all necessities. Pleasant café with a good reputation and including breakfast. Bar. Swimming pool (walled and gated). Play areas and field with goal posts. Nature trail. Family entertainment such as magic shows, bingo, folk and rock music. Off site: Fishing 1 mile. Golf 0.5 miles. Riding and boat launching 3 miles. Other beaches such as Watergate Bay, Mawgan Porth and Porth beach are a short car journey.

At a glance

Welcome & Ambience	✓✓✓✓	Location	✓✓✓✓
Quality of Pitches	✓✓✓✓	Range of Facilities	✓✓✓✓✓

Directions

From A39 St Columb Major take the B3059 for Newquay. Park is signed after about 4 miles.
O.S.GR: SW858625. GPS: N50:25.972 W005:00.75

Charges 2005

Per person	£ 4.00 - £ 6.50
child (3-14 yrs)	£ 1.50 - £ 4.00
pitch incl. electricity	£ 2.50

Reservations

Made with deposit (£20 per pitch per week).
Tel: 01637 872 063. Email: treloy-tp@btconnect.com

Open

20 May - 15 September.

UK0310 Trekenning Tourist Park

St Columb Major, Newquay TR8 4JF (Cornwall)

Trekenning's new owners are working hard to develop a popular park with a range of good facilities. Easy access just off the A39 roundabout at St Columb Major leads to a large sloping field with neatly cut grass and all the facilities tucked into the top corner. There are 75 pitches, 68 with 10A electricity. Some have been levelled, others are tucked away at a lower level shaded by tall trees. A well hidden tent field with just a water point is edged by a wooded small stream. The star of the show is undoubtedly the kidney shaped pool and paddling pool which are in a garden-like setting with gazebos and sun loungers surrounded by lawn and overlooked by the patio bar at the top – lovely for summer evenings. The 'olde worlde' upstairs bar is a cosy feature for cooler times with a useful 'eatery' underneath. Entertainment is provided every night in the main season (for example, singers, quiz nights, Connect-4 nights, discos on Fridays). The A39 runs parallel to one side of the site, so there may be road noise.

Facilities

Two toilet blocks, one providing normal showers and vanity style washbasins, the other with two en-suite bathrooms (50p) and six large family showers, well refurbished. Laundry room. Covered dishwashing sinks. Shop for basics. Free freezer service. Play area. Outdoor pool with poolside bar(Whitsun - end Aug). Games room with table tennis and pool and some amusement machines. Characterful bar with curries, etc. served. New takeaway including breakfasts (BHs and July/Aug). Off site: Fishing 1 mile. Riding and golf 2 miles. Bicycle hire 6 miles.

At a glance

Welcome & Ambience	✓✓✓✓	Location	✓✓✓✓
Quality of Pitches	✓✓✓✓	Range of Facilities	✓✓✓✓✓

Directions

Take A3059 turning to Newquay from St Columb Major then turn immediately left; park is signed (this was the old road). O.S.GR: SW907625.

Charges 2005

Per adult	£ 4.20 - £ 6.20
child (3-15 yrs)	£ 1.50 - £ 4.00
electricity	£ 3.50
extra vehicle	£ 1.50
dog	£ 2.00

Reservations

Made with deposit (£20) and fee (£2). Tel: 01637 880462. Email: enquiries@trekenning.co.uk

Open

All year.

UK0355 Saint Minver Holiday Park

St Minver, Near Rock, Wadebridge PL27 6RR (Cornwall)

This holiday village, part of the Parkdean Group, is based in the grounds of a former manor house near the well known Cornish coastal resorts of Rock and Padstow. There are over 200 privately owned caravan holiday homes which merge into landscape, with a further 145 for rent. A sloping grass field has now been developed to take lodges, leaving just 33 touring pitches, all with 16A electricity, with toilet facilities based in the far corner and rural views across the fields. A central village area, providing reception and most of the facilities including an indoor swimming pool with waterslide, is the hub of the site. The manor house itself is home to a bar/bistro and all the entertainment with cabaret, live music, disco and quiz nights. A children's club ensures there is something for everyone. A footpath through the woods takes you to the village of St Minver. You can take the passenger ferry from Rock to Padstow with its harbour where Rick Stein has his cookery school and restaurants. The Camel Trail is nearby for cycling enthusiasts. The nearby beach at Rock and Daymar beach are renowned for swimming, windsurfing and sailing.

Facilities

Fully equipped toilet block. Baby bath. En-suite unit for disabled people. Dishwashing sinks. Launderette. Shop. Bar, restaurant and takeaway. Indoor pool with lifeguards. Indoor soft play area and outdoor play area. Crazy golf. All amenities open when site is open. Entertainment programme. Sports programme with aqua-aerobics and scuba diving and laser clay pigeon shooting (high season only).

At a glance

Welcome & Ambience	✓✓✓✓	Location	✓✓✓✓
Quality of Pitches	✓✓✓	Range of Facilities	✓✓✓✓✓

Directions

From Wadebridge take B3314 for Port Isaac. Follow for 3 miles then turn left for Rock and park is 250 yds on right. O.S.GR: SW965768.

Charges 2005

Per unit incl. 4 persons	£ 7.00 - £ 27.00
extra person	free - £ 2.00
dog	£ 1.00 - £ 2.50

Reservations

Made with £25 deposit or full amount if less. Tel: 01208 862305. Email: enquiries@newquay.com

Open

Mid-March - October.

UK0306 Ruthern Valley Holidays

Ruthernbridge, Bodmin PL30 5LU (Cornwall)

This is a little gem of a site set in 7.5 acres of woodland, tucked away in a peaceful little valley not far from Bodmin. The park was landscaped over 30 years ago with an amazing range of trees and shrubs now all carefully tended by its present owners, Tim and Eileen Zair. This lends itself to the informal layout of the level touring pitches and the self catering accommodation. Twelve wooden chalets and six caravan holiday homes blend into the natural wooded environment. There are 16 touring pitches informally spaced but numbered in the main, tree-lined field, 6 with electricity, and a further 13 in smaller fields and alcove areas amongst the woods with a small stream meandering through. A very good adventure-type play area is set away from the pitches, and there is a small, basic toilet block and a little shop. This is a site for relaxing with time to enjoy the simpler pastimes of walking or birdwatching.

Facilities

The small toilet block provides everything necessary including a shower each per sex plus washing machines, dryer, laundry sink and dishwashing sinks (H&C). The shop with basic provisions shares with reception (reduced hours in low season). Barbecue hire. Play area with excellent equipment including five-a-side goal posts. Dogs are not accepted in touring areas during July/Aug. Bicycle hire (delivered to site). Off site: Nearest pub 3-4 miles. Riding 4 miles.

Open

April - October.

At a glance

Welcome & Ambience	✓✓✓✓✓	Location	✓✓✓✓✓
Quality of Pitches	✓✓✓	Range of Facilities	✓✓✓

Directions

Approaching Bodmin from A30 or A38 go anti-clockwise round the inner ring road. Go straight over double mini-roundabout, leaving Bodmin on A389/A391 towards St Austell. Ignore first sign for Nanstallon/Ruthernbridge. In1.5 miles, at top of hill, turn right. At Nanstallon village sign (0.75 miles), turn left then filter left for 1 mile to Ruthernbridge. Turn left before bridge. Site is 300 yards. O.S.GR: SX012668. GPS: N50:27.873 W04:48.114

Charges 2005

Per unit incl. 2 persons	£ 9.00 - £ 11.00
with electricity	£ 11.50 - £ 13.50
extra person over 4 yrs	£ 2.00 - £ 2.50
pet (low season only)	£ 1.00

Reservations

Contact park. Tel: 01208 831395. Email: ruthern.valley@btconnect.com

UK0430 Padstow Touring Park

Trerethern, Padstow PL28 8LE (Cornwall)

Under new ownership (and renamed) Padstow Touring Park is a traditional park made up of wide open fields covering 13 acres. However, some hedging and bushes are surviving despite the rabbits and the elements. There is room for 300 units but only 150 are taken so there is plenty of open space and the views across Bodmin Moor and the estuary are marvellous. The grass is neatly cut and the pitches mostly level, although there is a gentle slope in parts. Electricity (10A) is available on 64 pitches, there are ten water points and nine hardstanding places for motorcaravans, seven of these with electricity plus an emptying point (the site can accommodate 32-34 ft motorhomes). The 'Kernow' pitches have access to private, en-suite facilities. The owners live on site and, along with site wardens, ensure a well run and orderly park. Padstow itself is a mile away either by public footpath through the fields (20-30 minutes) downhill or for bicycles by the road. A bus service passes (the site is a request stop) and reception holds timetables. Rick Stein's restaurant or bistro may tempt you – if you can get a reservation!

Facilities

One toilet block has been refurbished with extra showers and two toilet washrooms. The other block is more basic, but clean and tidy, with a toilet washroom with ramped access is provided at the back. Six individual en-suite washrooms for use with the 'Kernow' pitches. Full laundry facilities. Reception/shop for gas, camping equipment and provisions (peak season). Play area. Off site: Nearest beach is at Padstow, others are within 5 miles. Access to the Camel Trail cycle route. Riding or fishing 2 miles, golf 5 miles.

Open

All year.

At a glance

Welcome & Ambience	✓✓✓	Location	✓✓✓✓
Quality of Pitches	✓✓✓✓	Range of Facilities	✓✓✓

Directions

Park is signed from the A389, SSW of Padstow. Follow tarmac approach road, then turn into park. O.S.GR: SW912739. GPS: N50:31.623 W04:56.951

Charges 2005

Per unit incl. 2 persons	£ 9.50 - £ 13.00
incl. electricity	£ 12.25 - £ 15.75
Kernow pitch	£ 16.00 - £ 21.00
child (3-15 yrs)	£ 1.50 - £ 2.00
dog	£ 1.00 - £ 1.50
No credit cards.	

Reservations

Made with non-refundable deposit (£15 p/week). Tel: 01841 532061. Email: mail@padstowtouringpark.co.uk

UK0230 **Glenmorris Park**

Longstone Road, St Mabyn PL30 3BY (Cornwall)

The beaches of north Cornwall and the wilds of Bodmin Moor are all an easy drive from Glenmorris Park. The park is being gradually improved and carefully maintained by its new, young owners and it provides a spacious and relaxed atmosphere. There are 80 level pitches, 60 with 16A electricity, on well drained and well mown grass with 20 hardstandings. There are some caravan holiday homes to let. A nice, sheltered outdoor pool is an added attraction. There is no bar although the local village inn has a good reputation for food. The Camel Trail is only two miles, providing a means to cycle or walk all the way to Bodmin, Wadebridge or Padstow. Bodmin and Wadebridge are only five or six miles for shopping.

Facilities	Directions
The fully equipped modern toilet block includes 1 en-suite unit per sex. Dishwashing sinks and laundry. Heated outdoor swimming pool and paddling pool (late May - early Sept), surrounded by a sheltered, paved and grass sunbathing areas. Good, fenced adventure play area with bark safety base. Tiny tots play area. Refurbished Games room for teenagers. Caravan storage. Off site: Fishing, riding or golf 3 miles, bicycle hire 5 miles.	From Bodmin or Wadebridge on A389, take B3266 north signed Camelford. At village of Longstone turn left signed St Mabyn and brown camping sign. Site is 400 yds. on right. Ignore all other signs to St Mabyn. O.S.GR: SX053732. GPS: N50:31.668 W04:44.711

Open

Easter - 31 October.

Charges 2005

Per adult	£ 3.70 - £ 4.95
child (3-15 yrs)	£ 1.20 - £ 1.40
electricity (16A)	£ 2.25 - £ 2.75
dog	£ 1.00

Reservations

Made with deposit (£10 per week per unit). Tel: 01208 841677. Email: info@glenmorris.co.uk

At a glance

Welcome & Ambience	✓✓✓✓	Location	✓✓✓✓
Quality of Pitches	✓✓✓	Range of Facilities	✓✓✓✓

UK0500 **Trewince Farm Holiday Park**

St Issey, Wadebridge PL27 7RL (Cornwall)

This well established and popular park four miles from Padstow has been developed around a dairy farm with magnificent countryside views. Careful attention has been made to the development of the park, maintaining trees and adding flowering shrubs and plants. There are 35 caravan holiday homes discreetly terraced, some privately owned, some to let. Two touring areas on higher ground provide both hardstanding and level grass pitches with a sheltered tent area. Over half of the 120 touring pitches have electricity (10A) and 34 have water and drainage. The park's main feature is an excellent sheltered, walled and heated swimming pool with paddling pool, and paved sunbathing area. Farm rides and pasty suppers in the barn are organised in the high season.

Facilities	Directions
Two fully equipped, well maintained toilet blocks include washbasins in cabins, hair care rooms, dishwashing under cover and laundry rooms. Also children's room with bath (20p) and facilities for disabled visitors. Well stocked shop (all season) by reception. Fish and chip van calls twice weekly, a butcher once a week. Swimming pool. Play area. Games room. Crazy golf. Off site: Pubs and restaurants in nearby village of St Issey. Camel Trail nearby for walking or cycling (goes to Padstow).	From Wadebridge follow A39 towards St Columb and pick up the A389 for Padstow. Site signed on left in 2 miles. Follow for short distance to park entrance on right. O.S. GR: SW937715.

Open

23 March - 31 October.

Charges guide

Per unit incl. 2 persons	£ 8.00 - £ 13.00
incl. electricity	£ 9.75 - £ 14.50
hardstanding, drainage and electricity	£ 10.25 - £ 15.00
extra adult	£ 3.20
child (3-15 yrs)	£ 1.60 - £ 2.65
dog	£ 1.10

Reservations

Made with £40 p/week deposit (non-refundable); balance on arrival. Tel: 01208 812830.

At a glance

Welcome & Ambience	✓✓✓✓	Location	✓✓✓✓
Quality of Pitches	✓✓✓✓	Range of Facilities	✓✓✓✓

45

UK0302 **South Penquite Farm**

South Penquite, Blisland, Bodmin PL30 4LH (Cornwall)

South Penquite offers real camping with no frills, set on a 80 hectare hill farm high on Bodmin Moor between the villages of Blisland and St Breward. The farm achieved organic status in 2001 and runs a flock of 300 ewes and a herd of 40 cattle. You will also find horses, ponies, chickens, geese, ducks and, when we visited, a pair of turkeys which had escaped the Christmas cull and showed their approval or not by the skin around their necks changing colour! A farm walk of some two miles takes you over most of the farm and some of the moor taking in a Bronze Age hut settlement, the river and a standing stone. It is also possible to fish for brown trout on the farm's stretch of the De Lank river – a tributary of the Camel. The camping is small scale and intended to have a low impact on the surrounding environment. Tents or simple motorcaravans can pitch around the edge of three walled fields, roughly cut in the midst of the moor. You can find shelter or a view. Three Yurts – round Mongolian tents, are available to rent in one field, complete with wood burning stoves – quite original. Take a look at the farm's website which offers a fascinating insight into life and work at South Penquite.

Facilities

Simple but adequate, there are separate toilets and washbasins for men and women, plus 4 new large showers. Two outside Belfast sinks. LPG gas available. Facilities for field studies and opportunities for educational groups and schools to learn about the local environment. Fishing (requires an EA rod licence and tokens available from the Westcountry Rivers Trust). Dogs are not accepted. Off site: Walking, riding and cycling. Sustrans Route 3 passes close by. North and south coasts within easy reach.

Open

14 May - mid October.

At a glance

Welcome & Ambience	✓✓✓	Location	✓✓✓✓
Quality of Pitches	✓✓✓	Range of Facilities	✓✓✓

Directions

Travelling into Cornwall on A30 over Bodmin Moor pass Jamaica Inn and sign for Colliford Lake and watch for St Breward sign (to right) immediately at end of dual-carriageway. Follow this narrow road over the open moor for about 2 miles ignoring any turns to left or right. Also ignore right turn to St Breward just before you arrive at the South Penquite sign. Follow track over stone bridge beside ford through farm gate and then bear to left to camping fields. Walk back to book in at Farm House.
O.S.GR: SX104752. GPS: N50:32.67 W04:40.31

Charges 2006

Per person	£ 4.00
child (5-16 yrs)	£ 3.00
Less 10% for stays of 5 nights or more.	

Reservations

Contact site. Tel: 01208 850 491.
Email: thefamr@bodminmoor.co.uk

UK0360 **Lakefield Caravan Park**

Lower Pendavey Farm, Camelford PL32 9TX (Cornwall)

Lakefield is a small, simple touring park on what was a working farm. Now the main focus is on the BHS approved equestrian centre. With only 30 pitches, it is no surprise that the owners, Maureen and Dennis Perring, know all the campers. The well-spaced pitches backing onto hedges and with 24 electricity hook-ups (16A) are in view of the small lake (fenced) and its feathered inhabitants. The white-washed shop/reception, converted from one of the old barns and including a picture gallery, is open all day and all season which impressed us for such a small site. It incorporates a tea room offering cream teas. A dozen colourful picnic tables are dotted about the site. Children will love the animals and 'Wabbit World'. With over 30 horses, from Shetlands to thoroughbreds, the riding school is very much part of the site, offering lessons and hacks with qualified supervision and instruction. You can even bring your own horse. All abilities are catered for with a very large indoor centre, outdoor sand ménage, show jumping paddock, beginners cross-country course and pony rides. This is the Riding for the Disabled Centre for the area . Nearby, Tintagel, Boscastle, Bodmin Moor and numerous beaches wait to be explored.

Facilities

The refurbished toilet block is simple but adequate. Washing machine and dryer in the ladies' and a dishwashing sink and a laundry sink outside but under cover. No facilities for disabled visitors. Shop and tea room. Gas supplies. Torches may be useful. Off site: Fishing (sea 4 miles, coarse 5 miles). Golf 2 miles.

Open

1 April - 31 October.

At a glance

Welcome & Ambience	✓✓✓✓	Location	✓✓✓
Quality of Pitches	✓✓✓	Range of Facilities	✓✓✓

Directions

Follow B3266 north from Camelford. Park access is directly from this road on the left just before the turning for Tintagel, clearly signed.
O.S.GR: SX097852.

Charges 2005

Per unit incl. 2 adults	£ 6.00 - £ 10.00
extra adult or child (5 yrs and over)	£ 1.00
electricity	£ 2.50

Reservations

Made with £ 30 deposit per week. Tel: 01840 213279. Email: lakefield@pendavey.fsnet.co.uk

UK0300 **The Colliford Tavern Campsite**

Colliford Lake, St Neot, Liskeard PL14 6PZ (Cornwall)

Colliford Tavern is quietly situated high on Bodmin Moor near Colliford Lake, hidden and protected by tall pines with a camping area and a tavern. The Cooper family run the free house with home cooked food and ale in an old world atmosphere. The tavern is open to campers and the public. The camping area is quiet and simple and kept very natural with short grass and sheltered from the moor by tall pines. The main field provides 40 fairly level pitches with 19 electric hook-ups and 6 hardstandings backing on to the pine trees. Ideally situated for Colliford Lake and the Moor, be it for walking, fly fishing (permits available) or birdwatching, the park is also good for excursions to both the north or south coast.

Facilities	Directions
The pine-fitted, heated toilet block is fully equipped. Baby room and unit for disabled people (no shower). Restaurant and bar. Play area. Occasional family entertainment.	On the A30 travelling south, pass the Jamaica Inn and site is signed a further 1-1.5 miles on the left. O.S.GR: SX168730. GPS: N50:32.216 W04:34.936

Open	Charges 2005	
Easter - end September.	Per unit incl. 2 adults	£ 10.00
	electricity (16A)	£ 3.00

At a glance			Reservations
Welcome & Ambience	✓✓✓✓	Location ✓✓✓✓	Advised for high season and made with £10 deposit,
Quality of Pitches	✓✓✓	Range of Facilities ✓✓✓	plus £5 for electric hook-up. Tel: 01208 821335. Email: info@colliford-tavern.co.uk

UK0380 **Wooda Farm Park**

Poughill, Bude EX23 9HJ (Cornwall)

Wooda Farm is spacious and well organised, with some nice touches. A quality, family run park, it is part of a working farm, under two miles from the sandy, surfing beaches of Bude. In peaceful farmland with plenty of open spaces (and some up and down walking), there are marvellous views of sea and countryside. The 200 large pitches are spread over four meadows on level or gently sloping grass. There are 142 with electricity connections (10A), 58 hardstanding hedged 'premier' pitches (electricity, water, waste water) and 5 premier pitches with Sky TV, linked by tarmac roads. A late arrivals area has electricity. Beside the shop and reception at the entrance are 55 caravan holiday homes for let. A few friendly farm animals welcome assistance at feeding time! Tractor and trailer rides, archery and clay pigeon shooting with tuition are provided according to demand, plus woodland (to find the pixies) and orchard walks and excellent coarse fishing. There is much to do in the area - sandy beaches with coastal walks, and Tintagel with King Arthur's Castle and Clovelly nearby. A member of the Best of British group.

Facilities	Directions
Three well maintained toilet blocks, one heated, include a unit suitable for disabled people, two baby rooms and five en-suite family bathrooms for hire (small charge). Two laundry rooms. Motorcravan service point. Self-service shop with off-licence. Attractive courtyard bar with bar meals and pleasant restaurant with home cooking (reduced hours out of season). Play area in separate field with plenty of room for ball games, 9 hole 'fun' golf course (clubs provided). Games room with TV, table tennis and pool. Coarse fishing in 1.5 acre lake (permits from reception). Certain breeds of dogs not accepted. Caravan storage. Off site: Village inn is five minutes walk. Leisure Centre and Splash Pool in Bude.	Park is north of Bude at Poughill; turn off A39 on north side of Stratton on minor road for Coombe Valley, following camp signs at junctions. O.S.GR: SS225080.

	Charges 2005	
	Per unit incl. 2 adults, electricity	£ 10.50 - £ 16.00
	Camping Cheques accepted.	

	Reservations
	Made with £20 p/week deposit Tel: 01288 352069. Email: enquiries@wooda.co.uk

At a glance			Open
Welcome & Ambience	✓✓✓✓✓	Location ✓✓✓✓✓	1 April - October.
Quality of Pitches	✓✓✓✓✓	Range of Facilities ✓✓✓✓	

UK1140 Lobb Fields Caravan & Camping Park

Saunton Road, Braunton EX33 1EB (Devon)

Braunton village, Saunton Sands, the famous Tarka Trail for cycling, Baggy Point for walking, the biosphere at Braunton Burrows (one of only 13 similar special reserves in the country), Marwood Gardens, and wind surfing and water skiing on the Taw estuary are just some of the many attractions within a short distance of Lobb Fields. If you just want to sit and relax, then the pitches at the park offer views of the Taw estuary and Saunton, as well as magnificent sunsets. Lobb Fields has two camping areas providing 180 pitches on sloping grass, with a few hardstandings. Twelve pitches are reserved for seasonal caravans, and 61 have 16A electricity hook-ups. A third field is open for campers for 28 days only in high season. The pitches are marked and grass roads lead to the amenities. As the two toilet blocks are at the very bottom or very top of the fields, some up and down walking is inevitable. A small play area with wooden adventure equipment is located in the lower field. Managers, Robert and Diana Gleed, assisted by Bruce and Maureen Reeves, offer their guests a friendly welcome and are pleased to give information about the area. Lobbs Fields may be close to many holiday activities, but it is also a peaceful retreat for those wanting a quiet holiday.

Facilities

Two elderly toilet blocks (one in each field) have all the usual facilities. Baby room (upper block only). Laundry. Dishwashing sinks under cover. Cleaning and maintenance can be variable. The lower block can be heated and has good facilities for disabled visitors in a recently built unit. Hair dryers and irons available from reception (£5 returnable deposit). Adventure play area. Off site: Nearest shops less than a mile.

Open

28 March - 26 October.

At a glance

Welcome & Ambience	✓✓✓✓	Location	✓✓✓✓
Quality of Pitches	✓✓✓	Range of Facilities	✓✓✓

Directions

Take A361 Barnstaple to Braunton road, then B3231 (signed Croyde) to Braunton. Park is 1 mile from Braunton on the right - take care through Braunton as roads are quite narrow and busy. O.S.GR: SS474370. GPS: N51:06.699 W04:10.874

Charges 2005

Per unit incl. 2 persons	£ 7.50 - £ 16.50
prime pitch	£ 10.00 - £ 19.00
extra person	£ 1.00 - £ 2.00
dog	£ 1.00

Reservations

£10 deposit for each week, non refundable - min. stay 3 nights during B.Hs. Tel: 01271 812090. Email: info@lobbfields.com

UK1150 Ruda Holiday Park

Parkdean Holidays, Croyde Bay, Croyde EX33 1NY (Devon)

Ruda Holiday Park is the latest addition to Parkdean Holidays, now comprising 12 parks in Scotland, Wales and southwest England. Ruda is right beside a Blue Flag beach and provides 313 camping and touring pitches in two distinct areas. A large camping area divided into four sections is reserved for tent campers and motorcaravans (there are some electricity hook-ups around the perimeter and it is served by two toilet blocks that are aging but clean). Touring caravan and motorcaravan pitches, all with 13A connections, are in a separate field across the road and have direct access to the beach. Here, the toilet facilities are modern with coded entry to stop day visitors using them. A central complex (well away from the camping fields) houses a supermarket, laundry, food outlets, and all of the entertainment clubs and bars. The Cascade Tropical Pool, a fun pool with flume and water features is supervised at all times (children under five must wear arm bands which are provided free of charge). A large adventure play area, a tennis court and a sports field are also a short distance from the camping fields so that visitors are not disturbed. There's plenty of walking on the sand dunes and around the park, and Croyde Bay is renowned for surfing.

Facilities

Two blocks in the camping fields provide toilets, showers with preset controls, and communal washbasins; these are aging but were clean at the time of visit. A separate bathroom with toilet has a door wide enough for wheelchairs (key from reception), however there are no aids for visitors with disabilities. A third, modern building provides all facilities in the touring field. Dishwashing sinks under cover. Laundry with washing machines, dryers and irons. Bar, restaurant, snack bar and takeaway. Amusement arcade. Cascade Tropical pool. Adventure playground. Tennis court. Sports field. Fishing lake. Supermarket, boutique and hire centre. Surfing equipment for hire. Direct access to sheltered beach. Caravan holiday homes and lodges for hire. Off site: Surfing. Lundy Island excursion.

At a glance

Welcome & Ambience	✓✓✓✓	Location	✓✓✓✓✓
Quality of Pitches	✓✓✓✓	Range of Facilities	✓✓✓✓✓

Directions

From Barnstaple, take A361 signed Braunton and Ilfracombe. At Braunton, take sharp left (narrow road) towards Croyde (signed) and follow the road all the way to the beach. Entrance to Ruda is on the right. O.S.GR: SS561331. GPS: N51:08.111 W04:14.112

Charges 2005

Per pitch	£ 7.00 - £ 27.00
pitch with services	£ 10.00 - £ 31.00

Prices are for pitch and up to four persons; maximum of eight persons per pitch.

Reservations

Made with £25 deposit or full amount if less. Tel: 01271 890477. Email: enquires@ruda.co.uk

Open

March - November.   *see advert on pg 43*

UK0690 Stowford Farm Meadows

Berry Down, Combe Martin, Ilfracombe EX34 0PW (Devon)

Stowford Farm is set in 500 acres of the rolling North Devon countryside, available for recreation and walking, yet within easy reach of five local beaches. The touring park and its facilities have been developed in the fields and farm buildings surrounding the attractive old farmhouse and provide a village like centre with a comfortable spacious feel. There are 710 pitches (including 238 used by seasonal units) on five slightly sloping meadows separated by Devon hedges of beech and ash. Unseparated, the numbered and marked pitches are accessed by tarmac or hard-core roads, most have electricity (10/16A) and there are well placed water points. The Old Stable Bars, refurbished to a high standard offers entertainment in high season including barn dances, discos, karaoke and other musical evenings. Children will also be entertained by the indoor heated pool and under cover mini-zoo (Petorama) where they can handle many sorts of animals (on payment). In low season some facilities may only open for limited hours. Stowford provides plenty to keep families occupied without leaving the park, including woodland walks and horse riding from the park's own stables. This is a friendly family, countryside base for exploring the North Devon coast and Exmoor.

Facilities

Five identical toilet blocks, each looked after by resident wardens, are fully equipped and provide good, functional facilities, each block with laundry facilities and dishwashing sinks under cover. The newest block (in field 5) has under-floor heating and includes facilities for disabled visitors. Extra good facilities for disabled visitors and private family washrooms are beside reception. Well stocked shop (with holiday goods and gas). Good value takeaway with restaurant area. Bars and entertainment in season. Swimming pool (22 x 10 m; heated Easter - Oct) at a small charge (£1.25). Riding. 18-hole pitch and putt. Crazy golf. Bicycle hire. 'Kiddies kar' track (all charged). Games room. Large play area. Games and activities organised in high season. ATM. Dogs welcome in three sections (max. 2 per pitch). Summer parking and winter caravan storage. Caravan workshop, sales accessories and repair centre. Off site: Fishing and boat launching 4 miles.

At a glance

Welcome & Ambience	✓✓✓✓	Location	✓✓✓✓
Quality of Pitches	✓✓✓✓	Range of Facilities	✓✓✓✓✓

Directions

From Barnstaple take A39 towards Lynton. After 1 mile turn left on B3230. Turn right at garage on A3123 and park is 1.5 miles on the right. O.S.GR: SS565438. GPS: N51:10.499 W04:03.285

Charges 2005

Per unit and car incl. 2 persons	£ 7.80 - £ 21.00
extra person	free - £ 3.00
child (5-12 yrs)	free - £ 2.00
awning with groundsheet	£ 2.00 - £ 3.00
dog	£ 1.50 - £ 2.50

Low and mid season discounts for over 50s.

Reservations

Any length, deposit £2 per night, £12 per week, £20 per fortnight. Balance due 28 days before arrival. Tel: 01271 882476. Email: enquiries@stowford.co.uk

Open

Easter - end October.

49

UK0720 Easewell Farm Holiday Parc

Mortehoe, Woolacombe EX34 7EH (Devon)

Near the sandy beaches of Woolacombe, Easewell Farm is now part of the Woolacombe Bay Holiday Parc group who own the Woolacombe Bay, Golden Coast and Twitchen parks. A shuttle bus runs between the four parks and to the beach (tickets £1 per person per holiday). This is a traditional style touring park which during the day is a hive of activity, but the nights are quiet and peaceful. The largest of the camping fields is sloping with superb views across the headland to the sea. Two smaller fields are terraced and one area has hardstandings. Together they provide 302 pitches, 124 with electricity connections (15A) and 20 also with TV and water connections. Also available are a lovely four bedroomed farmhouse (sleeping ten), a pretty two bedroomed cottage (five beds) and a caravan holiday home. The shop is well stocked (gas available), there is a takeaway and restaurant and an attractive bar with patio overlooking a small duck pond. The park has its own very well maintained nine hole golf course with reduced fees for campers. One of the huge redundant farm buildings has been put to excellent use: divided into three areas, it provides table tennis and pool, a skittle alley and two lanes of flat green bowling with changing rooms. Walks to the local village and along the coastal path are easy from the site and a bus to Ilfracombe and Barnstaple stops 100 yards from the entrance.

Facilities

The central toilet block has been regularly upgraded and can be heated. Two washbasins in the ladies have hoses for hair washing, controllable showers (no dividers). Small area with baby bath facilities. Dishwashing sinks under cover. Laundry. These facilities are arranged around the farmhouse area and include a very well equipped unit for disabled people with everything in one large room including a hairdryer. Motorcaravan service point. Shop. Bar. Golf. Small heated indoor swimming pool is well used, as are games and TV rooms. Fenced play area with bark base. Indoor skittle alley, bowls, and table tennis. In high season only one dog per pitch is allowed. Off site: Fishing or riding 1 mile, bicycle hire 3 miles. Tarka Trail for walking and riding. Boat trips to Lundy Island.

At a glance

| Welcome & Ambience | ✓✓✓✓ | Location | ✓✓✓✓ |
| Quality of Pitches | ✓✓✓✓ | Range of Facilities | ✓✓✓✓ |

Directions

From Barnstaple, take A361 Ilfracombe road through Braunton. Turn left at Mullacott Cross roundabout on B3343 to Woolacombe, turning right after 2-3 miles to Mortehoe. Park is on right before village. O.S.GR: SS455455. GPS: N51:11.118 W04:11.936

Charges 2005

Per caravan or motorcaravan	£ 14.00 - £ 45.00
with services	£ 17.50 - £ 47.50
tent - adult	£ 4.50 - £ 15.00
tent - child (5-15 yrs)	£ 2.25 - £ 7.50
dog	£ 1.50

Reservations

Made with £2 deposit per night booked (camping and touring). Tel: 01271 870343. Email: goodtimes@woolacombe.com

Open

Easter - end October.

UK0730 Twitchen Parc

Mortehoe, Woolacombe EX34 7ES (Devon)

Set in the grounds of an attractive Edwardian country house, Twitchen Parc is owned by Woolacombe Bay Holiday Parcs. Its main concern lies in holiday caravans and apartments, although it also provides marked pitches for tourers at the top of the park, with some views over the rolling hills to the sea. With a more recently developed touring field, they include 228 pitches with 16A electricity, many with tarmac hardstanding (not always level), mostly arranged around oval access roads in hedged areas. Further non-electric pitches are behind in two open, unmarked fields which are sloping (blocks are thoughtfully provided, stored in neat wooden boxes next to water points). A smart, modern entertainment complex incorporates a licensed club and family lounge with snacks, a restaurant, teenage disco room, cartoon lounge, outdoor pool and indoor pool complex. Twitchen is very popular for families with children. If they become bored, there are always the excellent beaches nearby with a footpath down to the sea. All the facilities of Golden Coast and Woolacombe Bay Holiday Villages and Easewell Farm are free to visitors at Twitchen, with a bus (small charge) running regularly between each one to the beach.

Facilities

There are two toilet blocks. Dishwashing and laundry facilities at each block plus a good modern launderette at the central complex. Motorcaravan service point. Shop and takeaway. Club, bars, restaurant and entertainment for adults and children, day and evening. OFSTED approved creche for children (charge). Outdoor pool (heated mid-May - mid-Sept). Attractive indoor pool with sauna, paddling pool, fountain and a viewing area. Games rooms for table tennis, pool and arcade games. Good adventure play area. ATM. American motorhomes are accepted (up to 30 ft). Off site: Beach 1 mile. Golf 1 mile. Fishing, riding and bicycle hire 2 miles.

Open

Easter- end October.

At a glance

| Welcome & Ambience | ✓✓✓✓ | Location | ✓✓✓✓ |
| Quality of Pitches | ✓✓✓✓ | Range of Facilities | ✓✓✓✓✓ |

Directions

From Barnstaple take A361 towards Ilfracombe and through Braunton. Turn left at Mullacott Cross roundabout towards Woolacombe and then right towards Mortehoe. Park is on the left before village. O.S.GR: SS465451. GPS: N51:11.081 W04:11.862

Charges 2005

Per caravan or motorcaravan	£ 14.00 - £ 45.00
with services	£ 17.50 - £ 47.50
tent - adult	£ 4.50 - £ 15.00
tent - child (5-15 yrs)	£ 2.25 - £ 7.50
dog	£ 1.50

Special offers available.

Reservations

Made with deposit (£2 per pitch per night). Tel: 01271 870343. Email:goodtimes@woolacombe.com

UK1070 **Woolacombe Bay Holiday Village**

Sandy Lane, Woolacombe EX34 7AH (Devon)

Woolacombe Bay Holiday Village, and its sister site Golden Coast Holiday Village nearby, are well known holiday parks providing a range of holiday accommodation from caravan holiday homes to luxury lodges, apartments and villas, with many on site amenities including pools, restaurants and bars, and providing a wide range of entertainment. A camping section at the Woolacombe Bay park caters for tents and trailer tents only, so touring visitors can enjoy all the activities and entertainment of both parks. Partly terraced out of the hillside and partly on the hill top with some existing pine trees but with many more trees planted for landscaping, the site has magnificent views out across the bay. Marked and numbered pitches have been provided on grass for 150 tents, 97 with electricity (10/16A). All should be level, having been terraced where necessary and they are connected by gravel roads. Some up and down walking is needed for the toilet block. A bus service (small charge) runs between the two parks, the third and fourth parks in the group (Twitchen Parc and Easewell Farm) and the beach during the main season, although there is a footpath to the beach from the site. The three larger parks have varied entertainment programmes and children's clubs and Woolacombe Bay also boasts a health spa and beauty suite.

Facilities

A super central toilet block has excellent facilities, including en-suite shower and washrooms and separate toilets, baby facilities, and also a sauna and sun bed - unusual but nice. Separate dishwashing and laundry rooms. Two units for disabled visitors. Supermarket. Bars, restaurant and entertainment. Indoor (heated) and outdoor pools with flumes and slides. Sauna and gym. Tennis courts. ATM. Dogs are welcome at Woolacombe Bay but not at Golden Coast. Off site: Fishing and riding 1 mile. Beach 1 mile.

Open

11 May - 21 September (camping) statics Mar-Oct.

At a glance

Welcome & Ambience	✓✓✓✓	Location	✓✓✓✓
Quality of Pitches	✓✓✓✓	Range of Facilities	✓✓✓✓✓

Directions

Take A361 Barnstaple - Ilfracombe road through Braunton. Turn left at Mullacott Cross roundabout towards Woolacombe then right towards Mortehoe. Now follow the camping signs by turning left and park is on the left. O.S.GR: SS469443.
GPS: N51:10.627 W04:11.479

Charges 2005

Per caravan or motorcaravan	
with all persons	£ 14.00 - £ 45.00
serviced pitch	£ 17.50 - £ 47.50
tent - adult	£ 4.50 - £ 15.00
tent - child (5-15 yrs)	£ 2.25 - £ 7.50
dog	£ 1.50

Reservations

Advised for peak season; contact park Tel: 01271 870343. Email: goodtimes@woolacombe.com

UK1075 **Golden Coast Holiday Village**

Station Road, Woolacombe EX34 7HW (Devon)

The Golden Coast Holiday Village is part of the Woolacombe Bay Holiday Parcs group that includes Woolacombe Bay, Twitchen Parc and the recently acquired Easewell Farm Holiday Parc. It predominantly comprises brick-built holiday accommodation, however, there are two small camping areas providing 91 pitches, 18 of which are fully serviced. The toilet block is adequate rather than good, and was quite clean at the time of our visit. Campers can enjoy an extensive program of entertainment for children and adults, and qualified nursery nurses run an OFSTED approved crèche. A shuttle bus runs between the four parks and to the beach several times a day (it costs £1 per person per holiday). A visit to the Old Mill Inn should not be missed; it serves bar meals, and has an excellent beer garden with adventure play area for the children. The range of amenities and facilities at this large park will suit families looking for a lively holiday filled with activities and entertainment.

Facilities

A new building provides good facilities including good showers. One washing machine and a dryer in the ladies' section. Dishwashing sinks inside. Large, well stocked supermarket, boutique and beauty salon. Indoor and outdoor swimming pools, outdoor flume, sauna and solarium. Bar, club, Old Mill Inn, restaurant and takeaway. Floodlit tennis court. Adventure playgrounds. Snooker. Games room. Soft play area and crèche. 9-hole golf course. Indoor and outdoor bowls, ten-pin bowling complex. Fishing. Woodland walks. Off site: Woolacombe beach is about 2 miles, and for walkers there is the coastal path. Amenities at sister parks available to all visitors.

At a glance

Welcome & Ambience	✓✓✓✓	Location	✓✓✓✓
Quality of Pitches	✓✓✓	Range of Facilities	✓✓✓✓✓

Directions

From Barnstaple, take A361 (signed Braunton and Ilfracombe). Turn left on B3343 (signed Woolacombe) and follow the road towards the town. The park is on the left near the top of the hill. O.S.GR: SS480435.
GPS: N51:10.350 W04:10.366

Charges 2005

Per caravan or motorcaravan	£ 14.00 - £ 45.00
with services	£ 17.50 - £ 47.50
tent - per adult	£ 4.50 - £ 15.00
tent - per child (5-15 yrs)	£ 2.25 - £ 7.50

Reservations

Made with £2 deposit per pitch per night (camping and touring). Tel: 01271 870343. Email: goodtimes@woolacombe.com

Open

12 February - 2 January.

UK0735 Woolacombe Sands Holiday Park

Beach Road, Woolacombe EX34 7AF (Devon)

With sea views and within walking distance of Woolacombe's lovely sandy beach, this family park has been terraced out of the valley side as you drop down into the village. Apart from its smart entrance, it has been left natural. The pond and stream at the bottom are almost hidden with gated access to the National Trust fields across the valley. The 200 terraced level grass pitches all with 10A electricity are accessed by gravel roads with some good up and down walking needed to the toilet blocks (probably not the best environment for disabled people). Some 50 mobile homes and 14 bungalows are in the more central area, and tents tend to be placed on the bottom terraces. The park boasts both indoor and outdoor pools (accessed by code) with a full time attendant. Evenings see Woolly Bear emerge from his 'shack' to entertain children, with adult family entertainment later. A good plus factor is the fact that all facilities open when the site opens. A useful path leads from the site to the beach via the car park and the walk is said to take 15 minutes.

Facilities

Four basic toilet blocks with good hot water are spread amongst the terraces. The newer shower block has separate toilets opposite. Shop (open 07.00 - 22.00). Self service food bar providing good value meals and breakfast (main season and BHs). Two bars and entertainment area. Indoor and outdoor pools both with paddling pool areas. Fenced play area on bark with plenty of equipment'. Ball area with nets. Crazy golf. 'Kingpin' bowling Off site: Beach 15 minutes walk. Riding next door. Golf 0.5 miles. Fishing (fresh water) 0.5 miles.

At a glance

Welcome & Ambience ✓✓✓✓ Location ✓✓✓✓
Quality of Pitches ✓✓✓ Range of Facilities ✓✓✓✓✓

Directions

Follow A361 from Barnstaple through Braunton towards Ilfracombe. At Mullacott Cross roundabout turn left for Woolacombe (B3343). Site clearly signed on left as you go down the hill into the village. O.S.GR: SS468436.

Charges 2005

Per unit incl. 6 persons
(max. 4 adults) and electricity £ 13.75 - £ 37.50
dog £ 5.00

Reservations

Advised for peak season and made with deposit (£30 per pitch/week). Tel: 01271 870569.

Open

1 April - 1 November.

UK0710 Hidden Valley Touring & Camping Park

West Down, Ilfracombe EX34 8NU (Devon)

The owners, Martin and Dawn Fletcher, run this aptly named award-winning, family park to high standards. In a sheltered valley setting between Barnstaple and Ilfracombe beside a small stream and lake (with ducks), it is most attractive and is also convenient for several resorts, beaches and the surrounding countryside. The original part of the park offers some 74 level pitches of good size on three sheltered terraces. All have hardstanding, electricity hook-ups (16A) and free TV connections (leads for hire), with a water point between each pitch. Kingfisher Meadow, a little way from the main facilities and reached by a tarmac road, provides a further 60 pitches entirely on grass (so suitable for campers with tents), all with electricity, water, waste water and TV hook-ups. Two good adventure play areas have wooden equipment and safe bark surfaces (one near a fast flowing stream). There is a well stocked shop with off-licence, a coffee shop, bar with good value food three times a week (high season) including takeaway, plus a games room. Essentially this is a park for those seeking good quality facilities in very attractive, natural surroundings, without too many man-made distractions - apart from some traffic noise during day time. It provides a relaxed setting with woodland walks direct from the site.

Facilities

Two modern toilet blocks (one for each area, one heated) are tiled and have non-slip floors. Some washbasins in cubicles, some en-suite with toilets in the Kingfisher Meadow block. Bathroom (tokens). Baby room. Laundry facilities including washing machine, dryer and iron. Dishwashing sinks under cover. Complete facilities for people with disabilities. Supplementary clean 'portacabin' style facilities in the original area. Motorcaravan service facilities. Gas supplies. Shop, bar and takeaway. Coffee shop open to the public. Play areas. Up to two dogs are accepted (otherwise by prior arrangement). Caravan storage. Off site: Fishing or golf 2 miles. Bicycle hire 4 miles. Riding 5 miles. Beach 5 miles.

At a glance

Welcome & Ambience	✓✓✓✓	Location	✓✓✓✓
Quality of Pitches	✓✓✓✓	Range of Facilities	✓✓✓✓

Directions

Park is on A361 Barnstaple - Ilfracombe road, 3.5 miles after Braunton. O.S.GR: SS499408. GPS: N51:08.792 W04:08.733

Charges 2006

Per unit incl. 2 persons	£ 7.00 - £ 22.50
extra adult	£ 1.50 - £ 4.00
child (5-15 yrs)	free - £ 2.00
dog	free - £ 1.00

Discounts for over 50s.

Reservations

Essential in high season and accepted with deposit (low season £20, high £35). Tel: 01271 813837. Email: relax@hiddenvalleypark.com

Open

All year.

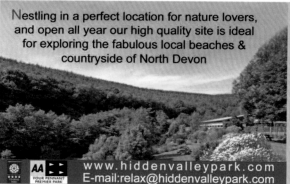

Nestling in a perfect location for nature lovers, and open all year our high quality site is ideal for exploring the fabulous local beaches & countryside of North Devon

www.hiddenvalleypark.com
E-mail:relax@hiddenvalleypark.com

Hidden Valley
TOURING & CAMPING PARK
For more information
PHONE 01271 813837

Hidden Valley Park
West Down
Near Ilfracombe
North Devon
EX34 8NU

For more
site inspiration
see our directory ON PAGE 314

UK0700 Greenacres Touring Caravan Park

Bratton Fleming, Barnstaple EX31 4SG (Devon)

A neat, compact, rural park on the edge of Exmoor, Greenacres is managed and run alongside, but separately from, the working farm owned by the family. Drive through the farm access to the park (clearly signed) - you will need to go back and call at the house to book in. No tents are taken. The site has 30 very large , well drained pitches (all with 16A electric hook-ups) with connecting gravel paths to the road - in theory you can get to your unit without stepping on the grass. The top area is level, the lower part next to the beech woods is semi-terraced to provide six hardstandings and some hedged places. There are marvellous views outside the beech hedge that shelters the site. To the west of Exmoor, the park is very suitable for the coast at Ilfracombe and Combe Martin, or for exploring the moor. The family has opened up a woodland walk through newly planted trees and across the fields to a secluded valley picnic area beside a stream to take advantage of the marvellous views and surroundings. The West Country cycle way passes within a mile of the park and the area is the setting for the classic novel, 'Lorna Doone'.

Facilities

The toilet block, kept very clean and tidy, is in the centre of the horseshoe layout with showers (1M, 1F) on payment (20p). Units for disabled visitors (and general use in peak times) . Laundry room, with sink, spin dryer, iron and board, and dishwashing room. Washing lines provided. Gas supplies. Tourist information kiosk . Area for children with football and volleyball nets and swings, separated by a Devon bank from the 2 acre dog exercise field. Recycling centre. Off site: Fishing 3 miles. Riding 6 miles. Golf 12 miles. Pubs, restaurants and takeaways within 3 mile radius.

Open

Easter/1 April - 31 October.

At a glance

| Welcome & Ambience | ✓✓✓✓ | Location | ✓✓✓✓ |
| Quality of Pitches | ✓✓✓✓✓ | Range of Facilities | ✓✓✓ |

Directions

From North Devon link road (M5, exit 27) turn north at South Molton onto A399. Continue for 9 miles, past turning for Exmoor Steam Centre and on to Stowford Cross. Turn left towards Exmoor Zoological Park and Greenacres is on the left. O.S.GR: SS660404. GPS: N51:08.858 W03:55.051

Charges 2005

Per unit incl. 2 persons	£ 5.25 - £ 8.50
incl. electricity	£ 6.75 - £ 10.00
extra person	£ 1.25 - £ 1.75
child (under 7 yrs)	free
dog	free
No credit cards.	

Reservations

Made with £5 deposit. Tel: 01598 763334.

UK1145 Hele Valley Holiday Park

Hele Bay, Ilfracombe EX34 9RD (Devon)

Hele Valley is a well-established park which has been in the same family for over 30 years. Located a mile from Ilfracombe in a wooded valley, it is only a few minutes walk from Hele Bay beach. Here, quaint coves and coastal paths reveal a genuine smuggler's cave. Apart from the 60 attractively laid out caravan holiday homes (20 available for rent), the park caters for tents and motorcaravans only because of the difficult access. Some 50 unmarked pitches are set in two lush green fields surrounded by trees and hedges. Being in a valley, some of the pitches are terraced. Eight dedicated grass pitches for motor-caravans are fully-serviced but tents have no hookups. This is a great centre for touring North Devon with Lynmouth, Porlock (Lorna Doone country), Exmoor, the pretty market town of Barnstaple and Great Torrington, famous for Dartington Glass. Nature lovers can enjoy walks on Exmoor or along the coast, including the Tarka Trail and, for bird watchers, Lundy Island is but a boat ride away (trips from Ilfracombe). A path leads from the park to nearby Chambercombe Manor with its association with Lady Jane Grey, a tunnel and a mysterious visitor - open to the public.

Facilities

The bright, airy and modern toilet block (access by key with deposit required) provides a mixture of open and enclosed washbasins; plus long mirrors and free hairdryers. Separately, a deluxe baby changing room, complete with pretty freize and chiming mobiles and a well-fitted unit for disabled visitors. Dishwashing and laundry areas, both enclosed. Modern reception with tourist information. Two good adventure play areas and a play field. Parents must keep children away from the steep-sided stream running the length of the park. Off site: Mini-market, pubs and cafés 5 minutes walk. Fishing, sea fishing, sailing, many shops in Ilfracombe 1 mile. Beach and golf 400 yards. Riding 4 miles. Bus service in main road.

Open

Whitsun - 31 August.

At a glance

| Welcome & Ambience | ✓✓✓✓ | Location | ✓✓✓✓ |
| Quality of Pitches | ✓✓✓✓ | Range of Facilities | ✓✓✓ |

Directions

From Ilfracombe, take A399 east towards Combe Martin. With Ilfracombe swimming pool on the left, proceed down the hill for a further 400 m. and, at brown Hele Valley sign, take sharp right turn. Go down steep road and continue to T-junction. Turn right to the park. From Combe Martin follow A399 west for 8 miles, past Ilfracombe golf course on left. Continue down the hill and turn left at the brown Hele Valley sign and continue as above. O.S. GR: SS533474. GPS: N51:12.667 W04:06.000

Charges 2005

Per tent or motorcaravan	
incl. 2 persons	£ 10.00 - £ 19.00
extra person	£ 3.00 - £ 5.00
child (5-14 yrs)	£ 2.00
dog	£ 2.50

Reservations

Made with 50% deposit for min. 3 nights. Tel: 01271 862460. Email: holidays@helevalley.co.uk

UK1120 **Napps Touring Holiday Park**

Old Coast Road, Berrynarbor, Ilfracombe EX34 9SW (Devon)

Set in an idyllic location in North Devon, this popular, family-run site offers peace and quiet on site, with plenty to see and do off site. A path just outside the gates leads down to a private beach with safe bathing; although it is only 200 yards to the gate, there are 200 steps down to the beach. Combe Martin and Ilfracombe beaches are also close by. The local pub (300 yards down the lane) offers snacks, a garden, restaurant and entertainment. The 170 touring pitches, most with views of Watermouth Bay, are terraced and spacious, 60 are serviced with electricity, water tap and waste point, and a further 70 have a 10A hook-up. An outdoor heated pool is unsupervised, but there is a terrace with table and chairs for non-swimmers to watch or enjoy a light meal from the snack bar. In high season, a ceramics studio is organised for older children. Light entertainment is organised during the high season. All the services are at the bottom of the site and it can be quite a climb back up, especially to the terraces and tent area.

Facilities

The modern toilet block includes open plan washbasins. Laundry. Licensed shop. Gas supplies. Bar with entertainment during high season. Takeaway. Heated outdoor pool with paddling pool and small toddlers' slide. Tennis. Ceramic studio. Games room. Adventure play area and five-a-side football pitch. Caravan storage. Off site: Beach and fishing 200 yds. Golf and boat launching 1.5 miles. Bicycle hire and riding 5 miles. Coombe Martin 1.5 miles.

Open

1 March - 15 November.

At a glance

| Welcome & Ambience | ✓✓✓✓ | Location | ✓✓✓✓✓ |
| Quality of Pitches | ✓✓✓✓ | Range of Facilities | ✓✓✓✓ |

Directions

Leave M5 at junction 27, take A361 to South Molton and then A399 to Combe Martin. Site is 1.5 miles west of Combe Martin on the A399 (signed). O.S.GR: SS559475. GPS: N51:12.511 W04:03.845

Charges 2005

Per unit incl. 2 persons	£ 6.00 - £ 14.00
incl. electricity	£ 8.00 - £ 17.00
extra person over 5 yrs	free - £ 2.00
dog	free - £ 2.00

Reservations

Made with £30 deposit per week or part week (non-refundable). Tel: 01271 882557. Email: info@napps.fsnet.co.uk

Yeatheridge Farm *Caravan & Camping Park*
01884 860330
www.yeatheridge.co.uk
If you are a country lover, there is everything to interest you here.
2 ½ miles of wood & riverside walks. If you wish to explore beautiful Devon,
then there could not be a better location.

NEW ON-SITE RESTAURANT

UK1060 **Yeatheridge Farm Caravan Park**

East Worlington, Crediton EX17 4TN (Devon)

Yeatheridge is a friendly, family park with riding, fishing lakes, and indoor pools. Based on a 200-acre farm, 9 acres have been developed over many years into an attractive touring park. Around the site there are views of the local hills and Dartmoor away to the south, and Exmoor lies to the north. You can explore three woodland walks ranging from 1 to 2.5 miles and the banks of the River Dalch. There are two deep coarse fishing lakes (bring your own rod), the top one offering family fishing and the lower one for serious fishing (age 14 or over and free of charge). Horse riding is available on site (best to bring your own hat) with hour-long and park rides available. The ponies and goats are also popular with adults and children alike. The touring area is very neat and tidy with a spacious feel to it as units are sited around the perimeter or back onto hedges, leaving open central areas. The 85 numbered, grass pitches are flat, gently sloping or on terraces and are sufficiently large, 80 with electricity (10A). Seasonal tourers take up 25 pitches and there are 4 caravan holiday homes. The owners, Geoff and Liz, are constantly upgrading the park and they try very hard to make everyone feel at home.

Facilities

Two toilet blocks provide family rooms, washbasins in cubicles, showers and facilities for babies. En-suite room for disabled visitors. Dishwashing (hot water 10p) and laundry. Shop. Bar, restaurant and snack bar (hours vary acc. to season). Unsupervised indoor swimming pools, toddlers' pool and water slide open daily, 10 am - 8 pm. Fenced play area with fort for under 10s (parental supervision). Football field. TV room. Pool table, table tennis and skittles. Fishing. Riding.

Open

22 March - 29 September.

At a glance

| Welcome & Ambience | ✓✓✓✓ | Location | ✓✓✓✓ |
| Quality of Pitches | ✓✓✓✓ | Range of Facilities | ✓✓✓✓✓ |

Directions

Park is off the B3042 Witheridge - Chawleigh (not in East Worlington). From M5 take exit 27 onto A361 to Tiverton. Turn left onto A396 for 0.5 miles then right on B3137 almost to Witheridge, then left on B3042 for 3 miles to site, well signed down concrete roadway on left. O.S.GR: SS770114. GPS: N50:53.322 W03:45.006

Charges 2005

Per unit incl. 2 persons	£ 7.00 - £ 12.00
extra person over 4 yrs	£ 1.50 - £ 2.00
electricity	£ 1.00

Reservations

Advised for Bank and school holidays and made with £35 deposit. Tel: 01884 860330. Email: yeatheridge@talk21.com

57

UK0750 Minnows Touring Caravan Park

Sampford Peverell, Tiverton EX16 7EN (Devon)

Minnows is an attractive, neat small park with views across the Devon countryside, separated from the Grand Western canal by hedging. Easily accessible from the M5, it is suitable as an ideal touring centre for Devon and Somerset, for cycling or walking, or simply for breaking a long journey. A small, neat park, open for nine months of the year, it provides 45 level pitches all with 16A electricity. Of these, 35 are all weather (grass and gravel). A further 3.5 acres have been added providing space for more and larger pitches, a tent area, a playground and a large field for ball games, etc. The village of Sampford Peverell, with pub and farm shop, is only a half mile walk via the towpath, with Tiverton 7.5 miles. In fact, there are 12 miles of level walking on the towpath or one can take a trip on a horse-drawn barge. The site is on the Sustran cycle route (route 3). Tiverton Parkway station (BR) is one mile and buses run from the village. Coarse fishing permits for the canal are available from reception. A Caravan Club affiliated site, non-members are also very welcome. There could be some road noise from the adjacent A361.

Facilities

The heated toilet block has been refurbished with tiled floors, new pressurised showers and 2 cubicles for ladies. It is clean and comfortable with all modern facilities and constant hot water. Facilities for disabled visitors and babies. Covered dishwashing sinks. Laundry with washing machine, dryer and ironing. Motorcaravan service point. Gas supplies. Newspaper delivery arranged. Excellent tourist information. Play area. Bicycle hire (delivery to site). American RVs accepted (up to 38 ft), advance booking necessary. All year caravan storage. Site gates closed 9 pm. and locked 11 pm.- 7.30 am. Off site: Boat slipway and Golf driving range 400 yds, full course 4 miles. Riding 6 miles.

Open

6 March - 13 November.

At a glance

Welcome & Ambience	✓✓✓✓	Location	✓✓✓✓
Quality of Pitches	✓✓✓✓✓	Range of Facilities	✓✓✓

Directions

From M5 junction 27 take A361 signed Tiverton. After about 600 yds leave on the first exit signed Sampford Peverell. After about 200 yds turn right at roundabout and cross bridge over A361 to a second roundabout. Go straight ahead and park is immediately ahead. From North Devon on A361 go to M5 junction 27 and return back up the A361 as above. O.S.GR: ST042148.
GPS: N50:55.501 W03:21.871

Charges 2005

Per adult	£ 3.30 - £ 4.80
child (5-16 yrs)	£ 1.10 - £ 1.60
pitch	£ 4.00 - £ 7.00
dog	free

Credit cards accepted for £10 or more.

Reservations

Made with £10 deposit. Tel: 01884 821770.

UK0760 Barley Meadow Camping & Caravan Park

Crockernwell, Exeter EX6 6NR (Devon)

This peaceful little park is located on the northern edge of Dartmoor with easy access from the A30. It is sheltered from the weather by good hedging and, although not always visible from the pitches, there are open views across the moorland to the south. The site would be a suitable base for visiting Exeter, Okehampton and Plymouth, hiking over the moors, or just enjoying the local area. The Two Moors Way for walkers is only 400 yards from the site. The 40 pitches are mostly on level grass, well spaced, with 13 hardstandings (some taken by seasonal units), and 27 electric hook-ups (10/16A). The resident owners can provide packed lunches and cream teas to order.

Facilities

The single heated toilet block is well maintained and provides all facilities including a well equipped room for disabled campers and babies. Laundry. Small shop for basic groceries, small camping items and gas. Games room with pool table and TV. Playground. Small library and information chalet. Only small American RVs (up to 30 ft.) accepted. Off site: Fishing 1 mile (river) or 2 miles (lake). Golf 2.5 miles. Riding 2 miles. Nearby is Castle Drogo, the youngest castle in the U.K. At Fingle Bridge there are walks and an Inn. Further afield is Canonteign Falls, home of England's highest waterfall. Okehampton 15 minutes.

Open

15 March - 15 November.

At a glance

Welcome & Ambience	✓✓✓✓	Location	✓✓✓✓✓
Quality of Pitches	✓✓✓✓	Range of Facilities	✓✓✓

Directions

From M5 exit 31, take A30 towards Okehampton. After 10 miles turn left towards Cheriton Bishop. Pass through village, and continue for 1 mile towards Crockernwell, and site is on your left. From the west on A30, at the 'Merry Roundabout' at Whiddon Down, take first left towards Cheriton Bishop. Continue for 2 miles and site entrance is on right. O.S.GR: SH742924. GPS: N50:43.052 W03:46.995

Charges guide

Per unit incl. 2 persons	£ 7.50 - £ 9.00
incl. electricity	£ 9.50 - £ 11.00
extra adult	£ 2.00
child (1-14 yrs0	£ 1.50
dog	£ 0.50

Reservations

Advised for peak season and B.Hs. Tel: 01647 281629. Email: angela.waldron1@btopenworld.com

UK0790 Harford Bridge Park

Peter Tavy, Tavistock PL19 9LS (Devon)

Harford Bridge has an interesting history - originally the Wheal Union tin mine until 1850, then used as a farm campsite from 1930 and taken over by the Royal Engineers in 1939. It is now a quiet, rural, mature park inside the Dartmoor National Park. It is bounded by the River Tavy on one side and the lane from the main road to the village of Peter Tavy on the other, with Harford Bridge, a classic granite moorland bridge, at the corner. With 16.5 acres, the park provides 120 touring pitches well spaced on a level grassy meadow with some shade from mature trees and others recently planted; 40 pitches have electrical hook-ups and 5 have 'multi-services'. Out of season or by booking in advance you may get one of the delightful spots bordering the river (these are without electricity). Some holiday caravans and chalets are neatly landscaped in their own area. At the entrance to the park a central grassy area is left free for games, which is also used by the town band, village fete, etc. While the river (unfenced) will inevitably mesmerise youngsters, a super central adventure play area on a hilly tree knoll will claim them. In early summer there are chicks to watch (Mr Williamson's hobby) and the park ducks are a feature. With its own and the local history, plus its situation, this is a super place to stay.

Facilities

The single toilet block is older in style but fully equipped and well kept. Facilities for disabled visitors double for babies. Good launderette and drying room. Freezer. Motorcaravan services. Games room and separate TV room. Play area. Tennis court (free). Two communal barbecue areas. Fly fishing (by licence, £3 p/day, £10 p/week). Off site: Bicycle hire, riding and golf, all within 2.5 miles.

Open

Late March - early November (all year for caravans).

At a glance

Welcome & Ambience	✓✓✓✓✓	Location	✓✓✓✓✓
Quality of Pitches	✓✓✓✓	Range of Facilities	✓✓✓

Directions

Two miles north of Tavistock, off A386 Tavistock - Okehampton road, take the road to Peter Tavy. O.S.GR: SX504768.

Charges 2005

Per person incl. 2 persons	£ 7.50 - £ 11.75
with electricity	£ 10.50 - £ 14.75
with services	£ 11.00 - £ 15.25
child	free - £ 1.90

Less 10% for over 7 days (not electricity or fishing).

Reservations

Made for any length with first night's fees. Tel: 01822 810349. Email: enquiry@harfordbridge.co.uk

HARFORD BRIDGE HOLIDAY PARK

ROSE AWARD

Peter Tavy, Tavistock, Devon PL19 9LS
Tel: 01822 810349 Fax: 01822 810028
Email: enquiry@harfordbridge.co.uk
Website: www.harfordbridge.co.uk

• Level sheltered park set in Dartmoor beside the River Tavy, with beautiful views of Cox Tor
• Riverside camping and other level spacious pitches - Open end Mar to Nov
• Self-catering luxury caravan holiday homes - Open all year
• Childrens play area, tennis and table tennis, fly fishing, dog exercise field
• Nearby pony-trekking and golf • Cinema/Theatre • Swimming Pool • Bellamy and Rose Award

Just 2 miles from Tavistock off A386 Okehampton Road, take Peter Tavy turn

UK0802 Langstone Manor Holiday Park

Moortown, Tavistock PL19 9JZ (Devon)

On the southwest edge of Dartmoor, this park is in the grounds of the old Langstone Manor house. The pitches are tucked into various garden areas with mature trees and flowering shrubs, or in the walled garden area with views over the moor. In all there are 42 level grass pitches which vary in size (20 with 10A electricity). You pass through an area of holiday caravans on the way to reception and the touring pitches where there are also some cottages for rent. The bar and restaurant in the Manor, with a terrace that catches the evening sun, is open in high season and on demand in low season. Approaching over a short section of the moor, you realise how well the park is situated to explore Dartmoor.

Facilities

The toilet block is set to one side of the walled garden area, fully equipped and well maintained. Showers on payment. Fully equipped laundry room. Basic supplies kept in reception. Bar/restaurant. Play area. Off site: Golf 1 mile. Fishing 2 miles. Bicycle hire 3 miles.

Open

15 March - 29 October.

At a glance

Welcome & Ambience	✓✓✓✓	Location	✓✓✓✓✓
Quality of Pitches	✓✓✓✓	Range of Facilities	✓✓✓✓

Directions

From Tavistock take B3357 Princetown road. After about 2 miles turn right (site signed). Pass over cattle grid onto the moor and follow site signs, leaving the moor to shortly find site on right. O.S.GR: SX524738

Charges 2006

Per unit incl. 2 persons	£ 8.00 - £ 10.00
electricity and water	£ 2.00

Reservations

Made with deposit (£10 per week). Tel: 01822 613371. Email: web@langstone-manor.co.uk

UK0800 Higher Longford Caravan Park

Moorshop, Tavistock PL19 9LQ (Devon)

This attractive well organised, family run park is situated within the Dartmoor National Park boundaries with views up to the higher slopes of the moor. A neat, sheltered field provides 40 level pitches arranged on each side of a circular access road, with three smaller touring areas for a further 12 units, a small terraced camping field with good views and a seasonal camping field for a further 40. Facilities include 65 electrical hook-ups (16A), several multi-serviced pitches and an area of hardstanding for motorcaravans in poor weather. Some attractive converted cottages form a courtyard area with the farmhouse and reception. Within the 14th century farmhouse is a small licensed shop with gas and some farm produce, and a takeaway including breakfast items and fresh bread. It adjoins a pleasant, cosy campers' lounge with pool table and TV which is open all day. Higher Longford is an ideal centre for touring Dartmoor, either by car, on foot, or astride a local pony. Plymouth and the cross-channel ferries are a 30 minute drive, Tavistock is 3 miles, with a good market and Goose Fair in October.

Facilities

A super new toilet block provides excellent full en-suite facilities (amongst the best we have seen) plus extra toilets and washbasins. Bathroom and baby changing. Full laundry facilities. Indoor dishwashing sinks. Motorcaravan services. Ice block service. Shop and takeaway (hours limited in winter). Campers' lounge with pool and TV . Large recreation field with adventure play area in centre. Caravan storage. Off site: Bus service outside park. Game or coarse fishing 3 miles, Tavistock golf course 1 mile. Bicycle hire 2.5 miles. Riding 5 miles. Beach 15 miles.

At a glance

Welcome & Ambience	✓✓✓✓✓	Location	✓✓✓✓✓
Quality of Pitches	✓✓✓✓✓	Range of Facilities	✓✓✓✓

Directions

Park is clearly signed from the B3357 Princetown road, 2 miles from Tavistock. O.S.GR: SX520747. GPS: N50:33.210 W04:05.623

Charges 2005

Per unit incl. 2 persons	£ 11.00 - £ 13.00
incl. electricity	£ 13.00 - £ 15.00
extra adult	£ 2.50
child	£ 1.50

Reservations

Made with deposit of one nights fee. Tel: 01822 613360. Email: stay@higherlongford.co.uk

Open

All year.

UK0805 Woodovis Park

Woodovis House, Gulworthy, Tavistock PL19 8NY (Devon)

Woodovis Park nestles in a sheltered wooded position covering 14 acres, by the edge of the Tamar Valley on the border of Devon and Cornwall. John and Dorothy Lewis have been running Woodovis Park since 1999 , helped by their very welcoming staff. There are 50 good sized pitches, 42 with 10A electricity and 16 with hardstanding. Split over two fields, most are on level, neatly mown grass, some are gently sloping. Landscaped in between are 35 caravan holiday homes, 20 privately owned and 14 for hire. The whole area is sheltered by thick hedges and woodland but in places you can see across the valley to Cornwall. An indoor heated swimming pool complete with spa pool and sauna are a welcome attraction, as are the freshly baked morning croissants or bread ordered the night before at reception. The approach to the site is down a tree lined lane with passing places. This is a peaceful spot with some nice touches. Try exploring Dartmoor and become addicted to 'Letterboxing'.

Facilities

A purpose built, modern toilet block is fully equipped. One washbasin in cabin for ladies. Bathroom (coin operated) could be used by disabled people or for babies. Toilet for disabled visitors at the pool. Dishwashing sinks. Fully equipped laundry. Shop for basics with off licence doubles with reception. Indoor heated swimming pool (no swimming alone). Good games room including pool table and large size 'Connect 4'! Fenced play area. Minigolf. Special frames for disposable barbecues. Off site: Pub within walking distance. Fishing 1.5 miles. Golf, riding and bicycle hire 3 miles. Boat launching 6 miles. Tavistock 4 miles.

Open

1 April/Easter - 4 November.

At a glance

Welcome & Ambience	✓✓✓✓✓	Location	✓✓✓✓✓
Quality of Pitches	✓✓✓✓	Range of Facilities	✓✓✓✓

Directions

From Tavistock follow A390 for Liskeard. After 3 miles turn right at Gulworthy crossroads signed Chipshop, Lammerton and Caravan Park. After 1 mile entrance is signed on left. O.S.GR: SX431743. GPS: N50:32.932 W04:12.951

Charges 2005

Per person (over 5 yrs)	£ 4.50
caravan, trailer tent	
or motorcaravan	£ 8.00 - £ 10.00
tent	£ 6.00 - £ 8.00
awning	£ 1.50
electricity	free

Reservations

Made with non-refundable deposit of £25 at time of booking. Tel: 01822 832968. Email: info@woodovis.com

UK0810 Riverside Caravan Park

Leigham Manor Drive, Marsh Mills, Plymouth PL6 8LL (Devon)

As you leave the A38 for Plymouth and negotiate the Marsh Mills roundabout you can have no idea that there is a lush green touring park tucked away from the modern, out-of-town shopping units in a quiet green valley. Twenty seven years ago it was a corn field but, with careful development by its owner, it now provides a welcome oasis from which to explore Dartmoor, to enjoy the amazing views from Plymouth Hoe or even to overnight quietly before catching the ferry to France. The wooded valley sides give way to level grass where the trees and shrubs planted all those years ago have matured to give a park-like feel. The River Plym runs down one side of the site but it is carefully fenced. There are 232 pitches for caravans or motorcaravans, 150 of which have electricity (10A) and 60 are on hard-standing – especially useful as the site is open all year round. There is further provision for 60 tents. Hidden behind a high, evergreen hedge are an attractive swimming pool and children's pool. A play area is nearby and a pleasant restaurant with bar and games room provide welcome facilities and entertainment in high season.

Facilities

Three modern, fully equipped toilet blocks include cubicles with toilets and washbasins. Laundry room. Dishwashing room. Motorcaravan service point. Gas supplies. Basics are kept in reception (more in high season). Bar, restaurant and takeaway (B.Hs and high season) with family entertainment included. Heated swimming pool and children's pool. Games room with TV and pool table. Play area. Off site: Fishing possible in River Plym. Sea fishing 3.5 miles. Golf and riding 5 miles. Bicycle hire and boat launching 3.5 miles. Beach 10 miles. Dry ski slope and supermarket within walking distance. Bus stop 10 minutes.

Open

All year.

At a glance

| Welcome & Ambience | ✓✓✓✓ | Location | ✓✓✓✓ |
| Quality of Pitches | ✓✓✓✓ | Range of Facilities | ✓✓✓✓ |

Directions

From the A38 Marsh Mills roundabout for Plymouth take the third exit. After a few yards turn left following caravan signs, then right alongside the River Plym to the park. O.S.GR: SX518576.

Charges 2005

Per adult	£ 2.75 - £ 3.75
child (3-10 yrs)	£ 1.25 - £ 1.50
pitch incl. electricity	£ 5.50 - £ 7.00
tent pitch	£ 3.50 - £ 5.00
awning	£ 1.50 - £ 2.00
dog, extra car or boat	£ 1.00

Reservations

Made with deposit (£15 for each week or part week). Tel: 01752 344122.
Email: info@riversidecaravanpark.com

UK0820 Moor View Touring Park

California Cross, Modbury PL21 0SG (Devon)

Moor View has a gently sloping position with terraced, individual, fairly level grass pitches with marvellous views across to the Dartmoor Tors. It provides 68 pitches of varying size, connected by hard-core roads. All are on hardstanding with 10A electricity, water and drainage. Bushes and shrubs on planted between the pitches are growing well giving the park a more mature feel. A two acre field provides space for the odd rally. The amenities have been designed in one block near the entrance, not too far from the furthest pitches. The block includes reception with a shop stocking fresh local produce and some camping accessories. Burgh Island and Bigbury Bay are nearby, Dartmoor is within striking distance. This is a park in a lovely corner of Devon, run personally by the enthusiastic owners, Edward and Liz Corwood. A member of the Countryside Discovery group and an 'adults only' park.

Facilities

Traditional style, heated toilet facilities have access from a courtyard area and are kept clean, providing all necessary facilities including a laundry room and sink, and covered dishwashing sinks. Shop. Takeaway in season (to order, 18.30 - 20.30). TV room. Off site: Golf 5 miles, riding and fishing 6 miles. A local country pub is within walking distance, the small town of Modbury is 3 miles.

Open

15 March - 15 November.

At a glance

| Welcome & Ambience | ✓✓✓✓ | Location | ✓✓✓✓ |
| Quality of Pitches | ✓✓✓✓ | Range of Facilities | ✓✓✓ |

Directions

On the A38 from Exeter, pass exit for A385 (Totnes) and continue for a further 2 miles. Just past Woodpecker Inn leave the A38 at Wrangaton Cross, signed Ermington, Modbury and Yealmpton (site signed from here). Turn left and follow straight on at crossroads (Kitterford Cross) signed Modbury, Loddiswell, Kingsbridge for 3 miles to California Cross. Leave garage on left and follow towards Modbury (B3207). Park is 0.5 miles on left. O.S.GR: SX705533.

Charges 2005

Per unit incl. 2 persons	£ 7.85 - £ 12.85
premier pitch	£ 9.85 - £ 13.85
extra adult	£ 2.85 - £ 4.85
electricity	£ 1.00
dog	£ 0.40

Reservations

Made with £10 deposit. Tel: 01548 821485.
Email: info@moorviewtouringpark.co.uk

UK0825 Karrageen Caravan & Camping Park

Bolberry, Malborough, Kingsbridge TQ7 3EN (Devon)

Karrageen is to be found in a wonderful area of Devon, near Kingsbridge and Salcombe, with a mixture of rolling countryside, hidden coves, cliff tops and sandy beaches. You can walk, sail, surf or just relax and enjoy the wonderful scenery. This is a small family park run personally by the Higgin family situated in the hamlet of Bolberry, one mile up the lane from Hope Cove. The family home across the road from the site provides reception, a licensed shop and a takeaway facility which includes vegetarian, Indian or Oriental options. You can also hire or buy a range of wetsuits or body boards. The main camping field slopes gently with either sea or rural views. It has been terraced with hedging to provide 70 grassy pitches with 54 electricity connections (10A). There are some 20 places specifically designed for touring caravans. Nineteen caravan holiday homes to let complete the provision in a separate field which houses the modern toilet block.

Facilities

The attractively decorated toilet block includes two curtained washbasins for privacy. En-suite provision for disabled visitors doubles as a family shower room. Parent and baby room. Laundry room. Separate dishwashing (water metered as it is spring water - 20p). Freezer for ice packs. Shop including some basic camping equipment. Fresh baguettes and croissants daily. Calor and camping gas. Takeaway (evenings only, last orders 7.00). No play area as such but two open areas for ball games. Off site: Fishing, boat launching and beach 1 mile. Golf 4 miles. Riding 6 miles. Salcombe, sailing Mecca and fishing port with sandy beaches 3.5 miles. Kingsbridge, ancient market town 6 miles.

Open

15 March - 30 September.

At a glance

Welcome & Ambience	✓✓✓✓	Location	✓✓✓✓✓
Quality of Pitches	✓✓✓	Range of Facilities	✓✓✓

Directions

Travelling south from Exeter on the A38, take the A3121 (signed Ermington and Modbury). Follow signs to Kingsbridge and Salcombe. At Malborough, turn sharp right through the village, following signs for Bolberry for 0.6 mile. Turn right to Bolberry, then after 0.9 miles the park is on the right. On the left is a concrete drive to Karrageen House and reception. Take care with single track lanes, although there are plenty of passing places. O.S.GR: SX692391.

Charges 2005

Per unit incl. 2 adults, 2 children	£ 8.00 - £ 14.00
extra adult	£ 2.00 - £ 3.00
child (under 17 yrs)	£ 1.00
electricity	£ 2.00
awning	£ 2.00 - £ 3.00
dog	free - £ 1.00
No credit cards.	

Reservations

Made with deposit of £20 per week or part week.
Tel: 01548 561230. Email: phil@karrageen.co.uk

UK0826 Higher Rew Caravan & Camping Park

Malborough, Kingsbridge TQ7 3DW (Devon)

The Squire family have developed this rural park on their farm which is located about a mile up a single track lane from South Sands, near Salcombe. South Sands is ideal for boating, sailing and windsurfing as well as providing safe bathing. A ferry runs to Salcombe town. The five miles of estuary which stretches between Salcombe and Kingsbridge is a local nature reserve famed for its unique marine habitats and its bird watching opportunities. You can travel the length of it by the 'Rivermaid' ferry. The rural views from the park are amazing but you have to climb a little higher to see the sea. The coastal path can be reached by footpaths from the park. There used to be a dairy herd on the farm but the buildings are now used to provide camping facilities which include a covered play area for children under 11 years. For older children there is a play barn with table tennis, skittle alley and a pool table. A tennis court is available to hire. A large, sloping, open field has been terraced to provide 90 grass pitches, 60 of which have 16A electricity.

Facilities

Toilet facilities are a little basic, with rafter beams. Unisex showers are in a separate, light and airy part with the laundry and dishwashing sinks. Showers are metered (20p for 4 minutes). Freezer for ice packs. Tourist information. Reception with shop for basics and some camping bits (open main season). Play area. Tennis court. Skittle alley. Caravan storage. Off site: Beach, fishing and sailing 1 mile. Boat launching 3 miles. Riding 5 miles. Golf 4-5 miles.

Open

Easter - October half term.

At a glance

Welcome & Ambience	✓✓✓✓	Location	✓✓✓✓✓
Quality of Pitches	✓✓✓	Range of Facilities	✓✓✓

Directions

Park is clearly signed from Malborough. Follow signs to Soar for 1 mile. Turn left at Rew Cross, then first right for Higher Rew. Take care with single track roads, although there are always plenty of passing places. O.S.GR: SX73381.

Charges 2005

Per unit incl. 2 persons	£ 7.00 - £ 12.00
extra adult	£ 2.00 - £ 3.00
child (under 12 yrs)	free - £ 0.50
child (12-17 yrs)	£ 0.50 - £ 1.00
electricity	£ 2.00
dog	free - £ 0.50

Reservations

Made with deposit (£25 per week) and fee (£1).
Tel: 01548 842681. Email: enquiries@higherrew.co.uk

UK0840 **Woodlands Leisure Park**

Blackawton, Totnes TQ9 7DQ (Devon)

Woodlands is a pleasant surprise – from the road you have no idea of just what is hidden away deep in the Devon countryside. To achieve this, there has been sympathetic development of farm and woodland to provide a leisure centre, open to the public and with a range of activities and entertainment appealing to all ages, plus a touring caravan park. Children will thoroughly enjoy a huge variety of imaginative adventure play equipment, amazing water toboggan runs, the 'Rock and Roll Tug Boat', the new 'Avalanche' and much more, hidden amongst the trees. Those more peacefully inclined can follow woodland walks around the attractive ponds. The 'Empire of the Sea Dragon', an indoor play centre, provides marvellous wet weather facilities comprising five floors of play areas and amazing slides. With a two night stay, campers on the touring park are admitted free of charge to the leisure park. The camping and caravan site overlooks the woodland and the leisure park, taking 320 units on three sloping, grassy fields, the original terraced one maturing nicely. One of the others has been fully terraced to provide groups of four to eight flat, very spacious pitches (90% with 10A electricity, a shared water tap, drain and rubbish bin). The newest field has 120 pitches (with electricity) designed with a more open feel to provide space for larger groups or rallies. A popular park, early reservation is advisable.

Facilities

Three modern, heated toilet blocks, well maintained and kept very clean, include private bathrooms (coin-operated, 20p) and 16 family shower cubicles. Two laundry rooms, dishwashing areas and freezer for ice packs. Baby changing facilities. The leisure park café, with terrace, provides good value meals and a takeaway service for campers. Café opening hours and the adjoining gift shop (with gas and a few basic food supplies) vary according to season and demand. TV and games room. Dogs are accepted on the campsite but not in the leisure park (kennels available). Caravan storage Off site: The charming town of Dartmouth and the South Hams beaches are near. Fishing 4 miles. Golf 0.5 miles. Riding 5 miles. Beach 4 miles.

Open

7 April - 5 November.

At a glance

Welcome & Ambience	✓✓✓✓	Location	✓✓✓✓
Quality of Pitches	✓✓✓✓✓	Range of Facilities	✓✓✓✓✓

Directions

From A38 at Buckfastleigh, take A384 to Totnes. Before the town centre turn right on A381 Kingsbridge road. After Halwell turn left at Totnes Cross garage, on A3122 to Dartmouth. Park is on right after 2.5 miles. O.S.GR: SX813521.

Charges 2005

Per unit incl. 2 persons	£ 11.00 - £ 17.50
extra person over 2 yrs	£ 6.25
awning or extra small pup tent	£ 2.50
large tent or trailer tent (120 sq ft plus)	£ 2.50
electricity	£ 2.50
dog (contact site first)	£ 2.50

Free entry to leisure park for stays 2 nights or more.

Reservations

Accepted for min. 2 nights with £35 deposit, except July/Aug. when min. 7 days and £50 deposit. Balance in full 21 days before arrival. Tel: 01803 712598. Email: fun@woodlandspark.com

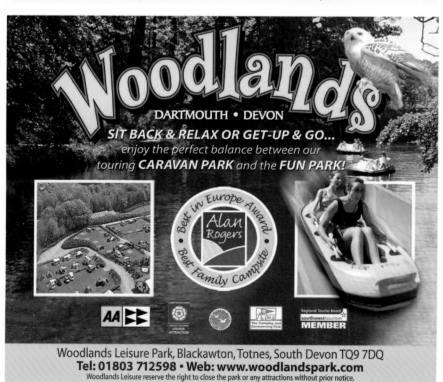

UK0830 Slapton Sands Camping & Caravanning Club Site

Middle Grounds, Slapton, Kingsbridge TQ7 2QW (Devon)

Slapton is a charming village with tiny lanes and cottages, a shop and two historic pubs, one dominated by the ruined tower of an old monastery. The village (unsuitable for camping traffic) is about half a mile inland from the shingle beach of Slapton Sands and the fresh water Ley which is administered as a nature reserve by the Field Studies Council. The Camping and Caravanning Club site is situated on the road which leads from the Sands, on a well kept meadow overlooking the bay – the sea views are panoramic from most areas of the site, with shelter provided by some large bushes and the surrounding hedge. There are 115 grass pitches, some with a slight slope, and electrical connections (16A) are available for 46 (including 10 with hardstanding). Motorcaravans, trailer tents and tents are accepted without problems but the planners will only permit 8 caravan pitches which are kept for club members. This area was used for rehearsals for the WW2 Normandy landings, when the whole population was evacuated – there are memorials, including a tank in the village of Torcross. The quaint port of Dartmouth is 7 miles, Kingsbridge 8 miles and a variety of beaches and coves around the beautiful South Hams coastline are within easy reach.

Facilities

The modern toilet block is central, can be heated and is kept very clean, with washbasins in private cabins. Useful parent and child room and separate unit for disabled visitors (with key). Dishwashing facilities, laundry sinks, washing machine and dryer (and outside lines). Motorcaravan service point. Reception has a small library, gas and freezer for ice blocks. Small play area. Off site: Riding 0.5 miles. The Field Studies Centre arranges guided walks and short study courses on a wide variety of interests and can issue fishing permits for the Ley (perch and pike, of legendary size, in the summer months). Beach fishing is also popular.

Open

March - October.

At a glance

Welcome & Ambience	✓✓✓✓	Location	✓✓✓✓✓
Quality of Pitches	✓✓✓✓	Range of Facilities	✓✓✓

Directions

From A38 Exeter - Plymouth road, take A384 to Totnes. Just before town, turn right on A381 to Kingsbridge, then A379 through Stokenham and Torcross to Slapton Sands. Half way along the beach road turn left to Slapton village and site is 200 yds on right. Note: Avoid the very narrow Five Mile Lane from the A381 which is signed Slapton (just after a filling station) 6 miles from Kingsbridge. O.S.GR: SX825450.

Charges 2005

Per adult	£ 4.30 - £ 6.40
child (6-18 yrs)	£ 1.90
pitch (non-member)	£ 5.00

Reservations

Necessary and made with deposit; contact site or Central Reservations 0870 243 3331. Tel: 01548 580538.

UK0850 Galmpton Park

Greenway Road, Galmpton, Brixham TQ5 0EP (Devon)

Within a few miles of the lively amenities of Torbay, Galmpton Park lies peacefully just outside the village of Galmpton, overlooking the beautiful Dart estuary just upstream of Dartmouth and Kingswear. A family park, some 120 pitches (60 marked for caravans) are arranged on a wide sweep of grassy, terraced meadow, each pitch with its own wonderful view of the river. Situated on the hillside, some parts have quite a slope, but there are flatter areas (the owners will advise and assist). There are 90 electrical connections (10A) and 19 pitches have water and drainage. There is a separate tent field. Galmpton is a quiet and simple park (the gates close 11.15 pm - 7.30 am) in a most picturesque setting, within easy reach of all the attractions of South Devon. A member of the Countryside Discovery group.

Facilities

A central, substantial looking toilet block provides clean facilities including three washbasins in cabins, a very attractive under 5's bathroom (key), baby unit and hair care areas. Dishwashing room also with washing machine, dryer, iron and ironing board. Reception/shop sells a wide range of basics including gas. Bread to order. Good adventure play equipment. Dogs (max. 2 per unit) are accepted at the owner's discretion and not mid-July and Aug. Motorhomes over 21 ft. are not accepted. Off site: Local pub is 5 minutes walk.

Open

Easter - 30 September.

At a glance

Welcome & Ambience	✓✓✓✓	Location	✓✓✓✓✓
Quality of Pitches	✓✓✓✓	Range of Facilities	✓✓✓

Directions

Take A380 Paignton ring road towards Brixham until junction with the Paignton - Brixham coast road. Turn right towards Brixham, then second right into Manor Vale Road. Continue through the village, past the school and site is 500 yds on the right. O.S.GR: SX885558.

Charges 2005

Per unit incl. 2 persons and awning	£ 10.30 - £ 15.00
de-luxe pitch plus	£ 12.30 - £ 17.80
extra adult	£ 2.50
child (5-16 yrs)	£ 1.20
Various discounts available.	

Reservations

Made with £20 deposit p/week booked. Tel: 01803 842066. Email: galmptontouringpark@hotmail.com

UK0860 Whitehill Country Park

Stoke Road, Paignton TQ4 7PF (Devon)

Whitehill Country Park is beautifully situated in rolling Devon countryside, just 2.5 miles from the nearest beaches. Extending over 40 acres, a definite sense of space characterises this park and ten acres of ancient woodland are available for walks and attract a great deal of wildlife. Whitehill is a friendly park with 329 large grassy pitches which are located in separate fields around the site with evocative names, such as Nine Acres, Sweethill and Coombe Meadow. Most pitches have electrical connections (16A). Around 60 pitches are used for caravan holiday homes. The park boasts an attractive swimming pool (max. depth 1.3m) with a children's paddling pool alongside, as well as a good range of other leisure facilities, notably The Hayloft bar (with satellite TV), a café and a well-stocked shop.

Facilities

Two well maintained sanitary blocks include private, individual washing facilities for ladies. Ample laundry facilities. Gas supplies. Shop. Bar. Café (29/5-4/9). Swimming and paddling pools (heated 29/5-4/9). Three play areas. Dogs and other pets are not accepted. Off site: Paignton 2.5 miles. Beach 3 miles. Fishing, golf and riding 2 miles. Torquay, Dartmoor, Quay West Aqua Park. Bus stop at park entrance.

Open

Easter - 30 September.

At a glance

Welcome & Ambience	✓✓✓✓	Location	✓✓✓✓✓
Quality of Pitches	✓✓✓✓	Range of Facilities	✓✓✓✓

Directions

Turn left at The Parkers Arms off the A385 Paignton to Totnes road, signed Stoke Gabriel. Site is 1 mile along this road. O.S.GR: SX857587.

Charges 2006

Per unit incl. 2 persons, elecricity	£ 10.50 - £ 20.00
tent pitch (no electricity)	£ 8.50 - £ 17.00
extra person	£ 3.50
child (4-14 yrs)	£ 2.50
awning or pup tent	£ 2.50

Reservations

Contact site. Tel: 01803 782338. Email: info@whitehill-park.co.uk

UK0845 **Hillhead Caravan Club Holiday Park**

Hillhead, Brixham TQ5 0HH (Devon)

Hillhead is a fully refurbished Caravan Club park set in 22 acres of beautiful Devon countryside. Originally developed in the 1960s within what is now a coastal protection area two miles from Brixham, the park has benefited from a £3 million redevelopment. Unusually for a Caravan Club site, it offers a full entertainment programme in peak season. Hillhead comprises 243 pitches, most with electrical hook-ups and many with fine views. Amenities are to a uniformly high standard, notably the main complex based around an attractive courtyard, and housing a shop, bar, games room and restaurant. The children's play area is outstanding with a range of imaginative items including a large wooden fort. Hillhead is rightly proud of its strong commitment to sound environmental practice, with a plan to promote species diversity and the encouragement of good practice by site workers and visitors alike.

Facilities
The two sanitary blocks are new and maintained to a high standard. Each block includes 3 special private family bathrooms (key from reception) and facilities for disabled visitors. Laundry facilities. Motoraravan service point. Shop. Bar and restaurant. Swimming pool (heated May – Sept) with children's pool adjacent. Large play area. Skateboard ramp. Games room. TV. Entertainment in season. Games field. Dog walking area. Off site: Nearest beach and coastal path 2 miles. Bus stop at site entrance. River Dart boat trips. Paignton, Torquay and Brixham. Golf (18 holes) and riding 2 miles. Bicycle hire 2.5 miles.

At a glance
Welcome & Ambience	✓✓✓✓	Location	✓✓✓✓
Quality of Pitches	✓✓✓✓	Range of Facilities	✓✓✓✓✓

Directions
Site is well signed from the A379 Paignton – Dartmouth road and is located on the B3205 (Slappers Hill Road). Entrance is on the left after 400 yards. O.S.GR: SX904534.

Charges 2005
Per person	£ 3.50 - £ 5.00
child (5-16 yrs)	£ 1.00 - £ 3.00
pitch incl. electricity	£ 10.00 - £ 16.00

Reservations
Required for peak season - contact site. Tel: 01803 853204. Email: enquiries@caravanclub.co.uk

Open
30 April - 31 October.

UK1130 **Hoburne Torbay**

Goodrington, Paignton TQ4 7JP (Devon)

Situated to the south of central Paignton, with a short, signed walk to the sea and some sea views of Torbay, this Hoburne-owned park's major interest is a complex of 504 holiday homes (135 to let) which totally dominate the higher of the two touring sites. However, there are 137 touring pitches (no tents) in two sections, each with a resident warden. One, probably the quieter of the two, is on flat grass by the entrance. The other is on higher ground, through the holiday homes at the top of the park with the sites large shop and café (with bakery) close by. It is on a gentle slope with some views. Pitches are of reasonable size, though with some variation, and all have 10A electricity. For those who like entertainment, the central club complex is the park's best feature, with a good sized heated outdoor pool (80 x 40 ft.) and a super indoor pool with views across the bay, complete with flume, sauna and steam room. The clubhouse has a large club lounge with dance floor, a separate bar/restaurant (with views of Torbay). Entertainment is organised for adults and children from Spr. B.H to end Sept. and at Easter.

Facilities
Three toilet blocks, two of modern design in lower touring field, third block is of older design at the top touring field. Large launderette. Dishwashing area. Recycling bins. Chemical disposal. Motorcaravan service point. Well stocked shop. Gas available. Club room. Restaurant/bar. Takeaway. Café. Heated outdoor pool. Indoor pool with flume and fountain, sauna and steam room (all free). Mini two lane bowling alley. Pool and snooker tables. Amusement arcade. TV room showing cartoons. Crazy golf. Adventure playground. Indoor soft adventure play area. Daily children's entertainment. Reception is busy but efficient. Up to 30 American motorhomes accepted (25 ft. max). No dogs or pets are accepted.

At a glance
Welcome & Ambience	✓✓✓✓	Location	✓✓✓✓
Quality of Pitches	✓✓✓✓	Range of Facilities	✓✓✓✓✓

Directions
Park is signed from the outer Paignton ring road. Look for left turn into Goodrington Road, then left into Grange Road. O.S.GR: SX890585.

Charges 2005
Per unit incl. up to 6 persons	£ 10.00 - £ 27.00

Reservations
Advised for high season. Made for 1-6 nights with payment in full, for 7 nights or over with £50 deposit p/week. Min. 7 days in high season. Tel: 01803 558010. Email: enquiries@hoburne.co.uk.

Open
14 February - 15 January excl. 2 weeks at Xmas.

UK0870 Beverley Park Holiday Centre

Goodrington Road, Paignton TQ4 7JE (Devon)

Beverley Park is a quality holiday centre, attractively landscaped, with marvellous views over Torbay. The pools, a large dance hall, bars and entertainment, are all run in an efficient and orderly manner. The park has 195 caravan holiday homes and 23 lodges, mainly around the central complex. There are 189 touring pitches in the lower areas of the park, all reasonably sheltered, some with views across the bay and some on slightly sloping ground. All pitches can take awnings and have 16A electricity (15 m. cable), 38 have hardstanding and 21 are fully serviced. Tents are accepted and a limited number of tent pitches have electrical connections. The park has a long season and reservations are essential for caravans. Entertainment is organised at Easter and from early May in the Starlight Cabaret bar. There are indoor and outdoor pools, each one heated and supervised. The Oasis fitness centre provides a steam room, jacuzzi, sun-bed and an excellent fitness room. The park is in the heart of residential Torbay, with views across the bay to Brixham and Torquay, and sandy beaches less than a mile away. This popular park has lots to offer and is well maintained and run. A member of the Best of British group.

Facilities

Good toilet blocks adjacent to the pitches, well maintained and heated, include roomy showers, some with washbasins en-suite. Baths on payment. Unit for disabled visitors. Facilities for babies. Laundry. Gas supplies. Motorcaravan service point. Large general shop (21/3-31/10). Restaurant, bars and takeaway (all Easter, then 30/5-26/10, and Autumn half-term). Swimming pools. Fitness centre. Tennis court. Crazy golf. Playground. Nature trail. Amusement centre with pool, table tennis and amusement machines. Soft play area. Dogs are not accepted. Off site: Regular minibus service to Paignton (timetable at reception) or normal services from outside the park. Fishing, bicycle hire, riding and golf all within 2 miles.

Open

January - December.

At a glance

Welcome & Ambience	✓✓✓✓✓	Location	✓✓✓✓
Quality of Pitches	✓✓✓✓✓	Range of Facilities	✓✓✓✓✓

Directions

Park is south of Paignton in Goodrington Road between A379 coast road and B3203 ring road and is well signed on both. O.S.GR: SX882584.

Charges 2006

Per serviced pitch incl. 2 persons and electricity	£ 12.50 - £ 27.50
incl. mains services and awning	£ 12.50 - £ 33.80
tent pitch incl. 2 persons	£ 8.50 - £ 24.50
extra adult	£ 4.50
child (4-14 yrs)	£ 3.00
awning or pup tent	£ 3.00
Max. 6 persons per reservation.	

Reservations

Made with £30 deposit (7, 14 or 21 days 17/7-3/9, min. 2 nights all other times); balance payable more than 28 days before arrival. Tel: 01803 661978. Email: info@beverley-holidays.co.uk

UK0880 **Dornafield**

Two Mile Oak, Newton Abbot TQ12 6DD (Devon)

The entrance to Dornafield leads into the charming old courtyard of a 14th Century farmhouse giving a mellow feeling that is complemented by the warm welcome from the Dewhirst family. The reception, shop, tourist information/ecology room have been sympathetically converted from farm outbuildings, with the games room from the old milking parlour, complete with stalls. Having booked in, continue down the lane (overlooked by a tree covered bank and alive with wild flowers) to the Buttermeadow, a tranquil valley providing 75 individual, numbered pitches on flat grass, separated by grassy ridges and in some places, wild rose hedges. You pass the walled orchard area, secluded and cosy for tents. Or take the road up the hill to Blackrock Copse with large luxury pitches with all facilities including a chemical disposal point for each pitch and TV connections, very cleverly concealed and 61 with hardstanding. Electricity points are 10A. Whilst having been carefully designed, the environment remains natural. Both Buttermeadow and Blackrock have super, well maintained woodland adventure play areas. Dornafield is a member of the Caravan Club's 'managed under contract' scheme, with both members and non-members made welcome. This park's rural situation is delightful, away from the coast and without any evening activities, it is a haven for those seeking a quiet, restful holiday and well worth consideration.

Facilities

Both modern toilet blocks are excellent and heated, with some washbasins in cubicles and comfortable roomy showers, but the new block up the hill could be said to be 'state of the art' with under-floor heating and a heat recovery system. Both blocks have facilities for disabled visitors and babies, laundry rooms and covered washing up areas. Shop, Gas supplies. All-weather hard tennis court. Games room with table tennis. Play areas. All year caravan storage. Off site: Local inn 0.5 miles. Fishing 2.5 miles. Golf 1 mile.

Open

18 March - 1 November.

At a glance

Welcome & Ambience	✓✓✓✓✓	Location	✓✓✓✓✓
Quality of Pitches	✓✓✓✓✓	Range of Facilities	✓✓✓

Directions

Park is northwest of A381 Newton Abbot - Totnes road. Leave A381 at Two Mile Oak Inn, opposite garage, and turn left at crossroads after about half a mile. Entrance is on the right. O.S.GR: SX848683.

Charges 2005

Per standard serviced pitch	£ 4.50 - £ 8.00
de-luxe pitch	£ 5.50 - £ 9.00
tent pitch (no services)	£ 4.00 - £ 6.00
extra adult	£ 3.50 - £ 5.00
dog	£ 1.00

Reservations

Any length, £10 p.w. low season, £30 p/week high season. Tel: 01803 812732.
Email: enquiries@dornafield.com

UK0910 **Ross Park**

Park Hill Farm, Ipplepen, Newton Abbot TQ12 5TT (Devon)

Ross Park has to be seen to appreciate the amazing floral displays with their dramatic colours, that are a feature of the park. These are complemented by the use of a wide variety of shrubs which form hedging for most of the 110 pitches to provide your own special plot, very much as on the continent. Many pitches have wonderful views over the surrounding countryside and for those who prefer the more open style, one small area has been left unhedged. The owners, Mark and Helen Lowe, continue to strive to provide quality facilities and maintain standards, and this is reflected in the awards they have won. The New Barn provides a comfortable lounge, a mezzanine bar with bar snacks and a restaurant with extra seating in the conservatory which is home to some exotic and colourful plants. The touring area is divided into bays or groups by hedging and shrubs and provides 110 pitches all with electricity (16A). Some 82 of these have a hardened surface, some made larger with a further gravel area. An orchard area alive with daffodils in the spring and a conservation area with information on wild flowers and butterflies, and with extended views, completes these environmentally considered amenities. Barn dances are organised on Sundays in high season. A well cared for park worthy of consideration, now a member of the best of British group.

Facilities

Seven well equipped, heated en-suite units, one with baby facilities, two suitable for disabled people. Further separate shower, washbasin and toilet facilities. Extra heated block with toilets, washbasins in cabins and hair-care centre. Fully equipped laundry room. Utility room with dishwashing, freezer and battery charging. Dog shower. Motorcaravan services. Recycling bins. Reception with licenced shop. Gas supplies. Bar, bar snacks and restaurant with a la carte menu (all April - end Oct, plus Christmas and New Year). New conservation and tourist information room. Games room (table tennis, snooker, pool). 7-acre park area for recreation. Croquet green. Badminton. Volleyball. Large well equipped playground. Caravan storage. Off site: Dainton Park 18 hole golf course is adjacent. Fishing 3 miles. Riding 1 mile. Beach 6 miles.

At a glance

Welcome & Ambience	✓✓✓✓✓	Location	✓✓✓✓
Quality of Pitches	✓✓✓✓✓	Range of Facilities	✓✓✓✓

Directions

From A381 Newton Abbot - Totnes road, park is signed towards Woodland at Park Hill crossroads and Jet filling station. O.S.GR: SX845671.

Charges 2006

Per unit incl. 2 persons	£ 10.50 - £ 16.95
incl. electricity	£ 11.50 - £ 17.95
extra adult	£ 3.25 - £ 5.00
child (4-16 yrs)	£ 1.50 - £ 1.85
Christmas packages available. No credit cards.	

Reservations

Made with £20 deposit. Tel: 01803 812983.
Email: enquiries@rossparkcaravanpark.co.uk

Open

All year excl. January and February.

UK0930 Ashburton Caravan Park

Waterleat, Ashburton TQ13 7HU (Devon)

For tents and motorcaravans only, Ashburton Park's four acres nestle in a hidden valley below Dartmoor, bordered by mature woodland. The Ashburn, a shallow stream with rocky pools, evenly divides and screens two acres of holiday homes from the two acre camping area. Sheltered and south facing, the park is a tranquil retreat, although for the energetic a half mile steep uphill walk brings you to the moor or by 1.5 miles of Devon lanes to Ashburton village. There are 35 level or gently sloping pitches, 8 with electricity connections (16A), on either side of a tarmac road that culminates in a small field area.

Facilities

First class, purpose built toilet block provides washbasins in cabins for ladies and a toilet and washbasin for disabled visitors (baby bath, etc. available). Washing machine and dryer, plus free spin dryer and iron. Reception/information centre provides gas, a freezer pack service, maps and walks and a daily weather report. Off site: Shops, a small heated pool and pubs, etc. are in Ashburton, a pleasant walk away by the river. Bicycle hire 1 mile. Riding and golf 3 miles.

Open

Easter - mid October.

At a glance

Welcome & Ambience	✓✓✓✓	Location	✓✓✓✓✓
Quality of Pitches	✓✓✓✓	Range of Facilities	✓✓✓

Directions

In the centre of Ashburton turn northwest into North Street. As built-up area thins out bear right before bridge following signs for 'Waterleat' for approx. 1.5 miles. Park is on the left. O.S.GR: SX752721.

Charges 2005

Per unit incl. 1 person	£ 5.50 - £ 7.00
incl. 2 persons	£ 9.00 - £ 12.00
extra person (over 1 yr)	£ 1.50 - £ 2.25
electricity	£ 2.00

No credit cards.

Reservations

Made for min. 3 nights with £15 deposit. Tel: 01364 652552. Email: info@ashburtoncaravanpark.co.uk

UK0960 Parkers Farm Holiday Park

Higher Mead Farm, Ashburton, Newton Abbot TQ13 7LJ (Devon)

Well situated with fine views towards Dartmoor, Parker's Farm is a modern touring site on a working farm. Close inspection reveals a unique chance to experience Devon country life at first hand, with pigs, sheep, goats and calves and rabbits to feed and touch. The Parker family have added a family bar which provides entertainment during the season (quiz night, bingo, guitar player). Farm walks are popular and take place four evenings a week in high season, on request at other times. The 100 touring pitches, with electricity (12A), are set directly above the farm buildings on terraces giving broad, flat groups of pitches, all with good views across the valley (to the A38 which may give some road noise). Hardstandings are available. Parker's Farm will suit those who don't seek the sophisticated amenities of more developed parks and a warm welcome awaits - in the words of one camper, 'You come here and feel you belong'.

Facilities

Two modern and clean shower and toilet blocks provide good facilities with two family shower rooms, baby bathroom, en-suite room for disabled visitors, dishwashing and laundry. Small shop (Whitsun - mid Sept). Restaurant, comfortable bar with family room (Whitsun - mid Sept.) and entertainment. Games room with table tennis, pool and amusement machines. Indoor play and TV area. Large outdoor play area. Trampolines. Caravan storage. Rallies welcome. American motorhomes accepted by prior arrangement. Off site: Bicycle hire 5 miles. Golf 4 miles. Riding 5 miles.

At a glance

Welcome & Ambience	✓✓✓✓✓	Location	✓✓✓✓
Quality of Pitches	✓✓✓✓	Range of Facilities	✓✓✓✓

Directions

From Exeter on A38, 26 miles from Plymouth, turn left at Alston Cross signed 'Woodland Denbury'. Site is 400 yards. O.S.GR: SX757702.

Charges 2005

Per unit incl. 2 persons	£ 6.00 - £ 12.50
incl. electricity	£ 8.00 - £ 14.50
extra person	£ 2.00
child (3-15 yrs)	£ 1.70
dog	£ 1.00

Reservations

Made with £20 deposit. Tel: 01364 652598. Email: enquiries@parkersfarm.co.uk

Open

Easter - 31 October.

UK0940 Holmans Wood Holiday Park

Harcombe Cross, Chudleigh TQ13 0DZ (Devon)

Close to the main A38 Exeter - Plymouth road, with easy access, this attractive, neat park makes a sheltered base for touring south Devon and Dartmoor. The hedged park is arranged on well kept grass surrounding a shallow depression, the floor of which makes a safe, grassy play area for children. Many attractive trees are growing and the park is decorated with flowers. In two main areas and accessed by tarmac roads, there are 125 level pitches (including a number of seasonal pitches) and 25 mobile homes. There are 100 pitches with electrical hook-ups (10A) and 70 with hardstanding, electricity, water and drainage. A picturesque 8 acre meadow is provided for tents. Adventure play equipment is provided for children, with badminton and tennis nets and an extra meadow for recreation. There may be some traffic noise on pitches to the west of the park. This is a pleasant, well run park and with no other on-site amenities would suit couples or families who prefer a peaceful stay.

Facilities

The single, good quality toilet block includes facilities for babies and disabled visitors, a dishwashing room and a laundry room. Children's play area. Caravan storage. Dogs are not accepted. Off site: Pub/restaurant nearby in Chudleigh village. The beach or Dartmoor are 7 miles and Haldon Forest for walks is 2 miles. Sunday market at Exeter Racecourse (2 miles). Fishing 1 mile. Golf or riding 4 miles.

Open

Mid-March - end October.

At a glance

Welcome & Ambience	✓✓✓✓	Location	✓✓✓✓
Quality of Pitches	✓✓✓✓	Range of Facilities	✓✓✓

Directions

From Exeter on A38 Plymouth road, 0.5 miles after the racecourse and just after a garage, take Chudleigh exit (signed). Park is immediately on the left. From Plymouth turn off A38 for Chudleigh/Teign Valley, then right for Chudleigh. Continue through the town and park is 1 mile. O.S.GR: SX882811.

Charges 2005

Per unit incl. 2 persons, awning and electricity	£ 10.50 - £ 14.75
de-luxe pitch	£ 11.50 - £ 15.75
extra adult	£ 1.95 - £ 2.50
child (4-14 yrs)	£ 1.60 - £ 1.80

Reservations

Any length, £30 deposit per week. Tel: 01626 853785. Email: enquiries@holmanswood.co.uk

"So easy to get to - so easy to explore from"

Our park is surrounded on all sides by rolling Devon countryside. Ideally situated for Dartmoor, Exeter, Torbay & Newton Abbot. Storage/seasonal pitches available.

Tel: 01626 853785   **www.holmanswood.co.uk**

UK0980 Lemonford Caravan Park

Bickington, Newton Abbot TQ12 6JR (Devon)

Lemonford is a well run, neat and tidy site for all ages and families on the southern edge of the National Park, some three miles from both Ashburton and Newton Abbot. It has the look and atmosphere of the 'cultivated' caravan park, close to the main road, yet set in a sheltered, peaceful dip bordered by the pretty River Lemon. Well mown grass and smart, trimmed hedges create the tranquil, attractive atmosphere the owners work hard to maintain. There are 85 pitches (45 used as seasonal pitches) on level grass and grouped in four areas according to whether they are to be used by families, couples or individuals. Most pitches have 10A electricity, about 55 have hardstanding. The park is well located for excursions and a good pub is within walking distance, along the banks of the river.

Facilities

Two modern toilet blocks, one new, can be heated and provide some private cabins, a ladies' bathroom (£1 payment) and a family bathroom. The new block has facilities for disabled visitors. Dishwashing area under cover. Laundry facilities. Shop. Gas supplies. Freezer service. Play area. Putting green. No commercial vehicles are accepted. Off site: Fishing 4 miles. Riding and bicycle hire 3 miles. Golf 2 miles. Leisure pool in Newton Abbot.

Open

End March - 31 October.

Reservations

Advised for July/Aug. and made with £20 deposit (min. 3 nights July/Aug). Tel: 01626 821242. Email: mark@lemonford.co.uk

At a glance

Welcome & Ambience	✓✓✓✓✓	Location	✓✓✓✓
Quality of Pitches	✓✓✓✓✓	Range of Facilities	✓✓✓✓

Directions

Travelling from Exeter, turn off A38 Plymouth road at A382 (Drumbridges) exit signed Newton Abbot, Bovey Tracey, Mortonhampstead. At roundabout take third exit to Bickington. Continue for 1 mile to Toby Jug Inn in the village and park is on left at the bottom of the hill. From Plymouth, take A383 (Goodstone) exit, cross A38 and take first left to Bickington to site on right. O.S.GR: SX793723.

Charges 2005

Per unit incl. 2 persons	£ 7.50 - £ 11.50
extra person	£ 2.00
child (3-15 yrs)	£ 1.50
electricity	£ 2.00
awning	£ 1.00
dog	£ 1.00

Special low season offers. No credit cards.

UK0950 River Dart Adventures

Holne Park, Newton Abbot TQ13 7NP (Devon)

The park is marketed as 'River Dart Adventures', where campsite and adventure experiences are enjoyed by old and young from all over Europe. Once part of a Victorian estate with mature woodland on the edge of Dartmoor in the beautiful Dart valley, the park and its activities are now open to the general public on payment. It features a variety of unusual adventure play equipment (e.g. a giant spider's web) arranged amongst and below the trees, 'Lilliput Land' for toddlers, Jungle Fun, and woodland streams and a lake with a 'pirate ship' for swimming and inflatables, fly fishing and marked nature and forest trails – all free to campers except fishing. It does become busy at weekends and school holidays with supervised activities for 7 year olds and upwards, such as climbing and canoeing. The camping and caravanning area is in the more open parkland overlooking the woods and is mainly on a slight slope with some shade from mature trees. There are 185 individual pitches of very reasonable size, marked by lines on the grass, some slightly sloping, with 105 electrical connections (10/16A) and 12 hardstandings.

Facilities

Two wooden toilet blocks, one quite smart, the older a little tired, can both be heated. Washbasins in cubicles, baby facilities, laundry and dishwashing, freezer, en-suite unit for disabled visitors (access by key), family bathroom and drying room. Motorcaravan service point. Shop (all season). Restaurant (recently improved), bar (all season) and takeaway (20/7-31/8). Large TV and games room. Indoor climbing room (some of these open all year for the activities on offer). Small, heated swimming pool (all season). Tennis. Max. two dogs per pitch. Off site: Bicycle hire or riding 4 miles. Golf 6 miles.

Open

1 April - 30 September.

At a glance

Welcome & Ambience	✓✓✓✓	Location	✓✓✓✓✓
Quality of Pitches	✓✓✓✓	Range of Facilities	✓✓✓✓✓

Directions

Signed from the A38 at Peartree junction, park is about 1 mile west of Ashburton, on the road to Two Bridges. Disregard advisory signs stating 'no caravans' as access to the park is prior to narrow bridge. O.S.GR: SX734701.

Charges 2005

Per unit incl. 2 persons	£ 9.50 - £ 17.00

Camping Cheques accepted.

Reservations

Advised for high season and made with £10 deposit per pitch (additional high season deposit £30 for 7 nights or less, £40 for longer). Balance due 21 days before arrival. All deposits non-returnable.
Tel: 01364 652511. Email: enquiries@riverdart.co.uk

Set in 90 acres of spectacular parkland

Self Catering

Play Lake

Family touring site with cafe, bar, tennis courts and heated outdoor pool
Extensive adventure playground
& pirate play lake
Instructor led activities in summer holidays

River Dart Adventures
at Holne Park, Ashburton, Devon
Follow the brown tourist signs from the A38

www.riverdart.co.uk   01364 652511

71

UK0970 **Cofton Country Holidays**

Starcross, Dawlish EX6 8RP (Devon)

About 1.5 miles from a sandy beach at Dawlish Warren this popular, family site takes over 400 touring units on a variety of fields and meadows with beautiful country views. Although not individually marked, there is never a feeling of overcrowding. The smaller, more mature fields, including a pleasant old orchard for tents only, are well terraced. While there are terraces on most of the slopes of the larger, more open fields, there are still some quite steep gradients to climb. There are some 300 electrical connections (10A) and a few hardstandings. One area has 66 park-owned, holiday homes. A well designed, central complex overlooking the pool and decorated with flowers and hanging baskets, houses reception, a shop and off-licence and a bar lounge, the 'Cofton Swan', where bar meals are usually available (all Easter - 30 Sept). A family room and bar are on the first floor of this building and there is an outdoor terrace and some light entertainment in season. The adjacent supervised kidney-shaped heated pool with paddling pool, has lots of grassy space for sunbathing. Coarse fishing is available in three lakes on the park and there is a woodland trail towards Dawlish Warren.

Facilities

Toilet facilities comprise four blocks, one on each side of the road dividing the park for the touring pitches and the third near the holiday home area. The newest, at the top of the larger fields is first rate, with laundry and facilities for disabled visitors and babies. Hair dryers. Dishwashing facilities under cover. In addition three 'portacabin' style units with basic toilet facilities are provided for the peak season. Two launderettes. Gas available. Ice pack hire service. Bar lounge. Shop. Fish and chip shop - breakfast possible. Swimming pool (overall length 100 ft. open Spr. B.H - mid Sept). Games room (busy in high season). Adventure playground in the woods overlooking the pools and two other well equipped play areas. Pony rides in high season. Coarse fishing (from £20 per rod for 7 days, discount for senior citizens outside July). Winter caravan storage. Off site: Golf 3 miles. Beach 1.5 miles. Woodland walks/pub 0.5 miles.

At a glance

Welcome & Ambience	✓✓✓✓✓	Location	✓✓✓✓
Quality of Pitches	✓✓✓✓✓	Range of Facilities	✓✓✓✓✓

Directions

Access to the park is off the A379 road 3 miles north of Dawlish, just after Cockwood harbour village. O.S.GR: SX965797. GPS: N50:36.756 W03:27.628

Charges 2005

Per unit incl. 2 persons and electricity	£ 12.00 - £ 19.80
hardstanding pitch	£ 14.00 - £ 21.50
tent incl. 2 persons	£ 8.50 - £ 15.00
extra adult	£ 1.70 - £ 3.00
child (2-13 yrs)	£ 1.50 - £ 2.80

Camping Cheques accepted.
Small low season discount for Senior Citizens.

Reservations

Made for min. 3 nights, 4 nights in peak season with £20 deposit. Tel: 01626 890111.
Email: info@coftonholidays.co.uk

Open

1 April - 31 October.

UK1010 Lady's Mile Touring & Camping Park

Dawlish EX7 0LX (Devon)

Lady's Mile is a popular, large family touring park that caters well for children. It has extensive grassy fields (with some trees for shade), in addition to the main, landscaped camping area which is arranged in broad terraces. There are 486 pitches, mostly marked by lines but with nothing between them, and most with electricity (10A). It is a 20 minute walk to a good sandy beach at Dawlish Warren and 10 minutes to Dawlish beach, but the park also has a good sized, free outdoor swimming pool with 200 ft. plus slide, paddling pool and a paved surround, plus a super heated indoor pool (20 x 10 m.) with 100 ft. flume and separate paddling pool (both with lifeguards). A large and attractive bar complex has a family area overlooking the indoor pool and an entertainment programme. Below is a spacious games room including pool tables and video games, and a new separate disco and bar. A sloping recreation field is ideal for kite flying and the large fenced adventure playground has a safe, sand surface. A nine hole golf course is on site (free but with small charge for hire of clubs) and a multi-sports pitch. The park is popular over a long season, with reservation necessary for high season.

Facilities

Four toilet blocks of various ages and styles, but of a good standard, are well spaced around the main areas of the park with an additional shower block. Facilities for disabled people. Four family bathrooms (50p). Dishwashing sinks under cover. Two launderettes. Mini-market. Fish and chip takeaway (both Easter - mid Sept). Bars. Indoor (Easter - Oct) and outdoor (May - Sept) pools. Adventure play area. Games room. Golf (9 hole). Ball area with nets. Tarmac area at reception for late arrivals. Winter caravan storage. Off site: Riding and bicycle hire 1 mile. Fishing 3 miles.

Open

13 March - 31 October.

At a glance

Welcome & Ambience	✓✓✓✓	Location	✓✓✓✓
Quality of Pitches	✓✓✓✓	Range of Facilities	✓✓✓✓✓

Directions

Park is 1 mile north of Dawlish with access off the A379 (Exeter - Teignmouth) road. O.S.GR: SX969778. GPS: N50:35.715 W03:27.568

Charges 2005

Per unit incl. 2 adults	£ 11.00 - £ 20.00
extra person over 2 yrs	£ 1.50 - £ 3.00
extra child's tent	£ 1.50 - £ 3.00
electricity	free - £ 1.00
dog	£ 1.50 - £ 3.00

Low season special offers.
Low season discount for OAPs.

Reservations

Made for Sat to Sat only in peak seasons, with £15 deposit. Tel: 01626 863411. Email: info@ladysmile.co.uk

UK1090 Peppermint Park

Warren Road, Dawlish Warren, Dawlish EX7 0PQ (Devon)

First impressions of this extensive family run park are perhaps somewhat formal. However, this is quickly dispelled by the friendly reception staff, abundant flowers and the way the level, terraced pitches have been laid out on the slightly sloping ground. There are 250 pitches, ranging in size, each with electricity (10A), with at least another 60 hook-ups available for tent campers. Tarmac roads thread through the site giving easy access to all areas, each pitch being marked and numbered. Visitors to Peppermint Park out of season can use the full facilities at the adjacent sister site (Golden Sands), which include a large indoor pool. Peppermint Park's own pool complex includes a water slide in the larger pool. Nightly entertainment is staged in the Peppermint Club in high season and at Golden Sands at other times. This site's 'jewel in the crown' is the walking distance (700 yds) to the large, safe beaches of Dawlish Warren and its associated pleasure complex - ideal for families. For others, there is the adjacent coastal footpath or the city of Exeter (7 miles) with its cathedral, museums and historic Quay complex. A passenger ferry operates from Starcross (2 miles) across the estuary to Exmouth during high season. Dawlish Warren nature reserve is adjacent and includes an 18 hole links golf course.

Facilities

The two modern sanitary blocks are kept in spotless condition and can be heated. Two units (WC, washbasin and shower) are provided for disabled visitors. Fully equipped mother and baby room. Laundry (washing machines, dryers and free irons) and dishwashing. Shop with gas. Restaurant, bar and takeaway (28/5-10/9). Entertainment. Swimming pool (28/5-10/9). Playground on a hill. Field for ball games. Small coarse fishing lake (£2.50 for adult day ticket). Off site: Golf at Dawlish Warren (links course), 9-hole course at Starcross.

Open

15 April - 28 October.

At a glance

Welcome & Ambience	✓✓✓✓	Location	✓✓✓✓
Quality of Pitches	✓✓✓✓	Range of Facilities	✓✓✓✓✓

Directions

Leave M5 at junction 30 and take A379 Dawlish road. After passing through Starcross (7 miles) turn left to Dawlish Warren just before Dawlish. Continue for 1.5 miles down hill and park is on left in 300 yards. O.S.GR: SX978788.
GPS: N50:35.962 W03:26.818

Charges 2005

Per unit incl. 2 persons, electricity	£ 10.00 - £ 16.00
awning or gazebo	£ 2.50 - £ 3.00
extra adult	£ 1.50 - £ 3.00
child (2-13 yrs)	£ 1.50 - £ 3.00
dog	£ 1.50 - £ 5.00

Reservations

Made with £15 deposit (Sat. - Sat. only 24 July - 28 Aug). Tel: 01626 863436.
Email: info@peppermintpark.co.uk

UK1100 Webbers Caravan & Camping Park

Castle Lane, Woodbury, Exeter EX5 1EA (Devon)

Set in a lovely location in East Devon, with rural views, this family run park has developed over 20 years to one that can boast spacious, modern facilities, yet still retain its relaxed, rural atmosphere. The 115 marked, grass pitches are large, with the majority level and a few gently sloping. Some of the higher pitches have marvellous views across the Exe river valley. There are 100 electricity connections (10/16A). The park is surrounded by fields and visitors can watch the wildlife and grazing sheep from a fenced walk around the park perimeter. Within the park is a 'pets paddock' with a friendly donkey, Shetland pony and goats. A short drive takes you to the two miles of glorious sand at Exmouth or the delightful pebble beach at Budleigh Salterton. Woodbury Common for excellent heathland walks is just over a mile away whilst, for a little city life, Exeter is also nearby. A member of the Countryside Discovery group.

Facilities

There are two modern toilet blocks, the newest (completed in 2002) a light and airy building with 4 family shower rooms, a bathroom (£1) and a unit for disabled visitors (WC, shower and washbasin). Dishwashing and laundry facilities. Unusual in terms of number, are seven chemical disposal points, located at each water point (and adequately separated). Motorcaravan service point. Small shop at reception for essentials. Ice pack service. Gas supplies. Play area and games field. All year caravan storage. Off site: Woodbury village within walking distance with excellent pub/restaurant, post office, etc. Exeter 6 miles. Fishing or golf (Woodbury Park Golf Club) 1 mile. Riding 4 miles. Bicycle hire or boat launching 5 miles.

Open

Mid March - end October.

At a glance

Welcome & Ambience	✓✓✓✓	Location	✓✓✓✓✓
Quality of Pitches	✓✓✓✓	Range of Facilities	✓✓✓

Directions

From M5 exit 30 take A3052 (Sidmouth) for 5 miles and turn right at Halfway Inn. From A30, Daisymount exit, take B3180 for 3 miles to Halfway Inn and go straight across at crossroads. All routes then follow B3180 (Budleigh Salterton/Exmouth). After 2 miles turn right into lane (signed Woodbury, golf and caravan parks). Follow downhill for 1 mile to park on left just before Woodbury village. O.S.GR: SY017874.
GPS: N50:40.685 W03:23.521

Charges 2005

Per unit incl. 2 persons, electricity	£ 11.00 - £ 16.00
tent pitch incl. 2 persons	£ 28.50 - £ 12.50
extra person (over 2 yrs)	£ 2.00
pup tent	£ 4.00

Reservations

Essential for peak periods and made with £20 deposit. Tel: 01395 232276.
Email: reception@webberspark.co.uk

UK1520 Waterrow Touring Park

Wiveliscombe, Taunton TA4 2AZ (Somerset)

Beside the River Tone in a pretty part of South Somerset, Tony and Anne Taylor have enthusiastically developed Waterrow into a charming, landscaped touring park for adults only. Nestling in a little sheltered valley, it is very peaceful and possible for an overnight stop (just over 30 minutes from M5) or ideal as a base for exploring nearby Exmoor and the Brendon Hills. There are 45 touring pitches, 27 of which are on level hardstandings, including 4 with full services. The remainder are on flat or gently sloping grass with little shade as yet but bushes and trees are maturing. All have electricity (16A), spring and mains water are available and TV aerial points have been installed (your own lead is required, sometimes quite long). A small area has been set aside for tent campers. Converted barns have been put to good use, providing local tourist information, a small library and a visual record of the park's development. Further down the park, below the touring area, wide steps lead to a private nature reserve where you can find the Otter Holt, go fly fishing for wild brown trout (tuituion available), take a riverside walk or just relax and watch the birds. This 'adult only' site is open all year.

Facilities

A modern, clean toilet unit, well fitted out and with heating, provides WCs and washbasins, some in curtained cubicles. New heated shower block. Facilities for disabled people (key). Dishwashing. Washing machine and dryer. Limited provisions are available in reception. Order jacket potatoes before lunchtime for the evening for just 80p. The Taylors will 'dog sit' if you are visiting somewhere your pet is not allowed (£5 per day). Water colour and drawing holidays arranged at certain times. Caravan storage with 'store and stay' system. Site is not suitable for American motorhomes. Off site: Golf and fishing 7 miles. Bicycle hire 10 miles. Riding 12 miles. The Rock Inn is a short walk and provides good meals and real ales. Wiveliscombe 3 miles.

At a glance

Welcome & Ambience	✓✓✓✓✓	Location	✓✓✓✓✓
Quality of Pitches	✓✓✓✓✓	Range of Facilities	✓✓✓✓

Directions

From M5 exit 25 take A358 (signed Minehead) round Taunton for 4 miles, then at Staplegrove onto the B3227 for 11.5 miles to Wiveliscombe where straight over at lights to Waterrow (still on B3227). Park is on left shortly after the Rock Inn. O.S.GR: ST052250. GPS: N51:00.990 W03:21.163

Charges 2006

Per unit incl. 2 persons (adults only, 18 years and over)	£ 11.00 - £ 16.00
extra adult	£ 4.00

Reservations

Advised for B.Hs. and high season and made with £20 deposit. Tel: 01984 623464.

Open

All year.

UK1590 Exe Valley Caravan Site

Bridgetown, Dulverton TA22 9JR (Somerset)

Occupying a prime position in a wooded valley alongside the River Exe, Exe Valley Caravan Site is ideally situated for visiting the Doone Valley, Tarr Steps, Dulverton and many other beautiful venues in the area. This four acre 'adult only' campsite is owned and managed by Paul and Christine Matthews, and reception forms part of their home. This is an old mill, complete with water wheel and grindstones which are in working order. Reception also houses a small shop stocking basic provisions. They hope to install CCTV so campers may watch the bat colony in the loft from a screen in the shop. Set beside the River Exe or the millstream, there are 30 large pitches (mostly grass but with some hardstandings at the top end), all with 16A electricity and TV hook-ups. Fly fishing along the River Exe is possible from the site or at Wimbleball Reservoir just over four miles away. Travellers find this part of Somerset is a haven for walkers, cycling, pony trekking, or as a place to just sit and relax.

Facilities

The refurbished toilet block houses the usual facilities and an en-suite room for disabled visitors (quite short steep ramp to enter). Excellent laundry with domestic washing and drying machines, plus a microwave (free). Small shop with basic provisions. Bicycle hire. Gas supplies. Free fly fishing. This is an adult-only park. Off site: Riding 4 miles. Golf 12 miles. Pub at Bridgetown. Winsford village has a general stores, pub and tea rooms.

Open

17 March - 16 October.

At a glance

Welcome & Ambience	✓✓✓✓	Location	✓✓✓✓
Quality of Pitches	✓✓✓✓	Range of Facilities	✓✓✓

Directions

Bridgetown is roughly midway between Dunster and Tiverton on the A396. As you enter Bridgetown from Tiverton, look for site sign and turn left in minor road; the site is 100 yards on the right. O.S.GR: SS923332. GPS: N51:05.292 W03:32.325

Charges 2006

Per unit incl. 2 adults	£ 7.50 - £ 12.50
extra adult	£ 3.00
electricity (16A) and TV hook-up	£ 2.50
awning	£ 1.00
dog	£ 1.00

Reservations

Made for any length with no deposit. Tel: 01643 851432. Email: paul@paulmatt.fsnet.co.uk

UK1370 Burrowhayes Farm Caravan & Camping Site

West Luccombe, Porlock, Minehead TA24 8HT (Somerset)

This delightful park with riding stables on site, is on the edge of Exmoor. The stone packhorse bridge over Horner Water beside the farm entrance sets the tone of the park, which the Dascombe family have created over the last thirty years having previously farmed the land. The farm buildings have been converted into riding stables with escorted rides available (from 7/4). Touring and tent pitches are on partly sloping field with marvelous views or a flatter location in the clearing by the river, while 20 caravan holiday homes are in a separate area. Electrical hook-ups are available (10A), although some long leads may be needed. With walking, birdwatching, plenty of wild life to observe, pretty Exmoor villages and Lorna Doone country nearby there is much to do. Children can ride, play in the stream or explore the woods at the top of the site. Limited trout fishing is available in Horner Water (NT permit) alongside the park.

Facilities

A new heated toilet block provides controllable hot showers, one washbasin cubicle for each sex, hairdressing and shaving areas. In the reception and stable block area are a laundry room, unit for disabled visitors and babies, and an indoor dishwashing room. A second older block is opened in high season with extra WCs and washbasins. Motorcaravan service point. Well stocked shop doubles with reception (from 22/3). Off site: Beach 2 miles. Fishing 2 miles. Bicycle hire 5 miles. Golf 6 miles. Minehead 5 miles. Local pub 20 minutes walk.

Open

15 March - 31 October.

At a glance

Welcome & Ambience	✓✓✓✓	Location	✓✓✓✓✓
Quality of Pitches	✓✓✓✓	Range of Facilities	✓✓✓✓

Directions

From A39, 5 miles west of Minehead, take first left past Allerford to Horner and West Luccombe. Site is on right after 400 yards. O.S.GR: SS899461. GPS: N51:12.212 W03:34.668

Charges 2005

Per unit incl. 1 or 2 persons	£ 7.50 - £ 12.00
extra person	£ 2.50 - £ 4.00
child (3-15 yrs)	£ 1.25 - £ 2.00
dog	free

Reservations

Made with deposit (£10 per week or part week, per pitch). Tel: 01643 862463. Email: info@burrowhayes.co.uk

IN THE HEART OF EXMOOR COUNTRY
Burrowhayes Farm
Popular family site in delightful National Trust setting on Exmoor. A walkers paradise. Pony trekking from site. Sites for touring caravans, tents & motorhomes. Caravans for hire. Heated toilet & shower block with disabled facilities.
Tel: 01643 862 463 www.burrowhayes.co.uk
AA

UK1360 Halse Farm Touring Caravan & Camping Park

Winsford, Minehead TA24 7JL (Somerset)

A truly rural park with beautiful, moorland views, you may be lucky enough to glimpse red deer across the valley or be able to see ponies and foals grazing outside the main gate which is adjacent to the moor. Two open, neatly cut fields (level at the top) back onto traditional hedging and slope gently to the middle and bottom where wild flowers predominate. One field provides electricity points (10A) and is used for motorcaravans and caravans, the other is for tents. There is no reception - you leave your unit by the toilet block and walk down to the farm kitchen to book in. Mrs Brown has laminated maps available (at a small cost) detailing six walks, starting and finishing at the farm. Also available is a list of the wild birds, flowers, etc. to be found on the site. The pretty village of Winsford is one mile (footpath from farm) with a post office, shop, pub and restaurant. A member of the Countryside Discovery group.

Facilities

The central toilet block is of good quality and heated. Well equipped and maintained, it includes a toilet, washbasin and shower for visitors with disabilities, washing machine, dryer and iron, and tourist information. Gas is available at the farm. Play equipment. Well behaved dogs are accepted (free). Off site: Fishing 4 miles, bicycle hire 5 miles, riding 2 miles. Tarr Steps and Barle Valley 3 miles. Winsford village 1 mile.

Open

18 March - 1 November.

At a glance

Welcome & Ambience	✓✓✓	Location	✓✓✓✓
Quality of Pitches	✓✓✓	Range of Facilities	✓✓✓

Directions

Turn off A396 Tiverton - Minehead road for Winsford (site signed). In Winsford village turn left in front of the Royal Oak (not over ford) and keep on uphill for 1 mile (go slowly round the sharp bend at the bottom). Cross cattle grid onto moor and turn immediately left to farm. Caravans should avoid Dulverton - keep to the A396 from Bridgetown (signed). O.S.GR: SS898342. GPS: N51:05.863 W03:34.799

Charges 2006

Per unit incl. 2 adults	£ 9.00 - £ 11.00
with electricity	£ 11.00 - £ 12.80

Less 10% for 7 days paid in advance 10 days before arrival.

Reservations

Advised for July/Aug. and made with £15 deposit. Tel: 01643 851259. Email: ar@halsefarm.co.uk

UK1380 **Hoburne Blue Anchor**

Blue Anchor Bay, Minehead TA24 6JT (Somerset)

With almost 300 caravan holiday homes, Blue Anchor nevertheless offers good facilities for 103 touring units. Trailer tents are accepted but not other tents (other than pup tents with a touring booking). Virtually in a separate touring area, the level pitches all have 16A electricity and hardstanding for cars and motorcaravans. A feature of the park is a good sized, irregularly shaped indoor pool. With views of the sea from the pool, it is heated and supervised. There are restaurants and takeaways within easy walking distance. The park's situation, directly across the small road from the beach, is unusual and gives some beautiful views across the Bristol Channel to South Wales. Part of the Hoburne Group.

Facilities	Directions
Toilet facilities provide large hot showers (with push-button). Fully equipped launderette. Indoor heated pool (free). Excellent adventure-style play area. Note: an unfenced river runs along one boundary of the park. Crazy golf. Small shop with coffee shop. American motorhomes accepted (max. 36 ft). Dogs are not accepted. Off site: Beach 100 yds. Riding and bicycle hire 5 miles. Golf 6 miles.	From M5 exit 25, take A358 signed Minehead. After 12 miles turn left on A39 at Williton. In 4 miles turn right on B3191 at Carhampton to park (1.5 miles). O.S.GR: ST024535. GPS: N51:10.932 W03:23.837

Open	Charges 2005
1 March - 31 October.	Per unit incl. up to 6 persons, electricity and awning £ 9.00 - £ 19.00

Reservations

For stays of 1-6 days, payment required in full at time of booking; for 7 nights or more £50 deposit. Min. bookings at B.Hs. Tel: 01643 821360.
Email: enquiries@hoburne.com

At a glance

Welcome & Ambience	✓✓✓✓	Location	✓✓✓✓✓
Quality of Pitches	✓✓✓✓	Range of Facilities	✓✓✓✓

UK1350 **Quantock Orchard Caravan Park**

Crowcombe, Taunton TA4 4AW (Somerset)

The old adage 'small is beautiful' certainly fits Quantock Orchard, nestling at the foot of the Quantocks in quiet countryside, yet close to many of the attractions of the area. Attractively developed, mature apple trees, shrubs and pretty flower beds, make a very pleasant environment and the clock tower on the toilet block adds interest. With access from gravel roads, there are 55 touring pitches, part separated by growing shrubs and hedging, of which 20 are for tents. Of various sizes, all touring pitches have 10A electricity, 20 have hardstanding, 4 have TV hook-up and 5 are fully serviced (two extra large, with patio and barbecue). Only 'air-flo' style groundsheets are permitted. A leisure suite provides a sauna, steam room, jacuzzi, mini-gym and conservatory rest area (this is also open to the public; visitor membership optional with a range of tariffs; children under 16 not admitted). It is complemented by the outdoor heated pool, open to all, which is walled with paved sunbathing surrounds.

Facilities	Directions
The central, heated sanitary block, refurbished in 2005, is very well maintained. Some washbasins in cubicles for ladies, excellent family bathroom and separate baby room. Good dishwashing provision, microwave. Laundry facilities. Drain for motorcaravan tanks. Well stocked licensed shop includes camping accessories. Mountain bike hire (some with buggies for children). Fish and chip van (twice weekly in summer). Swimming pool (40 x 20 ft. and open May - Sept). Leisure suite. Games room, Sky TV. Fenced safe-based play area. Caravan storage Oct. - March. Off site: The Carew Arms serving meals is within walking distance.	Park is west off A358 road (Taunton - Minehead), about 1 mile south of Crowcombe village. O.S.GR: ST140363. GPS: N51:06.504 W03:13.587

Charges 2006

Per unit incl. 2 adults, electricity	£ 10.95 - £ 17.95
tent pitch and car incl. 2 adults	£ 8.95 - £ 15.95
child (3-15 yrs)	£ 1.49 - £ 2.49

Reservations

Made with £20 per week deposit, per booking (non-returnable). Tel: 01984 618618.
Email: qocp@flaxpool.freeserve.co.uk

Open

All year.

At a glance

Welcome & Ambience	✓✓✓✓	Location	✓✓✓✓
Quality of Pitches	✓✓✓✓	Range of Facilities	✓✓✓✓

UK1570 Northam Farm Touring Caravan Park

Brean Sands, Burnham-on-Sea TA8 2SE (Somerset)

Brean has been a popular holiday destination for decades and many large campsites have evolved. Northam Farm is one of them; it is a large family park with good facilities and an ongoing programme of improvements. Of the 850 pitches, 400 are for seasonal units and these are separated from the four tourist fields. Pitches are large so you won't feel cramped and 154 have block paved hardstanding. There are two play areas for youngsters, a sports field with mobiliser swing, football, bicycle track, and cricket pitch for teenagers, and fishing on the lake for adults. The owners and staff are always available to help visitors enjoy their stay. About 500 yards down the road is The Seagull, which is also owned by Northam Farm. Here you'll find an excellent restaurant, bar and nightly live entertainment, even during the low season. A bus stops at the park entrance, or visitors can book a free ride on the bus to Cheddar, famous for its gorge and caves. Alternatively, just down the road is Brean Leisure Park with its swimming complex, funfair, golf and much more.

Facilities

Three good toilet blocks, well maintained and within reasonable distance of all pitches, provide ample toilets and washbasins (mostly open plan). The blocks have large showers (50p pull cord operation). Baby room, hair washing and drying, and slatted bench seats. Rooms for visitors with disabilities (opened by key). Dishwashing. New laundry. Dog shower. Licensed shop well stocked with food, holiday gear and accessories. Snack bar/takeaway. Free entry to live entertainment at The Seagull. Games room. Two play areas. Sports field. Fishing lake. Caravan workshop for repairs and servicing. Caravan storage. Dogs are not accepted in one field.

At a glance

Welcome & Ambience	✓✓✓✓	Location	✓✓✓✓
Quality of Pitches	✓✓✓✓✓	Range of Facilities	✓✓✓✓

Directions

Leave M5 motorway at junction 22 and follow the signs to Burnham-on-Sea, Berrow and then Brean. Continue through Brean and Northam Farm is on the right, half a mile past Brean Leisure Park. O.S.GR: ST297556. GPS: N51:17.694 W03:00.610

Charges 2005

Per unit incl. 2 persons	£ 5.50 - £ 17.50
extra adult	£ 1.00 - £ 2.50
child	£ 0.75 - £ 1.00
Dog and awning free.	

Reservations

Contact park for details; made with deposit to cover two night's fees. Tel: 01278 751244. Email: enquiries@northamfarm.demon.co.uk

Open

March - October.

UK1480 Home Farm Holiday Park & Country Club

Edithmead, Burnham-on-Sea TA9 4HD (Somerset)

Home Farm is neatly and attractively laid out covering 44 acres, and is convenient for those using the M5. The 780 level pitches (including 180 privately owned holiday homes) laid out on level mown grass are all clearly marked, accessed by tarmac roads and divided into various sections, for example an area for those with pets. Including 183 pitches with hardstanding, there are 20 serviced pitches for RVs and motorcaravans with water and grey water drainage. Electrical connections (10A) are available everywhere with plenty of water points in all the sections, but one central refuse area. A large, modern pool with paved surrounds and a paddling section is neatly walled. There is a well equipped playground, early evening children's entertainment, plus amusement machines and pool tables for those interested. The club house (with free membership) is a feature of the site providing carvery meals, a range of entertainment, a function room, wide screen TV, an attractive conservatory and outside barbecue area. In all, it is an excellent provision and Burnham-on-Sea is only a mile away – there is a footpath from the site crossing the railway line. With Berrow Sands and Brean Down there is over seven miles of beach to choose from! There is some road and rail noise but this quietens at night. Tents are not accepted.

Facilities

Two main, refurbished toilet blocks are heated and well situated for touring areas. Hot showers in one block are larger, but minus dividers. Bathrooms (key with £5 deposit). Baby changing room. Dishwashing facilities under cover and a well equipped laundry room. Facilities for disabled visitors. Dog shower. Shop with groceries, camping accessories and camping gaz. Bar. Restaurants, takeaway (open BHs, weekends and high season). Swimming pool (May-Sept, lifeguard at w/ends, B.Hs and school holidays). Play area. ATM. Security patrols at night. Barrier card (£2).
Off site: Boat launching 1 mile. Golf 2 miles. Riding 3 miles. Beach 3 miles.

Open

10 February - 6 January.

At a glance

Welcome & Ambience	✓✓✓✓	Location	✓✓✓
Quality of Pitches	✓✓✓✓	Range of Facilities	✓✓✓✓

Directions

Home Farm is 400 yards from M5 junction 22 and the A38. It is signed from the B3140 into Burnham-on-Sea. O.S.GR: ST328493
GPS: N51:14.325 W02:57.850

Charges 2005

Per pitch incl. 2 persons, electricity and awning	£ 7.50 - £ 18.50
extra person	£ 3.00 - £ 5.00
child (4-17 yrs)	£ 1.50 - £ 4.00
hardstanding	£ 2.00 - £ 3.00
dog	£ 1.00 - £ 2.00
Club membership free.	
Special breaks available.	

Reservations

Contact park for details Tel: 01278 788888. Email: SITE@hfhp.co.uk

UK1575 Holiday Resort Unity

Coast Road, Brean Sands TA8 2RB (Somerset)

Holiday Resort Unity offers everything for everyone, from young children to the 'young at heart'. Apart from the extensive on-site amusements and entertainment programme, campers can also use the swimming pools, funfair and other leisure pursuits at the adjoining Brean Leisure Centre (owned by the same family), some free of charge and others by paying a small fee. Access to the five-mile stretch of sandy beach is via a footpath opposite the site entrance. Fishing (with a licence) is permitted from Unity Lake in the Yellow Field. RJ's is a club with bars, food and nightly entertainment for the whole family. Sarah's Pantry offers takeaway or sit-down meals (including the Sunday roast), while fish and chips are available at Porkers Bar. Three large touring fields provide pitches that are flat and open, mostly grass but some on concrete hardstandings (motorcaravans up to 30 ft can be accommodated). Most pitches have 16A electricity hook-ups. A separate warden looks after each camping field. Ready equipped tents and a substantial number of caravan holiday homes are available for rent.

Facilities

Four toilet blocks provide ample showers. Some toilets and washbasins have been adapted for people with disabilities (key from reception). Dishwashing and hair care rooms, well-equipped laundries. Motorcaravan service point. Well stocked shop. Gas exchange. RJ's Club, Sarah's Pantry and Porkers fish and chip bar. Large adventure play area. Cyber Zone (high season; £1 for 10 minutes). Buster's Work Out Gym, Sally's sun beds. Monday market, Sunday car boot sales. All facilities open during high season, most open during mid season, and most facilities available during the weekends in low season. Torches advisable at night. Off site: Walking access from park to Brean leisure Centre (swimming pool, funfair etc); riding, cycling, cinema, walks, golf all within walking distance from park. Bus and land-train services vary according to season. Bus to Weston Super Mare and Cheddar stops at park gates. Beach 100 m.

At a glance

Welcome & Ambience	✓✓✓	Location	✓✓✓✓
Quality of Pitches	✓✓✓	Range of Facilities	✓✓✓✓✓

Directions

From M5, exit 22, follow signs for Burnham on Sea (B3140), Berrow and Brean. Holiday Resort Unity is right on the main street of Brean - it is well signed. Take care as road through Berrow and Brean is rather narrow. O.S.GR: ST290539.
GPS: N51:16.829 W03:00.733

Charges 2005

Per standard pitch	£ 6.00 - £ 175.00
serviced pitch	£ 8.00 - £ 189.00
with hardstanding	£ 10.00 - £ 210.00

Price includes unit, 4 persons, awning, entertainment/swimming and 'Piglet Club'.

Reservations

Made with full payment if arrival within 6 weeks; deposit of £20 if more than 6 weeks. Tel: 01278 751235. Email: rjh@hru.co.uk

Open

14 February - 25 November.

UK1580 Warren Farm Touring Park

Warren Road, Brean Sands, Burnham-on-Sea TA8 2RP (Somerset)

Warren Farm is a popular venue for family campers who want the beach, fun and entertainment. With over 1,000 pitches, the park is divided into several fields, with touring and seasonal pitches kept apart; Sunnyside, part of Warren Farm, is about 200 yards down the road and has its own warden. Access roads are wide and the 565 touring pitches are grassy and level, with 16A electricity. There are no hard-standings. Play equipment is located in a line through the centre of the camping fields - ranch-style wooden fences break up the fields and couples usually park around the perimeter with views of the Mendip Hills. A fabulous Play Barn incorporates an indoor play centre, bowling alley, large-screen TV and electronic games. The Beachcomber Inn offers a bar, restaurant (good food), Pirate's Cove for youngsters, and live entertainment. With its direct access to the beach, this holiday park caters for everyone.

Facilities

Several toilet blocks of varying styles provide WCs, showers (on payment) and mostly communal washbasins. Facilities vary depending on which block you are using. Showers are of adequate size – only one block with no dividers; the newest building in field 5 has larger ones. Facilities for disabled visitors in the block in field 5 (plus pitches which may be reserved nearby). Three laundries. Supermarket, snack bar and takeaway. Chinese takeaway at Sunnyside. Fish bar. Beachcomber Inn. Play barn. Sports field. Fishing lake. Two 'no dog' fields. Off site: Golf and riding 1.5 miles.

At a glance

Welcome & Ambience	✓✓✓✓	Location	✓✓✓✓✓
Quality of Pitches	✓✓✓✓	Range of Facilities	✓✓✓✓

Directions

Leave M5 at exit 22 and follow B3140 to Burnham-on-Sea, then Berrow and Brean. Go through Brean and Warren Farm is 1.5 miles past Brean Leisure Park. O.S.GR: ST297564. GPS: N51:18.149 W03:00.590

Charges 2005

Per unit incl. 2 persons	£ 6.00 - £ 12.50
extra person over 3 yrs	£ 2.00
electricity (16A)	£ 2.00

Reservations

Made with deposit.Tel: 01278 751227.
Email: enquiries@warren-farm.co.uk

Open

28 March - 13 October.

South West England

UK1530 Slimeridge Farm Touring Park

Links Road, Uphill, Weston-super-Mare BS23 4XY (Somerset)

This small touring site is next to the beach in Uphill village at the southern end of Weston Bay. There are 56 pitches (24 taken on seasonal lets), on level grass with electricity (16A) available, separated from the beach by stone walling. The view across the bay is quite something, with Brean Down and Steep Holm Island standing out. However it is worth noting that, because of its close proximity to the beach, the site could be affected by the tide in extreme adverse winter weather conditions. A circular tarmac road connects the marked and numbered pitches (allocated by the wardens) which include eight hard-standings for motorcaravans. Arrive betweeon 11.00 and 17.00 hrs only. Weston-super-Mare with all its leisure activities and entertainment is 2 miles, Cheddar Gorge, Wooky Hole and Glastonbury are within easy driving distance.

Facilities

A modern toilet block with electronic code entry system is well equipped and includes en-suite shower facilities that are also provided for handicapped visitors. Laundry room and washing up sinks. Chemical disposal unit also used for waste water. Off site: Post office, general stores and pubs within close walking distance. Golf (note: golfers have right of way to cross the park as the golf course is split by the site).

Open

1 March - 30 October.

At a glance

| Welcome & Ambience | ✓✓ | Location | ✓✓✓✓✓ |
| Quality of Pitches | ✓✓✓ | Range of Facilities | ✓✓✓ |

Directions

Site is south of Weston-super-Mare. From A370 follow sign for Uphill village and sands. O.S.GR: 312588. GPS: N51:19.433 W02:59.342

Charges guide

Per unit incl. 2 adults, electricity and awning	£ 10.00 - £ 20.00
extra adult	£ 1.50 - £ 3.00
child (4-9 yrs)	£ 1.00 - £ 2.50
dog	£ 0.50 - £ 1.00

Min. stay 2 nights at B.Hs. No credit cards.

Reservations

Made with deposit of £5 p/night; no refunds given. Tel: 01934 641641.

UK1460 Newton Mill Camping Park

Newton Road, Bath BA2 9JF (Somerset)

In a peaceful valley two miles from the centre of the historic city of Bath and with direct access to the local cycle track network, Newton Mill is an excellent base from which to explore the city and the area. The site has been created around an old mill, the bar and restaurant now occupying part of the original building, and there is a modern timber chalet style reception building with a small, well stocked shop. The restaurant (lunches/evenings all year) serves speciality meals including ostrich and lobster, and breakfasts are available (weekends Easter - October, daily in summer). The tent meadow is in an elevated position, or alternatively you may prefer the paddock, a small field alongside the stream which is a car free zone with a separate parking area. The site accepts 105 tents and also has 90 caravan pitches (with 30 long stay) which are located at the other end of the valley. All of these have hardstandings, with 16A electricity and satellite TV hook-ups. This end of the park is closest to the main Bristol - London railway line, not visually obtrusive but occasional rail noise may be noticeable.

Facilities

Two new heated toilet blocks provide excellent modern facilities with some washbasins in cubicles, free hot showers, bathrooms (on payment), baby rooms, dishwashing rooms and a good suite for disabled campers. Launderette. Basic motorcaravan service point. Shop, bar, restaurant with garden seating area. Play area. Boules court. Fishing. Off site: Bus service into Bath runs every 10 minutes from Twerton village which is a 10 minute walk. Nearby Bristol and Bath Railway Path (a traffic free cycle way) links to the West Bath Riverside Path, and the Kennet and Avon towpath.

Open

All year.

At a glance

| Welcome & Ambience | ✓✓✓✓ | Location | ✓✓✓✓ |
| Quality of Pitches | ✓✓✓✓ | Range of Facilities | ✓✓✓✓ |

Directions

Site is 2 miles west of Bath city centre, about 1 mile southeast of the roundabout where the A4 meets the A39. From the north take M4 exit 19, turn on to M32 and almost immediately take A4174 (Avon ring road) for 7.5 miles to the A4. Turn left towards Bath and after 5 miles at second roundabout, take second exit signed Newton St Loe and pass The Globe public house. Site entrance is on the left after about 1 mile. O.S.GR: ST713647. GPS: N51:22.688 W02:24.649

Charges 2005

Per adult	£ 4.00 - £ 5.00
child (3-16 yrs)	£ 2.00
pitch incl. car	£ 3.00 - £ 6.00
awning	£ 2.00
dog	£ 0.75

Reservations

Advised for peak season and B.Hs. Tel: 01225 333909. Email: newtonmill@hotmail.com

UK1510 Bath Chew Valley Caravan Park

Ham Lane, Bishop Sutton BS39 5TZ (Somerset)

A small and secluded garden site for adults only, Chew Valley has been developed with much tender love and care by Ray and Val Betton. The result is that caravans are sited by neat lawns amongst colourful beds of flowers and the cars are tucked away on the nearby car park, providing a tranquil and restful atmosphere. The warden will assist you in placing your caravan. Groundsheets are not permitted on the grass in order to protect it. There are neat hardstandings and 17 spacious, fully serviced pitches and, again to protect the lawns, motorcaravans must always use them. This park will particularly appeal to garden lovers; a very nice touch is the small nursery 'Gone to Pot' where those staying on the site can purchase some of the plants found on-site. Next to reception there is a good library, also providing tourist information. Chew Valley lake is a walk of about half a mile with trout fishing available and Blagdon lake is popular for birdwatching. There are several circular walks in the area - visitors may borrow the route plans and a walking stick from reception. Bristol and Bath are within an easy distance and Cheddar Gorge or Longleat make excellent days out. A Best of British group member.

Facilities

The heated toilet block (it has a 'home from home' feel), provides washbasins in cubicles and all the other fittings that make life comfortable. Two separate en-suite units. Useful utility room for dish or hand washing with a spin drier, together with a washing machine and tumble drier for service washes only. Motorcaravan service point. Off site: The village is 100 yds up the road with a useful general store, newsagent, two pubs and a post office. Supermarkets are within 15 minutes drive. Fishing 1 mile. Golf 4 miles. Riding 8 miles. Beach 15 miles.

Open

All year.

At a glance

Welcome & Ambience	✓✓✓✓✓	Location	✓✓✓✓
Quality of Pitches	✓✓✓✓✓	Range of Facilities	✓✓✓

Directions

From Bath direction on A368 turn right opposite the Red Lion pub in Bishop Sutton. Road appears a little narrow but continue past a small track to the left (50 yds) for a further 50 yds. Park entrance appears on your left with neat, clear entrance.
O.S.GR: ST584599. GPS: N51:20.195 W02:35.831

Charges 2005

Per adult	£ 4.00
standard pitch incl. electricity, awning and pets	£ 8.00
serviced pitch	£ 10.00

Reservations

Advisable for B.Hs and made with £20 non-refundable deposit. Tel: 01275 332127.
Email: enquiries@bathchewvalley.co.uk

Bath Chew Valley Caravan Park

NE Somerset's only 5 Star Park, **exclusively for adults.**
Units pitched between shrubs & flowers. Excellent toilets
& facilities. Booking advisable. **Call 01275 332 127** or email
enquiries@bathchewvalley.co.uk for a brochure or to book.

UK1440 Baltic Wharf Caravan Club Site

Cumberland Road, Bristol BS1 6XG (Somerset)

This excellent, city centre site is operated by the Caravan Club. In Bristol's re-developed dockland, it is well laid out and maintained with access via a lockable gate to the Baltic Wharf dockside. It is screened from the road by a high wall with a boatyard on one side and residential apartments on the other, and is well designed with a good use of trees. The view across the dock towards Clifton village and Bristol is unique and you can even glimpse the suspension bridge. The 58 pitches are accessed by a circular tarmac road, the central 9 on grass (not used in the winter), the rest on stone chippings and ideal for all year round use (steel pegs are sold at reception). All are supplied with 16A electricity. It is a 30 minute walk to the city centre, a ferry runs daily or there's a regular bus service (not Sundays). An extra ferry runs from the SS Great Britain to Templemeads. TV reception is poor but a booster is available. This is a well serviced situation and a very popular site so advance booking is necessary. Arrive between 12 noon and 8 pm. Space for large units and RVs is very limited and there is no space for trailers, boats, etc.

Facilities

The toilet block provides good clean facilities including controllable showers and washbasins in cubicles (heated in winter). Good facilities for disabled visitors, plus toilets for the walking disabled and showers in main block. Dishwashing under cover. Fully equipped laundry room. Motorcaravan service point. Tourist information room. Dogs are welcome but there is no dog walk. Wardens live on the site. Off site: Fishing (licences from Harbour Master's office).

Open

All year.

At a glance

Welcome & Ambience	✓✓✓✓	Location	✓✓✓✓✓
Quality of Pitches	✓✓✓✓✓	Range of Facilities	✓✓✓

Directions

Easiest access is to follow signs for the 'Historic Harbour' and SS Great Britain. Site is just west of the SS Great Britain, on the right behind a high wall - look carefully for the club sign (no brown signs to follow). O.S.GR: ST574721.
GPS: N51:26.792 W02:36.855

Charges 2005

Per adult	£ 3.80 - £ 5.00
child (5-16 yrs)	£ 1.10 - £ 1.80
pitch incl. electricity (non-member)	£ 9.50 - £ 15.00

Reservations

Essential at all times and made with £10 deposit; contact the Wardens with SAE for confirmation.
Tel: 0117 926 8030.

85

UK1450 **Bath Marina & Caravan Park**

Brassmill Lane, Bath BA1 3JT (Somerset)

British Waterways have taken the lease for the Bath Marina and Caravan Park. Conveniently located alongside the Bath to Bristol cycle path, the site is within walking distance of the city and a park-and-ride facility. There are 88 pitches of varying sizes pleasantly interspersed with grass, flowering trees and bushes; every pitch has a concrete hardstanding with a 16A electricity connection. Two wooden cabins provide clean facilities and amenities (accessed with a security code). Television reception is poor so future development will include an aerial and connections to every pitch. There is no shop (except postcards, some basic camping equipment and gas exchange), however visitors can order newspapers, milk, and bread at the reception to be delivered to their pitches the next morning. Meals are available at the Boathouse Inn, just a two-minute walk along the river path.

Facilities

Two fan-heated buildings provide toilets, washbasins (with privacy curtain in ladies), showers and hairdryers. Some toilets have been modified for use by visitors with disabilities. Dishwashing sinks under cover. Large laundry. Recycling bins. Gas exchange. Drain for motorcaravan waste water. Tourist information. Children's play park adjacent to park. Boat launching (free) from Marina. Off site: Bath 2 miles. Bristol 8 miles. Bristol-Bath cycle path.

Open

All year.

At a glance

Welcome & Ambience	✓✓✓✓	Location	✓✓✓✓
Quality of Pitches	✓✓✓✓	Range of Facilities	✓✓✓

Directions

Park is off the A4 Bristol to Bath road. From Bristol, stay on the A4 towards Bath, at roundabout (junction with A39) continue for 1.3miles (keep left as the road forks), cross the river and turn right just past the garage into Brassmill Lane and park is 100 yards on the right. O.S. GR: ST720655.
GPS: N51:23.295 W02:24.195

Charges guide

Per pitch all inclusive	£ 15.00

Reservations

Advised for B.Hs. and school holidays and made with £15 deposit. Tel: 01225 424301.

UK1430 **Cheddar Camping & Caravanning Club Site**

Priddy, Wells BA5 3BP (Somerset)

Historic Priddy is the highest village in the Mendips and is famed for its annual Sheep Fair in August. Nearby are extensive Roman lead-workings, Bronze Age burial mounds, the Priddy Circle and access to Swildons Hole, one of the popular cave systems in the Mendips. Formerly Mendip Heights Caravan Park, this well kept site is half a mile from the village with tranquil views across the Mendip fields, characterised by dry stone walling. It has a simple charm with field margins left natural to encourage wildlife and nest boxes in the mature trees edging the three fields which comprise the site. These provide space for 92 units on mostly level short grass with 51 electric hook-up, 26 with hardstanding and 5 seasonal pitches. A range of activities can be enjoyed in the area covering canoeing, abseiling, archery, caving, mountain biking and others. The park is also on the Padstow-Bristol Sustran Route 3. Many tourist attractions are within a 20 mile radius.

Facilities

The refurbished toilet block with all facilities is bright, cheerful and heated. Two family rooms (one with high and low toilet and shower). Dishwashing and laundry facilities. The reception/shop doubles as the village shop and is therefore open all season selling groceries, Calor gas, etc. with an off licence and tourist information. Wendy house, swings and table tennis for children. Torches useful. Off site: Two traditional village pubs with very different characters stand by the village green within walking distance (0.5 miles). Bicycle hire and golf 5 miles. Fishing 6 miles, riding 2 miles.

Open

1 March - mid-November.

At a glance

Welcome & Ambience	✓✓✓✓	Location	✓✓✓✓
Quality of Pitches	✓✓✓	Range of Facilities	✓✓✓

Directions

From M5 exit 21 take A371 to Banwell. Turn left on A368, right on B3134 and right on B3135. After 2 miles turn left at camp sign. From M4 westbound exit 18, A46 to Bath, then A4 towards Bristol. Take A39 for Wells and right at Green Ore traffic lights on B3135; after 5 miles turn left at camp sign. From Shepton Mallet, follow A37 north to junction of B3135 and turn left. Continue on B3135 to traffic lights at Green Ore. Straight on and after 5 miles turn left at camp sign. O.S.GR: ST522518.
GPS: N51:15.816 W02:41.123

Charges 2005

Per adult	£ 5.60 - £ 7.80
child (4-16 yrs)	£ 2.10 - £ 4.45
non-member pitch fee	£ 5.00

Reservations

Contact site. Tel: 01749 870241.
Email: cheddar@campingandcaravanningclub.co.uk

UK1550 Bucklegrove Caravan & Camping Park

Wells Road, Rodney Stoke, Cheddar BS27 3UZ (Somerset)

Bucklegrove is set right in the heart of Somerset on the southern slopes of the Mendip Hills and close to the tourist attractions of Cheddar Gorge, Wookey Hole, and Wells. The 125 touring pitches are split between two fields joined by a woodland walk. The top slightly undulating field is more suitable for tents and caravans, while the lower field with some short hardstandings is a little more level and would be suitable for caravans and smaller motorhomes. The play area (for under 14s) includes a fort, swings and obstacle course. Campers also have a games room and a heated indoor swimming pool (adult only sessions 10.00 - 11.00 daily). Adjoining the pool is a licensed bar with terrace providing simple bar menus and low-key entertainment mainly during high season or depending on the number of campers on site.

Facilities

Two bright and cheerful toilet blocks house all the usual amenities including some washbasins in cubicles and some spacious showers. The larger, heated block near reception also provides bathrooms (50p) with baby changing facilities, and a room for visitors with disabilities. Dishwashing and laundry rooms. Freezer for ice packs. Well stocked shop. Indoor swimming pool and paddling pool with terrace bar. Games room with pool table, video and electronic games. Play area. Dogs are accepted in low season only. Off site: Riding 2 miles. Golf 3 miles. Fishing 5 miles. Beach at Weston-Super-Mare 12 miles. Wookey Hole 2 miles, Wells Cathedral 4 miles, Cheddar 7 miles. A bus to Wells and Cheddar stops at the park entrance.

At a glance

Welcome & Ambience	✓✓✓✓	Location	✓✓✓✓
Quality of Pitches	✓✓✓✓	Range of Facilities	✓✓✓✓

Directions

Take A371 Wells to Cheddar road. Park is on right about 1 mile past Westbury village. Take care as the road between Wells and Cheddar is rather narrow through some of the villages. O.S.GR: ST490496. GPS: N51:14.599 W02:43.938

Charges 2005

Per unit incl. 2 persons, electricity	£ 7.50 - £ 17.50
pup tent	£ 0.50 - £ 1.50
extra adult	£ 2.00
child (4-14 yrs)	£ 0.50 - £ 1.50
dog (off peak only)	£ 1.00

Reservations

Special offers are available at certain times of the year if booking in advance. Tel: 01749 870261. Email: info@buckglegrove.co.uk

Open

1 March - 2 January.

UK1490 Greenacres Camping

Barrow Lane, North Wootton, Shepton Mallet BA4 4HL (Somerset)

Greenacres is a rural site in Somerset countryside for tents, trailer tents and small motorcaravans only. Hidden away below the Mendips and almost at the start of the 'Levels', it is a simple green site - a true haven of peace and quiet. The grass is neatly trimmed over the 4.5 acres and hedged with mature trees, though there is a view of Glastonbury Tor in one direction and of Barrow Hill in the other. All of the 30 pitches are around the perimeter of the park, leaving a central area safe for children to play. At the narrower neck end, 5 pitches have electricity hook-ups (16A) and are ideal for those without children or birdwatchers. Wild life abounds. A speciality of the park is the 'Turf Rider' that tows the cart used to give children an evening ride. There are many nearby attractions should you tire of the peace and quiet, such as Wookey Hole, Cheddar Caves and Gorge, Longleat, the beautiful small city of Wells (with leisure centre), Clarks Village, etc. You can cycle into both Wells and Glastonbury using Sustran Route 3.

Facilities

The central wooden toilet block is simple but perfectly acceptable and kept clean. Hot showers are accessed directly from the outside. Two dishwashing sinks, two laundry sinks (H&C) and a spin dryer, with and iron, board and hairdryer available from the park office. A selection of play equipment, a badminton net and a play house. The park office is across the lane (gate is usually keep shut), at the owner's bungalow. Here too are fridges and freezers for campers' use (free), a library, tourist information and bicycle hire. Batteries may be charged or borrowed. Dogs are not accepted. Off site: North Wootton (under 1 mile) with large pub/restaurant and a vineyard. Fishing and riding nearby.

At a glance

Welcome & Ambience	✓✓✓✓	Location	✓✓✓✓
Quality of Pitches	✓✓✓✓	Range of Facilities	✓✓✓

Directions

From A39 Glastonbury - Wells road turn east at Brownes Garden Centre and follow camping signs. From A361 Glastonbury - Shepton Mallet road follow camp signs from Pilton or Steanbow. O.S.GR: ST553416. GPS: N51:10.342 W02:38.513

Charges 2005

Per adult	£ 6.00
child (4-16 yrs)	£ 2.00
electricity	£ 2.00
No credit cards.	

Reservations

Made with £2 deposit. Tel: 01749 890497.

Open

March - October.

UK1540 Batcombe Vale Campsite

Batcombe Vale, Shepton Mallet BA4 6BW (Somerset)

Set in a secluded valley with fields gently rising around it, contented cows grazing with watchful buzzards cruising above and views across the distant hills, this is a very special place. Home to Donald and Mary Sage, Batcombe Vale House is a mellow, attractive building covered with wisteria, to one side of the valley overlooking the lakes and the 'wilder' landscape. Trees and shrubs have been skilfully placed to enhance the natural environment providing a range of colour and shape. Designated an 'area of outstanding natural beauty', there are 120 acres around the valley where you are welcome to wander and picnic in the fields – a haven for wild flowers, birds and butterflies. For those who fish, two of the lakes have carp and tench up to 18lbs but you must have a current licence. Descending slowly down the narrow entrance drive you see the pitches, attractively set and terraced where necessary, in an oval with the lakes below. The grass is left natural around the 32 pitches (20 have 10A electricity) and paths mown where needed. If you tire of the views and the fishing there is a range of circular walks from the site or you can potter about in one of the four small rowing boats. There are many places to visit nearby, from Glastonbury with the Tor, to Cheddar Gorge and the Caves.

Facilities

The small rustic toilet block covered in honeysuckle meets all needs, including a freezer and dishwashing sinks. Groundsheet awnings must be lifted daily. Fishing. Caravan storage. One dog per pitch is welcome (no dangerous breeds). Bed and breakfast available in Batcombe Vale House. Off site: Golf, riding and bicycle hire 5 miles. Bruton (for shops, etc.) is 2 miles. Launderettes at Shepton or Frome.

Reservations

Only essential for B.Hs. (min. 3 nights) and school holidays; made with £10 deposit and £1 fee (min. 2 nights at other times). Tel: 01749 830246. Email: DonaldSage@compuserve.com

Open

Easter - September.

At a glance

| Welcome & Ambience | ✓✓✓✓✓ | Location | ✓✓✓✓✓ |
| Quality of Pitches | ✓✓✓✓ | Range of Facilities | ✓✓✓ |

Directions

Bruton is south of Shepton Mallet and Frome and north of Wincanton where the A359 intersects the B3081. About 2 miles north of Bruton on B3081 turn on bend (site signed) into narrow lane. Turn left at T-junction and follow signs to site 500 yds on left. Access drive is steep. O.S.GR: ST684376.
GPS: N51:08.188 W02:27.190

Charges 2005

Per unit incl. 2 adults	£ 13.00
extra adult	£ 4.00
child (4-18 yrs)	£ 1.50 - £ 2.50
electricity	£ 2.00
dog	£ 1.00

Coarse fishing (up to 20 lbs) adults £3 p/day (child £1.50) or £2 p/day times length of stay. No commercial vehicles or motorcycle 'packs' - family groups only.

UK1390 The Old Oaks Touring Park

Wick Farm, Wick, Glastonbury BA6 8JS (Somerset)

The Old Oaks, an 'adults only' park, is tucked below and hidden from the 'Tor', in a lovely secluded setting with views across to the Mendips. There are 40 extra large pitches in a series of paddocks, all with 10A electricity, 18 with hardstanding and 4 fully serviced (including sewage). Mainly backing on to hedges, they are attractively arranged and interspersed with shrubs and flowers in a circular development or terraced with increasing views. A quiet orchard area or a separated hedged paddock for camping and a larger field with chemical disposal facilities complete the provision. Mature trees and hedging combine with the mellow farm buildings to give a sense of timelessness, tranquillity and peace. Whether you fish or not, the pond which is well stocked with carp, roach and tench is worth a visit not only for its view of the Tor, but also to see the ducks and the chickens on your way. There is parking for disabled visitors within 25 yards of the pond. In an area steeped in history and legend, this is a very well equipped and maintained park which should meet the needs of the discerning camper or caravanner. A member of the Best of British group.

Facilities

The heated toilet block, converted from the old stables, is of excellent quality and well equipped. Neatly paved outside, it has digital security locks (a public footpath from the Tor passes through the farm). Some washbasins are in cubicles. Two en-suite rooms and a bathroom (£1). Disabled visitors have two rooms, one with a toilet and basin, the other with a shower, toilet and basin. Fully equipped laundry room. Dishwashing under cover. Motorcaravan service facilities. Two recycling points. Freezer for ice packs (free). Useful dog wash. Shop for basics and locally baked bread in the main season and an off licence (limited hours). Bicycle hire (together with hire of helmets). Fishing. Adults only accepted (18 yrs and over). Internet access available at reception. Off site: Riding 5 miles and golf 6 miles. Market day is Tuesday.

At a glance

| Welcome & Ambience | ✓✓✓✓✓ | Location | ✓✓✓✓✓ |
| Quality of Pitches | ✓✓✓✓✓ | Range of Facilities | ✓✓✓✓ |

Directions

Park is north off A361 Shepton Mallet - Glastonbury road, 2 miles from Glastonbury. Take unclassified road signed Wick for approx. 1 mile and the park is on the left. O.S.GR: ST521394.
GPS: N51:09.158 W02:40.818

Charges 2005

Per unit with 2 persons	£ 11.00 - £ 14.00
with electricity (10A)	£ 13.00 - £ 16.00
awning with breathing groundsheet	£ 1.00
dog	£ 1.00

Reservations

Advised for high season and made with £20 non-refundable deposit Tel: 01458 831437. Email: info@theoldoaks.co.uk

Open

17 March - 31 October.

UK1400 The Isle of Avalon Touring Caravan Park

Godney Road, Glastonbury BA6 9AF (Somerset)

This modern park is under new ownership. It has a friendly atmosphere and is only a short walk from the centre of Glastonbury. Developed on flat, grassy ground, the park has been landscaped, part with trees and shrubs, part open, to provide 70 individual pitches. Well spaced and connected by hard roads, they have hardstanding with adjacent grass for awning and electricity points (5/10A). A further 50 tent spaces are on the adjoining field, the top corner being left clear as a play area. Water and refuse points are well distributed around and attractively surrounded by trees and shrubs. All visitors are personally seen to their pitches. A well stocked shop with takeaway and some camping accessories and reception with gas and tourist information is at the entrance. The nearby town of Street boasts 'Clarks Village' comprising a range of factory outlets including shoes!

Facilities

The single, tiled toilet block is comfortable, spacious and can be heated. Some washbasins in cubicles for women and excellent units for disabled visitors (plus ramps to the shop and reception). Large laundry room and dishwashing area. Motorcaravan point. Shop and takeaway. Bicycle hire. Dogs are accepted but by prior arrangement only on tent pitches. American motorhomes are welcome. Winter caravan storage. Off site: Glastonbury centre, with shops, restaurants and cafés, and the Abbey 10 minutes walk. Indoor and outdoor swimming pools at Street. Riding or golf 2 miles, fishing 200 yds.

At a glance

Welcome & Ambience	✓✓✓✓	Location	✓✓✓✓
Quality of Pitches	✓✓✓✓	Range of Facilities	✓✓✓✓

Directions

Park is on west side of the town bypass (A39), just off B3151 (Wedmore Road) with good signs from the bypass. O.S.GR: ST494397.
GPS: N51:09.227 W02:43.518

Charges 2005

Per adult	£ 2.00
child (3-14 yrs)	£ 1.50
pitch	£ 8.00 - £ 11.00
incl. electricity	£ 8.00 - £ 9.00
dog	£ 1.50

Reservations

Any length with £10 deposit. Tel: 01458 833618.

Open

All year.

UK1420 Southfork Caravan Park

Parrett Works, Martock TA12 6AE (Somerset)

Don't be put off by the address which is historic – this was once a 17th century flax mill. Michael and Nancy Broadley now own and run this excellent, modern, well drained site just outside the lovely village of Martock. With 25 touring pitches on grass with a gravel access road (21 with 10A electrical hook-ups), it is an orderly, quiet park on two acres of flat, tree lined meadow near the River Parrett. All the expected facilities are close to the entrance and as the owners live on the premises, the park is open all year. Most things are available, including an NCC approved caravan repairs/servicing centre. Despite the rural setting, the A303 trunk road is just five minutes away. This area of South Somerset contains so much of interest, including gardens, historic houses and sites, the Fleet Air Arm Museum, Haynes Motor Museum and Cricket St Thomas Wildlife Park. Information about access to many cycle routes and numerous walks, including the Parrett Trail, is available from reception.

Facilities

The heated well maintained toilet block is fully equipped and includes some washbasins in cabins. Laundry room with washing machine and dryer, plus dishwashing sink. Shop and limited off licence with gas and comprehensive camping accessories. Play area. Off site: Fishing (with licences) on the River Parrett a few yards from the park. Golf 5 miles. Bicycle hire 8 miles. Riding 10 miles. Pubs with good food in South Petherton and Martock, less than 2 miles in each direction.

At a glance

Welcome & Ambience	✓✓✓✓	Location	✓✓✓✓
Quality of Pitches	✓✓✓✓	Range of Facilities	✓✓✓✓

Directions

From A303 between Ilchester and Ilminster take signs for South Petherton or Martock; park is mid-way on the road between the two villages (follow signs). O.S.GR: ST446187. GPS: N50:57.922 W02:47.389

Charges 2005

Per unit incl. 2 persons	£ 8.00 - £ 13.50
extra person	£ 1.50

Reservations

Advisable for B.Hs. and peak season and made with £15 deposit. Tel: 01935 825661.
Email: southforkcaravans@btconnect.com

Open

All year.

UK1500 Long Hazel Park

High Street, Sparkford, Yeovil BA22 7JH (Somerset)

Pamela and Alan Walton are really enthusiastic about their neat, small park in the Somerset village of Sparkford where they will make you most welcome. With level grass, attractive beech hedging, silver birches and many other assorted trees, the park has a comfortable feel. It provides 75 touring pitches for all types of units, 50 with 16A electricity, 40 pitches with hardstanding, some extra long with grass lawns at the side, and the entrance has been widened for easier access. Part of the park near the road is being developed with pine lodges, which should lessen the noise from the A303 bypass. The village pub serves good food. Sparkford is also home to the Haynes Motor Museum and the Fleet Air Arm Museum is nearby at Yeovilton. Details of safe cycle routes and walks are available at reception.

Facilities

The well equipped heated toilet block is immaculate. Well planned en-suite facilities for visitors with disabilities. Washing machine and dryer. Motorcaravan discharge point. Gas from reception. Central area with play equipment and games area. The long hardstanding pitches are large enough for American style motorhomes. Off site: Spar mini-market 400 yards. Riding or fishing 8 miles. Golf 5 miles.

Open

16 February - 16 January.

At a glance

| Welcome & Ambience | ✓✓✓✓ | Location | ✓✓✓✓ |
| Quality of Pitches | ✓✓✓✓ | Range of Facilities | ✓✓✓ |

Directions

From Yeovil direction on A303 take road into village of Sparkford and park is signed on the left 100 yds before the Inn. O.S.GR: ST604263. GPS: N51:02.064 W02:34.118

Charges 2005

Per unit incl. 2 persons, electricity	£ 13.00 - £ 15.00
extra person (over 4 yrs)	£ 2.00
dog	£ 1.00

No credit cards.

Reservations

Contact park. Tel: 01963 440002.
Email: longhazelpark@hotmail.com

UK1630 Brokerswood Country Park

Brokerswood, Westbury BA13 4EH (Wiltshire)

This countryside campsite is located in an 80 acre country park, with ancient broadleaf woodland, plenty of marked walks, a woodland railway which also runs 'Santa Specials' (bookings taken from 1 August). The gift shop has a special Christmas theme from the end of October. The park also has adventure playgrounds and play trails amongst its many activities for the family. Most are free for campers, except for the train. Fishing in the lake is available, ask at reception. Cycling in the park is forbidden. The campsite has 65 pitches arranged around an open meadow area, served by a gravel roadway, with low level lighting. There are 25 hardstanding pitches, and 36 electric hook-ups (10A). Although recently laid out, the site is maturing well. In the interest of environmental conservation it has its own biological waste management system. American RVs and other large units should use the coach entrance and they (and all other arrivals after 6pm) are asked to phone ahead to make arrangements for the barrier.

Facilities

A recently constructed, well insulated and heated, timber clad building provides the usual facilities including large, controllable hot showers. Fully equipped suite for disabled people with ramped approach and alarm. Laundry. Motorcaravan services. Gas available. Milk, bread and papers to order. Broadleaf Café serving meals and refreshments all day. Entry barrier (key code). No cycling on site. Off site: Golf 6 miles. Pub with excellent meals (400 yds). Nearest shops are at Dilton Marsh. Longleat 6 miles.

At a glance

| Welcome & Ambience | ✓✓✓✓ | Location | ✓✓✓✓✓ |
| Quality of Pitches | ✓✓✓✓ | Range of Facilities | ✓✓✓✓ |

Directions

From Trowbridge take A361 south for 2 miles, turning left (east) at Southwick, and follow signs to Country Park. O.S.GR: ST840524. GPS: N51:16.217 W02:13.885

Charges 2005

| Per pitch | £ 9.00 - £ 19.00 |
| incl. electricity | £ 11.00 - £ 21.00 |

Reservations

Made with non-refundable deposit; contact site. Tel: 01373 822238. Email: woodland.park@virgin.net

Open

All year.

UK1660 Piccadilly Caravan Park

Folly Lane West, Lacock, Chippenham SN15 2LP (Wiltshire)

Piccadilly Caravan Park is set in open countryside close to several attractions in northern Wessex, notably Longleat, Bath, Salisbury Plain, Stourhead, and Lacock itself. It is a small, quiet family owned park that is kept neat and tidy. Landscaped shrubs and trees are maturing, giving the impression of three separate areas. There are 40 well spaced, clearly marked pitches, 12 of which have hardstanding. Electrical connections (10A) are available on 34 pitches. Lacock Abbey was once the home of Henry Fox-Talbot, pioneer of photography, and there is now a museum in the village. A bus service runs from Lacock village to Chippenham (entry to the Chippenham museum and Heritage centre is free of charge).

Facilities

The one toilet block is well maintained and equipped, should be adequate in size for peak periods and can be heated in cool weather. Dishwashing area. Laundry room with baby changing facilities. Ice pack service. Small, bark-based playground and a large, grass ball play area. Limited gas supplies. Papers can be ordered. Off site: Fishing 1 mile. Bicycle hire 6 miles. Riding 4 miles. Golf 3 miles.

Open

Easter/1 April - October.

At a glance

Welcome & Ambience	✓✓✓✓	Location	✓✓✓✓
Quality of Pitches	✓✓✓✓	Range of Facilities	✓✓✓

Directions

Park is signed west off A350 Chippenham - Melksham road (turning to Gastard with caravan symbol) by Lacock village. 300 yds. to park. O.S.GR: ST911683. GPS: N51:24.828 W02:07.781

Charges guide

Per unit incl. 2 persons	£ 10.00
extra person over 5 yrs	£ 1.00
electricity	£ 2.00

No credit cards.

Reservations

Any length; deposit of 1 nights fee. Tel: 01249 730260. Email: piccadillylacock@aol.com

UK1690 Longleat Caravan Club Site

Warminster BA12 7NL (Wiltshire)

What a magnificent situation in which to find a caravan park, amidst all the wonders of the Longleat Estate including the Elizabethan House, gardens designed by Capability Brown and the Safari Park. Visitors can roam the woodlands (leaflets are available on a range of walks) and enjoy the views, watch the wildlife and marvel at the azaleas, bluebells, etc. according to the season or listen to the occupants of the Safari Park. The site itself is situated in 10 acres of lightly wooded, level grassland within walking distance of the house and gardens. There are 165 generous pitches (101 with hardstanding and 64 on grass), all with 16A electricity. Water points and re-cycling bins are neatly walled with low night lighting. Two new buildings provide immaculate facilities, whilst the former toilet block now houses further services, a family room and tourist information. The wardens will help you to get the best out of your stay at Longleat. Tents are not accepted (except trailer tents).

Facilities

Two heated toilet blocks provide washbasins in cubicles, controllable showers and a vanity section with shelf, mirrors and hairdryers. Baby/toddler room, suite for disabled visitors, laundry and dishwashing room and a family room with a DVD player. Two motorcaravan service points. Play area. Office is manned 9 am - 6 pm and stocks basic food items, papers can be ordered and gas is available. Paperback exchange library. Fish and chip van calls. Late arrivals area. Off site: Longleat House and its attractions. Frome 7 miles.

Open

31 March - 30 October.

At a glance

Welcome & Ambience	✓✓✓✓✓	Location	✓✓✓✓✓
Quality of Pitches	✓✓✓✓✓	Range of Facilities	✓✓✓✓✓

Directions

The main entrance to Longleat which caravans must use is signed from the A362 Frome - Warminster road near to where it joins the A36 Warminster bypass. Turn into the estate and follow the Longleat House route through the toll booths for 2 miles then follow caravan club signs for 1 mile. There are shorter ways to leave the site. O.S.GR: ST806434 GPS: N51:11.442 W02:16.711

Charges 2005

Per adult	£ 3.80 - £ 5.00
child (5-16 yrs)	£ 1.10 - £ 1.80
pitch incl. electricity (non-member)	£ 9.50 - £ 15.00

Reservations

Advisable for B.Hs. and school holidays and made with £5 deposit. Tel: 01985 844663.

UK1680 **Plough Lane Caravan Site**

Plough Lane, Kington Langley, Chippenham SN15 5PS (Wiltshire)

Catering for adults only, this is a good example of a well designed, quality, modern touring site. The 50 pitches (all for touring units) are atrractively laid out over four acres, access roads are gravel and the borders are stocked with well established shrubs and trees. The pitches are half grass, half hardstanding and all have electricity (16A). Eight pitches are fully serviced. The site entrance has a barrier system for security. This site is an ideal base for visiting Bath, Westonbirt Arboretum, Abbey House and Gardens at Malmesbury, Castle Combe and the attractive villages of north Wiltshire and south Gloucestershire.

Facilities

The sanitary building is heated, spacious, light and airy, and has all the usual facilities including some washbasins in cubicles, with a hairdressing area for ladies. Separate en-suite room for disabled visitors with ramp access. Dishwashing sinks under cover. Fully equipped laundry with two further dishwashing sinks. Max. 2 dogs per unit, a gravel dog walking path is provided. This park is for adults only (over 18 yrs). Barrier card deposit £10. Off site: Local facilities include a supermarket, two public houses, and two garages (both with gas). Golf less than 1 mile.

Open

Mid March - mid October.

At a glance

Welcome & Ambience	✓✓✓✓	Location	✓✓✓✓
Quality of Pitches	✓✓✓✓	Range of Facilities	✓✓✓

Directions

From M4 junction 17 turn south on A350 for 2 miles, then left at traffic lights where site is signed. From Chippenham head north on A350 (towards M4), approaching traffic lights (signed for site and Kington Langley) you need the right hand lane.
O.S.GR: ST914764. GPS: N51:29.182 W02:07.542

Charges 2005

Per unit incl. 2 adults and electricity	£ 12.00
incl. services	£ 14.00
extra adult (max. 2 extra)	£ 3.00

No credit cards.

Reservations

Made with £ 12 deposit. Tel: 01249 750795.
Email: ploughlane@lineone.net

UK1700 **Devizes Camping & Caravanning Club Site**

Spout Lane, Seend, Melksham SN12 6RN (Wiltshire)

First opened in 1998, this site occupies a level field with gravel roads and centrally located facilities. It is also adjacent to the Kennet and Avon Canal (opened in 1810 and recently extensively restored) and the towpath now provides a traffic-free route passing the Caen Hill flight of 29 locks into Devizes (4 miles). In the other direction the towpath runs towards Melksham (also 4 miles). There are 50 hardstanding and 45 grass pitches, 77 with electricity (16A). The Millennium Wood on the site contains more than 1,000 trees. The site is central for visiting many places of interest including the stone circles at Stonehenge and Avebury. A more unusual outing is to Sandridge Farm, renowned for its speciality bacons, hams and sausages. The farm shop is open daily, May to Sept. and visitors can see the pigs and piglets (admission free - wellies advisable). The Vale of Pewsey cycle route can be accessed from the canal towpath to the east of Devizes, and runs for 41 miles between Great Bedwyn and Corsham.

Facilities

The modern, heated toilet block provides spacious hot showers, washbasins in cubicles, laundry, dishwashing room, and a baby room. Facilities for disabled visitors are in a suite (with alarm system) by reception. Motorcaravan services (in the late arrivals area). Small playground. Reception opens 09.00-10.00 and 16.00-17.30, and stocks basic foods and drinks, snacks and gas supplies, fishing licences and local tourist information.

Open

All year.

At a glance

Welcome & Ambience	✓✓✓✓	Location	✓✓✓✓
Quality of Pitches	✓✓✓✓	Range of Facilities	✓✓✓

Directions

From Devizes take A361 westbound, and 0.5 miles before Seend village, take A365 towards Melksham. Cross the canal bridge, take next left by 'Three Magpies' and the site entrance is on your right. Approaching from the M4 junction 17, use A350 to Melksham and A365 to the site. O.S.GR: ST950620. GPS: N51:21.390 W02:04.335

Charges 2005

Per adult	£ 5.55 - £ 6.40
child	£ 1.90
pitch fee (non-members)	£ 5.00

Reservations

Advised for B.Hs. and peak season; contact site or Central Reservations 0870 243 3331.
Tel: 01380 828839.

UK1640 Greenhill Farm Camping & Caravan Park

New Road, Landford, Salisbury SP5 2AZ (Wiltshire)

Located on the northern edge of the New Forest, this is an attractive, uncommercialised, hide-away for adults only (over 18 yrs), set around two small lakes, one of which is reserved for coarse fishing. The 100 level pitches, 35 hardstanding (the rest on grass), come complete with 16A electric hook-ups, and are attractively spread around the 14 acre site. An area for tents is in a separate hill-top meadow with views over the nearby forest and its own fishing lake. There is also a separate area set aside for pets. Several local pubs serving meals are close by and a bus stop outside the site entrance provides services to Salisbury or Southampton. Local attractions include Paultons Park, Breamore House, Downton Moot and the New Forest.

Facilities

Portacabin-type units of varying ages located around the site perimeter provide basic facilities and can be heated when necessary. Showers are free, but a token is issued with a refundable £1 deposit. No dedicated facilities for disabled persons. Laundry with washing machine and dryer. Gas supplies. Milk, eggs, gifts, maps etc. stocked. Tourist information from public telephone. Coarse fishing lakes (£3 per rod per day). Torches useful. One vehicle only per camping unit (others to remain in car park). CCTV on access road and car park areas. American motorhomes not accepted. Off site: Landford village has a bakery, post office, off licence and general stores (15 minute walk). Golf 3 miles.

At a glance

Welcome & Ambience	√√√√	Location	√√√√√
Quality of Pitches	√√√√	Range of Facilities	√√√

Directions

From M27 exit 2 take A36 north towards Salisbury for about 6 miles. Pass through West Wellow and after passing a B.P. garage on left, take next left into New Road, and continue for under 1 mile to site entrance on left. O.S.GR: SU264184. GPS: N50:57.867 W01:37.545

Charges 2005

Per unit incl. 2 persons, awning and electricity	£ 12.00
tent incl. 2 persons	£ 10.00
extra person	£ 4.00

Reservations

Required for B.Hs; contact park. Tel: 01794 324117.

Open

All year.

Greenhill Farm Camping & Touring Park Open All Year

Adult only hideaway site on the edge of the New Forest with level hard standings and hookups. Access to the Commons and New Forest and within easy reach of the cities Salisbury, Southampton and Winchester. Onsite toilets, showers, laundry, purchasable gas and fishing. Offsite facilities close by, including food shop, bar, restaurant, swimming pool, beaches and golf course. Separate area for visitors without dogs.

Landford, Nr Salisbury, Wiltshire • **Contact Mrs Jenny Osman on 01794 324117**

UK1650 Coombe Touring Park

Coombe Nurseries, Race Plain, Netherhampton, Salisbury SP2 8PN (Wiltshire)

A true touring park with outstanding views over the Chalke Valley, Coombe is adjacent to Salisbury racecourse. There are 100 spacious pitches all on level, well mown grass, 50 with electric hook-ups (10A). The tent pitches are generally around the outer perimeter. Many pitches are individual and sheltered by hedging, with picnic tables provided on many. Reception also has a small shop, there are supermarkets in Salisbury (4.5 miles), and pubs in Netherhampton and Coombe Bissett (2 miles) both serving meals.

Facilities

A well built, modern, centrally heated sanitary unit, provides an ample supply of WCs, spacious press button showers, washbasins in cubicles for the ladies, and a family room (with bath) has facilities for disabled persons, babies and toddlers. Dishwashing room. Laundry with washing machines, dryers and ironing stations. Small shop (May-Sept). Open grass play area. Gas available. Off site: Nearby attractions include Wilton House, Wilton Carpet Factory and the Wilton Shopping Village, Salisbury Cathedral, Stonehenge. Golf 400 yards. Riding and tennis in Wilton 2.5 miles. Indoor pool, leisure centre and cinema in Salisbury 4.5 miles.

Open

All year.

At a glance

Welcome & Ambience	√√√√	Location	√√√√
Quality of Pitches	√√√√	Range of Facilities	√√√

Directions

From A36 two miles west of Salisbury (just east of Wilton roundabout), turn south on A3094 towards Netherhampton and Harnham. After 0.5 miles on sharp left hand bend, turn right to Stratford Tony and Racecourse (site signed). Continue to top of hill by racecourse entrance, and turn left (signed) on narrow lane behind racecourse for 700 yards to site entrance. O.S.GR: SU098282. GPS: N51:03.340 W01:52.104

Charges 2005

Per unit incl. 2 persons	£ 11.00
extra adult	£ 3.00
child 13-17 yrs	£ 2.00
child 3-12 yrs	£ 1.00
electricity	£ 1.50
dog	£ 0.20

No credit cards.

Reservations

Advisable for B.Hs and July/August. Tel: 01722 328451.

UK1655 Church Farm Caravan & Camping Park

Sixpenny Handley, Salisbury SP5 5ND (Wiltshire)

Church Farm offers 20 spacious pitches (including two hardstandings), all with 16A electricity hook-ups, arranged around the perimeter of two fields, plus a tent field. Although the site is fairly open the farm buildings and thick hedges do give some shelter from the prevailing wind. Breakfasts are available in the main season from a recently created snack bar. Sixpenny Handley is a Saxon hilltop village and St Mary's church dates back some 900 years. From the site you can hear the bells and the chimes of its clock. The Roebuck Inn in the High Street offers a varied menu. This is a quiet corner right on the Wiltshire - Dorset border but within day trip distance of many of the area's finest attractions. There are some fine country walks available on nearby Cranborne Chase.

Facilities

A small modern building provides clean facilities and a dedicated room for disabled campers. Laundry with washing machine and dryer in a separate building. Breakfast snack bar. Rather basic motorcaravan service point (may be difficult to access for some units). Recycling centre just outside the main gate. Off site: The village has a bus stop, a number of small shops including a butchers where fresh meat, sausages and deli foods, a small supermarket and Post Office. Gas available in village. Golf 4 miles. Riding 5 miles. Fishing 10 miles.

At a glance

Welcome & Ambience	✓✓✓✓	Location	✓✓✓✓
Quality of Pitches	✓✓✓✓	Range of Facilities	✓✓✓

Directions

Sixpenny Handley is 1 mile west of the A354, about 11 miles southwest of Salisbury. Site is on the B3081 at the western end of the village by the church, on sharp bend turn into lane. O.S.GR: ST996173. GPS: N50:57.319 W02:00.413

Charges 2005

Per person	£ 4.50
child (3-14 yrs)	£ 1.50
serviced pitch	£ 2.00
awning	£ 1.00

Reservations

Essential for peak season and B.Hs. Tel: 01725 552563.

Open

All year.

UK1670 Alderbury Caravan & Camping Park

Southampton Road, Whaddon, Salisbury SP5 3HB (Wiltshire)

At the southern end of Alderbury/Whaddon village, this small, simple touring park is conveniently located for visiting Salisbury and the New Forest. Situated on level ground, there is a gravel access road to the 39 numbered pitches; 26 with electricity (16A) and 12 on hardstanding. The park has some mature trees for shade, as well as younger trees, shrubs and flowers. More recently a small playground has been added. The village shop and post office, a pub serving meals and a bus stop are within easy level walking distance of the entrance. There are hourly bus services to Salisbury, Southampton and Romsey. The country lanes around the area are good for cycling and walking. Salisbury Museum, the Cathedral and its Close are all well worth a visit. There is some road noise, most noticeable at the far end of the park.

Facilities

The central toilet block is practical, but has hard use all year round and would benefit from some refurbishment. Showers in cubicles with curtain, separate unit for disabled visitors, dishwashing sink, freezer, washing machine and microwave also in a separate room. Gas supplies. American motorhomes accepted by prior arrangement. Off site: Fishing 1 mile. Bicycle hire 3 miles. Riding 2 miles. Golf 5 miles.

Open

All year.

At a glance

Welcome & Ambience	✓✓✓	Location	✓✓✓
Quality of Pitches	✓✓✓	Range of Facilities	✓✓

Directions

From Salisbury take A36 towards Southampton and, after 3 miles (at far end of the dual-carriageway), turn left (Alderbury and Whaddon), then right, over bridge, and left for park entrance. From Southampton on A36 towards Salisbury, continue past A27 (Romsey) junction and over Pepperbox Hill. At end of a downhill straight, left on slip road marked Alderbury, park is signed. O.S.GR: SU198263. GPS: N51:02.072 W01:43.169

Charges 2005

Per unit incl. 2 adults	£ 9.50 - £ 11.50
with 16A electricity	£ 12.00 - £ 14.00
extra adult	£ 2.00 - £ 2.50
child (under 14 yrs)	£ 1.00 - £ 1.50
awning	£ 1.25 - £ 2.00
No credit cards.	

Reservations

Contact park. Tel: 01722 710125. Email: alderbury@aol.com

UK1810 Newlands Caravan Park

Charmouth DT6 6RB (Dorset)

Newlands is well situated on the Jurassic Coast, the first natural world heritage site in England. A family owned park, it is run with care and enthusiasm, occupying a prominent position beside the road into Charmouth village with rural views southwards to the hills across the valley. The terrain is terraced in two fields to provide over 200 well spaced places for touring units, some for seasonal units and over 80 for caravan holiday homes (some for hire). The mainly sloping tent field also has super views towards the sea and Lyme Regis. Electricity (10A) is provided on 160 pitches and 30 have hardstanding, water and drainage. Five special 'Millennium' pitches have a washing machine and dryer for individual use. Other accommodation includes smart pine lodges, apartments and motel rooms. All the facilities are located in a modern building to one side of the wide tarmac entrance. The club bar opens each evening and lunch times to suit. Family entertainment includes a children's club during school holidays with Dino Dan dinosaur. The indoor pool and an adjacent outdoor pool are walled, paved and sheltered. A large play area in the field below the tent field is open dawn to dusk. This is a comfortable site for families with the beach and village within easy walking distance, with some evening and family activity.

Facilities

Two modern, heated toilet blocks provide roomy showers and adjoining covered dishwashing areas and laundry rooms. Well stocked shop (March-Nov). Licensed club bar (limited hours Nov-March). Restaurant (open evenings 6-9 pm. March-Nov plus Xmas/New Year) including takeaway. Outdoor heated pool (supervised in high season; the entrance is key coded). Indoor pool and jacuzzi (small charge, open all year, limited hours Nov-March). Nine-pin bowling alley for hire at £5 per half hour. Play area. Off site: Beach 0.5 miles. Fishing 1 mile. Riding 3 miles. Golf 2 miles. Charmouth is known for its fossil finds and its connection with Jane Austen.

At a glance

Welcome & Ambience	✓✓✓✓✓	Location	✓✓✓✓
Quality of Pitches	✓✓✓✓	Range of Facilities	✓✓✓✓✓

Directions

Approaching from Bridport leave the A35 at first sign for Charmouth at start of the bypass and site almost directly on your left. O.S.GR: SY373935.

Charges 2005

Per unit incl. up to 6 persons	
and awning	£ 10.00 - £ 22.00
incl. electricity	£ 13.00 - £ 24.00
dog (max. 2)	£ 1.00 - £ 3.00
serviced pitch	£ 12.00 - £ 26.00
extra pup tent	£ 4.00

Only one van or tent per pitch.
Camping Cheques accepted.

Reservations

Made with £30 deposit per week. Tel: 01297 560259. Email: enq@newlandsholidays.co.uk

Open

All year.

UK1730 Monkton Wyld Farm Caravan Park

Monkton Wyld Farm, Charmouth DT6 6DB (Dorset)

Since Simon and Joanna Kewley opened Monkton Wylde in 1991, it has matured into an attractive, comfortable, garden-like park, with trees and flowering shrubs such as hydrangea and lavender creating a colourful, scented backdrop. A woodland walk has been created in 80 acres of the beautiful countryside surrounding the park. Mature trees around the perimeter of the park provide shade and plenty of space between the 60 pitches gives a feeling of spaciousness. All pitches have 16A electricity and around 35 have hardstanding. On site facilities are limited but an area at the top of the park has been turned into a play area, with a good space for ball games, a climbing frame, trampoline, etc. A separate site has been developed next to the existing park for the Camping and Caravanning Club (open to non-members), managed by resident wardens. Bread, milk, groceries and papers may be obtained from here in the main season (09.00-19.00 hrs). If you fancy a holiday with a difference, try staying in a 'yurt' – the site offers one of these fully equipped, Mongolian style tents for rent.

Facilities

The well built, heated toilet block is fully equipped. Family room with baby changing facilities (can also be accessed by wheelchairs). Washing machine and dryer. Dishwashing is under cover. Gas supplies. Play area. Caravan storage. Gate locked at 11 pm. Off site: Fishing or riding 2 miles, bicycle hire, golf and boat launching 3 miles. Shops and local pubs are within a mile's walking distance and Charmouth and Lyme Regis are only 3 miles (buses leave from just along the road to both towns). The X53 Jurassic Coast bus stops at the end of the lane.

Open

Easter - end October.

At a glance

Welcome & Ambience	✓✓✓✓	Location	✓✓✓✓
Quality of Pitches	✓✓✓✓	Range of Facilities	✓✓✓

Directions

Park is signed on A35 between Charmouth and Axminster, approx. 2.5 miles west of Charmouth. Turn right at Greenway Head (B3165 signed Marshwood) and park is 600 yds on the left past the Club site. Don't go to Monkton Wylde hamlet - the road is very steep. O.S.GR: SY329966.
GPS: N50:45.920 W002:57.15

Charges 2005

Per unit incl. 2 persons	£ 8.00 - £ 13.90
incl. electricity	£ 10.50 - £ 16.40
extra adult	£ 2.50
child (5-16 yrs)	£ 0.70 - £ 1.85
pup tent	free - £ 1.00
dog	free - £ 1.10

Reservations

Made with deposit of £5 per night booked.
Tel: 01297 34525.
Email: holidays@monktonwyld.co.uk

UK1760 Wood Farm Caravan Park

Axminster Road, Charmouth DT6 6BT (Dorset)

Wood Farm is an excellent, family run park, maintained to high standards and with an indoor swimming pool. Situated on the western side of Charmouth beside the A35 (some road noise may be expected) but only a mile or two from Lyme Regis and its beaches. This area is now part of England's first natural World Heritage site, the Jurassic Coast. Wood Farm is part of the Caravan Club's 'affiliated' scheme (non-members are also very welcome). On sloping, well landscaped ground, it has splendid rural views across the Marshwood Vale. There are 200 pitches for touring units of which 180 are neat, level all-weather pitches with hardstanding, electricity (10A) and TV connections, and provision for awnings. Some are divided by neat, box-like leylandii hedging, some are terraced. Water and waste water hook-ups are also available. One grassy terraced field takes about 25 tents and there are 80 caravan holiday homes in separate areas. Wood Farm makes excellent provision for disabled visitors, although there is considerable up and down walking due to the terrain. A member of the Best of British group.

Facilities

Four modern, well equipped toilet blocks can be heated and include some washbasins in cubicles, en-suite family rooms, 3 with showers and 1 with bath (charged). Excellent facilities for disabled people including low sinks for wheelchair access both for laundry and dishwashing. Baby care unit. Two laundry rooms. Covered dishwashing sinks. Motorcaravan service point. Shop by reception. Fish and chip van opens 2-4 times a week (acc. to season). Good heated indoor pool (27 x 54 ft; £2 per session, under 3s free). Recreation hall with two pool tables and family games area with table tennis, TV, 'soft play' and table football. Internet access. Bridge club. Outdoor draughts. Outdoor tennis court. Play field. Two coarse fishing ponds (carp, rudd, roach, tench, perch) adjacent - day and weekly tickets (rod licence required, also available from park). Dog wallk area Off site: Golf 1 mile. Riding 4 miles. Beaches and shops 1 and 2 miles. Use the X53 Jurassic Coast bus to explore the coast.

At a glance

Welcome & Ambience	✓✓✓✓✓	Location	✓✓✓✓✓
Quality of Pitches	✓✓✓✓✓	Range of Facilities	✓✓✓✓

Directions

Park is 0.5 miles west of Charmouth village with access near the roundabout at the A35 and A3052 (Lyme Regis) junction. O.S.GR: SY356940.

Charges 2005

Per adult	£ 3.50 - £ 5.00
child (5-16 yrs)	£ 1.50 - £ 1.75
pitch incl. 10A electricity, awning	£ 5.00 - £ 9.00
incl. water and drainage	£ 9.00 - £ 13.00
pup tent, dog, extra car	£ 1.50

Special senior citizens low season discounts.

Reservations

Made with £30 deposit (non-returnable), min. 5 nights in high season. Tel: 01297 560697.
Email: holidays@woodfarm.co.uk

Open

1 April - 31 October.

UK1780 Freshwater Beach Holiday Park

Burton Bradstock, Bridport DT6 4PT (Dorset)

Family run parks for families with direct access to a beach are rare in Britain and this one has the added advantage of being in beautiful coastal countryside in West Dorset. The site is next to the sea and a beach of fine pebbles, sheltered from the wind by pebble banks. The River Bride edges the park and joins the sea here. Approached by a fairly steep access road, the park itself is on level, open ground. The 500 plus touring pitches, 400 with 10A electricity, are on an open, undulating grass field connected by tarmac or hard-core roads. Caravan pitches (10 x 11 m.) are marked and evenly spaced in lines. Some tent pitches are in the main field, with others well spaced on a newly terraced extra field. In separate areas there are 270 caravan holiday homes, with 40 for hire. This lively holiday park has an extensive range of facilities which include an outdoor pool, a good value licensed restaurant and three bars with an evening entertainment programme in season. Daytime entertainment caters for all ages - don't miss the donkey derby! Footpaths lead to the thatched village of Burton Bradstock or West Bay. The overall impression is of a large, busy holiday park with a friendly reception and happy atmosphere.

Facilities

Toilet facilities are in two refurbished blocks, plus another with washbasins and toilets only. A third luxurious block was added in the tent field for 2004. In all, it is a good provision for a busy beach park. The main blocks have facilities for disabled people (Radar key), and a baby care room (key system). Laundry and dishwashing sinks cope well at peak times. Launderette. Bars with entertainment. Licensed restaurant (weekends only in late season; closed Mondays all season). Good value supermarket and takeaway. Heated and supervised outdoor swimming and paddling pools (15/5-30/10) with lessons available. New indoor games room with pool table, music, TV and soft drinks bar. Adventure play area. Pony trekking (stables on site). Off site: Golf course adjacent. Fishing possible from Chesil Bank. Abbotsbury Sub-Tropical Gardens and Swannery 17 miles.

At a glance

Welcome & Ambience	✓✓✓✓✓	Location	✓✓✓✓✓
Quality of Pitches	✓✓✓✓	Range of Facilities	✓✓✓✓✓

Directions

Park is immediately west of the village of Burton Bradstock, on the Weymouth - Bridport coast road (B3157). O.S.GR: SY980898.

Charges 2005

Per unit incl. up to 6 persons, car and awning	£ 8.00 - £ 28.00
extra person, car or boat	£ 2.00
electricity	£ 2.00
small tent incl. 2 persons walking or cycling	£ 4.00 - £ 15.00
dog	£ 2.50

Single sex groups not admitted.

Reservations

Made for min. 1 week with £20 deposit p/week, plus £1 fee. Short break reservations available - ring for details. Tel: 01308 897317.
Email: enquiries@freshwaterbeach.co.uk

Open

17 March - 12 November.

UK1740 Golden Cap Holiday Park

West Dorset Leisure Holidays, Eype, Bridport DT6 6AR (Dorset)

Golden Cap, named after the adjacent high cliff (the highest in southern England) which overlooks Lyme Bay, is only 150 metres from a shingle beach at Seatown and is surrounded by National Trust countryside and the Heritage Coastline. The park is arranged over several fields on the valley floor, sloping gently down towards the sea. It is in two main areas, having once been two parks, each separated into fields with marvellous views around and providing 108 touring pitches. All have electricity and 29 also have hardstanding with drainaway and gravel awning area. An extra sloping tent area is used for peak season (torch useful), although it is a five minute walk from here to the toilet blocks and shop. There are 219 caravan holiday homes in their own areas. A coarse fishing lake has recently been opened and the heated indoor pool at Highlands End (under the same ownership, 3 miles away) is open for campers at Golden Cap on payment. Beaches are nearby, sea fishing, boat launching, riding or fossil hunting are possible in the area, plus good walks including access to the coastal path. A well run park and a member of the Best of British group.

Facilities

The modern toilet block is of good quality with spacious shower cubicles (some with toilet and washbasin). Baby room. Two other smaller blocks around the park. Laundry room. Motorcaravan service point. Useful and well stocked shop (8 am - 6 pm, or 9 pm in high season). Gas supplies. Small play area. Fishing lake (day tickets from shop). American motorhomes are not accepted. Off site: Pub with food service close. Golf 2 miles. Beach 150 yds.

Open

17 March - 5 November.

At a glance

Welcome & Ambience	✓✓✓✓	Location	✓✓✓✓
Quality of Pitches	✓✓✓✓	Range of Facilities	✓✓✓✓

Directions

Turn off A35 road at Chideock (a bigger village with shops and restaurants) 3 miles west of Bridport, at sign to Seatown opposite church. Park is less than 1 mile down narrow lane. O.S.GR: SY423919.

Charges 2005

Per unit incl. 2 persons awning	
and electricity	£ 10.75 - £ 16.50
extra adult	£ 3.25 - £ 3.50
child (4-17 yrs)	£ 1.75 - £ 2.25
all service pitch	£ 13.25 - £ 20.00

Reservations

Essential in high season and made with £20 deposit (min. 3 days in high season). Contact: West Dorset Leisure Holidays, Eype, Bridport, Dorset DT6 6AR. Tel: 01308 422139. Email: holidays@wdlh.co.uk

UK1770 Binghams Farm Touring Park

Melplash, Bridport DT6 3TT (Dorset)

Binghams is a small park, for adults only. In a pleasant, rural situation two miles from the market town of Bridport, with views seaward towards West Bay and inland across Beaminster Downs and Pilsdon Hill. The park provides an area of individual pitches with 10A electricity and over 40 hardstandings, nicely landscaped with shrubs and trees growing between the pitches, plus an open sloping field overlooking the valley with 20 electrical hook ups. A path is provided to the river which links with the main footpaths for Bridport. The Brit Valley is an unspoilt area of West Dorset and coastal West Bay is only three miles.

Facilities

The toilet block, with under floor heating provides well fitted showers, a separate, fully equipped room for disabled people and a laundry room. Five luxury shower rooms with washbasins (four with a toilet as well). Restaurant serving home cooked food (open according to season). Gas available. Off site: Bus service from entrance. Sea fishing and golf 3 miles.

At a glance

Welcome & Ambience	✓✓✓✓	Location	✓✓✓✓
Quality of Pitches	✓✓✓✓	Range of Facilities	✓✓✓✓

Directions

From A35 roundabout on east side of Bridport, follow signs for Beaminster on A3066. After 2 miles watch for site entrance on the left. O.S.GR: SY482963.

Charges 2005

Per unit incl. 2 adults, electricity	£ 11.80 - £ 16.80

Reservations

Made with deposit. Tel: 01308 488234. Email: enquiries@binghamsfarm.co.uk

Open

March - October, Xmas and New Year.

UK2030 Wareham Forest Tourist Park

North Trigon, Wareham BH20 7NZ (Dorset)

Under the enthusiastic ownership of Tony and Sarah Birch, this peacefully located, spacious park on the edge of Wareham Forest continues to improve. Reception and the shop have been relocated to beside the pool, making this area the central focus of the park. There is a choice of formal pitching, with or without hardstanding, for caravans or natural pitches for tents in pine wood or open field. There is space for 200 units on large pitches with electrical connections (16A), including 102 with hardstanding and 8 luxury pitches on hardstanding with water, drainage, TV aerial, dustbin and light (available 1/3-31/10 only). It is possible to walk in the forest or use the seven miles of the Sika cycle trail. The lovely market town of Wareham is accessible by bike without having to use the roads. This park has an almost continental feel, with plenty of space. Even when it is busy, it is calm and peaceful in its forest setting. In low season you may be lucky enough to spot the herd of Sika deer which live in the forest. The park is well situated to explore the Dorset coast and Thomas Hardy country.

Facilities

Two well maintained toilet blocks are of a good standard with some washbasins in cubicles for ladies. The block used in the winter months is centrally heated. Facilities for disabled people. Well equipped laundry rooms and deep sinks for washing up. Motorcaravan service point. Small licensed shop with gas. Open-air swimming pool (60 x 20 ft), heated Spring B.H. to early Sept. Large adventure play area. Entrance closed 11 pm. - 7 am. Resident wardens on site. Caravan storage. Off site: Fishing 5 miles. Bicycle hire and golf 3 miles. Riding 8 miles. Cycle trail and walking in the forest.

Open

All year.

At a glance

Welcome & Ambience	✓✓✓✓✓	Location	✓✓✓✓✓
Quality of Pitches	✓✓✓✓	Range of Facilities	✓✓✓✓

Directions

Park is north of Wareham between Wareham and Bere Regis, located off the A35 road.
O.S.GR: SY899903. GPS: N50:43.304 W02:09.373

Charges 2005

Per adult	£ 2.00 - £ 3.50
child 5-15 yrs	£ 1.50 - £ 2.50
standard pitch	£ 5.50 - £ 9.00
serviced pitch	£ 8.00 - £ 11.00
'superior' pitch	£ 10.00 - £ 12.00
dog, extra tent, awning, boat	£ 0.60 - £ 1.50

Couples and families only.

Reservations

Made with £40 non-returnable deposit and £2 admin. fee, balance 28 days before arrival.
Tel: 01929 551393.
Email: holiday@wareham-forest.co.uk

For further details and free colour brochure write or phone:
Tel: (01929) 551393 Fax: (01929) 558321
Tony and Sarah Birch, Wareham Forest Tourist Park, North Trigon, Wareham, Dorset BH20 7NZ
email: holiday@wareham-forest.co.uk
www.wareham-forest.co.uk
Credit cards accepted.

UK2100 Sandford Caravan Park

Holton Heath, Poole BH16 6JZ (Dorset)

Sandford Park is an 'all singing, all dancing' park with a wide range of facilities near the popular coastal areas of Dorset. It has a large permanent section with 248 static holiday homes and lodges. However, the touring section in an attractive secluded area and can accommodate around 500 units of any type, mainly on distinctive individual pitches, on level grass with mature evergreen hedging, or in a more open style area broken up by shrubs all with 10A electrical connections. Early booking is advisable. Sandford is a large, very busy holiday park with a wide range of entertainment. The clubhouse (free membership) is spacious with dance floor, bar and seating area, and caters for different tastes and age groups. There is also a large air-conditioned ballroom for entertainment and dancing. Both are open over a long season. There is a variety of bars, restaurants (book in busy periods) and simple hot meals, breakfasts and takeaway elsewhere in peak season. The heated outdoor swimming pool (25 m. long, open May-Oct. and supervised) and a very large play pool with a sandy beach, ideal for children, are attractively situated with a snack bar, terraced area and go-kart track. There is also an impressive, heated and supervised indoor pool.

Facilities

The main toilet block in the touring area also provides facilities for disabled visitors and a baby room. A new block was added for 2004. Large launderette. Ladies' hairdresser. Bars, restaurants. TV lounges. Outdoor swimming pool (May-Sept) and indoor pool. Large supermarket and other shops, including well stocked camping accessory shop (all peak season only). Soft indoor play area (April - Oct and Christmas, supervised). Playground. Two tennis courts. New multi-sports court. Table tennis. Two short mat bowling greens (outdoor). Crazy golf. Mountain bike hire. Riding lessons available at stables on site. Dogs or pets are only permitted in the touring section in low or mid season (phone site to advise). Off site: Beach 9 miles. Golf 3 miles.

At a glance

Welcome & Ambience	✓✓✓✓	Location	✓✓✓✓
Quality of Pitches	✓✓✓✓	Range of Facilities	✓✓✓✓✓

Directions

Park is just west off A351 (Wareham - Poole) road at Holton Heath. O.S.GR: SY940913.
GPS: N50:43.204 W02:05.132

Charges 2005

Per pitch	£ 12.50 - £ 25.00
incl. electricity	£ 15.50 - £ 28.50
serviced pitch	£ 17.00 - £ 30.00
dog (1 only, after 2 Sept)	£ 5.00

Reservations

Early booking advisable (min. 3 days). Tel: 0870 0667793. Email: touring@weststarholidays.co.uk

Open

February - January.

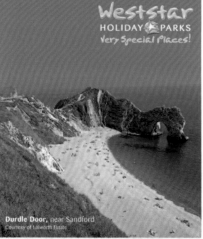

UK2180 Beacon Hill Touring Park

Blandford Road North, Poole BH16 6AB (Dorset)

Beacon Hill is located in a marvellous, natural environment of partly wooded heathland, with certain areas of designated habitation for protected species such as sand lizards and the Dartford Warbler, but there is also easy access to main routes. Wildlife ponds encourage dragonflies and other species but fishing is also possible. Conservation is obviously important in such a special area but one can ramble at will over the 30 acres, with the hilltop walk a must. Grassy open spaces provide 170 touring pitches for all units, 120 with 16A electricity, on sandy grass which is sometimes uneven. The undulating nature of land and the trees allows for discrete areas to be allocated for varying needs, e.g. for young families near to the play area, families with teenagers close to the bar/games room, those with dogs near the dog walking area, and for young people further away. The park provides a wide range of facilities including an open air swimming pool and a tennis court, with something for everyone and is well situated for beaches, Poole harbour and ferries for France or the Channel Isles.

Facilities

Two fully equipped toilet blocks include facilities for disabled people. Laundry facilities and washing up sinks. Well stocked shop at reception. Coffee bar and takeaway (main season). Bar (on demand outside the main season). Heated swimming pool. All weather tennis court (charges). Adventure play areas including a hideaway. Games room with pool tables and amusement machines. Fishing (charges). Off site: Brownsea Island, Studland beach with Sandbanks ferry and the Purbecks near. Poole harbour and ferries 3 miles.

Open

Easter/16 April - end September.

At a glance

Welcome & Ambience	✓✓✓	Location	✓✓✓✓
Quality of Pitches	✓✓✓	Range of Facilities	✓✓✓✓

Directions

Park is approx. 3 miles north of Poole, 400 yards north of the junction of the A35 and A350 towards Blandford. O.S.GR: SY977945.

Charges 2005

Per adult	£ 3.50 - £ 6.00
child (under 16 yrs)	£ 2.50
pitch	£ 3.00 - £ 18.00
awning	£ 1.00 - £ 2.50
electricity	£ 2.00
dog	£ 1.50

Reservations

Made with £20 non-refundable deposit per pitch; balance 21 days before arrival. Tel: 01202 631631. Email: bookings@beaconhilltouringpark.co.uk

UK2080 Merley Court Touring Park

Merley, Wimborne BH21 3AA (Dorset)

Merley Court is a credit to the Wright family. All aspects of this well planned, attractively landscaped park are constantly maintained to the highest of standards. The historic walled garden dating back to the 18th century provides ideal surroundings for a pleasant stroll or a family picnic with the opportunity to play croquet, crazy golf, boule, volleyball, short tennis or basketball. Tarmac roads connect 160 touring pitches (all with 16A electricity) on neat lawns or one of the many hardstandings. This provision includes 18 neat all-service pitches with water, waste disposal and satellite TV. The entire park is interspersed with a variety of shrubs, plants and the odd ornamental urn. Some attractive tent pitches are to be found in a small wooded valley. A well-furnished club complex provides a lounge bar where meals are available, snack bar, takeaway, large games room with pool tables and a family room leading onto a spacious sheltered patio. This in turn leads to the paved walled swimming pool area. There are woodland walks (including dog walks) directly from the site connecting to the disused railway line where nature has returned with an abundance of wild flowers, which in turn leads to Delph woods with designated nature trails. A member of the Best of British group.

Facilities

Three heated toilet blocks, two with showers, are of good quality. Separate facilities for disabled visitors and babies. Dishwashing and laundry facilities. Motorcaravan service point. Shop with caravan accessories and gas. Café and takeaway. Bar with food (limited hours in low and mid season). Outdoor pool (30 x 20 ft) with children's section open mid May - Sept. Tennis court. Table tennis. Play areas. Games room with pool tables. Tourist information. Conference/meeting venue in the Leisure Garden Orangery. Dogs are not accepted in high season (14/7-31/8). Barrier card £5 deposit. Off site: Fishing, riding and golf all within 5 miles. Poole 5 miles, Bournemouth 8 miles. Tower Park leisure and entertainment centre is nearby, Kingston Lacy House, Knoll Gardens, Brownsea Island and the Moors Valley Country Park are also near.

At a glance

Welcome & Ambience	✓✓✓✓✓	Location	✓✓✓✓✓
Quality of Pitches	✓✓✓✓✓	Range of Facilities	✓✓✓✓✓

Directions

Site clearly signed at the junction of A31 and A349 roads (roundabout) on the Wimborne bypass. O.S.GR: ST008984. GPS: N50:47.144 W01:59.115

Charges 2005

Per standard pitch incl. 2 persons and electricity	£ 11.00 - £ 16.00
all service pitch	£ 14.50 - £ 19.50
extra adult	£ 3.50
child (3-13 yrs)	£ 2.50
dog (outside 16/7 - 2/9)	£ 1.00

No extra pup tent as well as awning.

Reservations

Made with deposit (£40 p/w). Tel: 01202 881488. Email: holidays@merley-court.co.uk

Open

All year excl. 8 January - 28 February.

UK2110 **Pear Tree Touring Park**

Organford Road, Holton Heath, Poole BH16 6LA (Dorset)

Pear Tree is a neat, well cared for park welcoming families with young children and couples only. The new management has done much work to improve the landscaping of the park. Set in 7.5 acres, with mature trees and views across to Wareham Forest, there are 120 grass pitches with 10A electricity, 50 with full services (water, waste water and electricity) of which 26 have hardstanding. Only breathable groundsheets are permitted for awnings. The tent area is a tranquil secluded spot with many mature trees. Reception, tourist information and a small shop supplying milk, bread, gas and other basics is at the park entrance where the gates (with key) are closed at dusk, although latecomers are admitted. A large, hedged, separate play field is at the top of the park with swings, climbing frame, trampolines and ball games area, all for younger children. A bus service stops outside for Wareham (2.5 miles) or Poole (5 miles).

Facilities

The main heated toilet block (opened by key) has been refurbished and provides some washbasins in cubicles. Baby changing unit and two WCs for disabled visitors. Separate small block near the tent area. All is kept spotlessly clean. Motorcaravan service point. Shop (basics only). Play area. All year caravan storage. Off site: The Clay Pipe Inn 500 m. Bicycle hire 0.5 miles. Golf 2.5 miles. Riding 5 miles.

Open

Easter - early October.

At a glance

Welcome & Ambience ✓✓✓✓✓ Location ✓✓✓✓
Quality of Pitches ✓✓✓✓✓ Range of Facilities ✓✓✓✓

Directions

Park is just west off A351 (Wareham - Poole) road at Holton Heath. O.S.GR: SY940915. GPS: N50:43.442 W02:05.218

Charges 2006

Per unit incl. 2 persons, electricity and awning	£ 10.50 - £ 18.00
incl. services	£ 12.50 - £ 19.00
extra adult	£ 3.00 - £ 4.00

Security key deposit £10-£20 (refundable).

Reservations

Made with £40 deposit (min. 5 nights in high season). Tel: 01202 622434. Email: info@visitpeartree.co.uk

Pear Tree TOURING PARK
- Small family touring park
- Close to beaches and Poole
- Peaceful (no bar or entertainment)
- Quiet after 10.30 in the evening
- Excellent facilities, include modern toilets & showers
- Large play area for young children
- Well controlled dogs are welcome
- On local bus routes
- Low season discounts

☎ **01202 622 434**
✉ info@visitpeartree.co.uk www.visitpeartree.co.uk
AA DE LUXE PARK

UK2000 Swanage Coastal Holiday Park

Priestway, Swanage BH19 2RS (Dorset)

With wonderful views over the Swanage bay and the Purbeck hills, this park (formerly Priestway) is now part of Shorefield Holidays who already own parks in the New Forest. It is a popular park offering a quiet holiday but with easy access downhill to the town of Swanage with its lovely sandy beach. The only provision on site is a children's play area but it is possible to use the facilities at the holiday park next door which include an indoor pool, gym, bar and restaurant. Over 100 holiday caravans are terraced up the hillside (with over 50 available to rent). The rest of the site consists of bays, nooks and crannies on various levels, randomly split by naturally growing trees and shrubs providing shelter or views. The largest bay has six hardstandings with electricity (10A) with a further four grass pitches for touring units. The other 52 grass pitches are unnumbered. A further field at the top of the site is opened in high season on a 28 day license. Swanage is the start of the Jurassic Coast World Heritage Site and there is direct access to the coastal paths and to Durlston Country Park and Castle which is being developed as a 'Jurassic Centre'.

Facilities

Two older type toilet blocks are clean but basic. Laundry facilities. Dishwashing sinks. Play area. Membership of the Health and Fitness Club at the next door park allows use of the indoor pool, gym, sauna, solarium, bar and restaurant open all year. It also has a shop (open BHs and high season). Off site: Beach and town 1 mile. Golf 3 miles. Bicycle hire, fishing and boat launching 1 mile. 'Hop on Hop off' bus allows you to explore the whole of the Jurassic Coast.

Open

March - October.

At a glance

Welcome & Ambience	✓✓✓✓	Location	✓✓✓✓
Quality of Pitches	✓✓✓	Range of Facilities	✓✓✓

Directions

From A351 Wareham - Swanage road turn right just after 'Welcome to Swanage' sign into High Street then immediately right again into Bell Street. At the top turn left into Priests Road then first right up hill towards Priestway. O.S.GR: SZ018783.
GPS: N50:36.363 W01:58.499

Charges 2005

Per hardstanding pitch incl. electricity	£ 15.00 - £ 19.50
tent pitch	£ 12.50 - £ 15.00
dog	£ 1.50

Reservations

Necessary for B.Hs and made with deposit (£7 per night). Tel: 0800 214080.
Email: enquiries@shorefield.co.uk

see advert on pg 113

UK2130 Grove Farm Meadow Holiday Park

Meadowbank Holidays, Stour Way, Christchurch BH23 2PQ (Dorset)

Grove Farm Meadow is a quiet, traditional park with caravan holiday homes and a small provision for touring caravans. The grass flood bank which separates the River Stour from this park provides an attractive pathway. The river bank has been kept natural and is well populated by a range of ducks and a resident swan family and early in the season they parade their young through the park. It is also popular with bird watchers. There are just under 200 caravan holiday homes (117 privately owned, 75 for hire), regularly sited in rows. For touring units 41 level grass pitches, all with 15A electricity, are clearly numbered, backing on to fencing or hedging and accessed by tarmac roads. Some are fully serviced (with hardstanding, shingle base for awnings and chemical disposal point), the other grass pitches sharing service points. The impressive modern reception has a good collection of tourist information. The Littledown Centre, said to be the south coast's premier leisure facility is nearby. Bournemouth is 10 minutes by car, Christchurch 5.

Facilities

The well kept toilet block provides a bathroom for each sex (50p). Separate toilet and washbasin with ramped access for disabled visitors. Baby room. Dishwashing sinks, together with spin dryer, iron and board and washing lines provided. Launderette near reception. Well stocked shop (limited hours in low season). Games room with pool table and video games. Adventure play area beside the river bank. Fishing (permits from reception). No dogs or other pets are accepted. Off site: Boat launching 4 miles. Golf nearby. St Catherine's nature reserve.

Open

1 March - 31 October.

At a glance

Welcome & Ambience	✓✓✓✓	Location	✓✓✓✓
Quality of Pitches	✓✓✓✓✓	Range of Facilities	✓✓✓

Directions

From A388 Ringwood - Bournemouth road take B3073 for Christchurch. Turn right at the first roundabout and Stour Way is the third road on the right. O.S.GR: SZ136946.

Charges 2005

Per 'luxury' pitch incl. 2 persons and electricity	£ 13.00 - £ 25.00
large pitch	£ 10.50 - £ 21.00
standard pitch (no awnings)	£ 7.00 - £ 16.00
extra person over 5 yrs	£ 1.00 - £ 2.00
extra car or boat	£ 1.00 - £ 2.00

Reservations

Made for Sat-Sat or Sun-Sun in high season, min. 3 nights at other times, with £30 deposit. Contact Meadowbank Holidays at above address. Tel: 01202 483597.
Email: enquiries@meadowbank-holidays.co.uk

UK2150 Woolsbridge Manor Farm Caravan Park

Three Legged Cross, Wimborne BH21 6RA (Dorset)

Adjacent to the Moors Valley Country Park, this family run site is conveniently close to the holiday resort and beaches of Bournemouth and Poole, and the ancient market town of Wimborne Minster. The 7-acre camping meadow has 60 large level pitches, 45 with 10A electricity hook-ups, arranged on either side of a central tarmac road with a modern, centrally located toilet block. A nice touch here are the bicycle racks outside. Reception has a well stocked shop and a good selection of tourist information, again there are cycle racks outside. The site is part of a working beef cattle farm, so parents should be aware of moving farm machinery and tractors. A cycleway/footpath crosses the fields to the Country Park – very safe for children – where amenities include coarse fishing, golf, steam railway, bicycle hire, a tea room and a country shop.

Facilities

The neat, white, modern toilet block is well maintained and has ample facilities. Two newly built family rooms each with shower, WC, basin, handrails and ramped access provide for disabled people, babies and toddlers. Washing machine, dryer and ironing facilities. Covered dishwashing sinks. Shop. Gas available. Playground. Fishing. Recycling of aluminium cans. American RVs accepted, advance booking appreciated. Torches useful. Caravan storage. Off site: Old Barn Farm inn and restaurant 400 yds. Riding, golf and bicycle hire 0.5 miles.

Open

Easter - 31 October.

At a glance

Welcome & Ambience	✓✓✓✓	Location	✓✓✓✓
Quality of Pitches	✓✓✓✓	Range of Facilities	✓✓✓

Directions

From Ringwood take A31 southwest towards the large Ashley Heath roundabout, avoid underpass and take left hand slip road up to roundabout, and turn right on unclassified road signed Three Legged Cross, Ashley Heath, Horton and Moors Valley Country Park. Follow signs to Country Park (2 miles), pass the park entrance on right, continue for another 400 yards to campsite entrance (well signed on right). O.S.GR: SZ 099052.

Charges guide

Per unit incl. 2 persons, electricity	£ 10.00 - £ 15.00
extra adult	£ 3.00 - £ 3.50
child (under 16 yrs)	£ 2.00 - £ 2.50
awning or extra car	£ 1.25
dog	£ 1.00 - £ 1.25

Reservations

Advised for B.Hs and July/Aug. Made with deposit of 50% of total fees. Tel: 01202 826369. Email: woolsbridge@btconnect.com

UK2060 Wilksworth Farm Caravan Park

Cranborne Road, Wimborne BH21 4HW (Dorset)

First opened 34 years ago by the parents of the present owners, the careful and sympathetic development of Wilksworth continues with the aim of providing all the 'mod cons' yet remain in keeping with the environment. It is a spacious, quiet park, well suited for families with a heated outdoor pool. The rural situation is lovely, just outside Wimborne and around 10 miles from the beaches between Poole and Bournemouth. With a duck pond at the entrance, the park has been well planned on good quality ground with fairly level grass and some views. It takes 65 caravans and 25 tents mainly on grass. All pitches have electrical connections, 10 also have water and drainage. There are some 77 privately owned caravan holiday homes in a separate area. Facilities are in attractively converted farm buildings designed to be in keeping with the listed status of the other buildings. The heated swimming pool and a tennis court are on the far side of the touring area.

Facilities

The central, well equipped toilet block has under-floor heating, washbasins in cubicles, a family bathroom and a shower/bath for children with baby changing. Facilities for disabled visitors. Covered dishwashing sinks. Laundry room. Modern reception and shop (basics only, limited hours, Easter - 30 Sept). Gas supplies. Freezer for ice packs. Attractive coffee shop serving simple meals with full menu and takeaway service (weekends and B.Hs. only outside the main season). Heated 40 x 20 ft. swimming pool (unsupervised, but fenced and gated, open May-Sept) with small paddling pool. Football ground. Volleyball. Adventure play area. BMX track. Golf practice net. Two tennis courts, one full and one short size. Games room with table tennis, pool, some games machines. Security barrier. Winter caravan storage. Off site: Golf, fishing and riding 3 miles. Kingston Lacy (NT) 3 miles and Wimborne town centre (with its Minster) 1 mile. Beach 12 miles.

At a glance

Welcome & Ambience	✓✓✓✓	Location	✓✓✓✓	
Quality of Pitches	✓✓✓✓	Range of Facilities	✓✓✓✓	

Directions

Park is 1 mile north of Wimborne, west off the B3078 road to Cranborne. O.S.GR: SU010019. GPS: N50:49.002 W01:59.424

Charges 2006

Per unit incl. 2 persons, electricity	£ 10.00 - £ 20.00
extra adult	£ 3.00
child (3-16 yrs)	£ 1.50
full services	£ 2.00
dog	£ 1.00

No credit cards.

Reservations

Advised for July/Aug. and B.Hs. Made with £20 per week deposit; balance more than 28 days beforehand (min. 5 days at B.Hs, 7 days in summer holidays). Tel: 01202 885467.
Email: rayandwendy@wilksworthfarmcaravanpark.co.uk

Open

Easter/1 April - 30 October.

UK2020 Ulwell Cottage Caravan Park

Ulwell, Swanage BH19 3DG (Dorset)

Nestling under the Purbeck Hills in this unique corner of Dorset on the edge of Swanage, Ulwell Cottage is a family run holiday park with an indoor pool and wide range of facilities. A good proportion of the park is taken by caravan holiday homes (140), but an attractive, undulating area accessed by tarmac roads is given over to 77 numbered touring pitches. There are 68 electricity hook-ups (16A) and 18 hard-standings, 8 of which are serviced. The mixture of level and sloping pitches, interspersed with trees and shrubs, is quite pretty. The colourful entrance area is home to the Village Inn with a courtyard adjoining the heated, supervised indoor pool complex (both open all year and open to the public) and modern reception. The hill above the touring area, Nine Barrow Down, is a Site of Special Scientific Interest for butterflies overlooking Round Down. It is possible to walk to Corfe Castle this way. With Brownsea Island, Studland Bay, Corfe village and the Swanage Railway, Ulwell Cottage makes a marvellous centre for holidays.

Facilities

The modern, cheerful toilet block can be heated and includes a unit for disabled visitors. Supplemented by an older block in the holiday home section. Both are well equipped. Laundry room and baby sinks in the lower block. Dishwashing under cover. Well stocked shop with gas (Easter - mid Sept). Bar snacks and restaurant meals with family room. Indoor pool with lifeguard (times vary acc. to season). Playing fields and play areas. Off site: Bicycle hire or riding 2 miles. Fishing and golf 1 mile. Beach 1 mile.

Open

1 March - 7 January.

At a glance

Welcome & Ambience	✓✓✓✓	Location	✓✓✓✓✓	
Quality of Pitches	✓✓✓✓	Range of Facilities	✓✓✓✓✓	

Directions

From A351 Wareham - Swanage road, turn on B3351 Studland road just before Corfe Castle, follow signs to right for Swanage and drop down to Ulwell. O.S.GR: SZ019809.

Charges 2005

Per unit incl. up to 6 persons	£ 14.25 - £ 30.00
full services with hardstanding	£ 15.00 - £ 32.00
extra tent, car or boat	£ 2.00

Less £2 for two persons only, less £1 for three persons.

Reservations

Made with 25% deposit (min. £20); balance 2 weeks prior to holiday. Tel: 01929 422823.
Email: enq@ulwellcottagepark.co.uk

UK2340 Shamba Holidays

Ringwood Road, St Leonards, Ringwood BH24 2SB (Hampshire)

Although Shamba has new owners, the family run business has connections with the previous owners of the park and family members continue to run Shamba alongside a new team. There has been much redevelopment, but the aim remains to create a relaxed, pleasant atmosphere. The site has 150 pitches with 128 used for touring, the remainder let on a seasonal basis. Surrounded by trees, the camping area is on flat, open grass with 10A electricity available to all. A brand new clubhouse built in Scandinavian style at the entrance provides reception, a bar, takeaway, shop and amusements room. The second phase of the redevelopment will see new toilet facilities and an indoor pool. Bournemouth with its beaches is 8 miles, while the delights of the New Forest are within easy reach. The proximity of the A31 could mean some road noise. The access road is rather rough, but persevere and you will find a pleasant park.

Facilities

The old facilities are being totally replaced and will include showers, washbasins and toilets, facilities for families and disabled visitors, a launderette and dishwashing. It will also incorporate a new 40 ft. indoor swimming pool and toddlers' pool. Shop. New bar with snacks and takeaway. Amusements room. Large play area. Off site: Riding stables and fishing lake 500 yds. Ringwood 2.5 miles. Moors Valley Country Park 1 mile. Beach 8 miles.

Open

1 March - 31 October.

At a glance

| Welcome & Ambience | ✓✓✓✓ | Location | ✓✓✓✓ |
| Quality of Pitches | ✓✓✓✓ | Range of Facilities | ✓✓✓✓ |

Directions

Site is signed directly off the A31 Ringwood - Wimborne Road, 400 yds. down a small lane. Approaching from the east, after passing Little Chef, you will need to go round the next roundabout back on yourself, then immediately left down lane. O.S.GR: SU104026. GPS: N50:49.504 W01:51.187

Charges 2005

Per unit incl. 2 persons, electricity	£ 13.00 - £ 17.00
extra person	£ 3.00
child (6-11 yrs)	£ 2.00
Camping Cheques accepted.	

Reservations

Made with non-returnable deposit of £25. Tel: 01202 873302. Email: enquiries@shambaholidays.co.uk

UK2270 Oakdene Forest Park

St Leonards, Ringwood BH24 2RZ (Hampshire)

Set in 55 acres of park and woodland, with direct access to the Avon Forest and near the New Forest, Oakdene provides 420 caravan holiday homes to let and 150 pitches for all types of touring unit. These include 'premier' pitches with hardstanding, 10A electricity, water, drainage and pitch light (no tents on these pitches). The Leisure and Country Club provides a bar, restaurant and a range of entertainment. Super additions are an indoor pool with flume, sauna, spa bath and gym, plus an outdoor pool. Oakdene is owned by Shorefield Country Park at Milford on Sea and recent investment here includes a new reception, coffee shop, restaurant, ballroom, supermaket and bars. The aim is for the quality, standard and range of facilities and entertainment found at Shorefield and Lytton Lawn (UK2280).

Facilities

The new fully equipped, purpose built toilet block includes some washbasins in cabins, but 'portacabin' style facilities remain for the Meadow area. Launderette and dishwashing sinks. Shop. Restaurant and bars. Takeaway. Indoor pool (all year). Outdoor pools (May - Sept). Gym. Table tennis and pool table. Crazy golf. Compact bowling. Amusement arcade. Play area. Free Squirrel's Kids Club. Bicycle hire. ATM. Off site: Forest Pines Riding Centre (10% reduction). Forest walks. Golf 3 miles. Fishing 5 miles. Beach 9 miles.

At a glance

| Welcome & Ambience | ✓✓✓✓ | Location | ✓✓✓✓ |
| Quality of Pitches | ✓✓✓ | Range of Facilities | ✓✓✓✓✓ |

Directions

Park access leads off the main A31 westbound carriageway about 2.5 miles west of Ringwood. O.S.GR: SU101016. GPS: N50:48.774 W01:51.568

Charges 2005

Per pitch incl. all persons	£ 7.50 - £ 23.00
Min. stays at B.Hs.	

Reservations

Contact Shorefield Country Parks, Shorefield Road, Milford on Sea, nr Lymington, Hampshire SO41 0LH. Tel: 01590 648331. Email: holidays@shorefield.co.uk

Open

All year excl. January.   *see advert on pg 113*

Red Shoot Camping Park

Set in the heart of the New Forest and close to Bournemouth and Ringwood, this is a first class family-run park. Excellent facilities, cycle hire service, children's play area and adjacent to Red Shoot Inn. See our website for full details and saving discounts.

www.redshoot-campingpark.co.uk 01425 473789

UK2350 Red Shoot Camping Park

Linwood, Ringwood BH24 3QT (Hampshire)

Red Shoot is set on three acres of open, slightly sloping, level grass, in the heart of the New Forest. A simple, rural retreat with panoramic views of the surrounding countryside and forest, it is very popular in high season. There are around 130 good sized pitches, 45 with electrical hook-ups (10A), served by a circular gravel road. There is no site lighting so a torch would be useful. The adjacent Red Shoot Inn (under separate ownership) serves hot or cold meals and brews its own real ales - Forest Gold and Tom's Tipple. There are ample opportunities for walking, cycling and naturalist pursuits in the area, and nearby Ringwood has a market on Wednesday. Local attractions include watersports at the New Forest Water Park near Ringwood, a Doll Museum in Fordingbridge, cider making in Burley, and Breamore House just north of Fordingbridge.

Facilities

The sanitary facilities are fairly modern, well maintained and practical, but not luxurious (refurbishment is planned). Dishwashing sinks under cover. Laundry plus baby bath facility. Good unit for disabled visitors. Very well stocked, licensed shop. Fenced adventure style playground. Mountain bike hire. Off site: Fishing 5 miles. Riding 6 miles. Golf 7 miles. Beach 12 miles.

Open

1 March - 31 October.

At a glance

Welcome & Ambience	✓✓✓✓	Location	✓✓✓✓✓
Quality of Pitches	✓✓✓✓	Range of Facilities	✓✓✓

Directions

From A338 about 1.75 miles north of Ringwood, turn east (signed Linwood and Moyles Court). Follow signs, over a staggered crossroads, and continue straight on for another 1.75 miles to Red Shoot Inn. O.S.GR: SU188095 GPS: N50:53.035 W01:44.082

Charges 2005

Per adult	£ 5.50
child (5-14 yrs)	£ 3.50
child (0-4 yrs)	£ 1.25
pitch incl. car	£ 1.70 - £ 4.20
electricity	£ 3.20
dog	£ 1.00
Min. pitch charge £11.50.	

Reservations

Advised for w/ends, B.Hs and peak season (school holidays) and made with £18 deposit per week or part week. Tel: 01425 473789. Email: enquiries@redshoot-campingpark.com

UK2360 Hill Cottage Farm Caravan Park

Sandleheath Road, Alderholt, Fordingbridge SP6 3EG (Hampshire)

First opened in 2000, this is a newly constructed, modern site set in 47 acres of beautiful countryside on the Dorset and Hampshire border. The 32 pitches, all on hardstandings with electric hook-ups (16A) and water taps are arranged around a circular gravel roadway. Secluded and sheltered, they have views across the surrounding countryside. A field alongside the camping area is used for tents and rallies, and has space for ball games and a small playground. Also on site are a tennis court and a lake for coarse fishing, and there are many woodland walks in the area. Overall this site is more suitable for adults and younger children – it is not really designed for active teenagers.

Facilities

A large modern barn-style building provides excellent heated facilities, including covered dishwashing sinks, a laundry room with washing machines and dryers, plus facilities for disabled people and babies - in all, a very generous provision. The first floor has a games room with a full size snooker table, two pool tables and a darts board, plus a separate function room. Motorcaravan services. Playground. Off site: The village centre with pub, church, Post Office and store is a 20 minute woodland walk. Local attractions include Rockbourne Roman Villa, Cranborne Chase, The Dolls Museum at Fordingbridge, Salisbury, and Ringwood with its Wednesday market.

Open

All year (ring first in low season).

At a glance

Welcome & Ambience	✓✓✓✓	Location	✓✓✓✓
Quality of Pitches	✓✓✓✓	Range of Facilities	✓✓✓

Directions

From Fordingbridge take B3078 westwards for 2 miles to Alderholt. On entering the village, at left hand bend, turn right towards Sandleheath (site signed) and site entrance is about 300 yards on the left. O.S.GR: SU120130. GPS: N50:55.141 W01:49.967

Charges 2005

Per unit incl. 2 adults, electricity	£ 12.00 - £ 14.00
extra adult	£ 5.00
child (0-8 yrs)	£ 1.50
child (9-15 yrs)	£ 3.00
dog	£ 1.00
awning	£ 1.00 - £ 2.00

Reservations

Made with minimum £20 deposit. Advised for B.Hs and peak season. Tel: 01425 650513.

UK2280 Lytton Lawn Touring Park

Lymore Lane, Milford-on-Sea SO41 0TX (Hampshire)

Lytton Lawn is the touring arm of Shorefield Country Park, a holiday home park and leisure centre. Set in eight acres, Lytton Lawn provides 135 marked pitches. These include 53 'premier' pitches (hard-standing, 16A electricity, pitch light, water and waste water outlet) in a grassy, hedged area – this section with its heated toilet block is open for a longer season. The rest of the pitches, all with electricity, are in the adjoining, but separate, gently sloping field, edged with mature trees and hedges and with a further toilet block. The new larger reception and a well stocked shop make this a good, self-sufficient, comfortable site. Visitors to Lytton Lawn are entitled to use the comprehensive leisure facilities at Shorefield itself (2.5 miles away). These include a very attractive indoor pool, solarium, sauna and spa, fitness classes and treatments, all weather tennis courts, outdoor pools, restaurant facilities including a bistro (Easter - 2 Nov), and entertainment and activity programmes. The comprehensive facilities at Shorefield are of a very good standard and are mostly free (extra charges are made for certain activities).

Facilities

Two purpose built, modern toilet blocks are tiled and well fitted. Dishwashing, washing machine and dryer in each block. Baby changing facilities in one block and facilities for disabled visitors (Radar key). New shop (all year). Small fenced play area and hedged field with goal posts. Only one dog per pitch is accepted. Off site: Village pub 10 minutes walk. Golf, riding, coarse fishing (all within 3 miles), sailing, windsurfing and boat launching facilities (1.5 miles). The New Forest, Isle of Wight, Bournemouth, Southampton and the beach at Milford on Sea are near.

Open

All year excl. 4 January - 9 February.

At a glance

Welcome & Ambience	✓✓✓✓	Location	✓✓✓✓✓
Quality of Pitches	✓✓✓✓✓	Range of Facilities	✓✓✓

Directions

From M27 follow signs for Lyndhurst and Lymington on A337. Continue towards New Milton and Lytton Lawn is signed at Everton; Shorefield is signed at Downton. O.S.GR: SZ293937.

Charges 2005

Per pitch incl. all persons and electricity,	£ 9.50 - £ 28.00
premier pitch incl. water, drainage and TV connection	£ 11.50 - £ 31.00
pup tent or awning free, both together	£ 4.00
dog (1 only)	£ 1.50 - £ 3.00

Less 40% Mon - Thurs in certain periods.
Min. weekly charge at busy times.

Reservations

Made with deposit and cancellation insurance; contact Shorefield Holidays Ltd, Shorefield Road, Milford on Sea, nr. Lymington, Hampshire SO41 0LH. Tel: 01590 648331. Email: holidays@shorefield.co.uk

UK2285 Forest Edge Touring Park

229 Ringwood Road, St Leonards, Ringwood BH242SD (Hampshire)

This popular family park is the latest addition to the Shorefield Group. Offering touring and tenting holidays, it is complemented by the leisure facilities available at Oakdene Forest Park (which is now taking fewer touring units). There is easy access here to 205 level, marked pitches which include 4 'premier' serviced pitches, 20 with hardstanding and 165 with 16A electricity hook-ups. The cheerful, flowery reception and well stocked shop help create a friendly and relaxed atmosphere. Next to reception are a small bar, play area, swimming pool and one toilet block. A further toilet block is in the next field and a fenced ball game area. Picnic tables are dotted about the park giving it a country feel. A short walk through Hurn Forest (less than a mile) leads to Oakdene and its new clubhouse and entertainment centre. Visitors at Forest Edge may use the bar, restaurant, large pools, games room and other entertainment free of charge which is ideal for families not wishing to travel too far. The location of Forest Edge is ideal for visiting Bournemouth (beaches, shops and shows), the New Forest and all the attractions of Dorset.

Facilities

The two toilet blocks provide clean but fairly standard facilities. Unit for disabled visitors. Baby area. Dishwashing. These facilities may be under pressure in high season. Laundry in a separate room near the play area. gas supplies. Shop with off-licence. Small swimming pool (1 m. deep throughout). Quaint bar serving bar snacks (high season). Two Euro-style tents for rent. Off site: Riding 1 mile. Fishing 2 miles. Golf 3 miles. Beach 5 miles.

Open

All year except 4 January - 9 February.

At a glance

Welcome & Ambience	✓✓✓✓	Location	✓✓✓✓
Quality of Pitches	✓✓✓✓	Range of Facilities	✓✓✓

Directions

Take the A31 westbound from Ringwood. After 3 miles and two roundabouts, turn left at the second roundabout into Boundary Lane (before you get to Oakdene). Site is signed. O.S.GR: SU105024.

Charges 2005

Per unit incl. 6 persons	£ 7.50 - £ 23.00
incl. electricity	£ 9.50 - £ 28.00
incl. full services	£ 11.50 - £ 31.00
dog	£ 1.50 - £ 3.00

Reservations

Made with deposit and cancellation insurance; contact Shorefield Holidays Ltd, Shorefield Road, Milford on Sea, Lymington, Hampshire SO41 0LH. Tel: 01590 648331. Email: holidays@shorefield.co.uk

Best of both worlds
South Coast and New Forest

All four of our touring parks are set in peaceful, unspoilt parkland in the beautiful South Coast area.

There are comprehensive leisure facilities available and great entertainment for the whole family.

Pamper yourself in our new 'Reflections' Day Spa at Shorefield Country Park or explore Britain's latest National Park - the New Forest.

For full details, ask for our brochure or browse on-line.

For a really memorable family holiday

01590 648331
e-mail: holidays@shorefield.co.uk

Oakdene Forest Park
St. Leonards, Ringwood, Hampshire

Lytton Lawn Touring Park
Milford on Sea, Hampshire

Forest Edge Touring Park
St. Leonards, Ringwood, Hampshire

Swanage Coastal Park
Swanage, Dorset (formerly Priestway)

Ref: AR

SHOREFIELD
HOLIDAYS LIMITED

www.shorefield.co.uk

UK2250 **Hoburne Bashley**

Sway Road, New Milton BH25 5QR (Hampshire)

This is an attractive, well run park with many holiday homes (380), but it also has a very sizeable tourist section and can take 300 touring units. However, tents, trailer tents and pup tents are not accepted. Spread over three flat meadows the numbered touring pitches are large, divided by hedging or low fencing, and include 20 'super' pitches. These are of mixed grass and hardstanding with electricity. Set in pleasant park-like surroundings not far from beaches, Bournemouth and the New Forest, the park has a good clubhouse with excellent facilities. This overlooks an 18 m. circular outdoor swimming pool and 18 m. paddling pool, a sensible size and great fun with its geysers, clown and beach effect. An impressive indoor pool complex houses a water flume, sauna, solarium, spa bath and steam room, all well supervised by lifeguards. The club facilities are comprehensive, with a ballroom, large lounges and bars, and a wide range of entertainment from cabaret, talent shows, bingo, quizzes and competitions to discos (Spring B.H. to mid-Sept). Children's entertainment covers sports and games for the teens and Sammy the Seahorse club for under 12s. The Hungry Woodcutter provides simple hot food and takeaway all day. A popular park with lots going on, Bashley is part of the Hoburne group.

Facilities	Directions
Three well constructed toilet blocks, one central to each area, are fully tiled with modern fittings in cheerful yellow and blue with washbasins in cabins. Showers are pre-set (no dividers, but shower heads are set fairly low). Baby changing facilities. Covered dishwashing sinks. Launderette. Clubhouse with bars, restaurant and takeaway (1/3-31/10). 10-pin bowling. TV room. Video arcade and games room with snooker tables, plus two pool tables, table tennis and darts in other rooms. Children's club. Shop (1/3-31/10). Indoor pool. Outdoor pools (June - mid-Sept). Crazy golf. Golf course (9 hole, par 3). Tennis courts (3). Adventure play area. Soft ball play area. Only one dog or pet permitted per unit. American motorhomes accepted. Off site: Fishing and riding 1 mile. Mudeford beach 8 miles.	Park is on the B3055 about 400 yards east of the crossroads with the B3058 in Bashley village. O.S.GR: SZ246969.

Directions

Park is on the B3055 about 400 yards east of the crossroads with the B3058 in Bashley village. O.S.GR: SZ246969.

Charges 2005

Per unit incl.up to 6 persons and electricity	£ 10.50 - £ 35.00
multi-service pitch	£ 13.00 - £ 37.00
2 car pitch	£ 13.00 - £ 37.00
pet (1 only)	£ 2.00
Weekend breaks available.	

Reservations

Necessary for peak season and made for any length: £50 p/w deposit, balance 6 weeks before arrival. Tel: 01425 612340. Email: enquiries@hoburne.co.uk

Open

10 February - 30 October plus weekends.

At a glance

Welcome & Ambience	✓✓✓✓✓	Location	✓✓✓✓✓
Quality of Pitches	✓✓✓✓✓	Range of Facilities	✓✓✓✓✓

UK2300 **Ashurst Caravan & Camping Site**

The Forestry Commission, Lyndhurst Road, Ashurst SO40 7AR (Hampshire)

An attractive Forestry Commission site on the fringe of the New Forest, Ashurst is set in a mixture of oak woodland and grass heathland which is open to the grazing animals of the Forest. Smaller than the Hollands Wood site (23 acres), it provides 280 pitches, 180 of which have been gravelled to provide semi-hardstanding; otherwise you pitch where you like, applying the 20 ft. rule on ground that can be uneven. There are no electricity connections. Some noise must be expected from the adjacent railway line - the station is just five minutes walk away. Reception is run by the very helpful site managers who provide a freezer pack service, charging service for mobile phones and batteries and sell various camping accessories. Charcoal and disposable barbecues are for sale (but barbecues are not permitted in dry weather). There is a late arrivals area and separate car-parking area for those arriving or returning after the gate has closed (22.30 hrs).

Facilities	Directions
The single central toilet block has been refurbished and provides everything necessary, including hairdryers, a well equipped unit for visitors with disabilities (key required) and a good laundry room. It could be under pressure when the site is full in the main season. Motorcaravan service point. Bread and milk to order. Dogs are not accepted. A torch is useful. Off site: Local garage sells gas. Nearby pub by footpath across an adjacent field. Shops and local buses within a five minute walk. Guided forest walks are organised during the main season. Golf 4 miles.	Site is 2 miles east of Lyndhurst, set back from the A35 Southampton - Bournemouth road, 5 miles southwest of Southampton. O.S.GR: SU334099.

Directions

Site is 2 miles east of Lyndhurst, set back from the A35 Southampton - Bournemouth road, 5 miles southwest of Southampton. O.S.GR: SU334099.

Charges 2005

Per unit incl. up to 4 persons	£ 7.20 - £ 15.70
extra person (over 5 yrs)	£ 1.50
extra car, gazebo or pup tent	£ 5.00

Less 20% all year for disabled guests and outside 7/7-28/8 for senior citizens.

Reservations

Necessary for B.Hs and peak times (min. 2 nights or 3 nights at B.Hs) with £30 deposit. Contact (at all times): Forest Holidays, Forestry Commission, 231 Corstorphine Road, Edinburgh EH12 7AT. Tel: 0131 3146505. Email: info@forestholidays.co.uk

Open

March - September.

At a glance

Welcome & Ambience	✓✓✓✓	Location	✓✓✓✓
Quality of Pitches	✓✓✓	Range of Facilities	✓✓✓

UK2290 **Sandy Balls Holiday Centre**

Godshill, Fordingbridge SP6 2JZ (Hampshire)

Sandy Balls, probably one of the best known and one of the oldest 'campsites' in the UK, sits high above the sweep of the Avon River amongst woodland which is protected as a nature reserve. The history and development of the park, and how it came to get its name is interesting and it deserves the entry it has maintained in these guides for over 30 years. A very well run and progressive park set within 120 acres and open all year, it covers an extensive area in a series of fields or woodland. This provides 131 lodges and caravan holiday homes (many for rent), some tent areas with unmarked pitches, and 233 serviced pitches for touring units separated by hedging with part-hardstanding, part-grass (10A electricity and TV connection). In winter only 50 pitches are available. The central village area with all the amenities is designed to blend with the forest surroundings and provides for all round family entertainment. It includes a large indoor pool and a solar heated outdoor pool both with lifeguards and free at all times (in high season, sessions are timed according to demand). In all there are 120 acres of woodland to explore with a woodland leisure trail where wild animals and birds can be observed in their natural surroundings. We understand that the thatched gift shop is a must for children! The attractions of the New Forest are close at hand, together with Paultons Park and Beaulieu House and Motor Museum.

Facilities

Three modern toilet blocks have under-floor heating and washbasin cubicles. One 'portacabin' style unit remains as an overflow in the tent field (28 day). One block has a bath in each section (M&F). Toilets for disabled visitors and baby facilities. Excellent central launderette plus washing machines in all toilet blocks. Motorcaravan service point. Supermarket with bakery. Takeaway. Restaurants, bars and family room. Pizzeria. Gift shop with internet terminal. Wide screen TV and entertainment (high season only). Indoor pool (66 x 30 ft). Outdoor pool (25/5-30/8). Well equipped gym, jacuzzi spa bath, steam room, toning tables, sauna and solarium and dance studios. Games room. Adventure playground and play areas. Soft play area. Clay modelling tuition and story telling. River fishing on permit. Riding stables. Bicycle hire. Archery. Orienteering. Dogs allowed on certain fields. Off site: Golf 6 miles. Beach 20 miles.

At a glance

Welcome & Ambience	✓✓✓✓✓	Location	✓✓✓✓✓
Quality of Pitches	✓✓✓✓✓	Range of Facilities	✓✓✓✓✓

Directions

Park is northwest off B3078 (Fordingbridge - Cadnam) just west of Godshill village, and about 1.5 miles east of Fordingbridge. O.S.GR: SU168147. GPS: N50:55.816 W01:45.612

Charges 2005

Per pitch	£ 12.75 - £ 19.50
adult	free - £ 3.50
young adult (12-17 yrs)	free - £ 2.00
child (3-11 yrs)	free - £ 1.50
dog	free - £ 2.00

Reservations

Made with deposit and compulsory cancellation insurance. Tel: 01425 653042.
Email: post@sandy-balls.co.uk

Open

All year.

UK2310 Hollands Wood Caravan & Camping Site

The Forestry Commission, Lyndhurst Road, Brockenhurst SO43 7QH (Hampshire)

Hollands Wood is a large, spacious 168-acre secluded site in a natural woodland setting (mainly oak). It is set in the heart of the New Forest, with an abundance of wildlife, including the famous New Forest ponies. The site is arranged informally with 600 level unmarked pitches but it is stipulated that there must be at least 20 feet between each unit. There are no electrical connections and traffic noise is possible from the A337 which runs alongside one boundary. One area of the site is designated a dog free zone. Brockenhurst village is only about half a mile where there are shops for supplies and gas, etc, plus trains and buses. Reception offers a freezer pack service and sells batteries, maps and guides. Barbecues are not permitted in dry weather. The site can get very busy and we include the smaller Ashurst site as an alternative.

Facilities

Two large utilitarian toilet blocks (and a third smaller, older one) are full equipped if somewhat basic. Facilities for disabled people and baby changing surfaces. Two laundry rooms with washing machines and dryers. These facilities are under pressure at peak times. Motorcaravan service point. Bread and milk to order. Night security with the barrier closed 22.30 - 07.30 hrs (overnight area). Torches essential. Off site: Bicycle hire and riding 2 miles. Golf 3 miles.

Open

26 March - 27 September.

At a glance

Welcome & Ambience	✓✓✓✓	Location	✓✓✓✓
Quality of Pitches	✓✓✓	Range of Facilities	✓✓✓

Directions

Site entrance is on east side of A337 Lyndhurst - Lymington road, half a mile north of Brockenhurst. O.S.GR: SU303038.

Charges 2005

Per unit incl. up to 4 persons	£ 7.90 - £ 16.40
extra person (over 5 yrs)	£ 1.50
extra car, gazebo or pup tent	£ 5.00

Less 20% all year for disabled guests and outside 7/7-28/8 for senior citizens.

Reservations

Necessary for B.Hs and peak times (min. 3 nights with £30 deposit). Contact (at all times): Forest Holidays, Forestry Commission, 231 Corstorphine Road, Edinburgh EH12 7AT. Tel: 0131 3146505. Email: info@forestholidays.co.uk

UK2320 Chichester Camping & Caravanning Club Site

345 Main Road, Southbourne PO10 8JH (Hampshire)

This small, neat site is just to the west of Chichester and north of Bosham harbour. Formerly an orchard, it is rectangular in shape with 58 pitches on flat, well mown lawns on either side of gravel roads. All pitches have 16A electricity, 42 with level hardstanding. Although the A27 bypass takes most of the through traffic, the site is by the main A259 road so there may be some traffic noise in some parts (but not too busy at night). Opposite the park are orchards through which paths lead to the seashore. Unfortunately there is no parking outside or overnight area for late arrivals. Arrival must be before 8 pm. unless prior arrangements have been made with the site manager. Portsmouth is nearby with its ferry port and historic Naval Dockyard. Other attractions include Goodwood (racing), Chichester (Festival Theatre) and Fishbourne Roman palace, with Southampton and the New Forest a little further afield.

Facilities

The well designed, brick built toilet block is of first class quality. Fully tiled and heated in cool weather, with facilities for people with disabilities (access by key). Washing machines and dryers. Gas supplies. No ball games permitted on the park. Dogs can be walked in the lane opposite the entrance. Off site: Shops, restaurants and pubs within easy walking distance in the nearby village and the park is on a main bus route. Chichester has a leisure centre and market day is Wednesday. Excellent caravan shop nearby. Bicycle hire 1 mile. Fishing or golf 5 miles, riding 6 miles.

At a glance

Welcome & Ambience	✓✓✓✓	Location	✓✓✓✓
Quality of Pitches	✓✓✓✓	Range of Facilities	✓✓✓

Directions

Park is on A259 Chichester - Havant road at Southbourne, 750 yards west of Chichester Caravans. Coming from the west, it is 2.8 miles from the A27/A259 junction near Havant. O.S.GR: SU774056.

Charges 2005

Per adult	£ 5.55 - £ 7.40
child (6-18 yrs)	£ 1.90 - £ 2.00
pitch (non-member)	£ 5.00

Reservations

Necessary and made with deposit; contact site or Central Reservations 0870 243 3331. Tel: 01243 373202.

Open

February - November.

UK2315 Riverside Holidays

Satchell Lane, Hamble, Southampton SO31 4HR (Hampshire)

What makes Riverside so special is its location; close to the River Hamble, Mecca for the international yachtsman. Hamble village, one mile away, with its cobbled streets, pubs and restaurants, is famed the world over for its association with yachting. This is an ideal base for the Southampton Boat Show, Cowes Week and its very own Hamble Week Regatta. It is also home to the Royal Yachting Association. On the marina adjacent to the site, a mere two minutes walk, is Oyster Quay with a bar and restaurant over-looking hundreds of yachts worth millions. Where the Hamble river enters Southampton Water, visitors can see all the great liners as they pass in and out of nearby Southampton port. The site is family-owned and covers five acres surrounded by trees and hedges; it has 114 pitches of which 75 are level for touring caravans and tents with 53 electricity hook-ups (16A). The remaining pitches are used for lodges and residential and static caravans on slightly rising ground, but so well spaced and with plenty of grass they are not too obtrusive. A warden-run log cabin reception, with tourist information, including local bus and rail times, is at the entrance. Currently the amenities block comprises an old 'Portakabin', screened by fencing and butterfly shrubs. It is clean but not quite up to standard. However, the owners have already received planning permission to replace this with a totally new reception, shop, clubroom, toilet block and a pool in the next two years.

Facilities

The old 'Portakabin' unit is clean but not quite up to standard, with a baby changing area but no unit for the disabled. Small laundry room alongside. All these facilities could be under pressure in high season. Bicycle hire. Caravan storage. Off site: Buses and trains 1 mile. Fishing, sea fishing, sailing, supermarket, 1 mile in village. Riding 2 miles. Golf 5 miles. You can catch a small ferry across to Warsash on the other bank or take a boat up to the Upper Hamble Country Park. The New Forest, Winchester and Portsmouth are nearby.

Open

1 March - 31 October.

At a glance

Welcome & Ambience	✓✓✓✓	Location	✓✓✓✓✓
Quality of Pitches	✓✓✓✓	Range of Facilities	✓✓✓

Directions

From the M27 take exit 8 and follow signs for Hamble. Taking B3397 with Tesco on the left, continue 1.9 miles through traffic lights until Hound roundabout. After 50 yds turn left into Satchell Lane (signed Mercury Marina) and site is on left in 1 mile. Q,S. GR: SU484082. GPS: N50:52.200 W01:18.667

Charges 2005

Per unit incl. 2 persons	£ 10.00 - £ 18.00
extra person	£ 3.00
child (4-16 yrs)	£ 2.00
awning	£ 3.00
dog	£ 1.50
Camping Cheques accepted.	

Reservations

Made with £10 deposit. Tel: 023 8045 3220.
Email: enquiries@riversideholidays.co.uk

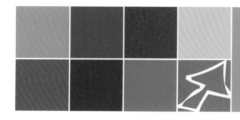

Planning your
next holiday?

don't forget to look at our directory
ON PAGE 314

UK2500 **Heathfield Farm Camping**

Heathfield Road, Freshwater PO40 9SH (Isle of Wight)

Heathfield is a pleasant contrast to many of the other sites on the Isle of Wight, in that it is a 'no frills' sort of place, very popular with tenters, cyclists and small camper vans. Despite its name, it is no longer a working farm. A large, open meadow provides 60 large, level pitches, 30 with electricity (10A). Two small fenced areas provide traffic free zones for backpackers and cyclists' tents. A play field for ball games also has two picnic tables and two barbecues, and there is a wild flower meadow with the perimeter mown for dog walking. There is no shop as you are only eight minutes walk from the centre of Freshwater. The site overlooks Colwell Bay and across the Solent towards Milford-on-Sea and Hurst Castle. It is ideal for visiting attractions on the western side of the island including Totland and Freshwater Bays, The Needles and Old Battery, Compton Down, and Mottistone Manor Garden. The Military road which runs from Freshwater Bay to St Catherine's Point gives spectacular coastal views.

Facilities

The main toilet unit is housed in a modern, ingeniously customised, 'portacabin' type unit including one washbasin cubicle for ladies and a baby room. Showers are slightly different in that they have two pushbutton controls, one for pre-mixed hot water, the other for cold only (provided at the special request of some of the regular customers). A second similar unit has WCs and washbasins in cubicles, plus facilities for disabled visitors. Laundry with washing machine and dryer, ironing facilities and dishwashing sinks. Motorcaravan service point. Gas supplies. Ice pack service. Play field. Bicycle hire. No commercial vehicles are accepted. Gate locked 22.30-07.00 hrs. Off site: Bus stop 200 m. Beach 0.5 miles. Fishing 0.5 miles. Golf 1.25 miles. Riding 3 miles.

At a glance

Welcome & Ambience	✓✓✓✓✓	Location	✓✓✓✓✓
Quality of Pitches	✓✓✓✓✓	Range of Facilities	✓✓✓

Directions

From A3054 north of Totland and Colwell turn into Heathfield Road where site is signed. Site entrance is on right after a short distance. O.S.GR: SZ336879.

Charges 2005

Per adult	£ 4.00 - £ 5.00
child (3-15 yrs)	£ 1.50 - £ 2.50
pitch	£ 0.50 - £ 1.00
with electricity	£ 2.00 - £ 3.00
dog (max. 1, 16/7-31/8)	£ 1.00

Min pitch fee July/Aug £12.00. One night booking supplement £2.00. No credit cards.

Reservations

Advisable for B.Hs and peak season. Tel: 01983 756756. Email: web@heathfieldcamping.co.uk

Open

1 May - 30 September.

UK2510 **Whitecliff Bay Holiday Park**

Hillway, Whitecliff Bay, Bembridge PO35 5PL (Isle of Wight)

Whitecliff Bay is a very large complex divided by a lane, with a holiday home and chalet park on the right hand side, and a touring site on the left hand side. The large touring site is on a sloping hillside with commanding views over the surrounding countryside. The 429 pitches are spread over three fields, the top and second fields are terraced, but field three (the only one in which dogs are permitted in low season only) is quite level. Half of the pitches have electric hook-ups (10A), and there are around 44 gravel hardstandings, 12 in the top field, the remainder in lowest field. There are 13 individual hedged multi-serviced pitches available, so book early. On the opposite side of the lane, in the holiday home park, you will find all the main entertainment and leisure facilities. These include The Culver Club with a bar and evening entertainment, several snack bars and takeaways, supervised swimming pools (indoor and outdoor), jacuzzi, a sauna and sun-bed, small gym and soft 'playzone' (under 8s). Close to the outdoor pool a very steep path leads down to a sandy beach, where there is a small café. It is possible to launch a boat from this beach (4-wheel drive vehicle essential, advance booking necessary).

Facilities

Three sanitary units, one on the lower part of the site. The other two are fairly close together, not far from reception and both of these have been refitted to a good standard. Showers (on payment) and a suite (with shower) for disabled people. A second suite with a hip bath/shower is at the lower block with a similar facility to serve as a baby/family room. Laundry with ironing facility. Motorcaravan service point. Small mini-market with reception. Playground. At the holiday home park: Launderette, hairdresser and second larger shop. The Culver Club. Snack bars. Swimming pool (18 x 18 m, Whitsun - end Aug). Indoor funpool with jacuzzi, a sauna and sunbed, small gym, a soft playzone (under 8 yrs). Most facilities open March - Oct. Dogs only accepted in lower field outside 20/7 - 31/8. Off site: Normal bus service from park entrance on weekdays, site runs a courtesy minibus at weekends to Bembridge and Sandown. Local airfield adjacent offering gliding and flying lessons. Golf 5 miles. Bicycle hire 4 miles. Riding 2 miles.

At a glance

Welcome & Ambience	✓✓✓✓✓	Location	✓✓✓✓✓
Quality of Pitches	✓✓✓✓	Range of Facilities	✓✓✓✓✓

Directions

Bembridge is at the eastern end of the island. From the A3055 between Ryde and Sandown, turn east at Brading on B3395 for approx. 2 miles passing the Airfield and Propeller Club, fork right (site signed). Follow signs to site, first entry on right is static area, touring entrance is on left immediately after. O.S.GR: SZ635865.

Charges 2005

Per pitch incl. 2 persons	£ 8.40 - £ 14.70
incl. electricity	£ 11.30 - £ 18.10
incl. full services	£ 13.90 - £ 21.70
extra adult	£ 3.70 - £ 5.70
child (5-13 yrs)	£ 2.40 - £ 3.90
dog (excl. 18/7-31/8)	£ 1.00

Reservations

Made with deposit of £40 per week (£80 if special offer package). Tel: 01983 872671. Email: holiday@whitecliff-bay.com

Open

22 March - 26 October.

UK2450 The Orchards Holiday Caravan Park

Newbridge, Yarmouth, Isle of Wight PO41 0TS (Isle of Wight)

In a village situation in the quieter western part of the island, The Orchards, 'a park for all seasons', is a busy and lively family holiday park combining 63 caravan holiday homes (in a separate area) with a neat touring area. A good place from which to explore, the beaches and Yarmouth are only four miles away. There are 171 marked touring pitches, arranged on gently sloping meadow, broken up by apple trees, mature hedges and fences. All have electricity and 84 have hardstanding. In addition, there are 20 'all-service' pitches, 10 with hardstanding. The large reception provides useful tourist information. A meeting room (up to 50 persons) is suitable for small rallies. Golfing and walking holidays are arranged. Part of the Caravan Club's 'managed under contract' scheme, non-members are also very welcome, the park is also a member of the Best of British group.

Facilities

Three toilet blocks are ample. A few washbasins are in private cabins. Baths on payment. The latest block, a smart mobile unit, provides en-suite facilities. Facilities for disabled visitors (a hardstanding pitch close by can be reserved). Full laundry facilities. Motorcaravan services. Ice pack and battery services. Gas supplies. Well stocked shop. Takeaway (mid-March - Oct). Indoor pool (Feb - Dec). Outdoor heated pool (late May - Sept). Multi-court. Exercise stations. Pool, table tennis, TV and amusements. Coarse fishing (no closed season). Bicycle hire arranged. Off site: Bus stop at entrance. Membership of village social club and small discount at Freshwater golf course (4 miles) - ask at reception. Boat launching 4 miles. Riding 1 mile.

At a glance

Welcome & Ambience	✓✓✓✓✓	Location	✓✓✓✓
Quality of Pitches	✓✓✓✓✓	Range of Facilities	✓✓✓✓

Directions

Park is in Newbridge village, signed north from B3401 (Yarmouth - Newport) road. O.S.GR: SZ411878. GPS: N50:41.278 W01:25.198

Charges 2005

Per unit incl. 2 adults, electricity £ 11.40 - £ 15.90
No pitch fee for hikers or cyclists.
Packages incl. ferry travel available - ring park for best deal.
Camping Cheques accepted.

Reservations

Made for min. 5 days with £30 p/wk deposit. Tel: 01983 531331.
Email: info@orchards-holiday-park.co.uk

Open

All year excl. 3 January - 15 February.

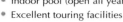
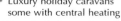
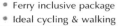

UK2470 Southland Camping Park

Newchurch, Sandown, Isle of Wight PO36 0LZ (Isle of Wight)

Southland is in the grounds of a former nursery and it has matured nicely with many attractive shrubs and trees. The pleasant surroundings have won many awards. In the peaceful country setting of the Arreton valley, it is a sheltered and well run park with 120 large, level pitches backing on to and separated by high hedging. Comfortable and spacious, all have electricity (10/16A) and some water points. Two acres of land overlooking the valley have been developed as a nature area. Sandown and Shanklin are 3 miles, the beach at Lake, 2.5 miles. A member of the Countryside Discovery group.

Facilities

The excellent toilet block is well maintained - the ladies' is modern, with washbasins in spacious cubicles, three en-suite basin and shower cubicles, and a bathroom (on payment). Baby room. Good unit for disabled people, and two family shower rooms also suitable for disabled visitors. Laundry. Motorcaravan service point. Shop (4/4-30/9). Fenced play area. More than one dog per pitch by prior arrangement only. Off site: Main bus route stops at the top of the road. Fishing 1 mile. Riding 2 miles. Bicycle hire and golf 3 miles. Beach 2.5 miles.

At a glance

Welcome & Ambience	✓✓✓✓	Location	✓✓✓✓
Quality of Pitches	✓✓✓✓✓	Range of Facilities	✓✓✓

Directions

Park is signed from A3055/6 Newport-Sandown road, southeast of Arreton. O.S.GR: SZ558848. GPS: N50:39.588 W01:12.718

Charges 2005

Per adult	£ 5.00 - £ 7.35
child (3-15 yrs)	£ 1.85 - £ 3.85

Packages incl. ferry travel. Special low season offers.

Reservations

Made for any length; contact park.
Tel: 01983 865385. Email: info@southland.co.uk

Open

Easter - end September.

UK2530 Waverley Park Holiday Centre

51 Old Road, East Cowes PO32 6AW (Isle of Wight)

This pleasant small family owned and run site is set in the grounds of an old country house, once owned by Dr Arnold, the author of Tom Brown's Schooldays. There are magnificent views over the Solent and just five minutes from the Cowes ferry terminal. The 45 touring pitches are in short rows, back to back on sloping grassland, whilst tents are pitched on the lower half nearer to the promenade and sea. The 28 electricity hook-ups (10A) are tightly packed at the top. To one side of the site is an area housing 75 private and rental holiday homes. At the bottom of the park a gate leads onto the promenade which provides good walks, and the pebble beach which is popular with sailors, windsurfers, etc. The site is an ideal vantage point for Cowes Week, and has good views of liners sailing in and out of Southampton.

Facilities

At the top of the park, a recently built toilet block provides the usual facilities, including some spacious cubicles with washbasins en-suite. Good suite for disabled people with a baby changing deck. Basic chemical disposal point in the static area. Laundry facilities. Dishwashing room. Small well stocked shop. Heated outdoor pool and paddling pool with sun terrace. Club with restaurant and bar serving good value meals, plus family entertainment in season (all Whitsun - early Sept). Small adventure style playground. Games room. Nine hole putting green. Boats accepted by prior arrangement - public slipway nearby. Off site: Tennis courts close to lower end of site, key available, ask at reception. Public slipway. East Cowes, with its basic shops and services is within walking distance. A chain ferry across the Medina River operates between East Cowes and the famous West Cowes with its altogether better shops and tourist attractions. Bus stop outside the site entrance.

At a glance

Welcome & Ambience	✓✓✓✓	Location	✓✓✓✓✓
Quality of Pitches	✓✓✓	Range of Facilities	✓✓✓✓

Directions

Immediately after leaving Southampton - Cowes ferry, take first left, then right into Old Road, and park entrance is 300 yds on left. O.S.GR: SZ505958.

Charges 2005

Per adult	£ 4.00 - £ 6.00
child (5-13 yrs)	£ 2.00 - £ 3.00
pitch incl. free electricity	£ 2.50
dog	£ 0.50 - £ 1.20

During Cowes Week min. pitch fees apply (£12.00 - £14.50). Packages incl. ferry travel and other offers available.

Reservations

Made with deposit (25%) and essential for B.Hs, peak season and Cowes Week (1st week August). Tel: 01983 293452. Email: sue@waverley-park.co.uk

Open

29 March - 30 September (statics all year).

UK2475 Lower Hyde Holiday Park

Landguard Road, Shanklin PO37 7LL (Isle of Wight)

This site is located on the edge of Shanklin within walking distance of shops and services and only 1.5 miles from the beach. Lower Hyde is a large holiday park complex with around 200 rental and 114 privately owned holiday homes. The separate touring area has 115 well spaced and numbered pitches, 85 with electric hook-ups (16A) of which 26 are multi-service with hardstanding, water, drain, electricity and TV hook-up. The touring area has recently been redeveloped, and is now in an elevated position with some good views over the surrounding countryside. There are good surfaced roads, low level site lighting, toilet and shower facilities in modern 'portacabin' style units, a late arrivals area, and a permanent warden. Outdoor sporting activities on-site include a multi-court, soccer, archery, fencing and tennis. The small indoor pool and spa pool and outdoor fun pool provide snorkelling, scuba diving and adult only swimming sessions. There is evening entertainment for all the family, with some 'big name' stars and a variety of supporting events. For children there is an adventure playground, Sparkys Krew Club (5-11 yrs), and for older children the 'Mix' (12-16 yrs) has a variety of challenging activities. 'Day Camp Action' is for 7-16 year olds, (extra charge, only run during school holidays) with high ropes, abseiling, climbing tower and quad bikes.

Facilities

A group of several modern 'portacabin' style units standing on a new concrete base currently provide all services, although a permanent building is in the planning stage. Current provision is adequate and well looked after, providing some good showers, open washbasins, dishwashing sinks, and an easily accessible suite for disabled campers. Launderette near reception. Shop. Takeaway. Hudson's bar and diner. Squires celebrity show bar. Games arcade. Indoor and outdoor pool complex with lifeguards. Adventure playground. Sparkys Krew Club, the Mix for teenagers. ATM. Off site: Fishing and boat launching 1.5 miles. Golf 2.5 miles. Riding and bicycle hire 5 miles.

Open

2 April - 29 October.

At a glance

Welcome & Ambience	✓✓✓✓	Location	✓✓✓✓
Quality of Pitches	✓✓✓✓	Range of Facilities	✓✓✓✓

Directions

From East Cowes ferry terminal take A3021 for about 2.5 miles to roundabout and turn right on A3054 to Newport. From Newport take A3020 towards Sandown and Shanklin. After 1.5 miles (at Blackwater) continue straight on joining A3056 to Sandown. Keep on this road until you pass Safeway on the left, and shortly afterwards, turn right into Whitecross Lane (signed Landguard Camping). Keep straight on, past Landguard and site is on right after 1 mile. O.S.GR:SZ576817
GPS: N50:37.999 W01:10.859

Charges 2005

per unit incl. up to 6 persons	£ 6.00 - £ 26.00
tent pitch	£ 3.00 - £ 23.00
hardstanding	£ 5.00

Reservations

Essential for B.Hs and peak season. Made with deposit of £5 per pitch per night for less than 7 nights, or £35 per pitch per week. Tel: 01983 866131.

UK2520 Thorness Bay Holiday Park

Thorness Bay, Cowes PO31 8NJ (Isle of Wight)

Spread over a large area of rural down and woodland that slopes down to the beach at Thorness Bay, this is a large site with more than 500 holiday homes. The touring site has around 90 marked pitches, most with electricity (16A) including 27 multi-serviced pitches on gravel hardstandings with electricity, water, drain and TV points. These and some grass pitches are on newly created terraces served by tarmac roads. The remainder are on sloping open grassland either divided by ranch style rails or in an open tent area, and all have views of the surrounding countryside. The main activity centre is located in the holiday home area, a short walk from the touring site. Outdoor sporting activities on-site include a multi-court, soccer, archery, and fencing. The indoor pool provides snorkelling, scuba diving and adult only swimming sessions. There is evening entertainment for all the family, with some 'big name' stars and a variety of supporting events. Children will be entertained by an adventure playground, Sparkys Krew Club (5-11 yrs) and for older children the 'Mix' (12-16 yrs) has a variety of challenging activities. 'Day Camp Action' is for 7-16 year olds (extra charge, only run during school holidays) with high ropes, abseiling, climbing tower and quad bikes.

Facilities

Several 'portacabin' style buildings provide the usual showers, WCs, and open washbasins. Separate units contain a suite for disabled persons (note: very steep short ramp, impractical for wheelchairs) and dishwashing sinks. Tower Diner and bar which also serves breakfasts. Indoor playroom for small children. Shop. Launderette. ATM machine. Takeaway. Games arcade. Indoor fun pool, with lifeguards. Regatta View show bar with entertainment programme including cabarets. Large adventure playground. Multi-sports court. Off site: The beach is easily accessed from the main entertainment complex. All the attractions of the Island are within easy day-trip distances. Golf 4 miles.

Open

2 April - 29 October.

At a glance

Welcome & Ambience	✓✓✓	Location	✓✓✓✓
Quality of Pitches	✓✓✓✓	Range of Facilities	✓✓✓✓

Directions

Thorness Bay is southwest of Cowes. From East Cowes ferry terminal follow signs to Newport. From centre follow A3054 towards Yarmouth. Continue for about 2.5 miles to crossroads, turning right (north) to Thorness Bay. After approx. 2 miles, on a sharp right hand bend, turn left where site is signed. After 400 yds. entrance on right leads to parking area and reception in main building.
O.S.GR: SZ452926. GPS: N50:43.868 W01:21.628

Charges 2005

Per pitch incl. up to 6 persons	£ 6.00 - £ 25.00
hardstanding pitch	£ 5.00
tent pitch	£ 3.00 - £ 22.00

Reservations

Essential for B.Hs and peak season. Made with deposit of £5 per pitch per night for less than 7 nights, or £35 per pitch per week. Tel: 01983 523109.

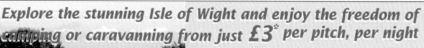

UK2570 Lincoln Farm Park

High Street, Standlake, Witney OX29 7RH (Oxfordshire)

From its immaculately tended grounds and quality facilities, to the efficient and friendly staff, this park is a credit to its owner. Situated in a small, quiet village, it is well set back and screened by mature trees, with wide gravel roads, hedged enclosures, attractive brick pathways and good lighting. All 90 numbered, level touring pitches are generously sized and have electrical connections (10/16A), 75 with gravel hardstanding and adjacent grass for awnings, and 22 are fully serviced (fresh and waste water, electricity and satellite TV). Gazebos or extra tents are not permitted on pitches. Although only a relatively small site its leisure facilities are quite outstanding. The indoor leisure centre boasts two heated pools plus a toddlers' pool, spa pools, saunas, steam room, sun bed and a fitness suite. Charges for all of these are modest, and outside of the open sessions everything can be hired privately by the hour. Oxford and the Cotswolds are conveniently close. A member of the Best of British group.

Facilities

The two heated toilet blocks are of notable design and quality, well maintained and exceptionally clean, with showers (sensibly sized and designed), and washbasins in cubicles. A well equipped, separate unit for disabled people is adjacent to a specially reserved pitch with direct access. Two family bathrooms (incorporating baby bath and changing facilities). Each block also contains a laundry room, dishwashing sinks under cover (more throughout the site), freezers, fridges and microwaves. Motorcaravan service point. Shop (basic supplies). Information kiosk. Outdoor chess/draughts, putting green and sizeable adventure play area (bark chipping and rubber base). Indoor swimming pools. Up to two dogs are welcome with allocated walks. Off site: Fishing (lake and river) 300 yds - 5 miles, riding centre and water sports nearby.

At a glance

| Welcome & Ambience | ✓✓✓✓ | Location | ✓✓✓✓ |
| Quality of Pitches | ✓✓✓✓✓ | Range of Facilities | ✓✓✓✓✓ |

Directions

Take A415 Witney - Abingdon road and turn into Standlake High Street by garage; park is 300 yds on the right. O.S.GR: SP396029.
GPS: N51:43.392 W01:25.727

Charges 2006

Per unit incl. 2 persons	£ 11.00 - £ 19.00
electricity	free - £ 2.75
extra adult	£ 2.25
child (5-14 yrs)	£ 1.50
dog	£ 1.25
Low season offers.	

Reservations

Made with £15 non-returnable deposit. Tel: 01865 300239. Email: info@lincolnfarm.touristnet.uk.com

Open

1 February - mid November.

UK2580 Cotswold View Caravan & Camping Park

Enstone Road, Charlbury OX7 3JH (Oxfordshire)

On the edge of the Cotswolds and surrounded by fine views, this well-run family site offers a warm welcome. It successfully combines a working farm, touring site and self catering country cottages. Wide gravel or tarmac roads ensure easy access to the 132 pitches (all with 10A electricity) in the 10-acre touring area. Part of this area has been carefully developed more recently to a high standard and will naturally take some time to mature. The small reception also serves as a licensed shop selling freshly baked bread, home-made cakes and eggs from their own hens. Farmhouse breakfasts (ordered the night before) are served in the farmhouse itself with B&B also offered. The farm's animals (sheep, hens, pigs, rabbits, ducks, goats, ponies and a donkey) add great interest to one's stay. Well defined and maintained trails around the enclosures enable the animals to be safely observed, whilst additional trails and woodland plantations provide more walking opportunities, particularly for dogs which can be allowed off the lead. Convenient for touring the Cotswolds, there is also a good train service for day trips to London.

Facilities

Two well maintained toilet blocks provide excellent facilities including washbasins in cubicles, showers with ample changing space, two family rooms, baths (50p), hairdryers, central heating and even soft piped music! Both blocks have good units for disabled people. Baby changing facilities, laundry room, freezers for ice packs and dishwashing sinks under cover. Motorcaravan service point. Shop. Children have a two sheltered grass areas in which to play and a games room with table tennis, pool table and football table. Hard tennis court. Latest addition is an under 5s fenced, rubber surfaced play area. Outdoor chess. Bicycle hire. Skittle alley is for hire. American motorhomes accepted. Security barrier system (£5 deposit). Off site: Fishing 1 mile, riding 10 miles, golf 7 miles.

At a glance

| Welcome & Ambience | ✓✓✓✓ | Location | ✓✓✓✓✓ |
| Quality of Pitches | ✓✓✓✓ | Range of Facilities | ✓✓✓✓ |

Directions

From A44 Oxford - Stratford-on-Avon road, take B4022 to Charlbury, just south of Enstone. Park is 2 miles on left. O.S.GR: SP365210.
GPS: N51:53.170 W01:28.248

Charges 2005

Per unit incl. 2 persons and electricity	£ 14.00 - £ 18.00
extra adult	£ 2.25
child (6-16 yrs)	£ 2.00
dog	free

Reservations

Advisable for B.Hs and peak season. Tel: 01608 810314. Email: bookings@cotswoldview.f9.co.uk

Open

Easter - 31 October.

UK2600 **Barnstones Caravan & Camping Park**

Great Bourton, Banbury OX17 1QU (Oxfordshire)

Three miles from Banbury and open all year round, this small, neat park provides an excellent point from which to explore the Cotswolds, Oxford and Stratford-upon-Avon. The 49 level pitches all have gravel hardstanding with a grass area for awnings (no groundsheets are allowed) and 10A electricity; 20 of these are fully serviced. Shrubs, flowers and an oval tarmac road convey a tidy impression throughout and the low level lighting is subtle but effective. A 36 pitch rally field (with 10A hook-ups) is near the main road, so some traffic noise is to be expected. New arrivals should report to the warden's caravan at the park entrance. The church in Great Bourton (250 m.) has a most unusual lych gate and there is a canal-side walk to Banbury (3 miles).

Facilities

The upgraded toilet block is small, but it can be heated and is quite adequate for the number of people it serves. Adjustable, unisex showers. Separate dishwashing and laundry rooms. Gas supplies. Small, fenced play area (grass and bark chipping base) adjacent to the entrance road. American motorhomes accepted by prior arrangement. Off site: Nearest shop 1 mile, supermarket 3 miles, pub 150 yds. Fishing, bicycle hire, golf and riding, all within 3 miles.

Open

All year.

At a glance

Welcome & Ambience	✓✓✓✓	Location	✓✓✓✓
Quality of Pitches	✓✓✓✓	Range of Facilities	✓✓✓

Directions

From M40 take exit 11 for Banbury. Turn off following signs for Chipping Norton, straight on at two small roundabouts. At third roundabout turn right on A423 signed Southam and in 2.5 miles turn right signed Great Bourton. Site entrance is 100 yds on right. O.S.GR: SP454454.

Charges 2006

Per unit incl. 2 persons and electricity	£ 8.50
extra person	£ 1.50
child (5-12 yrs)	£ 1.00
awning	£ 1.00 - £ 1.50
1 man tent	£ 5.50

OAPs less 50p per night. No credit cards.

Reservations

Contact park. Tel: 01295 750289.

UK2610 **Bo Peep Caravan Park**

Aynho Road, Adderbury, Banbury OX17 3NP (Oxfordshire)

Set amongst 85 acres of farmland and woodland, there is an air of spacious informality about this peaceful, friendly park and it blends perfectly with the surrounding views. Part of the Caravan Club's affiliated site scheme, non-members are also very welcome. All of the 112 numbered, pitches are large, have 16A electricity and, with the exception of eight that slope gently, are otherwise quite level. Gravel roads connect the various areas, such as Poppy Field, The Paddocks and The Warren, with reasonable shelter provided by hedges and trees. Pitches are mostly grassy and set around the perimeters, leaving central areas free for a liberal sprinkling of picnic tables. A separate 4 acre field is reserved for tents and 28 seasonal units occupy the hardstandings and some other pitches. Children are welcome but there is no play area. A network of circular walks around the site, including the pleasant river walk, has wide, well-kept paths and is being continually extended and developed; even bench seats and waste bins are provided. Dogs are also welcome on these walks. A 15 acre field is available for recreation use.

Facilities

The original toilet block has been supplemented by a larger, purpose-built unit, all clean and heated. Large showers with changing space, hairdryers. Dishwashing sinks under cover. Laundry rooms. Motorcaravan service point. Low level lighting. Small shop with off licence, gas and basic supplies. Information centre (with maps, leaflets, sample menus from local pubs, etc). Fishing (apply to office). Caravan storage. Caravan cleaning area. Log cabin information centre with internet access. Off site: Golf course next door. Banbury is just 3 miles, the famous Blenheim Palace 15 and Silverstone 16. Great day trips to Stratford upon Avon and Warwick and its castle.

At a glance

Welcome & Ambience	✓✓✓✓	Location	✓✓✓✓
Quality of Pitches	✓✓✓✓	Range of Facilities	✓✓✓✓

Directions

Adderbury village is on the A4260 Banbury - Oxford road. At traffic lights in Adderbury turn on B4100 signed Aynho; park is clearly signed, 0.5 miles on the right (0.5 mile drive). O.S.GR: SP482355.
GPS: N52:00.951 W01:17.966

Charges 2006

Per adult	£ 3.50 - £ 4.75
child (over 5 yrs)	£ 2.00

No credit cards.

Reservations

Advised and made with £10 deposit.
Tel: 01295 810605. Email: warden@bo-peep.co.uk

Open

18 March - 31 October.

UK2620 Wysdom Touring Park

The Bungalow, Burford School, Burford OX18 4JG (Oxfordshire)

You'll have to go a long way before you find anything else remotely like this site! The land is owned by Burford School and the enterprising caretaker and his wife, caravanners themselves, suggested that they create this wonderful place to raise money for the school (hence cheques payable to Burford School). It is really like putting your caravan or motorcaravan (tents are not accepted) into their own private garden. The 25 pitches (6 seasonal) are separated by hedges, all have electricity (16A) and a picnic table and some have their own tap. When we visited, the site was a true riot of colour. This is a lovely location for exploring the Cotswolds - Burford calls itself the 'Gateway to the Cotswolds'. The turn into the site off the school drive is narrow and the site is not therefore considered suitable for large motorhomes. It is also best to avoid school pick-up and drop-off when the drive can be congested. This is now an 'Adults Only' park.

Facilities

The small sanitary building offers all you need although, whilst it meets statistical requirements, with only one shower per sex (20p token) there may be a queue at times. Dogs permitted (max 2 per pitch). Off site: Burford is yards away with its famous shop lined hill full of antique shops, old coaching inns and all those 'interesting' shops it is so much fun rooting about in. Burford Golf Club is next door and you can walk from your caravan to the first tee.

Open

All year.

At a glance

Welcome & Ambience	✓✓✓	Location	✓✓✓✓
Quality of Pitches	✓✓✓✓	Range of Facilities	✓✓

Directions

From roundabout on A40 at Burford, take A361 and site is a few yards on the right signed Burford School. Once in school drive watch for narrow entrance to site on right in about 100 yards. O.S.GR: SP250115. GPS: N51:48.119 W01:38.362

Charges 2006

Per unit incl. 2 adults and electricity	£ 8.00 - £ 9.00
extra adult	£ 1.50
dog (max. 2)	free

No credit cards.

Reservations

Contact park. Tel: 01993 823207.

UK2690 Wellington Country Park

Riseley, Reading RG7 1SP (Berkshire)

Wellington Country Park is open to all on payment of an entry fee (entry for campers included in pitch fee) and many visit it for a day out. It contains a boating and fishing lake, a large adventure playground and other activities for children, nature trails, deer park, crazy golf, miniature railway and animal farm. The camping site is situated in a wood within the 350 acre park. It has 72 pitches, 10 with hardstanding and 56 with electricity hook-ups (10A). Some 'Premium' pitches are larger and have barbecues and picnic tables. There are several individual pitches and some small groups all within woodland clearings which gives a very rustic and casual feel to this site. It is a very pleasant setting and once the Country Park closes at 5.30 pm. all is very quiet. You should aim to arrive before 5.30 pm when the main park reception centre closes. Access to the site is through a locked gate (key from reception).

Facilities

The toilet block provides comfortable facilities including washbasins in cubicles and well equipped showers with good dry areas. Dishwashing sinks, and ample laundry. Shop stocks basics (from 1/5). Gas supplies. Fishing. Family events. Torch useful. Off site: Bus service at Risley 2 miles. Legoland and Windsor 30 minutes drive. Riding 1 mile. Golf 6 miles.

Open

Mid-February - early November.

At a glance

Welcome & Ambience	✓✓✓✓	Location	✓✓✓✓✓
Quality of Pitches	✓✓✓✓	Range of Facilities	✓✓✓

Directions

Park is signed at Riseley, off A32/A33 road between Reading and Basingstoke, and from M4. It is 4 miles south of M4 exit 11 and 7 miles north of M3 exit 5. O.S.GR: SU727628. GPS: N51:21.552 W00:57.670

Charges 2005

Per unit incl. up to 2 adults and 2 children	£ 10.00 - £ 20.75
extra adult	£ 2.00
child	£ 1.50
electricity	£ 1.75
dog	free

Reservations

Made with £16 non-returnable deposit (min 2 nights June, July or Aug. or 3 nights at B.Hs). Tel: 01189 326444. Email: info@wellington-country-park.co.uk

Wellington Country Park, Riseley, Reading, RG7 1SP
For further information please call: 0118 932 6444
Email: info@wellington-country-park.co.uk
www.wellington-country-park.co.uk

UK2930 Sheepcote Valley Caravan Club Site

East Brighton Park, Brighton BN2 5TS (East Sussex)

Brighton is without doubt the South of England's most popular seaside resort and the Caravan Club's Sheepcote Valley Site is a first class base from which to enjoy the many and diverse attractions both in the town and this area of the south coast. The site occupies a quiet situation in an almost fully enclosed valley in the South Downs, a mile north of the town's interesting Marina which has a super-store and good variety of shops and restaurants. A wide tarmac road winds its way through the site from reception, with gravel pitches on either side, leading to terraces with grass pitches on the lower slopes of the valley. With a total of 275 pitches, 169 have electricity (16A), 85 have hardstanding and 11 have water, drainage and TV sockets. Three grass terraces are for tents and these have hard parking nearby as a low fence prevents cars being taken onto the camping areas. Although there are a number of trees, many are young so do not yet provide shade. Flower beds add to the attractiveness of the site. The site fully lives up to the very high standards expected from the Caravan Club and provides a first class venue both for a quiet holiday and as a base from which to explore.

Facilities

Two well built, brick, heated sanitary blocks have excellent facilities including all washbasins in private cabins. In the main season a third timber clad building provides additional services near the tent places. Well equipped room for wheel chair users, another one for walking disabled and two baby and toddler wash rooms. Laundry facilities. Motorcaravan service point. Gas available. Milk and bread from reception. Play area with safety base. Off site: Brighton is 2 miles with a bus service from the entry road. Extensive recreation grounds adjacent.

Open

All year.

At a glance

Welcome & Ambience	✓✓✓✓	Location	✓✓✓✓
Quality of Pitches	✓✓✓✓	Range of Facilities	✓✓

Directions

Site is in eastern part of Brighton and signed from A259 coast road. From west on A259: at Palace Pier roundabout continue on A259 towards Newhaven for 1.25 miles, join dual carriageway and after 100 yards turn left at sign into Arundel Road. At mini-roundabout turn right into Wilson Avenue. After 100 yards, turn right into East Brighton Park. Continue for 0.5 miles, site on left. From east on A259: immediately after Roedean School take right hand slip road and turn into Roedean Road. Continue towards traffic lights and turn right into Wilson Avenue, then as above. O.S.GR: TQ341043.

Charges 2005

Per adult	£ 3.80 - £ 5.00
child (5-16 yrs)	£ 1.10 - £ 1.80
pitch incl. electricity (non-member)	£ 9.50 - £ 13.00

Reservations

Advised for high season with £5 deposit.
Tel: 01273 626546.

UK2900 Horam Manor Touring Park

Horam, Heathfield TN21 0YD (East Sussex)

In the heart of the Sussex countryside, this rural touring park is part of (but under separate management from) Horam Manor which has a farm museum, nature trail and several fishing lakes. The 90 pitches, 54 with electrical connections, are on two open meadows joined by a tarmac/gravel access road. The field nearer reception has an undulating surface, the second field is flatter but slopes - levelling blocks are needed for motorcaravans. Pitches are of generous size, those with electricity being numbered and marked. Both areas are ringed with a variety of mainly tall trees. The whole park, back from the main Eastbourne to Tunbridge Wells road, is a haven of peace and tranquillity. The site has no shop but the village is close, with supermarkets in Heathfield (3 miles). Two inns are within walking distance and the Lakeside cafe at the Farm Centre serves drinks and snacks (9.30 am. - 5 pm). The Craft Centre to the side of the site has some interesting exhibits, farm machinery and riding stables. The nature trail (with free access for campers) has walks ranging from 30 to 90 minutes in length (written guide available). Fishing is possible in 10 lakes on the estate (adults £4).

Facilities

The modern, well built toilet block (unheated) is fully equipped and is said to be cleaned four times daily. There are some curtained cubicles. Family room (access by key from reception) with shower, washbasin, toilet and baby bath, suitable also for disabled visitors (not ideal for wheelchairs). Laundry and dishwashing sinks. Washing machine. Gas supplies. Simple fenced play area. Up to two dogs per unit are accepted. Off site: Tennis (small fee) 200 yds. Golf within 1 mile. The coastal towns of Brighton, hastings and Eastbourne are within easy reach, as is the famousw Pantiles at Tunbridge Wells.

Open

1 March - 31 October.

At a glance

Welcome & Ambience	✓✓✓✓✓	Location	✓✓✓✓
Quality of Pitches	✓✓✓✓	Range of Facilities	✓✓✓

Directions

Horam is on the A267 between Tunbridge Wells and Eastbourne and entry to the park is signed at the recreation ground at southern edge of the village. O.S.GR: TQ577169. GPS: N50:55.907 E00:14.410

Charges 2005

Per unit incl. 2 adults and 2 children under 18)	£ 13.50
extra adult	£ 4.50
extra child	£ 1.50
electricity	£ 1.95 - £ 2.85
dog (max. 2)	free
No credit cards.	

Reservations

Contact park. Tel: 01435 813662.
Email: camp@horam-manor.co.uk

UK2920 Bay View Park

Old Martello Road, Pevensey Bay BN24 6DX (East Sussex)

Under new ownership, this friendly beach-side park is located at the end of a private road right beside the beautiful Sussex coast. There are 5.5 acres of grass (some areas are a little uneven) divided into two separate areas and surrounded by a low bank and hedges to give shelter if it is windy. The 50 touring pitches (80 sq.m, most with 10A electricity and some with hardstanding) are neatly marked by numbered posts, the majority divided by low wooden rails. Several caravan holiday homes for hire are at the back of the park. It is an ideal site for a family beach holiday. A newly developed cycle/walking path leads to Pevensey Bay and Eastbourne.

Facilities
Toilet facilities are housed in two superior 'portacabin' style buildings which are kept very clean and are heated when necessary. Showers on payment (20p). Laundry room. Motorcaravan services. Well stocked shop (open long hours as the managers live next to it). Gas available. Well made and fenced play area (10 years and under). Winter caravan storage. Off site: Sailing club. Sea fishing. Indoor swimming pool 1 mile. Golf 2 miles.

At a glance
Welcome & Ambience ✓✓✓✓✓ Location ✓✓✓✓
Quality of Pitches ✓✓✓✓ Range of Facilities ✓✓✓

Directions
Park is about 1 mile west of Pevensey Bay and 2 miles east of Eastbourne, off the A259 Pevensey Bay road. O.S.GR: TQ648028. GPS: N50:48.000 E00:20.279

Charges 2005
Per unit incl. 2 persons	£ 11.00 - £ 15.00
child (2-16 yrs)	£ 2.00

Reservations
Made with deposit (£25). Tel: 01323 768688. Email: holidays@bay-view.co.uk

Open
14 April - 31 October.

UK2960 Crazy Lane Tourist Caravan Park

Crazy Lane, Sedlescombe, Battle TN33 0QT (East Sussex)

Formerly known as Whydown Farm, this peaceful, traditional style, two acre park has just 36 pitches arranged on grassy terraces, all with electric hook-ups (5/10A) and 4 with hardstanding. It may be best to phone to make sure space is available before travelling long distances. Set in the heart of '1066 country' with its historical links, other local attractions within easy reach include the very pretty village of Sedlescombe, two steam railways, an organic vineyard, Rye with its quaint cobbled streets and of course Battle itself. This is an ideal park for couples.

Facilities
The tiny but well maintained sanitary unit (unheated) includes controllable hot showers (on payment), laundry facilities, dishwashing sinks and a suite for disabled visitors. Shop at reception. Caravan storage. Off site: Bus stop and pub in the village. Hastings with its beaches 6.5 miles.

Open
March - October.

At a glance
Welcome & Ambience ✓✓✓✓ Location ✓✓✓✓
Quality of Pitches ✓✓✓✓ Range of Facilities ✓✓✓

Directions
From A21, 100 yards south of junction with B2244 (to Sedlescombe) turn into Crazy Lane, where site is signed on the right hand side. O.S.GR: TQ782170.

Charges 2005
Per unit incl. 2 adults, electricity	£ 13.00 - £ 16.00
extra person over 12 yrs	£ 1.50
No credit cards.	

Reservations
Contact site. Tel: 01424 870147. Email: info@crazylane.co.uk

UK2965 Brakes Coppice Park

Forewood Lane, Crowhurst, Battle TN33 9AB (East Sussex)

Brakes Coppice Park is a small and secluded site set in woodland just a mile away from historic Battle. Reached by an uneven, winding private track, it is signed to prevent visitors taking a wrong turn to the nearby farm of the same name. The site has 30 grassy pitches, 21 with 6A electricity and TV aerial points, in a gently sloping field. An area of 15 small pitches has been set aside for adults only. A further area near a small fishing lake provides a few extra pitches. As well as fishing, visitors can enjoy walking in the surrounding woods and there is an attractive wooden play area for younger children in the centre of the main field. The reception building at the site entrance also doubles as the shop.

Facilities
The single toilet block is very basic but clean with coin operated showers (one for men, one for ladies). There are plans to add new facilities for disabled visitors. Washing machine, dryer, iron and board. Dishwashing sinks with hot water are outside but under cover. Shop. Gas supplies. Fishing permits from reception. Off site: Pubs and shops in Crowhurst and Battle. Crowhurst station 10 minutes walk.

Open
1 March - 31 October.

At a glance
Welcome & Ambience ✓✓✓✓✓ Location ✓✓✓✓
Quality of Pitches ✓✓✓ Range of Facilities ✓✓✓

Directions
From Battle follow A2100 towards Hastings for about 2 miles. Turn right on Telham Lane (Crowhurst). Continue into Foreword Lane and turn left on private track shortly after passing sign for Crowhurst village. O.S.GR: TQ764131. GPS: N50:53.439 E00:30.425

Charges 2005
Per pitch with 2 persons	£ 11.00 - £ 12.00
incl. electricity	£ 12.75 - £ 13.75
child (5-15 yrs)	£ 0.50

Reservations
Bookings are advisable and are made with deposit. Tel: 01424 830322. Email: brakesco@btinternet.com

UK3120 Gate House Wood Touring Park

Ford Lane, Wrotham Heath, Sevenoaks TN15 7SD (Kent)

This sheltered park, which opened for its first season in '98, has been created in a former quarry where all the pitches are on well drained grass. A spacious paved entrance with a new reception building and well stocked shop, leads on to the park itself. The 60 pitches are level and open with a few small trees, two brick built barbecue units, and 40 electric hook-ups (10A). A playground has swings, seesaw and a slide, all set on a safety base, and the entire site is enclosed by grassy banks on three sides, with a wild flower walk around the top. Local attractions include the nearby Country Park at West Malling.

Facilities

Comprehensive toilet facilities are well maintained, including a well equipped family room, also designed for disabled people. Laundry and dishwashing room. No dogs or other pets. Units greater than 25' overall are not admitted. Off site: Within walking distance are three pubs. Golf 1 mile. Riding 3 miles. Foshing 7 miles.

Open

1 March - 30 November.

At a glance

Welcome & Ambience	✓✓✓✓	Location	✓✓✓
Quality of Pitches	✓✓✓✓	Range of Facilities	✓✓✓

Directions

From M26 junction 2a, take A20 eastwards towards Wrotham Heath and Maidstone. Just past junction with A25, and opposite the Royal Oak pub, turn left into Ford Lane, and park is immediately on left. O.S.GR: TQ630580. GPS: N51:18.008 E00:20.723

Charges 2005

Per unit incl. 2 adults	£ 10.00 - £ 13.50
child (3-12 yrs)	£ 1.00

No credit cards.

Reservations

Made with deposit. Tel: 01732 843062. Email: liane_allsop@gatehousewood.freeserve.co.uk

UK3030 Tanner Farm Touring Caravan & Camping Park

Goudhurst Road, Marden TN12 9ND (Kent)

Tanner Farm is a top class, quality park, developed as part of a family working farm in the heart of the Weald of Kent. It is surrounded by orchards, oast houses, lovely countryside and delightful small villages and the owners are much concerned with conserving the natural beauty of the environment. Visitors are welcome to walk around the farm. The park extends over 15 acres, most of which is level. The grass meadowland has been semi-landscaped by planting saplings, etc. which units back onto, as the owners do not wish to regiment pitches into rows. Places are numbered but not marked, allowing plenty of space between units which, with large open areas, gives a pleasant, comfortable atmosphere. There are 100 pitches, all with 16A electricity, 26 with hardstanding, 20 with water and 1 with waste water point. The farm drive links the park with the B2079 and a group of oast houses (listed heritage buildings) with a duck pond in front, along with rare pigs, pygmy goats, lambs, etc. make a focal point. The park is a member of the Caravan Club's 'managed under contract' scheme; non-members are also welcome.

Facilities

Two heated, well cared for sanitary units include some washbasins in private cubicles in both units. Purpose built facilities for disabled visitors. Bathroom (£1 token) and baby facilities in the newer block (this block is not opened Nov - Easter). Small launderette. Dishwashing sinks. Motorcaravan service point. Small shop/reception (opening hours and stock limited in winter) and reception. Gas supplies. Play area. Fishing on site (on payment). Torches may be useful. Caravan storage all year. Off site: Riding and golf within 6 miles, leisure centres and sailing facilities near. Many National Trust attractions in the area.

At a glance

Welcome & Ambience	✓✓✓✓	Location	✓✓✓✓✓
Quality of Pitches	✓✓✓✓✓	Range of Facilities	✓✓✓✓

Directions

Park is 2.5 miles south of Morden on B2079 towards Oakhurst. O.S.GR: TQ732417.

Charges 2005

Per unit incl. electriciry	£ 5.00 - £ 8.00
adult	£ 3.30 - £ 4.80
child (5-16 yrs)	£ 1.10 - £ 1.60

Only one car per pitch permitted.

Reservations

Essential for high season and B.Hs, recommended for other times. Made with deposit £10. Tel: 01622 832399. Email: enquiries@tannerfarmpark.co.uk

Open

All year.

(131)

Pine Lodge

We are open all year round for Touring and Camping

01622 730018

Ashford Road
Hollingbourne
Kent ME17 1XH

for more information visit: www.pinelodgetouringpark.co.uk

UK3050 Pine Lodge Touring Park

Ashford Road, Hollingbourne, Maidstone ME17 1XH (Kent)

Set in the heart of Kent on the outskirts of the county town of Maidstone, Pine Lodge is central for many of the historical and scenic attractions of this county. Surrounded by rolling hills, farmland and trees, the rectangular field is on a slight slope. A tarmac, one-way road circles the site with pitches set against hedges around the perimeter and in a figure of eight in the centre with picnic areas. Attractive trees have been planted for decoration and shade. There are 88 pitches, all with electricity (16A), 35 with gravel hardstanding and 2 fully serviced. This is a useful park near the main London - Folkestone - Dover M20 and access from the A20 road is wide. However, there is some background traffic noise. The park is very convenient for events staged at Leeds Castle and is a useful overnight stop between London and the Channel ports.

Facilities

Good sanitary facilities at the entrance to the park include metered showers (20p coin), laundry and dishwashing facilities, plus a shower and toilet room for disabled visitors. Motorcaravan services. Basic supplies and gas are available from reception plus tourist information. Small play area. Dogs are not accepted. Off site: Golf 0.5 mile. Local shops 1 mile (Bearsted) or 3.5 miles (Maidstone). Riding 2 miles. Fishing 5 miles.

Open

All year.

At a glance

Welcome & Ambience	✓✓✓✓	Location	✓✓✓
Quality of Pitches	✓✓✓✓	Range of Facilities	✓✓✓

Directions

From M20 junction 8, at A20 roundabout, turn towards Maidstone and Bearsted. Park is about 0.5 miles on the left. O.S.GR: TQ808548.
GPS: N51:15.855 E00:06.222

Charges 2005

Per unit incl. 2 adults, electricity	£ 13.00 - £ 15.25
extra adult	£ 4.00
child (3-14 yrs)	£ 1.50
awning or extra tent	£ 1.00 - £ 1.50

Less 10% for 7 nights or more.

Reservations

Advised for bank holidays and special events at Leeds Castle, contact park. Tel: 01622 730018.
Email: booking@pinelodgetouringpark.co.uk

UK3040 Broadhembury Caravan & Camping Park

Steeds Lane, Kingsnorth, Ashford TN26 1NQ (Kent)

In quiet countryside just outside Ashford and within easy reach of Dover, Folkestone and the Kent coast, this sheltered park is attractively landscaped. It takes 65 touring units of any type with several seasonal units and 25 caravan holiday homes (5 for hire) in separate areas. The well kept pitches are on level grass and backed by tall, neat hedges, with over 50 electricity connections (10A). In addition, 4 pitches are fully serviced including16A electricity and 8 more have double hardstanding plus a grass area for an awning. The welcome is friendly at this popular park and it is often full in the main season, with a good proportion of continental visitors, so reservation is advisable. Thoughtfully considered amenities include a very good toilet block, well equipped campers' kitchen and provision for children of all ages. Security arrangements are excellent – the gates are closed at 11 pm. in high season with coded entry. For those who would like a trip to France, the International railway terminal is at Ashford (Paris in two hours) - take your passport. A member of the Best of British group.

Facilities

The recently upgraded toilet block is well equipped including under-floor heating and is kept very clean. Private cabins. High quality facilities for disabled visitors (can also be used as a family bathroom). Well equipped laundry room. Good campers' kitchen, fully enclosed with dishwashing sinks, microwaves, fridge and freezer, all free of charge. Motorcaravan service point. Well stocked shop (bread and papers to order) and comprehensive tourist information. Internet access. TV and pool room, games room with video games, table football and table tennis. Two play areas (one for children under 7 yrs). Play field away from the touring area. Dog exercise field - up to two dogs per pitch are accepted. Off site: Fishing 300 m. Golf 1 mile. Riding 2 miles. Bicycle hire 3 miles. Beach 12 miles.

At a glance

Welcome & Ambience	✓✓✓✓✓	Location	✓✓✓✓
Quality of Pitches	✓✓✓✓✓	Range of Facilities	✓✓✓✓

Directions

From M20 junction 10 take A2070. After 2 miles follow sign for Kingsnorth. Turn left at second crossroads in Kingsnorth village. O.S.GR: TR010382.

Charges 2005

Per unit incl. 2 persons	£ 12.00 - £ 17.00
with services	£ 18.00 - £ 20.00
extra person	£ 5.00
child (5-16 yrs)	£ 3.50

Less 10% excl. July/Aug. 7 nights or more (booked).

Reservations

Essential for B.Hs and peak season and made with deposit (min. 3 nights at Easter or Spr. B.H). Tel: 01233 620859.
Email: enquiries@broadhembury.co.uk

Open

All year.

UK3070 Canterbury Camping & Caravanning Club Site

Bekesbourne Lane, Canterbury CT3 4AB (Kent)

Situated just off the A257 Sandwich road, about 1.5 miles from the centre of Canterbury, this site is an ideal base for exploring Canterbury and the north Kent coast, as well as being a good stop-over to and from the Dover ferries, and the Folkestone Channel Tunnel terminal. There are 200 pitches, 86 with electric hook-ups (10/16A) and, except at the very height of the season, you are likely to find a pitch, although not necessarily with electricity. Most of the pitches are on well kept grass with hundreds of saplings planted, but there are also 21 pitches with hardstanding. Some pitches do slope so blocks are advised. A good sized overnight area for late arrivals can be reached even when the barriers are down. The site is adjacent to Bekepond nature reserve and within walking distance of Howletts Zoo. Although the busy A257 is close, there is minimal noise from the traffic. Note: power lines cross the site.

Facilities

Two modern toilet blocks, the main one with a laundry room, a room for dishwashing, an outside vegetable preparation area, and recycling bins. Motorcaravan service point. Reception stocks a small range of essential foods, milk and gas. Excellent tourist information room. Children's play area with equipment on bark chippings. Off site: Golf adjacent. Bicycle hire 2 miles.

Open

All year.

At a glance

Welcome & Ambience	✓✓✓✓✓	Location	✓✓✓✓
Quality of Pitches	✓✓✓✓	Range of Facilities	✓✓✓

Directions

From A2 take Canterbury exit and follow signs for Sandwich - A257. After passing Howe military barracks turn right into Bekesbourne Lane opposite golf course. O.S.GR: TR172577.
GPS: N51:16.614 E01:06.812

Charges 2005

Per adult	£ 4.30 - £ 6.40
child (6-18 yrs)	£ 1.90
non-member pitch fee	£ 5.00

Reservations

Necessary and made with deposit; contact site or Central Reservations 0870 243 3331.
Tel: 01227 463216.

UK3130 Sandwich Leisure Park

Woodnesborough Road, Sandwich CT13 0AA (Kent)

A pleasant well kept site, with modern facilities, this park is in one of England's historic old Cinque ports and within walking distance of all its attractions, shops and services. From the entrance barrier by reception, you drive through the area of privately owned holiday homes, to reach the two touring fields which have 190 pitches, all on grass with electric hook-ups (10A). There are 80 multi-service pitches with electricity, TV, water and waste water drain, nine of which have hardstandings. The site is encouraging wildlife in the newer second field by planting hedges of native varieties and these will give greater privacy as they develop. A railway runs along one side of the site and there is a little rail noise at times during the day but it is quiet at night. The site is well lit at night and all roads are well surfaced. Children will love the large, fenced adventure playground with its tube slides etc. which is on a bark surface.

Facilities

Stylish sanitary building provides washbasins in cubicles, controllable hot showers, plus a room which can be heated with some family suites and a full suite for disabled people (radar key). Dishwashing sinks under cover at each end of the building. Laundry in reception building with washing machines, dryers, spin dryer and ironing facility. Adventure playground. Note; skateboarding, rollerblading, skating, scooters and cycling are not permitted on site. Off site: Supermarket 5 minutes walk from the site entrance. Sandwich has a market on Thursdays. In and around the town are a folk museum, Roman fort, nature reserve, swing bridge, the old gaol, weavers, a sports and leisure centre and further afield is the Dreamland Fun Park. Fishing 3 miles, golf and beach 2 miles.

At a glance

Welcome & Ambience	✓✓✓	Location	✓✓✓✓
Quality of Pitches	✓✓✓✓	Range of Facilities	✓✓✓

Directions

Sandwich is mid-way between Ramsgate and Deal, with access from the A256. The town's streets are narrow and there is a one-way system in operation. Follow the brown campsite signs from anywhere in the town centre, the site is to the west of town, just after a railway level crossing. O.S.GR: TR 330575.
GPS: N51:16.443 E01:19.935

Charges 2005

Per pitch incl. up to 5 people and electricity	£ 9.50 - £ 14.75
extra person	£ 1.50
multi-service pitch, plus	£ 4.00
awning	£ 1.00
one man tent	£ 6.50 - £ 9.00

Reservations

Advisable for BHs and peak season. Tel: 01304 612681. Email: info@coastandcountryleisure.com

Open

1 March - 31 October.

(133)

UK3060 **Yew Tree Park**

Stone Street, Petham, Canterbury CT4 5PL (Kent)

Yew Tree Park is a small, quiet site located in the heart of the Kent countryside overlooking the Chartham Downs. Just 5 miles south of Canterbury and 8 miles north of the M20, it is ideally placed either to explore the delights of the ancient city or the many attractions of eastern and coastal Kent. Its nearness to the Channel ports also makes it useful for a night stop on the way to, or on return from, the continent. If catching a late evening ferry you may remain on site after 12 noon for a small payment. With some caravan holiday homes, the site also has 45 pitches for tourers and tents. The 20 with electricity (10A) are marked on mainly level grass either side of the entrance road, the remainder unmarked on a rather attractive, sloping area, left natural with trees and bushes creating cosy little recesses in which to pitch. This neat, tidy for park, created by resident proprietors Derek and Dee Zanders, makes an excellent base away from the hurly-burly of life where you can enjoy the scenery and have the opportunity for walking, riding, visiting local places of interest or for Cross-Channel excursions.

Facilities

Two brick-built sanitary blocks (one for each sex) can be heated. Washbasins with warm water from a single tap, and four showers (on payment). Extra toilets on the edge of the camping area. Recently added is a toilet/shower room for families or disabled visitors. Laundry and dishwashing sinks, plus a washing machine, dryer and iron. Gas supplies. Outdoor swimming pool (60 x 30 ft. open June-Sept). Torches may be useful. Dogs are not accepted. Off site: Riding 4 miles. Golf 6 miles. Bicycle hire 5 miles. The County cricket ground is 4 miles.

Open

Easter - early October.

At a glance

Welcome & Ambience	✓✓✓	Location	✓✓✓✓
Quality of Pitches	✓✓✓✓	Range of Facilities	✓✓✓

Directions

Park is on B2068 Canterbury-Folkestone road. From south, take exit 11 from the M20. From Canterbury, ignore signs to Petham and Waltham on B2068 and continue towards Folkestone. From either direction, turn into road beside the Chequers Inn, turn left into park and follow road to owners' house/reception. O.S.GR: TR138507. GPS: N51:13.008 E01:03.491

Charges 2005

Per unit incl. 2 adults	£ 10.00 - £ 15.00
small tent	£ 9.00 - £ 14.00
extra adult	£ 2.00 - £ 3.00
child (2-16 yrs)	£ 1.00 - £ 2.00
serviced pitch	£ 12.50 - £ 17.00

Reservations

Made with deposit of £5 per night.
Tel: 01227 700306. Email: info@yewtreepark.com

UK3090 **Black Horse Farm Caravan Club Site**

385 Canterbury Road, Densole, Folkestone CT18 7BG (Kent)

This neat, tidy and attractive six-acre park, owned by the Caravan Club, is situated amidst pleasant farming country in the village of Densole on the Downs just 4 miles north of Folkestone, 8 northeast of Dover and 11 south of Canterbury. This makes it ideal for an overnight stop travelling to or from the continent via the Channel Ports or the Tunnel, or as a base for visiting the many attractions of this part of southeast England. Accessed directly from the A260, the tarmac entrance road leads past reception towards the top field which has gravel hardstanding pitches with a grass area for awnings (possibly some road noise), past hedging to the smaller middle area with 8 hardstandings, then to the large bottom field which has been redeveloped to give 140 large pitches, all with electricity (16A). A late arrivals area and pitches for 'one-nighters' are now located in the top field. Opposite the entrance is a general store and newsagent and within 100 m, a pub and filling station.

Facilities

The carefully thought out and well constructed toilet blocks, one below reception and the other at the far end of the site, have washbasins in private cabins with curtains, good sized shower compartments, a baby room and facilities for disabled visitors, laundry and washing-up facilities, all well heated in cool weather. Motorcaravan service point. Gas supplies. Play area. A fish and chip van calls April to September. Caravan storage. Off site: Riding 1 mile. Golf and fishing 5 miles.

At a glance

Welcome & Ambience	✓✓✓✓✓	Location	✓✓✓✓✓
Quality of Pitches	✓✓✓✓✓	Range of Facilities	✓✓✓

Directions

Directly by the A260 Folkestone - Canterbury road, 2 miles north of junction with A20. Follow signs for Canterbury. O.S.GR: TR211418. GPS: N51:07.957 E01:09.509

Charges 2005

Per adult	£ 3.30 - £ 4.80
child (5-16 yrs)	£ 1.10 - £ 1.60
pitch incl. electricity (non-member)	£ 9.00 - £ 14.00

Reservations

Advised at all times - contact the Warden.
Tel: 01303 892665.

Open

All year.

UK3325 The Oaks Caravan Park

Chapel Road, Bucklesham, Ipswich IP10 0BT (Suffolk)

Situated between Felixstowe and Ipswich and with views over open farmland, this pleasant adult only touring park provides access to the surrounding countryside and towns, including the River Deben, Woodbridge and the Suffolk Heritage coast. Since opening in the summer of 2003, the park has quickly established many repeat visitors. Many newly planted trees and shrubs around the perimeter and across the length of the site, already provide screening and shade for the 89 marked touring pitches. The well maintained grass pitches are laid out either side of an oval gravel path. A summer house in the centre contains local information, newspapers and a small patio area with tables and chairs where visitors can sit and read. The site provides a minibus service in the evenings to local pubs and restaurants (by prior arrangement).

Facilities

The single modern sanitary block provides bright and clean toilet and shower facilities, as well as a covered dishwashing area and motorcaravan point. Facilities for disabled people are planned. Gas is available at reception. Bicycle hire. Off site: Bus service outside park. Minibus service in the evenings by prior arrangement to nearby local pubs/restaurants. Riding 1 mile. Fishing and golf 4 miles. Beach 5 miles.

Open

1 April - 31 October.

At a glance

Welcome & Ambience	✓✓✓✓	Location	✓✓✓✓
Quality of Pitches	✓✓✓✓	Range of Facilities	✓✓✓

Directions

Site is situated between Bucklesham and Kirton. From the A12 (south) or A14(12) (north) take A14 towards Felixstowe. Continue for about 5 miles and turn left signed Bucklesham and Brightwell. Continue for 1 mile, past Tenth Road on the left, take next right signed Kirton and Newbourne. Park is on the right in 550 yds O.S.GR: TM261411.

Charges 2005

Per unit incl. 2 adults, electricity	£ 14.00
tent incl. 2 adults	£ 12.00
extra adult	£ 1.50
dog	free

Reservations

Contact site. Tel: 01394 448837.
Email: oakscaravanpark@aol.com

UK3345 The Dell Caravan & Camping Park

Beyton Road, Thurston, Bury St Edmunds IP31 3RB (Suffolk)

Close to the A14 and surrounded by farmland, this small touring site, four miles east of Bury St Edmunds, provides a convenient base to explore the nearby town and surrounding villages or as a stopover point. The site has been much improved by the present owners, including the addition of an excellent, newly fitted sanitary block in 2005. Two additional unisex private toilet and shower cubicles should also be opened by 2006. The site has 100 pitches, 80 with electricity. This number includes a separate field with up to 12 pitches set under trees available for either tourers working locally, as well as any visitors who prefer shaded areas. The main touring field has some shade from well maintained hedges and the trees bordering the site. All pitches have access to the site's facilities. Food is available from local village pubs within two miles of the park. There is some noise from the nearby A14, especially to the south side of the park, but otherwise the site provides a quiet base for tourers to explore the area.

Facilities

Excellent and ample toilet and spacious shower facilities are provided within a purpose built sanitary block. Ladies' toilets include a private bathroom and toilet. Family bathroom with bath, shower and baby changing facilities. Toilet/shower for disabled people. Laundry room (£5 deposit for keys). Dishwashing facilities (free). Off site: Bus service 1 mile. Fishing, golf and riding 3 miles. Local pubs and restaurants in Thurston and neighbouring villages.

At a glance

Welcome & Ambience	✓✓✓✓	Location	✓✓✓
Quality of Pitches	✓✓✓✓	Range of Facilities	✓✓✓

Directions

From the A14 take exit for Thurston and Beyton, 4 miles east of Bury St Edmunds. Follow signs to Thurston. Park is on the left, shortly after arriving at Thurston and signed from Beyton. O.S.GR: TL928640.

Charges 2006

Per unit incl. 2 persons	£ 10.00
incl. electricity	£ 12.00

Reservations

Contact site. Tel: 01359 270121.
Email: thedellcaravanpark@btinternet.com

Open

All year.

UK3330 Moat Barn Touring Caravan Park

Dallinghoo Road, Bredfield, Woodbridge IP13 6BD (Suffolk)

Mike Allen opened this small, new touring park in April 2000. Family run, it provides just 25 level pitches, all with electricity hook-ups (10A) and a circular roadway has been added. As yet, the hedges have not matured, but the pitches are spacious and the park provides a tranquil environment making it very pleasant to use as a base. Walkers and cyclists will enjoy this location - the park is on the Suffolk Heritage Cycle Route, and also the Hull - Harwich National Cycle Route. Moat Barn also offers bed and breakfast.

Facilities	Directions
The well equipped sanitary block can be heated. A separate unit houses a dishwashing sink. Laundry and shop planned. Motorcaravan service point.	From Ipswich on A12 to Lowestoft, after Hasketon roundabout take first left signed Bredfield. At village pump turn right and follow road past public house and church. Continue through S-bends and, after 200 yards, site entrance is on left, just after farm buildings. From Lowestoft, take right turn to Bredfield just before Hasketon roundabout, then as above. O.S.GR: TM 270537
Reservations	
Advised, especially for B.Hs and made with £10 deposit. Tel: 01473 737 520.	
Open	**Charges 2006**
1 March - 15 January.	Per unit incl. 2 adults and electricity £ 12.00
At a glance	extra person or car £ 1.00
Welcome & Ambience ✓✓✓✓✓ Location ✓✓✓✓✓	
Quality of Pitches ✓✓✓✓ Range of Facilities ✓✓✓✓	

UK3340 Polstead Touring Park

Holt Road, Polstead, Colchester CO6 5BZ (Suffolk)

This lovely 30-pitch touring park in the peaceful Suffolk countryside (in the heart of 'Constable Country') is an ideal base from which to explore many places of interest. These include Flatford Mill, the scene for Constable's famous painting, Sudbury (the birthplace of Gainsborough), Long Melford with its Hall and Colchester, Britain's oldest town. The very neat and well cared for park offers really good facilities, its 30 level pitches all having electricity. Well established hedges separate the pitches and 25 have gravel hardstanding. There is little on-site to occupy younger visitors.

Facilities	Directions
The toilet block offers large spacious showers. Facilities for disabled visitors are provided in both men's and ladies' rooms (showers large enough for wheelchair access). Enclosed dishwashing area. Laundry. Reception sells basic supplies. Rally field. Caravan storage. Off site: Fishing and golf nearby. Pub serving food, 3 minutes walk.	From A1071 Hadleigh - Sudbury road, just past the 'Brewers Arms' public house, turn left just before a water tower towards Polstead; park is 250 yards on the right. O.S.GR: TL985403.
	Charges guide
	Per adult £ 3.00 - £ 3.50
	child (4-16 yrs) £ 1.50 - £ 2.00
Open	pitch £ 2.00 - £ 4.00
All year.	No credit cards.
At a glance	**Reservations**
Welcome & Ambience ✓✓✓✓✓ Location ✓✓✓✓✓	Made with £10 deposit. Tel: 01787 211969.
Quality of Pitches ✓✓✓✓ Range of Facilities ✓✓✓✓	

UK3350 Church Farm Holiday Park

Church Farm Road, Aldeburgh IP15 5DW (Suffolk)

This area of the Suffolk coast has always been a popular destination for visitors, with properties such as the beach huts at Southwold fetching prices the same as terraced houses further inland. The coast with its shingle beaches is a haven for birds and other wildlife. The town of Aldeburgh is only 15 minutes walk from this site where one can find good food and drink and many gift and food shops. The famous Aldeburgh lifeboat station is open to visitors and there are many other places of interest within easy reach. Church Farm is mainly for caravan holiday homes but the large front field is used for tourers, with 85 pitches all offering full services including 16A electricity. Many pitches are surrounded by young hedges giving shelter and creating a sun trap. This is a quiet park with no facilities for children (for example, a play area) although it is close to the beach. It will appeal to older couples or young families.

Facilities	Directions
The single toilet block has spacious cubicles with free showers and adequate hot water at washbasins. Laundry room. Gas supplies. Off site: Bus service 0.5 - 1 mile. Shops, pubs, etc. 15 minutes walk. Beach 5 minutes walk. Fishing and bicycle hire 1 mile. Riding 2 miles.	On arrival at Aldeburgh, site is signed at roundabout towards Thorpeness. Where road meets seafront, site is on left. From town centre follow seafront to site on left at end of town. O.S.GR: TM465572.
	Charges 2005
Open	Per pitch £ 12.00 - £ 14.00
Easter - 31 October.	with services £ 16.00 - £ 18.00
At a glance	**Reservations**
Welcome & Ambience ✓✓✓✓ Location ✓✓✓✓✓	Contact site. Tel: 01728 453433.
Quality of Pitches ✓✓✓✓ Range of Facilities ✓✓✓	Email: aldeburgh@amberleisure.com

UK3370 Kessingland Beach Holiday Park

Near Lowestoft NR33 7RN (Suffolk)

Set near to the most easterly point in the UK, this park offers all you need for that total family holiday experience. If you so wish you need never leave Kessingland Beach until your holiday ends. Children will be kept busy with swimming and games of all description, there is evening entertainment for all ages and a selection of bars and restaurants. Although mainly a park for static caravan holiday homes, there is a good touring area here with quite spacious pitching. Electricity hook-ups are available. The toilet block is old but it is kept in good condition and was remarkably clean and tidy at the time of our visit (August). There are plans to rebuild the block. If you do venture further afield, there is lots to see and do here on the Suffolk coast. Pleasurewood Hills Theme Park is less than 30 minutes away (a day out for the whole family), Oulton Broad is nearby with its weekly power boat racing.

Facilities

The toilet block is old but is well maintained and cleaned (a new block is planned). Dishwashing and laundry. Bars, restaurants and entertainment complex. Indoor and outdoor swimming pools. Play area. Shop. Tennis courts. Amusements. Crazy golf. Bicycle hire. Off site: Beach and sea fishing 100 yds. Golf and riding 3 miles.

Open

April - 19 September.

At a glance

Welcome & Ambience	✓✓✓✓✓	Location	✓✓✓✓✓
Quality of Pitches	✓✓✓	Range of Facilities	✓✓✓✓

Directions

From roundabout on A12 near Lowestoft signed Kessingland village, follow road through village. At beach take sharp right then follow road to end into site (narrow road). O.S.GR: TM535859

Charges 2005

Per unit	£ 5.00 - £ 23.00
tent pitch	£ 2.00 - £ 20.00
dog	free - £ 3.00

Reservations

Essential for high season and made with deposit (£5 per night). Tel: 01502 740636.

UK3480 Little Lakeland Caravan Park

Wortwell, Harleston IP20 0EL (Norfolk)

This peaceful hideaway with its own fishing lake is tucked behind the houses and gardens that border the village main street. It is a traditional, mature little park with just 58 pitches. There are several caravan holiday homes and long stay units, but there should always be around 22 places for tourers. The pitches are mostly individual ones separated by mature hedges and trees. Fishing in the attractive lake is free of charge and solely for the use of campers (bream, tench, roach, perch and carp). Places to visit nearby include The Cider Place at Ilketshall St Lawrence, The Otter Trust at Earsham, and there are many local way-marked walks around Wortwell and nearby Harleston (which has a market every Wednesday). A member of the Countryside Discovery group.

Facilities

A modern, heated toilet block provides washbasins all in cubicles for ladies, and one for men. Fully equipped laundry. Separate en-suite room for disabled visitors also has facilities for baby changing. A further unit (also heated) by reception provides a shower, WC and basin per sex and is used mostly in the colder months. Reception stocks gas and some basic essentials. Small play area. Library in the summer house. Fishing (max. 4 rods per unit). Off site: Bus service on the main road 250 yds. Riding 6 miles. Golf 4 miles.

Open

15 March - 31 October.

At a glance

Welcome & Ambience	✓✓✓✓✓	Location	✓✓✓✓✓
Quality of Pitches	✓✓✓✓	Range of Facilities	✓✓✓✓

Directions

Approaching from Diss, leave A143 at roundabout signed Wortwell. Continue to village, pass 'The Bell' public house then a garage on the right, after which turn right at first bungalow (Little Lakeland Lodge) watching carefully for signs. Site is down lane, 250 yards on right. O.S.GR: TM270850.

Charges 2005

Per unit incl. 2 adults	£ 9.30 - £ 11.60
incl. electricity	£ 11.30 - £ 13.60
child (4-16 yrs)	£ 1.20

No credit cards.

Reservations

Advisable for B.Hs and peak season; made with £20 deposit or full fee if less. Tel: 01986 788646. Email: information@littlelakeland.co.uk

UK3390 **The Dower House Touring Park**

Thetford Forest, East Harling NR16 2SE (Norfolk)

Set on 20 acres in the heart of Britain's largest forest on the Suffolk and Norfolk borders, the Dower House provides quiet woodland walks and cycle ways, with an abundance of wildlife. David and Karen Bushell, owners for many years, continue to upgrade the facilities without compromising the park's natural features. There are now 120 really large pitches with electricity available (10A). Most are level, although given the forest location there are a few tree roots. A fourth field provides 60 pitches for tents. Six pitches for visitors with mobility problems are linked by a path to the main facilities. The Dower House, as well as being the owners' home, houses a pleasant bar that also serves bar food (weekends only in low season) and a takeaway. A pleasant patio area is used for occasional entertainment at weekends and there is a small swimming pool. A torch is necessary as there is no site lighting other than at the facilities.

Facilities

Two toilet blocks - a small, refurbished one near the entrance, and a larger one with a baby room. A separate building houses the showers (5 for each sex and 20p) and a unit for disabled people. Dishwashing room, including a lower sink for children or disabled people. Laundry room with washing machine and dryer. Separate licensed shop doubling as reception and open daily in the season, on request at other times. Gas supplies. Information room. TV and quiet rooms (no games machines). A smallish swimming pool (only 1.1 m. deep, late May - early Sept), with a paddling pool alongside, is near the house. Caravan storage. Off site: Fishing nearby (1.5 miles). Snetterton motor racing circuit and Sunday market (2-3 miles).

Open

15 March - 29 September.

At a glance

| Welcome & Ambience | ✓✓✓✓✓ | Location | ✓✓✓✓✓ |
| Quality of Pitches | ✓✓✓✓ | Range of Facilities | ✓✓✓✓✓ |

Directions

From A11 (Thetford - Norwich) road, 7 miles from Thetford, turn right on B1111 towards East Harling. Turn right at church and right at T junction; park is on right. From A1066 Thetford-Diss road take left fork signed East Harling. Ignore signs for Forestry Commission site and park is next on left. Follow long drive (unmade road) for approx. 1 mile - keep speed down. O.S GR: TL969853.

Charges 2005

Per unit incl. 2 persons	£ 10.30 - £ 16.95
with electricity	£ 12.80 - £ 19.80
extra adult	£ 0.75 - £ 2.25
child (4-17 yrs)	£ 0.50 - £ 1.00

No charge for awnings or dogs.

Reservations

Accepted by phone; deposit of £10 required for electricity. Tel: 01953 717314. Email: info@dowerhouse.co.uk

UK3490 **The Grange Touring Park**

Ormesby St Margaret, Great Yarmouth NR29 3QG (Norfolk)

The appealing appearance of this family touring site is that of a garden, with hanging baskets, flower beds, bluebells and daffodils under the trees in spring, and all carefully tended by the resident wardens. The 70 level pitches are on well trimmed grass arranged around tarmac access roads, 60 with electricity (10A). Adjacent to the campsite is The Grange itself - a free house offering a wide range of meals, beers and real ale, plus children's play equipment (open all year). The site owner also has a holiday campsite at Hemsby (4 miles) with its own wide sandy beach, which guests at The Grange are welcome to use. The nearest beach is a mile away and local attractions include Caister Castle and Motor Museum, Norfolk Rare Breed Centre, Yarmouth greyhound stadium and ten pin bowling.

Facilities

A modern toilet building is spacious and well maintained, housing all the usual facilities including free showers, a baby changing room in the ladies' and a laundry room with washing machine and dryer. Washing lines are provided at the rear of the building. Gas supplies. Swings for children. Off site: Bus service 250 yds. Shops and supermarket 1 mile. Fishing 4 miles. Golf 3 miles. Beach 1 mile.

Open

20 March - 1 October.

At a glance

| Welcome & Ambience | ✓✓✓✓✓ | Location | ✓✓✓✓✓ |
| Quality of Pitches | ✓✓✓✓ | Range of Facilities | ✓✓✓✓ |

Directions

From A149 Great Yarmouth - North Walsham road, on the Caister bypass, at roundabout take B1159 road signed Hemsby. Park is on left just before next roundabout. O.S.GR: TG515140.

Charges 2005

Per unit incl. up to 4 persons	£ 7.00 - £ 12.50
extra person	£ 2.00
awning	£ 3.00
electricity	£ 2.00
first dog free, extra dog by arrangement	free - £ 2.00

No credit cards.

Reservations

Advisable for B.Hs (min. 3 nights), school holidays and peak season and made with deposit (£20 for under 7 days or £40 per week). Tel: 01493 730306. Email: info@grangetouring.co.uk

UK3485 **Clippesby Hall**

Clippesby, Great Yarmouth NR29 3BL (Norfolk)

Set in the heart of the Broads National Park this is an unusual park in the grounds of a private estate where one can wander at will. Clippesby offers the choice of pitching amongst the shady woodland or on the gently sloping lawns of the hall with colourful mature trees and shrubs. The 100 pitches are well spaced and clearly numbered (70 have 10A electricity). Hardstanding is available in the car parking area. There is a friendly welcome from the Lindsay family who have lived in the single storey Hall for many years and the opportunity to enjoy the mature gardens and facilities. These include a sunken grass tennis court, a small heated pool with mellow flagstone patio area behind the Hall, a timber adventure playground, and putting and recreation greens. The Muskett Arms with an attractive and comfortable family bar and a sheltered courtyard outside, provides evening meals, music nights and other family entertainment and the Beachcomber café has a good selection of foor during the day. Children can roam at will, and in safety, and parents can relax and unwind at this comfortable park, never mind all the attractions of the Broads and Great Yarmouth on your doorstep and only the peacocks to disturb you!

Facilities

Three timbered heated toilet blocks (two refurbished in 2005) provide clean and modern facilities. Some washbasins in cabins and 10 showers in total. New en-suite room for disabled visitors. Family room with bath and baby changing. Hot water for dishwashing is charged (20p) – the park is not on mains services. Laundry. Gas. Shop (Easter, then from 4/5). Café and family bar (from 19/5). Swimming pool (27/5-23/9). Adventure play area. Football field. Bicycle hire. Dog walk (max. 1 per pitch). Off site: Bus service 1.5 miles. Fishing 2 miles. Riding 3 miles. Golf 5 miles. Great Yarmouth 7 miles. Norwich 15 miles. Beach 5 miles.

Open

Easter - 20 September.

At a glance

Welcome & Ambience	√√√√√	Location	√√√√√
Quality of Pitches	√√√√	Range of Facilities	√√√√

Directions

From the A47 Norwich – Great Yarmouth road at Acle roundabout take exit for Filby (A1064). After 1.5 miles take left fork on B1152 signed Potter Heigham. Take first left and park is 100 yards on the right. O.S.GR: TG423145.

Charges 2005

Per unit incl. 2 persons	£ 13.00 - £ 19.50
extra adult	£ 1.50 - £ 2.00
child or student	£ 0.95
dog (max. 1)	£ 1.50 - £ 2.00
electricity	£ 2.00

Reservations

Advised for peak periods and made with deposit (£20 per week or part week). Tel: 01493 367800. Email: holidays@clippesby.com

UK3510 Breydon Water Holiday Park

Butt Lane, Burgh Castle, Great Yarmouth NR31 9QB (Norfolk)

Newly aquired by the Park Resorts group, these well established holiday parks (formerly Liffens Holiday Park and Welcome Holiday Centre) are in a semi-rural area on the edge of the Norfolk Broads within easy reach of Great Yarmouth. Breydon Water Holiday Park comprises the two parks, now named Bure Village (holiday homes only) and Yare Village, which are just a short walk apart along a country lane. Visitors at each park may use the facilities at the other. Yare Village has over 300 pitches which include 178 touring pitches (123 with 16A electricity, 2 fully serviced) on a separate open, grassy area, slightly sloping in parts. The remaining pitches are used for caravan holiday homes, most privately owned, 35 for rent. A large restaurant/bar providing club style entertainment in season and a takeaway service (noon-7 pm) overlook a heated outdoor pool. Campers can also use the indoor pool and other facilities at Bure Village close by. The amenities here would contribute to an enjoyable family holiday.

Facilities

Two toilet blocks offer clean, spacious, but fairly standard facilities. Unit for disabled persons. Baby room. Dishwashing sinks. Laundry. Shop and post office. Entertainment complex with restaurant, two bars and takeaway. Swimming pool (60 x 30 ft; open 29/5-31/8) with water slide and paddling pool. Play area and play field. Tennis. Off site: At Bure Village: indoor pool, gym, solarium, amusements and supermarket. Fishing 400 yds. Golf 3 miles. Riding 8 miles. Bus stop outside gate.

Open

1 March - 31 October.

At a glance

| Welcome & Ambience | ✓✓✓✓ | Location | ✓✓✓✓ |
| Quality of Pitches | ✓✓✓✓ | Range of Facilities | ✓✓✓✓✓ |

Directions

From Great Yarmouth take A143 signed Beccles. From the dual-carriageway at Bradwell turn right signed Burgh Castle into New Road. At mini-roundabout turn right into Butt Lane and follow this road for 1 mile to park on the left (care needed due to parked vehicles). O.S.GR: TM490050.

Charges 2005

| Per unit incl. 4 persons, electricity | £ 9.00 - £ 23.00 |
| extra person | £ 1.00 |

Special offer breaks available.

Reservations

Essential for high season and made with £20 p/week deposit. Tel: 01493 780357.
Email: breydon.water@park-resorts.com

UK3382 Rose Farm Touring Park

Stepshort, Belton, Great Yarmouth NR31 9JS (Norfolk)

This part of Norfolk is well known for its seaside attractions and the campsites which combine caravan holiday homes and touring pitches. Rose Farm caters for another type of camping holiday, offering space with the peace and tranquillity that you may not be expecting in this particular area! Sue and Tora Myhra are very proud of Rose Farm and what they have achieved in the few years since taking over what was quite a run-down campsite. Spread over eight acres, the park is split into two separate fields. The first is large and open, surrounded by fencing and hedges, with pitches around the edge. It is very spacious with a very good toilet block. The second field is long and narrow with pitching on either side.

Facilities

The two excellent blocks offer super facilities. The newer block is in Norwegian style, with modern fresh and spacious interior. Showers are good, washbasins are open or in cubicles. Laundry. Facilities for disabled visitors. Adventure playground. Pool table. TV room, library and tourist information. Off site: Shops nearby. Fishing and golf 3 miles. Riding and bicycle hire 4 miles. Beach 5 miles.

Open

All year.

At a glance

| Welcome & Ambience | ✓✓✓✓✓ | Location | ✓✓✓✓✓ |
| Quality of Pitches | ✓✓✓✓ | Range of Facilities | ✓✓✓✓ |

Directions

From Great Yarmouth and Gorleston take A143 signed Beccles/Diss. At dual carriageway (Bradwell) take immediate right to Burgh Castle and next right to site on right in 25 yds. O.S.GR: TG486033

Charges 2005

| Per unit incl. 2 persons, electricity | £ 12.00 - £ 14.00 |
| extra person | £ 1.50 - £ 2.00 |

Special offers available. No credit cards.

Reservations

Essential in high season. Tel: 01493 780896.
Email: myhra@rosefarmtouringpark.fsnet.co.uk

UK3420 **Two Mills Touring Park**

Yarmouth Road, North Walsham NR28 9NA (Norfolk)

Two Mills is a quiet site for adults only. Set in the bowl of a former quarry, the park is a real sun trap, both secluded and sheltered, with bird song to be heard at all times of the day. Neatly maintained with natural areas, varied trees, wild flowers and birds, the new owners, Barbara and Ray Barnes, want to add their own touches to this popular park. There are 55 level marked pitches for tourers, 48 all weather gravel, including 8 serviced pitches (hardstanding, patio area, water and waste water drainage). All are generously sized and have electricity (10/16A). This is a good centre from which to explore the north Norfolk coast, the Broads or for visiting Norwich and a footpath from the park joins the Weavers Way. A member of the Best of British group.

Facilities	Directions
Neat, clean central toilet block can be heated and includes some washbasins in cabins, en-suite facilities for disabled people, laundry and dishwashing rooms. Small shop at reception. TV room with tea and coffee facilities. Dogs are accepted by arrangement only. Only adults are accepted. Off site: Hotel/pub 100 yds. Town 20 minutes walk. Fishing or golf 5 miles. Bicycle hire 1.5 miles. The coast is 5 miles.	From A149 Stalham - North Walsham road, watch for sign 1.5 miles before North Walsham (also signed White Horse Common). The road runs parallel to the A149 and site is on right after 1.25 miles. From North Walsham take Old Yarrmouth road past hospital, and park is on left after 1 mile. O.S.GR: TG292287.

Open

All year excl. 2 January - 1 March.

At a glance

Welcome & Ambience	✓✓✓✓✓	Location	✓✓✓✓✓
Quality of Pitches	✓✓✓✓✓	Range of Facilities	✓✓✓✓

Charges 2005

Per unit incl. 2 adults	£ 12.54 - £ 17.50
extra person	£ 2.50
Senior citizen discounts.	

Reservations

Made with £10 deposit (£30 for B.Hs); balance payable on arrival. Tel: 01692 405829. Email: enquiries@twomills.co.uk

UK3500 **Woodhill Park**

Cromer Road, East Runton, Cromer NR27 9PX (Norfolk)

Woodhill is a seaside site with good views and a traditional atmosphere. It is situated on the cliff top, in a large gently sloping open grassy field, with 300 marked touring pitches. Of these, 216 have electricity (16A), 7 are fully serviced and many have wonderful views over the surrounding countryside. A small number of holiday homes which are located nearer to the cliff edge unfortunately have the best sea views, although perhaps at times a little bracing! Although the site is fenced there is access to the cliff top path (watch young children). Nearby attractions include boat trips to see the seals off Blakeney Point, the Shire Horse Centre at West Runton, the North Norfolk Steam Railway, and at Sheringham you can find 'The Splash' fun pool complex with wave machine.

Facilities	Directions
The three sanitary units (the newest part of the reception building) are fully equipped. Laundry with washing machines and dryer (iron from reception). Fully equipped unit for disabled persons. Well stocked mini-market plus gas exchange (19/3-31/8). Good, large adventure playground and plenty of space for ball games. Crazy golf. Giant chess. 9 hole golf course adjacent to the site. Off site: Bicycle hire, golf and riding 2 miles. Fishing 1 mile. Beach 0.5 miles.	Site is beside the A149 coast road between East and West Runton. O.S.GR: TG190420.

Open

19 March - 31 October.

At a glance

Welcome & Ambience	✓✓✓✓✓	Location	✓✓✓✓✓
Quality of Pitches	✓✓✓✓✓	Range of Facilities	✓✓✓✓

Charges 2005

Per adult	£ 1.50
child (4-16 yrs)	£ 1.00
small pitch (no electricity)	£ 5.80 - £ 8.00
pitch with electricity	£ 8.90 - £ 11.00
multi-service pitch	£ 11.90 - £ 14.20
dog	£ 2.00

Reservations

Accepted for min. 3 nights with £30 p/week non-returnable booking fee. Tel: 01263 512242. Email: info@woodhill-park.com

(151)

UK3450 Little Haven Caravan & Camping Park

The Street, Erpingham, Norwich NR11 7QD (Norfolk)

Within easy reach of the coast and the Broads, this is an attractive, peaceful little site with good facilities. Only adults are accepted. There are 24 grassy pitches, all with electricity (16A) and 6 with hardstanding. They are arranged around the outside of a gravel access road with a central lawn and decorative pergola, a neat little garden and a seating area. There is no shop, but two pubs serving food and traditional ales are within walking distance. An ideal base for cycling, walking, riding, or just relaxing, the Weavers Way footpath is within half a mile. Also close by is magnificent Blickling Hall with its superb state rooms, gardens and park, or a short drive takes you to the historic market town of Aylsham.

Facilities

The well maintained toilet unit is heated and includes spacious hot showers and two covered dishwashing and laundry sinks. Facilities for disabled people are planned. Gas available. Site is unsuitable for American motorhomes. Note: This is an adults only park. Off site: Bus service on the main A140 road. Riding 1 mile. Fishing 3 miles. Bicycle hire 5 miles. Golf 10 miles. Beach 6 miles.

Open

1 March - 31 October.

At a glance

Welcome & Ambience	✓✓✓✓	Location	✓✓✓✓
Quality of Pitches	✓✓✓	Range of Facilities	✓✓✓

Directions

From A140 Cromer - Norwich road, going south towards Aylsham and 3 miles south of Roughton, past the Horseshoes pub and Alby crafts, take first turning right signed Erpingham 2 miles (narrow road). Site is 175 yards on right. O.S.GR: TG190320.

Charges 2005

Per unit incl. 2 adults, electricity and awning	£ 10.00

No credit cards.

Reservations

Advisable for B.Hs and peak season and made without deposit. Tel: 01263 768959. Email: patl@haven30.fsnet.co.uk

UK3455 Deer's Glade Caravan & Camping Park

White Post Road, Hanworth, Norwich NR11 7HN (Norfolk)

As it's name suggests, you would not be surprised to wake and see deer wandering on this park and in the surrounding woodland areas. If you do miss them, a short walk will take you to Gunton Park where deer are bred and wander in herds. In 2003, David and Heather Attew decided that they had an area that would make a superb setting for a caravan park and that they could give up farming. In early 2004 after much hard work, they opened this top quality park and it has since developed into a very popular site. Not far from the Norfolk Broads and close to the East Anglian coast, the park is open all year round. There are 125 level, grass pitches, all with 16A electricity and 100 with TV aerial points. Internet access is possible from all the pitches. Amenities are of a high standard and include two toilet blocks, a play area, small shop and a popular, well stocked fishing lake.

Facilities

Two spacious new toilet blocks are of a high standard and include vanity style washbasins for ladies, a room for disabled visitors or families, dishwashing room and a laundry. Motorcaravan service point. Licensed shop (all year). Play area. Fishing lake (charge). Off site: Bus service under 1 mile. Pub 1.5 miles. Woodland walks. Riding 2 miles. Golf and bicycle hire 5 miles. Beach 5 miles.

Open

All year.

At a glance

Welcome & Ambience	✓✓✓✓✓	Location	✓✓✓✓✓
Quality of Pitches	✓✓✓✓✓	Range of Facilities	✓✓✓✓

Directions

From Norwich take A140 towards Cromer and 5 miles after Aylsham turn right towards Suffield Park (White Post Road). Park is 0.5 miles on the right. O.S.GR: TG214340.

Charges 2005

Per person	£ 4.50 - £ 7.00
child	£ 1.50 - £ 2.50
awning	£ 1.50
dog	£ 1.00

Family deals available.

Reservations

Contact park. Tel: 01263 268633. Email: info@deersglade.co.uk

UK3430 **Kelling Heath Holiday Park**

Weybourne, Holt, Sheringham NR25 7HW (Norfolk)

Not many parks can boast their own railway station and Kelling Heath's own halt on the North Norfolk Steam Railway gives access to shopping in Holt or the beach at Sheringham. Set in 250 acres of woodland and heathland overlooking the north Norfolk coast, this spacious holiday park offers freedom and relaxation with 300 touring pitches, all with electricity (16A) in four different zones. Pitching is good on quite firm, level grass (no hardstanding). Together with 384 caravan holiday homes (36 to let, the rest privately owned), they blend easily into the part-wooded, part-open heath. A wide range of facilities provides activities for all ages. 'The Forge' has an entertainment bar, an adult only bar and a family room, with comprehensive entertainment all season. 'Fitness Express' provides an indoor pool, spa pool, sauna, steam rooms and gym. An adventure playground with assault course is near. The central reception area is attractively paved to provide a 'village store' and an open air bandstand where one can sit and enjoy the atmosphere. The park's natural environment allows for woodland walks, a nature trail and cycling trails, and a small lake for free fishing (permit holders only). Other amenities include two hard tennis courts, a small, outdoor heated fun pool and play areas (some rather hidden from the pitches).

Facilities

Three toilet blocks serve the touring pitches, one heated and with a conservatory providing covered access all year to disabled people, baby room and dishwashing and laundry sinks. All blocks have a few washbasins in private cubicles, baby baths and in season a nappy disposal service. Washing machines and dryers, with irons to hire. Shop. Gas supplies. Bar, restaurant and takeaway. Indoor leisure centre with pool (19 x 9 m), gym, etc. with trained staff (membership on either daily or weekly basis). Outdoor pool (main season). Adventure play area. Tennis. Fishing. Bicycle hire. Entertainment programme. Special environmental 'Acorn Club' for children. Torches useful. Off site: The Norfolk coast, Felbrigg Hall, the Walsingham Shrine and the Norfolk Broads National Park are nearby.

At a glance

Welcome & Ambience	✓✓✓✓	Location	✓✓✓✓
Quality of Pitches	✓✓✓✓	Range of Facilities	✓✓✓✓✓

Directions

On A148 road from Holt to Cromer, after High Kelling, turn left just before Bodham village (international sign) signed Weybourne. Follow road for about 1 mile to park O.S.GR: TG117418.

Charges 2005

Per unit incl. electricity	£ 14.65 - £ 22.00
awning	£ 2.00
dog (max 2)	£ 3.00

Min 7 day stay in high season. No single sex groups.

Reservations

Necessary for July/Aug. on a weekly basis with £30 deposit. Tel: 01263 588181.
Email: info@kellingheath.co.uk

Open

14 February - 10 December.

UK3460 **The Garden Caravan Site**

Barmer Hall, Syderstone, Kings Lynn PE31 8SR (Norfolk)

An imaginative touring site in an enclosed, south facing, walled garden, this newly developed site has 30 spacious marked pitches, all on gently sloping grass in the most attractive setting behind the Hall itself. Levelling blocks may be needed. There are 30 electrical connections (16A), each with a TV hook-up as reception is variable, possibly due to the high wall and woodland surrounding the site. However, this does mean that the site is peaceful and a little sun-trap, a haven from the busy world outside. Attractive mature trees, shrubs and climbers provide shade at various times of the day. Reception is housed in a small kiosk (not always manned, so pitch yourself and pay later). Barmer Hall is not far from Sandringham, and there are plenty of peaceful lanes to explore on your bicycle or take a woodland walk from the little door in the wall at the rear of the site.

Facilities

Toilet facilities are in a new building (heated when necessary) including extremely spacious hot showers and free hot water. Dishwashing sinks are under cover at one end of the building. No shop, but gas, ices, soft drinks and free range fresh eggs are usually available. Off site: Bicycle hire 4 miles, riding 6 miles, golf 10 miles. Maybe visit Norfolk Lavender, Langham Glass or the Thursford Collection of steam engines, mechanical organs and Wurlitzer fame.

At a glance

Welcome & Ambience	✓✓✓✓	Location	✓✓✓✓✓
Quality of Pitches	✓✓✓✓	Range of Facilities	✓✓✓

Directions

About 6 miles west of Fakenham turn off A148 at Fourwinds Garage to Docking and Hunstanton on B1454. After a further 4 miles turn to Barmer Hall (site signed). Road is marked 'unsuitable for motor vehicles' but ignore and follow past and behind the Hall and farm buildings. O.S.GR: TF810330.

Charges 2005

Per unit incl. 2 adults	£ 11.00

No credit cards.

Reservations

Advised for B.Hs and peak season. Tel: 01485 578220. Email: nigel@mason96.fsnet.co.uk

Open

1 March - 1 November.

UK3400 **The Old Brick Kilns Caravan & Camping Park**

Little Barney Lane, Barney, Fakenham NR21 0NL (Norfolk)

This tranquil, family run park is under new ownership and further improvements are taking place. The park's development on the site of old brick kilns has resulted in land on varying levels. This provides areas of level, well drained pitches (e.g. the Dell, the Orchard) which include some hardstandings. There are 65 pitches in total, all with electricity (10/16A), including a new area with serviced pitches. Banks around the park and a wide range of trees and shrubs provide shelter and are home for a variety of wildlife. There are garden areas, including a butterfly garden, and a conservation pond is the central feature. Drinking water is supplied by a 285 ft. bore and excellent, roofed service areas provide water and waste disposal. Amenities include a large, comfortable bar area and restaurant, open at weekends. A friendly, helpful atmosphere prevails and as the park is 8 miles from the coast, it is ideally situated to explore North Norfolk. A member of the Best of British group.

Facilities

Smart, heated toilet blocks provide very good, clean facilities with washbasins in curtained cubicles and a baby room. Facilities for disabled people (unisex; Radar key). Laundry room. Motorcaravan service point. Good shop with gas supplies. Bar/restaurant (weekends) with patio area outside with barbecue. New TV and games room. Table tennis, giant chess and mini library. Fenced play area with bark surface. Fishing. Caravan storage. B&B also available. Off site: Riding 6 miles. Golf 5 or 8 miles.

Open

All year excl. 7 January - 1 March.

At a glance

Welcome & Ambience	✓✓✓✓✓	Location	✓✓✓✓✓
Quality of Pitches	✓✓✓✓✓	Range of Facilities	✓✓✓✓

Directions

From Fakenham take A148 Cromer road. After 6 miles, at Thursford, fork right on B1354 Melton Constable road. In 300 yds, turn right, signed Barney, and then first left along a narrow country lane with passing places, for 0.75 miles. O.S.GR: TG004332.

Charges 2005

Per pitch incl. 2 persons and electricity	£ 13.50 - £ 16.75
extra adult	£ 2.00
child (4-15 yrs)	£ 1.50
child (0-3 yrs)	£ 0.75
dog (max 2)	£ 0.75

Reservations

Advised and made with £15 deposit (non-refundable). Tel: 01328 878305. Email: enquiries@old-brick-kilns.co.uk

UK3520 **Searles Leisure Resort**

South Beach Road, Hunstanton PE36 5BB (Norfolk)

This 'all-in' family holiday park on the North Norfolk coast offers everything you need for that seaside family holiday. With the beach within walking distance, the new undercover 'town plaza' including sports bar, Chinese restaurant and Mediterranean café, pools, a golf course, fishing lakes and bowling greens, there should be something to entertain everyone. Although now a major caravan holiday home park, for more than fifty years touring pitches have remained important on this site. Spacious pitches separated by hedges, either fully serviced, with electricity or not, are set in seven different areas of the park, with three large toilet blocks providing good facilities. Being such a large site security is important for safety and peace of mind and 24 hour CCTV operates. The seaside resort of Hunstanton is under a mile away providing all the usual ice creams, buckets and spades. The Royal House of Sandringham with its gardens and parts of the house open to the public is within easy reach. For bird watchers a trip further round the coast brings some excellent spots to see some interesting species.

Facilities	Directions
Three large toilet blocks offer clean and tidy facilities with background music adding that little extra. Washbasins in cubicles. En-suite rooms in all blocks for disabled visitors. Baby room. Laundry. Dishwashing facilities on the side of each block. Food hall. Restaurants, bars and cafés. Hair and beauty salon. Indoor and outdoor swimming pools. Gym. Tennis. Soft play area. Golf (9 hole course, driving range and putting course). Fishing lake. Bicycle hire. Off site: Nearest beach 200 yards. Hunstanton 0.5 miles.	On the A149 from Kings Lynn take Hunstanton exit at roundabout. At next roundabout take second exit then immediate left into site. O.S.GR: TF670401.

Open

March - October.

Charges 2005

Per tent or tourer pitch	£ 10.00 - £ 27.00
pitch with electricity	£ 13.00 - £ 30.00
fully serviced pitch	£ 13.00 - £ 33.00
awning	£ 2.65
dog	£ 2.20

At a glance

Welcome & Ambience	✓✓✓✓	Location	✓✓✓✓✓
Quality of Pitches	✓✓✓✓✓	Range of Facilities	✓✓✓✓✓

Reservations

Max. permitted stay 2 weeks. Only proprietry makes of tourers and campers are accepted. Large caravans or tents by arrangement. Contact site for details. Tel: 01485 534211. Email: bookings@searles.co.uk

UK3440 **Gatton Waters Lakeside Touring Site**

Hillington, nr Sandringham, Kings Lynn PE31 6BJ (Norfolk)

Developed around two fishing lakes (formerly stone quarries), Gatton Waters has a peaceful, open aspect. Fishermen will delight in pitching at the lakeside, while other pitches are available away from the water at this adult only park. There are 60 level caravan pitches (all with electricity) and 30 tent pitches in quiet and very pleasant surroundings. With all but 25 pitches taken by seasonal units, there is still room for those looking either to fish (day tickets available) or for a quiet base to visit Sandringham or the north Norfolk coast (although reservations are essential). Everything is kept as natural as possible and skylarks, pheasants, ospreys and leverets are to be seen, in addition to the many types of ducks, etc. on the lakes. In general the site retains a natural look but the grass is well trimmed and cared for. The site is now run by the son of the original owners, who are still adamant that their best ever decision was only to take adults - this also seems popular with their visitors. Only people over 18 years are accepted.

Facilities	Directions
Three modern, heated toilet blocks provide good clean facilities including dishwashing. Extra facilities near reception. Bar with open fire – very welcoming and with the attraction of real ales and good food (booking required). Caravan storage. Torches are necessary. Off site: Riding or golf 8 miles. Within easy reach are Sandringham (2.2 miles) and the North Norfolk Coast (8 miles).	From Kings Lynn follow A148 Cromer road. Site is on left just after West Newton turn, but before Sandringham turn and Hillington village. O.S.GR: TF705255.

Open

Easter - 1 October.

Charges 2005

Per unit incl. 2 persons	
and electricity	£ 9.00 - £ 12.00
tent incl. 2 persons	£ 9.00 - £ 12.00
extra person	£ 1.00

At a glance

Welcome & Ambience	✓✓✓✓	Location	✓✓✓✓✓
Quality of Pitches	✓✓✓	Range of Facilities	✓✓✓✓

Reservations

Essential and made for min. 3 days at B.Hs. Tel: 01485 600643. Email: gatton.waters@virgin.net

UK3470 **Breckland Meadows Touring Park**

Lynn Road, Swaffham PE37 7PT (Norfolk)

Within walking distance of the historic market town of Swaffham, this is a pleasant little park for adults only with enthusiastic owners, that would make a good base to explore Norfolk and the local area. The 45 pitches are on fairly level, neat grass, all with electricity (16A), some with hardstanding. There may be some road noise at times but newly planted trees should reduce this as they mature. Adjacent to the site is the Swaefas Way, a seven mile circular walk which links to the better known Peddars Way. Local attractions include Cockley Cley Medieval Iceni Village and Saxon Church, Castle Acre Priory, Oxburgh Hall and the Therefore Collection of steam engines, mechanical organs and Wurlitzer fame. Swaffham (half a mile) has a popular Saturday market.

Facilities

The toilet block has been completely refurbished and is neat, clean and heated when necessary. It provides all the usual facilities, a separate toilet and washbasin unit for disabled visitors, and outside covered washing-up and laundry facilities. Gas. Off site: Fishing 5 miles. Riding 4 miles. Golf 2 miles.

Open

All year.

At a glance

Welcome & Ambience	✓✓✓✓✓	Location	✓✓✓✓
Quality of Pitches	✓✓✓✓	Range of Facilities	✓✓✓

Directions

Park is just west of Swaffham on the old A47, approx. 1 mile from town centre. O.S.GR: TF809094.

Charges 2005

Per unit incl. 2 adults and electricity	£ 11.00 - £ 13.00
extra adult	£ 2.50
awning	£ 2.00
dog	£ 0.50
No credit cards.	

Reservations

Essential for B.Hs and advised for peak season; made with non-refundable £10 deposit. Tel: 01760 721246. Email: info@brecklandmeadows.co.uk

UK3550 **Old Manor Caravan Park**

Church Road, Grafham, Huntingdon PE28 0BB (Cambridgeshire)

Situated within easy walking distance of Grafham Water, this small, well maintained and attractive park combines history with a natural charm. The old white cottage (now reception) was once owned by Oliver Cromwell's family and the grounds formed part of their garden. To this day the horse pond and part of the moat still remain, while the remnants of an old yew hedge provide an intriguing, natural sculpture. With the exception of seven all-weather pitches the remainder of the 92 numbered and good sized pitches are grass; 54 for touring and most with 10A electrical connections. A variety of mature trees and hedges provide good shade on some pitches. 24 pitches, used only in June, July and August, are in a separate meadow with limited toilet facilities. The main attraction of the area is the nearby Grafham Water – a large reservoir with a wide range of leisure activities.

Facilities

The main heated toilet block, recently refurbished, is thoughtfully planned and always extremely clean. Small baby room. Dishwashing and laundry rooms, plus a free freezer for ice blocks and food storage. Another block with limited facilities in the separate meadow. Basic provisions are available from reception (1/3-31/10). Small playground. Heated outdoor pool (extra charge; unsupervised). Off site: Grafham Water 550 yards. Buckden and West Perry with village store 3 miles. Bicycle hire, fishing, sailing, wind surfing and 10 miles of footpaths and cycle track around the reservoir. Nearby market towns of Huntingdon, St Ives and St Neots. Duxford War Museum. Cambridge, Peterborough.

Open

All year.

At a glance

Welcome & Ambience	✓✓✓✓	Location	✓✓✓✓
Quality of Pitches	✓✓✓	Range of Facilities	✓✓✓

Directions

Leave A1 at Buckden roundabout and follow B661 west towards Grafham Water for about half a mile. Turn right to Grafham following camping signs. In the village take the first left into Church Road, the park is on the right in a few hundred yards. From A14 at Ellington turn south towards Grafham and in the village right into Church Road. O.S.GR: TL157698.

Charges 2005

Per unit incl. 2 adults and electricity	£ 15.00 - £ 18.00
tent pitch incl. 2 adults	£ 13.00 - £ 16.00
extra adult	£ 3.50 - £ 4.00
child (5-15 yrs)	£ 2.00 - £ 2.25
awning	£ 1.50
dog (max 2)	£ 1.00

Reservations

Made with £10 non-returnable deposit (min 3 nights at B.Hs) Tel: 01480 810264. Email: camping@old-manor.co.uk

UK3690 Bainland Country Park

Horncastle Road, Woodhall Spa LN10 6UX (Lincolnshire)

A family park with many amenities, Bainland has 170 spacious, level pitches in hedged bays (130 pitches for touring) grouped in circles and islands and linked by curving roads. 51 pitches are fully serviced with hardstanding, honeycombed for awning, individual water, drainage and chemical disposal, electricity and TV aerial hook-ups. The remainder of the pitches are either on gravel hardstanding or level grass, all with 16A electricity. The friendly reception is housed in a pleasant Swiss-style building together with the heated indoor pool and jacuzzi, a bistro and spacious bar area. These overlook the 18 hole, par 3 golf course and outdoor bowls area. Bainland is 1.5 miles from Woodhall Spa, with its old fashioned charm and Dambusters associations, yet deep in the heart of the Lincolnshire Wolds, surrounded by mature trees and with direct access to woods for walking dogs. A member of the Best of British group.

Facilities

Three modern, well equipped, heated toilet blocks including a baby room, unisex en-suite shower rooms, family bathroom, fully equipped unit for disabled people. Laundry room. Enclosed dishwashing and separate laundry sinks. Motorcaravan service points. Licensed shop (Feb-Dec). Bistro and bar (all year). Indoor pool (under 16s must be accompanied by an adult). Adventure playground. Trampolines. Crazy golf. Croquet. TV and games room. Soft play area. Floodlit tennis dome with 3-4 courts including badminton (the dome comes off in the summer). Leisure activities, including the pool, are individually booked and paid for at reception. Some entertainment in high season. Winter caravan storage. Off site: Fishing 3 miles. Riding 6 miles.

At a glance

Welcome & Ambience	✓✓✓✓✓	Location		✓✓✓✓
Quality of Pitches	✓✓✓✓✓	Range of Facilities	✓✓✓✓✓	

Directions

Woodhall Spa is 18 miles southeast of Lincoln. Entrance to park is off B1191 Horncastle road 1.5 miles northeast of the village by 50mph sign. O.S.GR: TF214637. GPS: N53:09.517 W00:11.011

Charges 2005

Per unit incl. electricity and awning	£ 11.50 - £ 28.00
serviced pitch	£ 16.50 - £ 33.00
pup tent	free - £ 3.00

Special rate for firework display (min. 2 nights, 4/5 Nov). Discounts for senior citizens.

Reservations

Advised and made for any length. Deposit of one night's fee (non-refundable). Tel: 01526 352903. Email: bookings@bainland.com

Open

All year (in winter, 'super' pitches only).

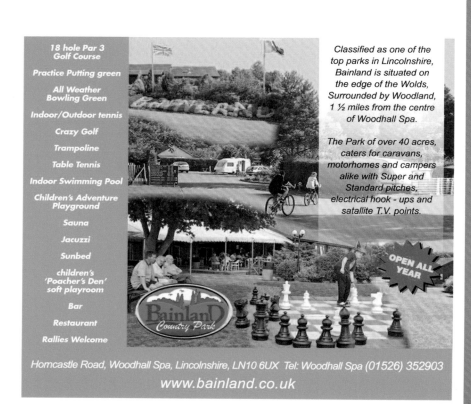

18 hole Par 3 Golf Course

Practice Putting green

All Weather Bowling Green

Indoor/Outdoor tennis

Crazy Golf

Trampoline

Table Tennis

Indoor Swimming Pool

Children's Adventure Playground

Sauna

Jacuzzi

Sunbed

children's 'Poacher's Den' soft playroom

Bar

Restaurant

Rallies Welcome

Classified as one of the top parks in Lincolnshire, Bainland is situated on the edge of the Wolds, Surrounded by Woodland, 1 ½ miles from the centre of Woodhall Spa.

The Park of over 40 acres, caters for caravans, motorhomes and campers alike with Super and Standard pitches, electrical hook - ups and satallite T.V. points.

OPEN ALL YEAR

Horncastle Road, Woodhall Spa, Lincolnshire, LN10 6UX Tel: Woodhall Spa (01526) 352903

www.bainland.co.uk

UK3692 Glen Lodge Touring Park

Glen Lodge, Edlington Moor, Woodhall Spa LN10 6UL (Lincolnshire)

This quiet, modern site is ideal for couples and families who enjoy the rural lifestyle, yet it is only just over a mile from the thriving village of Woodhall Spa which retains much of its old-fashioned charm. All 35 pitches have hardstanding and 10A electricity hook-ups (one or two appeared to need long leads) and are served by shingle roads with some street lighting. The grass and flowerbeds are obviously tended by someone who enjoys gardening. In fact, the whole park has a much-loved feel. Places to visit include the Battle of Britain Memorial Flight, Tattershall Castle, Horncastle with its antiques centre and the city of Lincoln. Skegness is only 26 miles away.

Facilities

The modern heated toilet block (key-pad access) is spotlessly clean with vanity style washbasins and piped music. Facilities for disabled visitors. Washing machine and dryer. Off site: Pub 0.5 miles, golf 2 miles, fishing 5 miles, riding 6 miles.

Open

1 March - 30 November.

At a glance

Welcome & Ambience	✓✓✓✓✓	Location	✓✓✓✓
Quality of Pitches	✓✓✓✓✓	Range of Facilities	✓✓✓✓

Directions

Woodhall Spa is 18 miles southeast of Lincoln. From mini-roundabout in village turn northeast towards Bardney on B1190 (Stixwould Road) past Petwood Hotel. In about 1 mile at sharp left bend, turn right. Site is 300 yards on left. O.S.GR: TF189647. GPS: N53:09.974 W000:13.20

Charges 2005

Per unit incl. 2 adults and electricity	£ 11.50
extra person (over 4 yrs)	£ 1.50

No credit cards.

Reservations

Contact site. Tel: 01526 353523.

GLEN LODGE TOURING PARK

Small family run park within a mile of Woodhall Spa, set in beautiful woodland surroundings. Heated toilet/shower block and utility room with washer, dryer and phone. A great combination of peace and tranquillity and yet within easy reach of the seaside town of Skegness. Discounts available Monday to Thursday for senior citizens.

Edlington Moor, Woodhall Spa, Lincolnshire LN10 6UL ▪ Tel/Fax No. 01526 353523

UK3700 Pilgrims Way Caravan & Camping Park

Church Green Road, Fishtoft, Boston PE21 0QY (Lincolnshire)

In a rural setting, this delightful, family run park is two miles from Boston and its famous church tower. There are 22 individual pitches of which 17 are for touring all with access to electricity (10A) and 6 with hardstanding. The park's facilities are housed in a good quality conversion at one end of what was once a workshop. Local attractions include the 'Boston Stump', the Pilgrim Fathers Memorial and Maud Foster Windmill, all in and around the town. Further afield is Heckington village and its unique eight- sailed windmill (6 miles) and the Aviation Heritage Centre (12 miles). Boston market days are on Wednesdays and Saturdays and the town also has a fine marina, two sport and leisure centres (one with swimming pools), a ten-pin bowling alley and a tennis centre.

Facilities

Heated in low season, the sanitary facilities are thoughtfully planned and exceptionally clean and well maintained. Entry is by keypad and all of the usual facilities are provided, including free hot showers, dishwashing and laundry sinks, and an excellent fully equipped unit for disabled persons. Laundry with washing machine and dryer. Motorcaravan service point. Gas available. Groundsheets, kite flying and ball games are not allowed. Dogs are only accepted by prior arrangement. Off site: Mini-market, baker and fuel station within 1 mile, supermarket 2 miles. Golf, fishing, bicycle hire and riding within 2 miles.

Open

1 April/Easter - 30 September.

At a glance

Welcome & Ambience	✓✓✓✓	Location	✓✓✓✓
Quality of Pitches	✓✓✓✓	Range of Facilities	✓✓✓

Directions

Boston is 35 miles southeast of Lincoln. From the A52, northeast of town, 1 mile east of junction with A16, turn south by the 'Ball House' public house, continuing past the Boston Bowl towards Fishtoft, where the site is on your left. (From town, ignore first campsite sign). O.S.GR: TF360420. GPS: N52:58.311 E000:01.27

Charges 2005

Per unit incl. 2 persons	£ 12.00

No credit cards.

Reservations

Advised for B.Hs and peak season. Tel: 01205 366646. Email: pilgrimswaylincs@yahoo.com

UK3730 Skegness Sands Touring Site

Winthorpe Avenue, Skegness PE25 1QZ (Lincolnshire)

This very well organised touring site is part of a much larger caravan holiday home park, but has its own entrance. It is a modern, well appointed site adjacent to the promenade and beach. There are 85 pitches, all level and with electricity (16A). 48 are grass (3 tents only) and 37 gravel hardstandings, four of which are fully serviced. Site lighting is good throughout and there are regular security patrols. The gate to the promenade is kept locked at all times, campers getting a key. Local attractions include Funcoast World, Fantasy Island, Hardy's Animal Farm, a seal sanctuary and Gibraltar Point National Nature Reserve. The site is a member of the Caravan Club's 'managed under contract' scheme, members and non-members are all made very welcome.

Facilities

The good quality, heated toilet block includes washbasins in curtained cubicles plus three family shower rooms with WC and washbasin and a well equipped room for disabled people. Two dishwashing sinks are outside under cover. Laundry room. Gas supplies on site. Hairdressing salon. Indoor heated swimming pool (Spr. B.H. - 30 Sept; adult £3, child £2). Small modern playground. Off site: Well stocked shop/post office 200 m. Pubs, fast food outlets and a supermarket are all within easy walking distance. 'Hail and ride' bus service to Skegness and Ingoldmells at 200 m. Fishing 1 mile. Golf 2 miles. Riding 5 miles. Also stock car racing and ten pin bowling.

Open

All year.

At a glance

Welcome & Ambience	✓✓✓✓	Location	✓✓✓✓
Quality of Pitches	✓✓✓✓	Range of Facilities	✓✓✓✓

Directions

Site is off the A52 Boston - Skegness - Mablethorpe road, 1.75 miles north of Skegness town centre. Turn east opposite 'Garden City' public house into Winthorpe Avenue and site entrance is on the left at far end of road. Note: This entrance is locked from 5pm - 8am. At other times, access is by the Roman Bank entrance, a short distance further north on A52. New arrivals please contact site if unable to arrive before 5pm. O.S.GR: TF570640.
GPS: N53:10.008 E000:20.97

Charges 2005

Per adult	£ 3.80 - £ 5.00
child (5-16 yrs)	£ 1.20 - £ 1.70
non-member pitch fee	£ 9.50 - £ 12.50
'super' pitch supplement	£ 3.00

Reservations

Advised for B.Hs, school holidays and peak season. Made with £10 deposit (non-refundable).
Tel: 01754 761484. Email: info@skegness-sands.com

UK3765 Woodland Waters

Willoughby Road, Ancaster, Grantham NG32 3RT (Lincolnshire)

This attractive holiday park occupies 70 acres of woodland, gently-sloping grassland and lakes, with the caravan park itself taking up about 20 of them. Although the site has a capacity of 120 pitches, only 60 (all with 10A electricity and water taps nearby) are regularly used. A further 20 with electricity are kept for rallies and there are areas for camping and those not requiring hook-ups. The main pitches are numbered but not marked (jockey-wheels go on the number pad). The land slopes gently down to the 14-acre lake and the pitches nearer the water are more level, although probably not suitable for those with younger children since there is no fencing. Reception is housed in a neat modem building at the entrance to the park, the welcome is warm, fishing tickets are sold and tourist information is available. The pleasant bar and restaurant (open to the public) occupy a chalet-style building near the lake; the menu seemed varied and reasonably-priced. There are four fishing lakes (plus a junior pool), with carp, tench, bream, roach, rudd and pike. Walking and bird-watching are other featured attractions of the park, while days out could include a visit to Nottingham, Lincoln or even Skegness (50 miles). Some aircraft noise is possible.

Facilities

A single, modern, heated toilet block provides clean, well maintained toilets, washbasins (in cubicles for ladies) and free showers (controllable for ladies, push-button for men). These facilities might possibly be under some pressure if the additional camping areas were fully occupied, but regular visitors had nothing but praise for them. Dishwashing sinks under cover. Small laundry room with washing machine, tumble dryer and iron, but no laundry sinks. Motorcaravan service point. Bar and restaurant with takeaway (all year). Play area. Off site: Limited bus service in Ancaster. Shop in village (1 mile). Go-karting and paint-ball 1 mile. Golf 3 miles. Riding 6 miles.

Open

All year.

At a glance

Welcome & Ambience	✓✓✓✓✓	Location	✓✓✓✓
Quality of Pitches	✓✓✓✓	Range of Facilities	✓✓✓✓

Directions

Ancaster is 8 miles northeast of Grantham and 19 miles south of Lincoln. The park entrance is off the A153 Grantham - Sleaford road, 600 yards west of the junction with 86403 High Dyke road (Ermine Street). O.S.GR: SK973437.

Charges 2005

Per unit incl. up to 4 persons	£ 9.00 - £ 11.00
incl. electricity	£ 11.50 - £ 13.50
extra person	£ 2.00
child	£ 1.00
awning	£ 2.00 - £ 2.25

Reservations

Made with deposit (£20-£30). Tel: 01400 230888.
Email: info@woodlandwaters.co.uk

Heart of England

163

www.alanrogers.com for latest campsite news

UK3750 Foreman's Bridge Caravan Park

Sutton St James, Spalding PE12 0HU (Lincolnshire)

Foreman's Bridge is an extremely pleasant and compact park and the owners are now well established. It makes an excellent base from which to explore the Fens, including Spalding, famous for its annual flower festival held in early May. Fishing and cycling are popular pastimes in the area, indeed fishing is possible in the river that runs just past the entrance. Occupying a large, level and grassy meadow surrounded by trees and high hedges which give it a secluded feel, the park has 40 level pitches, of which 28 are touring pitches, all with electricity (10A) and 20 with gravel hardstanding. Fruit trees, flower beds and hanging baskets provide bursts of vibrant colour. At times there can be noise from military aircraft.

Facilities
The modern, brick built toilet unit is spacious and kept very clean, with large shower rooms with seats and washbasins (showers on payment). Dishwashing room. Laundry room. Basic provisions and gas are kept. Fishing. Bicycle hire. Site barrier (£5 deposit for card). Winter caravan storage. Off site: Small shop in village 1 mile. Golf 5 miles, riding 8 miles. Coast 12 miles (The Wash); nearest beach 32 miles.

Open
1 March - 30 November.

At a glance
Welcome & Ambience	✓✓✓✓	Location	✓✓✓✓
Quality of Pitches	✓✓✓✓	Range of Facilities	✓✓✓

Directions
Sutton St James is 17 miles west of Kings Lynn. From A17 Spalding - Kings Lynn road turn south on B1390 at Long Sutton towards Sutton St James for 2 miles. Entrance is on the left immediately after the bridge. O.S.GR: TF410198. GPS: N52:45.471 W000:05.28

Charges 2005
Per unit incl. 2 persons	£ 8.50
electricity	£ 2.00
No credit cards.	

Reservations
Advisable for Flower Festival, B.Hs (min. 3 nights), and peak season; made with £10 deposit. Tel: 01945 440346. Email: ann@anegus.wanadoo.co.uk

UK3760 Tallington Lakes Caravan & Camping

Barholm Road, Tallington, Stamford PE9 4RJ (Lincolnshire)

This large, 160-acre site spreads around a series of lakes that provides for many watersport activities including water-ski (slalom and jump courses), jet-ski, sailing (sailboards and dinghies), and angling. The touring campsite has recently been brought up to date and now has around 120 pitches, of which 106 have electric hook-ups (10A), and 11 are on hardstandings. Major roads are tarmac, with gravel roads around the pitches, but the small hedges and shrubs separating the pitches are new and will need time to mature. The complex also has many permanent holiday homes.

Facilities
The heated sanitary unit includes facilities for babies and disabled visitors, plus room with dishwashing. Additional WCs and showers (also used by water skiers). Laundry. Excellent motorcaravan services. Bar and restaurant. Watersports. Fishing. Dry-ski slope. Tennis. Small playground (5-12 yrs). Key-card for toilet unit and barrier (£10 deposit).

Open
1 March - 31 January.

At a glance
Welcome & Ambience	✓✓✓✓	Location	✓✓✓✓
Quality of Pitches	✓✓✓✓	Range of Facilities	✓✓✓✓

Directions
From A16, between Stamford and Market Deeping, just east of railway crossing at Tallington, turn north into Barholm Road and site entrance is on the right. (site is signed). O.S.GR: TF085090.

Charges 2005
Per person	£ 1.50
pitch	£ 6.00
electricity	£ 2.00

Reservations
Accepted with full payment. Tel: 01778 347000. Email: info@tallington.com

UK3770 Low Farm Touring Park

Spring Lane, Folkingham, Sleaford NG34 0SJ (Lincolnshire)

This quiet secluded park is a lovely spot either just to relax or to tour the Lincolnshire countryside. Jane and Nigel Stevens are working hard to make this site a pleasant place to stay and have a well laid out park offering good quality facilities which are very clean and tidy. The site is on the edge of the village of Folkingham with a pub and a couple of small shops. There are some pleasant walks around the village which is set in attractive countryside. The site has 36 touring pitches, 35 of which have electric hook-ups.

Facilities
Controllable free showers. Dishwashing and laundry sinks. Washing machine. Tourist information. Large field where children can play (also sometimes used by tenters). Off site: Fishing 2 miles. Golf 6 miles. Riding 7 miles.

Open
Easter - 30 September.

At a glance
Welcome & Ambience	✓✓✓✓	Location	✓✓✓✓
Quality of Pitches	✓✓✓	Range of Facilities	✓✓✓

Directions
Folkingham is on the A15 Lincoln - Peterborough road, 2 miles south of roundabout junction with the A52 (Nottingham/Grantham - Boston). Park is on southern edge of village. O.S.GR: TF070333. GPS: N52:53.211 W000:24.67

Charges 2005
Per unit incl. 2 persons	£ 8.00 - £ 10.00
electricity	£ 2.00
No credit cards.	

Reservations
Contact park. Tel: 01529 497322.

UK3800 Highfields Farm

Fenny Bentley, Ashbourne DE6 1LE (Derbyshire)

This caravan and camping park is set on high, flat ground in the Peak District National Park with marvellous views. Run by the Redfern family, it takes up to 50 touring units and a considerable number of seasonal units in open, hedged fields accessed by tarmac roads. For touring units there is a large field with concrete slabs for jockey wheels, 80 electricity connections (16A) and 8 full hardstandings. There is another small field for adults only and a sloping, rather uneven field for tents. Privately owned caravan holiday homes (54) occupy further fields. An indoor, heated swimming pool is open all season (restricted times if the park is not very full, not supervised at all times but monitored from reception by CCTV). A room with table and chairs, is available for hire. The park is in the heart of the Peak District - Dovedale and Ilam are only a mile or two by footpath and the Tissington Trail with access to the High Peak Trail passes by the park. Days out could include trips to Buxton, Chatsworth House, the Crich Tram Museum or the Alton Towers theme park.

Facilities

The three heated toilet blocks are kept locked (deposit for key) and are well maintained. Hot water is metered for laundry and dishwashing, and to the showers. Baby bath. Washing machine and dryer. Shop for basics and gas. Good playground with new rubber base. Swimming pool (£1 per session). American motorhomes accepted. Winter caravan storage. Torches are useful. Off site: Pub and restaurant close. Riding 2 miles. Fishing and bicycle hire 3 miles. Golf and boat launching 5 miles.

Open

1 March - 31 October.

At a glance

Welcome & Ambience	✓✓✓✓	Location	✓✓✓✓✓
Quality of Pitches	✓✓✓	Range of Facilities	✓✓✓✓

Directions

Park is west off A515 Buxton - Ashbourne road, just north of Fenny Bentley village; the entrance is 100 yards south of old railway bridge (take care at sharp turn to site road when approaching from Ashbourne). O.S.GR: SK170510. GPS: N53:03.335 W01:44.935

Charges 2005

Per unit incl. 2 persons	£ 12.00
extra adult	£ 5.00
child (under 17 yrs)	£ 1.00
electricity (16A)	£ 3.00
awning	£ 1.00
dog	£ 1.00

Reservations

Made with payment of one night's fee; min. stay at B.Hs 3 nights. Tel: 0870 741 8000.

UK3815 Lickpenny

Lickpenny Lane, Tansley, Matlock DE4 5GF (Derbyshire)

This spacious new caravan park on a hill above Matlock has 103 terraced pitches, all on hardstandings (no tents) and with electricity (16A). Of these, 82 are touring pitches and 13 are fully serviced. Looking at the rows of mature trees and bushes, it seems hard to believe that this site was only created for the 2003 season; the enthusiastic owners have taken full advantage of the fact that this was previously a market garden and are continuing to work very hard to maintain high standards and improve facilities. Pitches are large and separated by shrubs and bushes. Buildings are of natural stone and well equipped. Recreational grassy areas and attractive flower borders are well tended, whilst the top corner of the park has been kept as woodland. Reception incorporates a small shop (basics only at present) and tourist information. Local attractions include Matlock Bath and the Heights of Abraham, Chatsworth House, Haddon Hall, Hardwick Hall, Eyam and Castleton.

Facilities

Two well equipped, heated toilet blocks include free controllable showers and some washbasins in cubicles. Good facilities for disabled people. Family room with small bath, toilet and washbasin. Laundry room with washing machines, dryers, irons and ironing boards. Chemical disposal points. Motorcaravan service point. Security barrier with keypad access at all times. Off site: Bus service from end of the road. Riding 1 mile. Fishing 3 miles. Golf 4 miles. Bicycle hire 6 miles. Woodland walk to Garden Centre with restaurant serving snacks and lunches (200 yards).

Open

All year.

At a glance

Welcome & Ambience	✓✓✓✓	Location	✓✓✓✓
Quality of Pitches	✓✓✓✓	Range of Facilities	✓✓✓

Directions

Matlock is 18 miles west of the M1 at exit 28. From motorway, follow signs for Matlock on A38, A61 and A615. After 5 miles on A615 turn north on Lickpenny Lane to site (signed). From Matlock take A615; after Tansley fork left on B6014 (Clay Cross) and turn right at top of hill after Garden Centre. O.S.GR: SK339598. GPS: N53:08.072 W01:29.429

Charges 2005

Per unit incl. 2 persons	£ 13.50 - £ 17.00
extra person	£ 2.00
child (0-14 yrs)	£ 1.00

Reservations

Contact park. Tel: 01629 583040. Email: lickpenny@btinternet.com

UK3840 Lime Tree Park

Dukes Drive, Buxton SK17 9RP (Derbyshire)

A select park with high quality, modern facilities, Lime Tree is in a convenient, edge of town location that makes a very good base for touring the Peak District. There are 99 pitches including some for seasonal and rental units, the 64 for tourists with 10A electricity (there are hardstandings available) and an area for tents (some terracing but mainly sloping ground) are on the two upper terraces which have the best views but are slightly more exposed. Below are areas set aside for late arrivals and the caravan holiday homes (most privately owned, some for rent). On site is a small shop for gas and basic provisions, and a recently extended children's playground. Buxton town centre is just a comfortable stroll away. A member of the Best of British group.

Facilities

A modern toilet building serves the caravan and motorcaravan area, including some washbasins in cubicles, controllable showers, a baby room with the very latest design of baby bath, and a family room with facilities for disabled people, whilst the refitted original unit serves the tent area. Both units can be heated and have top quality fittings. Dishwashing sinks are outside under cover. Laundry room with washing machine and dryer. Motorcaravan service area. Shop. Play area. Games/TV room. Off site: The nearest pub serving food is just around the corner. Riding and golf 1 mile, fishing, bicycle hire, sailing and boat-launching 5 miles. Alton Towers 22 miles.

Open

1 March - 31 October.

At a glance

Welcome & Ambience	✓✓✓✓	Location	✓✓✓✓
Quality of Pitches	✓✓✓	Range of Facilities	✓✓✓

Directions

Park is on outskirts of Buxton and is signed from A515 Buxton - Ashbourne road 1 mile south of town. From town, immediately after hospital bear sharp left into Dukes Drive, go under railway viaduct and site is on the right. From south watch out for sharp turn right at foot of hill (signed in advance). O.S.GR: SK069725.

Charges 2005

Per unit incl. 2 adults	£ 12.00
extra adult	£ 5.00
child (5-15 yrs)	£ 2.00
electricity	£ 3.00
awning	£ 2.00
dog	£ 1.00

Reservations

Made with £10 deposit, £30 for Bank Holidays (both non-refundable). Tel: 01298 22988. Email: limetreebuxton@dukes50.fsnet.co.uk

UK3864 The Firs Farm

Crich Lane, Nether Heage, Ambergate, Belper DE56 2JH (Derbyshire)

This is a pleasant, compact, adult-only park on a ridge above the valley of the River Derwent. About half of the 60 pitches are usually available for touring units, the rest being used as seasonal pitches. There are a few level grass pitches (on which the use of groundsheets is discouraged) but most are on hardstandings with grass verges. All have access to 10A electricity. Reception is housed in a wooden cabin next to the warden's caravan and has local information; new arrivals are taken to their pitch. The owner also lives on site. The park is clearly well cared for, and every year wins awards for its presentation and its hanging baskets (sadly not yet in evidence when we visited in early June). Despite its location, there are no views from the site itself, though there are, of course, plenty in the Derwent Valley below. The historical mills between Matlock and Derby have led to this becoming a World Heritage Site. The magnificent scenery of the Peak District National Park is just a short drive away: Dove Dale, Matlock Bath and the Heights of Abraham, the Crich Tram Museum, the Tissington Trail, Bakewell and Chatsworth House all within a 20 mile radius.

Facilities

The heated toilet block has controllable showers, some washbasins in cubicles and dishwashing and a laundry sink under cover. The facilities appear to be well maintained. Water and waste-water points and chemical disposal point. Off site: Bus from site gate (4 daily), train 1 mile. Pub and shop nearby. Fishing 1 mile. Riding 2 miles. Golf 4 miles. Bicycle hire 6 miles. Sailing and boat launching 7 miles.

Open

All year.

At a glance

Welcome & Ambience	✓✓✓	Location	✓✓✓✓
Quality of Pitches	✓✓✓	Range of Facilities	✓✓✓

Directions

Nether Heage is east of the A6, 10 miles north of Derby, between Belper and Matlock. Turn east 1.7 miles south of Ambergate at campsite sign onto Broadholme Lane (take care of the sharp turn if approaching from the north) and follow signs to site in 1 mile. If coming from M1 via A610, ignore any signs for Nether Heage; continue to Ambergate, then as above. O.S.GR: SK354510. GPS: N53:02.967 W01:28.408

Charges 2005

Per unit incl. 2 adults and electricity	£ 12.00
tent and 2 adults	£ 10.00
extra adult	£ 2.00

Reservations

Contact park. Tel: 01773 852913. Email: thefirsfarmcaravanpark@b.t.internet.co.uk

UK3850 **Rivendale Caravan & Leisure Park**

Buxton Road, Alsop-en-le-Dale, Ashbourne DE6 1QU (Derbyshire)

This is an unusual park, recently developed in the bowl of a hill quarry that was last worked 50 years ago. The steep quarry walls shelter three sides with marvellous views over the Peak National Park countryside to the south. A wide access road passes the renovated stone building which houses the reception, a shop, bar and a café/restaurant. It gently climbs to a horseshoe shaped area providing 100 pitches, most of generous size, with 16A electricity. The pitches, a mixture of hardstanding and half grass, half hardstanding, are divided by shrubs which are now maturing well with a further, open, marked grass area accessed by hard core roads. All pitches are within easy reach of the central stone-built toilet block which is in keeping with the environment and thoughtfully provided with under-floor heating. The park takes up about 11 acres and a further 26 acres belong to the owners with certain parts suitable for walking – a must to appreciate the Derbyshire countryside with its dry stone walls, wild flowers and a little more of the quarry history. The park is situated almost on the Tissington Trail for walking or off road cycling and linking with the High Peak and Monsal Dale Trail. Other spectacular walks and cycle rides run along the Manifold, Wye and Dove valleys.

Facilities

First rate toilet facilities include some washbasins in cubicles for ladies, and an excellent en-suite room for disabled visitors. Laundry room. Glass and paper recycling bins. Bar (evenings) and café with home-made and local food (open mornings, lunch times and evenings, both with limited opening in low season). Special events monthly and games in main season. Shop (all essentials). Off site: Bicycle hire and riding 5 miles. Sailing and boat-launching 8 miles. Fishing and golf 10 miles. Alton Towers 35 minutes drive. Chatsworth House and Gardens, Heights of Abraham and Guillivers Kingdom near.

At a glance

Welcome & Ambience	✓✓✓✓	Location	✓✓✓✓
Quality of Pitches	✓✓✓	Range of Facilities	✓✓✓✓

Directions

Park is about 7 miles north of Ashbourne on the A515 to Buxton, on the eastern side of the road. It is well signed between the turnings east to Alsop Moor and Matlock (A5012), but take care as this is a very fast section of the A515. O.S.GR: SK161566. GPS: N53:06.383 W01:53.933

Charges 2005

Per pitch incl. 2 adults, electricity	£ 11.40 - £ 13.60
extra adult	£ 2.00
child (4-15 yrs)	£ 1.50
dog	£ 1.00

Camping Cheques accepted.

Reservations

Made with £10 deposit. Tel: 01335 310311. Email: enquiries@rivendalecaravanpark.co.uk

Open

All year excl. 9 January - 2 February.

Beautiful surroundings in the Peak District National Park. Open all year **except** 9th January - 2nd February. Ideal for cycling, walking, outdoor and adventure sports. Convenient for Chatsworth, Alton Towers & Dove Dale. Holiday homes for sale.

www.Rivendalecaravanpark.co.uk **Tel: +44 (0)1335 310311 or 310441**

167

UK3904 Greendale Farm Caravan & Camping Park

Pickwell Lane, Whissendine, Oakham LE15 7LB (Rutland)

This is a delightful little, adult only park set in rolling countryside, ideal for those seeking peace and tranquillity. It is very eco-friendly and extremely well appointed for such a small site. Reception, the shop and the toilet facilities are housed in a modern building adjoining the owners' house. The shop is well stocked with essentials and local produce and operates on an 'honesty' basis: visitors are given a code for the lock and can use it at any time. It also has one of the best-presented and most comprehensive information displays we have seen on any campsite. This includes charts for visitors to record birds seen on the park – the list is most impressive – walking and cycle routes and pub menus. There are weekly meetings for birdwatchers, would-be artists (the office is decorated with the paintings produced by visitors over the past four years) and photographers, all free in April and May. Cooked breakfasts are available on Sundays. There are only 15 pitches, 14 with 10 or 16A electricity, and three of these are usually occupied for the season, so it's worth checking availability!

Facilities

Each of the two rooms of the toilet 'block has a power-shower, WCs and two washbasins (cubicles for the ladies). All is beautifully appointed and immaculately kept. Small open-air swimming-pool (6 x 3 m; £1 charge), heated by solar-panels, with summer house. Outdoor dishwashing sink plus one in the shop which can also be used for laundry. Washing machine, tumble dryer and spin dryer. Chemical disposal and nearby sluicing point. Recycling bins (glass, paper, cardboard, batteries, green waste). Two bicycles for hire. Off site: Village with bus service 0.5 miles. Riding 4 miles. Fishing 6 miles. Golf 8 miles. Sailing, bird-watching, walking, cycling (and bicycle hire) and fishing at Rutland Water 8 miles.

Open

Easter - end September.

At a glance

| Welcome & Ambience | ✓✓✓✓✓ | Location | ✓✓✓✓ |
| Quality of Pitches | ✓✓✓✓ | Range of Facilities | ✓✓✓✓ |

Directions

Oakham is 20 miles east of Leicester and Whissendine is just off the A606 Oakham - Melton Mowbray road. Approach park from this road and NOT through the village. From Oakham ignore the first turning to Whissendine, continue 2 miles and turn right at campsite sign. From Melton ignore first two turnings to Whissendine; turn left 0.6 mile after Rutland sign (at campsite sign). Park is on right in 0.6 mile. O.S.GR:SK819133. GPS: N52:42.710 W00:47.317

Charges 2005

Per adult	£ 4.00
pitch incl. electricity	£ 5.00 - £ 8.00
dog	£ 1.00

Reservations

Made with deposit (£10 - £25); contact park. Tel: 01664 474516. Email: enq@rutlandgreendale.co.uk

UK3920 Riverside Caravan Park

Central Avenue, Worksop S80 1ER (Nottinghamshire)

A town centre touring park, adjacent to the Worksop cricket ground, this excellent park is attractive and surprisingly peaceful. Riverside is within easy walking distance of the town centre pedestrian precinct and shops, and the Chesterfield Canal runs close to its northern side offering delightful tow-path walks or fishing (children would need to be watched). For those who cannot resist the thwack of leather on willow, this site is ideal. Of the 60 marked level pitches, 50 are for touring, mainly on gravel hard-standing, others are on grass and some are separated by trees and low rails, and all have electric hook-ups (10A). There is excellent site lighting. Attractions in the area include Creswell Crags, Clumber Park, the Dukeries Cycle Trail, Thoresby Park and Gallery and Rufford Mill Craft Centre and Country Park.

Facilities

The modern sanitary unit near reception can be heated and has all the usual facilities, although showers are on payment (20p). No laundry, but a launderette is close by in the town. Off site: Fishing 0.5 miles. Several golf courses 1 mile. Bicycle hire 4 miles. Squash and flat or crown green bowling nearby. Campers are made very welcome at the cricket ground clubhouse. One of Worksop's most interesting buildings, the medieval Priory Gatehouse, is open free of charge. Market days are Wednesday, Friday and Saturday.

Open

All year.

At a glance

| Welcome & Ambience | ✓✓✓✓ | Location | ✓✓✓✓ |
| Quality of Pitches | ✓✓✓✓✓ | Range of Facilities | ✓✓✓ |

Directions

Worksop is 7 miles west of the M1 at junction 30 and 4 miles east of the A1. Easiest approach to Park is from A57/A60 roundabout west of the town - third roundabout from the A1. Turn east (at Little Chef) on B6024 towards Town Centre. Site is well signed: in 400 yds, turn left into Stubbing Lane, then right into Central Avenue and left into Cricket Ground taking care at sharp left turn after bridge. Site entrance is to the left of clubhouse. O.S.GR: SK580790. GPS: N53:18.360 W001:07.72

Charges 2005

Per pitch incl. 2 adults, awning and electricity	£ 10.00
extra person	£ 4.50
child (5-13 yrs)	£ 1.50

No credit cards.

Reservations

Advised for B.Hs, peak season and weekends, with £5 deposit. Tel: 01909 474118.

UK3910 **Shardaroba Caravan Park**

Silverhill Lane, Teversal, Sutton-in-Ashfield NG17 3JJ (Nottinghamshire)

In a peaceful village location, and yet surprisingly close to the motorway network, this attractive, six acre campsite has 100 pitches (25 seasonal). It is beautifully kept and has recently won awards. Many of the spacious touring pitches are on hardstandings, arranged in well spaced rows surrounded by areas of grass and flower beds. All have electric hook-ups (16A), and 20 are multi-serviced. A grassed area for campers has a covered patio nearby with tables and chairs. Picnic tables are provided around the site. The owners live on site and their attention to detail is evident everywhere. Adjacent is an attractive country park - the highest point in Nottinghamshire. Nearby attractions include Hadwick Hall, Crich Tramway Museum, Newstead Abbey and the Pleasley Trails.

Facilities

Excellent, well equipped, heated toilet block with spacious showers, and brand new family room. Disabled shower room and toilet/wash room designed with visually impaired visitors in mind. Separate laundry has modern washing machines, dryers and free spin dryers. New covered dishwashing sinks. Separate building with six full suites (WC, washbasin, shower) and unisex toilet/washbasin next to camping area. Motorcaravan service point. Shop with basics. Calor gas. Tourist information cabin. Playground. American RVs accepted. Security barrier. Off site: Riding 200 yds. Golf 800 yds. Fishing, bicycle hire, pub, bakery, chip shop and general stores within 1 mile. Sailing 2 miles.

Open

All year.

At a glance

Welcome & Ambience	✓✓✓✓✓	Location	✓✓✓✓
Quality of Pitches	✓✓✓✓✓	Range of Facilities	✓✓✓✓

Directions

Teversal is central in a triangle formed by junctions 28 and 29 of the M1 and Mansfield. Site is signed off B6014 at western end of the village, turning north by the Carnarvon Arms into Silverhill Lane. Site entrance is 300 yds on left. O.S.GR: SK485625.
GPS: N53:08.911 W001:17.75

Charges 2005

Per unit incl. 2 adults	£ 12.00 - £ 16.00
extra adult	£ 4.00
child (3-14 yrs)	£ 2.00
electricity	£ 2.00
awning or pup tent	£ 1.00

Reservations

Advisable for B.Hs and July/August. Made with £10 non-refundable deposit. Tel: 01623 551838.
Email: stay@shardaroba.co.uk

UK3940 **Smeaton's Lakes Touring Caravan & Fishing Park**

Great North Road, South Muskham, Newark-on-Trent NG23 6ED (Nottinghamshire)

This 82-acre site is really ideal for anglers, with four fishing lakes (coarse, carp and pike) and river fishing on the Trent. Smeaton's Lakes has tarmac access roads and a modern building near the entrance housing reception and the original sanitary facilities. There are 130 pitches of which 50 are on hardstanding and 100 have electricity connections (16A). Non-anglers might choose this park if visiting events at nearby Newark Showground, or Newark town (1 mile) with its castle and various weekly markets. The park is only two minutes from DMG Newark Antique Fairs and Arthur Swallow's Swinderby Antique Fairs. During your stay, you might enjoy a visit to Southwell Cathedral, Lincoln with its castle and cathedral or Nottingham with its Lace Hall, Castle or Caves. For people who like to look at motorhomes, Brownhills is close by.

Facilities

Two toilet blocks (with keypad access) are heated and include a good unit for disabled people, but no laundry room. Laundry and dishwashing sinks are outside. Reception keeps gas, soft drinks, dairy produce, etc. and newspapers can be ordered. On-site concessions for lake and river fishing. Security cameras and night-time height barrier (about 6 ft). Off site: Bus stop at the end of the entry lane – buses run into Newark every hour until 10 pm. Riding 2 miles.

Open

All year.

At a glance

Welcome & Ambience	✓✓✓	Location	✓✓✓
Quality of Pitches	✓✓✓	Range of Facilities	✓✓✓

Directions

Park is just over a mile north of Newark on the Great North Road (to the east). From south on A1, take A46 west (signed Newark, then Leicester) and at next roundabout turn north on A6065/A616 (Ollerton) towards South Muskham. From the southwest on the M1/A46 turn north off the Newark bypass on the A6065/A616 as above. From the north on A1 leave B6325 (Newark) continue south through South Muskham and follow signs for Newark.
GPS: N53:05.616 W000:49.24

Charges 2005

Per unit incl. 2 adults	£ 11.00 - £ 12.00
extra adult	£ 1.50
child (over 5 yrs)	£ 1.00
Credit cards accepted.	

Reservations

Essential for electric hook-ups. Tel: 01636 605088.
Email: lesley@smeatonslakes.co.uk

UK3950 **Orchard Park**

Marnham Road, Tuxford, Newark NG22 0PY (Nottinghamshire)

This well established family run touring and caravan park has been created in an old fruit orchard in a quiet location, yet is very convenient for the A1. It has a friendly feel, with just 65 pitches, including 34 with hardstanding, 20 of which were occupied by seasonal units at the time of our visit. All pitches have access to electricity (10A). There is a spacious camping field with views and plenty of room for ball games. Reception is at the owner's house with a nearby information cabin and at the far end of the park is a picnic area, an excellent children's adventure trail and a nature walk with wild flowers, birds and butterflies. Local attractions include Sundown Adventureland theme park for children, Laxton Medieval village and Victorian Times, Sherwood Forest and the Robin Hood Centre and Clumber Park.

Facilities

The heated toilet block (with piped music) includes a well equipped room for disabled persons. Laundry with washing machines, dryer and dishwashing sinks, free spin dryer, iron and freezer for ice-packs. Small shop with basics and gas. Apples, pears and blackberries can be picked in season. Entrance barrier (£5 deposit for key). Off site: Pub 0.5 miles, shops 1 mile. Riding 3 miles. Fishing 4 miles. Bicycle hire and golf 10 miles.

Open

March - October.

At a glance

| Welcome & Ambience | ✓✓✓✓ | Location | ✓✓✓✓ |
| Quality of Pitches | ✓✓✓✓ | Range of Facilities | ✓✓✓ |

Directions

Tuxford is 15 miles north of Newark and 18 miles west of Lincoln. The Park lies to the east of the A1. Leave at signs for Tuxford and turn east on A6075 towards Lincoln (A57), continue through village to the outskirts and turn south towards Marnham. Site is on right 0.5 miles after railway bridge (well signed in village). O.S.GR: SK750710. GPS: N53:13.776 W000:52.17

Charges 2005

Per unit incl. 2 adults, electricity	£ 14.00
extra adult	£ 2.00
child (4-15 yrs)	£ 1.00
awning or child's pup tent	£ 1.00

Reservations

Advised for B.Hs (min. 3 nights) with £50 deposit and peak season with £10 deposit. Tel: 01777 870228. Email: info@orchardcaravanpark.co.uk

UK3970 **Glencote Caravan Park**

Station Road, Cheddleton, Leek ST13 7EE (Staffordshire)

At the entrance to the Churnet Valley, three miles south of the market town of Leek, Glencote is a pleasant, family run park of six acres. It has 74 numbered pitches set on flat grass, all with patio style hardstandings, with tarmac access roads. There are 40 pitches for touring units and all have electrical connections (10A) and a dedicated water supply. Pretty flower-beds and trees make a very pleasant environment. An attractive, sunken children's play area, on grass and bark with an abundance of shrubs and flowers, sits alongside the small (fenced) coarse fishing pool, together with a barbecue area with a tented cover. Attractions nearby include a renovated Flint Mill powered by two giant water wheels and Cheddleton railway centre. The Churnet Valley, an Area of Outstanding Natural Beauty is good for walking, the Staffordshire Way is also near. For the more energetic visitor, canoeing, climbing and hang-gliding opportunities are close. Alton Towers is 10 miles away.

Facilities

The toilet block is centrally situated and can be heated. Facilities include one private cabin for ladies, a small laundry room, and two dishwashing sinks under cover. Gas supplies. Max. 2 dogs per unit. Off site: In the village of Cheddleton, 0.5 miles away, is a small supermarket and a post office. A variety of inns are within easy walking distance - the Boat Inn beside the canal is very good value. Riding 10 miles, bicycle hire 5 miles, golf 4 miles.

Open

Mid March - end October.

At a glance

| Welcome & Ambience | ✓✓✓✓✓ | Location | ✓✓✓✓ |
| Quality of Pitches | ✓✓✓✓ | Range of Facilities | ✓✓✓ |

Directions

Park is signed off A520 Leek - Stone road, 3.5 miles south of Leek on northern edge of Cheddleton Village. O.S.GR: SJ982524.

Charges 2005

Per unit incl. 2 persons and electricity (10A)	£ 14.50
extra adult	£ 4.00
child (3-16 yrs)	£ 2.00
dog	free - £ 0.50
Min. stay of 3 nights at B.Hs.	

Reservations

Advised for peak season. Made with deposit (£ 30 for 4 nights or more, full payment for up to 3 nights). Tel: 01538 360745. Email: canistay@glencote.co.uk

UK3980 Longnor Wood Caravan & Camping Park

Longnor, nr. Buxton SK17 0NG (Derbyshire)

A secluded rural location, deep in the heart of the Peak District, Longnor Wood is an ideal environment for a relaxing break from the outside world. It is a good base for walking, red deer and bird watching (barn owls) and serious cycling - the area is very hilly. There are 47 pitches, of which 14 are taken by holiday homes, the remaining 33 touring pitches are level, some on small terraces, all with 10A electric hook-ups. Thirteen are multi-serviced with electricity, water, waste water and TV connections. Twelve are on hardstandings. The tenting area is at the top of the site with wonderful views over the National Park, but you may have a problem with tent pegs as the topsoil can be rather thin in places. There is a well appointed late arrivals area at the entrance. Reception has a brochure with the history of the old market town of Longnor (where 'Peak Practice' was filmed), which includes several places worth visiting. This is an adult only park (over 18 yrs).

Facilities

The single heated building has been recently refurbished and includes cubicles with a toilet and washbasin, spacious showers and has dishwashing sinks under cover, and a microwave oven (donations to charity). Laundry with washing machine, tumble dryer and spin dryer. Reception is licensed and stocks basic requirements. Gas supplies. Putting green, badminton and boules courts. Dogs accepted, max. 2 per unit. Site is not suitable for American RVs. Off site: Markets in Buxton (Tues/Sat), Leek (Wed). Sightseeing opportunities include Dove dale and the Manifold Valley, Arbor Low Stone Circle, and Flash, at 1,580 ft. is the highest village in England. Fishing 5 miles, golf 8 miles, riding 8 miles.

Open

1 March - 31 October.

At a glance

Welcome & Ambience	✓✓✓✓✓	Location	✓✓✓✓✓
Quality of Pitches	✓✓✓✓	Range of Facilities	✓✓✓

Directions

Longnor village is on the B5053, about 6 miles south of Buxton. Site is west of village (where it is signed) on a minor road (1 mile). Also signed from the A53 between Leek and Buxton, turning next to the Winking Man public house. O.S.GR: SK072640.

Charges 2005

Per pitch incl. 2 persons and electricity	£ 13.50
serviced pitch (electricity, water and drainage) incl 2 persons	£ 15.00
extra person	£ 2.00
tent incl 2 persons	£ 11.50
No credit cards.	

Reservations

Advisable for weekends, B.Hs and peak season. Made with £10 deposit. Tel: 01298 83648. Email: info@longnorwood.co.uk

UK4040 Clent Hills Camping & Caravanning Club Site

Fieldhouse Lane, Romsley, Halesowen B62 0NH (West Midlands)

Conveniently close to Birmingham and only a couple of miles or so off the M5/M42 intersection, this site is a real surprise in terms of being quiet and peaceful and very pretty with good views. Its only disadvantage is that it is on sloping ground, but the present, very helpful holiday site managers are happy to assist in pitching anyone who has a problem in getting level (mainly motorcaravanners); in fact, there are some level pitches and these are all earmarked for motorcaravans. The 95 pitches are all of a good size, 74 with electrical connections (10/16A) and 17 with hardstanding. The modern reception building with excellent tourist information, arrivals area and larger car parking area are at the entrance. Generally this is a well run and attractive site, very usefully situated.

Facilities

The central sanitary toilet block can be heated and provides the latest facilities, including washbasins in cabins, hairdryers, baby room and a toilet and shower for disabled people. It was spotless when last visited. Washing machine, dryer and ironing facilities. Small play area with rubber safety surface. Gas supplies. Caravan storage. Off site: Riding 1 mile. Fishing 3 miles. Golf 7 miles.

Open

March - November.

At a glance

Welcome & Ambience	✓✓✓✓✓	Location	✓✓✓✓
Quality of Pitches	✓✓✓✓	Range of Facilities	✓✓✓

Directions

From M5 junction 3 take A491, branch right to Romsley on B4551 and watch for site signs in Romsley village by shops. Site is on left. O.S.GR: SO955795.

Charges 2005

Per adult	£ 4.30 - £ 6.40
child (6-18 yrs)	£ 1.90
non-member pitch fee	£ 5.00

Reservations

Necessary and made with deposit; contact site or Central Reservations 0870 243 3331. Tel: 01562 710015.

Planning your
next holiday?

don't forget to look at our directory
ON PAGE 314

UK4070 Somers Wood Caravan Park

Somers Road, Meriden CV7 7PL (Warwickshire)

Somers Wood is attractively located and edged by pine woods, with views of the adjacent 18 hole golf course (including a driving range) and coarse fishing lake, both of which can be used by visitors. The park is near Birmingham and also close to the National Exhibition Centre. Log buildings that blend comfortably into their surroundings provide reception, the owners' home at the entrance and separate sanitary facilities. An oval, gravel road provides access to 48 large pitches, all on hardstanding with 10A electricity connections. This is a very useful park for those visiting the NEC. For certain shows, such as the National Boat, Caravan and Leisure Show in February, it can be busy, although at other times it is quiet and peaceful. Only adults are accepted and the park does not take tents.

Facilities	Directions
The central, heated sanitary block is fully equipped. Two dishwashing sinks on the veranda area. Laundry service at reception. Off site: Local shops and restaurant less than 1 mile and visitors also welcome to use the bar and restaurant at the golf club next door.	From M42 junction 6 (NEC) take A45 towards Coventry. Keep in left lane down to roundabout and exit on A452 (signed Leamington/Meriden), then turn left into Hampton Lane at the next roundabout. Site is signed with golf and fishing centres on the left. O.S.GR: SP228819.

Open

1 February - 12 December.

Charges 2006

Per pitch incl. 2 persons and electricity	£ 17.00
extra adult	£ 3.00
Special offers for some weeks.	

At a glance

Welcome & Ambience	✓✓✓	Location	✓✓✓✓
Quality of Pitches	✓✓✓✓	Range of Facilities	✓✓✓

Reservations

Advised for B.Hs and certain NEC exhibitions; made with deposit of £5 per night booked. Tel: 01676 522978. Email: info@somerswood.co.uk.

UK4075 Hollyfast Caravan Park

Wall Hill Road, Allesley, Coventry CV5 9EL (Warwickshire)

Hollyfast is situated in beautiful countryside on the outskirts of Coventry, part of the park being set within a lovely woodland area giving peace and tranquillity all year round. Located on the Birmingham side of Coventry, this means a five minute drive into the centre of Coventry and just a ten minute drive to Birmingham's National Exhibition Centre. You will receive a friendly welcome and be directed to a very clean and well spaced site with 35 pitches of varying sizes with 6A electricity connections. You may be asked to park your car on a nearby car park. A new toilet block provides very clean facilities, along with a laundry room and games room. Rallies are welcome and a club house is provided with a stage, television and kitchen areas for these groups. Under the same ownership, a motorcaravan sales centre with caravan and motorhome storage, LPG and a children's play area are reached through the site.

Facilities	Directions
The modern toilet block provides simple clean facilities with good sized showers (3 per sex) and open washbasins. Toilet and shower for disabled campers. Laundry. Games room. Club house for rallies. Deposit for barrier (£25). Off site: The local area has shops, three pubs (hot and cold food), a golf course and a riding centre. Bus stop 1 mile for Coventry. Interesting British Road Transport museum. Birmingham, Stratford upon Avon, Leamington Spa and Warwick are within driving distance.	From M1/M45 (or the M40/A46, or M69/A46) take A45 towards Birmingham. Turn right on A4114 and follow brown and white caravan signs. After turning by the Jolly Farmers pub, site is 0.5 miles on the left. From the north take M6 north of Birmingham or the M1 north (Nottingham) follow the M42 to the NEC, A45 towards Coventry and onto A4114 and as above. O.S.GR: SP303831

Open

All year.

Charges 2005

Per unit incl. 2 persons and electricity	£ 11.00 - £ 15.00
extra adult	£ 2.50
child (5-15 yrs)	£ 1.50
awning	£ 2.75
dog	£ 1.00

At a glance

Welcome & Ambience	✓✓✓✓	Location	✓✓✓✓
Quality of Pitches	✓✓✓✓	Range of Facilities	✓✓✓

Reservations

Contact site. Tel: 024 7633 6411. Email: sales@hollyfastcaravanpark.co.uk

UK4080 Riverside Caravan Park

Tiddington Road, Tiddington, Stratford-upon-Avon CV37 7AB (Warwickshire)

On the bank of the River Avon, this spacious site has about 250 pitches in total, and about 100 privately owned mobile homes. The 125 touring pitches (no tents) are on level grass, all with electric hook-ups (16A) and some with TV aerial sockets. There is a small shop and cafe on site, which serves breakfasts and takeaways in addition to stocking a good selection of basic supplies. A clubhouse with a restaurant, bar, playground, games room and TV is on the adjacent Rayford Park which is under the same management. There is a possible flood risk during periods of inclement weather. A river taxi runs to Stratford.

Facilities

The main toilet unit has been re-fitted to modern standards and is bright and comfortable with central heating. Spacious pre-set showers, some washbasins in cubicles, with a child-size toilet and shower in the ladies. Facilities for disabled guests. Utility room with dishwashing and laundry sinks, washing machines and dryers. Slipway and fishing on-site. Courtesy river launch to Stratford. Gas supplies. No commercial vehicles are accepted. Off site: Shakespeare.

At a glance

Welcome & Ambience	✓✓✓✓	Location	✓✓✓✓
Quality of Pitches	✓✓✓✓	Range of Facilities	✓✓✓

Directions

From Stratford take B4086 towards Wellesbourne. Site entrance is on left, after one mile, just before Tiddington village (ignore entrance to Rayford Park C.P.) O.S.GR: SP219559.

Charges 2005

Per caravan or motorcaravan incl. 4 persons   £ 14.00

Reservations

Advisable for weekends, B.Hs, and peak season and made with £10 non-refundable deposit. Tel: 01789 292312. Email: info@stratfordcaravans.co.uk

Open

1 April - 31 October.

UK4090 Island Meadow Caravan Park

The Mill House, Aston Cantlow B95 6JP (Warwickshire)

This peaceful, traditional, family run site is in a rural location, surrounded by the River Alne and its mill race. A good base for walking, cycling and birdwatching, it has 80 pitches in total, with 56 holiday homes (4 for rent) located around the perimeter. The 24 touring pitches are on the spacious, central grassy area of the site, all have 10A electric hook-ups. Only environmentally friendly groundsheets are permitted. The small shop has an adequate stock of basic requirements and gas supplies, and a good stock of local visitor information. Note: The site is on an island with obvious hazards for small children. There is an excellent playground in the village centre (five minutes walk via footpath across Mill Meadow).

Facilities

Two sanitary units, both heated. The original provides adequate WCs and washbasins for men, and the more modern unit has been provided for women, with a separate access shower unit for the men, and a suite for disabled people on one end. Dishwashing sink. Laundry with washing machine, sink and ironing facility. The millpond and its weir offer good coarse fishing. Off site: The village has its own 'club' (campers welcome) and the local pub serves a good range of meals. Golf 3 miles, riding 4.5 miles, bicycle hire 6 miles. Warwick Castle. Stratford-upon-Avon. Mary Arden's house in Wilmcote is only 1 mile from the site. Buses from village to Alcester and Stratford, including a late night service.

At a glance

Welcome & Ambience	✓✓✓✓	Location	✓✓✓✓
Quality of Pitches	✓✓✓✓	Range of Facilities	✓✓✓

Directions

Site is well signed from the A46 mid-way between Alcester and Stratford-upon-Avon, and also from the A3400 at Wootton Wawen. O.S.GR: SP136598.

Charges 2005

Per unit incl. 2 persons and electricity	£ 15.00
extra person	£ 1.00
child (5-10 yrs)	£ 0.50
tent (2 man)	£ 11.00

Gazebos only by prior arrangement. No credit cards.

Reservations

Advised for B.Hs (3 nights minimum) and July/August. Tel: 01789 488273. Email: holiday@islandmeadowcaravanpark.co.uk

Open

1 March - 31 October.

(173)

UK4100 **Hoburne Cotswold**

Broadway Lane, South Cerney, Cirencester GL7 5UQ (Gloucestershire)

Since this park is adjacent to the Cotswold Water Park, those staying will have easy access to the varied watersports there which include sailboarding and water ski-ing. On the park itself there is a lake with pedaloes and canoes for hire. Its wide range of other amenities include an outdoor heated swimming pool and an impressive, large indoor leisure complex. There are 340 well marked touring pitches for any type of unit, all with hardstanding (only fairly level) and a grass surround for awning or tent; 40 are serviced 'super' pitches. Of good size but with nothing between them, all have electricity (some need long leads). There are also 210 holiday units, mainly for letting. The large clubhouse has a big general lounge with giant TV screen, entertainment at times, food service (or food bar in lounge), big games room and a lounge bar which overlooks the pool and lake with a patio. Part of the Hoburne group.

Facilities

Six toilet blocks, all quite small, but clean and well maintained with pre-set showers and background heating. Baby changing facilities. Basic facilities for disabled visitors are in toilet block 4 and at the clubhouse. The site has heavy weekend trade. Launderette. Supermarket. Indoor leisure complex including pool with flume, spa bath, sauna, steam room (all free) and sun bed (charged). Outdoor pool (open Whitsun - early September; 44 x 22 ft). Clubhouse with bar, food and entertainment. Football field. Tennis courts. Good quality adventure playground with bark base. Crazy golf. Fishing lake (permits from reception). No dogs or pets are accepted.

At a glance

Welcome & Ambience	✓✓✓	Location	✓✓✓✓
Quality of Pitches	✓✓✓✓	Range of Facilities	✓✓✓✓✓

Directions

Three miles southeast of Cirencester on A419, turn west towards Cotswold Water Park at new roundabout on bypass onto B4696. Take second right and follow signs. O.S.GR: SU055957.

Charges 2005

Per pitch incl. max. 6 persons	
and electricity	£ 13.00 - £ 27.50
serviced 'super' pitch	£ 14.00 - £ 29.00

Weekly rates and weekend breaks available.

Reservations

Bookings of 1-6 nights payable in full at time of reservation; caravans with £50 deposit for 1 week. Min. 4 nights booking at B.Hs. Tel: 01285 860216. Email: enquiries@hoburne.co.uk

Open

March - October.

UK4150 **Croft Farm Water & Leisure Park**

Bredon's Hardwick, Tewkesbury GL20 7EE (Gloucestershire)

Croft Farm is an AALA licensed Watersports Centre with Royal Yachting Association approved tuition available for windsurfing, sailing, kayaking and canoeing. The lakeside campsite has around 96 level pitches, with 80 electric hook-ups (10A), but there are many seasonal units, leaving around 36 pitches for tourists, plus some tent pitches. There are 22 gravel hardstandings but very little shade or shelter. 'Gym & Tonic' is a fully equipped gymnasium with qualified instructors, sun bed and sauna. Sports massage, aromatherapy and beauty treatments are available by appointment. The 'Playzone' has a soft play area, play structure, bouncy castle table football and a Playstation. In school holidays supervised activities the 'Playzone Pirates' are run on weekday mornings, and afternoon Funtimes for parents and children. Activity holidays for families and groups are also organised. Campers can use their own non-powered boats on the lake with reduced launch fees and there is free fishing. A new clubroom, bar and reception building was added in 2004.

Facilities

A new building (open in summer months) on the far side of the lake, has excellent modern facilities with spacious hot showers, plus some dishwashing sinks outside to the rear. A heated unit at the back of the gymnasium in the main building (near the reception/watersports shop) is always open and best for cooler months, this provides further WCs, washbasins and showers, laundry and includes facilities for disabled persons. Gas available. Cafe/bar (Friday-Sunday in low season, daily at other times). Takeaway. Gym. Indoor 'Playzone' for under 10s. Outdoor playground. River fishing. Key for barrier and toilet block £5 deposit. Off site: The Cross Keys Inn opposite the site entrance serves meals. Supermarkets in Tewkesbury 1.5 miles, where the Black Bear Inn claims to be the oldest in Gloucestershire. Climb Bredon Hill (2 miles) for a panoramic view of the Severn and Avon Valleys. Places of interest include Bredon Barn, pottery and church, Beckford Silk Mill and Tewkesbury Abbey. Golf 3 miles. Riding 8 miles.

At a glance

Welcome & Ambience	✓✓✓✓	Location	✓✓✓✓
Quality of Pitches	✓✓✓✓	Range of Facilities	✓✓✓✓

Directions

Bredons Hardwick is midway between Tewkesbury and Bredon on B4080. Site is well signed at western end of village, site entrance opposite 'Cross Keys Inn'. From M5 exit 9 take A438 toward Tewkesbury, at first traffic lights turn right into Shannon Way. Turn right at next lights, cross motorway bridge, and turn left (housing estate), and cross second motorway bridge. At T-junction turn right on B4080, site entrance is immediately on your left. O.S.GR: SO 912353. GPS: N52:00.958 W02:07.816

Charges 2005

Per unit incl. 2 persons and awning	£ 10.00
extra person (over 3 yrs)	£ 3.00
electricity	£ 2.00
extra pup tent	£ 1.00

Discount 10% for 8 nights or more (excl. July, August and B.Hs).

Reservations

Essential for weekends. B.Hs. and July/Aug. Made with £10 deposit. Tel: 01684 772321. Email: enquiries@croftfarmleisure.co.uk

Open

All year, excl. January and February.

174

UK4110 Tewkesbury Caravan Club Site

Gander Lane, Tewkesbury GL20 5PG (Gloucestershire)

There are two important reasons why the Caravan Club site at Tewkesbury is so popular: firstly, it is within five minutes walk of the town centre and is overlooked by the Norman Abbey, the focal point of the town and secondly, it is a good base for exploring the eastern end of the Cotswolds as well as some of the country's most delightful towns. The Malvern hills are also within driving distance. Covering nine acres, the site has 170 pitches reached by tarmac roads. All are on grass, but some slope so blocks are essential, and all have electric hook-ups (16A). There is a late arrivals area just outside. A popular site and one of the largest sites operated by the Caravan Club with friendly and helpful wardens.

Facilities

There are three toilet blocks, all maintained to the Club's high standards and they can be heated. One block has facilities for disabled visitors and two have laundry rooms. Motorcaravan services. Reception sells basic supplies and gas. Off site: Fishing 400 yds. Riding 5 miles. Golf 1 mile.

Open

April - October.

At a glance

Welcome & Ambience	✓✓✓✓	Location	✓✓✓✓✓
Quality of Pitches	✓✓✓	Range of Facilities	✓✓✓

Directions

From all directions follow signs for town centre and head for the Abbey (easily distinguished). Turn by the Abbey into Gander Lane, follow passing two car parks to site at end of the lane. O.S.GR: SO894324.

Charges 2005

Per adult	£ 3.30 - £ 4.80
child (5-16 yrs)	£ 1.10 - £ 1.60
pitch incl. electricity (non-member)	£ 9.00 - £ 14.50

Reservations

Accepted and are essential for all B.Hs. and June-Aug. Tel: 01684 294035.

UK4130 Moreton-in-Marsh Caravan Club Site

Bourton Road, Moreton-in-Marsh GL56 0BT (Gloucestershire)

This excellent, busy, but rural, tree-surrounded site in the heart of the Cotswolds is only 250 yards from the town. The site has 182 pitches, all with electricity (16A) and TV sockets, 172 with hardstanding. Milk, and ice-cream are available from reception. A large play field provides a climbing frame with bark base and space for football, volleyball, boules and crazy golf. Kite flying is not allowed because of low power cables. Moreton-in-Marsh is famous for its Tuesday street market and is always busy , being only a few miles from the pretty villages of Bourton-on-the-Water and Stow-on-the-Wold, just two of the many interesting Cotswold villages worthy of a visit in this lovely area of England. Tents are not accepted.

Facilities

Two toilet blocks offer very good facilities with spacious showers, washbasins in cabins, with facilities in each block for the walking disabled (4 inch step). Excellent en-suite room for disabled visitors in another building, baby room and large laundry. Play area. Boules. Internet access. Off site: Shops, pubs and restaurants 400 yards. Golf 7 miles.

Open

All year.

At a glance

Welcome & Ambience	✓✓✓✓	Location	✓✓✓✓✓
Quality of Pitches	✓✓✓✓✓	Range of Facilities	✓✓✓✓

Directions

From Evesham on A44, site on left after Bourton-on-the-Hill, 150 yards before town sign. From Moreton-in-Marsh take A44 towards Evesham and site is on right, 150 yards past the Wellington museum. O.S.GR: SP200323. GPS: N51:59.325 W01:42.650

Charges 2005

Per adult	£ 3.80 - £ 5.00
child (5-16 yrs)	£ 1.10 - £ 1.60
pitch incl. electricity (non-member)	£ 9.50 - £ 14.50

Reservations

Contact site. Tel: 01608 650519.

UK4140 Winchcombe Camping & Caravanning Club Site

Brooklands Farm, Alderton, Tewkesbury GL20 8NX (Gloucestershire)

This is a popular, quiet site in a rural location, close to the Cotswold attractions. Some pitches surround a small coarse fishing lake, with others in an area with open views over the surrounding countryside. In total there are 80 pitches, 53 with electric hook-ups (10A) and 42 with gravel hardstandings. The reception building flanks a small gravel courtyard car park and late arrivals area approached from a tarmac drive. Places to visit include Gloucester Docks and the National Waterways Museum, whilst south of Gloucester are Owlpen Manor near Uley, and the Painswick Rococo Garden. Much closer to the site is the GWR (Gloucester Warwickshire Railway) at Toddington or Winchcombe.

Facilities

The main, heated sanitary units well equipped. To the rear of the site is a small, 'portacabin' style sanitary unit (also heated). Well equipped unit for disabled people. Laundry with washing machine and dryer. Gas supplies. Large games room. Small outdoor play area

Open

March - January.

At a glance

Welcome & Ambience	✓✓✓✓	Location	✓✓✓✓✓
Quality of Pitches	✓✓✓✓	Range of Facilities	✓✓✓✓

Directions

From M5 exit 9, take A46 Evesham road for 3 miles to Toddington roundabout, then take B4077 towards Stow-on-the-Wold, for a further 3 miles to site O.S.GR: SP 007324. GPS: N51:59.424 W01:59.441

Charges 2005

Per adult	£ 5.55 - £ 6.40
child (5-16 yrs)	£ 1.90
non-member pitch fee	£ 5.00

Reservations

Advised; contact site or Central Reservations 0870 243 3331. Site tel: 01242 620259.

(175)

UK4160 **Forestry Commission - Christchurch Campsite**

Bracelands Drive, Christchurch, Coleford GL16 7NN (Gloucestershire)

With 280 unmarked pitches, this 20 acre site is on an undulating, open grassy area in the heart of the Forest of Dean. There are around 60 seasonal units, seven hardstandings, and 95 pitches have electric hook-ups (10A). The reception also houses a well stocked licensed shop (including hot pies and pasties) and has a good selection of tourist information, including a leaflet about the local forest trails (55p). Tenters will appreciate the large pavilion in the centre of the site, a large common room with a wood burning stove (logs supplied), tables and chairs, an ideal retreat if the weather proves inclement. Symonds Yat Rock is within walking distance, with spectacular views over the Wye Valley and also nearby are Clearwell Caves, ancient iron mines and Dean Forest Railway.

Facilities

Four sanitary units, two fairly modern with spacious well equipped showers, some vanity style basins with dividers, plus two much older units with WCs and washbasins only. The central block has a laundry with washing machines and dryers and dishwashing room. Units for disabled people and baby changing in two blocks. Shaded adventure playground on a bark surface. Dogs are not accepted. Off site: Shops and other services in Coleford - 1.5 miles. Ross-on-Wye 8 miles. Fishing 1 mile. Swimming 1 mile. Golf 2 miles. Bicycle hire 3 miles. Riding 10 miles.

Open

21 March - 4 November.

At a glance

| Welcome & Ambience | ✓✓✓✓ | Location | ✓✓✓✓✓ |
| Quality of Pitches | ✓✓✓✓ | Range of Facilities | ✓✓✓ |

Directions

From Monmouth take A4136 east for approx. 5 miles turning north at crossroads at Pike House Inn (site signed), site entrance on left after 0.5 miles. From centre of Coleford take road towards Monmouth, turning right to Symonds Yat and Berry Hill (site is signed). O.S.GR: SO569129.
GPS: N51:48.800 W02:37.641

Charges 2005

Per unit incl. 2 persons	£ 6.80 - £ 12.60
extra adult	£ 3.00
child (5-14 yrs)	£ 2.00

Less 20% all year for disabled guests and outside 23 /7-31/8 for senior citizens.

Reservations

Necessary for B.H.s and peak times (min 2 nights with £30 deposit). Contact the Forestry Commission, 231 Corstorphine Road, Edinburgh EH12 7AT.
Tel: 0131 314 6505. Tel: 0131 3146505.
Email: info@forestholidays.co.uk

UK4170 **Tudor Caravan & Camping Park**

Shepherds Patch, Slimbridge GL2 7BP (Gloucestershire)

This traditional style campsite is adjacent to the Gloucester - Sharpness Canal, and behind the Tudor Arms public house. It has 75 pitches, all with electric hook-ups (16A), and 35 with hardstanding. It is divided into two separate fields, the old orchard for long stay or adults only units, with some concrete wheel track hardstands, and a more open grassy meadow for family touring units. The Wildfowl and Wetlands Centre at Slimbridge, founded in 1946 by artist and naturalist Sir Peter Scott, has an incredible variety of different species which visit each year. This site is an obvious choice if you are at all interested in ornithology, being only 800 yards from the Centre. Other local attractions include Berkeley Castle, Frampton with its half timbered buildings and Stroud, famous for alternative medicine, homeopaths, reflexologists, herbalists, acupuncturists, chiropractors and cranial masseurs.

Facilities

The toilet building located to one side of the orchard, provides all the usual facilities including push-button hot showers and it can be heated in cool weather. Dishwashing sinks outside under cover. No facilities for disabled persons. Gas available. Some site lighting but a torch would be useful. Gate locked 22.30 - 07.00. Off site: Meals at the Tudor Arms pub. Shop and cafe in boatyard opposite the site (Easter-Sept), also serves breakfasts. Fishing adjacent. Towpath walks.

Open

All year.

At a glance

| Welcome & Ambience | ✓✓✓✓ | Location | ✓✓✓✓✓ |
| Quality of Pitches | ✓✓✓✓ | Range of Facilities | ✓✓✓ |

Directions

From A38 by the junction with A4135 (Dursley), turn west, signed WWT Wetlands Centre Slimbridge. Continue for 1.5 miles turning left into car park of the Tudor Arms. Site entrance is at rear of car park. O.S.GR: SO728042. GPS: N51:44.132 W02:23.749

Charges 2005

Per unit incl. 2 persons	£ 9.00
extra adult	£ 1.00
child (under 12 yrs)	£ 0.50
awning	£ 1.50
electricity	£ 2.25 - £ 1.50
dog	£ 0.50

Supplement for B.Hs and school holidays.
No credit cards.

Reservations

Advisable for B.Hs and July/Aug. Tel: 01453 890483.
Email: info@tudorcaravanpark.co.uk

UK4180 Ranch Caravan Park

Honeybourne, Evesham WR11 7PR (Worcestershire)

The Vale of Evesham is noted for being a sheltered area growing fruit and other produce from early spring through to late autumn. Ranch lies not far from both Evesham and Broadway in quiet rural surroundings of 50 acres and is also only half an hour's drive from Stratford-on-Avon. A free swimming pool is open and heated from June - September. The park takes 120 touring units - motorcaravans, caravans or trailer tents, but not other tents - on flat, partly undulating, hedged meadows with well mown grass and a spacious feel. Pitches are not marked but the staff position units. All have electrical connections (10A) and there are 20 hardstandings including 8 fully serviced pitches (electricity, TV, water and sewer connections). There are 169 caravan holiday homes in their own section.

Facilities

Two very well appointed, modern sanitary blocks, with free hot showers and heating, make a good provision. Motorcaravan service point. Shop. The comfortable clubhouse (weekends only in early and late season) offers a wide range of value for money meals and entertainment is arranged at B.H. weekends and Saturdays in school holidays. Swimming pool (55 x 30 ft; June - Sept). Small games room with TV (incl. Sky), video machines and pool table. Playground. Off site: Riding stables and bicycle hire 2 miles. Fishing 4 miles. Golf 6 miles.

Open

1 March - 30 November.

At a glance

Welcome & Ambience	✓✓✓✓✓	Location	✓✓✓✓✓
Quality of Pitches	✓✓✓✓	Range of Facilities	✓✓✓✓✓

Directions

From A46 Evesham take B4035 towards Chipping Campden. After Badsey and Bretforton follow signs for Honeybourne down unclassified road (Ryknild Street, Roman road). Park is through village on left by station. O.S.GR: SP112444.

Charges 2005

Per unit incl. 2 persons, electricity	£ 14.50 - £ 18.75
with water and drainage	£ 17.50 - £ 21.75
extra person (over 5 yrs)	£ 2.50
dog	£ 2.50

One free night for every 7 booked.

Reservations

Advised for peak weeks and essential for B.Hs. (when min. 3 days). Made with £5 per night deposit. Tel: 01386 830744. Email: enquiries@ranch.co.uk

UK4190 Kingsgreen Caravan Park

Kingsgreen, Berrow, Malvern WR13 6AQ (Worcestershire)

A friendly, comfortable, farm site with views of the Malvern Hills, Kingsgreen has an attractive rural location. An ideal site for adults who like the quiet life, there are no amusements for children. The countryside is ideal for walking or cycling, and the small, fenced fishing lake on the site is well stocked (£4 per day). There are 45 level, grass and gravel pitches, all with electricity (16A), plus an additional area for tents. Some old orchard trees provide a little shade in parts. The site is 7 miles from the market town of Ledbury with its half timbered buildings and within easy driving distance of Malvern, the Three Counties showground, Cotswolds, Forest of Dean or Tewkesbury with its 12th century Abbey.

Facilities

Modern toilet facilities (key on deposit) provide hot showers (25p token from reception) and a separate unit for disabled people (WC and washbasin). Dishwashing sinks under cover. Laundry room with washing machine, dryer, sink and iron and board (all metered). Gas and barbecue fuels are stocked and a milkman calls daily with milk, eggs, bread, soft drinks, etc. Off site: Nearest shop and pub 1.5 miles. Bicycle hire 2 miles. Riding 3 miles. Golf 5 miles.

Open

1 March - 31 October.

At a glance

Welcome & Ambience	✓✓✓✓✓	Location	✓✓✓✓
Quality of Pitches	✓✓✓✓	Range of Facilities	✓✓✓

Directions

From M50 junction 2, take A417 towards Gloucester, then first left, where site is signed, also signed the Malverns, back over the motorway. Site is 2 miles from the M50. O.S.GR: SO767338.

Charges 2005

Per unit incl. 2 adults	£ 7.00 - £ 8.00
extra person over 2 yrs	£ 1.00
electricity	£ 1.50
dog	£ 1.00

No credit cards. VAT not included.

Reservations

Essential for peak season and B.Hs. Tel: 01531 650272.

UK4210 Lickhill Manor Caravan Park

Lower Lickhill Road, Stourport-on-Severn DY13 8RL (Worcestershire)

Lickhill Manor is a well managed touring or holiday site within easy walking distance (15 minutes) of the town centre via a footpath along the River Severn which lies a short distance below the site. There are opportunities for fishing and boating. The touring field has 90 marked, level, grassy pitches accessed via tarmac roads, all with electricity (10/16A). The 124 holiday homes, well screened from the touring area amongst tree lined avenues, are not visually intrusive. There is a separate rally field (with 50 electricity hook-ups). There is an excellent children's playground and the site has recently created wildlife ponds and planted over 1,000 native trees and shrubs. With its new sanitary block, roads and landscaping and friendly welcoming staff, this park has matured into one of the best in the area. Stourport is a lively bustling town with some splendid public parks, amusements and sports facilities. Kidderminster, the Forestry Commission Visitor Centre at Bewdley, the Severn Valley Railway and West Midland Safari Park are a short drive from the site.

Facilities

A second sanitary building was added in '98 to serve the touring pitches and complement the older unit at the other end of the park. This heated building provides very good, modern facilities including a comprehensively equipped suite for disabled guests which also double as a family washroom with facilities for baby changing. Excellent drive over motorcaravan service point. Recycling bins. Gas supplies. New children's play park in separate family area. Off site: Riding 1 mile. Bicycle hire 3 miles. Six golf courses within 5 miles. A small parade of shops and the nearest pub are 10 minutes walk.

At a glance

Welcome & Ambience	✓✓✓✓	Location	✓✓✓✓✓
Quality of Pitches	✓✓✓✓	Range of Facilities	✓✓✓✓

Directions

From centre of Stourport take B4195 northwest towards Bewdley. After 1 mile turn left at crossroads (traffic lights), into Lickhill Road North where site is signed. O.S.GR: SO790730

Charges 2005

Per unit incl. 4 persons, electricity	£ 11.00 - £ 16.50
extra person over 2 yrs	£ 1.50
awning	£ 2.00
dog	£ 0.75

Weekly rates available. Senior citizen discounts.

Reservations

Advised for B.Hs. and peak season. Tel: 01299 871041. Email: excellent@lickhillmanor.co.uk

Open

All year.

UK4220 Riverside Caravan Park

Little Clevelode (on B4424), Malvern WR13 6PE (Worcestershire)

A traditional, older style site, Riverside at Little Clevelode is set in the picturesque Severn Valley four miles east of Great Malvern, and close to the Malvern Hills. The main touring site is located on high ground above the river near the site entrance, and has around 70 grassy pitches, with a good many seasonal units, but there is usually space for tourists. There are two playgrounds and an area for football and ball games and a tennis hard-court. The lower level of the site near the river has an area for holiday homes and a clubhouse /bar, games room with pool table, electronic machines and TV, a well stocked shop plus a further sanitary unit and a small laundry. No dogs, washing lines, children's cycles, roller skates, skateboards, or scooters are permitted on site.

Facilities

The modernised toilet block serving the touring site provides controllable hot showers, vanity style washbasins and a small dishwashing room. Whilst not luxurious these basic facilities are adequate and kept clean. Clubhouse/bar (weekends only). Shop (09.00-09.30 and 17.30-18.00 weekdays plus 14.00-15.00 at weekends). Coarse river fishing. Off site: Riding and bicycle hire 3 miles. Golf 4 miles.

Open

Easter - 1 November.

At a glance

Welcome & Ambience	✓✓✓	Location	✓✓✓✓
Quality of Pitches	✓✓✓✓	Range of Facilities	✓✓✓

Directions

Little Clevelode is due east of Great Malvern on the B4424. From Great Malvern take B4211 east for 2 miles, turning north on B4424 for about 0.5 miles to site entrance. From Worcester (north) take A449 south and fork left on B4424 for 2 miles to site entrance. O.S.GR: SO830460.

Charges 2005

Per unit incl. 2 persons	
incl. electricity and water	£ 13.00
extra person (over 4 yrs)	£ 3.50
awning	free

No credit cards.

Reservations

Advised for B.Hs (min. 3 nights) and school holidays and made with one nights pitch fee. Tel: 01684 310475.

UK4200 The Boyce Caravan Park

Stanford Bishop, Bringsty, Worcester WR6 5UB (Herefordshire)

The Boyce is a very peaceful park on rolling downland, with distant views of the Malvern Hills. Within its 17 acres are 20 touring pitches (with 10A electrical connections), 150 permanent caravan holiday homes and three cottages for hire. There is a fenced and gated playground for smaller children, plus plenty of open space for ball games (no cycling on the park). The adjacent disused railway line is now the dog walk (dogs accepted by arrangement, no dangerous breeds). Coarse fishing is available across a meadow and the area is rich in wildlife. Nearby Shortwood Farm has Jacob sheep, cider making, sheep shearing and a farm trail. The new reception building offers good tourist information including maps of local walks. Bromyard with its shops and restaurants is 4 miles, and the cathedral cities of Hereford and Worcester are within easy driving distance.

Facilities

The modern toilet unit, built to serve the touring section, can be heated and provides controllable hot showers (10p for 4 minutes) and a hairdressing area. Facilities for disabled visitors. Utility room housing dishwashing and laundry sinks, a washing machine, dryer, iron, and a freezer for campers' use. Gas supplies. Off site: Riding 5 miles. Several golf courses in the area.

Open

1 March - 31 October.

At a glance

Welcome & Ambience	✓✓✓✓	Location	✓✓✓✓✓
Quality of Pitches	✓✓✓✓	Range of Facilities	✓✓✓✓

Directions

From A44 (Worcester - Leominster), turn on the B4220 1 mile east of Bromyard. After 1.5 miles, turn opposite 'Herefordshire House' inn (signed Linley Green), site is 400 yards and signed. O.S.GR: SO696526. GPS: N52:10.267 W02:26.771

Charges 2006

Per unit incl. 2 adults	£ 10.00
extra person over 5 yrs	£ 1.00
1 person tent	£ 5.00
awning/pup tent	£ 1.50
extra car	£ 1.00

No tent pitches at B.H. weekends. No credit cards.

Reservations

Made with deposit of one night's fee. Tel: 01886 884248. Email: ah.richards@btopenworld.com

UK4300 Poston Mill Caravan Park

Peterchurch, Golden Valley HR2 0SF (Herefordshire)

Poston Mill Park is a pleasant, neat park in farmland a mile from Peterchurch in the heart of the Golden Valley. It has seen some redevelopment recently with the balance changing towards pitches for caravan holiday homes (there are now 100 with more planned). There are currently 70 touring pitches which are set on level grass or hardstanding, including some very pleasant ones near the River Dore, with mature trees and conifers around the perimeter. All pitches have electricity (10/16A), water and TV connections (leads to hire), and a few have waste water and sewage outlets. An attractive walk along one side of the park, edging the River Dore (fishing available), follows the line of the old Golden Valley railway and there is a footpath from the park over the fields. Next to the park is 'The Mill' restaurant for lunches, evening meals, takeaway meals and a TV room. Peterchurch village is only one mile. A member of the Best of British group.

Facilities

There is one central sanitary block with a smaller block near the holiday home area. Of reasonably modern construction and fully equipped, they include a unit for disabled people (toilet and basin only) and a baby changing room. Motorcaravan service point. Small, well equipped laundry room housing a campers' fridge and a freezer for ice packs. Gas supplies. Mobile shop calls 10 am. Mondays and Thursdays. Large play area. Pitch and putt. Tennis court. Petanque and croquet. Golf driving range. Football pitch. Games room with snooker and darts. Winter caravan storage. Off site: Riding 3 miles.

At a glance

Welcome & Ambience	✓✓✓✓	Location	✓✓✓✓✓
Quality of Pitches	✓✓✓✓	Range of Facilities	✓✓✓✓

Directions

Park is 1 mile southeast of Peterchurch on the B4348 road. O.S.GR: SO356371.

Charges 2006

Per unit incl. 2 adults, electricity	£ 12.00 - £ 16.00
extra person	£ 2.00
child (4-10 yrs)	£ 1.00
awning	£ 2.00
dog	£ 1.00

Min. charge at B.Hs. 5 nights.

Reservations

Made with £20 deposit, min. 5 nights for B.Hs. Tel: 01981 550225. Email: enquiries@poston-mill.co.uk

Open

All year.

UK4310 **Lucksall Caravan & Camping Park**

Mordiford, Hereford HR1 4LP (Herefordshire)

Set in around 17 acres on the bank of the River Wye and benefiting from improvements by the new owners, Lucksall has 80 large, well spaced and level touring pitches, of which 72 have 16A electricity and 30 have hardstanding. The river is open to the site but lifebelts and safety messages are in evidence. Canoes are available for hire (or bring your own) and fishing permits may be obtained from reception. A small, fenced playground and a large grassy area for games are provided for children. The site shop has basic supplies and gas (a mini-market is within 1.5 miles). Amongst the local places worthy of a visit are the Cider Museum and King Offa Distillery in Hereford, Belmont Abbey and Queenswood Country Park. The park is also a good base for touring the Wye Valley. A member of the Countryside Discovery group.

Facilities

The main sanitary facilities, in a new building, provide showers (20p) and a separate unit for disabled visitors with ramped entrance, WC, washbasin, shower and hand-dryer. Dishwashing sinks. A smaller, older unit near the entrance provides extra facilities for peak periods and a fully equipped laundry room. Shop (basics only). Fishing. Canoeing. Winter caravan storage. Site barrier (2.13 m. height limit) locked 21.00 - 09.00 hrs. Only 'breathable' groundsheets are permitted. Off site: Golf 5 miles. Bicycle hire 9 miles.

Open

Easter/1 March - 30 November.

At a glance

Welcome & Ambience	✓✓✓✓	Location	✓✓✓✓
Quality of Pitches	✓✓✓✓	Range of Facilities	✓✓✓

Directions

Between Mordiford and Fownhope, 5 miles southeast of Hereford on B4224, the park is well signed. O.S.GR: SO571355.

Charges 2006

Per unit incl. 2 adults	£ 10.00 - £ 12.50
extra person over 5 yrs	£ 2.00
awning	£ 1.25 - £ 2.00
pup tent on same pitch	£ 2.00
small 1 man tent	£ 6.00 - £ 6.75
dog	£ 0.75

Reservations

Essential for B.Hs. and peak season and made with £25 deposit. Tel: 01432 870213. Email: enquiries@lucksallpark.co.uk

A family run park situated alongside a large woodland & the River Wye...

Lucksall ☘ **01432 870213**
CARAVAN & CAMPING PARK
www.lucksallpark.co.uk
Mordiford, Hereford, Herefordshire HR1 4LP

UK4320 **Broadmeadow Caravan & Camping Park**

Broadmeadows, Ross-on-Wye HR9 7BH (Herefordshire)

This modern, spacious park, with open views and its own fishing lake, is convenient for the town of Ross-on-Wye. The approach to the site is unusual, but persevere and you will find one of the best laid out, immaculately maintained sites with facilities of the very highest quality. Opened in 1996, it is level and has good lighting. There are 150 large pitches on open grass, and the site is especially good for tents. Each set of four pitches has a service post with water, drain, electricity points (16A) and lighting, and is within view of the clock-tower on one of the heated sanitary buildings. The town centre is within easy walking distance. Although the A40 relief road is at the eastern end of the site, the traffic noise should not be too intrusive (but tenters be aware). This is a good base for touring Herefordshire, the Wye Valley or the Forest of Dean.

Facilities

Two superb modern sanitary buildings are fully equipped, including hairdryers, baby rooms, family bathrooms each with WC, basin and bath, and a comprehensive unit for disabled visitors with alarm and handrails. Dishwashing room and laundry with sinks, washing machine, dryer, iron (tokens from reception), at each building. Basic motorcaravan service point. New entrance barrier and keypad entry system on this and all external doors. Small part-fenced playground. Well fenced fishing lake (coarse fishing £5.50 per day). Off site: Supermarket 200 m. Bicycle hire in town. Riding 8 miles. Golf 3 miles.

At a glance

Welcome & Ambience	✓✓✓✓	Location	✓✓✓✓
Quality of Pitches	✓✓✓✓	Range of Facilities	✓✓✓

Directions

From A40 relief road turn into Ross at roundabout, take first right into industrial estate, then right in 0.5 miles, before Safeway supermarket, where site is signed. O.S.GR: SO610240.

Charges 2005

Per adult	£ 2.50
child (4-14 yrs)	£ 2.00
pitch	£ 6.50 - £ 10.75
awning or pup tent	£ 1.75
dog	£ 1.00

Reservations

Made with £10 deposit. Tel: 01989 768076. Email: broadm4811@aol.com

Open

Easter/1 April - 30 September.

UK4330 The Millpond Touring Caravans & Camping

Little Tarrington, Hereford HR1 4JA (Herefordshire)

This peaceful little site with its own fishing lake is set in 30 acres of countryside. Opened for the first time in 1997, it has 40 large pitches on open grassland, all with electricity hook-ups (10A) and 15 pitches for tents in an adjacent field. The large fishing lake (unfenced) is well stocked with a good mix of coarse fish, has facilities for disabled fishermen and offers reduced rates for campers. The large acreage surrounding the campsite has a variety of well-established trees that have been supplemented with many new plantings, and well-mowed paths encourage you to wander and enjoy the many trees, wild flowers, birds and the peaceful surroundings. Site lighting is minimal (local authority regulations) so a torch might be useful, but it is an ideal site for amateur astronomers. A railway track is at the rear of the site, so there may be a little noise at times. The site is just seven miles from the city of Hereford with its cathedral, the fascinating Mappa Mundi and chained library, seven miles from Ledbury and close to the Black and White Village Trail.

Facilities

A modern building houses heated sanitary facilities, laundry and dishwashing sinks, baby changing surface, a unit for disabled persons and a 'common room' with a massive supply of tourist information, wildlife charts and walking guides. The site is currently not really suitable for American motorhomes. Off site: The local pub is a 10 minute walk, but there is no shop in the village.

Open

1 March - 31 October.

At a glance

Welcome & Ambience	✓✓✓✓	Location	✓✓✓✓
Quality of Pitches	✓✓✓✓	Range of Facilities	✓✓✓

Directions

Little Tarrington is midway between Hereford and Ledbury. The site is just north of A438 on eastern edge of Tarrington village (signed). O.S.GR: SO627409.

Charges 2006

Per unit incl. 2 adults, awning, electricity and pets	£ 12.50 - £ 15.50
extra person	£ 3.00

Reservations

For 2 nights - payment in full, 3-6 nights - £25, £30.00 per week. 50% of total for B.Hs. Advised for B.Hs and peak season. Tel: 01432 890243. Email: enquiries@millpond.co.uk

UK4345 Townsend Touring & Caravan Park

Townsend Farm, Pembridge, Leominster HR6 9HB (Herefordshire)

Recently created and opened for the first time in 2002, this is a good example of a modern, family run campsite. It provides tarmac roads, good site lighting, well spaced pitches and a drive-over motor-caravan service point, with plenty of open space and a small fishing lake. There are 60 pitches in total, 20 with gravel hardstanding, the remainder on grass, and all have access to multi-service facilities (electricity hook-up 16A, water and waste water drain). Reception is at the Farm Shop by the entrance. This is a real treat as it stocks a wide variety of fresh fruit and vegetables, eggs and has a butchery section with farm produced meats.

Facilities

A modern timber clad building with blown air heating, is accessed through a foyer with a public telephone and tourist information. The building is surrounded by wide decking with ramps giving good access for wheelchairs to all facilities including the dishwashing area, laundry room and chemical disposal point at the rear. Inside are spacious controllable showers, some washbasins in cubicles, a suite for disabled guests, family bathroom and baby changing facilities. Off site: Pembridge is known as the capital of the Black & White Villages and holds its Farmer's Market on the first Saturday of each month. This is a short stroll from the site. Kington 5 miles, Leominster 7 miles. Riding and bicycle hire 0.5 miles. Golf 7 miles.

At a glance

Welcome & Ambience	✓✓✓✓	Location	✓✓✓✓✓
Quality of Pitches	✓✓✓✓	Range of Facilities	✓✓✓✓

Directions

Site is beside the A44, 7 miles west of Leominster. Site is just inside the 30 mph speed limit on the eastern edge of Pembridge village. O.S.GR: SO385580.

Charges 2005

Per unit incl. 2 persons	£ 9.00 - £ 13.00
electricity, water and drainage	£ 12.00 - £ 16.00
extra adult	£ 3.00
child (5-15 yrs)	£ 1.50
awning or pup tent	£ 2.00
dog	£ 1.00

Reservations

Made with £2 per night non-refundable deposit. Tel: 01544 388527. Email: info@townsend-farm.co.uk

Open

1 March - 18 January.

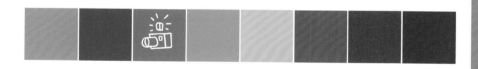

UK4360 Doward Park Camp Site

Great Doward, Symonds Yat West HR9 6BP (Herefordshire)

Created around 1997 in a disused quarry, this is a very pleasant, peaceful little site, partially terraced, and in a sheltered location. The access roads and the physical proportions of the site make it suitable only for tents, trailer tents and camper vans. This is a site that is popular with couples and young families, but has nothing to offer teenagers. The 33 pitches are mostly on grass (with 6 hardstandings used by seasonal units when we visited) and there are 8 electricity hook-ups (16A) for tourers. There are two new motor-caravan hardstanding pitches for units up to 23 feet, otherwise the site is unsuitable for large units, double axle caravans, and American RVs. Visit King Arthur's Caves, and Seven Sisters Rocks. Walk to Symonds Yat Rock and cross the River Wye on the suspension bridge. In nearby Symonds Yat West you will find The Amazing Hedge puzzle, and The Splendour of the Orient with gardens, waterfalls, tea-rooms and gift shop.

Facilities

A neat timber clad building provides the usual facilities including hot showers, dishwashing sinks and a freezer for ice packs. Small shop selling basic supplies. Torches are advisable. Off site: Variety of inns at both Symonds Yat West and East all offering meals. Shops and services in Monmouth 4 miles.

Open

Mid March - 31 October.

At a glance

| Welcome & Ambience | ✓✓✓✓ | Location | ✓✓✓✓✓ |
| Quality of Pitches | ✓✓✓✓ | Range of Facilities | ✓✓✓ |

Directions

From A40 between Ross-on-Wye and Monmouth, turn for Symonds Yat West, and follow signs for Doward Park and Biblins. Turn into a fairly narrow lane for about 1 mile (passing places) and site entrance is on right, on a sharp left hand bend. O.S.GR: SO548157. GPS: N51:50.311 W02:39.420

Charges 2005

Per unit incl. 2 persons and electricity	£ 12.00 - £ 14.00
extra person	£ 2.00 - £ 2.50
child (4-15 yrs)	£ 1.00 - £ 1.50
dog	£ 1.00

Reservations

Advised for B.Hs. (min. 3 nights) and made with £10 deposit and S.A.E. Tel: 01600 890438. Email: enquiries@doward-park.co.uk

UK4400 Stanmore Hall Touring Park

Stourbridge Road, Bridgnorth WV15 6DT (Shropshire)

This good quality park is situated in the former grounds of Stanmore Hall, where the huge lily pond, fine mature trees and beautifully manicured lawns give a mark of quality. There are 135 generously sized pitches, 130 with 16A electricity including 30 hardstanding 'super' pitches with TV connections. A limited number of 'standard' hardstanding pitches are also available, but the majority are on grass. Some pitches are reserved for adult only use (over 18 years). Access and internal roads are tarmac; site lighting is adequate and reassuring. Reception is located within the shop. The adjacent conservatory and patio overlook the lake, accommodating everything from humbler ducks to the resident peacocks who strut proudly around their domain. But there's something else too; this is a peaceful site with personality. Little wonder it needs advance booking and people keep returning to enjoy its atmosphere. Open all year round, there are even groups who spend Christmas and New Year at Stanmore Hall. The Severn Valley is full of interest - Bridgnorth nearby, the Clee Hills and Ironbridge Gorge Museum are just a few suggestions. The site is a member of the Caravan Club's managed under contract scheme but non-members are also very welcome.

Facilities

Access to the centrally heated sanitary block is by key. Facilities are excellent and provide washbasins in cubicles and a room for disabled people (which includes equipment for baby care) demonstrating thoughtful design. Full laundry facilities. Motorcaravan service points. Licensed shop (open all year) is well stocked, including caravan accessories and repair items. Limited, bark based play area. Dogs are limited to two per unit Off site: Fishing at Bridgnorth (1.5 miles). Golf 2 miles. Riding 2 miles.

Open

All year.

At a glance

| Welcome & Ambience | ✓✓✓✓ | Location | ✓✓✓✓✓ |
| Quality of Pitches | ✓✓✓✓✓ | Range of Facilities | ✓✓✓✓✓ |

Directions

Site is 1.5 miles from Bridgnorth on the A458 (signed Stourbridge). O.S.GR: SO744922. GPS: N52:31.629 W02.22.717

Charges 2005

Per adult	£ 4.45 - £ 5.70
child (5-15 yrs)	£ 1.95
pitch	£ 5.95 - £ 8.20
awning or pup tent	£ 1.25
full services	£ 2.50 - £ 3.00
dog (max. 2)	£ 1.00

Reservations

Advisable and made with £10 deposit. Tel: 01746 761761. Email: stanmore@morris-leisure.co.uk

UK4380 Fernwood Caravan Park

Lyneal, Ellesmere SY12 0QF (Shropshire)

Fernwood is set in an area known as the Shropshire 'Lake District' – the mere at Ellesmere is the largest of nine meres – and the picturesque Shropshire Union Canal is only a few minutes walk. The park itself is a real oasis of calm and rural tranquillity with its floral landscaping, the setting and the attention to detail, all of a very high standard with planted and natural vegetation blending harmoniously. In addition to 165 caravan holiday homes, used normally only by their owners, the park takes 60 caravans, motorcaravans or trailer tents (but not other tents) in several well cut, grassy enclosures (including 27 seasonal long stay). Some are in light woodland, others in more open, but still relatively sheltered situations. All 60 pitches have electricity (10A). One area is set aside for units with adults only. Siting is carried out by the management and there is always generous spacing, even when the site is full.

Facilities

The small toilet block for tourers has background heating for cooler days and includes some washbasins in cabins and a unit for disabled people, but no dishwashing sinks. Basic motorcaravan services. Laundry room near the shop and adjacent are WCs for ladies and men. Small shop doubling as reception (from 1/4, hours vary). Coarse fishing lake. Forty acres of woodland for walking. Play area on grass.

Open

1 March - 30 November.

At a glance

Welcome & Ambience	✓✓✓✓	Location	✓✓✓✓
Quality of Pitches	✓✓✓✓	Range of Facilities	✓✓✓

Directions

Park is just northeast of Lyneal village, signed southwest off the B5063 Ellesmere - Wem road, about 1.5 miles from junction of the B5063 with the A495. O.S.GR: SJ452338.
GPS: N52:53.950 W02:48.961

Charges 2005

Per unit incl. electricity	£ 14.50 - £ 18.75
awning	free - £ 2.75

One night free for every 7 booked in advance.

Reservations

Necessary for peak season and B.Hs (min. 3 nights) with deposit of £5 per night. Tel: 01948 710221. Email: fernwood@caravanpark37.fsnet.co.uk

- ESTABLISHED FAMILY-RUN PARK
- PEACEFUL WOODLAND SETTING
- TOURERS WELCOME
- ALL PITCHES HAVE ELECTRICAL HOOK-UPS
- PICTURESQUE LAKE
- CHILDRENS PLAY AREA
- SHOP
- LAUNDRY

LYNEAL
NR. ELLESMERE
SHROPSHIRE SY12 0QF

www.ranch.co.uk/fernwood.htm

TEL: (01948) 710221

UK4390 Westbrook Park

Little Hereford, Ludlow SY8 4AU (Shropshire)

A beautifully kept, traditional, quiet touring campsite in a 'working' cider apple orchard, Westbrook Park is bordered on one side by the River Teme and within walking distance of the village and pub. There are 52 level pitches with 16A electric hook-ups, some on well mown grass, and 23 on gravel or concrete/gravel all-weather hardstandings with water and waste water drain. Satellite TV hook-ups are available to all pitches. A footpath along the river bank in one direction leads to the Temeside Inn which serves hot meals. There is a pleasant riverside walk and dog walk in the other direction.

Facilities

A modern, timber clad, heated toilet block provides spacious hot showers (20p for 5 minutes), washbasins in curtained cubicles, a basic laundry room with washing machine, dryer and dishwashing sinks. Limited facilities for disabled people (WC and basin) - the current steps need to be replaced with a ramp. Gas supplies. Playground. Fishing (£3 per day). Riverside walks. Caravan 'storage and use'. Gazebos are not permitted. No cycling on the park.
Off site: Local attractions include Burford House Gardens and Croft Castle. Golf 3 miles. Riding, bicycle hire 5 miles.

Open

1 March - 30 November.

At a glance

Welcome & Ambience	✓✓✓✓✓	Location	✓✓✓✓✓
Quality of Pitches	✓✓✓✓✓	Range of Facilities	✓✓✓

Directions

From A49 mid-way between Ludlow and Leominster, turn east at Woofferton on A456 signed Tenbury Wells, Kidderminster. After 2 miles turn right just before bridge over river and the Temeside Inn. Turn left after 150 yds, and park entrance is on your left. O.S.GR: SU547679. GPS: N52:13.440 W02:39.955

Charges 2005

Per unit incl. 2 adults, electricity	£ 12.00 - £ 16.00
extra person	£ 2.00
child (3-10 yrs)	£ 1.00
dog	£ 1.00

No credit cards.

Reservations

Advised for B.Hs (min. 3 nights) and made with £10 deposit per night. Tel: 01584 711280.

UK4410 Beaconsfield Farm Caravan Park

Battlefield, Shrewsbury SY4 4AA (Shropshire)

Just north of the historic market town, a drive of half a mile through open fields lead to this purpose-designed park for adults only (21 yrs). It is neatly laid out in a rural situation, with a well stocked trout fishing lake and a small coarse pool forming the main feature. The ground is levelled and grassed to provide 60 well spaced pitches, 35 are 'de-luxe' hardstanding pitches with 16A electricity (with 10A hook-ups to the other pitches). Two further areas accommodate 34 caravan holiday homes. The park is well lit with a circular tarmac access road. A large timber chalet-style building provides the reception and a coffee shop that opens during reception hours. Recent additions are the bowling green (use is free and woods may be hired by those without such essential caravanning kit) and the 'Bothy' restaurant. Limousins and pedigree Suffolk sheep graze in neighbouring fields and a 'park and ride' scheme operates nearby for those interested in Shrewsbury and its medieval past, bought to life by the Brother Cadfael novels. This is a top class park, maturing by the year. A member of the Best of British Group.

Facilities

Heated toilet facilities (£2 key deposit) are of excellent quality, with curtained, roomy, pre-set showers and free hairdryers. Excellent unit for disabled visitors. Dishwashing room. Laundry with washing machines, dryers, free irons and boards. Motorcaravan services. Restaurant. Indoor heated swimming pool, available all year, with daily open sessions (£2.50 per person) and to hire privately at other times. Bowling green. Small library. Bicycle hire. Security barrier in operation. Only two dogs per unit are accepted. An adult only park. Off site: Golf 2 miles. Riding 7 miles.

Open

All year.

At a glance

Welcome & Ambience	✓✓✓✓	Location	✓✓✓✓✓
Quality of Pitches	✓✓✓✓✓	Range of Facilities	✓✓✓✓

Directions

Site is north of Shrewsbury and off the A49 Whitchurch road just before the village of Hadnall. Turn opposite the New Inn at brown camping sign towards Astley and park entrance is 400 m. on right. O.S.GR: SJ525195. GPS: N52:46.255 W02:42.289

Charges 2006

Per grass pitch incl. unit, 2 persons and electricity	£ 14.00 - £ 16.00
hardstanding pitch	£ 16.00 - £ 19.00
extra adult	£ 4.00
awning	£ 1.50

No credit cards. Last arrivals 7 pm. (8 pm. Fridays).

Reservations

Advised for weekends, B.Hs and July/Aug. and made with £20 deposit. Tel: 01939 210370. Email: mail@beaconsfield-farm.co.uk

UK4420 Severn Gorge Park

Bridgnorth Road, Tweedale, Telford TF7 4JB (Shropshire)

This six acre touring park, in a woodland setting, has 50 pitches, all with hardstanding and electricity (10/16A) and including a few seasonal tourers. A development of park homes has been constructed on one side of the park and a tent area with hardstanding for campers' cars. There could be some road noise from the A442 which runs down one boundary. A barrier is locked at 11.45 pm. but parking and a late arrivals area is outside. The main local attraction has to be the Ironbridge Museums, featuring the Blists Hill Victorian Town, where you can discover and enjoy a working Victorian town. Hawkstone Park, with its walks and follies, is very popular and the Cosford Aerospace Museum is essential visiting for those interested in aviation. A short distance from the park is the Silkin Way cycle path which runs into Telford town centre or to the attractions at Ironbridge.

Facilities

The sanitary buildings can be heated and have been upgraded to provide comprehensive facilities including facilities for disabled visitors and a baby room. Dishwashing conservatory leading to an ample laundry (8 am.- 9 pm). Motorcaravan services. Small, limited shop (8.30 am - 5.30 pm daily). Gas supplies. New adventure play area. Kite flying is discouraged because of nearby overhead cables. Only two dogs per pitch are accepted. Off site: Two pubs within walking distance, one with a tempting 'Ale and Hearty' menu served until 9 pm. Golf 1 mile, riding 3 miles.

Open

All year.

At a glance

Welcome & Ambience	✓✓✓✓	Location	✓✓✓✓✓
Quality of Pitches	✓✓✓✓✓	Range of Facilities	✓✓✓

Directions

From M54 junction 4 follow signs (A442) onto the A442 signed Kidderminster. Take slip road signed Bridgnorth to Brockton roundabout, turn right and pick up park signs. O.S.GR: SJ702051. GPS: N52:38.578 W02:26.526

Charges 2005

Per unit incl. 2 persons	£ 10.15 - £ 12.15
extra adult	£ 2.95 - £ 3.55
child (5-15 yrs)	£ 1.30 - £ 1.55
awning	£ 1.30
dog (max 2)	£ 1.25

Reservations

Contact park for details. Tel: 01952 684789. Email: info@severngorgepark.co.uk

UK4532 Middlewood Farm Holiday Park

Misslewood Lane, Fylingthorpe, Robin Hood's Bay YO22 4UF (North Yorkshire)

Middlewood Farm is set on a sloping hillside with views of the sea from some of the pitches. A short walk through the farm fields and wild flower conservation areas leads to the picturesque old fishing village of Robin Hood's Bay and sea. The park has 150 touring pitches 34 with hardstanding and 13A electricity, the rest on grass. There are two areas for tents and 30 caravan holiday homes to rent. A good beach is only ten minutes walk through the fields and the nearby village of Fylingthorpe has shops and a pub. This is a very tidy farm site. The access roads are not really suitable for very large units.

Facilities

The central toilet block has clean facilities and is modern, heated and tiled with free showers. Another new block is planned for 2006. Fully equipped laundry room incl. iron and board. Facilities for babies and disabled persons. Two private family shower rooms to rent. Play area with bark base set amongst the tents. Off site: Sandy beach with fishing 0.5 miles. Boat launching 2 miles. Golf 7 miles. Shops in village 5 minutes walk.

Open

Easter - early November.

At a glance

Welcome & Ambience	✓✓✓✓	Location	✓✓✓✓
Quality of Pitches	✓✓✓	Range of Facilities	✓✓✓

Directions

From the A171 Scarborough - Whitby road turn right signed Robin Hood's Bay and Fylingthorpe. Just past 30 mph sign bear right (site signed) and after 100 yds turn right into Middlewood Lane (site signed). From Whitby on the A171 turn left on B1447 signed Robin Hood's Bay and Fylingthorpe. After 1.5 miles turn right signed Fylingthorpe and brown site sign. Follow for 1 mile to crossroads and shops and straight on to Middlewood Lane (site signed). O.S.GR: NZ945045. GPS: N54:29.503 W00:38.566

Charges 2005

Per unit incl. 2 persons, electricity	£ 10.00 - £ 15.50
extra person	£ 3.00
awning	£ 2.00
dog	£ 1.50

Reservations

Made with deposit (£ 20). Tel: 01947 880414.

St Helens in the Park
250 Spacious pitches set in 30 acres of parkland.
Adventure playground, excellent shop,
games room & amusements
Nearby there is excellent fishing, diving,
windsurfing & sailing
Tel: 01723 862771

UK4540 St Helens in the Park

Wykeham, Scarborough YO13 9QD (North Yorkshire)

St Helens is a high quality touring park with pleasant views, set within 30 acres of parkland. The 250 mainly level pitches have a spacious feel and the 52 pitches with hardstanding are used by seasonal lets in the summer months, but are available for tourers in winter. Electrical hook-ups (16A) are available on 240 pitches, also in the late arrivals area. Set on a hillside (hence the views), the park's buildings are built in local stone and all is maintained to a high standard. The Downe Arms, a short stroll away, is known for its good food and it occasionally runs family discos in high season. Scarborough is only 5 miles with its beaches and summer shows and buses pass the site gates.

Facilities

Four heated toilet blocks are well equipped and maintained, three having been extended and refurbished. Some washbasins in cabins and baby baths. The new unit for disabled visitors is of a very high standard. All four blocks have dishwashing sinks under cover. Good laundry room. Well stocked shop with snacks and takeaway, and new restaurant (31/3-31/10). Adventure playground set on bark is part of a three acre area set aside for children with goal posts and a mountain bike track. Bicycle hire. Small games room with pool table and amusement machines. Caravan storage. Off site: Nearby Wykeham Lakes offer fishing (trout and coarse), scuba diving, windsurfing and sailing (in your own boat), 1 mile. Golf or riding 2 miles.

At a glance

Welcome & Ambience	✓✓✓✓	Location	✓✓✓✓
Quality of Pitches	✓✓✓✓	Range of Facilities	✓✓✓✓

Directions

Park access road leads off the A170 (Pickering - Scarborough) road in Wykeham village 2 miles west of junction with B1262. O.S.GR: SE963835. GPS: N54:14.282 W00:30.028

Charges 2005

Per unit incl. 2 persons	£ 9.60 - £ 12.10
electricity	£ 2.40
extra person (over 3 yrs)	£ 1.00
dog	£ 1.00

Reservations

Made with £20 deposit (min. 4 nights for Spr. and Aug. B.Hs). Tel: 01723 862771. Email: caravans@wykeham.co.uk

Open

All year excl. 15 January - 13 February.

UK4740 Jasmine Park

Cross Lane, Snainton, Scarborough YO13 9BE (North Yorkshire)

Jasmine is a very attractive, quiet and well manicured park with owners who go to much trouble to produce many plants to decorate a very colourful entrance. Set in the Vale of Pickering, the park is level, well drained and protected by a coniferous hedge. The 106 pitches (54 for touring units) are on grass, with electricity connections (10A) for all caravans and some tents. There is no play equipment for children, although a field is provided for games. Much tourist information is provided in a log cabin and the owners are only too happy to advise. The market town of Pickering and the seaside town of Scarborough are both 8 miles. Local attractions are within easy reach, including Castle Howard, Dalby Forest, Sledmere House, Nunington Hall, Goathland (the setting for ITV's 'Heartbeat') and the North York Moors Railway. Some privately owned log cabins and seasonal tourers are also on the site. This is an award-winning, peaceful park for a restful holiday. A member of the Countryside Discovery group.

Facilities

The heated toilet block has been refurbished to a high standard and is kept very clean. It includes a large room for families or disabled visitors containing a bath, shower, WC and washbasin (access by key). Laundry room with dishwashing sinks, washing machine, dryer and iron (hot water metered). Motorcaravan service point. Licensed shop selling essentials and gas. Dogs are welcome but there is no dog walk. Caravan storage. Off site: Bus service in village 0.5 miles. Riding 2 miles. Golf driving range 2 miles. Fishing and bicycle hire 5 miles.

Open

1 March - 31 December.

At a glance

Welcome & Ambience	✓✓✓✓	Location	✓✓✓✓
Quality of Pitches	✓✓✓✓	Range of Facilities	✓✓✓

Directions

Snainton is on the A170 Pickering - Scarborough road and park is signed at eastern end of the village. Follow Brakers Lane to park on left in 1 mile. O.S.GR: SE928813. GPS: N54:13.115 W00:34.534

Charges 2005

Per unit incl. 2 persons	£ 9.50 - £ 15.00
with electricity	£ 11.50 - £ 17.00
extra adult	£ 1.50
child (5-14 yrs)	£ 1.00
awning or tent over 150 sq ft	£ 2.00

Min. stay at Easter 4 nights, other B.Hs 3 nights.

Reservations

Made with £20 deposit and S.A.E. Tel: 01723 859240. Email: info@jasminepark.co.uk

UK4550 Cayton Village Caravan Park

Mill Lane, Cayton Bay, Scarborough YO11 3NN (North Yorkshire)

Cayton Village Caravan Park can only be described as a gem. Just three miles from the hustle and bustle of Scarborough, it is a peaceful, attractive haven. Originally just a flat field with caravans around the perimeter, years of hard work have produced a park which is very pleasing to the eye and of which the owner, Carol, can be justly proud. The entrance is a mass of flowers. The late arrivals area here has electrical hook-ups, very handy as the gates are locked at night and anyone leaving early is also expected to use it, so as not to disturb others. The 200 pitches are numbered and everyone is taken to their pitch. All of the 160 for touring units, have electricity (many with hardstanding) and there are 17 fully serviced pitches. A short walk across a field takes you to Cayton Village which has a popular pub providing excellent meals, a post office stores and a church, and Cayton Bay is half a mile. The North York Moors are a short distance away, as is the Forestry Commission's Dalby Forest with its scenic drive, mountain bike trails and way-marked walks.

Facilities

Three toilet blocks (key code locks) can be heated and have high quality tiling and fittings. Some showers are pre-set, others controllable. Two family shower rooms, family bathroom and baby changing facilities. Reception and shop, both open 8.30 am. to 8 pm. The shop's comprehensive range includes gas and caravan spares. Adventure playground with safety surface. Superb dog walk (an enormous well mown field, floodlit at night). Caravan storage. Off site: Fishing and bicycle hire 0.5 miles. Riding 4 miles. Golf 3 miles. Regular bus service from the village to Scarborough or Filey.

Open

1 March - 4 January.

At a glance

Welcome & Ambience	✓✓✓✓	Location	✓✓✓✓
Quality of Pitches	✓✓✓✓	Range of Facilities	✓✓✓

Directions

From A64 Malton - Scarborough road turn right at roundabout (with MacDonald's and pub) signed B1261 Filey. Follow signs for Cayton, in Cayton Village take second left after Blacksmiths Arms down Mill Lane (at brown caravan sign) and park is 200 yds. From roundabout to park is 2.25 miles. From A165 turn inland at Cayton Bay traffic lights and park is 0.5 miles on right. O.S.GR: TA057837. GPS: N54:14.144 W00:22.567

Charges 2005

Per unit incl. 2 persons, electricity and awning	£ 13.00 - £ 19.00

Special offers available.

Reservations

Advised and made for min. 3 nights (4 at B.Hs) with £20 deposit. Tel: 01723 583171. Email: info@caytontouring.co.uk

UK4590 Jacobs Mount Caravan Park

Stepney Road, Scarborough YO12 5NL. (North Yorkshire)

Situated just two miles from the centre of Scarborough, yet in the heart of the country, Jacobs Mount is well placed to meet many holiday needs. The sea and the sand are the main attractions, but this is also on the doorstep of the North York moors and the Dalby Forest Drive. In addition to caravan holiday homes in separate areas of the park, there are 142 touring pitches, all with electricity. Of these 131 are fully serviced (water, drainage) on well spaced gravel hardstandings. In sunny locations, some pitches have good views. There is a bar with a pleasant lounge (no children), plus a family room and a games and TV room. Bar meals and a quite extensive range of takeaways can be purchased. Footpaths lead into the surrounding woods and buses pass the gates.

Facilities
The heated toilet block is new and of a high standard. Washbasins in cubicles with WCs, large shower cubicles (free) and a family bathroom (metered hot water) and baby changing facilities. Separate unisex cubicles contain WC, washbasin and shower. Motorcaravan service point. Small shop in reception for basic needs. Bar with bar meals and takeaway. Two play areas for different ages. Caravan storage. No gazebo style tents allowed. Up to two dogs per pitch are accepted. Off site: Scarborough centre and beach 2 miles. Golf, fishing and bicycle hire 2 miles. Riding 5 miles.

Open
1 March - 31 October.

At a glance
Welcome & Ambience	✓✓✓✓	Location	✓✓✓✓
Quality of Pitches	✓✓✓✓	Range of Facilities	✓✓✓✓

Directions
Site entrance is on the A170 Pickering - Scarborough road, about 2 miles west of Scarborough (on the right as you start to drop down into the town). O.S.GR: TA021877. GPS: N54:16.037 W00:26.073

Charges 2005
Per unit incl. 4 persons and electricity (16A)	£ 10.50 - £ 16.00
extra person 3 yrs and over	£ 1.50
awning	£ 2.00
dog (max 2)	£ 1.00
No single sex parties.	

Reservations
Made with deposit (3 days charge); min. stay at B.Hs 3 nights. Tel: 01723 361178. Email: jacobsmount@yahoo.co.uk

UK4780 Lebberston Touring Park

Filey Road, Lebberston, Scarborough YO11 3PE (North Yorkshire)

Lebberston Park is a quiet, spacious touring site and is highly suitable for anyone seeking a quiet relaxing break, such as mature couples or young families (although tents are not accepted). There is no play area or games room, the only concession to children being a large central area with goal posts, so teenagers may get bored. The park itself has a very spacious feel – it is gently sloping and south facing and the views are superb. There are 125 numbered pitches with 75 for touring units. All have 10A electricity and 6 are on hardstanding. The circular access road is tarmac, the grass is well manicured and the entrance a mass of flowers. Reception is part of an attractive log cabin which is also the home of the owners and their young family. The resorts of Filey, Bridlington, Scarborough and Hornsea provide something for everyone, the moors and the Dalby forest are also within a short distance. This being such a popular area, we feel justified in adding another site to this guide, especially one of such quality.

Facilities
Recently upgraded toilet blocks are of high quality and kept very clean. Large shower cubicles and washbasins in cubicles with curtains. Both blocks have dishwashing sinks and one has a family bathroom (20p). Good room for disabled visitors. Laundry with washing machine, dryer, spin dryer, iron and board. A key is supplied for the laundry, bathroom, telephone booth and the disabled room (£10 deposit). Reception sells a few supplies, plus papers, ice cream and gas. Only 'breathable' groundsheets are permitted. Caravan storage. Off site: Hourly bus 5 minutes walk. Local pub within walking distance. Each new arrival is given details of parking in Scarborough including a parking disc.

At a glance
Welcome & Ambience	✓✓✓✓	Location	✓✓✓✓
Quality of Pitches	✓✓✓✓✓	Range of Facilities	✓✓✓✓

Directions
From A64 Malton - Scarborough road turn right at roundabout (MacDonald's, pub and superstore) signed B1261 Filey. Go through Cayton, Killerby and in 4.5 miles site is signed on right. O.S.GR: TA082823

Charges 2005
Per unit incl. 2 persons and electricity	£ 11.50 - £ 17.00
extra adult	£ 1.50
child (5-14 yrs)	£ 1.00
trailer tent over 8 sq.m.	£ 2.00
full awning	£ 2.00 - £ 2.00

Reservations
Made with £20 non-refundable deposit. Tel: 01723 585723. Email: lebberstontouring@hotmail.com

Open
1 March - 31 October.

UK4534 Overbrook Caravan Park

Maltongate, Thornton-le-Dale, Pickering YO18 7SE (North Yorkshire)

Situated in the very pretty village of Thornton-le-Dale, Overbrook has been developed on the site of the old railway station. With the line dismantled, the station building now provides holiday cottages and the caravan park toilet facilities. This is a level site with 50 pitches (20 for tourers, the remainder used for seasonal units) arranged either side of a tarmac access road and backed by trees. All are on hard-standing and all have electricity connections (16A). Neither children nor tents are accepted at this 'adult only' park. A half mile, level walk brings you to the village which is very convenient for shops, pubs, tearooms and even a chocolate factory. There is a good bus service to York, Pickering and Scarborough. The beck which runs through the village and down under the railway property is home to kingfishers, herons, ducks and trout. There are plenty of footpaths for walking in this lovely area. Many local attractions are within half an hour's drive from the park. Dalby Forest is nearby with a visitor centre, walks and mountain bike trails.

Facilities

Toilet facilities in the old station house are in need of refurbishment which will take place as soon as possible. They are old fashioned but kept very clean. Laundry facilities and provision for disabled visitors will be added in due course. Dishwashing sinks and laundry sink with ironing board. Gas supplies. Battery charging (£1). No tents accepted. Children are not admitted. Off site: Village with bus stop, shops, pubs, fish and chips 800 yds. Fishing 3 miles. Golf courses within 10 miles. Bicycle hire 800 yds.

Open

1 March - 31 October.

At a glance

Welcome & Ambience	✓✓✓✓	Location	✓✓✓✓
Quality of Pitches	✓✓✓✓	Range of Facilities	✓✓✓

Directions

Thornton-le-Dale is on the A170 Pickering - Scarborough road. In the village follow sign for Malton and park is 800 yds. on the left (follow the stream on the left). O.S.GR: SE833821.
GPS: N54:13.712 W00:43.374

Charges 2005

Per unit incl. 2 adults and electricity	£ 11.50 - £ 12.50
incl. awning	£ 13.00 - £ 14.00
extra person	£ 2.00
dog (max. 2)	free

No credit cards.

Reservations

Made with deposit (£10-£30); contact park.
Tel: 01751 474417.
Email: enquiry@overbrookcaravanpark.co.uk

UK4545 Wolds Way Caravan Park

West Farm, West Knapton, Malton YO17 8JE (North Yorkshire)

This new park, opened in 2004, is located along the top of the Yorkshire Wolds with super panoramic views across the Vale of Pickering to the North Yorks Moors. The one and a half mile gravel track from the road to the park is well worth while to reach this peaceful location set amongst glorious country-side. There are 80 level pitches (50 for touring units), most with 16A electricity and some with water points. There are 34 pitches with hardstanding. Seating areas, picnic benches and barbecues are provided on the park. As well as the obvious attractions of walking the Wolds Way national trail and the many other footpaths and cycle ways the area has to offer, the park is well placed for visiting all the local attractions which include Scarborough, Bridlington, Sledmere House and Scampston Hall.

Facilities

A brand new toilet block is very well appointed and heated. Family bathrooms. Laundry facilities. Very large heated room with dishwashing sinks and tourist information. Room for disabled visitors. Reception also provides a small shop selling basic supplies. Play area and football field for children and many places to walk dogs. Caravan storage. Off site: Fishing 3 miles. Golf and riding 5 miles. Beach 15 miles.

Open

1 March - 31 October.

At a glance

Welcome & Ambience	✓✓✓✓	Location	✓✓✓✓
Quality of Pitches	✓✓✓✓	Range of Facilities	✓✓✓

Directions

Park entrance is on the south side of the A64 York - Scarborough road, just past the B1258 turn off and it is well signed. O.S.GR: SE896744.
GPS: N54:09.969 W00:39.242

Charges 2005

Per unit incl. 2 persons, electricity	£ 11.00 - £ 13.00
tent incl. 2 persons and car	£ 9.00 - £ 11.00
extra person (over 10 yrs)	£ 1.00
awning	£ 1.50
dog	free

Reservations

Contact park. Tel: 01944 728463.
Email: info@ryedalesbest.co.uk

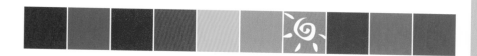

UK4570 Forestry Commission – Spiers House Campsite

Cropton Forest, Cropton, Pickering YO18 8ES (North Yorkshire)

The Spiers House site, run by the Forestry Commission, is set in a sunny clearing in the middle of Cropton Forest. It is an ideal location for a cycling or walking holiday without having to move your car. The site buildings, built in local stone, are set around a central courtyard with a pedestrian archway leading to the pitches. The welcoming reception also incorporates a well stocked shop. Sloping fields provide for 150 pitches, which include 74 with 10A electricity and 19 with hardstanding. The Moors bus calls at the site every Sunday from 1 May - 1 Sept, and daily in high season (21 July - 1 Sept) making journeys to Rosedale or beyond and Pickering possible. Reception provides leaflets for way-marked walks in the forest and orienteering.

Facilities

The tiled toilet block is spacious, if a little Spartan, with open plan washbasins and roomy, pre-set showers. Unit for disabled campers (WC and washbasin only). Dishwashing sinks under cover with free hot water, laundry room with washing machine, dryer and sinks (hot water charged). Well stocked shop. Large adventure playground and games field set under tall pines. Raised barbecues are permitted. Off site: Pub with home-brewed beer 1 mile. Riding 5 miles. Fishing 7 miles. Golf 12 miles.

Open

26 March - 27 September.

At a glance

Welcome & Ambience	✓✓✓✓✓	Location	✓✓✓✓✓
Quality of Pitches	✓✓✓✓	Range of Facilities	✓✓✓

Directions

From Pickering take A170 westwards towards Helmsley for about 2 miles. Just after delimited speed sign, take unnumbered road to the right signed Cropton and Rosedale. After 4 miles site is signed to the right into the forest (do not go into Cropton village). O.S.GR: SE758918.
GPS: N54:18.459 W00:50.776

Charges 2005

Per unit incl. 2 persons	£ 7.60 - £ 11.70
extra person over 5 yrs	£ 2.00

Prices are higher at weekends.
Less 20% all year for disabled guests and outside 7/7-28/8 for senior citizens.

Reservations

Necessary for B.Hs and peak times; made for min. 3 nights with £30 deposit. Contact site when open, otherwise Forest Holidays on 0131 314 6505.
Tel: 01751 417591. Email: info@forestholidays.co.uk

UK4560 Golden Square Caravan & Camping Park

Oswaldkirk, York YO62 5YQ (North Yorkshire)

Golden Square is a popular, high quality, family owned touring park. Mr and Mrs Armstrong are local farmers who have worked hard to turn an old quarry into a very attractive caravan park with a number of level bays that have superb views over the North York Moors. The 130 pitches are not separated but they do have markers set into the ground and mainly back on to grass banks. In very dry weather the ground can be hard, steel pegs would be needed (even in wet weather the park is well drained). All pitches have electrical connections (10A), 24 have drainage and 6 are 'deluxe' pitches (with waste water, sewage, electricity, water and TV aerial connection). The licensed shop is very well stocked, selling home-made fresh bread and cakes, dairy produce, fresh vegetables and groceries, newspapers, gas and gifts. Visitors may have membership of the Ampleforth College sports centre, with its indoor pool, tennis and gym, etc. The area abounds with footpaths and three well known long distance footpaths are near. Dog owners are well catered for with two or three enormous fields for exercising alongside the park.

Facilities

Two heated well cared for toilet blocks are of excellent quality, with some washbasins in private cabins. Showers are pre-set and metered (token) and a bathroom (token) also houses baby changing facilities. Both ladies and men have full facilities for disabled visitors. Dishwashing sinks under cover. Laundry with washing machines, dryers, spin dryer and iron and board. Motorcaravan service point. Tourist information room also houses a microwave and an extra iron and board. Shop. Two excellent play areas allow tiny tots to be kept separate from older children. Games field and a barn with table tennis and pool table. Bicycle hire. All year caravan storage. Off site: Riding 2 miles. Golf 3 miles. Fishing 5 miles. Outdoor pool at Helmsley, sports centre at Ampleforth, both have shops and pubs with food.

At a glance

Welcome & Ambience	✓✓✓✓✓	Location	✓✓✓✓✓
Quality of Pitches	✓✓✓✓	Range of Facilities	✓✓✓✓

Directions

From York take B1363 to Helmsley. At Oswaldkirk Bank Top turn left on B1257 to Helmsley. Take second left turn signed Ampleforth to site.
O.S.GR: SE605797. GPS: N54:12.560 W01:04.427

Charges 2005

Per unit incl. 2 persons	£ 9.50 - £ 13.50
incl. electricity	£ 11.50 - £ 15.50
incl. full services and awning	£ 18.50 - £ 23.50
extra person (10 yrs or over)	£ 2.00
awning	£ 1.50 - £ 2.00
hikers and bikers, per person	£ 4.25 - £ 4.75

No credit cards.

Reservations

Essential for B.Hs and made with £10 deposit (£20 for B.Hs). Tel: 01439 788269.
Email: barbara@goldensquarecaravanpark.com

Open

1 March - 31 October.

UK4620 Upper Carr Chalet & Touring Park

Upper Carr Lane, Malton Road, Pickering YO18 7JP (North Yorkshire)

With a central location in the Vale of Pickering, Upper Carr is well placed for the many attractions the area has to offer. The park is surrounded by a high, well trimmed hedge which protects it from the wind and deadens the road noise. There are colourful gardens and a pets corner with unusual breeds of poultry. Quiet and well maintained, Upper Carr's six acres provide 80 level pitches, 75 with electricity (10A) and some with hardstanding. Seasonal units use 25 pitches. Picturesque Thornton Dale can be reached on foot or by cycle along the Upper Carr nature trail. A member of the Countryside Discovery group.

Facilities

The heated toilet blocks are a little dated (in 'portacabin' style) but all is kept very clean and well decorated. Showers are charged for. Baby changing facilities. Separate room with WC and washbasin for disabled visitors. Laundry room. Motorcaravan service point. Small shop in reception supplies basic needs and gas. Good play area. Bicycle hire. Nature trail. Off site: Pub 100 yards. Golf (9 hole) or tennis adjacent to park. Riding 6 miles. Fishing 5 miles. Swimming pool 1.5 miles. Bus service passes entrance.

At a glance

| Welcome & Ambience | ✓✓✓✓ | Location | ✓✓✓ |
| Quality of Pitches | ✓✓✓ | Range of Facilities | ✓✓✓ |

Directions

Travelling on the Pickering - Malton A169 road, park is on the left about 1.5 miles south of Pickering. O.S.GR: SE804815. GPS: N54:13.378 W00:46.140

Charges 2006

| Per unit incl. 2 persons and electricity | £ 11.50 - £ 16.00 |

Reservations

Made with £15 deposit. Tel: 01751 473115. Email: harker@uppercarr.demon.co.uk

Open

1 March - 31 October.

UK4580 Foxholme Touring Caravan & Camping Park

Harome, Helmsley YO62 5JG (North Yorkshire)

Foxholme is now an 'adult only' park. With only 60 pitches for caravans and a small field for a few tents, it is unusual in that nearly all the pitches are individual ones in clearings in the quite dense coniferous plantation. The trees give much shade and quite a lot of privacy (manoeuvring may be difficult on some of the pitches). All pitches have electricity (6A, a few need long leads) and six places have hardstanding. Some picnic tables are provided. There are 30 pitches for tourers, the remainder being taken by seasonal units. The site is managed by a warden, with reception usually open 9 am. - 9 pm. (6 days). Very basic provisions are kept. The park is set in quiet countryside and would be a good base for touring, being within striking distance of the moors, the coast and York. There are no on site activities but campers may use the indoor pool at the Pheasant Hotel in Harome. There is lighting, but a torch would be useful.

Facilities

The toilet block is of good quality, built in local stone, with all washbasins in private cubicles, a bathroom (£3), laundry room with washing machine and sinks and a washing up room. Two further small blocks provide WCs only in other parts of the park. Motorcaravan service point. Caravan storage. Off site: The nearest shops are at Helmsley and Kirkbymoorside, both about 4 miles away, where there is also bicycle hire. Riding and golf also 4 miles.

Open

Easter - 31 October.

At a glance

| Welcome & Ambience | ✓✓ | Location | ✓✓✓ |
| Quality of Pitches | ✓✓✓ | Range of Facilities | ✓✓✓ |

Directions

Turn south off the A170 between adjoining villages of Beadlam (to west) and Nawton (to east) at sign to Ryedale School, then 1 mile to park on left (passing another park on right). From east ignore first camp sign at turn before Nawton. From west turn right 400 yards east of Helmsley, signed Harome, turn left at church, go through village and follow camp signs. O.S.GR: SE661831. GPS: N54:14.247 W000:59.42

Charges 2005

| Per unit incl. 2 persons and electricity | £ 12.00 |
| child | £ 1.00 |

No credit cards.

Reservations

Made for any dates with £20 deposit. Tel: 01439 771696.

UK4610 Moorside Caravan Park

Lords Moor Lane, Strensall, York YO32 5XJ (North Yorkshire)

Strensall is only a few miles from York, one of England's most attractive cities and Moorside Adult Touring Park will provide a peaceful haven after a day's sightseeing. It will impress you with its pretty fishing lake, masses of flowers and the tranquillity (except for the odd passing daytime train). There are 57 marked pitches on neat well trimmed grass, most with electricity (5/10A) and 18 with paved hard-standing. The whole park is very well maintained making it a very pleasant environment. The small lake is well stocked for coarse fishing and the pitches bordering the lake are the most popular. York golf course is almost opposite the site entrance. Children (under 16 years) are not accepted at this park.

Facilities

The purpose built toilet block can be heated and houses immaculately kept facilities with washbasins in cubicles for ladies. One WC is suitable for use by disabled visitors. Fully equipped laundry room. Dishwashing area. Tourist information and books to borrow. Coarse fishing (£2 per day). Caravan storage. Off site: Strensall village with shops and places to eat is less than a mile. Golf 0.5 miles. Riding 3 miles.

Open

March - end October.

At a glance

Welcome & Ambience	✓✓✓✓	Location	✓✓✓✓
Quality of Pitches	✓✓✓✓✓	Range of Facilities	✓✓✓

Directions

From A1237 York outer ring road follow signs for Earswick and Strensall. At Strensall follow Flaxton road. The park entrance is on the left past signs to Strensall village and York Golf Club. O.S.GR: SE647614. GPS: N54:02.564 W01:00.701

Charges 2005

Per unit incl. 2 persons	£ 7.50 - £ 11.00
extra person	£ 2.00
awning	£ 1.00
hardstanding	£ 0.50
electricity	£ 1.50

No credit cards.

Reservations

Contact park. Tel: 01904 491208.

UK4650 Fangfoss Old Station Caravan Park

Fangfoss, York YO41 5QB (North Yorkshire)

Fangfoss railway station stands on the old York – Beverley line (closed in 1965) and the Station House and its platform give this small, simple site plenty of character. Its rural situation amongst rolling farmland provides peace and tranquillity and its owners, a friendly welcome and clean and comfortable facilities. The grassed over track and sidings provide hardstanding and together with the adjacent fairly level grass field, give a total of 75 marked pitches, all with 10A electricity and 19 with hardstanding. York is 8 miles (with 'park and ride') and the Yorkshire Wolds 5 miles. There are nearby market towns and a variety of pubs and restaurants within a 6 mile radius. Fangfoss is 1 mile, Pocklington 4, with sports facilities, etc. This area will encourage walkers and cyclists.

Facilities

A modern, centrally situated toilet block provides free adjustable hot showers, vanity style washbasins (two cubicles for ladies). A separate wooden utility block, 'The Wendy House', provides covered washing up sinks and a laundry sink with free hot water and a food preparation bar (useful for tenters). No washing machine but a laundry service is offered. Reception carries food essentials with an off-licence and gas. Some play equipment on grass. Winter caravan storage. Off site: Fishing, bicycle hire, riding and golf within 4 miles.

Open

1 March - 30 November.

At a glance

Welcome & Ambience	✓✓✓✓	Location	✓✓✓
Quality of Pitches	✓✓✓	Range of Facilities	✓✓✓

Directions

Using the A1079 York - Hull road, follow site signs at Wilberfoss for 1.5 miles (in a northerly direction). On A166 York - Bridlington road, park is clearly signed at Stamford Bridge, on right just after crossing the river. O.S.GR: SE748527. GPS: N53:57.930 W00:51.710

Charges 2005

Per unit incl. 2 persons, electricity	£ 10.00 - £ 13.00
tent (no electricity)	£ 8.50 - £ 9.50
extra person	£ 1.50
awning	£ 2.50
Trailer or Family tent (4 persons)	£ 14.00 - £ 15.50

No credit cards.

Reservations

Made with £20 deposit. Tel: 01759 380491. Email: info@fangfosspark.co.uk

UK4640 Goose Wood Caravan Park

Sutton-on-the-Forest, York YO61 1ET (North Yorkshire)

A family owned park in a natural woodland setting, Goose Wood provides a quiet, relaxed atmosphere from which to explore York itself or the surrounding Yorkshire Dales, Wolds or Moors. The park has a well kept air and a rural atmosphere, with 95 well spaced and marked pitches on level grass, all with electricity (16A) and 95 with paved hardstanding and patio pitch. No tents are accepted. For children, there is a 'super plus' adventure playground in the trees at one side of the park and for adults, a small coarse fishing lake and attractive, natural woodland for walking, plus a large scale chess set. The park is popular with families in high season when it can be busy at weekends. A 'park and ride' scheme for York operates from nearby all year, six days a week or there is a local bus every two hours, six days a week. The park is just over a mile from Sutton village and only 7 miles from 'Water World' a water leisure centre with pool, slides, wave machines, etc. A member of the Best of British group.

Facilities

Tiled and heated, the modern toilet block is of excellent quality and well maintained. Bathroom (£1). An additional unit provides shower rooms, WC and washbasins in cubicles and extra dishwashing sinks. Full facilities for disabled visitors and a motorcaravan service point are planned. Laundry room. Small shop (with gas). Fishing lake. Large adventure playground. Games room with pool and TV. Outdoor table tennis. Dogs (max. two per pitch), to be exercised in nearby woodland. No tents are accepted. Off site: Riding or golf 1 mile. Bicycle hire 6 miles. York 6 miles.

Open

All year excl. 15-31 January.

At a glance

Welcome & Ambience	✓✓✓✓	Location	✓✓✓✓✓
Quality of Pitches	✓✓✓✓	Range of Facilities	✓✓✓✓

Directions

Park is 6 miles north of York; from the A1237 York outer ring-road take the B1363 for Sutton-on-the-Forest and Stillington, taking the first right after the Haxby and Wigginton junction and follow park signs. O.S.GR: SE595636.

Charges 2005

Per unit incl. 1 or 2 persons and car	£ 7.50 - £ 14.00
extra person	£ 1.50
awning or extra pup tent (1 only)	£ 2.00
electricity (16A)	£ 2.50
fully serviced pitch	£ 5.50

Reservations

Made with £20 deposit (min. 3 nights at B.Hs). Tel: 01347 810829. Email: edward@goosewood.co.uk

UK4638 Alders Caravan Park

Home Farm, Alne, York YO61 1RY (North Yorkshire)

The Alders is located in the village of Alne, only nine miles from the centre of the ancient city of York. Carefully developed on a working farm in historic parkland, the drive to reach the pitches gives a real feeling of space. On reaching the 40 level pitches (16 for tourers, the rest for seasonal units), you will find an area of well trimmed grass and a pitch layout designed to give as much privacy and space as possible. Arranged in small bays, each group is named after a Yorkshire Abbey. Newly planted woodland with woodland walks and a water meadow with wild flowers enhance the wonderful peace and tranquillity. The site overlooks the village cricket pitch where you can watch summer matches or enjoy a drink at the club bar at weekends. This park would suit couples or young families (no play area). The village centre is only a short stroll away. Alders is also well placed for visiting the many attractions of the area, for example York, Harrogate and Castle Howard.

Facilities

The central toilet block is heated with family sized shower rooms, one also has a bath (£1 charge). Dishwashing sinks but no laundry. Gas is sold at reception (shop in the village). Bicycle hire. Off site: Floodlit tennis courts in the village. Fishing 2 miles. Golf 3 miles. Riding 4 miles.

Open

1 March - 31 October.

At a glance

Welcome & Ambience	✓✓✓✓	Location	✓✓✓✓
Quality of Pitches	✓✓✓✓✓	Range of Facilities	✓✓✓

Directions

From the north on the A19: after leaving Easingwold bypass take next right turn signed Alne. From the south (A19), 5 miles north of Shipton turn left at sign for Alne. In 1.5 miles at T-junction turn left and in about 0.5 miles, site is signed in the centre of the village. O.S.GR: SE496651.
GPS: N54:04.911 W01:14.463

Charges 2005

Per unit incl. 2 persons, electricity	£ 10.00
extra person	£ 2.00
awning	£ 1.50
dog (max. 2)	free
No credit cards.	

Reservations

Made with £10 deposit. Tel: 01347 838722. Email: enquiries@homefarmalne.co.uk

UK4710 **Rudding Holiday Park**

Follifoot, Harrogate HG3 1JH (North Yorkshire)

The extensive part wooded, part open grounds of Rudding Park are very attractive, peaceful and well laid out. One camping area is sloping but terraces provide level pitches and further pitches are in the very sheltered old walled garden. All 141 touring pitches have electricity (10/16A) and 20 'super pitches' are fully serviced. Further pitches are let on a seasonal basis and a separate area contains 96 owner occupied caravan holiday homes and pine chalets. On the outer edge of the park is an 18 hole golf course and driving range, together with the 'The Deer House', a bar and restaurant open twice daily during B.Hs and school holidays, otherwise only at weekends. Tennis, markets, pubs and restaurants are within a few miles, and the majestic City of York is less than an hour away. This is an attractive park with something for all the family.

Facilities

Two tiled, well maintained toilet blocks are of a good standard (one completely refurbished), with central heating, some washbasins in cabins, a baby room and bathroom. Fully equipped laundry room at each block. Disabled people have well appointed facilities. Motorcaravan service point. Large, well stocked shop (all season, sometimes limited hours). Gas supplies. Restaurant and bar. Heated outdoor swimming and paddling pools with sunbathing areas (Spr. B.H.- early Sept), supervised at all times (extra charge). Adventure playground. Football pitch, games room. Golf. Off site: Buses pass the gate hourly to Harrogate and Knaresborough. Fishing 2 miles, riding 1 mile.

Open

1 March - 31 January.

At a glance

| Welcome & Ambience | ✓✓✓✓ | Location | ✓✓✓✓ |
| Quality of Pitches | ✓✓✓✓ | Range of Facilities | ✓✓✓✓✓ |

Directions

Park is 3 miles south of Harrogate clearly signed between the A658 and A661 roads. O.S.GR: SE333528.

Charges 2005

Per pitch	£ 6.00 - £ 18.00
with electricity	£ 14.50 - £ 21.00
'supersite' incl. awning and electricity	£ 19.00 - £ 28.00
awning	£ 1.50 - £ 2.50
tent per adult	£ 4.00 - £ 6.00
child (5-16 yrs)	£ 2.00 - £ 3.00

Special offers - contact park.

Reservations

Made with full advance payment (essential for B.H. w/ends). Tel: 01423 870439. Email: holiday-park@ruddingpark.com

UK4670 **Wood Nook Caravan Park**

Skirethorns, Threshfield, Skipton BD23 5NU (North Yorkshire)

Wood Nook is a family run park in the heart of Wharfedale, part of the Yorkshire Dales National Park. The access road is narrow for a short distance, but you will find it is well worth this slight rural inconvenience as the site includes six acres of woodland with quite rare flora and wildlife. Reception is in the farmhouse, as is the small shop. The gently sloping fields have gravel roads and provide 25 pitches with gravel hardstanding. All have electricity (10A, long leads may be required) and there are water and chemical disposal points. There is also room for 24 tents and the park has some caravan holiday homes to let. The Thompson family are very friendly, trying always to have time for a chat, although Wood Nook is still a working farm producing beef cattle. The park itself adjoins the fells, with direct access from the top of the site. A visit to the nearby village of Grassington is a must, with its cobbled main street and quaint gift shops. All in all, this is a peaceful park from which to explore the Yorkshire Dales.

Facilities

Farm buildings have been converted to provide modern, neat sanitary facilities which can be heated, are well maintained and kept very clean (opened by key). Washbasins in cubicles for ladies. Roomy showers (in another building) are coin operated. Fully equipped laundry with clothes lines. Dishwashing sinks under cover. Motorcaravan service points. Licensed shop for basics and a range of gifts (from Easter). Gas supplies. Small, attractive play area on top of a small hill. American motorhomes are taken by prior arrangement. Wi-Fi internet coverage installed (charged). Off site: Fishing and bicycle hire 2 miles. Riding 3 miles. Golf 9 miles. Good range of bar food available locally. Leisure centre with pool nearby.

At a glance

| Welcome & Ambience | ✓✓✓✓ | Location | ✓✓✓✓✓ |
| Quality of Pitches | ✓✓✓✓ | Range of Facilities | ✓✓✓✓ |

Directions

From Skipton take B6265 to Threshfield, then the B6160. After 50 yds turn left into Skirethorns Lane and follow signs for 600 yds, up narrow lane then 300 yds. O.S.GR: SD974641.

Charges 2006

Per adult	£ 3.00
child (5-15 yrs)	£ 1.00
young adult (16-17 yrs) as part of family unit	£ 1.50
serviced pitch incl. electricity	£ 7.50
tent and car	£ 6.50
awning	£ 1.50

Payment also accepted in Euros.

Reservations

Necessary for high season and B.Hs with £15 deposit. Tel: 01756 752412. Email: enquiries@woodnook.net

Open

1 March - 31 October.

UK4700 Nostell Priory Holiday Park

Nostell, Wakefield WF4 1QD (West Yorkshire)

This tranquil, secluded woodland park is within the Nostell Priory estate. Under new ownership, the site now provides just 25 touring pitches, plus 82 caravan holiday homes in a separate area. In a grassy, flat and sheltered area edged with mature trees, all the touring pitches have 5A electricity connections. There is a hardstanding area suitable for motorcaravans. Amenities are designed to blend into the environment in rustic wood, including the toilet block. Nostell Priory itself, with a collection of Chippendale furniture and attractive gardens, is well worth a visit. Fishing, golf and watersports are possible locally (details in reception). The park is well cared for and the natural environment is encouraged so there is an abundance of birds and wildlife. The Dales, York and the Peak District are all an easy drive away. Buses pass the end of the drive (a mile long).

Facilities	Directions
The toilet block, although older in style, has been refurbished and includes some washbasins in cubicles (coded entry). Separate room for dishwashing. Laundry with two washing machines and a dryer (opening times on the door). Gas supplies. Milk and papers can be ordered at reception. Play area. Fishing. Up to two dogs are accepted. No single sex groups or units over 21'6". Off site: Nearest shops 2 miles. Golf 5 miles. Boat launching 8 miles.	Park entrance is off A638 Wakefield - Doncaster road, 5 miles southeast of Wakefield. Follow drive for 0.5 miles keeping the rose nursery on your left. Approaching from the south on A638, the entrance is a mile past the entry to the Priory, on the right. O.S.GR: SE394181. GPS: N53:39.297 W000:23.91

Open

1 March - 31 October.

At a glance			
Welcome & Ambience	✓✓✓✓	Location	✓✓✓
Quality of Pitches	✓✓✓✓	Range of Facilities	✓✓✓

Charges 2005

Per unit incl. 2 persons	£ 12.50 - £ 17.50
extra person (over 5 yrs)	£ 1.00
dog (max 2)	£ 1.00

Reservations

Advised and made with deposit of one night's charge. Tel: 01924 863938.
Email: info@nostellprioryholidaypark.co.uk

UK4790 Bronte Caravan Park

off Halifax Road, Keighley BD21 5QF (West Yorkshire)

Bronte Caravan Park is now an 'adult only' site – a peaceful haven set in a 50-acre park with wonderful views. It is hard to believe that you are only 1.5 miles from the busy town of Keighley, as only the rolling hillsides with a village on the opposite side are visible. Ten acres of the land are devoted to the owners' own deer herd. A two acre lake is in a lovely setting with its island, weeping willows and several varieties of waterfowl, not to mention the local heron or kingfisher. It is well stocked to provide sport for both coarse and fly fishermen. The hillside has been terraced and a stream tumbles down into the lake. The River Worth runs alongside the site (well fenced). The level pitches have gravel surfaces and 10A electricity (some are a little small). There are also 25 pitches for tents. The Worth Valley railway, of 'The Railway Children' fame, running alongside the site is a big attraction and one of its smaller stations is only a short walk. Ingrow station with a railway museum and free parking is half a mile. Haworth and its Bronte heritage (2 miles) is a must with the museum, the parsonage where the sisters lived and the moorland walks. Further away at Bradford is the cinema and photography museum and Cliffe castle museum in Keighley is well worth a visit.

Facilities	Directions
The well appointed, heated, central toilet block of local stone includes showers and a large room for disabled visitors. Laundry with washing machine, dryer and iron. Dishwashing sinks under cover. This block is quite a walk from some pitches but two 'portacabin' style blocks nearer to the pitches are well equipped with toilets, washbasins and an outside dishwashing sink. Fishing (£3.50 per day). Barrier access (key £10 deposit). Caravan storage. Only two dogs per pitch. Off site: Supermarket 1.5 miles. Golf 3 miles.	Park is south of Keighley off the A629 Keighley - Halifax road, on the right approx. 1.75 miles from Keighley. O.S.GR: SE058385

Open

1 April - 31 October.

At a glance			
Welcome & Ambience	✓✓✓✓✓	Location	✓✓✓✓
Quality of Pitches	✓✓✓	Range of Facilities	✓✓✓

Charges 2005

Per unit incl. 2 persons	£ 10.00
extra person over 18 yrs	£ 2.50
electricity hook-up rental	£ 3.00
backpacker	£ 4.50
dog (max. 2)	£ 0.50
No credit cards.	

Reservations

Made with £10-£20 deposit (non-returnable). Tel: 01535 649111.
Email: bronte@brontecaravanpark.co.uk

MAP 5

The northwest region boasts a wealth of industrial heritage with undiscovered countryside, the vibrant cities of Manchester and Liverpool, the seaside resorts of Blackpool and Morecambe Bay, plus miles of glorious coastline, home to a wide variety of bird species.

THIS REGION INCLUDES: CHESHIRE, LANCASHIRE, MERSEYSIDE, GREATER MANCHESTER AND THE HIGH PEAKS OF DERBYSHIRE

The miles of beautiful, North West countryside offers endless opportunities for recreation. For the more active, the peaceful plains of Cheshire are a walker's haven with endless trails to choose from. Lancashire is also good walking country, with way marked paths passing through the outstanding forest of Bowland, which affords marvellous views over the Lake District in Cumbria and the Yorkshire Dales. Birdwatchers are catered for too, with the coast offering some of the best bird spotting activitiy in the country, most notably along the Sefton coast and around the Wirral Peninsula. The region's cities have their own charm. Manchester, with its fabulous shopping centres and vibrant nightlife, boasts a rich Victorian heritage; the maritime city of Liverpool has more museums and galleries than any other UK city outside London; Lancaster features fine Georgian buildings and an imposing Norman castle; while Chester is renowned for its medieval architecture and shopping galleries. And offering good, old-fashioned seaside fun is Blackpool. England's most popular seaside resort is packed full of lively entertainment and attractions, such as the white knuckle rides at the pleasure beach, amusement games on the pier and the observation decks in the famous Tower.

Places of interest

Cheshire: Tatton Park in Knutsford; Chester Cathedral and Zoo; Cheshire Military Museum; Lyme Park stately home in Macclesfield; Beeston Castle; Boat Museum at Ellesmere Port

Lancashire: Williamson Park, Castle and Leisure Park in Lancaster; Camelot Theme Park; Museum of Football in Preston; Morecambe Bay; Hoghton Tower and National Museum of Football in Preston

Merseyside: Liverpool Football Club Museum and Tour Centre; The Beatles Story Museum; Speke Hall Garden and Estate; The Wirral Country Park; Williamson Tunnels Heritage Centre

Greater Manchester: Imperial War Museum North; Manchester United Football Club Museum; The Lowry; Corgi Heritage Centre in Rochdale; Stockport Air Raid Shelter

Did you know?

The first public gallery to open in England was in Liverpool in 1877

Lancaster Castle is infamous as host to the Pendle Witch trials in 1612

The first passenger railway station was built in Manchester

Houghton Tower is where King James I knighted a loin of beef in 1617 – hence the name Sirloin

To date 300 bird species have been recorded within the boundaries of Sefton

Chester has the most complete set of city walls in Britain

Opened in 1894, the Blackpool Tower was copied from the Eiffel Tower; the height to the top of the flagpole is 518 feet 9 inches

UK5250 Capesthorne Hall Touring Caravan Park

Macclesfield SK11 9JY (Cheshire)

The approach to this site is impressive as you enter the main gates, pass the gatekeeper's cottage and proceed carefully up the drive (mind the speed bumps) through the parkland almost to the front door of this imposing stately home. The campsite is set on a five acre meadow to the right of the Hall and with only 30 pitches, everyone has plenty of space arranged around a series of small fenced copses. All have access to electric hook-ups (10A, long leads may be necessary) and most are on grass – there are just two hardstandings. The park, lakes, gardens and woodland walks extend to over 100 acres and caravanners have free access to these between 7am and 7pm. The Hall, Butler's Pantry and Grounds are open to the public on Wednesday, Sunday and Bank Holiday afternoons. A range of events are also held in the park adjacent to the campsite during the year. These include Craft Fairs, horse shows, open air theatre and opera. Wedding receptions are also staged. Site lighting is minimal so torches are useful and only 'breathable' groundsheets are permitted. Tents or trailer tents are not accepted.

Facilities

Toilet facilities are in some of the Hall's outbuildings around a courtyard to the side of the campsite. Only the ladies section is heated but they provide one huge shower room per sex, with free controllable hot water, and a generous supply of WCs and washbasins. Tiny laundry and dishwashing room. All are naturally in a very traditional period style but are very clean. Basic drive over drain for motorcaravans, neatly marked with a cone!
Off site: Jodrell Bank and Gawsworth Hall are nearby. Fishing and riding 1 mile. Golf 3 miles. Bicycle hire 10 miles. Shop and garage 1 mile.

At a glance

Welcome & Ambience	✓✓✓✓	Location	✓✓✓✓
Quality of Pitches	✓✓✓✓	Range of Facilities	✓✓✓✓

Directions

Capesthorne Hall is on A34, 3 miles south of Alderley Edge and 6 miles north of Congleton, just south of the crossroads with the A537. O.S.GR: SJ840730.

Charges 2005

Per unit incl. 2 persons and electricity	£ 15.00

Reservations

Essential for peak season and B.Hs.
Tel: 01625 861779.

Open

1 April - 31 October.

UK5240 Lamb Cottage Caravan Park

Dalefords Lane, Whitegate, Northwich CW8 2BN (Cheshire)

This quiet, family run 'adult only' park is set in the midst of the lovely Vale Royal area of Cheshire. Mike and Lynn Howard are making great improvements with a complete redevelopment of the touring section and new toilet and shower facilities. The entrance road is flanked by 22 privately owned residential caravan holiday homes which are not unduly obtrusive, and a second area beyond has 28 landscaped seasonal caravan pitches. Beyond this again is the touring area which has 30 large pitches, all with 16A electric hook-ups. There are 2 grass pitches, and 28 on gravel hardstandings, which are multi-serviced with electricity, water and waste water drain. Only 'breathable' groundsheets are permitted and tents and motorcycles are not accepted. Nearby are Delamere Forest with its walking and mountain biking trails, Whitegate Way walking trail, Oulton Park Motor Racing Circuit, castles at Peckforton and Beeston, and the city of Chester, which is 12 miles.

Facilities

Toilet and shower facilities are housed in a new custom built 'park home' style unit which includes washbasins in cubicles and facilities for disabled guests. Dishwashing area. Laundry room. Recycling of glass and paper. Calor gas stocked. Fenced dog walk (max. 2 dogs per unit permitted).
Off site: Pub serving food under 1 mile, supermarket 3 miles. Golf 2 miles. Fishing 3 miles. Riding 1.5 miles. Bicycle hire 4 miles.

Open

1 March - 31 October.

At a glance

Welcome & Ambience	✓✓✓✓	Location	✓✓✓✓
Quality of Pitches	✓✓✓✓	Range of Facilities	✓✓✓

Directions

From M6 exit 19 take A556 towards Chester. After about 12 miles turn left at traffic lights (signed Winsford and Whitegate) into Dalefords Lane. Continue for about 1 mile and site entrance is on right between white house and bungalow. O.S.GR: SJ614693.

Charges 2006

Per pitch incl. 2 persons and electricity	£ 17.00 - £ 20.00

Reservations

Essential for peak season and B.Hs.
Tel: 01606 882302. Email: lynn@lccp.fsworld.co.uk

UK5230 **Chester Southerly Caravan Park**

Balderton Lane, Marlston-cum-Lache, Chester CH4 9LF (Cheshire)

This is a well managed friendly campsite within three miles of the city of Chester. It is easily accessible from the Chester Southerly bypass and convenient for the new ferry terminal at Mostyn. It enjoys a quiet countryside environment, although there can be some road noise from the Chester bypass. The 90 pitches, mostly on hardstanding for touring units, are spaciously spread in bays around this mature site. Pitches are marked, numbered and level with 10A electricity connections. To the left of the card operated security barrier stands reception which incorporates a small shop selling basic food items. Chester is one of England's most historic cities and this site makes a convenient base for spending time discovering its famous rows, walls, gates and towers. There are many other touring possibilities from here such as the North Wales Coast, the Dee valley, Cheshire Plain, etc. making the park ideal for adults on a touring and sightseeing holiday.

Facilities

A single toilet block (key system), whilst not ultra modern is brightly decorated and kept clean. Open style washbasins; facilities for people with disabilities (washbasin and WC), laundry room with sinks, washing machine and dryer and dishwashing area. Shop. Adventure type play area. Off site: Bus stop 100 m. City centre 3 miles.

Open

Easter - end November.

At a glance

Welcome & Ambience	✓✓✓✓	Location	✓✓✓
Quality of Pitches	✓✓✓	Range of Facilities	✓✓

Directions

Park is on Dodleston - Kinnerton turn off from A483 and is signed from the junction of A55 and A483 roads. O.S.GR: SJ385624.

Charges 2005

Per unit incl. 2 persons and electricity	£ 14.00
extra adult	£ 4.00
child (3-16 yrs)	£ 2.00
awning	£ 2.00
dog	£ 1.00

Reservations

Contact site. Tel: 01244 671308.

UK5280 **Abbey Farm Caravan Park**

Dark Lane, Ormskirk L40 5TX (Lancashire)

This quiet, well equipped, family park beside the Abbey ruins has views over open farmland. It is an ideal base for a longer stay with plenty of interest in the local area, including Ormskirk parish church, unusual for having both a tower and a spire. Market days are on Thursday and Saturday. The park is divided into small paddocks, one of which is for 30 privately owned seasonal units, one for tents, the others for touring units, plus a rally field for special events. The 60 touring pitches, all with electricity (10/16A), are on neatly mown level grass, separated by small shrubs and colourful flower borders. Some mature trees provide shade in parts. Amenities include a farm walk and a small, free lending library with a good stock of tourist information. The owners organise two annual events – a barbecue in early June and a Bonfire Night in November. They have planned plenty of routes for walkers from the park. Southport with its beach and Pleasureland is 10 miles. Wigan Pier, Aintree for the Grand National, the annual Beatles Festival or Southport Flower Show and Martin Mere Nature reserve are some of the attractions within easy reach. A member of the Countryside Discovery group.

Facilities

The main toilet block is modern, heated and spotless, providing controllable hot showers. Dual purpose family bathroom that includes facilities for disabled people. A second smaller unit has individual shower/WC/washbasin cubicles. Dishwashing sinks under cover at both units. Laundry room with washing machine, dryer, spinner, ironing board and airing cupboard. Small well stocked shop shares space with reception, with a butcher calling twice weekly. Indoor games room with table tennis and football games machine. Small adventure playground and large field for ball games. Fishing lake (£2 per rod, per day).

Open

All year.

At a glance

Welcome & Ambience	✓✓✓✓✓	Location	✓✓✓✓
Quality of Pitches	✓✓✓✓	Range of Facilities	✓✓✓✓✓

Directions

From M6 junction 27 take A5209 (Parbold) road. After 5 miles turn left (just before garage) onto B5240, and then first right into Hob Cross Lane, following signs to site. O.S.GR: SD433099. GPS: N53:34.188 W02:51.399

Charges 2005

Per unit incl. 2 adults	£ 8.00 - £ 13.60
serviced pitch	£ 13.80 - £ 15.30
extra adult	£ 2.50
child (5-15 yrs)	£ 1.50
electricity	£ 1.90 - £ 2.30

Less 10% for 7 nights booked on or before arrival.

Reservations

Essential for high season or B.Hs. Min charge 3 nights for B.Hs. + £10 deposit. Tel: 01695 572686. Email: abbeyfarm@yahoo.com

UK5510 The Larches Caravan Park

Mealsgate, Wigton CA7 1LQ (Cumbria)

Mealsgate and The Larches lie on the Carlisle - Cockermouth road, a little removed from the hectic centre of the Lake District, yet with easy access to it (and good views towards it) and to other attractions nearby - the Western Borders, Northumberland, etc. It is a quality, family run park which takes 73 touring units of any type and also accommodates 100 privately owned holiday homes. Touring pitches are in different grassy areas with tall, mature trees, shrubs and accompanying wildlife. Some are sloping and irregular, others on marked hardstandings, with electricity (10A), water and drainage. Events in the surrounding district each day displayed prominently in the window of the shop. On arrival visitors are loaned very comprehensive tourist information brochures. There are bus routes to Carlisle and Keswick, walks from the park and good restaurants nearby. The Elliott family provide a warm welcome at this peaceful, well organised park which is undergoing some redevelopment. This is an ideal haven for couples - only adult visitors are accepted.

Facilities

Toilet facilities, in two purpose designed blocks, are of good quality providing en-suite facilities for both sexes. Washbasins for ladies are in cubicles, those for men set in flat surfaces. Separate unit for disabled visitors can be heated. Campers' kitchen with cooker and microwave (metered). Laundry room. Well stocked shop incl. camping accessories, gas and off licence. Small indoor heated pool. Table tennis. Wildlife pond. Caravan storage. Off site: Golf 3.5 miles. Bicycle hire 7 miles. Fishing 8 miles. Riding 10 miles.

Open

1 March - 31 October.

At a glance

| Welcome & Ambience | ✓✓✓✓ | Location | ✓✓✓✓ |
| Quality of Pitches | ✓✓✓✓ | Range of Facilities | ✓✓✓✓ |

Directions

Park entrance is south off A595 (Carlisle - Cockermouth) road just southwest of Mealsgate. O.S.GR: NY206415. GPS: N54:45.796 W03:14.148

Charges guide

Per unit incl. 2 adults	£ 9.00 - £ 12.90
incl. electricity	£ 11.90 - £ 14.90
extra person	£ 2.00 - £ 2.50
awning or extra car	£ 1.00
backpacker	£ 5.50 - £ 6.50

Discounts for senior citizens and bookings over 7 nights. No credit cards.

Reservations

Made with £1 per night deposit, balance on arrival. Tel: 01697 371379. Email: info@larchescaravanpark.co.uk

UK5660 Castlerigg Hall Caravan & Camping Park

Keswick CA12 4TE (Cumbria)

This well laid out park was started in the late 1950s by the Jackson family, who over the years have developed and improved the site whilst maintaining its character. Good use has been made of the traditional stone buildings to house the reception and shop, whilst another building houses a modern amenity block along with a really excellent campers' kitchen. Tarmac roads wend their way around the site to the separate tent area of 110 pitches. Gently sloping with some shelter, these pitches have fine views across Keswick, Derwentwater and the western Fells. The 45 caravan pitches tend to be on terraces, again overlooking the lake. Each terrace has a maximum of seven pitches, all on hardstanding and with 10A electricity and nearly all with a water tap and grey water drain. Places to visit include Keswick (about 20 minutes walk), Derwentwater, Ullswater, Penrith, Carlisle, Hadrian's Wall, Rhegad (the village in the hill) and, quite close to the site, Castlerigg stone circle which is believed to be some 4,000 years old, and of course as much walking as you might want. The Jacksons are committed to conservation.

Facilities

The main toilet block is beautifully fitted out, fully tiled and heated, with showers, vanity style washbasins (2 in cabins) and hair care areas. Unit for disabled visitors (key). Baby area. Fully equipped laundry and dishwashing area. Games room and campers' kitchen complete with microwave, toasters, kettle and hot plates. Two other toilet blocks are older in style but newly decorated and clean. Reception houses tourist information, internet point and a well stocked shop (with gas). Off site: Hotel/pub for meals adjacent to site. Fishing, golf, riding. bicycle hire and boat launching, all 1.5 miles.

Open

Mid-March - November.

At a glance

| Welcome & Ambience | ✓✓✓✓✓ | Location | ✓✓✓✓✓ |
| Quality of Pitches | ✓✓✓✓ | Range of Facilities | ✓✓✓✓✓ |

Directions

From Penrith take A66 towards Keswick and Cockermouth. Leave at first sign for Keswick on the A591 and follow to junction (A5271). Turn left on A591 signed Windermere and after 1 mile, take small road on right signed Castlerigg and Rakefoot. Park entrance is on right after 400 yards. O.S.GR: NY282227. GPS: N54:35.586 W03:06.755

Charges 2006

Per caravan incl. 2 persons	£ 13.20 - £ 15.80
per motorcaravan incl. 2 persons	£ 11.95 - £ 14.20
awning (strong steel pegs required)	£ 1.60 - £ 2.00

Reservations

Accepted for caravans or motorcaravans only with £10 deposit. Tel: 017687 74499. Email: info@castlerigg.co.uk

211

UK5615 Hill of Oaks Caravan Park

Tower Wood, Windermere LA12 8NR (Cumbria)

This park on the banks of Lake Windermere lives up to its name 'Hill of Oaks'. Set on a hillside in mature woodland, the park offers families a safe natural environment with nature walks through the managed ancient woodlands, as well as six jetties for boat launching and access to watersport activities (jet skis are not allowed). The road into the park passing the farmhouse is long, winding and narrow, so care should be taken especially with long outfits, reception being about half a mile from the entrance. The entrance barrier is open from 08.00 till dusk with a security code being provided for exit. The reception and shop selling basics with a tourist information room adjacent are on the lakeside in wooden chalet-type buildings with an abundance of hanging baskets and flowers. Privately owned caravan holiday homes have been built into the hillside on terraces and are quite unobtrusive, screened by hedges and trees. Although the park is situated on Lake Windermere the touring pitches nestle within the trees, not actually by the lake. All 43 have electricity (16A), digital TV hook-up and hardstanding, most large enough to take a car and boat. Three large super pitches, all hardstanding, have 16A electricity, drain, water and digital TV. Tents are not accepted at Hill of Oaks.

Facilities

The central tiled toilet block, recently refurbished, is very clean and heated. Vanity style washbasins, controllable showers and free hair dryers. Baby changing areas. Fully equipped laundry. Dishwashing area under cover. New unit for disabled visitors (combination lock). Recycling bins. No motorcaravan service point. Shop for basics. Two fenced play areas, one for toddlers and adventure type for over 5s. Picnic areas and nature trails. Fishing (licence required). Off site: Fell Foot Park and Gardens 1 mile, with rowing boat hire or ferry rides to Lakeside or Ambleside. Aquarium of the Lakes (3.5 miles) at Newby Bridge. Golf 4 miles. Riding and bicycle hire 6 miles.

At a glance

Welcome & Ambience	✓✓✓✓	Location	✓✓✓✓
Quality of Pitches	✓✓✓✓	Range of Facilities	✓✓✓✓✓

Directions

From M6 exit 36 head west on A590 towards Barrow and Newby Bridge. Follow A590 to roundabout signed Bowness and turn right on A592 for about 3 miles. Site is signed on left. O.S.GR: SD384903. GPS: N54:18.453 W02:56.724

Charges 2006

Per unit	£ 12.50 - £ 25.00

Reservations

Contact site. Tel: 015395 31578. Email: enquiries@hillofoaks.co.uk

Open

1 March - 14 November.

UK5605 Woodclose Caravan Park

Kirkby Lonsdale LA6 2SE (Cumbria)

Woodclose is an established, nine-acre park with new owners. Situated in the Lune Valley and just one mile from the market town of Kirkby Lonsdale, this park offers a peaceful and secluded setting catering for walkers, tourers and people who just want to relax. Access to the park is narrow, so care should be taken. The whole park has a very well cared for appearance with well mown grass, flowering tubs and neat hedges. The upper part contains many privately owned holiday homes with neat terraces built from local stone. Screened by a hedge and placed around the perimeter are several seasonal pitches with touring units being placed in the centre. These pitches are numbered and mostly level, some on hardstanding, some on grass, with 16A electricity and digital TV hook-ups. More seasonal pitches and holiday homes on the lower part of the park, again most attractively terraced with stone walling and paths. Reception is part of the well stocked shop which includes local produce and fresh baked bread; an information room is adjoining with tables and chairs.

Facilities

Two toilet blocks, the main one central to the touring area. These facilities are all unisex in large, heated, individual rooms with toilets, washbasin and toilet or washbasin and shower, all well equipped and very clean. Indoor dishwashing, well equipped laundry and chemical disposal within the same building. The second block is in the lower part, again all unisex in cubicles together with an indoor dishwashing area. No motorcaravan service point, but facilities for disabled visitors have been installed. Shop. Small adventure play area. Table tennis table. American style motorhomes accepted (limited space). Gates locked 12.00 - 07.30, warden and telephone on site for emergencies. Off site: Golf 1 mile. Fishing 7 miles. Beach 20 miles.

At a glance

Welcome & Ambience	✓✓✓✓	Location	✓✓✓✓
Quality of Pitches	✓✓✓✓	Range of Facilities	✓✓✓✓

Directions

From M6 exit 36 take A65 to Kirkby Lonsdale. Site is off the A65 in 6 miles. O.S.GR: SD620781. GPS: N54:11.901 W02:35.101

Charges 2006

Per unit incl. 2 persons and electricity	£ 10.00 - £ 20.00
tent incl. 2 persons	£ 11.50 - £ 13.50

Reservations

Contact site. Tel: 015242 71597. Email: info@woodclosepark.com

Open

1 March - 1 November.

Waterfoot Park, Ullswater
ETC 5★

Ideal parkland location for touring caravans & motorhomes overlooking Ullswater.
Quiet family park with good facilities, bar, shop & laundry.
Ullswater, Pooley Bridge, Penrith, Cumbria, CA11 0JF Tel: 017684 86302
email: enquiries@waterfootpark.co.uk • web: www.waterfootpark.co.uk

Hill of Oak, Windermere
ETC 5★

Beautiful secluded lakeside estate with long shoreline, launching, licensed shop & other excellent
facilities. Outstanding location for both touring caravans & motorhomes. Windermere, Cumbria,
LA12 8NR Tel: 015395 31578 email: enquiries@hillofoaks.co.uk • web: www.hillofoaks.co.uk

Woodclose Caravan Park
ETC 5★

Exclusive site offering touring caravans, motorhomes & tent facilities in between
the Lakes and the Dales. Short walk to Kirby Lonsdale's attractive shops & Inns.
Kirkby Lonsdale, Cumbria, LA6 2SE Tel: 015242 71597
email: info@woodclosepark.com • web www.woodclosepark.com

UK5610 Waterfoot Caravan Park

Pooley Bridge, Penrith CA11 0JF (Cumbria)

Waterfoot is a quiet family park for caravans and motorcaravans only. It is set in 22 acres of partially wooded land, developed in the fifties from a private estate. The 146 private caravan holiday homes are quite separate from the 37 touring pitches. Lake Ullswater is only about 400 yards away and a half mile stroll through bluebell woods brings you to the village of Pooley Bridge. Waterfoot's touring pitches are arranged very informally in a large clearing. Most are level, there are some hardstandings and all have 10A electricity. The park no longer accepts American RVs. There is a bar in a large, imposing mansion, in the past a family home then a golf hotel. Public footpaths lead straight from the park. The regular lake steamer service calls at Pooley Bridge, the Ullswater yacht club is only 10 minutes drive and the market town of Penrith is 5 miles. The historic house and gardens of Dalemain are a short walk.

Facilities
The heated toilet block includes washbasins and preset showers in cubicles. New facilities for disabled visitors. Large, light and airy dishwashing room and fully equipped laundry. Small shop selling basics, gas and newspapers. Bar with strictly enforced, separate family room open weekend evenings in low season and every evening in high season. Large fenced field with play equipment to suit all ages and goal posts for football and a new play park. Off site: Fishing 0.5 miles. Riding 1.5 miles. Golf 5 miles. Pooley Bridge has a post office/general store, hotels and restaurants.

At a glance
Welcome & Ambience	✓✓✓✓✓	Location	✓✓✓✓✓
Quality of Pitches	✓✓✓✓	Range of Facilities	✓✓✓✓

Directions
From M6 junction 40, take A66 signed Keswick. After 0.5 miles at roundabout take A592 signed Ullswater and site is on right after 4 miles. O.S.GR: NY460245. GPS: N54:36.841 W02:49.869

Charges 2006
Per unit incl. all persons and electricity	£ 14.00 - £ 19.50
No credit cards.	

Reservations
Essential for B.Hs and summer holidays. Tel: 017684 86302. Email: enquiries@waterfootpark.co.uk

Open
1 March - 14 November.

UK5560 Sykeside Camping Park

Brotherswater, Patterdale, Penrith CA11 0NZ (Cumbria)

This small touring park is located in a really beautiful, quiet spot in the northern Lakes area (it is just 400 yards from Brotherswater). Surrounded by the fells, it is ideal for active outdoor holidays. With views up the Dovedale valley, the park has 100 pitches in the valley floor, including several hardstandings. The pitches are not marked and campers arrange themselves to best enjoy the superb views. There are just 19 electrical connections (5/10A). The stone-built building, an original barn, near the entrance, 200 yards from the field, houses all the facilities. These include the Barn End bar where meals are served.

Facilities
The toilet block includes hot showers and has been refurbished, with a chemical disposal point added. Small launderette and dishwashing room. Self-service shop with camping equipment, gas and an ice-pack service, doubles as reception. Cosy, licensed bar and restaurant (daily in summer, weekends only in winter). Bunkhouse accommodation for 30 persons in various groupings. Fishing nearby. Off site: Bicycle hire 3 miles. Riding 8 miles. Golf 10 miles. The Brotherswater Inn is nearby.

Open
All year.

At a glance
Welcome & Ambience	✓✓✓✓✓	Location	✓✓✓✓✓
Quality of Pitches	✓✓✓✓	Range of Facilities	✓✓✓✓

Directions
On west side of A592 road about 2 miles south of Patterdale, which lies at the southwestern end of Ullswater - entrance is just behind the Brotherswater Inn. O.S.GR: NY396005. GPS: N54:29.910 W002:55.53

Charges 2005
Per adult	£ 3.00 - £ 3.75
child (4-14 yrs)	£ 1.50
car or motorcycle	£ 2.50 - £ 3.25
Min. charge for motorcaravan £15 per night.	

Reservations
Reservation is essential in peak seasons. Made with £15 per pitch deposit (not possible to book electricity hook-up). Tel: 017684 82239. Email: info@sykeside.co.uk

UK5620 Cove Camping Park

Ullswater, Watermillock, Penrith CA11 0LS (Cumbria)

Cove Camping is a delightful small site, some of the 50 pitches having great views over Lake Ullswater. A separate area behind the camping field holds 38 privately owned caravan holiday homes, plus one for hire. The grass is well trimmed, there are ramps to keep speeds down to 5 mph and the site is well lit. At the top of the park are 17 level pitches with electric hook-ups and 13 with hardstanding suitable for touring caravans and motorcaravans. The rest of the park is quite sloping. Rubbish bins are hidden behind larch lap fencing, as are recycling bins. The park is well situated for walking, boating, fishing and pony trekking activities. The road up from the A592 is narrow, but a self imposed one way system is generally adhered to and the warden will advise on a different way to leave the site.

Facilities

The tiled toilet block is immaculate and heated in cooler months, providing adjustable showers, some washbasins in cabins and, for ladies, a hairdressing area with stool and a baby changing unit. Foyer containing a freezer (free), coffee machine and tourist information. Laundry with washing machine, dryer and an iron. Dishwashing sinks in a separate area. Gas supplies. Small, grass based play area. Off site: Shop nearby. Fishing 1.5 miles. Riding 3 miles. Golf 6 miles. Bicycle hire 7 miles (will deliver).

Open

March - 31 October.

At a glance

Welcome & Ambience	✓✓✓✓✓	Location	✓✓✓✓
Quality of Pitches	✓✓✓✓	Range of Facilities	✓✓✓✓✓

Directions

From A66 Penrith - Keswick road, take A592 south, signed Ullswater. Turn right at Brackenrigg Inn (site signed) and follow road uphill for about 1.5 miles to park on left. This road is narrow so if you have a larger unit, telephone the park for advice about an alternative route. O.S.GR: NY431236. GPS: N54:36.257 W02:52.913

Charges 2005

Per unit incl. 2 persons and electricity	£ 13.00 - £ 16.00
tent incl. 2 persons	£ 11.00 - £ 13.00
extra person (over 4 yrs)	£ 3.00
dog	£ 1.00
No credit cards.	

Reservations

Made with deposit (caravans or motorcaravans £10, tents £5); contact park. Tel: 017684 86549. Email: info@cove-park.co.uk

Cove Park
"The Peaceful Park"

A small and quiet 5★ caravan and camping park in The Lake District. Pure tranquility and escapism. We are easy to find, only 7 miles from junction 40 on the M6, yet in the very heart of the Northern Lakes overlooking Ullswater.

www.cove-park.co.uk
01768 486549

UK5600 Pennine View Caravan & Camping Park

Station Road, Kirkby Stephen CA17 4SZ (Cumbria)

Suitable for night halts or longer breaks to visit the Lake District or the Yorkshire Dales, Pennine View is a super small park, well managed and well maintained. With a very attractive rockery at the entrance, the whole site is very neat and tidy. Level, numbered pitches with gravel hardstanding are arranged around the perimeter with grass pitches in the centre. The pitches are of a good size (some being especially large) and are all are supplied with electricity hook-ups (16A). Pennine View was opened in 1990 and is built on reclaimed land from a former railway goods yard. One end of the park adjoins the River Eden with steps leading down huge projecting stone slabs on the river bank (good for sunbathing). There are trout but a licence is needed for fishing.

Facilities

Built of local stone, the modern toilet block is accessed by a digital keypad and includes individual wash cubicles and deep sink for a baby bath. Both ladies and men have large en-suite units for disabled visitors. Well equipped laundry room. Dishwashing sinks under cover. Gas available. Off site: Nearby hotel offers bar meals. Kirkby Stephen 1 mile. Bicycle hire 300 m. Golf 4 miles.

Open

1 March - 31 October.

At a glance

Welcome & Ambience	✓✓✓✓✓	Location	✓✓✓✓
Quality of Pitches	✓✓✓✓✓	Range of Facilities	✓✓✓✓

Directions

Park is on the A685 on the southerly outskirts of Kirkby Stephen (just under a mile from the town centre). Turn left at small site sign opposite the Croglin Castle hotel. Site is 50 yds on right. O.S.GR: NY772075. GPS: N54:27.700 W02:21.202

Charges 2005

Per adult	£ 4.60 - £ 4.80
child (4-15 yrs)	£ 1.75 - £ 2.00
pitch	£ 11.20 - £ 12.60

Reservations

Made with £5 deposit; min. 3 days Easter and B.Hs. Tel: 017683 71717.

UK5630 The Quiet Site Caravan & Camping Park

Watermillock, Penrith CA11 0LS (Cumbria)

The Quiet Site is a secluded, family run park on a hillside in the National Park with views over the fells, just 1.5 miles from Lake Ullswater. There are 84 unmarked pitches, including some with hardstanding and 60 with electricity connections. Most have been terraced to provide level surfaces, but a few are very sloping (levelling blocks are supplied). The camping area is very undulating (we noticed that some tents were pitched amongst the caravans to find flatter ground). In a separate part of the park, screened by mature trees, are 23 privately owned caravan holiday homes and one for hire. In converted old farm buildings, the amenities are centred around the reception and shop and include a first floor 'Olde Worlde' bar with oak beams and barrel seats. Many beautiful walks start from right outside the park and the numerous activities and attractions of the Lake District are within a short drive. The owners, the Holder family, are continuing to develop this attractive, well maintained park and a new bathroom and two new shower rooms have been added.

Facilities

The upgraded toilet block provides pre-set showers and open style washbasins. Bathroom with facilities for disabled visitors (key from reception). Baby changing area. Dishwashing under cover. Laundry facilities. Well stocked shop at reception. Gas supplies. Bar (weekends only in low season), adult only room with pool and darts. TV and games room. Excellent adventure play area. Caravan storage. American motorhomes would find access very difficult. Off site: Fishing 1.5 miles. Riding and bicycle hire 3 miles. Golf 8 miles.

Open

1 March - 15 November.

At a glance

| Welcome & Ambience | ✓✓✓✓ | Location | ✓✓✓✓ |
| Quality of Pitches | ✓✓✓✓ | Range of Facilities | ✓✓✓✓ |

Directions

From M6, exit 40, take A66 (Keswick) for 1 mile, then A592 signed Ullswater for 4 miles. Turn right at Lake junction, still on A592 signed Windermere. After 1 miles turn right (at Brackenrigg Inn) and follow for 1.5 miles to site on right (large units should phone for an alternative route). O.S.GR: NY431236. GPS: N54:36.281 W02:52.967

Charges 2005

Per unit incl. 2 persons, awning and electricity	£ 14.00 - £ 22.00
tent incl. 2 persons	£ 10.00 - £ 18.00
extra person	free - £ 3.00
Camping Cheques accepted.	

Reservations

Made with deposit. Tel: 017684 86337. Email: info@thequietsite.co.uk

UK5670 Flusco Wood Touring Caravan Park

Flusco, Penrith CA11 0JB (Cumbria)

Flusco Wood Caravan Park is still being developed but everything is to a very high standard. Set amongst woodland with the touring pitches in bays, this park will meet the needs of those requiring a quiet holiday (with plenty of walks from the site) and also those travelling up or down the M6 looking for a quiet night's rest. There are pitches on grass and hardstanding, with an area near reception with hardstandings for motorcaravans. Recent additions here include 19 new log cabins (privately owned) with a further 11 planned. The area abounds with wildlife including deer and red squirrels, as well as many breeds of birds (we watched a woodpecker taking food from a bird feeder). For a wet day you are about 2.5 miles from Rheged, the 'village in the hill' and, if the weather improves, a short drive from Ullswater, Keswick, Penrith and Carlisle. Member of the Countryside Discovery group.

Facilities

A log cabin style building houses very clean, heated facilities including pre-set showers and vanity style washbasins (1 cubicle). Large en-suite shower rooms for families or disabled visitors, one in the ladies' and one in the men's. Dishwashing sinks under cover. Laundry, drying room and boot washing sink. Second log cabin serves as reception/shop with basic supplies, gas and daily newspapers. Play equipment on bark. Grass area for ball games. Off site: Pub and P.O. stores 2 miles. Fishing, bicycle hire and golf 4 miles. Riding 5 miles.

Open

Easter or 1 April - end October.

At a glance

| Welcome & Ambience | ✓✓✓✓ | Location | ✓✓✓✓ |
| Quality of Pitches | ✓✓✓✓ | Range of Facilities | ✓✓✓✓✓ |

Directions

From M6 take A66 towards Keswick. Go straight on at first roundabout, then third right at top of hill (signed Flusco, Recycling Centre, Pottery and caravan sign). After 0.5 miles road turns right up hill (narrow, so take care in large units), site is on left at the top. Site is 4 miles from M6. O.S.GR: NY457293. GPS: N54:59.381 W02:50.537

Charges 2005

| Per unit incl. 2 persons and electricity | £ 15.00 - £ 18.00 |
| extra person (over 3 yrs) | £ 2.00 - £ 2.25 |

Reservations

Made with deposit (£20 per week, £5 for single nights). Tel: 017684 80020. Email: admin@fluscowood.co.uk

215

UK5545 Park Cliffe Camping & Caravan Estate

Birks Road, Windermere LA23 3PG (Cumbria)

Set in the heart of the Lake District National Park, this attractive park has been recently acquired by the Holgates family. Sitting high in open countryside it has spectacular views over the Lakeland Fells and Lake Windermere. Well managed and maintained, the park is neat and tidy with attractive shrubs and plants in local, stone-built troughs set around the entrance. The touring pitches here have been redeveloped into numbered gravel hardstandings with electricity (10A), water and drainage services. There are also 24 seasonal pitches positioned high on the hillside with commanding views. Two areas have been set aside for tents, one unmarked and undulating on the hillside divided by an original stone wall and adjacent to the tourers and one across the road for tents that require electric hook-ups – these are marked and numbered. There is no automatic barrier, but gates closed to both campers and caravanners 11.00-07.30 with a warden on site for emergencies. A new development for caravan holiday homes is being constructed in a valley offset from the main park.

Facilities

The central main building includes two blocks of toilets and showers. These are tiled, heated and very clean with vanity style washbasins, hair drying areas, full facilities for disabled visitors and excellent baby room (both with combination lock). On the floors above five rooms with bath, WC and washbasin, 4 of which for hire (min. 3 days, £12 per day) and one available by the hour for refundable deposit. Fully equipped laundry. Covered dishwashing area. Bar and area with pool table for over 16s. Restaurant and takeaway. Small well stocked shop. Freezer for ice packs (20p). Games room with arcade machine and pool table. Large outdoor adventure type play area is set secluded to one side of the tourers, not fenced as a public footpath runs through to Moor How. Off site: Fellfoot Park with boat launching (sail), Walking, climbing, cycling and many other activities possible. Cruises on the lake. Many visitor attractions.

At a glance

Welcome & Ambience	✓✓✓✓✓	Location	✓✓✓✓✓
Quality of Pitches	✓✓✓✓	Range of Facilities	✓✓✓✓✓

Directions

From M6 exit 36 take A590 to Newby Bridge. Turn right on A592 for 3.6 miles and turn right. Site is signed shortly on the right. Note: Caravans and trailers must approach Park Cliffe from the direction of Newby Bridge on the A592. O.S.GR: SD391911. GPS: N54:18.469 W02:56.607

Charges 2005

Per unit incl. 2 persons and electricity	£ 20.00
tent incl. 2 persons	£ 17.00
extra adult	£ 4.00
child (2-14 yrs)	£ 2.00
awning	£ 4.00
dog	£ 2.00

Reservations

Made with 25% deposit. Tel: 015395 31344. Email: info@parkcliffe.co.uk

Open

1 March - 14 November.

UK5540 Fallbarrow Park

Rayrigg Road, Bowness, Windermere LA23 3DL (Cumbria)

Fallbarrow Park is most attractively situated alongside Lake Windermere with a lake frontage of about 600 yards; one can stroll among the lawns and gardens near the lake. The major part of the park is occupied by approximately 260 seasonal holiday homes, with about 90 for letting, the remainder privately owned. In the 'Lake' area (not actually by the lake, but some pitches have lake views), there are 38 fenced or hedged touring pitches, all with hardstanding, fresh and waste water points, electric hook-up (10/16A) and TV aerial connection. Reception is smart and comfortable, with lots of tourist information. The Boathouse pub has a spacious and comfortable lounge with bar meals and snacks, a separate restaurant section with varied menu and table service, and an attractive outdoor terrace. TV lounge with occasional entertainment and a large games room with pool table and games machines. The site has a boat park with winter storage and two launching ramps and three jetties can cater for craft up to 18 ft in length. The centre of Bowness is only a short walk and facilities for pony trekking and numerous visitor attractions are close.

Facilities

Two excellent toilet blocks serve the touring sections (combination locks) with top quality fittings and heating when required, controllable showers, make up and hairdressing areas and a baby washroom. Dishwashing sinks. Very well equipped laundry which also houses a freezer. Motorcaravan service point. Gas is available at the well stocked supermarket. Restaurant. Bar. Fishing. Adventure play area and sports field. American motorhomes are accepted by prior arrangement. Dogs are accepted, but only one per booking (exercise area provided). Off site: Bicycle hire 1 mile. Riding 2 miles. Golf 3 miles.

Open

8 March - 9 November.

At a glance

Welcome & Ambience	✓✓✓✓	Location	✓✓✓✓
Quality of Pitches	✓✓✓✓	Range of Facilities	✓✓✓✓

Directions

Park is beside the A592 road just north of Bowness town centre. O.S.GR: SD401971. GPS: N54:22.007 W02:55.246

Charges 2005

Per unit incl. 2 adults and 2 children	£ 17.00 - £ 24.00
extra person	£ 1.50 - £ 2.00
child	£ 1.00 - £ 1.50
awning	£ 3.00 - £ 4.00
dog	£ 2.00 - £ 3.00

Reservations

Essential for June - Sept. and B.Hs. Made for min. 3 nights (7 at Spring BH). Payment in full at time of booking. Bookings tel: 0870 774 4024. Tel: 015394 44422. Email: enquiries@southlakeland-caravans.co.uk

UK5520 Skelwith Fold Caravan Park

Ambleside LA22 0HX (Cumbria)

Skelwith Fold has been developed in the extensive grounds of a country estate taking advantage of the wealth of mature trees and shrubs. The 300 privately owned caravan holiday homes and 150 touring pitches are absorbed into this unspoilt natural environment, sharing it with red squirrels and other wildlife in several discrete areas branching off the central, mile long main driveway. Touring pitches (caravans, motorcaravans and trailer tents only) are on gravel hardstanding and metal pegs will be necessary for awnings. Electricity hook-ups (10A) and basic amenities are available in all areas. Youngsters and indeed their parents will find endless pleasure exploring over 90 acres of wild woodland and, if early risers, it is possible to see deer, foxes, etc. taking at the almost hidden tarn deep in the woods. This is a fascinating site where you feel at home with nature at any time of the year, but it is particularly beautiful in the spring with wild daffodils, bluebells and later rhododendrons and azaleas.

Facilities

Eight toilet blocks, well situated to serve all areas, have the usual facilities including laundry, drying and ironing. Some blocks have facilities for disabled visitors. Well stocked, licensed shop. Battery charging, gas and caravan spares and accessories. Adventure play area. Recreation area with picnic tables and goal posts in the Lower Glade. Bicycle hire. Off site: Ambleside village 1.5 miles. Pubs within walking distance. Fishing 200 m. Riding 3 miles.

Open

1 March - 15 November.

At a glance

Welcome & Ambience	✓✓✓✓	Location	✓✓✓✓
Quality of Pitches	✓✓✓✓	Range of Facilities	✓✓✓✓

Directions

From Ambleside take the A593 towards Coniston. Pass through Clappergate and on the far outskirts watch for B5286 to Hawkshead on the left. Park is clearly signed 1 mile down this road on the right. O.S.GR: NY358028. GPS: N54:25:029 W02:59.717

Charges 2005

Per pitch	£ 14.50 - £ 17.00
electricity	£ 2.50
awning	£ 3.00

Discounts for weekly or monthly stays.

Reservations

Essential for July/Aug and B.Hs. and made for min. 3 days with £10 deposit. Tel: 01539 432277. Email: info@skelwith.com

A jewel set in the heart of English Lakeland

The perfect haven for touring caravans. Skelwith Fold's 130 acres offers a tranquil setting - even in Lakelands peak season. Open from 1st March to 15th November.

Ambleside, Cumbria LA22 0HX • Telephone 015394 32277 • www.skelwith.com • E-mail: info@skelwith.com

UK5550 Limefitt Park

Windermere LA23 1PA (Cumbria)

Limefitt Park is located in a really beautiful valley with fine views and ideal for walking and cycling. Four miles from Windermere, it is also centrally located for the attractions of the southern Lake District. With various active pursuits on offer nearby and some evening entertainment, this park is for families and couples. Of the 151 touring pitches, many are on hardstanding and fully serviced. Tent pitches are in a separate area. Ground by the beck has been developed for 65 log cabins some caravan holiday homes. Fell walking and pony trekking are possible from the park. Away from the camping area by the river is a play field and an adventure playground on grass and a small riverside area with picnic tables.

Facilities

Sanitary facilities are of excellent quality with one large, central block for the tent area and a smaller block for the caravan area accessed by combination locks. Three toddlers' rooms with half-size bath and changing facilities. Campers' kitchen. Launderette. Motorcaravan service point. Gas supplies. Supermarket. Bar (real ales), bar meals and takeaway, all open all season. Weekly entertainment. Games room with many machines. Play area. Riding. Play area. Dogs are not accepted in tents or at all in high season. Off site: Fishing 2 miles. Bicycle hire 4 miles. Golf 5 miles.

At a glance

Welcome & Ambience	✓✓✓✓✓	Location	✓✓✓✓✓
Quality of Pitches	✓✓✓✓	Range of Facilities	✓✓✓✓

Directions

Limefitt is 2.5 miles north up the A592 from its junction with the A591 north of Windermere. O.S.GR: NY416030. GPS: N54:25.210 W002:54.21

Charges 2005

Per unit incl. 2 persons, electricity and TV hook up	£ 13.00 - £ 25.00
tent incl. 2 persons	£ 11.00 - £ 17.00
child (2-14 yrs)	£ 1.00 - £ 1.50

Reservations

Made with deposit; contact 0870 774 4024.

Open

1 March - 15 November.

Cumbria

UK5640 Green Acres Caravan Park

High Knells, Houghton, Carlisle CA6 4JW (Cumbria)

Green Acres is a small, family run park situated in beautiful, rural surroundings, yet only two miles from the M6/A74 – perfect for an overnight stop or a longer stay to enjoy Cumbria, Hadrian's Wall and the delights of Carlisle city (4 miles away). Mr and Mrs Brown have developed Green Acres over the last few years into an attractive, well maintained and level touring park. There are 30 numbered pitches arranged in a semi-circle, some on grass but most on large hardstandings. There are 19 electricity connections (10A). Divided by a long beech hedge is a large camping field including on one side 6 new hardstanding 'super' pitches for seasonal letting and, in one corner, a small play area.

Facilities

Small, very clean toilet block with open style washbasins and coin operated showers (50p for 10 minutes). No facilities for disabled people. Dishwashing sinks under cover. Laundry room in farm building. Car wash area. No shop but ices, drinks and sweets from reception. Play area. Caravan storage. Off site: Golf 3 miles. Fishing 8 miles. Riding and bicycle hire 10 miles.

Open

March - end October.

At a glance

Welcome & Ambience	✓✓✓✓	Location	✓✓✓✓✓
Quality of Pitches	✓✓✓✓✓	Range of Facilities	✓✓✓✓

Directions

Leave M6/A74 at junction 44 and take A689 for 1 miles. Turn left towards Scaleby (site signed) and site is 1 miles on left. O.S.GR: NY419615.

Charges 2005

Per unit incl. 2 persons	£ 7.50 - £ 8.75
extra person	£ 1.25
awning	£ 1.00
electricity	£ 2.00

Reservations

Contact park. Tel: 01228 675418.

UK5650 The Ashes

New Hutton, Kendal LA8 0AS (Cumbria)

The Ashes is a friendly, small, adult only park in an extremely peaceful setting in the rolling Cumbrian countryside, yet less than three miles from the M6, and only slightly further from Kendal. Thus it is not only a convenient night stop, but also a useful base from which to explore the Lake District and the Yorkshire Dales. A very tidy park, the central grass area is attractively planted with shrubs and bushes and there is an open vista (with little shade). There are 24 hardstanding gravel pitches, all with electrical connections (10A). These are neatly placed around the perimeter, with an oval access road. The whole area slopes gently down from the entrance, with some pitches fairly level and others with a little more slope. No tents are accepted other than trailer tents.

Facilities

A small, purpose built stone building with a slate roof houses two unisex, heated shower rooms and the washing and toilet facilities. New facilities for disabled visitors. Laundry service. No shop. New electronic barrier. Off site: Mr and Mrs Mason have prepared a full information sheet with details of shopping, eating and many other local venues. Fishing 2 miles. Golf and riding 3 miles. Bicycle hire 4 miles. Kendal 4 miles.

Open

1 March - 15 November.

At a glance

Welcome & Ambience	✓✓✓✓✓	Location	✓✓✓✓✓
Quality of Pitches	✓✓✓✓✓	Range of Facilities	✓✓✓✓✓

Directions

From M6 junction 37 follow the A684 towards Kendal for 2 miles. Just past a white cottage turn sharp left at crossroads signed New Hutton. Site is on right in 0.75 miles at a left bend. O.S.GR: SD560908. GPS: N54:18.788 W002:40.50

Charges 2005

Per unit incl. 2 adults and electricity	£ 11.00 - £ 13.00
extra person (over 18s only)	£ 3.50
awning	£ 2.00
extra car/trailer	£ 1.00

Reservations

Made with deposit 1 night £8, 2 or more nights £16. Advised for B.Hs and peak season. Tel: 01539 731833. Email: info@ashescaravanpark.co.uk

218

UK5930 Cwmcarn Forest Drive Campsite

Cwmcarn, Crosskeys, Newport NP1 7FA (Newport)

Set in a narrow, sheltered valley with magnificent wooded slopes (it's hard to believe it was once the site of the Cwmcarn Colliery), this park is not only central for the many attractions of this part of Wales, but there is now also much of the natural environment to enjoy including a small fishing lake. The seven mile forest drive (open daily in season) shares its Visitor Centre with the camp reception and has much to offer - bird watching, badger seeking, the Twmbarlwm ancient hill fort to visit with its magnificent views across the Severn to Somerset, Devon and Gloucestershire. The site has a slightly wild feel, but is stunningly located and has 40 well spaced, flat pitches (30 with 15A electricity, 3 with concrete hard-standing and with tarmac for the car) spread over three small fields between the Visitor Centre and the small lake (fishing permits available). Wardens are on hand daily and the Visitor Centre and reception are open 09.00 - 17.00 (18.00 at weekends, Oct - Easter Fridays 09.00 - 16.30 pm), so arrive before then.

Facilities

The single well equipped, heated toilet block (£5 deposit for key) includes toilet facilities for disabled visitors, laundry with washing machine, dryer, iron and board, and a kitchen with two washing up sinks, small cooker and fridge (hot water free). Visitor Centre has a coffee shop selling refreshments and snacks. Guided walks and the popular Twrch (15 km) mountain bike route are available. Numeracy trail and 'environmenteering' routes for children. Rallies accommodated. Dogs accepted by prior arrangement. Off site: Shops, a leisure centre, pubs and takeaway food are available in the village under a mile away. Riding 2 miles, golf 6 miles.

At a glance

| Welcome & Ambience | ✓✓✓✓ | Location | ✓✓✓✓✓ |
| Quality of Pitches | ✓✓✓ | Range of Facilities | ✓✓✓ |

Directions

Cwmcarn Forest Drive is well signed from junction 28 on M4. From the Midlands and the 'Heads of the Valleys' road (A465), take A467 south to Cwmcarn. O.S.GR: ST230935.

Charges 2005

Per unit	£ 8.00 - £ 9.00
large tent	£ 7.00 - £ 8.00
small ridge tent	£ 5.00 - £ 6.00
electricity	£ 2.00

Reservations

No stated policy. 14 day max. stay. Contact the Warden. Tel: 01495 272001.
Email: cwmcarn-vc@caerphilly.gov.uk

Open

All year excl. 23 December - 2 January.

UK5925 Cardiff Caravan Park

Pontcanna Fields, Via Sophia Close, Cardiff CF11 9LB (Cardiff)

Run by the city council, this popular site is in a fairly central location, ideal for visiting the many attractions of the city of Cardiff. The County Cricket Ground, sports facilities and swimming pool, the Millennium Stadium, Cardiff Castle, museums and many other attractions are within walking distance. The recently redeveloped Cardiff Bay area is a 2.5 mile cycle ride (a good city centre cycle route map is available from reception) or there is a bus service from just outside the gate. The campsite has 73 pitches which are on a fairly open area, attractively landscaped, with 43 on grassed grid surface having electric hook-ups (16A), the remainder are on grass. The site is not fenced and there is a public right of way through the site. However, security is good with an on-site warden 24 hours a day, and security cameras (infra red) constantly scanning the whole area. Remember though that you are in a city centre environment, so lock up your valuables.

Facilities

Two heated buildings each with key code entry systems, the one by reception has a laundry with washer and dryer, and facilities for disabled campers. Both have controllable hot showers, baby changing and dishwashing facilities. Bicycle hire - the site specialises in cycles adapted for disabled people. Riding can be arranged. Off site: The Millennium Stadium, Glamorgan County Cricket Ground, Cardiff Bay. Local shops and services within easy walking distance. Fishing 0.25 mile, golf 4 miles.

Open

All year.

At a glance

| Welcome & Ambience | ✓✓✓ | Location | ✓✓✓✓ |
| Quality of Pitches | ✓✓✓✓ | Range of Facilities | ✓✓✓ |

Directions

From the A48 turn south onto the A4119 (Cardiff Road). Follow round past church on left, following signs for Institute of Sport and at next set of traffic lights turn into Sophia Close and Sophia Gardens. Turn left at the Welsh Institute of Sport, and continue past the County Cricket Ground on your right, continue through an avenue of trees, and the site entrance is on your left. O.S.GR: ST171772.

Charges 2005

Per adult	£ 4.25
child (4-14 yrs)	£ 2.15
vehicle	£ 2.70

Reservations

Essential for peak season and B.Hs.
Tel: 02920 398362.

227

UK5927 Acorn Camping & Caravanning

Ham Lane South, Llantwit Major CF61 1RP (Vale of Glamorgan)

A well appointed and friendly site in a near coastal location, you will find a warm welcome here from the resident owners. The 105 pitches are mostly on grass, with a few private and rental mobile homes at the far end of the site, leaving around 90 pitches for tourers. Four have gravel based hardstandings and there are 44 electric hook-ups (10A). Reception also houses a very well stocked shop which includes groceries and essentials, souvenirs, children's toys, camping gear, a delicatessen, and takeaway meals available on demand. Site lighting is kept to a minimum to allow guests to enjoy the night sky - a torch might be useful. The Heritage Coastal path is a short walk from the site, and St Illtud's church in Llantwit Major is also worth a visit for its wall paintings, mediaeval altar, and collection of Celtic stones.

Facilities

A warm, modern building houses all the facilities. Dishwashing sinks and laundry facilities are in the central atrium which is accessed through a double glazed foyer, where there is a drinks machine. Inside are spacious shower cubicles with washbasins, ample WCs, a family/baby room, and a suite for disabled campers (key to the block £10 deposit). Shop. Gas available. Recycling of glass, paper and metal. Adjacent to reception is a snooker room (charged), a general games room and, just outside, a good playground on rubber and grass. Off site: Glamorgan Heritage Coastal footpath. Llanerch Vineyard. Cosmeston Lakes Country Park at Penarth has a reconstructed Mediaeval Village. Fishing 1 mile (sea), 4 miles (lake). Riding 2 miles. Golf 9 miles. Boat launching 9 miles.

Open

1 February - 8 December.

At a glance

Welcome & Ambience	✓✓✓✓✓	Location	✓✓✓✓✓
Quality of Pitches	✓✓✓✓	Range of Facilities	✓✓✓✓

Directions

From the east from M4 exit 33 follow signs to Cardiff airport, then take B4265 for Llantwit Major. Turn left at first traffic lights, pass through Broverton and turn left into Ham Lane East (between playing fields), finally turning left into Ham Manor Park and follow signs to campsite. From the west: M4 exit 35, turn south on A473 for 3 miles, then left on A48, turning right at Pentre Meyrick towards Llantwit Major on B4268/70. Left at first roundabout on B4265, straight on at mini-roundabout, right at traffic lights into Llanmaes Road, left at mini-roundabout, continue around back of the town, left at mini-roundabout, and right into Ham Lane East and continue as above. O.S.GR: SS974678.

Charges 2006

Per unit incl. 2 persons	£ 8.50 - £ 9.00
extra adult	£ 3.25 - £ 3.75
child	£ 3.25 - £ 3.75
electricity	£ 2.75
dog	£ 0.50

Reservations

Essential for peak season and B.Hs, and made with £10.00 non-refundable deposit. Tel: 01446 794024. Email: info@acorncamping.co.uk

UK5940 Pembrey Country Park Caravan Club Site

Pembrey, Llanelli SA16 0EJ (Carmarthenshire)

This very popular Caravan Club site reopened in 2002 following major changes and refurbishment to the club's high standards. The extended 12-acre grounds provide 50 large hardstanding pitches and 80 level, grass pitches, all with 16A electricity. Tents are not accepted. Thoughtful landscaping has included the planting of many species of tree and a circular, one-way tarmac road provides easy access. Sensibly placed service points provide fresh water and waste disposal of all types. Close to reception is a late arrivals area that includes electric hook ups. RAF jets do practice in this area (generally no flying at weekends). However, the real plus for this site is its proximity to the Country Park – access to this is free on foot or cycle direct from the site, or the Club has organised a special weekly car pass for £11. Within the 520 acres of parkland are delightful walks, cycle trails, unlimited flora and fauna, bird hides, an equestrian centre, children's play area, toboggan and ski runs, pitch and putt, narrow gauge railway and picnic areas, all fronted by Cefn Sidan, an eight mile stretch of golden sands. The nearest section of beach is a 20 minute walk, whilst car parks place you close to the visitor centre, gift shop and the lifeguard patrolled bathing area. At some distance, naturists frequent the extreme northern end of the beach.

Facilities

The refurbished toilet block gives the impression of a new building with the interior to the latest design and specification including washbasins in cabins. Full facilities for disabled visitors (with key). Baby room. Fully equipped laundry room. Dishwashing room and further sinks under cover. Motorcaravan service point. Gas available. Local delivery vans visit each morning selling milk, bread and newspapers. Play area. Off site: Dogs are restricted to one end of the beach May - Sept (follow signs).

Open

All year excl. 6 January - 30 March.

At a glance

Welcome & Ambience	✓✓✓✓✓	Location	✓✓✓✓✓
Quality of Pitches	✓✓✓✓✓	Range of Facilities	✓✓✓

Directions

Leave M4 at junction 48 onto A4138. After 4 miles turn right onto A484 at roundabout signed Carmarthen. Continue for 7 miles to Pembrey. The Country Park is signed off the A484 in Pembrey village; site entrance is on right 100 yds before park gates. O.S.GR: SN413006.
GPS: N51:40.909 W04:17.845

Charges 2005

Per adult	£ 3.80 - £ 5.00
child (5-16 yrs)	£ 1.10 - £ 1.60
pitch incl. electricity (non-member)	£ 9.50 - £ 14.50

Reservations

Essential for July/Aug. and B.Hs; contact the Warden. Tel: 01554 834369.

UK5974 **Pantglas Farm Caravan Park**

Tavernspite, Whitland SA34 0NS (Carmarthenshire)

A secluded, rural, family run park with a nice atmosphere, Pantglas Farm is four miles from the coast with extensive views over rolling countryside and down to the sea. Set in three gently sloping paddocks spread over 14 acres, there are 86 generous sized, fairly level pitches most with 10A hook-ups, 52 on gravel hardstanding. Around 46 are available for touring units. This is a popular and attractive site close to the main resorts but enjoying a more tranquil atmosphere. Amenities on site include a well equipped, partially fenced playground and activity centre which includes an aerial ropeway. A football field is located at the very end of the site. The on site clubhouse also has a non-smoking lounge with TV, a games room with pool table and video machines, and some simple entertainment activities are arranged at Bank Holidays, weekends and in high season. No kite flying or washing lines are allowed on the site and single sex groups are not accepted.

Facilities

Two toilet blocks (one can be heated) have a good standard of facilities including large controllable showers, some washbasins in cubicles, a laundry with washing machine, dryer, indoor washing lines and a baby deck. Washbasin and WC for disabled campers. Dishwashing sinks. Gas supplies. Battery charging and freezer pack services. Licensed clubhouse (evenings only every day for B.Hs and peak season, weekends only low season). Playground and games field. Games room. TV lounge. Caravan and boat storage. Off site: Supermarket and ATM at Whitland 3 miles. Beaches at Amroth or Pendine 4 miles. Also nearby are Whitland Abbey, Oakwood Adventure and Leisure Park and Colby Woodland Gardens. Fishing 1 mile. Golf 10 miles.

Open

Easter - 3rd Weekend in October.

At a glance

Welcome & Ambience	✓✓✓✓	Location	✓✓✓✓
Quality of Pitches	✓✓✓✓	Range of Facilities	✓✓✓

Directions

Site is 3 miles southwest of Whitland. From A477 Tenby - Pembroke road turn right at Red Roses crossroads to Tavernspite for 1.25 miles. At the village pump take the middle road and site is about 0.5 miles on left. O.S.GR: SN 176122.
GPS: N51:46.699 W04:38.725

Charges 2005

Per unit incl. 2 persons, electricity	£ 10.25 - £ 12.50
tent incl. 2 persons	£ 6.00 - £ 11.00
extra person	£ 1.50
child (2-15 yrs)	£ 1.25
dog	£ 1.25

No credit cards.

Reservations

Essential for peak season and B.Hs. Made for 5 or more nights with £20 non refundable deposit.
Tel: 01834 831618. Email: neil@pantglasfarm.co.uk

UK5975 **Little Kings Park**

Ludchurch, Amroth SA67 8PG (Pembrokeshire)

This superb family run park has a number of attributes to make your stay both comfortable and memorable. First there is the stunning view, at its best from the seat on the 9 hole putting green. From here on a good day you can look out over Carmarthen Bay to the Gower and on beyond to the coast of Somerset and North Devon. At night no fewer than seven lighthouses can be seen blinking out their warnings. Then there is the restaurant and bar, which has a conservatory overlooking the well presented, covered, heated swimming pool. The restaurant serves a good range of evening meals and has a children's menu. Last, but by no means least, is the comprehensively stocked shop which has just about everything you might need, including reception, tourist information and a bakery offering fresh bread daily and hot snacks (pasties, sausage rolls, etc.) cooked to order. The park itself provides 111 well spaced, large touring pitches all with 10A electricity, 23 with gravel hardstanding and 17 fully serviced. There are 40 pitches for tents arranged in two paddocks. An attractive playground is in the central open grass area of one of the paddocks, and a games field is at the back of the second. A separate well hedged and screened paddock contains 28 caravan holiday homes. This is an ideal site for a family holiday or for touring the area.

Facilities

The two toilet blocks are modern and well equipped, including controllable hot showers (20p. for 6 minutes 30p. for 9), open style washbasins, a family shower room with basin and WC, baby bath and full suite for disabled campers. Extras include paper towel and soap dispensers, perfumed air fresheners, and hand and hairdryers. Dishwashing and laundry rooms. Shop with bakery, Takeaway, bar and restaurant with conservatory (evenings only; low season at BHs and weekends only). Covered swimming pool. Games rooms. 9-hole pitch and putt. Playground. Ball games area. Gas supplies. Off site: Nearest supermarket and ATM at Kilgetty 2.5 miles. Tenby and Pendine Sands both 7 miles. Oakwood Adventure and Leisure Park 6 miles. Highly recommended is a day trip to the National Botanic Garden of Wales.

At a glance

Welcome & Ambience	✓✓✓✓✓	Location	✓✓✓✓✓
Quality of Pitches	✓✓✓✓	Range of Facilities	✓✓✓✓✓

Directions

Site is 5 miles southeast of Narberth. From A477 Carmarthen to Pembroke road turn left towards Amroth and Wiseman's Bridge. Take first right (signed Ludchurch) and park is 300 m. on left.
O.S.GR: SN146093. GPS: N51:45.091 W04:41.274

Charges 2005

Per unit incl. 2 persons, electricity	£ 13.30 - £ 20.00
tent incl. 2 persons	£ 10.00 - £ 20.00
extra person (over 2 yrs)	£ 2.00
awning	£ 2.00
dog (max. 2)	£ 2.00 - £ 3.00

Reservations

Essential for peak season and B.Hs. Made with £20 per week or part week non-refundable deposit.
Tel: 01834 831330.

Open

1 week before Easter - 30 September.

UK5880 **Springwater Lakes**

Harford, Llanwrda SA19 8DT (Carmarthenshire)

Set in 20 acres of Welsh countryside, Springwater offers a selection of fishing lakes to keep even the keenest of anglers occupied. However, it is not just anglers who will enjoy this site – it is a lovely base to enjoy the peace and tranquility of this part of Wales. Springwater offers 20 spacious, flat pitches either on grass or gravel hardstanding, all with electricity hook-ups (16A). Malcolm and Shirley Bexon are very proud of their site and welcome all visitors with a smile. This is not a site for children unless they enjoy fishing (no play areas). If you want to learn about fishing Malcolm will be happy to help.

Facilities	Directions
The modern toilet block is very clean and includes facilities for disabled visitors (there is also access to the lakes for wheelchairs). Dishwashing. Baker visits daily. Fishing; tackle/bait shop. Off site: Spar shop and garage 500 yards, other shops 5 miles. Bicycle hire and riding 2 miles. Golf 4 miles.	From A40 at Llanwrda take A482 to Lampeter. After 6 miles go through village of Pumsaint and site is 1 mile further on the left, just before garage shop. O.S.GR: SN642429. GPS: N52:04.045 W03:58.935

Open

March - 31 October.

Charges 2005

Per unit incl. 2 persons	£ 12.00
extra person (over 2 yrs)	£ 4.00
electricity	£ 2.00 - £ 2.00
dog	free - £ 1.00

At a glance

Welcome & Ambience	✓✓✓✓	Location	✓✓✓✓✓
Quality of Pitches	✓✓✓✓	Range of Facilities	✓✓

Reservations

Contact site. Tel: 01558 650788.

UK5960 **Abermarlais Caravan Park**

Llangadog SA19 9NG (Carmarthenshire)

Apart from the attractions of south or mid Wales for a stay, this sheltered, family run park could also double as a useful transit stop close to the main holiday route for those travelling to Pembrokeshire. In a natural setting, up to 88 touring units are accommodated in one fairly flat, tapering five-acre grass field edged by mature trees and a stream. Pitches are numbered, and generously spaced around the perimeter or on either side of a central, hedged spine at the wider end, with 42 electrical hook-ups (10A) and some hardstanding. Backpackers have a small, separate area. The park is set in a sheltered valley with a range of wildlife and nine acres of woodland walks. There is also an old walled garden, with some pitches and lawns for softball games, that screens the park, both audibly and visibly, from the A40 road. However, the most sought after pitches are beside the stream, loved by children and a haven for wildlife. A torch would be useful.

Facilities	Directions
The one small toilet block is older in style, but is clean, bright, cheerful and adequate with controllable showers. Two external, covered washing-up sinks but no laundry facilities (nearest about 5 miles). Motorcaravan service point. Shop doubling as reception. Gas supplies. Play area with tennis and volleyball nets and play equipment. Winter caravan storage. Off site: Restaurants nearby. Pubs, shops, etc. at Llangadog. Fishing 2 miles.	Park is on the A40, between the junctions with the A4069 and A482, between Llandovery and Llandeilo. O.S.GR: SN695298. GPS: N51:57.095 W03:54.018

Charges 2005

Per adult	£ 1.50
child (over 5 yrs)	£ 1.00
pitch	£ 5.50
awning	£ 0.75
electricity	£ 2.00

At a glance

Welcome & Ambience	✓✓✓✓	Location	✓✓✓✓
Quality of Pitches	✓✓✓✓	Range of Facilities	✓✓✓

Reservations

Any length, with £5 deposit. Tel: 01550 777868.

Open

14 March - 14 November.

UK6070 Rhandirmwyn Camping & Caravanning Club Site

Rhandirmwyn, Llandovery SA20 0NT (Carmarthenshire)

This is a popular site with those who like a peaceful life with no on-site entertainment, just fresh air and beautiful countryside. The site is only a short drive from the magnificent Llyn Brianne reservoir and close to the Dinas RSPB nature reserve, where a two mile trail runs through oak and alder woodland alongside the River Tywi and the wildlife includes many species of birds including red kites. The site is in a sheltered valley with 90 pitches on level grass, 51 electric hook-ups (16A) and 17 hardstandings. The village is within walking distance although there is a fairly steep hill to negotiate (but the return is much easier), and you can take a short cut through the woodland grove dedicated to John Lloyd, a former Chairman of the Club.

Facilities

The single heated sanitary block is kept very clean and tidy. Some washbasins in cubicles, dishwashing sinks and fully equipped laundry. Drive-over motorcaravan service point. Small playground with rubber base. Off site: The village has a Post Office and general store and the Royal Oak Inn serves good value meals. Farmers' market in Llandovery twice a month. Fishing 6 miles. Golf 7 miles. Riding 11 miles.

Open

March - October.

At a glance

| Welcome & Ambience | ✓✓✓✓✓ | Location | ✓✓✓✓✓ |
| Quality of Pitches | ✓✓✓✓ | Range of Facilities | ✓✓✓ |

Directions

From centre of Llandovery take A483 towards Builth Wells, after a short distance turn left by the fire station, signed Rhandirmwyn, continue for approx. 7 miles along country lanes. O.S.GR: SN779436. GPS: N52:04.621 W03:47.030

Charges 2005

Per adult	£ 4.30 - £ 6.40
child (6-18 yrs)	£ 1.90
non-member pitch fee	£ 5.00

Reservations

Advised for high season and made with deposit; contact site or Central Reservations 0870 243 3331. Site tel: 01550 760257.

UK5980 Moreton Farm Leisure Park

Moreton, Saundersfoot SA69 9EA (Pembrokeshire)

Moreton Farm has been developed in a secluded valley, a 10-20 minute walk from Saundersfoot and four miles from Tenby. It provides 30 caravan (all with 16A electricity, and including 17 with hardstanding) and 30 tent pitches on two sloping, neatly cut grass fields, with 12 pine holiday lodges and four cottages for letting occupying another field. The site is approached under a railway bridge (height 10 ft 9 ins, width across the top 6 ft 6 ins, but with alternative access over the railway line for slightly larger vehicles just possible). There are a few trains during the day, none at night. An attractive lake at the bottom of the valley is home to ducks, geese and chickens (fishing is no longer available) – pride of place must go to 'Missy'! Pembroke and Carew castles and a variety of visitor attractions are close. This is a quiet family site.

Facilities

The toilet blocks (which can be heated) are light and airy, providing pre-set hot showers (on payment), and a ramp to a unit for disabled visitors with toilet and washbasin, a baby bath, dishwashing sinks and laundry facilities. Fenced, outside clothes drying area. Small shop for basics and gas. Playground. Bicycle hire can be arranged. No dogs or other pets are accepted. Off site: Fishing and riding 1 mile. Golf 4 miles.

Open

1 March - 31 October.

At a glance

| Welcome & Ambience | ✓✓✓✓ | Location | ✓✓✓✓ |
| Quality of Pitches | ✓✓✓✓ | Range of Facilities | ✓✓✓ |

Directions

From A477 Carmarthen - Pembroke road take A478 for Tenby at Kilgelly. Park is signed on left after 1.5 miles. Watch carefully for sign and park is 0.5 miles up poorly made-up road and under bridge. O.S.GR: SN116050. GPS: N51:42.719 W04:43.661

Charges 2005

Per unit incl. 2 persons	£ 11.00 - £ 14.00
tent incl. 2 persons	£ 9.00 - £ 14.00
extra adult	£ 2.00
child (2-17 yrs)	£ 1.00
awning	£ 1.50
electricity	£ 2.50

No credit cards.

Reservations

Made with deposit (£20 p/week caravans, £15 p/week tents), balance 28 days before arrival. Tel: 01834 812016. Email: moretonfarm@btconnect.com

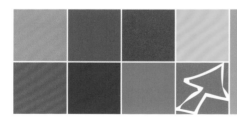

Planning your
next holiday?

don't forget to look at our directory
ON PAGE 314

UK5985 Manorbier Country Park

Station Road, Manorbier, Tenby SA70 7SN (Pembrokeshire)

This area of southwest Wales is quite attractive, with a variety of activities available, sandy beaches and an extensive coastal footpath. This campsite is relatively small, with 99 caravan holiday homes and 14 seasonal units, which leaves only around 35 pitches for tourists. From reception you pass through the area of holiday homes to the touring area which, although neat, is rather uninspiring. There are seven rows of concrete and gravel hardstanding pitches set into a level grass field; 32 pitches have electric hook-ups (16A), cable TV and a shared water tap, and 4 are multi-service pitches (electricity, water, waste water, sewage, TV). Additionally, 10 grass pitches are on the opposite side of the car park with electric hook-ups, and 4 grass pitches at the front of the main field with no services. Cars park away from the caravans on a wide tarmac parking area. A small grassy recreation area is at one end of the touring site, and a playground is behind the main complex. The complex offers a bar with family entertainment in season, a good value restaurant and an indoor pool. Larger units should book in advance and motorhomes over 23 ft. are not accepted. Some noise is possible as there is a Royal Artillery range nearby, and RAF jets fly in this area.

Facilities

A single building at one end of the car parking area provides all toilet facilities, it can be heated, and has controllable hot showers (on payment), a multi-purpose room suitable for families, babies and disabled campers. Small laundry room and dishwashing sinks outside under cover. Shop. Bar and restaurant. Indoor heated swimming and paddling pools. Jacuzzi. Sauna and steam room, vertical solarium, gym and tennis (all charged). Dogs are not accepted. Off site: Bicycle hire, boat launching and beach 1.5 miles. Golf and riding 3 miles. Adjacent garden centre restaurant serves cream teas and Sunday lunches. Fish and chip bar opposite. Manorbier Castle overlooks the sandy beach. Tenby 6 miles.

At a glance

Welcome & Ambience	✓✓✓✓	Location	✓✓✓
Quality of Pitches	✓✓✓✓	Range of Facilities	✓✓✓✓

Directions

From Tenby take A4139 towards Pembroke, passing through Penally and Lydstep. At crossroads (Manorbier signed to left) continue straight on following signs to the station. Turn right by Baptist Chapel into Station Road, and continue to site entrance (do not go into Manorbier village). O.S.GR: SS068991. GPS: N51:39.475 W04:47.657

Charges 2005

Per unit incl. up to 4 persons	£ 14.50 - £ 21.50
extra person	£ 2.00
awning	£ 1.50

Reservations

Essential for peak season and B.Hs. Gazebos, pup tents, dogs or single sex groups are not accepted. Tel: 01834 871952. Email: enquiries@countrypark.co.uk

Open

1 March - 31 October.

UK5992 Creampots Touring Caravan & Camping Park

Broadway, nr. Broad Haven, Haverfordwest SA62 3TU (Pembrokeshire)

This peacefully located and beautifully manicured, garden-like park is ideal for couples and families with very young children, and is a convenient base within easy reach of beaches or for touring the local area. Creampots has 72 spacious, level pitches all with 10A electric hook-ups, including 12 with gravel hard-standing, and 10 pitches for tents. These are in two neat well hedged and sheltered paddocks. Around 40 seasonal units and one caravan holiday home for rent are accommodated, and there is a separate rally field and an overflow area taking 30 touring units for the August peak holiday time. There is a grassy games area for children. Nearby there are bird sanctuaries and the Pembrokeshire Coastal Path.

Facilities

The single small white-washed sanitary unit is a modern building which can be heated. Two free hot showers per sex, open style washbasins. Washbasin and WC for disabled campers. These facilities were clean and tidy but may come under pressure at peak times. Tiny laundry room with just about space for one person at a time but with washing machine, dryer and sink. Outside are 2 covered dishwashing sinks at each end of the block. Gas supplies. Bread, milk, newspapers to order. Off site: Summer bus service (May-Sept) 500 m. from site entrance. Shop, post office, pub with hot food in Broad Haven 1 mile. Fishing and boat launching 1 mile. Beach 1.5 miles. Riding 4 miles. Sailing 6 miles. Golf 7 miles.

At a glance

Welcome & Ambience	✓✓✓✓	Location	✓✓✓✓
Quality of Pitches	✓✓✓✓	Range of Facilities	✓✓✓

Directions

Site is 5 miles west of Haverfordwest. From Haverfordwest take B4341 to Broad Haven, at Broadway turn left (signed Milford Haven) and park is second entrance on right in under half a mile. O.S.GR: SM882132. GPS: N51:46.640 W05:04.337

Charges 2005

Per unit incl. 2 persons	£ 10.00 - £ 12.50
extra person	£ 4.00
electricity (10A)	£ 2.50
dog	free

Reservations

Essential for peak season and B.Hs; contact park. Tel: 01437 781776. Email: info@creampots.co.uk

Open

March - October.

UK5990 Freshwater East Caravan Club Site

Freshwater East, Lamphey SA71 5LN (Pembrokeshire)

This Caravan Club site in the Pembrokeshire Coast National Park is open to non-members (for all units). At the bottom of a hill, it has 140 mainly level pitches which are bounded by trees, 128 with electrical hook-ups (16A) and around half on hardstanding. There are a further 12 pitches for tents. The beach and the Pembroke Coastal Path are about a five minute walk. This is an excellent area for walking with magnificent cliff views and birdwatching. You will find St David's, the smallest cathedral city, well worth a visit. Note: TV aerial connections are available, but you will need your own extension cable.

Facilities

The two heated toilet blocks are modern and clean with washbasins in cubicles, and free hairdryers or sockets for your own. Facilities for disabled visitors. Fully equipped laundry rooms. Waste point for motorcaravans. Gas supplies. Reception keeps basic food items. Information kiosk. Small play area. Off site: Shop 0.5 miles. Fishing within 5 miles.

Open

26 March - 1 November.

At a glance

| Welcome & Ambience | ✓✓✓✓ | Location | ✓✓✓✓ |
| Quality of Pitches | ✓✓✓✓ | Range of Facilities | ✓✓✓ |

Directions

From the east on A477, fork left 1.25 miles past Milton onto A4075 Pembroke road. After 2 miles in Pembroke immediately (after railway bridge) turn sharp left at roundabout on A4139 Tenby road. In 1.75 miles in Lamphey turn right onto B4584 signed Freshwater East. In 1.75 miles turn right signed Stackpole and Trewent and after 400 yds at foot of hill, right into lane at Club sign. Do not tow to the beach area. O.S.GR: SS014980.

Charges 2005

Per adult	£ 3.30 - £ 4.80
child (5-16 yrs)	£ 1.10 - £ 1.60
pitch incl. electricity (non-member)	£ 9.00 - £ 14.00

Reservations

Contact the Warden. Tel: 01646 672341.

UK5995 Caerfai Bay Caravan & Tent Park

St Davids, Haverfordwest SA62 6QT (Pembrokeshire)

About as far west as one can get in Wales, St David's is Britain's smallest city, noted for its Cathedral and Bishops Palace. This cliff-top park in West Wales has direct access to the Pembrokeshire Coastal Path and a magnificent sandy beach is just a few minutes away, down the path from the car park by the site entrance. The camping area is spread over three open and sloping fields, all with magnificent views over St Brides Bay. The caravan field also has a small number of holiday homes and is closest to reception. The second and third fields are for tents and motorcaravans, almost all on grass with a few hardstandings available. Main access roads are tarmac. Altogether there are 105 touring pitches and 45 electricity hook-ups (10A). Caerfai Farm Shop is just across the lane (opens end of May), and other shops and services are just 1 mile. Site lighting is deliberately minimal, so a torch would be useful.

Facilities

Two main buildings house the sanitary facilities, one by reception and the second in the tent field. The first, the newest and heated, contains a facility for disabled visitors, also suitable for families, baby changing facilities, and a room with dishwashing sinks, microwave and hot drinks machine. Also in this block is a useful 'storm shelter', a welcome haven for inclement weather. The second, a double block between the tent fields, is older, but well maintained and includes a dishwashing room. The adjacent part provides 4 family rooms with heating. A further elderly block near the entrance houses extra WCs and has been left open at the request of regular campers. Lockable bicycle shelter. Basic motorcaravan services. Wet suit washing facility and enclosed clothes drying area. Gas stocked. Barbecue stands for hire. Off site: Walk the Pembrokeshire coastal path, visit Ramsey Island Bird and Grey Seal Reserve. Sea fishing 0.25 miles. Indoor pool and bicycle hire 1 mile. Golf 2 miles. Riding 10 miles. Boat launching 1.5 or 3 miles.

At a glance

| Welcome & Ambience | ✓✓✓✓ | Location | ✓✓✓✓✓ |
| Quality of Pitches | ✓✓✓ | Range of Facilities | ✓✓✓ |

Directions

From Haverfordwest take the A487 to St David's. Pass the city boundary, turn left into lane immediately before National Park Visitor Centre (site signed), and continue on for 0.75 mile to site entrance on right. O.S.GR: SM759244. GPS: N51:52.379 W05:15.414

Charges 2005

Per unit incl. 2 persons	£ 10.00 - £ 14.00
tent incl. 2 persons	£ 8.00 - £ 10.00
extra person	£ 4.00
child (3-12 yrs)	£ 2.00
electricity	£ 2.50
dog	£ 1.00

Discounts for early payment, and for senior citizens in low season.

Reservations

Advised for peak season and B.Hs, and made with £20 non-refundable deposit. Tel: 01437 720274. Email: info@caerfaibay.co.uk

Open

1 March - 15 November.

UK5994 Redlands Caravan Park

Hasguard Cross, nr Little Haven, Haverfordwest SA62 3SJ (Pembrokeshire)

This peaceful, family run site is located in the heart of the Pembrokeshire countryside, close to a lovely sandy beach. Redlands takes around 85 touring units in three areas divided by banks topped with pine trees, 64 with 10A electricity. The first two areas take 60 caravans or motorcaravans and include 11 hard-standings, the third takes 25 tents on a level grassy meadow. There are fine views across rolling countryside to St Brides Bay. Adjacent to the site is the West Wales Diving Centre which runs diving courses. A nearby caravan holiday home park has a restaurant and bar which Redlands customers are welcome to use. Reception has a small shop with local produce which is open only in peak periods, with deliveries of meat, fish and milk in main season. Breathable groundsheets must be used. American RVs - advance booking only. A sandy beach and the Pembrokeshire Coastal Path are 1.5 miles away.

Facilities
The traditional style toilet block is well kept and heated early and late season. It has all the usual requirements including two shower, basin and WC suites. Large utility room with washing machine, dryer and spin dryer. Ironing is free, and there are sinks for laundry and dishes. Shop with fresh food deliveries. Freezers. Wet suit washing area. Off site: Shops and ATM in Broadhaven 2 miles. Summer bus service. Fishing and boat launching 1.5 miles. Riding and sailing 5 miles. Golf 6 miles.

Open

1 March - 31 December.

At a glance

Welcome & Ambience	✓✓✓✓	Location	✓✓✓✓
Quality of Pitches	✓✓✓✓	Range of Facilities	✓✓✓

Directions

Site 6.5 miles southwest of Haverfordwest. From Haverfordwest take the B4327 road towards Dale and site is on the right at Hasguard Cross. N.B. Do not approach via Broad Haven. O.S.GR: SM853109. GPS: N51:45.334 W05:06.743

Charges 2005

Per unit incl. 4 persons	£ 11.75 - £ 14.00
extra person	£ 4.00
hire of electric hook-up	£ 2.00
awning	£ 1.00 - £ 1.75
dog	free

Reservations

Essential for peak season and B.Hs. Made with non-refundable deposit of £3 per night (min. £10). Tel: 01437 781300. Email: jenny.flight@virgin.net

UK6010 Cenarth Falls Holiday Park

Cenarth, Newcastle Emlyn SA38 9JS (Ceredigion)

The Davies family have developed an attractively landscaped, part wooded holiday home park with 80 privately owned units and 7 for hire. However, a neat well cared for, sheltered grassy area at the top of the park provides 30 touring pitches, all with sunken grass grid hardstanding and electricity (16A). Accessed via a semi-circular tarmac road, they enjoy views across the Teifi valley. A sunken, kidney shaped outdoor pool with landscaped surrounds and sun-beds is very pleasant. The Coracles Health and Country Club provides an indoor pool, spa, sauna and steam rooms and fitness suite (reduced rates for campers). It also provides a bar, restaurant area, adult-only lounge and a large function room where live entertainment is organised weekly all season. A footpath leads to the village and the famous Cenarth Falls (with leaping salmon). The National Coracle Centre is well worth a visit. A member of the Best of British group.

Facilities
The excellent, heated sanitary block has easy ramped access, even to the chemical disposal unit. etc. Accessed by key, it uses a 'P.I.R.' system that controls heating, lighting, water and air-freshener on entry - very efficient. Tiled with non-slip floors, both men and ladies have an en-suite family room (doubling as provision for disabled visitors), an additional well equipped shower and also one washbasin in a roomy private cabin. Laundry room with two washing machines, two dryers and ironing facilities (used by the whole park). No laundry sinks, but two dishwashing sinks are under cover. Motorcaravan service point. Gas supplies. Outdoor pool (mid-May - mid-Sept). Coracles Health and Country Club (see above). Play area. Games room with pool table and video game machine. Off site: Shop within 0.5 miles. Fishing 0.25 miles. Bicycle hire 8 miles. Riding 7 miles. Golf 10 miles.

At a glance

Welcome & Ambience	✓✓✓✓	Location	✓✓✓✓✓
Quality of Pitches	✓✓✓✓	Range of Facilities	✓✓✓✓✓

Directions

Follow A484 Cardigan - Newcastle Emlyn road and park is signed before Cenarth village. O.S.GR: SN265421. GPS: N52:02.994 W04:31.903

Charges 2005

Per unit incl. up to 4 people and a car	£ 13.00 - £ 20.00
extra person	£ 2.00
awning	£ 2.00
extra pup tent (space permitting)	£ 2.50
dog	£ 2.00

Reservations

Made with 33% deposit; contact park. Tel: 01239 710345. Email: enquiries@cenarth-holipark.co.uk

Open

1 March - 9 January.

UK6280 **Aeron Coast Caravan Park**

North Road, Aberaeron SA46 0JF (Ceredigion)

Aeron Coast is a family holiday park with a wide range of recreational facilities, on the west coast of Wales. Although it has a high proportion of caravan holiday homes (200 privately owned), touring units of all types are provided for in two fields separated from the beach and sea by a high bank (although the best beach is on the south side of this traditional fishing village). Pitches are on level grass with all units regularly and well spaced in lines in traditional style. The main attraction of the park is its excellent provision for families, both in and out of doors. This includes two outdoor pools (one new) and a toddlers' pool (unsupervised) in a paved, walled area good for sunbathing, a tennis court and small half-court for youngsters, football and a sand pit. The indoor leisure area provides an under-5s room with slide, etc, teenagers-only room with juke box, table tennis, pool and games machines and TV room. In high season activities are organised nightly free of charge in the large entertainment and disco room. In low season reception is open 10.00-14.00 – choose a pitch from the numbers on the board and return to the office in the morning.

Facilities

Two modern toilet blocks offer excellent facilities including large family showers. Facilities for disabled people and babies are in one block. Basic motorcaravan service point. Swimming pools (1/6-30/9). Club house and bar (from Easter, 12-2 and from 7 pm) with family room serving bar meals and takeaway in school holiday periods. Reception keeps a wide range of tourist information. Shop at the petrol station at the entrance. Only one dog per unit is accepted. Off site: Beach, fishing and boat launching 0.5 miles. A steam railway, craft centre, woollen mills and potteries can be visited locally.

At a glance

Welcome & Ambience	✓✓✓✓	Location	✓✓✓✓
Quality of Pitches	✓✓✓✓	Range of Facilities	✓✓✓✓

Directions

Park is on northern outskirts of Aberaeron village with entrance on the right beside a petrol station - not too easily seen. O.S.GR: SN461631.
GPS: N52:14.670 W04:15.295

Charges 2005

Per unit incl. 2 persons and electricity	£ 10.50 - £ 14.00
extra person (over 18 yrs)	£ 3.00
child (over 12 yrs)	£ 1.00
child (over 2 yrs)	£ 0.50

Reservations

Made with £20 deposit. Tel: 01545 570349. Email: aeroncoastcaravanpark@aberaeron.freeserve.co.uk

Open

1 March - 31 October.

UK6290 **Glan-y-Mor Leisure Park**

Clarach Bay, Aberystwyth SY23 3DT (Ceredigion)

Follow the road to Clarach Bay and on the sea-front is Glan-y-Mor, a busy, holiday-style park with an enviable situation. On a wet day you may not wish to go far with the comprehensive leisure centre on site - it is open eight months of the year with reduced entry fee for campers. Although the balance of pitches is very much in favour of caravan holiday homes (3:1) which dominate the open park and bay, there are 60 touring pitches, 45 with electricity (10A) and 4 new 'super' pitches. They are rather small and are pressed together in two small sections on the lower part of the park. In high season, tents, tourers or motorcaravans can opt for space and fine views (but maybe winds) on a ridge of higher ground above the park. The well equipped leisure centre offers a heated pool, jacuzzi, solarium, sauna, steam room and gym. This complex also includes reception, a video and amusement room, 10-pin bowling, bar, buffet bar and dance room (free entertainment nightly, Easter and May-Oct). This is an ideal site for those seeking 'all the bells and whistles'!

Facilities

The heated toilet block is on the lower touring area with dishwashing facilities and laundry room, plus a toilet for disabled people. A 'portacabin' type block (high season only) is on the ridge ground. A suite including shower for disabled people is in a block in the upper static site, with further facilities at the leisure centre (RADAR key). Motorcaravan service point. Supermarket. Play area designed with younger children in mind. Large sports field. Swimming pool. Licensed restaurant and takeaway (from Easter). Freezer pack service and gas supplies. No dogs are accepted on touring pitches during B.H. and school summer holiday periods. Beware of prominent speed bumps on site. Off site: Reduced rates are available at local golf courses.

Open

1 March - 31 October.

At a glance

Welcome & Ambience	✓✓✓✓	Location	✓✓✓✓
Quality of Pitches	✓✓✓	Range of Facilities	✓✓✓✓✓

Directions

Clarach is signed west from the A487 (Aberystwyth - Machynlleth) in village of Bow Street (take care at narrow bridge). Follow signs over crossroads to beach and park. Access for caravans from Aberystwyth on B4572 is difficult. O.S.GR: SN587841.
GPS: N52:26.175 W04:04.815

Charges 2005

Per unit incl. 2 persons	£ 8.50 - £ 16.00
super pitch	£ 20.00
dog (not 7/7-4/9)	£ 2.00
awning	£ 3.00

Top camping area max. charge £10 plus £2 electricity. Club membership (but not Leisure complex) included.

Reservations

Any length, with £20 deposit; balance 28 days before arrival. Tel: 01970 828900.
Email: glanymor@sunbourne.co.uk

UK6040 Pencelli Castle Caravan & Camping Park

Pencelli, Brecon LD3 7LX (Powys)

Open all year round, this is a quality park with atmosphere and character which continues to improve. Set amidst the Brecon scenery, it offers excellent facilities in peaceful, rural tranquillity. The owners, Liz and Gerwyn Rees, have retained the country charm but have added an all embracing range of spacious, heated, luxury facilities, attractively enhanced by potted plants, etc. There are three touring fields. The 'Orchard' incorporates 15 fully serviced pitches with hardstanding, amongst shrubs, fruit trees and a stone cider mill. The 'Oaks' taking 20 caravans and tents and the 'Meadow' for 40 tents (with boot and bike wash) are bordered by majestic trees and the Monmouthshire and Brecon Canal, where gaily painted barges slip past. All the fields are level with neatly mown grass and tarmac access roads. The historic manor house, that dates back to 1583, is adjacent to arched barns that house an increasing collection of vintage farm machinery including carts and rare tractors. For mountain bikers and walkers, a path leaves the village to reach the top of the Brecon Beacons or there is an easy towpath ramble to Tal-y-Bont where there are pubs, tea rooms and a post office.

Facilities

The toilet block is very well designed and includes some private cubicles, two large fully equipped rooms for families or disabled visitors incorporating double showers, baby changing and bath facilities, all humorously decorated for the young at heart. Laundry. Drying room with lockers (a must as this is walking country). Information and planning room. Internet access and WiFi. Indoor dishwashing and food preparation room. Motorcaravan service point (with washbasin, soap and hand dryer). Small shop at reception (basics). Playground and nature trail for children. Bicycle hire. Dogs are not accepted (except 'assistance dogs'. Off site: The Royal Oak Inn with meals 100 m. Buses pass regularly for Brecon, Abergavenny. Golf and bicycle hire 5 miles. Riding 2 miles.

At a glance

Welcome & Ambience	✓✓✓✓✓	Location	✓✓✓✓✓
Quality of Pitches	✓✓✓✓✓	Range of Facilities	✓✓✓

Directions

From A40 south after Brecon bypass take B4558 at signs for Llanfrynach and later Pencelli (narrow bridge). If travelling north on A40, approach via Tal-y-Bont. Site at south end of Pencelli. O.S.GR: SO095249. GPS: N51:54.887 W03:19.072

Charges 2005

Per caravan or motorcaravan	
incl. 2 persons	£ 12.00 - £ 16.00
extra adult	£ 5.50
child (5-15 yrs)	£ 4.00 - £ 4.50
awning	£ 1.50
electricity	£ 2.75
tent - per adult	£ 7.00 - £ 8.00
No credit cards.	

Reservations

Advised for peak season and B.Hs.
Tel: 01874 665451. Email: pencelli.castle@virgin.net

Open

All year excl. 4th - 27th December.

UK6245 Morben Isaf Touring & Holiday Home Park

Derwenlas, Machynlleth SY20 8SR (Powys)

Machynlleth is a market town, home of Owain Glyndwr's fifteenth century Welsh Parliament building and the Celtica Centre, and is also close to the Tal-y-Llyn Steam Railway, the Centre for Alternative Technology, Corris Craft Centre and King Arthur's Labyrinth. This site is in a convenient location for an overnight halt, or a short stay whilst visiting all these attractions. It provides 26 multi-service touring pitches all with electricity (16A), water tap, waste water drain and a satellite TV hook-up. There is further grassy space below the touring pitches beyond the fishing lake which is normally used as a football pitch but can accommodate around 30 tents who do not need any services. On a lower level, behind the site manager's bungalow, and barely visible from the touring site, are 87 privately owned holiday mobile homes. Also on site is an unfenced coarse fishing lake which campers are free to use.

Facilities

A small but well equipped, heated modern toilet block includes spacious controllable showers, baby changing and child seats in both ladies' and men's, and a well equipped laundry and dishwashing facilities. There are no facilities for disabled campers. Powered motorcaravan service point suitable for American RVs. Gas available. Off site: Pub serving hot food 1.5 miles. Leisure Centre, shops and services in Machynlleth 3 miles (market on Wednesday). Centre for Alternative Technology 6 miles.

Open

Mid-March - 31 October.

At a glance

Welcome & Ambience	✓✓✓✓	Location	✓✓✓✓
Quality of Pitches	✓✓✓✓	Range of Facilities	✓✓

Directions

Site is 2.5 miles southwest of Machynlleth beside A487. O.S.GR: SN706986. GPS: N52:34.204 W03:54.687

Charges 2005

Per unit incl. 2 adults, 2 children	
and electricity	£ 12.50 - £ 15.00
extra person	£ 2.00
2-man tent	£ 10.50
tent (1-man, 2-man, family)	
on field	£ 7.50 - £ 12.50
dog	free - £ 1.00

Reservations

Essential for peak season and B.Hs.
Tel: 01654 781473.

UK6030 Brynich Caravan Park

Brecon LD3 7SH (Powys)

Brynich is a well kept, family run park with a picturesque setting and super views towards the Brecon Beacons, developed over the years by Colin and Maureen Jones to very high standards. Originally farmland near the Brecon bypass, there are now three level, hedged and neatly mown camping fields with tarmac roads and a mixture of hardwood trees and shrubs maturing nicely. These fields provide for 130 touring units of all types with hardstanding on many pitches, 108 electricity points (10/16A) and 39 multi-serviced pitches with grass or gravel hardstandings. In a sloping field leading down to a stream, is an extensive dog walk on one side of the Brynich Brook and, on the opposite side, an adventure play area. The stream is shallow and an added attraction along with the play equipment and there is a large recreation field for ball games. For smaller children there is some play equipment near reception and the Play Barn which provides extensive indoor entertainment for the under-12s (charges apply). In a beautifully converted barn adjacent to the campsite the fully licensed restaurant uses local produce in its good value menus. Being within the Brecon Beacons National Park, this is a good area for hill walking and climbing. A member of the Best of British group.

Facilities

Two modern, heated toilet blocks have well equipped showers, some washbasins in cubicles (one block only), dishwashing sinks and a laundry room. Two fully equipped units for disabled visitors in one block, one providing left handed toilet facilities, the other right handed (key system). Baby unit including bath. Family room with bath, shower, toilet and hand basin. Fridge, freezer and microwave for visitors' use. Motorcaravan service point with bike wash. Reception and well stocked shop (with gas). Play areas. Restaurant and indoor Play Barn open all year. Boules court. Off site: Local pub within walking distance. Access to the towpath of the Brecon and Monmouthshire Canal is 200 yds. Market days in Brecon on Tuesday and Friday. Fishing or bicycle hire 1.5 miles. Riding 2 miles. Golf 3 miles.

At a glance

Welcome & Ambience	✓✓✓✓✓	Location	✓✓✓✓
Quality of Pitches	✓✓✓✓✓	Range of Facilities	✓✓✓✓✓

Directions

From the A40 Abergavenny road, at roundabout on the Brecon bypass (A40/A470) take A470 and park is 150 yards on right. O.S.GR: SO069279. GPS: N51:56.526 W03:21.312

Charges 2005

Per unit incl. 2 persons, electricity	£ 13.00 - £ 16.00
with services	£ 15.00 - £ 18.00
tent incl. 2 persons	£ 10.00 - £ 13.00
extra adult	£ 3.00
child (4-16 yrs)	£ 2.00
dog	£ 1.00

Reservations

Advisable for hook-ups at B.Hs. and made with £20 deposit. Tel: 01874 623325. Email: holidays@brynich.co.uk

Open

18 March - 30 October.

UK6250 Dolswydd Caravan Park

Dolswydd, Pen-y-Bont, Llandrindod Wells LD1 5UB (Powys)

Dolswydd is on the edge of a pretty, traditional working farm. Peaceful and tranquil, with fine views of the Welsh hills, it has modern facilities and 25 good spacious pitches mainly on hardstandings, all with 16A electricity. The park is within walking distance of the local pub which offers good, home cooked food. The Hughes family extend a warm and friendly welcome to their little park, surrounded by hills and wandering sheep, which is ideal as a touring base or for a one night stop, but booking is advised, especially at peak times, Bank Holidays and during the Victorian Festival (last week in August).

Facilities	Directions
Modern and clean facilities include lots of hot water, dishwashing, laundry, and a WC/washroom for disabled people. Fishing in the river alongside the site (free, but licence required). Off site: Within walking distance are the local pub, Post Office and garage. Riding 1 mile. Golf 5 miles. Bicycle hire 5 miles.	Pen-y-bont is 2 miles east of the junction of the A44 and A483 roads at Crossgates. Take A44 signed Kington. Go through Pen-y-bont and site is on right after crossing cattle grid. O.S.GR: SO117639.

Open	Charges 2005	
Easter - end October.	Per unit with 2 adults and 2 children	£ 8.00
	extra person	£ 1.00
	electricity	£ 1.50

At a glance

				Reservations
Welcome & Ambience	✓✓✓✓	Location	✓✓✓✓	Contact site. Tel: 01597 851267.
Quality of Pitches	✓✓✓✓	Range of Facilities	✓✓✓	Email: Hughes@dolswydd.freeserve.co.uk

UK6305 Smithy Park

Abermule, Montgomery SY15 6ND (Powys)

Set in four acres of landscaped ground bordered by the River Severn and the Shropshire Union Canal in the tranquil rolling countryside of central Wales, Smithy has 60 privately owned caravan holiday homes. However, the touring area is separate and also has the benefit of being closest to the river with the best views. This area has 26 fully serviced hardstanding pitches (16A electricity, water, waste water and satellite TV hook-ups). A timber chalet provides all the sanitary facilities, and is located in one corner of the touring area. This is a well run site, which is under the same ownership as Westbrook Park, with a resident manager on-site here.

Facilities	Directions
The new timber clad chalet building provides two good sized showers per sex, washbasins in cubicles, a family room suitable for the less able (there is a step). Laundry with washing machine, dryer and dishwashing sink. Fishing in the river Severn. Fenced playground. Gas stocked. Off site: Bus stop in village. Supermarkets and all other services in Newtown 3 miles. Golf 3 miles. Riding 5 miles.	Site is 3 miles north of Newtown in the village of Abermule. Turn off the A483 into village, and turn off beside the Waterloo Arms. Site is at end of lane. O.S.GR: SO161948. GPS: N52:32.653 W03:14.323

Open	Charges 2005	
1 March - 30 November.	Per unit incl. 2 persons, electricity £ 12.00 - £ 16.00	
	extra person	£ 2.00
	child (4-10 yrs)	£ 1.00

At a glance

				Reservations
Welcome & Ambience	✓✓✓✓	Location	✓✓✓✓	Essential for peak season and B.Hs. Made with
Quality of Pitches	✓✓✓✓	Range of Facilities	✓✓✓	full amount payable. Tel: 01584 711280.
				Email: info@bestparks.co.uk

UK6310 Bacheldre Watermill Caravan Park

·Churchstoke, Montgomery SY15 6TE (Powys)

A delightful little site, Bacheldre has just 25 pitches arranged around the perimeter of a grass meadow, with no site roads and just one lamp on the outside of the toilet block. However, there are 18 electricity hook-ups (10A) and 5 hardstandings. Ideal for tents and small units, it is not really suitable for large units. The watermill is fully operational, producing high quality organic wheat flour, which can be purchased from reception. The mill is not normally accessible, although guided tours can be arranged. Note: there are obvious hazards for children – a deep partially fenced millpond, moving waterwheel and the stream.

Facilities	Directions
A portacabin provides the usual facilities including one controllable hot shower per sex. Calor gas stocked. Torches could be useful. Off site: Walking and cycling along Offa's Dyke 800 yards from site. Supermarket at Churchstoke 2 miles.	Bacheldre is just off the A489 between Newtown and Churchstoke, about 9 miles east of Newtown and 2 miles west of Churchstoke. Turn into narrow lane (signed Bacheldre Mill), over the bridge to site. O.S.GR: SO243929.

Open	Charges 2005	
All year.	Per unit incl. 2 adults	£ 8.00 - £ 10.00
	extra person	£ 2.00
	No credit cards.	

At a glance

				Reservations
Welcome & Ambience	✓✓✓✓	Location	✓✓✓✓	Contact park. Tel: 01588 620489.
Quality of Pitches	✓✓✓✓	Range of Facilities	✓✓✓	Email: info@bacheldremill.co.uk

UK6320 Fforest Fields Caravan & Camping Park

Hundred House, Builth Wells LD1 5RT (Powys)

This secluded 'different' park is set on a family hill farm in the heart of Radnorshire. Truly rural, there are glorious views of the surrounding hills and a distinctly family atmosphere. This is simple country camping and caravanning at its best, without man-made distractions or intrusions - a place to unwind and watch the stars. The facilities include 67 large pitches on level grass on a spacious and peaceful, carefully landscaped field by a stream. Electrical connections (mostly 16A) are available and there are 13 hardstanding pitches, also with electricity. Several additional areas without electricity are provided for tents. George and Kate, the enthusiastic owners, have opened up much of the farm for moderate or ample woodland and moorland trails which can be enjoyed with much wildlife to see. Indeed wildlife is actively encouraged with nesting boxes for owls, song-birds and bats, by leaving field margins un-mown to encourage small mammals and by yearly tree planting. George and Kate also run a para-gliding school where beginners are welcome.

Facilities
The toilet facilities are acceptable with baby bath, dishwashing and laundry facilities including washing machines and a dryer. Milk, eggs and orange juice are sold in reception and gas, otherwise there are few other on-site facilities, but the village of Hundred House, one mile away, has a pub, village stores and post office. Torches are useful. Off site: Fishing 3 miles. Bicycle hire and golf 5 miles. Riding 10 miles.

Open
Easter - 17 November.

At a glance
Welcome & Ambience	✓✓✓✓	Location	✓✓✓✓✓
Quality of Pitches	✓✓✓✓	Range of Facilities	✓✓✓

Directions
Park is 4 miles east of Builth Wells near the village of Hundred House on A481. Follow brown signs. O.S.GR: SO098535.

Charges 2005
Per unit	£ 2.00
extra adult	£ 3.00
child (4-16 yrs)	£ 1.50
electricity	£ 2.00

Special low season rates for senior citizens. No credit cards.

Reservations
Contact park. Tel: 01982 570406. Email: office@fforestfields.co.uk

Wonderful walks lead up into the hills from Fforest Fields

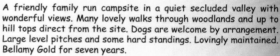

Fforest Fields
Caravan & Camping Park

A friendly family run campsite in a quiet secluded valley with wonderful views. Many lovely walks through woodlands and up to hill tops direct from the site. Dogs are welcome by arrangement. Large level pitches and some hard standings. Lovingly maintained. Bellamy Gold for seven years.

See lots of photos, prices & local info on
www.fforestfields.co.uk
Or phone 01982 570406 for brochure

Four miles from Builth Wells and the Wye Valley (On the A481)

UK6240 Cringoed Caravan Park

Cringoed, Llanbrynmair, Newtown SY19 7DR (Powys)

Cringoed is a pleasant, peaceful, small park with a river to one side, hills on the other and trees at either end. There are 50 spacious pitches of which 20 are occupied by seasonal units. These are in a level open field. Some of these have hardstanding and all have electricity (16A). The 31 caravan holiday homes are at both ends of the site, some amongst trees and some in a newer, more open area. There are also 10 tent pitches. This is a relaxing base where you can sit and listen to the river and watch the wildlife, but it is also within easy reach of some of mid-Wales' best scenery and not far from the coast. Paul and Sue Mathers will make you very welcome.

Facilities
The single toilet block is neat, modern and quite adequate. Laundry and dishwashing. Adventure play area. Small tourist information room. American motorhomes accepted (max. 36 ft). Off site: Shops 1 mile. ATM at Spar in Carno 6 miles. Fishing 5 miles. Golf 8 miles. Riding 12 miles.

Open
7 March - 7 January (ring first in low season).

At a glance
Welcome & Ambience	✓✓✓✓	Location	✓✓✓✓
Quality of Pitches	✓✓✓✓	Range of Facilities	✓✓✓

Directions
From the A470 between Newton and Machynlleth in the village of Llanbrynmair take the B4518 signed Staylittle (caravan signs). After 1 mile just before bridge turn right, go over site bridge and turn right into site. O.S.GR: SH887013.
GPS: N52:35.900 W03:38.663

Charges 2005
Per unit incl. 2 persons, electricity	£ 13.00 - £ 16.00
tent pitch incl. 2 persons	£ 10.00 - £ 13.00

Reservations
Contact site. Tel: 01650 521237.

(239)

UK6330 Daisy Bank Touring Caravan Park

Snead, Montgomery SY15 6EB (Powys)

For adults only, this pretty, tranquil park in the Camlad Valley has panoramic views, and is an ideal base for walkers. Attractively landscaped with 'old English' flower beds and many different trees and shrubs, this small park has been carefully developed. The Welsh hills to the north and the Shropshire hills to the south overlook the three fields which provide a total of 55 pitches. The field nearer to the road (perhaps a little noisy) is slightly sloping but there are hardstandings for motorcaravans, while the second field is more level. All pitches have 16A electricity, water and waste water drainage and most have TV hook up. With many walks in the area, including Offa's Dyke, a series of walk leaflets is available centred on Bishop's Castle three miles away. The owners will site your caravan for you and there is a late arrivals area with hook-up. A security bar at the entrance has to be lifted for motorcaravans. Although technically in Wales, the park is 500 yards from the Shropshire border, an area rich in history.

Facilities

The well equipped, heated toilet block now incorporates modern, en-suite units (6 with shower, WC and washbasin, 2 with WC and washbasin). Dishwashing sinks at the rear of the block are covered. Washing machine, laundry sink and drying room. Gas supplies. Brick built barbecues. Small putting green (free loan of clubs and balls). Off site: Supermarket 2 miles. Many eating places near. Bicycle hire and fishing 3 miles. Golf and riding 10 miles.

At a glance

Welcome & Ambience	✓✓✓✓✓	Location	✓✓✓✓✓
Quality of Pitches	✓✓✓✓✓	Range of Facilities	✓✓✓

Directions

Site is by the A489 road 2 miles east of Churchstoke in the direction of Craven Arms. O.S.GR: SO302930. GPS: N52:31.795 W03:01.782

Charges 2005

Per unit incl. 2 adults and all services	£ 14.00 - £ 20.00
extra person	£ 4.00
dog	£ 0.75

Reservations

An adult only park. Contact park. Tel: 01588 620471. Email: enquiries@daisy-bank.co.uk

Open

All year.

UK6340 Pen-y-Bont Touring & Camping Park

Llangynog Road, Bala LL23 7PH (Gwynedd)

This is a pretty little park with 59 pitches on hardstanding (34 for touring units) and 36 for tents mainly on sloping grass. Connected by circular gravel roads, they are intermingled with trees and tall trees edge the site. Electricity connections (16A) are available, including 11 for tents, and there are 24 new serviced pitches with hardstanding, electricity, water and drainage. There are also pitches for 25 seasonal units. The park entrance and the stone building that houses reception and the well stocked shop provide quite a smart image. With views of the Berwyn mountains, Pen-y-bont has a peaceful, attractive and useful location being the closest park to Bala town, 100 yards from Bala Lake and 3 miles from the Welsh National White Water Centre, with Snowdonia on hand.

Facilities

The toilet block includes washbasins in cubicles and spacious hot showers. Two new cubicles with washbasin and WC. Separate laundry room and an en-suite unit for disabled visitors, that doubles as a baby room, operated by key (£2 deposit). Outside covered area with fencing and concrete floor for dishwashing sinks and bins. Motorcaravan service point. Shop. Caravan storage. Off site: Fishing 200 yds. Boat launching, bicycle hire, golf and riding 2 miles. Bala market on Mondays.

Open

1 April - 31 October.

At a glance

Welcome & Ambience	✓✓✓✓	Location	✓✓✓✓
Quality of Pitches	✓✓✓✓	Range of Facilities	✓✓✓

Directions

Park is 0.5 miles southeast of Bala village on the B4391. Bala is between Dolgellau and Conwen on the A494. O.S.GR: SH932350. GPS: N52:54.103 W03:35.407

Charges 2005

Per unit incl. 2 persons	£ 11.50
with electricity	£ 14.00
extra person	£ 3.00
child (4-16 yrs)	£ 1.00 - £ 2.00
awning	£ 2.30

Reservations

Made for exact dates for particular pitches, with deposit of £10 per pitch. Tel: 01678 520549. Email: penybont@balalake.fsnet.co.uk

Planning your **next holiday?**

don't forget to look at our directory
ON PAGE 314

UK6345 Glanllyn Lakeside Caravan & Camping Park

Llanuwchllyn, Bala LL23 7ST (Gwynedd)

This 16-acre site lying alongside the southern end of Bala lake has 204 pitches. With around 40 seasonal units, this leaves 164 tourist pitches, 94 of which have electric hook-ups. In this location, virtually all the pitches have wonderful views of the lake or the surrounding mountain sides. The terrain is grassy, fairly open and level, but with natural terraces. There are around ten individual hardstandings and a further hardstanding area by the beach is a favourite with motorcaravanners. The site is served by main tarmac access roads with speed bumps. Lake swimming is possible and the private beach allows easy access for windsurfing. The park is also an ideal base for some serious walking.

Facilities

A complex of three modern buildings (one can be heated and is used in low season) is located centrally at the rear of the site. They provide a good supply of services including pre-set hot showers, hairdressing and shaver stations, a laundry and dishwashing room, facilities for babies and a suite for disabled people (key code access). Motorcaravan service point. Well stocked shop at reception (Easter - Oct) and plenty of tourist information. Freezer pack service. Gas supplies. Splendid, well fenced adventure style playground on bark surface. Only 2 dogs per unit permitted (fenced dog walk area). Breathable groundsheets only and only for min. 3 day stay. Off site: Bus stops outside site gate. Ideal for exploring the southern part of Snowdonia National Park. Bicycle hire, indoor swimming pool and golf in Bala 3 miles. Bala market on Mondays. Riding 18 miles.

At a glance

Welcome & Ambience	✓✓✓✓	Location	✓✓✓✓✓	
Quality of Pitches	✓✓✓✓	Range of Facilities	✓✓✓	

Directions

From Bala take A494 southwest towards Dolgellau for about 3 miles, entrance is on left, on right hand bend. O.S.GR: SH893324.
GPS: N52:52.660 W03:38.799

Charges 2005

Per unit incl. 2 persons	£ 11.00
incl. electricity	£ 14.00
extra adult	£ 3.00
child (9-16 yrs)	£ 2.00
child (3-8 yrs)	£ 1.00
dog (max .2)	£ 1.00

Reservations

Essential for peak season and B.Hs (when min. stay is 3 nights) and made with £20 deposit.
Tel: 01678 540227. Email: info@glanllyn.com

Open

Mid-March (Easter) - mid October.

UK6355 Woodlands Caravan Park

Harlech LL46 2UE (Gwynedd)

This delightful little site is lovingly tended by its owners and has just 18 pitches for tourists, all with gravel hardstanding and electric hook-up (10A) for caravans and motorcaravans only. Tents are not accepted. There are also 21 privately owned holiday homes, one for rent and a holiday cottage. However, the location of this site certainly makes up for its diminutive size, nestling under the massive rock topped by Harlech Castle, now a designated World Heritage Site. The narrow lane running alongside the site up to the old town above, is the steepest hill in Britain – no wonder the town is considering installing a funicular railway in the future. The coastal railway runs close to the site and the station is just 100 yards away. Railway noise should not be a problem (the small 'Sprinter' trains do not run at night). The 'Blue Flag' beach is only 500 yards, and the Leisure Centre with its indoor pool is 250 yards.

Facilities

The modern stone built toilet facilities are heated, clean and tidy with controllable showers (50p), vanity style washbasins, a small laundry with a baby changing area, but with no dedicated facilities for disabled visitors (£5 deposit for the key to the facilities). Chemical disposal point but no motorcaravan service point. Off site: Harlech Castle. The town also has a theatre and cinema. Nearby is Maes Artro Village with its Museum of Bygone Days. Portmeirion, location of the cult TV series 'The Prisoner', 8 miles. Barmouth (market Thursday and Sunday) 10 miles. Golf 0.25 mile. Fishing 3 miles. Riding 3 miles.

Open

1 March - 31 October.

At a glance

Welcome & Ambience	✓✓✓✓✓	Location	✓✓✓✓✓	
Quality of Pitches	✓✓✓✓	Range of Facilities	✓✓✓	

Directions

From Barmouth take A496 to Harlech and continue downhill past Royal St David's Golf Course. Fork right immediately before railway crossing, and site is 200 yards on right. DO NOT turn towards town centre which lies on B4573, it is very narrow and congested. O.S.GR: SH582314.
GPS: N52:51.693 W04:06.458

Charges 2005

Per unit incl. 2 persons and electricity	£ 11.50 - £ 13.00
extra person	£ 2.00
awning	£ 2.00
No credit cards.	

Reservations

Recommended at all times. Tel: 01766 780419.
Email: grace@woodlandscp.fsnet.co.uk

UK6370 Hendre Mynach Touring Caravan & Camping Park

Llanaber, Barmouth LL42 1YR (Gwynedd)

A neat and tidy family park, colourful flowers and top rate facilities make an instant impression on arrival down the steep entrance to this park (help is available to get out if you are worried). The 240 pitches are allocated in various areas, with substantial tenting areas identified. Forty gravel hardstandings are available and around the park there are 110 electricity hook-ups (10A), 20 fully serviced pitches and ample water taps. The quaint old seaside and fishing town of Barmouth is under a mile away, a 15-20 minute walk along the prom. Here you will find 'everything'. The beach is only 100 yards away but a railway line runs between this and the park. It can be crossed by pedestrian operated gates which could be a worry for those with young children. Reception will provide leaflets with maps of local walks. Snowdonia National Park and mountain railway, the famous Ffestiniog railway, castles and lakes everywhere provide plenty to see and do – this is a classic park in a classic area.

Facilities

Two toilet blocks, one modern and one traditional, both offer excellent facilities including spacious showers (free) and washbasins in cubicles. An extension to the traditional block has added a good unit for disabled visitors with ramp access. Motorcaravan service point. Well stocked shop incorporating a snack bar and takeaway (Easter - 1 Nov; 08.30-21.00 hrs. in peak season, less at quieter times). Off site: Beach 100 m. Fishing, boat launching and bicycle hire within 0.5 miles. Riding 5 miles. Golf 9 miles.

Open

All year excl. 10 Jan - 28 Feb.

At a glance

Welcome & Ambience	✓✓✓✓✓	Location	✓✓✓✓✓
Quality of Pitches	✓✓✓✓✓	Range of Facilities	✓✓✓✓

Directions

Park is off the A496 road north of Barmouth in village of Llanaber with entrance down a steep drive.
O.S.GR: SH606171. GPS: N52:43.980 W04:03.971

Charges 2005

Per caravan or large motorcaravan incl. 2 persons and electricity	£ 8.00 - £ 20.00
2 adults and up to 3 children	£ 15.00 - £ 25.00
extra adult	£ 3.00
child (2-15 yrs)	£ 1.00
first dog free, extra dog	£ 0.50

Plus £1 per night for certain weekends.
Mid-season and Christmas/New Year offers.

Reservations

Made with £20 deposit. Tel: 01341 280262.
Email: mynach@lineone.net

UK6580 Llanystumdwy Camping & Caravanning Club Site

Tyddyn Sianel, Llanystumdwy, Criccieth LL52 0LS (Gwynedd)

Overlooking mountains and sea, Llanystumdwy is one of the earliest Camping and Caravanning Club sites. Well maintained with good facilities, it is on sloping grass. However, the managers are very helpful and know their site and can advise on the most suitable pitch and even have a supply of chocks. There are 70 pitches in total (20 ft. spacing), 45 with 10A electricity connections, spaced over two hedged fields with mainly caravans in the top field with four hardstandings for motorcaravans, and with tents lower down. A little library with a supply of tourist information is next to the small reception. A shop and pub are in the village and a bus leaves each hour from outside the site to Pwllheli or Porthmadog. This is a good base from which to explore the Lleyn peninsula or Snowdonia National Park. Portmeirion with its Italianate village is near.

Facilities

A purpose-built toilet block to one side includes excellent, full facilities for disabled visitors including access ramp, one washbasin each in a cubicle for male and female and extra large sinks. Facilities for babies. Laundry (taps with fitting for disabled people). Gas supplies. Off site: Riding or fishing 0.5 miles. Golf 2.5 miles. Beach 3 miles.

Open

March - October.

At a glance

Welcome & Ambience	✓✓✓✓	Location	✓✓✓✓
Quality of Pitches	✓✓✓	Range of Facilities	✓✓✓

Directions

Follow A497 from Criccieth west and take second right to Llanystumdwy. Site is on the right.
O.S.GR: SH469384. GPS: N52:55.252 W04:16.731

Charges 2005

Per adult	£ 4.30 - £ 6.40
child (6-18 yrs)	£ 1.90
non-member pitch fee	£ 5.00

Reservations

Necessary and made with deposit (especially for hardstanding pitches); contact site or Central Reservations 0870 243 3331. Tel: 01766 522855.

UK6590 **Forestry Commission - Beddgelert Campsite**

Caernarfon Road, Beddgelert LL55 4UU (Gwynedd)

This well equipped Forestry Commission site is in the heart of Snowdonia. Set in a marvellous, natural, wooded environment on the slopes of Snowdon there is abundant fauna and flora, tumbling streams and always something to watch from the cheeky squirrels to the smallest bird in Britain. Well equipped and well managed, the site provides 280 pitches – tents in a semi-wooded field area and caravans amongst the trees with numbered hardstandings, and 105 places with 10A electricity. Tents may pitch where they like in their areas leaving 6 m. between units or there are 6 new grass pitches with electrical hook-ups for tents. Metal tent pegs may be best (available from the shop). Free maps of the forest walks are provided in reception and orienteering and fishing are possible. A bus service stops at the top of the entrance lane (two hourly for Caernarfon and Porthmadog).

Facilities

Two fully equipped modern sanitary toilet blocks clad in natural wood provide large, free hot showers (with good dry areas). Laundry equipment is in one block. A small unit provides extra washbasins and toilets in peak season and there is a toilet and washbasin for disabled visitors. Excellent drive-through motorcaravan service point. Recycling bins. Reception is central, as is a well provisioned shop (Easter - end-Sept. approx). Well equipped adventure playground. Log cabin common room. Off site: Pub within walking distance (under a mile) and other eating places nearby. Bicycle hire within 500 m. in forest.

At a glance

Welcome & Ambience	✓✓✓✓	Location	✓✓✓✓✓
Quality of Pitches	✓✓✓✓	Range of Facilities	✓✓✓

Directions

Site is clearly signed to the left 1 mile north of Beddgelert on A4085 Caernarfon road.
O.S.GR: SH579492. GPS: N52:01.245 W04:07.186

Charges 2005

Per unit incl. 2 persons	£ 7.20 - £ 12.20
extra adult	£ 2.80
child (5-14 yrs)	£ 2.00
electricity	£ 2.50 - £ 3.00

Less 20% all year for disabled guests and outside 23/7-31/8 for the over 60s.

Reservations

Necessary for B.Hs and peak times (min. 3 nights with £30 deposit). Contact site or phone: 0131 314 6505.
Tel: 0131 314 6505. Email: info@forestholidays.co.uk

Open

All year excl. 1 November - 16 December.

UK6600 **Bryn Gloch Caravan & Camping Park**

Betws Garmon, Caernarfon LL54 7YY (Gwynedd)

Bryn Gloch is a well kept and family owned touring park in the impressive Snowdonia area - an unusual feature is the mountain railway which passes through the park. Neat and quiet, it takes some 160 units on five flat, wide meadows with some breathtaking views. With tarmac access roads and free areas allowed in the centre for play, 100 pitches have electricity connections (10A). There are 80 all weather pitches, including 18 'super' pitches and 6 serviced pitches (shared), all with hardstanding. In addition, there are 12 caravan holiday homes. Fishing is possible on the river bordering the park with a barbecue and picnic area, adventure play area and field for ball games. Tourist information is provided in the complex by reception and the park is very popular with walkers and cyclists. Caernarfon with its famous castle is 5 miles.

Facilities

The two main toilet blocks (both recently refurbished) include washbasins in cabins, a family bathroom (hot water £1), baby room and complete facilities for visitors with disabilities (coded access). The far field has a 'portacabin' style unit containing all facilities, for use in peak season. Well equipped laundry and separate drying room. Motorcaravan service point and car wash. Shop (1/3-30/10). TV and games rooms with pool tables and amusement machines. Minigolf. Entrance barrier with coded access. Off site: Pub 1 mile. ATM at garage in Ceathro 3 miles. Riding 2.5 miles, bicycle hire or golf 5 miles.

Open

All year, limited facilities 1 November - 1 March.

At a glance

Welcome & Ambience	✓✓✓✓✓	Location	✓✓✓✓✓
Quality of Pitches	✓✓✓✓✓	Range of Facilities	✓✓✓✓

Directions

From Caernarfon take A4085 signed Beddgelert. Park is just beyond Waunfawr, 4.5 miles southeast of Caernarfon. At Betws Garmon, after crossing river bridge, watch for signs and entrance is opposite St Garmon church. O.S.GR: SH536576.
GPS: N53:05.711 W04:11.304

Charges 2005

Per unit incl. 2 persons	£ 13.00 - £ 15.00
incl. electricty	£ 16.00 - £ 18.00
serviced pitch, plus	£ 18.00 - £ 20.00
extra adult	£ 4.00
child (3-16 yrs)	£ 2.00
dog	£ 1.00

Reservations

Necessary for B.Hs. (min. 3 nights) with payment in full; other times with deposit of first night's fee.
Tel: 01286 650216. Email: eurig@bryngloch.co.uk

243

UK6620 Plas Gwyn Caravan & Camping Park

Llanrug, Caernarfon LL55 2AQ (Gwynedd)

In a beautiful location, this traditional touring site is within the grounds of a house that was built in 1785 in the Georgian style with a colonial style veranda. Of historical interest, Prime Minister Lloyd George was a frequent visitor to Plas Gwyn House. The site is just 2.5 miles from the Llanberis Pass, the Snowdon Mountain Railway, the Electric Mountain Visitor Centre, and this is also good walking country. The 27 touring caravan pitches are set around the perimeter of a slightly sloping grass field, and there are four hardstandings for motorcaravans. The separate tent field has 10 pitches. There are 30 electric hook-ups (16A), and with minimal site lighting on the caravan field and none on the tent field, a torch could be very useful. A further separate small field houses 18 caravan holiday homes. This site is not really suitable for American RVs. A member of the Countryside Discovery Group.

Facilities

An older style building houses the toilet facilities - although the fittings and tiling inside are modern and are kept neat and tidy. Controllable free hot showers, dishwashing sinks, a good laundry room (by reception), but no dedicated facilities for babies or disabled campers. Drive-over motorhome service point. Gas stocked. Reception stocks basic food items, etc. Breakfast 'butties' to order. Internet access possible (ask at reception). Off site: Llanberis and Snowdon Mountain Railway 2.5 miles, Golf 1 mile. Riding 2.5 miles. Bicycle hire 3 miles. Fishing 4 miles.

At a glance

Welcome & Ambience	✓✓✓✓	Location	✓✓✓✓✓
Quality of Pitches	✓✓✓✓	Range of Facilities	✓✓✓

Directions

Site is on A4086, 3 miles from Caernarfon, and 2.5 miles from Llanberis, well signed with easy access. O.S.GR: SH522634. GPS: N53:08.804 W04:12.734

Charges 2005

Per person	£ 2.00
child (5-15 yrs)	£ 1.50
child (under 5 yrs)	£ 1.00
pitch incl. awning and electricity	£ 6.50 - £ 10.00
tent pitch	£ 2.00 - £ 5.00

Reservations

Advised for peak season and B.Hs.
Tel: 01286 672619. Email: info@plasgwyn.co.uk

Open

1 March - 31 October.

UK6635 Fron Caravan & Camping Park

Brynsiencyn, Anglesey LL61 6TX (Isle of Anglesey)

A traditional, all touring campsite in a peaceful rural location, Fron has panoramic views over the surrounding countryside. From the entrance gate a tarmac drive passes through a two-acre level grass paddock, which is reserved for 35 large sized tent and trailer tent pitches. The drive leads up to the old farmhouse which houses reception, a well stocked shop, and plenty of tourist information. Behind the farmhouse is another two-acre sloping paddock with 40 caravan and motorcaravan pitches, 5 with hardstandings, and 45 electricity hook-ups (10A). An adventure style playground is located in the tent paddock, and by the farmhouse a well fenced outdoor heated swimming pool (30 x 14 ft. and open May - Sept, weather permitting) is well controlled by the owners.

Facilities

Toilet facilities are in three units of varying ages and designs located at both sides of the farmhouse. These include a new unit for ladies with some basins in cubicles, good hot showers with dividers (20p), hairdryers, a baby area with mat and a suite for disabled campers. Laundry with washing machine, dryer and dishwashing sinks (hot water 30p). Motorcaravan service point. Outdoor heated swimming pool. Gas stocked. Internet point. Recycling of glass and newspapers. Max. 2 dogs per pitch. No single sex groups are accepted. Torches useful. Breathable groundsheets only. Off site: Nearby are Anglesey Sea Zoo, Plas Newydd House, Foel Farm Park, Anglesey Transport and Agriculture Museum and the Menai Bridges. Brynsiencyn Village (0.5 mile) has a hotel and Spar shop (with ATM). Anglesey Model village 0.5 mile. Fishing 1.5 miles. Riding 3 miles. Golf 4 miles.

At a glance

Welcome & Ambience	✓✓✓✓	Location	✓✓✓✓
Quality of Pitches	✓✓✓✓	Range of Facilities	✓✓✓✓

Directions

After crossing the Britannia Bridge, take first slip road signed Llanfairpwll A4080, then next left signed Newborough and Brynsiencyn. Continue on A4080 for 5 miles, turning right in village at the Groeslon Hotel. Continue through Brynsiencyn to site at western end of village. O.S.GR: SH472668. GPS: N53:10.573 W04:17.271

Charges 2005

Per unit incl. 2 adults and 2 children	£ 12.50
extra adult	£ 2.50
extra child	£ 1.50
electricity	£ 2.50
single person tent	£ 7.00
No credit cards.	

Reservations

Essential for peak season and B.Hs, and made with 25% deposit. Tel: 01248 430310. Email: mail@troncaravanpark.co.uk

Open

Easter - end September.

UK6640 Home Farm Caravan Park

Marianglas, Anglesey LL73 8PH (Isle of Anglesey)

A tarmac drive through an open field leads to this neatly laid out quality park, with caravan holiday homes to one side. Nestling below what was once a Celtic hill fort, later decimated as a quarry, the park is edged with mature trees and farmland. A tarmac access road leads to 99 well spaced and numbered pitches. There are 20 hardstanding pitches all with 16A electric hook-ups, including 9 larger pitches with TV hook-ups, water and waste water drain, and 11 normal size pitches with water taps and waste water drain. All the remaining pitches have 10A hook-ups, 33 are on hardstandings, 45 on neatly cut grass. Some areas are slightly sloping. There is a separate area for tents and 15 seasonal units are taken. The 'piece de resistance' must be the indoor play area with super equipment, complete with tunnels and bridges on safe rubber matting, not to mention an outside fenced play area and fields for sports, etc. and walking. Various beaches, sandy or rocky, are within a mile. A member of the Best of British group.

Facilities

Two purpose built toilet blocks, one part of the reception building, are of similar design and can be heated. En-suite provision for people with disabilities (with key). Excellent small bathroom for children with baby bath. Family room (with key). Laundry room and good dishwashing facilities. Motorcaravan services. Ice pack service. Reception provides basic essentials, gas and some caravan accessories. Indoor and outdoor play areas. TV and pool table. Small library. Hard tennis (extra charge) with racquet hire.
Off site: Restaurants, shops and ATM at Benllech 2 miles. Beach 1 mile. Fishing and golf 2 miles. Riding 8 miles.

Open

April - October.

At a glance

Welcome & Ambience	✓✓✓✓	Location	✓✓✓✓
Quality of Pitches	✓✓✓✓✓	Range of Facilities	✓✓✓✓

Directions

From the Britannia Bridge take second exit left signed Benllech and Amlwch on the A5025. Two miles after Benllech keep left at roundabout and park entrance is approx. 300 yards on the left beyond the church. O.S.GR: SH499850. GPS: N53:20.433 W04:15.382

Charges 2005

Per unit incl. 2 persons	£ 10.50 - £ 18.25
dog (max. 2)	£ 1.00
incl. electricity and hardstanding	£ 13.00 - £ 19.00
incl. full services	£ 16.00 - £ 22.50
extra adult	£ 2.00 - £ 2.50
child (5-16 yrs)	£ 1.50 - £ 1.75

Reservations

Essential for peak season (min. 3 days at B.Hs) and made with £20 deposit. Tel: 01248 410614. Email: enq@homefarm-anglesey.co.uk

UK6650 Hunters Hamlet Caravan Park

Sirior Goch Farm, Betws-yn-Rhos, Abergele LL22 8PL (Conwy)

This small, family owned park is licensed for all units except tents (trailer tents allowed). On a gently sloping hillside providing beautiful panoramic views, one area provides 15 well spaced pitches with hardstanding and 10A electricity hook-ups, with access from a circular, hard-core road. A more recent area has been developed next to this of a similar design but with 8 fully serviced 'super pitches' (water, waste water, sewage, TV and electricity connections). Shrubs and bushes at various stages of growth enhance both areas. A natural play area incorporating rustic adventure equipment set amongst mature beech trees with a small bubbling stream is a children's paradise. Milk and papers can be ordered and the Hunters will do their best to meet your needs, even to survival rations! The park is well situated to tour Snowdonia and Anglesey and is within easy reach of Llandudno and Rhyl.

Facilities

The tiny heated toilet block has fully tiled facilities including showers en-suite with toilets for both sexes. A covered area to the rear houses laundry facilities, dishwashing, freezer and fridge. Family bathroom (metered) and basic toilet and shower facilities for disabled visitors. Play area. All year caravan storage. Max. 2 dogs per pitch. Off site: Fishing and golf 2 miles. Riding 10 miles.

Open

21 March - 31 October.

Reservations

Made with £20 deposit; B.H. bookings min. 4 nights. Tel: 01745 832237. Email: huntershamlet@aol.com

At a glance

Welcome & Ambience	✓✓✓✓	Location	✓✓✓✓
Quality of Pitches	✓✓✓✓	Range of Facilities	✓✓✓

Directions

From Abergele take A548 south for almost 3 miles; turn onto B5381 in direction of Betws-yn-Rhos and park is on left after 0.5 miles. To date there are no local authority caravan signs so watch carefully for the farm after turning - it can be identified by an artistically painted sign with the house and farm name: 'Sirior Goch Farm' and Hunter's Hamlet. O.S.GR: SH929736. GPS: N53:14.930 W03:36.408

Charges 2005

Per unit incl. 2 adults incl.	
electricity	£ 12.00 - £ 15.00
super pitch (fully incl.)	£ 17.00 - £ 20.00
extra adult	£ 2.00
child	£ 1.00

Less £5 on weekly bookings.
Aug. B.H. plus £1.00.

UK6655 Ty Mawr Holiday Park

Towyn Road, Towyn, Abergele LL22 9HG (Conwy)

Ty Mawr is located close to the many attractions of the North Wales Coast and the Snowdonia National Park. It is an easy walk into the town of Towyn with seaside facilities and Rhyl, some three miles along the coast is a busy resort with holiday amusements on its wide promenade. Ty Mawr is ideal for families seeking plenty of holiday park type activities, with organised children's clubs for 5-11 and 12-16 year olds. The outdoor all-weather multi-sports courts and the playground are excellent facilities for younger family members to let off steam and all are catered for in the entertainment complex which provides mini ten-pin bowling, pool and darts. In the evening there are live spectaculars and discos. The heated indoor pool complete with flume is the venue for organised water-based activities. There are two areas for touring units, one on open meadows with facilities provided in 'portacabin' style units, the other in a more well established area near the playgrounds and entertainment facilities. Both areas are flat with views of open countryside. There is some noise from the road adjacent to the meadow. A large proportion of private and rental caravan holiday homes are neatly sited on well manicured grass pitches.

Facilities
Two well maintained, functional blocks which can be heated serve the main touring area with 'portacabin' style units (unisex) on the open meadows. They are regularly cleaned. Washbasins are open style, preset showers have curtains and hooks, but no seats. Baby rooms. Facilities for disabled visitors (key). Launderette. Ice pack service. Shop. Bar with meals, cafeteria and takeaway. Indoor pool. Multi-sport courts. Excellent play areas and children's clubs. Evening family entertainment. Off site: Bicycle hire 0.5 miles. Golf, riding and boat launching 3 miles. Fishing 6 miles. Beach 0.25 miles.

At a glance

Welcome & Ambience	✓✓✓✓	Location	✓✓✓✓
Quality of Pitches	✓✓✓	Range of Facilities	✓✓✓✓

Directions
Take the A55 in a westerly direction into North Wales and take exit for Abergele. Follow signs for A548 Rhyl towards Towyn. Shortly after Towyn turn right into site. O.S.GR: SH965791

Charges 2005

Per unit incl. electricity	£ 6.00 - £ 30.00
tent	£ 3.00 - £ 27.00
dog	free - £ 3.00

Reservations
Contact site. Tel: 01745 832079.

Open
Easter - 30 October.

UK6690 Bron-Y-Wendon Touring Caravan Park

Wern Road, Llanddulas, Colwyn Bay LL22 8HG (Conwy)

Bron-Y-Wendon is right by the sea between Abergele and Colwyn Bay on the beautiful North Wales coast road. This is a quiet park which, by its own admission, is not really geared up for the family unit. It is manicured to the highest standards and caters for a large number of seasonal caravans on pitches with gravel bases which are kept very tidy. There are a further 65 grass based, and 20 hardstanding touring pitches, all with 16A electricity. All pitches have coastal views and the sea and beach are just a short walk away. There is some road noise and during our visit a small train passed on the track between the park and the sea. Trailer tents are accepted, but not other tents.

Facilities
Two toilet blocks, both with heating, provide excellent facilities. Good facilities for disabled visitors. Laundry. Mobile shop visits daily. Gas supplies. Off site: Llanddulas village with shops and several good pubs is very near. Fishing 1 mile. Golf 4 miles. Riding 6 miles. Bicycle hire 15 miles.

Open
All year.

At a glance

Welcome & Ambience	✓✓✓	Location	✓✓✓
Quality of Pitches	✓✓✓✓	Range of Facilities	✓✓✓

Directions
From A55 Chester - Conwy road turn at Llanddulas interchange (A547), junction 23. Turn right opposite Shell garage and park is 400 yards, signed on coast side of the road. O.S.GR: SH903785.

Charges 2005

Per unit incl. 2 persons, electricity	£ 13.00 - £ 16.00
extra person	£ 2.00
child (2 -12 yrs)	£ 1.00

Reservations
Made with £5 per night deposit. Tel: 01492 512903. Email: bron-y-wendon@northwales-holidays.co.uk

UK7030 Gibson Park Caravan Club Site

High Street, Melrose TD6 9RY (Borders)

This is an ideal transit park, close to the A68, but is also a perfect base for exploring this area or for a trip to Edinburgh (only 35 miles away by car). This small, three acre park has 60 touring pitches plus, unusually, an extra 12 tent pitches (summer only) next to the adjacent rugby pitch. All pitches have electricity (16A) and TV connections, 57 have hardstanding and 10 are serviced with water and drainage. This is Sir Walter Scott country - visit Abbotsford House, his romantic mansion on the banks of the River Tweed. Melrose's Abbey ruins are believed to be the final resting place of Robert The Bruce.

Facilities

First rate toilet facilities include spacious showers, washbasins in cabins, centrally heated. Laundry facilities. Separate room with shower and WC for disabled visitors. Motorcaravan service point. Gas is available. Security barrier (operated by card). Off site: Situated on the edge of the little town of Melrose, a five minute walk, shops, pubs and restaurants are all in easy reach. Play area next to site.

Open

All year.

At a glance

Welcome & Ambience	✓✓✓✓	Location	✓✓✓✓✓
Quality of Pitches	✓✓✓✓✓	Range of Facilities	✓✓✓✓✓

Directions

Turn left off A68 road at roundabout about 2.5 miles past Newton St Boswell on A6091 (Galashiels). In 3.25 miles at roundabout turn right on B6374 to Melrose. Site is on right, just before town centre. O.S.GR: NT545340. GPS: N55:35.881 W02:43.454

Charges 2005

Per adult	£ 3.80 - £ 5.00
child (5-16 yrs)	£ 1.10 - £ 1.60
pitch (non-member)	£ 9.50 - £ 14.50

Reservations

Advised at all times and made with £5 per night deposit. Tel: 01896 822969.

UK6870 Glenearly Caravan Park

Dalbeattie DG5 4NE (Dumfries and Galloway)

Glenearly is a new park (opened in 2000), owned and managed by Mr and Mrs Jardine. Rurally located, it has been tastefully developed from farmland into a touring and mobile home, all year park. There are 39 marked, open pitches, all with 16A electrical connections (and TV), mostly on level grass areas with 14 hardstandings available. Seasonal units use some pitches. Walls and shrubs divide the touring section from the caravan holiday homes (two for rent), with mature trees around the perimeter. There are attractive views over the hills and forest of Barhill and buzzards, yellow wagtails, woodpeckers and goldfinch are some of the birds that can be seen, along with the park's own donkeys, ponies and sheep. The large games room, once an old barn, is excellent - heated and with plenty of chairs and tables for parents to supervise the activities. A super play area suitable for all ages is located behind the touring area. A ten minute stroll brings you into the small town of Dalbeattie. Just 6 miles from the park along the Solway coast is Kippford, a well known sailing centre from which you can walk the Jubilee Path (1 mile) to Rockcliffe. Set in a bay, Rockcliffe has a small sandy beach, a good tea room and gift shop.

Facilities

Situated in the centre of the touring area, the toilets and showers are fitted out to a high standard. Unit for disabled visitors or families. Laundry room with washing machines and dryer and an outside drying area. Large games room. Play area. Off site: Shops, pubs, restaurants, etc. at Dalbeatie. Bicycle hire at Mabie Forest just 3 miles from Dumfries on the A710.

At a glance

Welcome & Ambience	✓✓✓✓✓	Location	✓✓✓✓
Quality of Pitches	✓✓✓✓	Range of Facilities	✓✓✓✓

Directions

From Dumfries take A711 towards Dalbeattie. Six miles beyond Beeswing, after passing sign for Edingham Farm, park is signed with entrance on right (beside a bungalow). O.S.GR: NX834626. GPS: N54:56.692 W03:49.337

Charges 2006

Per unit incl. 2 persons	£ 10.00 - £ 12.00

Reservations

Made with £10 deposit. Tel: 01556 611393.

Open

All year.

UK6950 **Brighouse Bay Holiday Park**

Brighouse Bay, Borgue, Kirkcudbright DG6 4TS (Dumfries and Galloway)

Hidden away within 1,200 exclusive acres, on a quiet, unspoilt peninsula, this spacious family park is only some 200 yards through bluebell woods from a lovely sheltered bay. It has exceptional all weather facilities, as well as golf and pony trekking. Over 90% of the 210 touring caravan pitches have electricity (10/16A), some with hardstanding and some with water, drainage and TV aerial. The three tent areas are on fairly flat, undulating ground and some pitches have electricity. There are 120 self-contained holiday caravans and lodges of which about 30 are let, the rest privately owned. On site leisure facilities include a golf and leisure club with 16.5 m. pool, water features, jacuzzi, steam room, fitness room, games room (all on payment), golf driving range and clubhouse bar and bistro. The 18 hole golf course extends onto the headland with superb views over the Irish Sea to the Isle of Man and Cumbria. A nine-hole family golf course is a popular attraction. Like the park, these facilities are open all year. The BHS approved pony trekking centre (April - Oct) offers treks for complete beginners, slow hacks for the nervous or inexperienced or gallops on the beach for the more experienced. This is a well run park of high standards and a member of the Best of British group.

Facilities

The large, well maintained main toilet block includes 10 unisex cabins with shower, basin and WC, and 12 with washbasin and WC, a launderette and covered dishwashing sinks. A second, excellent block next to the tent areas has en-suite shower rooms (one for disabled people) and bathroom, separate washing cubicles, showers, baby room, laundry sinks, and covered dishwashing sinks. One section is heated in winter. Motorcaravan service point. Gas supplies. Licensed supermarket. Bar, restaurant and takeaway (all year). Golf and Leisure Club with indoor pool (all year). Play area. Riding centre. Mountain bike hire. Quad bikes, boating pond, 10 pin bowling, playgrounds, putting. Nature trails. Coarse fishing ponds plus sea angling and an all-tide slipway for boating enthusiasts. Caravan storage.

At a glance

Welcome & Ambience	✓✓✓✓✓	Location	✓✓✓✓✓
Quality of Pitches	✓✓✓✓✓	Range of Facilities	✓✓✓✓

Directions

In Kirkcudbright turn onto A755 and cross river bridge. In 400 yards turn left onto B727 at international camping sign. Or follow Brighouse Bay signs off A75 just east of Gatehouse of Fleet. O.S.GR: NX630455. GPS: N54:47.250 W04:07.746

Charges 2006

Per unit incl. 2 persons	£ 11.90 - £ 16.75

Contact site for full charges.
Camping Cheques accepted.
Golf packages in low season.

Reservations

Advance booking is advised and made with £30 deposit. Tel: 01557 870267.
Email: info@gillespie-leisure.co.uk

Open

All year.

UK6900 **Seaward Caravan Park**

Dhoon Bay, Kirkcudbright DG6 4TJ (Dumfries and Galloway)

Seaward Caravan Park is little sister to the much larger Brighouse Bay Holiday Park, 3.5 miles away. Set in an idyllic location overlooking the bay, this park is suitable for all units. The terrain is slightly undulating, but most of the numbered pitches are flat and of a good size. There are 35 pitches (18 hardstandings) designated for caravans and motorcaravans, a further 14 for tents, plus 43 caravan holiday homes (6 for hire). Electric hook-ups (16A) are on 32 of the touring pitches and 12 are also serviced with water and drain. This is a quiet park with excellent views ideally suited for that relaxing holiday or for touring the region.

Facilities

The principal, fully equipped toilet block is to the rear of the park. Four rooms with en-suite facilities are also suitable for disabled campers. Well equipped baby room. Laundry and dishwashing room. No motorcaravan service point but the manager can lift a manhole cover to empty waste water tanks. The reception/shop stocks basic provisions, books, gifts, gas, and tourist information. Unsupervised heated outdoor swimming pool with sunbathing area (15/5-15/9). Central play area with bark surface, rocking horse, table tennis and picnic tables. Excellent games room. Pitch and putt. Off site: Beach and sea angling nearby. Riding or bicycle hire 3.5 miles. Kirkcudbright 2.5 miles.

Open

1 March - 31 October.

At a glance

Welcome & Ambience	✓✓✓✓✓	Location	✓✓✓✓
Quality of Pitches	✓✓✓✓	Range of Facilities	✓✓✓✓

Directions

In Kirkcudbright turn onto A755 signed Borgue. Go over river bridge and after 400 yards turn left onto B727 at international camping sign. Proceed with caution when turning right into site entrance as the turn is tight. O.S.GR: NX680510. GPS: N54:49.186 W04:04.927

Charges 2006

Per unit incl. 2 persons	£ 10.25 - £ 14.60
extra adult	£ 1.70
child (4-15 yrs)	£ 1.30
electricity	£ 3.20
awning	£ 1.10 - £ 1.90
dog	£ 1.50

Less 5-10% for bookings (not valid with some other discount schemes).

Reservations

Made with deposit of £30 per week booked, balance on arrival. Tel: 01557 870267.
Email: info@seaward-park.co.uk

UK6880 Sandyhills Bay Leisure Park

Sandyhills, Dalbeattie DG5 4NY (Dumfries and Galloway)

Sandyhills Bay is a small, quiet park beside a sheltered, sandy beach. Reception is on the left through a car park used by visitors either walking the hills or enjoying the beach. Beyond is a large flat camping area, above which, divided by a tree lined hedge, are 60 pitches, half taken by mobile homes situated around the perimeter. The 30 touring pitches, 28 with electricity (16A) are in the centre of the all grassed flat area. This is an excellent family park, with the beach and a play area at the site, whilst up the hill next to the park is an 18 hole golf course where you can enjoy a bar meal in the clubhouse and within walking distance at Barend is an approved riding centre suitable for all the family. There is a well stocked licensed shop and a takeaway with table and chairs outside from where you can enjoy the well kept garden and splendid views across the Solway.

Facilities

The sanitary facilities are of traditional design, situated in one central block to the side of the touring area. Laundry room (tokens from reception). Shop and small takeaway. New adventure play area by the beach. Visitors can also use the facilities at Brighouse Bay, the largest park in the Gillespie Group. Off site: Cliff top walk from Sandyhills to Rockcliffe approx. 10 miles. Pleasant drive to Rockcliffe and Kippford, a well known sailing centre.

Open

Easter - 31 October.

At a glance

Welcome & Ambience	✓✓✓✓	Location	✓✓✓✓
Quality of Pitches	✓✓✓✓	Range of Facilities	✓✓✓✓

Directions

From Dumfries take A710 Solway coast road (approx. 16 miles). Site is on left just after signs for Sandyhills. O.S.GR: NX890549. GPS: N54:52.741 W03:43.862

Charges 2006

Per unit incl. 2 persons	£ 9.75 - £ 14.00
extra adult	£ 1.70
child (4-15 yrs)	£ 1.10
electricity	£ 3.20
awning	£ 1.10 - £ 1.80
dog	£ 1.50

Reservations

Made with £30 deposit. Bookings tel: 01557 870267. Tel: 01387 780257. Email: info@sandyhills-bay.co.uk

UK6945 Barlochan Caravan Park

Palnackie, Castle Douglas DG7 1PF (Dumfries and Galloway)

Barlochan Caravan Park is situated on a hillside overlooking the Urr Estuary on the Solway Coast close to Dalbeattie and Castle Douglas, with the small village of Palnackie a short walk away. Set on terraces, level, marked and numbered, most of the touring and tent pitches are on grass with a limited number of hardstandings available. There are 12 with electricity(16A). In addition, 55 mobile homes (5 for rent) are positioned on terraces high above the touring areas and screened by mature shrubs and trees. Just to the left of the entrance there is minigolf course and an adventure play area. Through the village, there is a fishing lake which is free for visitors to the park. Castle Douglas is just 9 miles away.

Facilities

The toilet block is of traditional design with pine ceiling and tiled walls, kept spotlessly clean. Shower cubicles have recently been made larger suitable for wheelchair entry, but if required there is also a separate unit with WC and basin. Fully equipped laundry with outside drying area. Dishwashing under cover. Reception and well stocked shop. Large games/TV room. Off site: Fishing 400 yds. Bicycle hire 6 miles. Golf 7 miles. Riding 10 miles. Beach 10 miles.

Open

Easter - end October.

At a glance

Welcome & Ambience	✓✓✓✓✓	Location	✓✓✓✓✓
Quality of Pitches	✓✓✓✓	Range of Facilities	✓✓✓✓

Directions

From Dumfries take A711 west to Dalbeattie. Continue through Dalbeattie, bear left at T-junction signed Auchencairn and site is 2 miles on the right. O.S.GR: NX819571. GPS: N54:53.757 W03:50.601

Charges 2006

Per unit incl. 2 persons	£ 9.75 - £ 14.00
extra adult	£ 1.60
child (4-15 yrs)	£ 1.10
electricity	£ 3.20
dog	£ 1.50

Reservations

Bookings tel: 01557 870267. Tel: 01556 600256. Email: info@barlochan.co.uk

UK6910 Hoddom Castle Caravan Park

Hoddom, Lockerbie DG11 1AS (Dumfries and Galloway)

The oldest part of Hoddom Castle itself is a 16th century Borders Pele Tower, or fortified Keep. This was extended to form a residence for a Lancashire cotton magnate, became a youth hostel and was then taken over by the army during WW2. Since then parts have been demolished but the original 'Border Keep' still survives, unfortunately in a semi-derelict state. The site's bar and restaurant have been developed in the courtyard area from the coach houses, and the main ladies' toilet block was the stables. The park is landscaped and spacious, well laid out on mainly sloping ground with many mature and beautiful trees, originally part of an arboretum. The drive to the site is just under a mile long, with a one way system. Many of the 120 numbered pitches have good views of the castle and have gravel hard-standings with grass for awnings, most with electrical connections (16A). In front of the castle are flat fields for tents and caravans not needing electricity. Amenities include a comfortable bar lounge with a family room and TV. The park's nine hole golf course is in an attractive setting alongside the Annan river, where fishing is possible for salmon and trout (tickets available). Coarse fishing is also possible elsewhere on the estate. This is a peaceful base from which to explore historic southwest Scotland.

Facilities

The main toilet block can be heated and is very well appointed, with washbasins in cubicles, 3 en-suite cubicles with WC and basin (one with baby changing facilities) and an en-suite shower unit for disabled visitors. Two further tiled blocks, kept very clean, provide washbasins and WCs only. Each block has dishwashing sinks. Well equipped laundry room at the castle. Motorcaravan service point. Licensed shop at reception (gas available). Bar, restaurant and takeaway (restricted opening outside high season). Games room with pool tables, table tennis and video games. Large, grass play area. Crazy golf. Bicycle hire and mountain bike trail. Fishing. Golf. Guided walks organised in high season. Caravan storage. Off site: Tennis nearby.

At a glance

Welcome & Ambience	✓✓✓✓	Location	✓✓✓✓✓
Quality of Pitches	✓✓✓✓	Range of Facilities	✓✓✓✓✓

Directions

Leave A74M at junction 19 (Ecclefechan) and follow signs to park. Leave A75 at Annan junction (west end of Annan by-pass) and follow signs. O.S.GR: NY155725. GPS: N55:02.482 W003:18.66

Charges 2005

Per unit incl. 2 persons	£ 7.00 - £ 12.00
extra adult	£ 2.00
child (7-16 yrs)	£ 1.00
electricity (10A)	£ 2.50
small tent	£ 6.00 - £ 9.50
dog	£ 1.00

Reservations

Necessary for July/Aug and B.Hs. Any length with deductible £10 deposit. Tel: 01576 300251. Email: hoddomcastle@aol.com

Open

1 April - 30 October.

- Fishing
- Walking
- Golf
- Cycle Hire

ENQUIRIES: The Warden, Hoddom Castle, Hoddom, Lockerbie DG11 1AS
Tel: 01576 300251 • www.hoddomcastle.co.uk • Email: hoddomcastle@aol.com

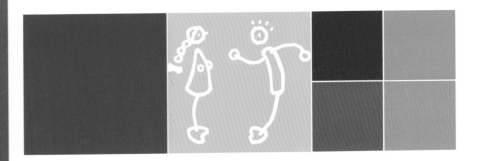

UK6930 **Park of Brandedleys**

Crocketford, Dumfries DG2 8RG (Dumfries and Galloway)

Brandedleys is a first class park providing pitches for some 75 caravans and a limited number of tents, plus 60 self-contained caravan holiday homes in three or four flat and variably sloping fields with tarmac access roads. It has excellent facilities and amenities. Caravan pitches are on lawns or terraced hard-standings, many with a pleasant outlook across a loch. There are 80 electrical connections (10A), 21 pitches with water and drainage, plus some 'premier' pitches with TV connections and a picnic bench. Improvements continue with more serviced pitches and a new fishing lake. A small, heated outdoor swimming pool is open when the weather is suitable and the heated indoor pool adjacent to the bar/restaurant is open all season with changing room (both pools free) and a sauna. The bar and licensed restaurant are open for lunch and dinner with full menus at reasonable prices and a patio area overlooking Auchenreoch Loch. Walks on the open moors or forest and beautiful sandy beaches 12 miles away from this popular, quality park.

Facilities

The main heated toilet block has been extensively modernised with clean, well appointed shower cubicles with toilet and washbasin (just one for men), in addition to the normal provision. Bathroom for disabled visitors. Laundry room, baby and hair care room. Covered dishwashing sinks. A second block of equal size and standard is in the lower field, also with laundry and dishwashing facilities. Bar and restaurant. Takeaway food to order (18.00-21.30 hrs). Swimming pools. All-weather tennis courts, outdoor badminton court. Play area. Games room, pool table and air-hockey table. Putting course and golf driving net. Fishing lake. Off site: Riding 5 miles. Golf 6 miles. Bicycle hire 9 miles. Beach 12 miles.

At a glance

Welcome & Ambience	✓✓✓✓✓	Location	✓✓✓✓✓
Quality of Pitches	✓✓✓✓	Range of Facilities	✓✓✓✓✓

Directions

Park is 9 miles from Dumfries on the south side of the A75 Dumfries - Stranraer road, just west of the village of Crocketford. O.S.GR: NX830725.
GPS: N55:01.966 W03:49.898

Charges 2005

Per unit incl. 2 persons and electricity	£ 12.50 - £ 18.00
family unit (5)	£ 15.50 - £ 21.00
serviced pitch	£ 2.00
awning	£ 2.00
pup tent	£ 3.00

No single sex groups.

Reservations

Advised for peak dates and made with £20 deposit per pitch. Tel: 0845 4561759.
Email: brandedleys@holgates.com

Open

All year.

www.**alanrogers**.com for latest campsite news

UK7020 **Aird Donald Caravan Park**

London Road, Stranraer DG9 8RN (Dumfries and Galloway)

Aird Donald is a good stopping off place when travelling to and from the Irish ferries, but it is also useful for seeing the sights around Stranraer. This tidy park comprises 12 acres surrounded by conifers, flowering trees and shrubs and the 300 yard drive is lit and lined with well trimmed conifers. There are grass areas for caravans or tents and hardstandings with electricity hook-up (these very handy for hardy winter tourers). A small play area caters for young children, but the local leisure centre is only a walk away and provides for swimming, table tennis, gym, etc, and a theatre that hosts everything from country and western to opera. It also has bar facilities. The area has three world famous gardens to visit, numerous golf courses, fishing, riding and watersports.

Facilities

Two toilet blocks, the new block modern and heated. Kept very clean with excellent, tiled facilities, this one is kept locked with a key deposit of £5. There are two types of shower, an electric one which is metered (20p) and two others which are free (strange, because they are all excellent). Washbasins are in vanity units, ladies having one in a cubicle. Unit for visitors with disabilities has a washbasin and WC. The original block is being renovated but is more basic with free showers and open all the time. Dishwashing sinks and a small laundry with sinks, dryer, washing machine, an old fashioned mangle and clothes lines. Motorcaravan services. Play area.

At a glance

Welcome & Ambience	✓✓✓✓✓	Location	✓✓✓✓	
Quality of Pitches	✓✓✓✓	Range of Facilities	✓✓✓✓	

Directions

Enter Stranraer on A75 road. Watch for narrow site entrance on left entering town, opposite school. O.S.GR: NX075605. GPS: N54:54.111 W05:00.373

Charges 2006

Per unit incl. 2 persons	£ 12.00
extra person (over 2 yrs)	£ 1.00
electricity	£ 2.00
No credit cards.	

Reservations

Contact park. Tel: 01776 702025.
Email: enquiries@aird-donald.co.uk

Open

All year.

UK7010 **Culzean Castle Camping & Caravanning Club Site**

Maybole KA19 8JJ (South Ayrshire)

With wonderful views of the Firth of Clyde and over to the Isle of Arran, this quiet Camping and Caravanning Club site is next door to Culzean Castle (pronounced Kullayne). Visitors are given a pass to walk in the grounds (when open) with their 17 miles of footpaths as many times as they wish. The 18th century, cliff top castle is built on the site of a former ancient castle and its armoury exhibition is superb. Besides the woodland walks, deer park and aviary, there are three miles of rocky shore and small sandy beaches. A full programme of events is staged at the castle over the season, including special children's weeks, sheepdog trials, bands, battle re-enactments, ranger walks and craft fairs. The campsite has 90 pitches, some level others slightly sloping, and 60 have electrical hook-ups (10A). A few level pitches are suitable for motorcaravans and 20 pitches have hardstanding. American style motorhomes (more than 27 ft.) must contact the site prior to arrival as large pitches are limited. Should you have your fill of the castle and its grounds, Maybole with shops, etc. is only four miles and the area has a wealth of places to visit.

Facilities

The toilet blocks, kept very clean, can be heated and include some washbasins in cubicles. Unit for disabled visitors has a WC, washbasin and shower - an excellent facility. Dishwashing sinks. Well equipped laundry with clothes lines. Small shop with very basic provisions opens for short periods morning and evening. Adventure playground. Units over 25 ft long only accepted by prior arrangement. Off site: Golf or bicycle hire 4 miles. Fishing 8 miles. Buses pass the gate.

Open

March - November.

At a glance

Welcome & Ambience	✓✓✓✓	Location	✓✓✓✓	
Quality of Pitches	✓✓✓✓	Range of Facilities	✓✓✓✓	

Directions

From Maybole follow signs for Culzean Castle and Country Park, turning in the town on B7023 which runs into the A719. Country Park entrance is clearly signed on right after 3.75 miles; entrance to caravan park is on the right in Country Park drive. O.S.GR: NS247103. GPS: N55:21.207 W04:46.167

Charges 2005

Per adult	£ 4.30 - £ 6.40
child (6-18 yrs)	£ 1.90
non-member pitch fee	£ 5.00
services	£ 2.40

Reservations

Advised for high season and made with deposit; contact site or Central Reservations 0870 243 3331. Tel: 01655 760627.

UK7015 The Ranch Holiday Park

Culzean Road, Maybole KA19 8DU (South Ayrshire)

This holiday park is situated in the Ayrshire countryside, four miles from the small town of Maybole. The Ranch, a Caravan Club Affiliated Site, is managed by the McAuley family who moved here in November 2003. The park is beautifully set out with 55 spacious touring pitches, all with 10-16A electricity connections and including 8 super pitches. Most are on level hardstanding with a few level, all grass pitches arranged open plan facing a huge playing field. There are also 65 caravan holiday homes, 2 for rent. The superb facilities include a private Leisure Centre with an indoor heated pool, sauna, solarium and well equipped gym, complete with changing room, toilets, shower and free hair dryers. To the rear is a small unfenced play park adjacent to the small camping area which has undercover seating for those rainy days. A 'Wee Honesty Shop' offers exchange books and magazines and a kiddies corner for the under 5s. This is an excellent park for relaxing and enjoying the amenities or for touring the area with nearby sandy beaches at Maybole Shore and Croy Bay plus the wonderful freak of nature, where the laws of gravity are turned upside down at the Electric Brae, where you can see water run uphill.

Facilities

The sanitary facilities are away from the touring area and older in style, but kept spotlessly clean. Washbasins in vanity units, four in cubicles with WCs for ladies. Large showers operated individually by gas geysers. Individual unit with WC and basin for disabled visitors. Purpose built wooden building housing well equipped laundry with dishwashing area on the end. No shop on site but reception has a good information area. Off site: Golf courses at Turnberry and fishing at Mochram Loch.

At a glance

Welcome & Ambience	✓✓✓✓	Location	✓✓✓✓
Quality of Pitches	✓✓✓✓	Range of Facilities	✓✓✓✓

Directions

From Maybole turn onto B7023 (signed Culzean Maidens) for 1 mile and site is signed on left.
O.S.GR: NS286102 GPS: N55:21.358 W04:42.368

Charges 2005

Per unit incl. 2 persons	£ 15.60 - £ 19.60
extra person	£ 3.30 - £ 4.80
child	£ 1.10 - £ 1.60

Reservations

Essential at all times. Tel: 01655 882446.

Open

March - October.

UK7000 Strathclyde Country Park Caravan Site

Strathclyde Country Park, 366 Hamilton Road, Motherwell ML1 3ED (North Lanarkshire)

The 1,200 acre Country Park is a large green area less than 15 miles from the centre of Glasgow. Well kept and open to all, it provides nature trails, children's adventure play area, sandy beaches and coarse fishing, with an 18 hole golf course two miles away. In addition there is a large water sports centre offering sailing, water skiing, windsurfing, canoeing, rowing (all with craft for hire), a water bus, a selection of family 'fun boats' and bicycle hire, plus Scotland's own theme park nearby. The touring site, part of the park, is suitable for both overnight or longer stays (max. 14 days) and has 80 numbered pitches for caravans or tents, 70 with electrical connections (10A). Arranged in semicircular groups on flat grass they are served by made-up access roads and the site is well lit. As it is close to the motorway so there may be some traffic noise.

Facilities

Four solidly built toilet blocks make a good provision. Enclosed sinks for dishwashing or food preparation. Laundry in two blocks (irons from reception). Block 4 has facilities for visitors with disabilities, block 3 has a baby changing room. Motorcaravan services. Shop within reception sells basic provisions. Play equipment. Bicycle hire. American motorhomes accepted up to 22 ft. Barrier card and toilet block key £10 deposit. Off site: Bar and restaurant facilities (100 yds) in the Country Park. Fishing 400 yards. Bus 1 mile.

Open

Easter - 18 October.

At a glance

Welcome & Ambience	✓✓✓✓	Location	✓✓✓✓
Quality of Pitches	✓✓✓✓	Range of Facilities	✓✓✓✓

Directions

Take exit 5 from the M74 and follow sign for Strathclyde Country Park. Turn first left for site.
O.S.GR: NS720584. GPS: N55:48.235 W04:02.804

Charges 2005

Per caravan pitch incl. 2 persons	£ 9.60
tent pitch	£ 4.25 - £ 8.20
extra adult	£ 1.15 - £ 8.20
child	£ 0.90
electricity	£ 2.85

No credit cards.

Reservations

Made for any period with deposit of one night's fee. Max. stay 14 nights. Tel: 01698 266155.
Email: strathclydepark@northlan.gov.uk

257

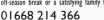
UK7060 Tantallon Caravan Park

Dunbar Road, North Berwick EH39 5NJ (East Lothian)

Tantallon is a large park with views over the Firth of Forth and the Bass Rock, which is a popular venue for bird-watchers with its world famous gannet colony. Tantallon and Dirleton Castles are also nearby. Access to the beach is through the golf course and then down the road or via cliff paths. The park has 147 quite large, grass touring pitches in two lower, more sheltered areas (Law Park), with the rest having good views at the top (Bass Park). Many have some degree of slope. There are 75 electrical connections (15A) and 10 pitches also with water and waste water. Each area has its own sanitary facilities, the top block a little way from the end pitches. About 55 caravan holiday homes for sale or hire are in their own areas. This is a mature, well managed park with good facilities.

Facilities

Bass Park has 8 unisex units with shower, washbasin and toilet. The other areas have open washbasins. Two heated units for disabled visitors. Dishwashing sinks. Good launderette with spin dryer and free iron. Motorcaravan service point. Reception combines with a small shop. Games room with pool table and TV. Internet access. Good playground and better than average putting green. Dogs are only accepted by prior arrangement. Off site: Golf next door, sea fishing, safe sandy beaches in walking distance. Town (with footpath) 1 mile. Riding 5 miles. Bicycle hire 1 mile.

At a glance

Welcome & Ambience	✓✓✓✓✓	Location	✓✓✓✓✓
Quality of Pitches	✓✓✓✓✓	Range of Facilities	✓✓✓✓✓

Directions

Park is beside the A198 just to the east of North Berwick, which lies between Edinburgh and Dunbar. O.S.GR: NT567850. GPS: N56:03.345 W002:41.45

Charges 2005

Per pitch	£ 8.00 - £ 15.00
with electricity	£ 10.00 - £ 17.00
with full services	£ 12.00 - £ 19.00
awning	£ 1.00 - £ 5.00
dog	£ 1.00

Reservations

Advisable in July and August. Tel: 01620 893348. Email: tantallon@meadowhead.co.uk

Open

20 March - 31 October.

UK7050 Edinburgh Caravan Club Site

Marine Drive, Edinburgh EH4 5EN (Edinburgh)

On the northern outskirts and within easy reach of the city of Edinburgh, this large, busy Caravan Club site (open to non-members) provides an ideal base. Buses (numbers 8A and 28A stop just outside the gates) take you right into the centre of the city and within walking distance of many of its attractions. Enter the site through rather grand gates to find reception to the left. There are 147 large flat pitches (103 hardstandings, 12 with water tap and waste water disposal) with electric hook-ups (16A) and TV aerial and provision for 50 tents in a separate field (hook-ups available) with a covered cooking shelter and bicycle stands close by. As the bushes planted around the site mature, there will be shade. The nearest hotel/restaurant is under a mile away.

Facilities

Two heated, well kept toilet blocks provide washbasins in cubicles, hair and hand dryers, an en-suite room for campers with disabilities, plus a baby and toddler room with child-size facilities. Laundries. Drying room. No shop, but milk, bread, and newspapers can be ordered, with ice creams and gas from reception. Fenced play area. Boules. Dog walk in the only natural wood in Edinburgh (part of the site). Off site: Bicycle hire. Health club (with internet access) 400 yds; ask at site for introduction card.

At a glance

Welcome & Ambience	✓✓✓✓✓	Location	✓✓✓✓✓
Quality of Pitches	✓✓✓✓✓	Range of Facilities	✓✓✓✓✓

Directions

From A720 (signed City Bypass North), turn right at Gogar roundabout on A8 and follow camping signs. O.S.GR: NT212768. GPS: N55:58.653 WOO3:15.87

Charges 2005

Per adult	£ 3.80 - £ 5.00
child (5-16 yrs)	£ 1.10 - £ 1.60
pitch (non-member)	£ 9.50 - £ 14.50

Reservations

Made with £5 deposit, balance on arrival. Tel: 0131 312 6874.

Open

All year.

UK6990 Mortonhall Caravan Park

38 Mortonhall Gate, Frogston Road East, Edinburgh EH16 6TJ (Edinburgh City)

The Mortonhall park makes a good base to see the historic city of Edinburgh and buses to the city leave from the park entrance every ten minutes (parking in Edinburgh is not easy). Although only four miles from the city centre, Mortonhall is in quiet mature parkland, in the grounds of Mortonhall mansion, and easy to find with access off the ring road. There is room for 250 units mostly on numbered pitches on a slight slope with nothing to separate them, but marked by jockey wheel points. Over 180 places have electricity (10/16A), several with hardstanding, water and drainage as well, and there are many places for tents. The park is very popular but only part is reserved and tourists arriving early may find space. An attractive courtyard development houses a lounge bar and restaurant, open all year and to all, with good value meals in pleasant surroundings. There are mobile homes (19) and wooden family camping cabins (Wigwams) for rent.

Facilities

Two modern toilet blocks with outside, but covered dishwashing sinks, but the only cabins are in the third excellent facility at the top of the park, which has eight unisex units incorporating shower, washbasin and WC. The courtyard area provides further standard facilities and 'portacabin' type units are added for the high season to serve the large number of tents. Facilities for disabled visitors. Laundry room with washing machines and dryer. Motorcaravan services. Bar/restaurant. Self-service shop. Games and TV rooms. Table tennis. Play area. Internet access. Late arrivals area with hook-ups. Torches useful in early and late season. Security lockers. Off site: Bus from site gate. Golf courses and driving range 2 miles. Riding 2 miles. Bicycle hire 4 miles.

At a glance

Welcome & Ambience	✓✓✓✓✓	Location		✓✓✓✓✓
Quality of Pitches	✓✓✓✓✓	Range of Facilities		✓✓✓✓

Directions

Park is well signed south of the city, 5 minutes from A720 city by-pass. Take the Mortonhall exit from the Straiton junction and follow camping signs. Entrance road is alongside the Klondyke Garden Centre. O.S.GR: NT262686. GPS: N55:54.200 W003:10.80

Charges 2005

Per unit incl. 2 persons and children under 5 yrs	£ 10.00 - £ 16.00
extra person (5 yrs and over)	£ 12.00 - £ 18.00
with water	£ 13.50 - £ 22.00
incl. electricity	£ 12.00 - £ 18.00
awning	£ 2.50 - £ 5.00
dog	£ 1.50

Reservations

Advised for August and made with 1 night's charge plus £1.50 fee. Tel: 0131 664 1533. Email: mortonhall@meadowhead.co.uk

Open

12 March - 4 January.

UK7065 Belhaven Bay Caravan & Camping Park

Belhaven Bay, West Barns, Dunbar EH42 1TU (East Lothian)

Located in the John Muir Country Park, Belhaven Bay Caravan Park is just one mile from the historic town of Dunbar, where the ancient castle ruin stands guard over the town's twin harbours. This is an excellent family park with easy access to the beach and to the cliff top trail which has spectacular views capturing the beauty of the countryside and seascapes. The park's 67 caravan holiday homes (8 for rent) are located quite separately from the touring and tent areas. These are surrounded by mature trees and are arranged in large open bays. There are 27 reasonably level, mostly grass touring pitches with 10A electricity connections. Two separate areas accommodate 25 pitches for tents. There is much to see nearby with Dunbar's Lifeboat and underground museums, golf courses, a local smokery and the Belhaven Brewery. Attractions for children include the John Muir Country Park, Lauderdale Park and a tropical leisure pool. During daytime some train noise may be heard on the park.

Facilities

Facilities are central, but are old, poor and in need of complete refurbishment. Replacement is planned before the 2006 season. The old facilities provide only two showers in each, WCs and open style washbasins with a separate room for the disabled visitors or baby changing. Laundry room. Motorcaravan service point and chemical disposal. No shop but reception sells ice cream and cold drinks together with tourist information and internet connection (metered). Play area and ball game area. Off site: Golf 1 mile. Riding and boat launching 2 miles. Bus stop at entrance.

Open

March - October.

At a glance

Welcome & Ambience	✓✓✓✓	Location		✓✓✓✓
Quality of Pitches	✓✓✓	Range of Facilities		✓✓✓

Directions

From the A1 (north or south) exit at the roundabout west of Dunbar. Park is about 1 mile down the A1087 towards Dunbar. O.S.GR: NT655784. GPS: N55:59.806 W02:32.707

Charges 2005

Per pitch incl. 4 persons	£ 9.00 - £ 14.00
incl. electricity	£ 11.00 - £ 16.00
extra person	£ 1.00
awning	£ 1.50 - £ 2.50
dog	£ 1.00

Reservations

Contact park. Tel: 01368 865956. Email: belhavenbay@meadowhead.co.uk

UK7040 Slatebarns Caravan Park

Slatebarns, Roslin EH25 9PU (Mid Lothian)

Slatebarns is a recently developed, well groomed park, perfectly located for that trip to Edinburgh, a night stop on the way north or for local walks, including the nearby Pentland Hills. It has only 30 pitches, all with electricity hook-ups (10A), some with hardstanding (with grass for awnings) and some on grass (steel awning pegs useful). Buses run from the village (five minutes walk) regularly into Edinburgh (30 minute journey, 6 miles), although they are less frequent in the evening. Slatebarns is a small park with little on site for children or teenagers. Managed under contract for the Caravan Club, non-members are also very welcome. An ideal base to get away from the bustle after a full day in Edinburgh, or equally attractive as a touring base or country hideaway, it can unsurprisingly get busy.

Facilities

Small purpose built toilet block with washbasins in cubicles for ladies and excellent separate provision for disabled visitors. Good launderette. Very practical motorcaravan service point. Gas supplies. Off site: Village shops, pubs and hotels.

Open

Easter - 31 October.

At a glance

Welcome & Ambience	✓✓✓✓✓	Location	✓✓✓✓✓
Quality of Pitches	✓✓✓✓✓	Range of Facilities	✓✓✓✓

Directions

From Straiton junction on A720 (Edinburgh bypass) go south on A701 signed Bilston, Penicuik. At roundabout in Bilston turn left on B7006 signed Roslin. After 1 mile, in Roslin continue over crossroads signed Rosslyn Chapel. Site entrance is immediately past Chapel. O.S.GR: NT275632.
GPS: N55:51.404 W03:09.823

Charges 2005

Per person	£ 3.50 - £ 4.25
child	£ 1.20 - £ 1.50
pitch incl. electricity	£ 10.00 - £ 11.00
No credit cards.	

Reservations

Contact park. Tel: 0131 440 2192.

UK6980 Drum Mohr Caravan Park

Levenhall, Musselburgh EH21 8JS (East Lothian)

This family owned, attractively laid out touring park is on the east side of Edinburgh. It is a secluded, well kept modern park, conveniently situated for visits to Edinburgh, the Lothian and Borders regions. It has been carefully landscaped and there are many attractive plants, flowers and hedging. There are 120 individual pitches, 40 with hardstanding, for touring units of any type, well spaced out on gently sloping grass in groups of 12 or more, marked with white posts. Most have electric hook-ups and 13 are fully serviced with water and waste water connections. Free space is left for play and recreation. Twelve chalets are available to rent. Musselburgh centre is 1.5 miles, Edinburgh 7, with a frequent bus service to the latter. Managed personally by the owner, Mr Melville, this is a well run park and is a member of the Best of British group.

Facilities

The two toilet blocks are clean, attractive, of ample size and can be heated. Free hot water to washbasins (one cabin for men, two for ladies in each block) and to four external washing-up sinks, but hot water is on payment for the showers (outside the cubicle) and laundry sinks. Laundry facilities in each block. Motorcaravan service point. Well stocked, licensed shop (gas available, bread and papers to order). Playground on sand. Excellent dog walk. Security barrier. Caravan storage. Off site: Golf course adjacent.

Open

1 March - 31 October.

At a glance

Welcome & Ambience	✓✓✓✓	Location	✓✓✓✓
Quality of Pitches	✓✓✓✓	Range of Facilities	✓✓✓✓

Directions

From Edinburgh follow A1 signs for Berwick on Tweed for 6-7 miles. Turn off for Wallyford and follow camp and Mining Museum signs. From south follow A1 taking junction after Tranent village (A199 Musselburgh) and follow signs.
O.S.GR: NT371732. GPS: N55:57.002 W003:00.70

Charges 2005

Per unit incl. 2 persons	£ 12.00 - £ 15.00
serviced pitch	£ 15.00 - £ 18.00
awning	£ 2.00
extra person (over 5 yrs)	£ 1.50 - £ 2.00
dog	£ 0.50

Reservations

Made for any length with deposit of one night's charge plus £1 fee. Tel: 0131 665 6867. Email: bookings@drummohr.org

UK7290 Craigtoun Meadows Holiday Park

Mount Melville, St Andrews KY16 8PQ (Fife)

This attractively laid out, quality park has individual pitches and good facilities and although outnumbered by caravan holiday homes, the touring section is an important subsidiary. Its facilities are both well designed and comprehensive. With 67 units taken on gently sloping land, caravans go on individual hardstandings with grass alongside for awnings on most pitches. All caravan pitches are large (130 sq.m) and are equipped with electricity (16A), water and drainage. There are 15 larger 'patio pitches' with summer house, barbecue patio, picnic table and chairs, partially screened. Tents are taken on a grassy meadow at one end, also with electricity available. The 157 caravan holiday homes stand round the outer parts of the site; 27 are owned and let by the park. Buses pass the entrance and Craigtoun park with boating pond and miniature railway, etc. is within walking distance. This is a well run park, two miles from St Andrews with its golf courses and long, sandy beaches, from where there is a picturesque view of St Andrews and its ruined Abbey and Castle.

Facilities

An excellent, de-luxe, centrally heated sanitary building serves the touring area. All washbasins are in cabins and each toilet has its own basin. Showers are unisex, as are two bathrooms, with hand and hair dryers, facilities for disabled people and babies. Dishwashing room. Launderette. Shop and attractive licensed restaurant (both restricted hours in low seasons), also providing takeaway. Games room. Well equipped playground, play field and 8 acres of woodland. Barbecue area. All weather tennis court. Small information room. Dogs and other pets are not accepted. Off site: Golf or bicycle hire 1.5 miles. Fishing 5 miles. Riding 6 miles.

Open

1 March - 31 October.

At a glance

Welcome & Ambience	✓✓✓✓✓	Location	✓✓✓✓✓
Quality of Pitches	✓✓✓✓✓	Range of Facilities	✓✓✓✓

Directions

From M90 junction 8 take A91 to St. Andrews. Just after sign for Guardbridge (to left, A919), turn right at site sign and sign for Strathkinness. Go through village, over crossroads at end of village, left at next crossroads, then 0.75 miles to park.
O.S.GR: NO482151. GPS: N56:19.477 W02:50.247

Charges 2005

Per unit incl. 3-6 persons and electricity	£ 16.50 - £ 23.00
tent incl. 2 persons	£ 15.50 - £ 22.00
backpacker's tent (1 person)	£ 13.50

Only 'breathable' type groundsheets may be used in awnings.

Reservations

Advised for main season; any length with full payment at time of booking. Tel: 01334 475959. Email: craigtoun@aol.com

UK7230 **Trossachs Holiday Park**

Aberfoyle FK8 3SA (Perth and Kinross)

Nestling on the side of a hill, three miles south of Aberfoyle, this is an excellent base for touring this famously beautiful area. Lochs Lomond, Ard, Venachar and others are within easy reach, as are the Queen Elizabeth Forest Park and, of course, the Trossachs. This park specialises in the sale and hire of top class mountain bikes. Very neat and tidy, there are 45 well laid out and marked pitches arranged on terraces with hardstanding. All have electricity and TV connections and most also have water and drainage. There is also a large area for tents. There are trees between the terraces and lovely views across the valley. The adjoining oak and bluebell woods are a haven for wildlife, with wonderful walks. You will receive a warm welcome from Joe and Hazel Norman at this well run, family park. A member of the Best of British group.

Facilities

A modern wooden building houses sanitary facilities providing a satisfactory supply of toilets, showers and washbasins, the ladies' area being rather larger, with two private cabins. Laundry room. Well stocked shop (all season) and bike shop. Games room with TV. Play equipment (on gravel). Off site: Nearby are opportunities for golf, boat launching and fishing (3 miles). A passport scheme arranged with a local leisure centre (10 miles, 8 passes) provides facilities for swimming, sauna, solarium, badminton, tennis, windsurfing, etc.

Open

1 March - 31 October.

At a glance

| Welcome & Ambience | ✓✓✓✓✓ | Location | ✓✓✓✓✓ |
| Quality of Pitches | ✓✓✓✓✓ | Range of Facilities | ✓✓✓✓ |

Directions

Park is 3 miles south of Aberfoyle on the A81 road, well signed. O.S.GR: NS544976. GPS: N56.08.408 W004.21.33

Charges 2005

Per unit incl. 2 persons and electricity	£ 12.00 - £ 16.00
with all services	£ 14.50 - £ 18.00
tent pitch incl. 2 persons	£ 10.00 - £ 14.00
extra adult	£ 2.00

Reservations

Advisable and made for min. 3 days with £25 deposit. Tel: 01877 382614. Email: info@trossachsholidays.co.uk

UK7270 **Auchterarder Caravan Park**

Nether Coul, Auchterarder PH3 1ET (Perth and Kinross)

This is a charming small park, purpose designed and landscaped by the owners Stuart and Susie Robertson. In a sheltered position, it is conveniently situated for exploring central Scotland and the Highlands with many leisure activities close at hand (particularly golf) and within walking distance of the village (1 mile). The 21 original pitches, all with electricity (6A) and hardstanding, 12 with drainage, are well spaced around the edge of the elongated, level grass park. Marked pitches with grass frontage back on to raised banks which are planted with trees. Further pitches have been developed to one side of the site, along with a trout fishing pond (exclusively for campers) and a woodland walk. A tarmac area at the entrance for late arrivals (with electricity) ensures that no one is disturbed. Also at the entrance, a modern pine chalet blending with the environment houses reception and a small library. There is easy access from the nearby A9 road which does create some background road noise, although it is peaceful at night.

Facilities

Toilet facilities (with key system) include controllable, well equipped hot showers. A toilet for disabled people is provided in both the male and female units. Laundry room with sink and washing machine; an iron can be provided. Dishwashing is under cover. Caravan storage. Off site: Village 1 mile. Golf 1 mile. Bicycle hire and riding 6 miles. The historic cities of Perth and Stirling are less than half an hour's drive away.

Open

All year.

At a glance

| Welcome & Ambience | ✓✓✓✓ | Location | ✓✓✓✓ |
| Quality of Pitches | ✓✓✓ | Range of Facilities | ✓✓✓ |

Directions

Park is between the A9 and A824 roads east of Auchterarder village, only 0.5 miles from the main road. It is reached by turning on to the B8062 (Dunning) road from the A824. O.S.GR: NN964138. GPS: N56:18.260 W003:40.57

Charges 2005

Per unit incl. up to 4 adults	£ 11.50
electricity and drainage	£ 1.50 - £ 2.50
extra person (over 5 yrs)	£ 1.00
awning	£ 1.00
No credit cards.	

Reservations

Advisable July/Aug. and made with deposit of one night's charge and booking fee (£1). Bookings held until 5 pm. on day reserved. Tel: 01764 663119. Email: info@prestonpark.co.uk

UK7280 Nether Craig Caravan Park

By Alyth, Blairgowrie PH11 8HN (Perth and Kinross)

Nether Craig is a family run touring park, attractively designed and beautifully landscaped, with views across the Strathmore valley to the long range of the Sidlaw hills. The 40 large pitches are accessed from a circular, gravel road; 26 have hardstanding (for awnings too) and 10A electrical connections. The majority are level and there are 9 large tent pitches on flat grass. There is a personal welcome for all visitors at the attractive wooden chalet beside the entrance (with a slope for wheelchairs) which doubles as reception and shop providing the necessary essentials, gas and tourist information. A one mile circular woodland walk from the park has picnic benches and a leaflet guide is provided. Otherwise you can just enjoy the peace of the Angus Glens by hill walking, birdwatching, fishing or pony trekking. Alyth with its Arthurian connections is only 4 miles away and Glamis Castle, the childhood home of the Queen Mother, is nearby, as is the beautiful Glenshee and Braemar with its castle.

Facilities

The central, purpose built toilet block is modern, well equipped and maintained, and can be heated. Unit for disabled visitors (entry by key). Separate sinks for dishwashing and clothes are in the laundry room (metered hot water), plus a washing machine, dryer and iron, and a rotary clothes line outside. Shop. Play area. Small football field. Bicycle hire. Caravan storage. Off site: Fishing 2 miles. Riding 4 miles. Three golf courses within 4 miles. Boat launching 6 miles.

Open

15 March - November.

At a glance

Welcome & Ambience ✓✓✓✓✓ Location ✓✓✓✓
Quality of Pitches ✓✓✓✓✓ Range of Facilities ✓✓✓

Directions

From A926 Blairgowrie - Kirriemuir road, at roundabout south of Alyth join B954 signed Glenisla. Follow caravan signs for 4 miles and turn right onto unclassified road signed Nether Craig. Park is on left after 0.5 miles. O.S.GR: NO265528. GPS: N56:39.684 W03:11.988

Charges 2005

Per unit incl. 2 persons and electricity	£ 13.50 - £ 15.50
tent per person	£ 4.50
extra person	£ 1.50 - £ 2.50

Reservations

Advisable for main season. Tel: 01575 560204. Email: nethercraig@lineone.net

UK7300 Blair Castle Caravan Park

Blair Atholl, Pitlochry PH18 5SR (Perth and Kinross)

This attractive, well kept park is set in the grounds of Blair Castle, the traditional home of the Dukes of Atholl. The castle is open to the public, its 32 fully furnished rooms showing a picture of Scottish life from the 16th century to the present day, while the beautiful grounds and gardens are free to those staying on site. The caravan park has a wonderful feeling of spaciousness with a large central area left free for children's play or for general use. There is space for 200 touring units with 190 electricity connections (10/16A), 144 hardstandings and 42 fully serviced pitches with water and waste water facilities also. Caravan holiday homes, 78 privately owned and 27 for hire, are in separate areas. The castle grounds provide many walking trails and the village is within walking distance with hotels, shops, a water mill craft centre and folk museum. A quality park, quiet at night and well managed. A member of the Best of British group.

Facilities

The five toilet blocks can be heated and are of excellent quality with very high standards of cleanliness. Large hot showers are free, some also incorporating WC and washbasin, and further cubicles with WC and washbasin. Four blocks have facilities for disabled visitors, two with bath, two with shower, all with WC and washbasins. Baby changing mats. Dishwashing. Motorcaravan service point. A new central development incorporates reception, a shop, games room, laundry and internet gallery. Gas supplies. American motorhomes are accepted (max. 30 ft or 5 tons). Off site: Mountain bike hire, riding, golf and fishing within 1 mile.

At a glance

Welcome & Ambience ✓✓✓✓✓ Location ✓✓✓✓✓
Quality of Pitches ✓✓✓✓✓ Range of Facilities ✓✓✓✓

Directions

From A9 just north of Pitlochry take B8079 into Blair Atholl. Park is in grounds of Blair Castle, well signed. O.S.GR: NN868659. GPS: N56:46.050 W03:50.644

Charges 2006

Per unit incl. 2 persons	£ 11.00 - £ 15.00
tent (no car)	£ 8.00 - £ 11.00
child (5-12 yrs)	£ 0.50
electricity	£ 2.00
dog (max 2)	£ 0.50

Reservations

Made for any length with deposit of 1 night's charge. Tel: 01796 481263. Email: mail@blaircastlecaravanpark.co.uk

Open

1 March - 27 November.

UK7310 **Twenty Shilling Wood Caravan Park**

Comrie PH6 2JY (Perth and Kinross)

Everyone gets a warm welcome from the Lowe family when they arrive at Twenty Shilling Wood. Set amongst 10.5 acres of wooded hillside, this unusual park has a few touring pitches for caravans and motorcaravans (no tents), plus a number of owner occupied caravan holiday homes. However, with terracing and landscaping, not many of these are visible and flowering trees and shrubs help to hide them. The lowest level is the entrance where there is a late arrivals area and visitor car park. You will be escorted to your pitch. There are just 16 level touring pitches on gravel with grass bays between them, all with electricity hook-ups (10A). Television reception is very poor. There are many walks in the area from strenuous Munros to a gentle stroll to the Devil's Cauldron waterfall.

Facilities

The clean and spacious toilet blocks have some washbasins in cubicles for both men and women. Dishwashing area and laundry. No shop but rolls, milk and papers can be ordered at reception. Games room with pool table, table tennis (both free) and lounge area with comfortable seating and well stocked library. Fenced adventure playground for all ages. Entrance barrier (£10 deposit for card). Only two dogs per pitch are accepted. Off site: Buses pass the gate. Comrie is 1 mile where most things can be purchased. Golf or fishing within 1 mile, riding or bicycle hire 6 miles. Glen Turret, Scotland's oldest distillery is at Crieff, 7 miles away, Auchingarrich Wildlife centre is 2.5 miles, there are watersports at Loch Earn, 11 miles.

At a glance

| Welcome & Ambience | ✓✓✓✓✓ | Location | ✓✓✓✓✓ |
| Quality of Pitches | ✓✓✓✓ | Range of Facilities | ✓✓✓✓ |

Directions

Park is on north side of A85 Crieff - Lochearmead road, about 0.75 miles west of B827 junction, 0.5 miles west of Comrie. O.S.GR: NN762222. GPS: N56:22.513 W004:00.39

Charges 2005

Per unit incl. 2 adults, electricity and TV hook-up	£ 14.50
extra person (over 2 yrs)	£ 1.50
awning (rock pegs required)	£ 1.00
dog (max. 2)	free

Reservations

Advised for B.Hs and July/Aug; made with £10 deposit. Tel: 01764 670411. Email: alowe20@aol.com

Open

23 March - 23 October.

UK7220 **The Gart Caravan Park**

Stirling Road, Callander FK17 8LE (Perth and Kinross)

Gart Caravan Park is situated within the Loch Lomond and Trossachs National Park, just a mile from the centre of Callander. Surrounded by mature trees, this attractive, family run park is peaceful and spacious. All is kept in a pristine condition and a very warm welcome awaits on arrival with a superb information pack given to all. The 128 all grass touring pitches are reasonably level, open plan and marked, with electricity (10A), water and drain. Tents or pup tents are not accepted, groundsheets are not permitted. Privately owned caravan holiday homes are located away from the touring section near to the river which runs for 200 m. along the park boundary. This is an area steeped in history with possible excursions including the Rob Roy Visitor Centre, the medieval Castle of Doune, or a sail on the steamship Sir Walter Scott on Loch Katrine. For the more active there are recommended local walks or fishing in the park's private stretch of river. There is some road noise during daytime.

Facilities

Modern heated central facilities are immaculate, kept spotlessly clean with toilets and showers, plus extra areas with showers, baby changing and hair washing basins. Separate facilities for disabled visitors. Fully equipped laundry. Dishwashing under cover. Chemical disposal points. Drive-over motorcaravan service point. Gas sales. No shop on site but a breakfast car arrives at 09.00 with papers and basic provisions. Large adventure play area, part undercover. Separate field for ball games. Fishing (not on Sundays). Max. two dogs permitted. Free fishing (not Sundays). Off site: Golf and bicycle hire 1 mile. Riding 6 miles. Bus 1 mile.

At a glance

| Welcome & Ambience | ✓✓✓✓✓ | Location | ✓✓✓✓ |
| Quality of Pitches | ✓✓✓✓ | Range of Facilities | ✓✓✓✓ |

Directions

From the south take M9. Near Stirling, leave at exit 10 and follow A84 through Doune. Park is on the left, 1 mile before Callander town centre. O.S.GR: NN643070. GPS: N56:14.190 W04:11.346

Charges 2005

Per pitch incl. services	£ 16.00
awning	£ 1.00
Reduced rates for the over 50s.	

Reservations

Made with £16 deposit. Tel: 01877 330002. Email: enquiries@gart-caravan-park.co.uk

Open

1 April - 15 October.

UK7320 **Witches Craig Caravan Park**

Blairlogie, Stirling FK9 5PX (Stirling)

Witches Craig is a neat and tidy park, nestling under the Ochil Hills and the friendly Stephen family take each visitor to their pitch to make sure that they are happy. All 60 pitches have electrical hook-ups (10A) and 14 have hardstanding, 7 of these being large (taking American style motorhomes easily). Reasonably level, the park covers five well maintained acres with the grass beautifully manicured. Seven residential park homes are well kept and surrounded by flowering shrubs. The area has a wealth of historic attractions, starting with the Wallace Monument which practically overlooks the park. Its 220 ft. tower dominates the surrounding area and the climb up its 246 steps gives spectacular views. Stirling is known as the 'Gateway to the Highlands' and its magnificent castle is world renowned. Being by the A91, there is some day-time road noise. Trees have been planted to try to minimise this but the further back onto the park you go, the less the traffic is heard, although the main touring section with the sanitary facilities is at the front.

Facilities

The modern, heated toilet block is well maintained, and includes one cubicle with washbasin and WC each for ladies and men. Free controllable showers. Baby bath and mat. Good unit for disabled campers. Dishwashing sinks. Laundry, with free fridge/freezer facilities. New reception. Bread, milk, drinks and papers are available daily (supermarket 2.5 miles). Large fenced play area. Field for team games. Off site: Riding or bicycle hire 2 miles, fishing 3 miles, golf 1 mile. Buses stop at the park entrance. Within 10 miles there are castles, museums, cathedrals and parks. There are many walks from the site into the Ochil Hills.

At a glance

Welcome & Ambience	✓✓✓✓✓	Location	✓✓✓✓
Quality of Pitches	✓✓✓✓✓	Range of Facilities	✓✓✓✓

Directions

Park is on the A91, 2 miles northeast of Stirling. O.S.GR: NS822968 GPS: N53:08.882 W003:53.92

Charges 2005

Per unit incl. 2 adults	£ 12.00 - £ 13.00
incl. electricity	£ 14.00 - £ 15.00
extra adult	£ 2.00
child (2-13 yrs)	£ 1.00
awning (no groundsheet)	£ 2.00

£5 deposit for key to facilities. No credit cards.

Reservations

Made without deposit. Tel: 01786 474947. Email: info@witchescraig.co.uk

Open

1 April - 31 October.

UK7400 **Lochlands Caravan Park**

Dundee Road, Forfar DD8 1XF (Angus)

Lochlands Caravan Park is situated just off the A90 road, near the town of Forfar. The entrance to the park is past the coffee shop and garden centre following the caravan sign. Mr and Mrs Delft moved to this garden centre and caravan park three years ago and during that time have created an excellent, well maintained park suitable for a night visit or a long stay to visit the east coast towns of Arbroath and Montrose. Attached to the large shop, which has various gifts for home and garden, there is a most unusual and attractive coffee shop which was originally a horse mill used in the 1800s. Homemade food is served at reasonable prices and for the gardening enthusiasts – a show of camellias during March and April. The park is level with 40 marked pitches, several with hardstanding and all with 10A electricity. Dividing the park is a mature hedge with a large grass area which could be used for recreation or camping and there is a well equipped play area.

Facilities

Toilets and showers are in two 'portacabin' style buildings near the entrance but are excellent and spotlessly clean. Dishwashing area divides units. No laundry. Shop and coffee shop/café (Thursday, Friday and Saturday, all year). Play area. Off site: Fishing 5 miles. Golf 3 miles. Riding 10 miles.

Open

All year.

At a glance

Welcome & Ambience	✓✓✓✓	Location	✓✓✓✓
Quality of Pitches	✓✓✓✓	Range of Facilities	✓✓✓✓

Directions

From Dundee take A90 north for 7 miles, turning right at Forfar sign (A932). Site is immediately on right at rear of garden centre. O.S.GR: NO444478. GPS: N56:37.148 W02:54.069

Charges 2005

Per adult	£ 2.00
child (5-16 yrs)	£ 1.25
pitch incl. 2 people	£ 8.00 - £ 11.00
with electricity	£ 11.00 - £ 14.25

Reservations

Made with £10 deposit. Tel: 01307 463621. Email: vandelft@btinternet.com

UK7240 **Lomond Woods Holiday Park**

Tullichewan, Old Luss Road, Balloch G83 8QP (West Dunbartonshire)

A series of improvements over the last few years has made this one of the top parks in Scotland. Almost, but not quite, on the banks of Loch Lomond, this landscaped, well planned park is suitable for both transit or longer stays. Formerly known as Tullichewan Holiday Park, it takes 120 touring units on well spaced, numbered pitches on flat or gently sloping grass. Most have hardstanding, 106 have electrical connections (10A) and 8 have water and waste water too. Watersport activities and boat trips are possible on Loch Lomond, with a visitor attraction, 'Lomond Shores' opened nearby. This is a well run park, open all year, with very helpful wardens and reception staff.

Facilities

The single large heated, well kept toilet block includes some showers with WCs, baths for ladies, a shower room for disabled visitors and two baby baths. Covered dishwashing sinks. Launderette. Motorcaravan service points. Games room with TV, table tennis and pool table. Playground. Caravan storage. American motorhomes accepted with prior notice. Off site: Fishing and boat launching 400 yards. Riding 4 miles. Golf 5 miles. Rail and road connections to Glasgow. Restaurants, bar meals and buses in Balloch (5 minutes).

Open

All year.

At a glance

Welcome & Ambience	✓✓✓✓✓	Location	✓✓✓✓✓
Quality of Pitches	✓✓✓✓✓	Range of Facilities	✓✓✓✓✓

Directions

Turn off A82 road 17 miles northwest of Glasgow on A811 Stirling road. Site is in Balloch at southern end of Loch Lomond and is well signed.
O.S.GR: NS389816. GPS: N56.00.093 W04.35.534

Charges 2005

Per unit incl. up to 2 persons	
and electricity	£ 15.00 - £ 20.00
incl. mains services and awning	£ 17.00 - £ 22.00
extra person	£ 2.00
awning	£ 2.00
dog	£ 0.50

Reservations

Made for any length with deposit of first night's charge and £2 fee. Tel: 01389 755000.
Email: lomondwoods@holiday-parks.co.uk

UK7260 **Ardgartan Forestry Commission Campsite**

Ardgartan, Arrochar G83 7AR (Argyll and Bute)

Ardgartan is a rugged Forestry Commission site in the Argyll Forest Park. Splendidly situated with mountains all around and lovely views of Loch Long, there are lots of opportunities for sightseeing and activity. At the northern end of the Cowal Peninsula, the site is on a promontory on the shores of Loch Long, with good sea fishing and facilities for launching small boats. The 70 touring pitches are in sections which are well divided by grass giving an uncrowded air. Most with hardstanding and marked by numbered posts, they are accessed from hard surfaced roads and 54 have electrical hook-ups. There are additional grass areas for tents. Midges can be a problem in this area of Scotland. Walking and climbing, as well as sea and river fishing (permits obtainable locally), are all possible nearby. The site gate is locked 22.00 - 07.30.

Facilities

The main toilet block is opposite the reception and shop. It is a basic, but clean provision with facilities for disabled visitors and a launderette. These facilities may be quite stretched when the park is busy. Play equipment (bark surfaces). Raised barbecues are allowed. Off site: Arrochar village (2 miles) has fuel, general stores and a restaurant.

Open

21 March - 24 October.

At a glance

Welcome & Ambience	✓✓✓	Location	✓✓✓✓
Quality of Pitches	✓✓✓✓	Range of Facilities	✓✓✓

Directions

From A82 Glasgow - Crianlarich road take A83 at Tarbet signed Arrochar and Cambletown. Site is 2 miles past Arrochar, the entrance on a bend.
O.S.GR: NN275030. GPS: N56:11.327 W004:46.90

Charges 2005

Per unit incl. 2 persons	£ 7.40 - £ 10.50

Less 20% all year for disabled guests and outside 22/7-30/8 for senior citizens.

Reservations

Necessary for B.Hs and peak times (min. 3 nights with £30 deposit); contact site. Brochure requests: Forest Holidays, Forestry Commission, 231 Corstorphine Road, Edinburgh EH12 7AT. Tel: (0131) 314 6505. Site tel: 01301 702293.
Email: fe.holidays@forestry.gsi.gov.uk

UK7790 Invercoe Caravan & Camping Park

Invercoe, Glencoe PH49 4HP (Argyll and Bute)

On the edge of Loch Leven, surrounded by mountains and forest, Iain and Lynn Brown are continually developing this attractively located park in its magnificent historical setting. It provides 60 pitches for caravans, motorcaravans or tents on level grass with gravel access roads (some hardstandings). You choose your own numbered pitch, those at the loch side being very popular. The only rules imposed are necessary for safety because the owners prefer their guests to feel free and enjoy themselves. There is much to do for the active visitor with hill walking, climbing, boating, pony riding and sea loch or fresh water fishing in this area of outstanding natural beauty. This is a park you will want to return to again and again.

Facilities

The well refurbished toilet block can be heated. Dishwashing under cover, excellent laundry facilities with a drying room. New large under-cover eating area. Motorcaravan service point comprising multi-drainage point, fresh water, dustbins, and chemical disposal point. Shop (Easter - end Sept). Play area with swings. Fishing. Off site: The village with pub and restaurant is within walking distance. Visitor's Centre at Glencoe 2 miles. Golf 3 miles. Bicycle hire 2 miles.

Open

All year excl. November.

At a glance

Welcome & Ambience	√√√√√	Location	√√√√√
Quality of Pitches	√√√√	Range of Facilities	√√√

Directions

Follow A82 Crianlarich - Fort William road to Glencoe village and turn onto the B863; park is 0.5 miles along, well signed. O.S.GR: NN098594.
GPS: N56:41.194 W05.06.359

Charges 2005

Per unit incl. 2 persons and electricity	£ 15.00
extra adult	£ 2.00
child (3-15 yrs)	£ 1.00
awning	£ 2.00
Senior citizens less £1 per person outside July/Aug.	

Reservations

Advised for electricity for peak season; made with £17 deposit and £3 fee. Tel: 01855 811210. Email: invercoe@sol.co.uk

UK7800 Resipole Farm Caravan & Camping Park

Loch Sunart, Acharacle PH36 4HX (Highland)

This quiet, open park is marvellously set on the banks of Loch Sunart, 8 miles from Strontian, on the Ardnamurchan peninsula. It is a must for anyone seeking peace and tranquillity and really worth the journey. With views across the water and regularly visited by wild deer, Resipole Farm offers a good base for exploring the whole of this scenic area or, more locally, for fishing, boating (launching from the site's own slipway) and walking in the unspoilt countryside. There are 60 touring pitches here, more than half with hardstanding and electric hook-ups (10/16A), and 4 with all services. Tents are sited by the hedges. This is a good location for day trips to Mull via the Lochaline ferry.

Facilities

The central, modern sanitary block can be heated and is kept very clean. Good dishwashing facilities. Excellent provision for visitors with disabilities. Laundry facilities. Adjoining the farmhouse is a well equipped bar and restaurant offering reasonably priced home made food in the evenings (vegetarians catered for). Caravan storage. Art gallery and studios. Off site: Riding 5 miles.

Open

1 April - 31 October.

At a glance

Welcome & Ambience	√√√√√	Location	√√√√√
Quality of Pitches	√√√√√	Range of Facilities	√√√√

Directions

From A82 Fort William road, take the Corran ferry located 5 miles north of Ballachulish and 8 miles south of Fort William. On leaving ferry, turn south along the A861. Park is on the north bank of Loch Sunart, 8 miles west of Strontian. The road is single track for 8 miles approaching Resipole and care is needed, but it is well worth it. O.S.GR: NM676740.
GPS: N56:42.656 W05.43.213

Charges 2005

Per unit incl. 2 persons	£ 10.00 - £ 12.50
extra adult	£ 3.00
child (5-16 yrs)	£ 1.00
serviced pitch incl. electricity (10A)	£ 2.00
backpacking or cyclist's tent	£ 7.50 - £ 8.00

Reservations

Advisable for hook-ups and made for any period with one night's fee. Tel: 01967 431235. Email: info@resipole.co.uk

UK7810 Oban Camping & Caravanning Club Site

Barcaldine, By Connel PA37 1SG (Argyll and Bute)

Owned by the Camping and Caravanning Club, this site at Barcaldine, 12 miles north of Oban, is a small, intimate site taking 75 units. Arranged within the old walled garden of Barcaldine House, the walls give it some protection from the wind and make it quite a sun trap. There are 23 level, fairly small pitches with hardstanding and 52 electrical hook-ups (16A). Being a small site, it has a very cosy feel to it, due no doubt to the friendly welcome new arrivals receive. Through the garden gate, one is immediately in the Barcaldine forest with its miles of forest tracks, absolutely perfect for both dog walking and mountain biking. Unusually for a club site there is a lounge bar selling very reasonably priced meals most evenings. This is a very comfortable area, only open until 10.30 pm. (no children after 8 pm) with bar meals served 6-8 pm. The loch across the road is handy for sea fishing and a 20 minute walk takes you to a freshwater lake for fishing.

Facilities

The central toilet block can be heated and is kept very clean with free hot showers, hair dryers and plenty of washbasins and WCs. Excellent unit for disabled visitors. Laundry. Motorcaravan service point. Small shop open a few hours each day for basic provisions and gas. Bar serving bar meals. Small play area with effective safety base. Off site: Sea Life Centre 2 miles. A not too frequent bus passes the gate.

Open

April - end October.

At a glance

Welcome & Ambience	✓✓✓✓	Location	✓✓✓✓
Quality of Pitches	✓✓✓✓	Range of Facilities	✓✓✓✓

Directions

Entrance is off the A828 road on south side of Loch Creran, 6 miles north of Connel Bridge. O.S.GR: NM966420. GPS: N56.31.590 W05.18.596

Charges 2005

Per adult	£ 3.70 - £ 5.15
child (6-18 yrs)	£ 1.65
non-member pitch fee	£ 4.60

Reservations

Necessary for high season; contact site or Central Reservations 0870 243 3331. Tel: 01631 720348.

UK7860 Glendaruel Caravan Park

Glendaruel PA22 3AB (Argyll and Bute)

Glendaruel is in South Argyll, in the area of Scotland bounded by the Kyles of Bute and Loch Fyne, yet is less than two hours by road from Glasgow and serviced by ferries from Gourock and the Isle of Bute. There is also a service between Tarbert and Portavadie. Set in the peaceful wooded gardens of the former Glendaruel House in a secluded glen surrounded by the Cowal hills, it makes an ideal centre for touring this beautiful area. The park takes 35 units on numbered hardstandings with electricity connections (10A), plus 15 tents, on flat oval meadows bordered by over 50 different varieties of mature trees. In a separate area are 28 privately owned holiday homes and 2 for rent. The converted stables of the original house provide an attractive little shop selling basics, local produce, venison, salmon, wines (some Scottish!) and tourist gifts. Glendaruel is a park for families with young children or for older couples to relax and to enjoy the beautiful views across the Sound of Bute from Tighnabruaich or the botanical gardens which flourish in the climate. The Craig family provide a warm welcome and will advise you where to eat and what to do - they are justifiably proud of their park and its beautiful environment. A member of the Best of British group.

Facilities

The toilet block is ageing but it is kept very neat and tidy and can be heated. Washing machine and dryer. A covered area has picnic tables for use in bad weather and dishwashing sinks. Shop (hours may be limited in low season). Gas available. Games room with pool table, table tennis and video games. Behind the laundry is a children's play centre for under 12s and additional play field. Fishing. Torches advised. Off site: Sea fishing and boat slipway 5 miles, adventure centre (assault courses, abseiling and rafting) and sailing school close. Golf 12 miles.

Open

28 March - 26 October.

At a glance

Welcome & Ambience	✓✓✓✓	Location	✓✓✓✓
Quality of Pitches	✓✓✓✓	Range of Facilities	✓✓✓

Directions

Entrance is off A886 road 13 miles south of Strachur. Alternatively there are two ferry services from Gourock to Dunoon, then on B836 which joins the A886 about 4 miles south of the park - this route not recommended for touring caravans. Note: the park has discount arrangements with Western Ferries so contact the park before making arrangements (allow 7 days for postage of tickets). O.S.GR: NS001865. GPS: N56:02.038 W005:12.77

Charges 2005

Per unit incl. 2 persons, electricity	£ 12.00 - £ 16.00
tent (person, no car)	£ 6.00
extra adult	£ 2.00
child (3-15 yrs)	£ 1.60
dog (max. 2)	free
Special weekly rates and senior citizen discount outside July/Aug.	

Reservations

Any length, with £10 deposit and £2 fee. Tel: 01369 820267. Email: mail@glendaruelcaravanpark.co.uk

UK7840 **North Ledaig Caravan Park**

Connel, Oban PA37 1RU (Argyll and Bute)

The views over the Sound of Mull here are magnificent and Mr and Mrs Weir have tried to ensure good views by staggering the pitches and not planting many trees. The park provides 260 pitches for caravans, motorcaravans and trailer tents only, all with electricity (10A) and 228 with hardstanding. A dog walk follows the disused railway track that runs through the park. An award winning 30 acre nature reserve with ponds and walks (strictly no dogs) to attract wildlife has been developed on land across the road. Being well organised and run, this is a quiet park which makes a good base for exploring the area, visiting the islands from Oban or simply relaxing on the shores of the loch. Fishing and sailing are possible from the site (there is a slipway for small boats), hill walking or pony trekking are close. A member of the Caravan Club's 'managed under contract' scheme, non-members are also very welcome.

Facilities

The main sanitary block is central - a bit of a walk depending on your pitch but a new, semi-underground block is planned. The current amenities are excellent and include full facilities for disabled visitors and for babies (access by key). Washbasins in cabins for ladies (one for men). Well equipped laundry with irons for hire, and dishwashing. Motorcaravan service area. Further, well renovated sanitary facilities are behind the reception block. Well stocked, licensed shop. Play area. Caravan storage. Off site: Bicycle hire and golf 6 km. Buses pass the gate five or six times a day.

At a glance

Welcome & Ambience	✓✓✓✓	Location	✓✓✓✓✓
Quality of Pitches	✓✓✓✓✓	Range of Facilities	✓✓✓✓

Directions

Park is about 1 mile north of Connel Bridge, on the A828 Oban - Fort William road, 7 miles from Oban. O.S.GR: NM913456. GPS: N56.28.654 W05.23.925

Charges 2005

Per adult	£ 3.30 - £ 4.80
child (5-17 yrs)	£ 1.10 - £ 1.60
pitch incl. electricity	£ 4.00 - £ 7.00

Reservations

Any length, with £10 deposit incl. £1 non-returnable fee. Tel: 01631 710291.

Open

27 March - 31 October.

UK7530 **Aden Country Park Caravan Park**

Station Road, Mintlaw AB42 8FQ (Aberdeenshire)

Aden Country Park is owned by the local authority and is open to the public offering several attractions for visitors including an Agricultural Heritage Centre, Wildlife Centre, Nature Trail and restaurant, as well as open and woodland areas with a lake, for walking and recreation. The caravan and camping site is on one side of the park. Beautifully landscaped and well laid out with trees, bushes and hedges, it is kept very neat and tidy. It provides 48 numbered pitches for touring units, with varying degrees of slope (some level) and all with electrical hook-ups (16A), plus an area for tents. There are also 12 caravan holiday homes in a row on the left as you enter. The park is in a most attractive area and one could spend plenty of time enjoying all it has to offer.

Facilities

The modern, fully tiled toilet block, with good facilities for disabled visitors, was very clean when we visited. It can be heated and provides free, pre-set hot showers, hairdryer for ladies, and a baby bath, but no private cabins. Dishwashing and laundry facilities are together, with washing machines, tumble and spin dryers and an iron - all metered. Small shop (sweets and ice-creams) in the reception area. Restaurant in the Heritage Centre. Two games areas and items of play equipment (with safety surfaces). Large dog exercise area. Off site: Mintlaw half a mile for shopping. Fishing 1 mile. Riding 2 miles.

At a glance

Welcome & Ambience	✓✓✓✓	Location	✓✓✓✓
Quality of Pitches	✓✓✓✓	Range of Facilities	✓✓✓✓

Directions

Approaching Mintlaw from the west on A950 road, park is shortly after sign for Mintlaw station. From the east, go to the western outskirts of the village and entrance is on left - 'Aden Country Park and Farm Heritage Centre'. O.S.GR: NJ985484. GPS: N57:31.485 W02:01.567

Charges 2005

Per unit incl. electricity	£ 12.40 - £ 13.90
small tent per person	£ 3.70 - £ 4.70
awning	£ 1.05

Reservations

Advisable for weekends; write for details. Tel: 01771 623460.

Open

Easter - 25 October.

UK7550 **Huntly Castle Caravan Park**

The Meadow, Huntly AB54 4UJ (Aberdeenshire)

Huntly Caravan Park was opened in '95 and its hard-working owners, the Ballantynes, are justly proud of their neat, well landscaped 15 acre site that is managed under contract for the Caravan Club (non-members welcome). The 76 level grass and 41 hardstanding touring pitches are separated and numbered, with everyone shown to their pitch. Arranged in three bays with banks of heathers and flowering shrubs separating them, 66 pitches have electric hook-ups (16A) and 15 are fully serviced with water and waste water. Two bays have central play areas and all three have easy access to a toilet block, as has the camping area. Campers are provided with a covered cooking shelter (with work tops) should the weather turn inclement. The park also has 33 privately owned caravan holiday homes (3 to hire). An Activity Centre near the entrance contains two indoor safe play areas (one for up to 2 yrs old, the other up to height 1.37 metres). There are snooker and pool tables, table tennis, badminton and short tennis. The area abounds with things to do, from forest trails to walk or cycle, a falconry centre, malt whisky distilleries and an all year Nordic ski track. A member of the Best of British group.

Facilities

The three heated toilet blocks are well designed and maintained, with washbasins (in cubicles for ladies) and large, free showers. Each block also has a family shower room (even larger), dishwashing sinks with free hot water and a good room for disabled visitors. Well equipped laundry room. No shop but milk and papers may be ordered at reception. Activity centre (there is a charge and the facilities are also open to the public, with tea, coffee and ices sold; open weekends and all local school holidays). Off site: The town of Huntly is only 10 minutes walk with shops and pubs and castle. Fishing, golf or bicycle hire within 1 mile, riding 5 miles

At a glance

Welcome & Ambience ✓✓✓✓✓   Location ✓✓✓✓✓
Quality of Pitches ✓✓✓✓✓   Range of Facilities ✓✓✓✓

Directions

Site is well signed from A96 Keith - Aberdeen road. O.S.GR: NJ526402. GPS: N57:27.123 W02:47.496

Charges 2006

Per unit incl. 2 persons, electricity	£ 13.50 - £ 17.50
extra adult	£ 3.00
child (5-16 yrs)	£ 1.50 - £ 1.90
awning	£ 1.00 - £ 1.75
pup tent	£ 2.00

Reservations

Contact park. Tel: 01466 794999.
Email: enquiries@huntlycastle.co.uk

Open

31 March - 29 October.

UK7670 **Grantown-on-Spey Caravan Park**

Seafield Avenue, Grantown-on-Spey PH26 3JQ (Highland)

John Fleming takes care of this excellent park which is managed under contract for the Caravan Club (non-members are welcome). Peacefully situated on the outskirts of the town, with views of the mountains in the distance, the park consists of well-tended gravel (raked so that it is perfect for each occupant) and grass pitches. Trees and flowers are a feature of this landscaped location. There are 100 pitches for caravans or motorcaravans, of which 14 offer fresh and waste water facilities and 16 have individual fresh water taps. A further 20 pitches are used for seasonal occupation, and there is space for 50 or more tents. More than 80 pitches have 10A electrical hook-ups. The wardens escort visitors to their pitch and will help to site caravans if necessary. Caravan holiday homes are located in a separate area of the park. Grantown is a pleasant touring base for the Cairngorms and for the Malt Whisky Trail. A peaceful park with a warden on site at all times.

Facilities

A new toilet an shower block was completed in 2004, complete with laundry and drying room. A further block provides good, clean toilet facilities, with new wash-cabins for ladies. Dishwashing sinks under cover. Laundry room. New motorcaravan service point planned. No shop because the town is just a short distance, however gas cylinders, ice creams, cold drinks and camping accessories can be purchased at reception. Games room with table tennis and pool table. New touring and motorcaravan secure storage. Off site: Fishing, golf and mountain bike hire within 1 mile. Riding 3 miles.

At a glance

Welcome & Ambience ✓✓✓✓✓   Location ✓✓✓✓
Quality of Pitches ✓✓✓✓   Range of Facilities ✓✓✓

Directions

Park is signed from the town centre.
O.S.GR: NJ028283. GPS: N57.20.088 W03.37.117

Charges 2005

Per pitch incl. 2 persons and 10A electricity	£ 14.00 - £ 17.00
small 2-man tent	£ 9.00 - £ 12.50
extra person	£ 1.50 - £ 2.50

Reservations

Advised for peak periods and made with £10 deposit. Tel: 01479 872474.
Email: team@caravanscotland.com

Open

28 March - 31 October.

UK7540 Aberlour Gardens Caravan & Camping Park

Aberlour-on-Spey AB38 9LD (Moray)

This pleasant park is within the large walled garden of the Aberlour Estate on Speyside. Mr and Mrs Moss, the owners, have made many improvements to the sheltered, five acre, family run park which provides a very natural setting amidst spruce and Scots pine. Of the 64 level pitches, 35 are for touring units leaving the remainder for holiday homes (1 for rent) and seasonal units. All pitches have electrical connections (10A) and 9 are 'all-weather' pitches. This is an ideal area for walking, birdwatching, salmon fishing and pony trekking or for following the only 'Malt Whisky Trail' in the world, while Aberlour has a fascinating old village shop - a 'time capsule'.

Facilities
The toilet block can be heated and has four large unisex showers on payment and facilities for visitors with disabilities (can be used as family or baby changing room). Laundry facilities. Motorcaravan service point. Small licensed shop stocking basics and with an information area. Play area. Caravan storage. Off site: Fishing 1 or 5 miles. Golf 4 miles. Riding 0.5 miles. Swimming and bicycle hire 1 mile.

Open
1 April - 31 October.

At a glance
Welcome & Ambience	✓✓✓✓✓	Location	✓✓✓✓✓
Quality of Pitches	✓✓✓✓✓	Range of Facilities	✓✓✓

Directions
Turn off A95 midway between Aberlour and Craigellachie onto unclassified road and site is signed in 500 yds. Vehicles over 10'6" high should use A941 Dufftown road (site signed). O.S.GR: NJ282432. GPS: N57:28.491 W03:11.916

Charges 2005
Per caravan, motorcaravan, trailer tent incl. 2 persons	£ 11.50 - £ 14.50
tent incl. 2 persons	£ 7.50 - £ 9.00
extra person	£ 2.00
child (under 5 yrs)	free
backpacker and tent (per person)	£ 5.00 - £ 6.00

Reservations
Advised for July/Aug; made with deposit (1 nights fee). Tel: 01340 871586. Email: Aberlourgardens@aol.com

UK7680 Forestry Commission – Glenmore Caravan & Camping Site

Aviemore PH22 1QU (Highland)

The site managers here have made tremendous improvements to this site and the opening of new toilet and shower blocks in July 2005 has greatly improved the facilities. The Glenmore Forest Park lies close to the sandy shore of Loch Morlich amidst conifer woods and surrounded on three sides by the impressive Cairngorm mountains. It is conveniently situated for a range of activities, including skiing (extensive lift system), orienteering, hill and mountain walking (way-marked walks), fishing (trout and pike) and non-motorized watersports on the Loch. The campsite itself is attractively laid out in a fairly informal style in several adjoining areas connected by narrow part gravel, part tarmac roads, with access to the lochside. One of these areas, the Pinewood Area, is very popular and has 32 hardstandings (some distance from the toilet block). Of the 220 marked pitches on fairly level, firm grass, 137 have electricity (10A). This site with something for everyone would be great for family holidays.

Facilities
New toilet and shower blocks. Next to the site is a range of amenities including a well stocked shop (open all year), a café serving a variety of meals and snacks, and a Forestry Commission visitor centre and souvenir shop. Barbecues are not permitted in dry weather. Off site: The Aviemore centre with a wide range of indoor and outdoor recreations 7 miles. Several golf courses within 15 miles. Fishing and boat trips.

Open
All year excl. 1 November - 19 December.

At a glance
Welcome & Ambience	✓✓✓✓✓	Location	✓✓✓✓
Quality of Pitches	✓✓✓✓	Range of Facilities	✓✓✓

Directions
Immediately south of Aviemore on B9152 (not A9 bypass) take B970 then follow sign for Cairngorm and Loch Morlich. Site entrance is on right past the loch. O.S.GR: NH976097. GPS: N57:10.022 W03:41.683

Charges 2005
Per unit incl. up to 4 persons	£ 8.20 - £ 12.90
extra person (over 5 yrs)	£ 2.00
electricity	£ 2.60
'select' pitch incl. electricity	£ 10.80 - £ 15.50
extra car, trailer or child's tent	£ 3.50

Less 20% all year for disabled guests and outside 7/7-28/8 for senior citizens.

Reservations
Made with £30 deposit (min. 2 days or 3 at B.Hs). Contact site when open, otherwise Forest Holidays, Forestry Commission, 231 Corstorphine Road, Edinburgh EH12 7AT. Tel: 0131 314 6505. Tel: 01479 861271. Email: info@forestholidays.co.uk

UK7690 **Torvean Caravan Park**

Glenurquhart Road, Inverness IV3 6JL (Highland)

Torvean is a small and neat, select touring park for caravans and motorhomes only. It is on the outskirts of Inverness beside the Caledonian Canal and is within easy reach of the town's amenities which include an ice rink, theatre and leisure sports centre. Excursions to the coast and Highlands, including Loch Ness, are possible in several directions. The pitches on level grass are clearly marked with a tarmac access road and street lighting giving a very neat appearance. There are 47 touring pitches (27 with 10A electricity connections, 18 are fully serviced with fresh water tap, waste water disposal and electricity).

Facilities

Two heated toilet blocks are of good quality - ladies have two cubicles with washbasin and toilet and a hair washing cubicle. Controllable hot showers on payment. Suite for disabled people with toilet and shower. Launderette. Motorcaravan service point. Gas available. Play area. Only one dog per unit is accepted. Off site: Golf adjacent, bicycle hire or fishing 3 miles.

Open

Easter - end-October.

At a glance

| Welcome & Ambience | ✓✓✓✓ | Location | ✓✓✓✓ |
| Quality of Pitches | ✓✓✓✓ | Range of Facilities | ✓✓✓ |

Directions

Park is off the main A82 on the southwest outskirts of the town by the Tomnahurich Canal Bridge. O.S.GR: NH638438. GPS: N57:27.924 W04:14.731

Charges guide

Per unit incl. 2 adults	£ 9.00 - £ 13.00
extra adult	£ 2.00
child (under 16 yrs)	£ 1.00
electricity	£ 2.50

No credit cards.

Reservations

Necessary for July/Aug. and made with first night's charge and £1 fee. Tel: 01463 220582.

UK7700 **Pitgrudy Caravan Park**

Poles Road, Dornoch IV25 3HY (Highland)

In a rural situation, Pitgrudy has superb views over the Dornoch Firth and the surrounding Ross-shire hills. There are 40 touring pitches, mostly on slightly sloping grass and with electricity (10A). A few have hardstanding (unfortunately still on a slope) and six are fully serviced. Located at the top of the park are 35 caravan holiday homes, of which 25 are privately owned. The whole park is on immaculately tended grass with tarmac roads. The pleasant little town of Dornoch is less than a mile away with restaurants, shops, plus the cathedral. A member of the Best of British group.

Facilities

Sanitary facilities are in a modern, superior 'portacabin' style unit which is very clean and well equipped. Laundry with washing machine, dryer and iron. Gas supplies. Off site: Safe sandy beach 1 mile. Good area for walking and golf (7 courses within 15 miles of the park). Fishing 1 mile, bicycle hire or boat launching 3 miles, riding 5 miles.

Open

25 April - 30 September.

At a glance

| Welcome & Ambience | ✓✓✓✓ | Location | ✓✓✓✓✓ |
| Quality of Pitches | ✓✓✓✓ | Range of Facilities | ✓✓✓ |

Directions

At the war memorial in Dornoch, turn north (park signed) on the B9168. Park is 0.5 miles on the right (45 miles north of Inverness). O.S.GR: NH795911.

Charges guide

Per unit incl. 2 persons	£ 7.50 - £ 12.00
child (under 16 yrs)	£ 0.75
electricity	£ 2.50

No credit cards.

Reservations

Bookings and enquiries to: GNR Sutherland, Caravan Sales, Edderton, Tain, Ross-shire IV19 1JY. Tel: 01862 821253.

UK7710 **Ardmair Point Caravan Park**

Ardmair Point, Ullapool IV26 2TN (Highland)

This spectacularly situated park, overlooking the little Loch Kanaird, just round the corner from Loch Broom, has splendid views all round. The 68 touring pitches are arranged mainly on grass around the edge of the bay, in front of the shingle beach. Electrical hook-ups (10A) are available and some gravel hardstandings are on the other side of the access road, just past the second toilet block. Tent pitches are in a large field behind the other sanitary facilities. Scuba diving is popular at Loch Kanaird because the water is so clear. Seals and otters are regularly seen in the bay and the whole area is full of interest, including visits to Inverewe Gardens and the Isle Martin bird and seal colonies.

Facilities

Two toilet blocks, both with good facilities. One block has wonderful views from the large windows in the launderette and dishwashing rooms, plus large en-suite rooms for disabled people. Motorcaravan service point. Limited shop. Play area. Off site: Ullapool for shopping 3 miles. Golf and bicycle hire 3 miles.

At a glance

| Welcome & Ambience | ✓✓✓✓ | Location | ✓✓✓✓✓ |
| Quality of Pitches | ✓✓✓✓ | Range of Facilities | ✓✓✓ |

Directions

Park is off the A835 road, 3 miles north of Ullapool. O.S.GR: NH109983. GPS: N57:56.038 W05:11.821

Charges 2005

| Per unit incl. 2 persons | £ 10.00 - £ 16.00 |

Less for 7 or more nights pre-paid.

Reservations

Recommended for July/Aug. (min. 2 nights). Tel: 01854 612054. Email: sales@ardmair.com

Open

1 May - late September, depending on the weather.

UK7720 Woodend Camping & Caravan Park

Achnairn, Lairg IV27 4DN (Highland)

Woodend is a delightful, small park overlooking Loch Shin and perfect for hill walkers and backpackers. Peaceful and simple, it is owned and run single-handedly by Mrs Cathie Ross, who provides a wonderfully warm Scottish welcome to visitors. On a hill with open, panoramic views across the Loch to the hills beyond and all around, the large camping field is undulating and gently sloping with some reasonably flat areas. The park is licensed to take 55 units and most of the 22 electrical hook-ups (16A) are in a line near the top of the field, close to the large, fenced play area which has several items of equipment on grass. There are opportunities for fishing and hill walking. The famous Falls of Shin with a Visitor Centre is an ideal place to see the salmon leap (about 10 miles).

Facilities

The sanitary facilities are of old design but kept very clean and are quite satisfactory. Laundry with two machines and a dryer. Kitchen with dishwashing sinks and eating room for tent campers. Reception is at the house, Sunday papers, daily milk and bread may be ordered. Fishing licences for the Loch (your catch will be frozen for you). Off site: Mountain bikes can be hired in Lairg, 5 miles. Several scenic golf courses within 20-30 miles.

Open

1 April - 30 September.

At a glance

Welcome & Ambience	✓✓✓✓✓	Location	✓✓✓✓
Quality of Pitches	✓✓✓	Range of Facilities	✓✓✓

Directions

Achnairn is near the southern end of Loch Shin. Turn off the A838 single track road at signs for Woodend. From the A9 coming north take the A836 at Bonar Bridge, 11 miles northwest of Tain. O.S.GR: NC558127. GPS: N58:04.816 W04:26.823

Charges 2005

Per unit incl. electricity	£ 8.00 - £ 9.00
tent	£ 7.00 - £ 8.00

No credit cards.

Reservations

Not considered necessary Tel: 01549 402248.

UK7730 Scourie Caravan & Camping Park

Harbour Road, Scourie IV27 4TG (Highland)

Mr Mackenzie has carefully nurtured this park over many years, developing a number of firm terraces with 60 pitches which gives it an attractive layout - there is nothing regimented here. Perched on the edge of the bay in an elevated position, practically everyone has a view of the sea and a short walk along the shore footpath leads to a small sandy beach. The park has tarmac and gravel access roads, with well drained grass pitches and some hard-core hardstandings with 10A electric hook-ups. A few are on an area which is unfenced from the rocks (young children would need to be supervised here). Reception, alongside the modern toilet block, contains a wealth of tourist information and maps. There are very good facilities for disabled visitors on the park and at the restaurant, although the ramps leading to them are a little steep. Mr Mackenzie claims that this is the only caravan park in the world from where, depending on the season, you can see palm trees, Highland cattle and Great Northern divers from your pitch. Red throated divers have also been seen. Trips to Handa Island (a special protection area for seabird colonies) are available from here and Tarbet. The clear water makes this area ideal for diving.

Facilities

The toilet facilities can be heated. Showers have no divider or seat. Fully equipped laundry and dishwashing sinks. Motorcaravan service point. The 'Anchorage' restaurant at the entrance to the park (used as reception at quiet times) is large and well appointed with meals at reasonable prices cooked to order (l/4-30/9). Boat launching facilities. Fishing permits (brown trout) can be arranged. Off site: The village has a well stocked shop with post office, gas is available from the local petrol station and mobile banks visit regularly.

Open

1 April - 30 September, but phone first to check.

At a glance

Welcome & Ambience	✓✓✓✓	Location	✓✓✓✓✓
Quality of Pitches	✓✓✓✓	Range of Facilities	✓✓✓✓

Directions

Park is by Scourie village on A894 road in northwest Sutherland. O.S.GR: NC153446. GPS: N58:21.085 E05:09.406

Charges guide

Per unit incl. 1-2 adults	£ 10.00
extra adult	£ 1.50
child (3-16 yrs)	£ 0.75
electricity	£ 2.00
extra tent, vehicle or awning	£ 1.00
hiker and tent	£ 4.00

No credit cards.

Reservations

Not made. Tel: 01971 502060.

UK7735 Sango Sands Oasis Caravan & Camping Site

Durness via Lairg IV27 4QB (Highland)

Sango Sands Oasis is a quiet, ten acre site overlooking the beautiful Sango Bay, a Blue Flag beach. The site was established by the family in 1978 and they have worked hard improving the facilities over the years. There are 82 pitches for tents and touring caravans, 30 with electricity hook-ups. The land is well drained and fairly level. It is possible to see whales, porpoise, dolphins and seals from the site plus a variety of sea birds which nest nearby. An ideal area for walkers, including the less adventurous, there are numerous marked paths and there is an excellent variety of angling, from rivers to the sea. The nearby Durness golf course with its superb views welcomes visitors. Smoo Cave with the waterfall down into the dramatic tidal gorge is close by and worth seeing also it is possible to visit Cape Wrath. A good value café, bar and licensed restaurant serves home cooked meals and malt whiskies and Scottish beers. There are occasional dances or discos in the bar and a TV.

Facilities

Traditional toilet and shower blocks are lit at night but a torch may be useful. Free showers with curtains. Showers and toilets are separate. With the beach so close don't be surprised to find sand in the showers. En-suite facilities for disabled visitors. Laundry with sinks, washing machines, dryers, irons and boards. Campers kitchen with cooking rings. Café, bar and licensed restaurant. TV. Games room with pool and darts. Off site: Two grocery stores, post office, ATM, petrol, diesel and gas supplies in the village. Nearby Visitor Centre with extensive information on the area.

Open

All year.

At a glance

Welcome & Ambience	✓✓✓✓✓	Location	✓✓✓✓✓
Quality of Pitches	✓✓✓	Range of Facilities	✓✓✓✓

Directions

From Thurso take the North Coast road (A836 as far as Tongue, where it continues on as the A838 to Durness). Site is on the right as you go through the village. From Ullapool follow A835 north to Ledmore Junction and turn left on the A837. After 8 miles turn right onto the A894 and continue to Laxford Bridge. Turn left on A838. Durness is 19 miles further on this road. Site is on the left going through the village. O.S.GR: NC420668.

Charges 2005

Per person	£ 4.40
child (5-15 yrs)	£ 1.10 - £ 2.20
electricity	£ 2.40

Reservations

Not usually necessary unless to ensure electricity. Tel: 01971 511726. Email: keith.durness@btinternet.com

UK7920 Laxdale Holiday Park

6 Laxdale Lane, Stornoway HS2 0DR (Isle of Lewis)

Whilst not in the most scenic of locations, this good park is well placed for touring. Surrounded by trees, it is on the edge of Stornaway (ferry port) and is well laid out with a tarmac road running through the centre. A level hardstanding area for touring caravans has 14 electricity hook-ups plus 2 for tents and a grassy area for the tents gently slopes away to the trees and boundary. There are 5 holiday caravans and a self catering holiday bungalow available for rent on the site, plus a bunkhouse. The site is centrally situated in an ideal spot for touring the Isle of Lewis with easy access to all parts of the island. The Butt of Lewis, the Callanish standing stones and the Black House Village are all within easy reach as well as many other attractions. Some parts have rocky coastal scenery but there are some lovely beaches around the island. The main road south leads to Harris passing through the mountainous area to the south of the Isle of Lewis. Ferries come into Stornoway from Ullapool and also Uig (Skye) to Tarbert (north Harris). Ferries to Berneray/North Uist go from Leverburgh in the south of Harris.

Facilities

The well maintained and modern toilet block is heated and raised above the hardstanding area. Access is via steps or a gravel path to the ramp. Good (but narrow) showers with dividing curtain (50p). Well equipped laundry with washing machine, dryer, iron and board, sink and clothes line. Indoor sink for dishwashing with hot water. Water and chemical toilet disposal points. Telephone. Off site: Bus stop 200 m. The busy fishing port of Stornoway has a comprehensive range of shops and restaurants. New sports centre with swimming pool. Library with free internet access.

Open

1 April - 31 October.

At a glance

Welcome & Ambience	✓✓✓✓	Location	✓✓✓
Quality of Pitches	✓✓✓✓	Range of Facilities	✓✓✓✓

Directions

From Stornoway take the A857 for 1 mile then take the second turning on the left past the hospital. O.S.GR: NB420348.

Charges 2005

Per person	£ 1.50 - £ 2.00
child (5-15 yrs)	£ 1.50
pitch	£ 4.50 - £ 7.00
electricity	£ 2.00
awning	£ 1.50

Reservations

Advised for July and August and made with deposit (1 night's fees). Tel: 01851 706966. Email: info@laxdaleholidaypark.com

UK7950 Point of Ness Caravan & Camping Site

Stromness (Orkney)

This quiet site is in an idyllic position bounded by the sea one side (an entrance to the harbour). It is sheltered by the land from the open sea and has views to the mountains and the island of Hoy. There is a rocky beach close by and walks from the site. It is a level, firm grassy site, protected from the small drop to the sea by a low fence. Access to the steps to the sea is gained by a gate in the fence. Whilst being located at one end of Orkney, it is still easy to visit the Churchill Barriers and the Italian Church as well as the closer Maes Howe and Scara Brae sites. Regular ferries come into Stromness from Thurso. Don't be surprised if the seals come to watch you. Ferries to other islands go from various ports and it is sometimes necessary to book in advance.

Facilities
The well maintained traditional style toilet block has good-sized showers (20p) with curtains separating the changing area. Well equipped laundry. Telephone and tourist information. Lounge with TV for campers is at one end of the block.

Open
2 May - 30 September.

At a glance
Welcome & Ambience	✓✓✓✓✓	Location	✓✓✓✓✓
Quality of Pitches	✓✓✓✓	Range of Facilities	✓✓✓✓

Directions
Site is just west of Stromness and is signed from the town. Campers can walk along the narrow high street to the site on the edge of the town. Caravans and motorcaravans are advised to take the road at the back of the town (about 2 miles) that is clearly marked. O.S.GR: HY256079.

Charges 2005
Per pitch	£ 6.20 - £ 9.55
small tent	£ 4.00
awning	£ 2.05
electricity	£ 2.05

Reservations
Booking and further information: Dept. of Education and Recreation Services, Orkney Islands Council, Council Offices, Kirkwall, Orkney KW15 1NY. Telephone: 01856 873535 Ext 2404. Maximum length of stay 21 days. Tel: 01856 873535.

UK7980 Clickimin Caravan & Camp Site

Clickimin Leisure Complex, Lochside, Lerwick ZE1 0PJ (Shetlands)

The caravan and camping site is in the grounds of the Clickimin leisure complex, but it is not dominated by the building with its swimming pool and restaurant, etc. The site is arranged in two tiers which are well laid out with a tarmac road in the centre of each tier. The lower grass tier is separated into areas by shrubs and provides a camping area fro 30 tents. The upper tier has 20 touring pitches, each with a large gravel area and divided from its neighbour by a wide impressed concrete section for sitting out. A small lamppost with electricity, water and waste disposal points is provided at each pitch. From the pitches there is a view across a lake with its ruined 'broche' that is floodlit at night. The site is on the edge of Lerwick (ferry terminal), but with easy access to the town and its facilities. Lerwick is ideal as a base to explore the Shetlands. Travel between the islands is exceptionally easy with drive on and off ferries running regularly between the islands and booking not essential. Daily ferries go to the Shetlands from The Orkneys and Aberdeen.

Facilities
The modern toilet block is clean and includes a toilet/shower cubical for disabled visitors. Large, warm and well equipped laundry and drying room with an area for food preparation.

Open
May - September.

At a glance
Welcome & Ambience	✓✓✓✓✓	Location	✓✓✓✓
Quality of Pitches	✓✓✓✓✓	Range of Facilities	✓✓✓✓✓

Directions
Site is on the west side of Lerwick and is signed as you start to leave Lerwick. Take the A969 north or south. Just before leaving the town is the road North Lochside (turn south) or South Lochside (turn north). Clickimin Leisure Centre is on this road. O.S.GR: HU464413.

Charges 2005
Per pitch	£ 6.70 - £ 10.20
one-person tent	£ 4.70

Reservations
Contact site. Tel: 01595 741000. Email: clickimin.centre@srt.org.uk

UK7740 Loch Greshornish Camping Site

Arnisort, Edinbane IV51 9PS (Isle of Skye)

Mr and Mrs Palmer took over this simple, spacious site with simple facilities in 1999. In a beautiful, peaceful setting with views over the loch to the low hills to the northwest of Skye, it is suitable for long or short stays. There are 30 level grass pitches for motorcaravans and caravans, 28 with 10A electric hook-ups. There are also places for up to 100 tents (but numbers never reach that level). A new building houses reception and a small, licenced shop selling basic essentials. A new launderette with washing machines, dryers and sinks will be completed this year. The owners offer bicycle hire (with safety helmets) and canoe hire.

Facilities

The refurbished toilet facilities are light, airy and spotlessly clean. The showers are a little cramped. Dishwashing sink in the ladies' and another in the men's. Launderette. Camper's shelter with seating, cooking and eating area. Small shop. Bicycle hire. Canoe hire. Off site: The local village has two hotels for drinks and meals; Portree, the nearest town, is 15 miles. Riding 2 miles. Golf 5 miles.

Open

Easter - 15 October.

At a glance

Welcome & Ambience	✓✓✓✓✓	Location	✓✓✓✓✓
Quality of Pitches	✓✓✓✓	Range of Facilities	✓✓✓

Directions

Site is 15 miles west of Portree on the A850 Dunvegan road by Edinbane. O.S.GR: NG343524.
GPS: N57:29.113 W06:26.097

Charges 2005

Per adult	£ 3.50
child (5-10 yrs) (11-15 yrs)	£ 1.25 - £ 2.25
caravan, motorcaravan or trailer tent	£ 1.75
tent	£ 1.00 - £ 1.50
electricity	£ 1.75

Reservations

Advised for high season. Tel: 01470 582230.
Email: info@skyecamp.com

UK7750 Staffin Caravan & Camping Site

Staffin IV51 9JX (Isle of Skye)

This simple camping site is on the side of a hill just outside Staffin, where the broad sweep of the bay is dotted with working crofts running down to the sea. A marked walk from the site leads to the seashore and slipway (good for walking dogs but too far to be taking a boat). With 50 pitches, the site is quite sloping but there are 18 reasonably level pitches with irregular hardstanding for caravans and motorcaravans, all with electrical hook-ups (16A). Skye has many activities to offer and for the truly dedicated walker the Cuillins are the big attraction but the hills above Staffin look demanding! However, the first section of road from Portree should be treated with caution by those with caravans and large motorhomes. The entrance to the site from the main road is by a single track road.

Facilities

The sanitary block includes large, controllable showers. Dishwashing sinks are unfortunately not under cover and have only cold water. An older block is only opened at very busy times. Large hardstanding area has a motorcaravan service point. Gas available. Off site: Fishing or boat launching 1 mile. Bicycle hire 5 miles. Riding 9 miles. Staffin village is 400 yards and has a large shop (open six days a week), a restaurant and a launderette (useful as the site has no laundry). The Columbia centre in the village provides internet access.

Open

1 April - 30 September.

At a glance

Welcome & Ambience	✓✓✓✓	Location	✓✓✓
Quality of Pitches	✓✓✓	Range of Facilities	✓✓✓

Directions

Site is 15 miles north of Portree on A855 (2 miles of single track at the start), just before 40 mph signs on the right. O.S.GR: NG496668.
GPS: N57:37.321 W06:11.760

Charges 2005

Per caravan or motorcaravan incl. 2 persons	£ 10.00
tent incl. 2 persons	£ 9.00 - £ 7.50
extra adult	£ 1.50
No credit cards.	

Reservations

Maybe necessary for peak periods (made with £10 deposit), but will always try to fit you in.
Tel: 01470 562213.
Email: staffin@namacleod.freeserve.co.uk

Visit the Isle of Skye for FREE

On Monday 21st December 2004 the Scottish Executive announced the removal of all tolls on the Skye Bridge.

First opened in 1995 the Skye Bridge was on the one hand welcomed as it provided a fixed connection between Skye and the mainland but the high level of tolls charged was the subject of many objections from the moment it opened. Tolls were based on the old ferry fares and as a result were the highest levied in Europe.

Built as a private finance initiative with the capital costs due to be recouped by the charging of tolls the intention was that the crossing would eventually be free once these costs were paid off. However, the Scotish Executive reached an agreement with the financiers to settle these costs and so from 21 December 2004 tolls were no longer payable. A Hogmanay party was planned on the bridge to celebrate!

UK8330 Sixmilewater Caravan & Camping Park

Lough Road, Antrim BT41 4DG (Co. Antrim)

Sixmilewater is located at the Lough Shore Park and is adjacent to the Antrim Forum leisure complex, a major amenity area that includes swimming pools, a bowling green, an adventure playground for children, fitness and health gyms and sports fields. Managed by Antrim Borough Council, the park is easily accessible when travelling to and from the ports of Belfast and Larne making it perfect for stop overs. It is also central for sightseeing in the area including for the Antrim Castle Gardens and Clotworthy Arts Centre or for shopping in Antrim town. The Lough Shore Park offers visitors boating and water activities and boat launching on the beautiful Lough Neagh, as well as walking and cycling the Longshore Trail which takes in 25 places of interest along its 128 mile cycle route. The nearby golf club also offers a 20 bay driving range. Sixmilewater Caravan and Camping Park provides 18 pitches with electricity, arranged in a herringbone layout of hardstandings with grass for awnings. There are 24 pitches for tents to one side, plus picnic and barbecue areas. Advance booking is advisable.

Facilities

The small, modern toilet block provides bright facilities including toilets, washbasins and showers. Facilities for disabled campers. Baby changing unit. Laundry room. Fishing and boat launching. Off site: The facilities of Lough Shore Park including a café in season. Antrim Forum leisure centre. Bus service 1 mile. Shops, pubs and restaurants within 1.5 miles. Golf 1.5 miles. Riding 6 miles.

Open

Easter - September.

At a glance

Welcome & Ambience	✓✓✓✓	Location	✓✓✓✓✓
Quality of Pitches	✓✓✓✓	Range of Facilities	✓✓✓

Directions

Site is 1 miles south of the city centre. Follow signs for Antrim Forum and Lough Shore Park. On the Dublin road, turn off into Lough Road. Pass Antrim Forum and park is at the end of the road.

Charges 2005

Per pitch	£ 10.00 - £ 11.50
incl. electricity	£ 13.00
awning	£ 1.50

Reservations

Max. stay 14 nights. Contact site.
Tel: 028 9446 4963. Email: info@antrim.gov.uk

Sixmilewater Caravan & Camping Park

Lough Road, Antrim, Northern Ireland, BT41 4DG

Situated on the shores of Lough Neagh. On-site facilities include: TV lounge, games room, modern toilet and shower block, payphone, fully equipped laundry, electric hook up for 18 pitches and 24 camping sites. Maximum stay 7 nights. Open Easter - October.

Tel: 028 9446 4963 Fax: 028 9446 2968 Email: info@antrim.gov.uk

UK8340 Drumaheglis Caravan Park

36 Glenstall Road, Ballymoney BT53 7QN (Co. Antrim)

A caravan park which continually maintains high standards, Drumaheglis is popular throughout the season. Situated on the banks of the lower River Bann, approximately 4 miles from the town of Ballymoney, it appeals to watersports enthusiasts or makes an ideal base for exploring this scenic corner of Northern Ireland. The marina offers superb facilities for boat launching, water-skiing, cruising, canoeing or fishing, whilst getting out and about can take you to the Giant's Causeway, seaside resorts such as Portrush or Portstewart, the sands of Whitepark Bay, the Glens of Antrim or the picturesque villages of the Antrim coast road. This attractive site is for touring units only and is well laid out with trees, shrubs, flower beds and tarmac roads. There are 53 serviced pitches with hardstanding, electricity (5/10A) and water points. Ballymoney is a popular shopping town and the Joey Dunlop Leisure Centre provides a high-tech fitness studio, sports hall, etc. There is much to see and do within this Borough and of interest is the Ballymoney museum in Charlotte Street.

Facilities

Modern toilet blocks were very clean when we visited. Individual wash cubicles. Facilities for disabled visitors. Baby room and four family shower rooms. Dishwashing sinks. Washing machine and dryer. Play area. Volleyball and table tennis. Barbecue and picnic areas. Barrier with key system. Off site: Bus servce from park entrance. Bicycle hire, riding and golf 4 miles.

At a glance

Welcome & Ambience	✓✓✓✓	Location	✓✓✓✓✓
Quality of Pitches	✓✓✓✓✓	Range of Facilities	✓✓✓✓

Directions

From A26/B62 Portrush - Ballymoney roundabout continue for approx. 1 mile on the A26 towards Coleraine. Site is clearly signed - follow International camping signs.

Charges 2005

Per unit incl. electricity	£ 14.50

Reservations

Essential for peak periods and weekends.
Tel: 028 2766 6466. Email: info@ballymoney.gov.uk

Open

Easter - 1 October.

281

UK8350 Bush Caravan Park

97 Priestland Road, Bushmills BT57 8UJ (Co. Antrim)

An ideal base for touring the North Antrim Coast, this family run, recently extended park is only minutes away from two renowned attractions, the Giant's Causeway and the Old Bushmills Distillery. This fact alone makes Bush a popular location, but its fast growing reputation for friendliness and top class facilities makes it equally appealing. Conveniently located just off the main Ballymoney - Portrush Road (B62), it is approached by a short drive. The site itself is partly surrounded by mature trees and hedging, but views across the countryside can still be appreciated. Tarmac roads around the site lead to 47 well laid out and spacious pitches, with hardstanding and electric hook-up (16A), or to a grass area for tents. Unique features on site are murals depicting the famed scenery, sight and legends of the Causeway Coast. The enthusiastic owners organise tours to the Distillery and coastal trips - a musical evening cannot be ruled out.

Facilities

The toilet block (opened by key-pad) is modern, clean and equipped to a high standard. Facilities include controllable showers with excellent provision for people with disabilities (can also be used by families). Washing machine, dryer and dishwashing sinks. Central play area. Recreation room for all ages. Off site: Riding 2 miles. Golf and fishing 3 miles. Bicycle hire and boat launching 4 miles. Beach 3 miles.

At a glance

Welcome & Ambience	✓✓✓✓✓	Location	✓✓✓✓
Quality of Pitches	✓✓✓	Range of Facilities	✓✓✓

Directions

From Ballymoney A26/B62 roundabout proceed north on B62 towards Portrush for 6.5 miles. Turn right onto B17 and site is 350 yds on the left.

Charges 2005

Per unit incl. all persons, electricity	£ 12.50
tent	£ 5.00 - £ 10.00
awning	£ 1.50

Reservations

Advised for high season or weekends. Tel: 028 2073 1678.

Open

Easter - 31 October.

UK8360 Ballyness Caravan Park

40 Castlecatt Road, Bushmills BT57 8TN (Co. Antrim)

Ballyness is immaculately cared for and is designed with conservation in mind. In keeping with the surrounding countryside, it is extensively planted with native trees and shrubs which attract local wildlife and birds and there are ponds with ducks and swans. The overall appearance of this site, with its entrance gate, white stone pillars and broad tarmac drive is attractive. The drive leads to 30 hardstanding pitches with electricity hook-ups, water and drainage. There is a dedicated area for tents and several caravan holiday homes, but these are placed away from the touring pitches. From the site you can enjoy a relaxing walk by way of the meadow ponds and winding pathway alongside the stream known as St Columb's Rill. The village of Bushmills, with its famous Whiskey Distillery, is within walking distance and the Causeway Coast a short drive.

Facilities

One spotlessly clean and well decorated, cottage style heated sanitary block (key coded) includes facilities for disabled visitors (toilet and shower), a bathroom and baby changing unit, laundry room and dishwashing area. Play area. Football field. Nature trail. Off site: Bus service 0.5 miles. Bicycle hire 0.5 miles. Beach and fishing 1 miles. Golf and boat launching 1.5 miles. Riding 5 miles.

Open

17 March - 31 October.

At a glance

Welcome & Ambience	✓✓✓✓✓	Location	✓✓✓✓
Quality of Pitches	✓✓✓✓	Range of Facilities	✓✓✓

Directions

From M2 follow A26 N. At Ballymoney turn right on B66 towards Dervock and turn left. Stay on B66 and site is 5.5 miles on right.

Charges 2005

Per unit incl. 2 persons, electricity, water and drainage	£ 15.00
extra person over 5 yrs	£ 0.50
awning or pup tent	free - £ 1.00
2 person tent	£ 10.00

Reservations

Contact site. Tel: 028 2073 2393. Email: info@ballynesscaravanpark.com

UK8405 Cranfield Caravan Park

123 Cranfield Road, Cranfield West, Kilkeel BT34 4LJ (Co. Down)

On the shores of Carlingford Lough with direct access to a blue flag beach, this friendly family run park immediately impresses with its well cared for flower beds, neat hedging, cordyline trees and the elegant building which incorporates the family home and reception. Situated at Northern Ireland's most southerly point, the surrounding scenery of the Mourne Mountains, the Lough and distant vistas is stunning. A focal point is the Haulbowline lighthouse, built in the 1800s, which sits in the middle of the sea. Despite the many privately owned caravan holiday homes on site, touring pitches are kept separate and situated towards the park entrance. Each pitch has a sea view, has hardstanding and all have tower units providing an electricity hook up (16A), water, waste water point and TV outlet; 19 have a main sewerage connection.

Facilities

A modern, heated toilet block (entrance by key) is well maintained with tiled walls/floors, pre-set showers (50p token) and open style washbasins. Excellent suite for disabled visitors doubles as a family room, also a night WC (by key). Dishwashing sinks and well equipped laundry in a separate building. Play area (outside park). Sea fishing, boat launching and beach (with lifeguard). Off site: Kilkeel town (3.5 miles). Golf, hill walking in the Mournes, Anglo Norman castle.

At a glance

Welcome & Ambience ✓✓✓✓✓   Location ✓✓✓✓
Quality of Pitches ✓✓✓✓   Range of Facilities ✓✓✓

Directions

Travelling southeast on A2 Newry/Kilkeel Road turn right approx. 5.5 miles after passing through Rostrevor onto local road, signed Cranfield/Greencastle. Site signed at end of road. GPS: N54:01.796 W06:04.098

Charges guide

Per unit incl. all persons and electricity	£ 12.00
awning	£ 1.50

Reservations

Contact park. Tel: 028 417 62572.
Email: jimchestnut@btconnect.com

Open

17 March - 31 October.

UK8420 Tollymore Forest Caravan Park

178 Tullybrannigan Road, Newcastle BT33 6PW (Co. Down)

This popular park, for tourers only, is located within the parkland of Tollymore Forest. It is discreetly situated away from the public footpaths and is noted for its scenic surroundings. The forest park, which is approached by way of an ornate gateway and majestic avenue of Himalayan cedars, covers an area of almost 500 hectares. It is backed by the Mourne mountains and situated two miles from the beaches and resort of Newcastle. The site is attractively laid out with hardstanding pitches, 72 of which have electricity (6A). The Head Ranger at Tollymore is helpful and ensures that the caravan site is efficiently run and quiet, even when full. Exploring the forest park is part of the pleasure of staying here, and of note are the stone follies, bridges and entrance gates. The Shimna and Spinkwee rivers flow through the park adding a refreshing touch and tree lovers appreciate the arboretum with its many rare species.

Facilities

Toilet blocks, timbered in keeping with the setting, are clean and modern with wash cubicles, facilities for disabled people, dishwashing and laundry area. Off site: Confectionery shop and tea room nearby. Small grocery shop a few yards from the exit gate of the park with gas available.

Open

All year.

At a glance

Welcome & Ambience ✓✓✓✓✓   Location ✓✓✓✓✓
Quality of Pitches ✓✓✓✓   Range of Facilities ✓✓✓

Directions

Approach Newcastle on the A24. Before entering the town, at roundabout, turn right on to A50 signed Castlewellan and follow signs for Tollymore Forest Park.

Charges 2005

Per unit incl. car and occupants	£ 9.00 - £ 13.00
electricity	£ 1.50
Low season mid-week special rates.	

Reservations

Advisable in high season and for B.Hs. and made with £10 deposit. Contact: Tollymore Forest Park (Administration), 176 Tullybrannigan Road, Newcastle, Co. Down BT33 0PW. Tel: 028 4372 2428.

283

UK8460 Delamont Country Park Camping & Caravanning Club Site

Delamont Country Park, Downpatrick Road, Killyleagh BT30 9TZ (Co. Down)

Within the boundaries of Delamont Country Park, it is an idyllic location for those seeking an away from it all feel, yet wanting to be within easy reach of major attractions. The country park is a designated area of outstanding natural beauty and commands from its highest point, breathtaking vistas of Strangford Lough and surrounding countryside. Facilities on the campsite itself are excellent and it has an orderly, neat and tidy appearance. Reception stands to the fore of the site and the sanitary block towards the rear. The 64 all weather pitches on level terrain all have electricity, plus water and waste hook-ups. Although the site is surrounded by trees and the rich vegetation of the country park, the young shrubs and trees around the pitches will take time to mature.

Facilities
The single modern toilet block, with heating, has wash cubicles and a baby bath. En-suite facilities for disabled visitors. Laundry sinks, washing machine and dryer; dishwashing inside. Small shop area selling basics. Adventure playground and miniature railway in country park. Free admittance to country park for campers. Off site: Tyrella beach 7 miles. Fishing and riding 1 mile. Golf 4 miles.

At a glance
Welcome & Ambience	✓✓✓✓✓	Location	✓✓✓✓✓
Quality of Pitches	✓✓✓✓✓	Range of Facilities	✓✓✓✓

Directions
From Belfast follow A22 southeast to village of Killyleagh. Pass through village and site entrance is on left after 1 mile.

Charges 2005
Per adult	£ 4.30 - £ 6.40
non-member pitch fee	£ 5.00

Reservations
Contact site or Central Reservations 0870 243 3331. Tel: 028 4482 1833.

Open
March - October.

UK8550 Dungannon Park

Moy Road, Dungannon BT71 6DY (Co. Tyrone)

This small touring park nestles in the midst of a 70-acre park with a multitude of tree varieties, brightly coloured flower beds and a 12 acre fishing lake. The 12 pitches, which are discreetly sited, some with lake views, are on hardstanding with water, waste and 16A electricity. There is also an unmarked grass area for tents. Run by Dungannon Council the park, which also incorporates tennis courts, football and cricket pitches lies about one mile south of the town. Walkers can enjoy three miles of walks which command from the high ground, views of the surrounding countryside and Lough Neagh. A modern Visitor Amenity Centre houses reception, sanitary facilities, a TV area and vending machines.

Facilities
Sanitary facilities which include showers (by token), washbasins, baby changing mat and spacious unit for disabled visitors are to the rear of the Amenity Centre. Laundry room Night watchman (until 6 am). Excellent play area. Tennis, fishing and walking. Off site: Bus stop and shop at main entrance to park. Tyrone Crystal (guided tours), walking and cycling in Clogher Valley, local markets.

At a glance
Welcome & Ambience	✓✓✓✓	Location	✓✓✓✓✓
Quality of Pitches	✓✓✓✓✓	Range of Facilities	✓✓✓

Directions
Leave M1 motorway at exit 15 to join A29 towards Dungannon. Turn left at second traffic lights signed Dungannon Park. GPS: N54:23.413 W06:45.478

Charges 2005
Per pitch	£ 8.00 - £ 10.00
with electricity	£ 12.00

Reservations
Contact park. Tel: 028 8772 7327. Email: dungannonpark@utvinternet.com

Open
1 March - 31 October.

UK8510 Mullynascarthy Caravan Park

Lisnaskea BT92 0NZ (Co. Fermanagh)

This well kept touring site on the banks of the Colebrooke River has instant appeal with a setting more like a mature garden. The pitches to the right of reception, which are grass on hardstanding, are mostly angled between the many tree varieties, also separated by low hedging and flowering shrubs. To the left of the facility block additional pitches are spread over meadow-like terrain and all have electricity. The attention and care this site obviously receives is due to the warden who also extends a friendly warm welcome to her guests. Lisnaskea makes an ideal base for exploring this lakeland county which abounds in historic treasures, stately homes, and is excellent for watersports enthusiasts.

Facilities
The toilet block (key operated) has showers, open style washbasins, facilities for disabled people (washbasin/WC). Laundry room. Games and sports area. Play area. River fishing (licences available). Off site: Bus service 1.5 miles.

Open
17 March - 31 October.

At a glance
Welcome & Ambience	✓✓✓✓✓	Location	✓✓✓
Quality of Pitches	✓✓✓✓	Range of Facilities	✓✓✓

Directions
From Enniskillen take A4 towards Dungannon for 8 miles, then turn right on A34 signed Lisnaskea. Continue on A34 for 2.5 miles and turn right onto B514 where site is signed Mullynascarthy.

Charges 2005
Per unit incl. 2 persons and electricity	£ 12.00
tent	£ 8.00 - £ 12.00

Reservations
Contact site. Tel: 028 6772 1040.

IR8750 Belleek Caravan & Camping Park

Ballina (Co. Mayo)

Belleek has a quiet woodland setting, only minutes from Ballina, a famed salmon fishing centre. With excellent pitches and toilet block, the family owners are committed to ensuring that it is immaculate at all times. From the entrance gate, the park is approached by a drive that passes reception and leads to 58 well spaced pitches. With a very neat overall appearance, 32 pitches have hardstanding, 45 have electricity hook-ups, and you may choose your pitch. Sports facilities within a short distance of the park include a swimming pool, tennis and bicycle hire. Other local attractions are the Blue Flag beach at Ross, Ceide Fields (Neolithic farm), Down Patrick Head, Mayo North Heritage Centre or a seaweed bath at Kilcullen's Bath House, Enniscrone.

Facilities

Spotlessly clean, tastefully decorated toilet block providing showers (€ 0.80 token), baby sink and facilities for disabled people. Laundry sink, two washing machines and two dryers. TV room and games room with table tennis and football game. Campers' kitchen and emergency accommodation with beds provided. Play area, ball game area, basketball and tennis courts. Barbecue area. Reception includes a shop (June-Sept) and a tea room that also serves breakfasts. Off site: Fishing 1 km. Bicycle hire 3 km.

Open

1 March - 1 October; by arrangement all year.

At a glance

Welcome & Ambience	✓✓✓✓✓	Location	✓✓✓✓
Quality of Pitches	✓✓✓✓✓	Range of Facilities	✓✓✓✓

Directions

Take R314 Ballina - Killala road. Park is signed on right after approx. 1.75 miles.
GPS: N54:08.051 W09:514

Charges guide

Per unit incl. 2 persons	€ 14,00 - € 16,00
extra adult	€ 4,00
child	€ 2,00
electricity (10A)	€ 2,50
hiker/cyclist and tent	€ 7,00

No credit cards.

Reservations

Contact park. Tel: 096 71533.
Email: lenahan@belleekpark.com

IR8770 Parkland Caravan & Camping Park

Westport House Country Park, Westport (Co. Mayo)

Located in the grounds of an elegant country estate, this popular park offers the choice of a 'pitch only' booking, or a 'special deal' (min. stay three nights). This includes free admission to Westport House and children's animal and bird park, plus other activities, such as boating and fishing on the lake and river, pitch and putt, 'slippery dip', ball pond and 'supabounce', new play adventure world, hillside train rides and a flume ride. Stay one week or more and all the above are free, plus tennis, a par-3 golf course and 20% discount on bar food in the Horse and Wagon bar on the site. From Westport Quay, you enter the grounds of the estate by way of a tree lined road that crosses the river and leads to the site. In an attractive, sheltered area of the parkland, set in the trees, are 155 pitches. There are 65 with hardstanding and 76 electric hook-ups. The gate is closed 11.30 pm. - 9 am. with good lighting around the site. If late, vehicles must be parked in the car park. Early in the season the site may not be fully prepared, and only minimal facilities may be available. Westport is an attractive town with splendid Georgian houses and traditional shop fronts. There are many good restaurants and pubs

Facilities

Toilet facilities are provided at various points on the site, plus a 'super-loo' located in the farmyard buildings. Facilities for disabled people. Dishwashing and laundry sinks, washing machines and dryers plus free ironing facilities. Fifties style function room and bar with food and musical entertainment (all 1/6-31/8). Dogs are not accepted. Off site: Within 5 km. of the estate are an 18 hole golf course and deep sea angling on Clew Bay.

Open

14 May - 5 September.

At a glance

Welcome & Ambience	✓✓✓✓	Location	✓✓✓✓✓
Quality of Pitches	✓✓✓	Range of Facilities	✓✓✓✓

Directions

Take R335 Westport - Louisburgh road and follow signs for Westport Quay, then turn right into Westport House. GPS: N53:48.32 W09:32.369

Charges 2005

Per unit with 2 persons excl.	
free facilities, pitch only	€ 23,00 - € 25,00
hiker or cyclist incl. 2 persons	€ 20,00 - € 22,00
Electricity incl.	

No credit cards.

Reservations

Contact park. Tel: 098 27766.
Email: camping@westporthouse.ie

Don't forget!

the international dialling code for the Republic of Ireland is **00 353**
(then drop the first '0' of the number)

289

IR8780 Knock Caravan & Camping Park

Claremorris Road, Knock (Co. Mayo)

This park is immediately south of the world famous shrine that receives many visitors. Comfortable and clean, the square shaped campsite is kept very neat with tarmac roads and surrounded by clipped trees. The pitches are of a decent size accommodating 50 caravans or motorcaravans, 20 tents and 18 caravan holiday homes (for rent). All pitches have hardstanding (5 doubles) and there are 52 electrical connections (13A), with an adequate number of water points. There is also an overflow field. Because of the religious connections of the area, the site is very busy in August and indeed there are unlikely to be any vacancies at all for 14-16 August. Besides visiting the shrine and Knock Folk Museum, it is also a good centre for exploring scenic Co. Mayo.

Facilities

Two heated toilet blocks have good facilities for disabled visitors and a nice sized rest room attached, hot showers (on payment) and adequate washing and toilet facilities. Laundry and dishwashing room. Gas supplies. Playground. Off site: Fishing 4.5 km. Golf and riding 11 km.

Open

1 March - 31 October.

At a glance

Welcome & Ambience	✓✓✓✓	Location	✓✓✓
Quality of Pitches	✓✓✓✓✓	Range of Facilities	✓✓✓

Directions

Exit from the N17 at the Knock bypass and from the roundabout follow signs to the site which is just south of the village. GPS: N53:47.262 W08:55.165

Charges 2005

Per adult	€ 2,00
child	€ 1,00
pitch	€ 14,00 - € 15,00
electricity (13A)	€ 2,50
hiker or cyclist incl. tent	€ 9,00 - € 10,00

No credit cards.

Reservations

Taken for any length, no deposit, but see editorial for August. Tel: 094 938 8100.
Email: info@knock-shrine.ie

IR8790 Carra Caravan & Camping Park

Belcarra, Castlebar (Co. Mayo)

This is an ideal location for those seeking a real Irish village experience in a 'value for money' park. Small, unpretentious and family run, it is located in Belcarra, a regular winner of the 'Tidiest Mayo Village' award. Nestling at the foot of a wooded drumlin, it is surrounded by rolling hills and quiet roads which offer an away from it all feeling, yet Castlebar the county's largest town is only an 8 km. drive. On the pleasant 1.5 acre park, the 20 unmarked touring pitches, 14 with electric hook-up (13A), are on flat ground enclosed by ranch fencing and shaded in parts by trees. An additional novel idea at Carra are eight horse-drawn caravans for hire. Also of interest are the talks that the owner Sean and daughter Deirdre give on the area. There are recommended walks and maps provided. New to the area is the National Museum of Country Life at Turlough (8 km) which is now a super attraction.

Facilities

The basic toilet block has adequate, well equipped showers (€ 0.40). Combined kitchen, dishwashing, laundry area with fridge/freezer, sink, table, chairs, washing machine and dryer. Comfortable lounge with TV, books and magazines located at reception. Off site: Village shops, a post office and 'Flukies' cosy bar which serves Irish breakfast and where Irish stew is a speciality. Leisure centre and tennis courts. Free fishing area and special walkway to the river. Golf 8 km.

At a glance

Welcome & Ambience	✓✓✓✓	Location	✓✓✓
Quality of Pitches	✓✓✓	Range of Facilities	✓✓✓

Directions

From Castlebar take N60 Claremorris road for 8.5 km. southeast and turn right at sign for Belcarra. Continue for 4.5 km. to village and site on left at end of village. GPS: N53:47.974 W09:12.989

Charges guide

Per unit incl. all persons	€ 8,00
electricity	€ 2,00

No credit cards.

Reservations

Contact park. Tel: 094 903 2054.

Open

5 June - 18 September.

IR8810 Lough Lannagh Caravan Park

Castlebar (Co. Mayo)

Lough Lannagh is an attractive holiday village on the lake shore and comprises quality accommodation, self catering cottages and a caravan park. It is within walking distance of Castlebar with its many restaurant, pubs and shops. County Mayo's main attractions are also within a short drive. The caravan park has 20 touring pitches, well laid out in a separate dedicated corner of the village, all on hardstanding with electric connections. One reception area serves all and is situated to the right of the security barrier. When not out and about, there are many on site activities for all the family. The main attraction is the fitness suite, sauna and steam room, plus reflexology and therapies available (over 18s only admitted to the gym). Popular with the young is the three times weekly club held in July/August. Anglers need only travel 500 metres, or if you prefer cycling, bicycles can be hired.

Facilities	Directions
One modern heated sanitary block provides washbasins and well equipped, pre-set showers. En-suite unit for disabled people. Laundry room with sink, washing machines and dryers; dishwashing area. Café (serving breakfast). Fitness suite. Tennis. Table tennis. Bicycle hire.	To get to Castlebar take the N5, N60 or N84. At Castlebar ring road follow directions for Westport. Site is signed on all approach roads to the Westport roundabout. GPS: N53:50.950 W09:18.713

Open	Charges 2005
All year, excl. 15 Dec - 8 Jan.	Per unit incl. 2 adults, electricity and hardstanding € 20,00 - € 26,00
	tent incl. 2 persons € 12,00 - € 14,00

At a glance				Reservations
Welcome & Ambience	✓✓✓✓	Location	✓✓✓✓	Advised for high season; contact site.
Quality of Pitches	✓✓✓✓	Range of Facilities	✓✓✓✓	Tel: 094 902 7111. Email: llv@eircom.net

IR8815 Willowbrook Camping & Caravan Park

Kiltybranks, Ballaghaderreen. (Co. Roscommon)

This is a campsite with a difference. Willowbrook is a small family run caravan and camping park, which offers a unique holiday in an unspoiled part of Ireland. It has 8 hardstanding pitches with electricity and a central level grass area without power, all with ample water points. An additional tenting area is available in the adjoining field. The main difference is that meditation, Tai Chi and other relaxation techniques, all adding to the tranquillity of the setting, are organised by Dave and Lin Whitefield whose aim is to ensure their guests relax and unwind in this idyllic hideaway. Archery and guided walks on the Suck Valley Way and in the Ox and Curlieu mountains, and coarse fishing for more active relaxation are also provided. A bunkhouse (for up to twelve), a library and reading room with a TV in a renovated 100 year old cottage add to the ambiance of the park. The camper's kitchen is spotless and homely. This clean and well cared for park is located in an area rich with archaeology and heritage, about 20 minutes from Knock airport. It is ideal as a holiday base or as a stop over on the Dublin - Mayo route to the west of Ireland.

Facilities	Directions
The toilet block is immaculate and lit at night, with separate shower cubicles and facilities for disabled campers. Laundry room. Campers' kitchen with microwave, kettle and toaster. Library and reading room with TV. Fishing. Torches useful. Off site: Local sporting activities available include tennis, golf and fishing.	Park is 6 km. from Ballaghaderreen. Take the R293 from Ballaghaderreen towards Castlerea and Ballyhaunis, then the R325 over the bridge. Bear left, still towards Castlerea and Ballyhaunis for 1.5 km. Turn right at sign to park in 500 m.

Open	Charges 2005
All year.	Per unit incl. 2 persons, electricity € 15,50

At a glance				Reservations
Welcome & Ambience	✓✓✓✓✓	Location	✓✓✓✓	Contact park. Tel: 094 9861307.
Quality of Pitches	✓✓✓✓	Range of Facilities	✓✓✓	Email: info@willowbrookpark.com

IR8825 Lough Key Caravan & Camping Park

Lough Key Forest Park, Boyle (Co. Roscommon)

This caravan and camping park is set deep in the 320 hectares of the Lough Key Forest Park. Comprising mixed woodland including giant red cedar, beech, ash and oak trees, the forest is bounded by Lough Key and incorporates several of its islands. The history of the parkland goes back to 1184. A visit to the Lough offers views of islands inhabited by monks and hermits in days gone by, ring forts and tunnels, and natural and historical features like the Temple, the Wishing Chair, the Bog Gardens and Rockingham House and harbour. The rustic design of the main building on the park (which houses reception, a camper's kitchen, a TV room with a log fire, and the sanitary and laundry facilities) blends well with the wooded environment. The well landscaped, 5-hectare site provides space for 52 touring units with electricity connections and ample water points. There is a separate area for tents. The location in Lough Key Forest Park offers a base for visiting Strokestown House, Boyle Abbey, Famine Museum and Garden, and the Elphin 18th century windmill. A fisherman's dream, there are pike, bream, roach and perch in Lough Key and brown trout at nearby Lough Arrow. Guided walking tours with Park Rangers combine the historical and the legend with wildlife, flora and fauna. Boat tours of the lake and boat hire are also available. Coillte, the Irish Forestry Board, who manage the amenity, strictly enforces the forest code.

Facilities

The main toilet block includes metered hot showers. Facilities for disabled campers (key required). Campers' kitchen and sheltered eating area. Laundry. TV room. Play area in the centre of the park with adventure type play equipment in a hedged area, plus seating for parents. Forest walks and trails. Boat tours and boat hire. Security barrier closed at night. Off site: Coffee shop at Rockingham harbour. Nearby town of Boyle for bars, restaurants and entertainment 3 km. Bicycle hire and golf 5 km.

At a glance

Welcome & Ambience	✓✓✓✓✓	Location	✓✓✓✓✓
Quality of Pitches	✓✓✓✓✓	Range of Facilities	✓✓✓

Directions

Site is 4 km. east of Boyle on the A4 Carrick-on-Shannon road.

Charges 2005

Per person	€ 2,00
child	€ 1,00
pitch	€ 9,00 - € 14,00
electricity	€ 2,00

Reservations

Contact site. Tel: 071 9662212.
Email: seamus.duignan@coillte.ie

Open

14 April - 10 September.

IR8960 Lough Ree (East) Caravan & Camping Park

Ballykeeran, Athlone (Co. Westmeath)

This touring park is alongside the river, screened by trees but reaching the water's edge. Drive into the small village of Ballykeeran and the park is discreetly located behind the main street. The top half of the site is in a woodland situation and after the reception and sanitary block, Lough Ree comes into view and the remaining pitches run down to the shoreline. There are 60 pitches, 20 with hardstanding and 52 with electricity. With fishing right on the doorstep there are boats for hire and the site has its own private mooring buoys, plus a dinghy slip and harbour. A restaurant and 'singing' pub are close.

Facilities

The toilet block is clean without being luxurious. Hot showers (€ 0.50). Dishwashing sinks outside. Laundry room. A wooden chalet houses a pool room and campers' kitchen. Off site: Golf and riding 4 km.

Open

1 April - 30 September.

At a glance

Welcome & Ambience	✓✓✓✓	Location	✓✓✓✓
Quality of Pitches	✓✓✓	Range of Facilities	✓✓✓

Directions

From Athlone take N55 towards Longford for 4.8 km. Park is in the village of Ballykeeran, clearly signed. GPS: N53:26.915 W07:53.460

Charges guide

Per adult	€ 4,00
child (under 14 yrs)	€ 2,00
pitch	€ 4,00 - € 6,00
electricity	€ 3,00
No credit cards.	

Reservations

Contact park for details. Tel: 090 6478561.
Email: athlonecamping@eircom.net

IR8965 Lough Ennell Camping & Caravan Park

Tudenham Shore, Mullingar (Co. Westmeath)

Nature and rustic charm is the visitor's first reaction on arrival at Lough Ennell Caravan Park. Set in 18 acres of mature woodland beside a Blue Flag lake, Eamon and Geraldine O'Malley run this sheltered and tranquil park with their family. Just an hour from Dublin, it provides a good holiday base or a useful stopover en-route to the West of Ireland. The watersports permitted on the lake include canoeing, sailing, windsurfing, boating, fishing and safe swimming. The woodlands offer ample opportunities for walking and cycling. Numerous other lakes in the area provide fishing for all varieties especially wild trout. Other activities might include tennis, horse riding, golf, dog racing and of course forest walks. Belvedere House and Tullynally Castle are nearby and the large town of Mullingar is just 6 km. The O'Malley family, who live on the site, receive a complimentary blend of visitors – seasonal residents in camping holiday homes (private and to rent), caravanners and motorcaravanners and there are ample areas for tents. Pitches are varied, sheltered with trees and natural shrubbery, and spacious with gravel or gravel and grass combinations (ideal for those with awnings). Electricity is available on 44 hardstanding pitches and there are water points on or near all the pitches.

Facilities

The toilet block provides toilets, washbasins and hot showers (€1 coin). Additional dishwashing areas are around the park. Laundry. Small shop. Café and coffee shop with takeaway. TV and games room. Play areas and area for ball games. Small lakeside beach. Fishing. Late arrivals area outside. Security including CCTV. Some breeds of dog are not accepted. Off site: Bus service 6 km. Golf 1.5 km. Riding 4 km. Bicycle hire 6 km.

Open

Easter/1 April - 30 September.

At a glance

Welcome & Ambience	✓✓✓✓✓	Location	✓✓✓✓✓
Quality of Pitches	✓✓✓✓	Range of Facilities	✓✓✓

Directions

From Mullingar town take the Tullamore road (N52) heading south for 5 km. Look out for sign and follow to site which is 1 km. off the N52 on the shores of Lough Ennell.

Charges 2005

Per person	€ 5,00
child	€ 3,00
pitch	€ 7,00 - € 10,00
electricity	€ 3,00

Reservations

Contact site. Tel: 044 48101.
Email: eamon@caravanparksireland.com

IR9080 Forest Farm Caravan & Camping Park

Dublin Road, Athy (Co. Kildare)

This site makes an excellent stopover if travelling from Dublin to the southeast counties. It is signed on the N78 and approached by a 500 m. avenue of tall pines. Part of a working farm, the campsite spreads to the right of the modern farmhouse, which also provides B&B. The owners have cleverly utilised their land to create a site which offers 64 unmarked touring pitches on level ground. Of these, 32 are for caravans, all with electricity connections and 10 with hardstanding, and 32 places are available for tents. Full Irish breakfasts are served at the farmhouse and farm tours are arranged on request.

Facilities

The centrally located, red brick toilet block is heated and double glazed, providing quality amenities including a spacious shower unit for disabled visitors, a family room with shower and WC. It also houses a laundry room, a campers' kitchen with dishwashing sinks, a fridge/freezer, cooker, table and chairs and a comfortable lounge/games room (a TV can be provided). Basketball net, sand pit and picnic tables. Off site: Golf courses nearby. Course and game fishing 4 km.

Open

All year.

At a glance

Welcome & Ambience	✓✓✓✓	Location	✓✓✓
Quality of Pitches	✓✓✓	Range of Facilities	✓✓✓

Directions

Site is 4.8 km. northeast of Athy town off the main N78 Athy - Kilcullen road.
GPS: N53:00.835 W06:55.534

Charges guide

Per adult	€ 1,50
child	€ 0,50
pitch	€ 10,00
1 or 2 person tent per person	€ 5,00
hiker, cyclist or motorcyclist incl. tent	€ 5,00
electricity (16A)	€ 2,00

Reservations

Contact site. Tel: 05986 31231.
Email: forestfarm@eircom.net

IR9100 Camac Valley Tourist Caravan & Camping Park

Naas Road, Clondalkin Dublin 22 (Co. Dublin)

Opened in 1996, this campsite is not only well placed for Dublin, but also offers a welcome stopover if travelling to the more southern counties from the north of the country, or vice versa. Despite its close proximity to the city, being located in the 300 acre Corkagh Park gives it a 'heart of the country' atmosphere. The site entrance and sign are distinctive and can be spotted in adequate time when approaching on the busy N7. Beyond the entrance gate and forecourt stands an attractive timber fronted building. Its design includes various roof levels and spacious interior layout, with large windows offering a view of the site. Housed here is reception, information, reading, TV and locker rooms plus shop and sanitary facilities. There are 163 pitches, 48 for tents placed to the fore and the hardstandings for caravans laid out in bays and avenues with electrical connections, drainage and water points. Young trees separate pitches and roads are of tarmac. After a day of sightseeing in Dublin, which can be reached by bus from the site, Camac Valley offers an evening of relaxation with woodland and river walks in the park or a number of first class restaurants and pubs nearby.

Facilities

Heated sanitary facilities include good sized showers (token), facilities for disabled people, baby changing room, laundry and washing up. Playground with wooden play frames and safety base. Shop and coffee bar (open June, July and August). Electronic gate controlled from reception and 24 hour security. Dogs are not accepted in July/Aug. Off site: Bicycle hire 1.5 km. Golf 6 km. Fishing 8 km. Riding 9 km.

Open

All year.

At a glance

Welcome & Ambience	✓✓✓✓✓	Location	✓✓✓✓
Quality of Pitches	✓✓✓✓✓	Range of Facilities	✓✓✓

Directions

From north follow signs for West Link and M50 motorway. Exit M50 at junction 9 onto N7 Cork road. Site is on right of dual carriageway (beside Green Isle Hotel) after 2 km. and is clearly signed. At City West business park, cross over bridge and return on dual-carriageway following camp signs - site is on left after 800 m. GPS: N53:18.285 W06:24.931

Charges 2005

Per unit incl. 2 adults	€ 19,00 - € 24,00
incl. 2 adults and up to 4 children	€ 21,00 - € 26,00
extra person	€ 5,00

Reservations

Advance bookings necessary (max. stay operates at certain times). Tel: 01 464 0644. Email: reservations@camacvalley.com

IR9380 Parsons Green Caravan & Camping Park

Clogheen (Co. Tipperary)

In a tranquil and scenic location, this small, family run park commands panoramic views toward the Vee Gap and Knockmealdown Mountains. In open style, surrounded by low ranch fencing, it offers 34 pitches with hardstanding for caravans and motorcaravans and 10 on grass, all with electrical connections (6A), plus 20 pitches for tents. There is a range of things to do and see including a garden area, river walks, picnic area, an extensive farm museum, a pet field with selection of domestic and rare animals and birds, pony and trap rides, boating on the small lake and trout fishing river. If not sitting back enjoying the scenic surroundings or participating in the many activities, there is much to see and do in this area. The manager at Parson's Green would be more than pleased to pinpoint places of interest. A large indoor play area has been added.

Facilities
Toilet facilities are near the top right of the site close to reception, and are kept clean and include good facilities for disabled people (shower and toilet). Laundry area with washing machines, dryer and sinks, plus dishwashing sinks. Coffee shop and takeaway. Playground. Minigolf. Fishing. TV/games room. Campers' kitchen and function room. Off site: Village within 500 m. (footpath and lighting) with shops, pubs, bank, post office, etc. Riding and golf 8 km.

At a glance
Welcome & Ambience	✓✓✓✓	Location	✓✓✓✓
Quality of Pitches	✓✓✓✓	Range of Facilities	✓✓✓✓

Directions
Site is in the village of Clogheen, 200 m. off the R665, 24 km. west of Clonmel, 19 km. east of Mitchelstown. GPS: N52:16.895 W07:59.399

Charges 2005
Per adult	€ 3,00
child	€ 2,00
caravan, family tent or motorcaravan	€ 7,00
small tent	€ 6,00

Reservations
Contact site. Tel: 052 65290.
Email: kathleennoonan@oceanfree.net

Open
All year.

IR9390 Carrick-on-Suir Camping & Caravan Park

Carrick-on-Suir (Co. Tipperary)

This memorable site is conveniently situated off the main N24 between Waterford and Clonmel. It is an ideal stop over en-route to Killarney and the west or a good base for touring the southeast. On this quiet, family run site campers are guaranteed the finest example of 'Cead Mile Failte' it is possible to encounter - personal attention and advice on where to go and what to see in the area is all part of the service given by its owner, Frank O'Dwyer. The entrance to the park is immediately past the O'Dwyers' shop/reception. The tarmac drive leads past tall hedges and well kept shrubs to the right and several caravan holiday homes (for hire) to the left. The touring park lies to the rear with scenic views to the wooded hills. At present there are 30 level pitches, 33 with electricity (6/10A) and several with hardstanding, but this number is to be extended. What makes this site distinctive is its excellent, well designed sanitary block which has a sparkling clean freshness. Within a short drive is the 'magic road', the Mahon Falls, a slate quarry or a romantic river walk. Carrick is well placed en-route to the west, only 90 minutes from Rosslare.

Facilities
Toilet facilities are kept clean and fresh with plenty of hot water. Showers cost €1. Laundry room with washing machine. Campers' kitchen with dishwashing area and TV (no cooker). Motorcaravan service point. Good grocery shop with hot snacks to take away and a selection of fine wines. Gas supplies. Good night lighting. Off site: Fishing 1 km. Riding 6 km. Golf 3 km. Carrick town centre is five minutes walk for shops, pubs, restaurants, etc. plus a castle which is open to the public.

Open
1 March - 1 November.

At a glance
Welcome & Ambience	✓✓✓✓✓	Location	✓✓✓✓
Quality of Pitches	✓✓✓✓	Range of Facilities	✓✓✓

Directions
Approaching town on N24 road, follow signs for the R696 in the direction of Kilkenny. Site is north of town, clearly signed at junction with R696. GPS: N52:21.119 W07:24.847

Charges 2006
Per adult	€ 4,00
child	€ 2,50
pitch	€ 18,00
electricity 6/10A	€ 3,00
hiker/cyclist incl. tent	€ 10,00

Reservations
Contact site. Tel: 051 640461.
Email: coscamping@eircom.net

IR9410 The Apple Camping & Caravan Park

Moorstown, Cahir (Co. Tipperary)

This fruit farm and campsite combination offers an idyllic country holiday venue in one of the most delightful situations imaginable. For tourers only, it is located off the N24, midway between Clonmel and Cahir. Entrance is by way of a 300 m. drive which follows straight through the heart of the farm. Apple trees guard the route, as do various non-fruit tree species, which are named and of interest to guests who are free to spend time walking the paths around the farm. When we visited, strawberries were being gathered - the best we had tasted all season – and apple juice, jams, etc. are also sold on the farm. Reception is housed with the other site facilities in a large farmyard barn. Although a rather unusual arrangement, it is very effective. The 32 pitches are in a secluded situation behind the barns and are mostly grass with a few hardstandings, with electricity connections to 25. The towns of Cahir and Clonmel are of historic interest and the countryside around boasts rivers, mountains, Celtic culture and scenic drives.

Facilities

Toilet facilities, kept very clean, quite modern in design and with heating, comprise showers, washbasins with mirrors, electric points, etc. in functional units occupying two corners of the large floor space. Facilities for disabled visitors. Also in the barn are dishwashing sinks, washing machine and a fridge/freezer for campers to use. Motorcaravan service point. Tennis court, basketball/football pitch and play area. Dogs are not accepted. Off site: Fishing, golf, bicycle hire and riding within 6 km.

At a glance

Welcome & Ambience	✓✓✓✓	Location	✓✓✓✓
Quality of Pitches	✓✓✓✓	Range of Facilities	✓✓✓

Directions

Park is 300 m. off main N24, 9.6 km. west of Clonmel, 6.4 km. east of Cahir.
GPS: N52:22.719 W07:50.509

Charges 2006

Per person	€ 5,50 - € 6,00
child (0-12 yrs)	€ 3,00
electricity (13A)	€ 2,00

No charge per unit.
Less 20% for groups of 4 or more.

Reservations

Contact site. Tel: 052 41459.
Email: con@theapplefarm.com

Open

1 May - 30 September.

IR9420 Streamstown Caravan & Camping Park

Streamstown, Roscrea (Co. Tipperary)

This family run site, set on a dairy farm in the centre of Ireland, is conveniently situated off the N7 Dublin - Limerick road. It makes a good overnight halt or for a longer stay if you are seeking a quiet, restful location with little to disturb the peace. This is a working farm and the owners, who are friendly and welcoming, are in the process of improving and developing their site. What impresses most here is the tidy overall appearance with neatly trimmed hedging, tables placed around the grass areas and with flower baskets a special feature. There are 27 touring pitches, 10 with hardstanding and separated by low hedges. The remainder are on grass and more suitable for units with awnings. Nearby pubs offer traditional music evenings and mountain walking and fishing can be enjoyed in the area.

Facilities

The sanitary facilities, which were clean when we visited, are housed in a modern block, although showers, toilets and washbasins are of the older type and slightly out of keeping with the outside appearance. Good campers' kitchen with fridge/freezer and electric cooker. Good quality play area with safety surface. TV and pool room. Off site: Fishing 1.8 km. Golf 5 km. Riding 8 km.

Open

1 April - 9 October.

At a glance

Welcome & Ambience	✓✓✓✓	Location	✓✓✓
Quality of Pitches	✓✓✓✓	Range of Facilities	✓✓✓

Directions

From Roscrea centre follow signs for R491 Shirone. Continue towards Shirone following camp signs for approx. 2.5 km and site entrance is on left.
GPS: N52:57.432 W07:50.362

Charges 2005

Per adult	€ 3,50
child (under 14 yrs)	€ 2,00
pitch	€ 10,00
electricity (10A)	€ 3,00

5 nights for the price of 4.

Reservations

Contact site. Tel: 0505 21519.
Email: streamstowncaravanpark@eircom.net

IR9455 **Adare Camping & Caravan Park**

Adare (Co. Limerick)

This attractive, family run park gains in popularity because of its location three kilometres from Adare, which is claimed to be Ireland's prettiest village. It also makes an ideal overnight halt on route to or from the southwest of the country. A small park, set back from the busy N21 Tralee – Limerick road, it has an open layout with young maturing shrubs and is screened by mature trees. There are 28 unnumbered, level pitches, of about 80-100 sq.m. Of these, 15 have hardstanding with 16A electricity hook-ups, whilst the remainder are on grass and used mainly for tents. An added facility for campers is a number of picnic tables. A modern building at the entrance houses reception and a shop area selling basic requirements.

Facilities

The heated toilet block is well tiled and clean when we visited. It houses spacious well fitted showers, washbasins, hand/hair dryers; baby changing room and facilities for disabled visitors (washbasin and WC); covered dishwashing sinks. Fridges. Laundry room with sink, washing machine, dryer, iron/ironing board. Campers' kitchen. Games room, hot tub and a play area for children. Night lighting: Off site: Adare village; old abbeys and ruins, park, heritage centre, etc. Fishing 2 km. Golf 3 km. Riding 3 km. Limerick city is 20 minutes drive.

Open

12 March - 30 September.

At a glance

Welcome & Ambience	✓✓✓✓	Location	✓✓✓
Quality of Pitches	✓✓✓✓	Range of Facilities	✓✓✓

Directions

Travel west from Limerick city on N21 to Adare and follow camp signs. GPS: N52:32.320 W08:47.574

Charges 2005

Per unit incl. 2 persons	€ 20,00
small tent incl. 2 persons	€ 18,00
extra adult	€ 4,00
child	€ 2,00
electricity (16A)	€ 3,50
awning	€ 2,00

Reservations

Contact site. Tel: 061 395376.
Email: dohertycampingadare@eircom.net

IR9460 **Corofin Village Camping & Caravan Park**

Main Street, Corofin (Co. Clare)

This compact green oasis in the centre of the village of Corofin occupies one acre and adjoins the family's hostel. The owners, Jude and Marie Neylon live on the site and have a policy of always having a family member on hand at all times. They are very environmentally aware and have excellent re-cycling facilities. The 20 pitches all have electricity and there are ample water points. A campers' kitchen, laundry room and the TV and games room are separate to the hostel facilities. This little site is neat and well maintained and makes an ideal base for sightseeing throughout Clare, especially for the world famous Burren and the Aillwee Caves, Craggaunown Megalithic Centre and Quinn and Knappogue Castles, as well as places of interest in Galway and Limerick. Public transport is available to the famous Lahinch beach and to the large town of Ennis. It is a peaceful location, yet central for the restaurants, takeaway, shops and pubs in the village. This area is renowned for its traditional music. There are several lakes in the immediate locality for boating and fishing enthusiasts.

Facilities

The sanitary block is bright and clean with free hot showers and separate facilities for disabled campers. Laundry room with washing machine and dryer. CCTV security. Torches useful. Site is not suitable for large units. Off site: Fishing and boat launching 2 km. Riding 8 km. Bicycle hire 10 km. Golf 20 km. Beach 20 km.

At a glance

Welcome & Ambience	✓✓✓✓	Location	✓✓✓✓✓
Quality of Pitches	✓✓✓✓	Range of Facilities	✓✓✓

Directions

Corofin village is 12 km. from Ennis. Take the N85 to Ennistymon and after 2 km. (well signed) turn on R476. Site is in the centre of the village. GPS: N52:56.442 W09:03.536

Charges 2005

Per unit, all inclusive	€ 20,00

Reservations

Contact site. Tel: 065 6837683. Email: corohost@iol.ie

Open

1 April - 30 September.

IR9480 Blarney Caravan & Camping Park

Stone View, Blarney (Co. Cork)

There is a heart of the country feel about this 'on the farm' site, yet the city of Cork is only an 8 km. drive. What makes this friendly, family run park so appealing is its secluded location and neatly laid out, open appearance. The terrain on the three acre park is elevated and gently sloping, commanding views towards Blarney Castle and the surrounding mountainous countryside. The 40 pitches, 30 of which have hardstanding and 10A electrical connections, are with caravans sited to the centre and left and tents pitched to the right. There are gravel roads, well tended young shrubs and a screen of mature trees and hedging marks the park's perimeter. In the Blarney area, apart from the castle, house and gardens, there are shops, restaurants, pubs with traditional music and an abundance of outdoor pursuits such as walking, riding and fishing.

Facilities

Well kept toilet areas, one new, are housed in converted farm buildings with reception and small shop. Facilities for disabled visitors. Laundry room with sinks, washing machine, dryer and ironing. Dishwashing area in the large campers' kitchen. Motorcaravan service point. Shop (1/6-31/8). TV lounge. 18 hole golf and pitch and putt course. Night lighting. Off site: Public bar and restaurant 100 m. serving food all day. Within easy reach of the ports of Cork and Rosslare.

Open

1 April - 31 October.

At a glance

| Welcome & Ambience | ✓✓✓✓✓ | Location | ✓✓✓✓ |
| Quality of Pitches | ✓✓✓✓ | Range of Facilities | ✓✓✓✓ |

Directions

Site is 8 km. northwest of Cork, just off the N20. Take N20 from Cork for approx. 6 km. and then left on R617 to Blarney. Site clearly signed at filling station in village, in approx. 2 km. GPS: N51:56.872 W08:32.776

Charges 2006

Per adult	€ 5,50
child (under 4 yrs)	€ 2,50
caravan, family tent or motorcaravan	€ 6,50 - € 8,00
small tent and car	€ 5,50 - € 6,50
electricity (10A)	€ 3,00
awning	€ 1,50 - € 2,00

Reservations

Contact park. Tel: 021 451 6519. Email: con.quill@camping-ireland.ie

IR9500 The Meadow Camping Park

Glandore (Co. Cork)

The stretch of coast from Cork to Skibbereen reminds British visitors of Devon before the era of mass tourism. This is rich dairy country, the green of the meadows matching the emerald colours of the travel posters. Thanks to the warm and wet Gulf Stream climate, it is also a county of gardens - and keen gardeners. The Meadows is best described not as a site, but as a one acre garden surrounded, appropriately, by lush meadows. It lies 1.5 km. east of the fishing village of Glandore. A further 5 km. west is the regional centre, Skibbereen, beyond which the landscape moves from unspoilt Devon to unspoilt Cornwall. The owners, who live on the park, have cunningly arranged accommodation for 19 pitches among the flower beds and shrubberies of their extended garden. Space is rather tight and only small caravans are encouraged. There are 10 hardstandings for motorcaravans with 6A electric hook-ups. Among the homely features are a sitting room and a well equipped kitchen. Note: tents, small caravans and motorcaravans only.

Facilities

Facilities are limited but well designed and immaculately maintained. Showers on payment. Washing machine and dryer. American motorhomes accepted with additional charge according to length. Off site: Fishing or riding 2 km, fishing, swimming, boat launching and sailing at Glandore (2 km).

Open

14 April - 18 September.

At a glance

| Welcome & Ambience | ✓✓✓✓ | Location | ✓✓✓ |
| Quality of Pitches | ✓✓✓ | Range of Facilities | ✓✓✓ |

Directions

Park is 1.5 km. east of Glandore, off N71 road, on R597 mid-way between Leap and Rosscarbery (coast road). GPS: N51:34.009 W09:05.818

Charges 2005

Per unit incl. 2 persons	€ 15,00
extra person	€ 5,00
child (under 12 yrs)	€ 2,00
electricity (6A)	€ 2,00
hiker or cyclist incl. tent (per person)	€ 7,00

No credit cards.

Reservations

Please phone site for details. Tel: 028 33280. Email: the_meadow@oceanfree.net

IR9505 The Hideaway Camping & Caravan Park

Skibbereen (Co. Cork)

A sister park to The Meadow at Glandore, the Hideaway is ideally situated as a touring base for the southwest of Ireland. It is a well run site under the constant supervision of the owners and although it enjoys tranquil surroundings, including preserved marshland, it is within a ten minute walk from the busy market town of Skibbereen. A touring only park, it has 60 pitches which include 45 with hardstanding and 6A electric hook-up. The remainder for tents and caravans are on grass. Shrubs and low hedges divide the park giving an open feel overall and with commanding views across the fields and hills. One long building houses reception, the toilet facilities and a games room.

Facilities
The modern toilet block has non slip floors, well equipped showers (on payment), a baby room with bath and an en-suite unit for disabled visitors. Dishwashing sinks. Laundry machines. Campers' dining room. Motorcaravan service point. Night lighting. Adventure play area. Dog walk. Off site: Fishing 1.6 km. Golf 2 km. Riding 4 km. Bicycle hire 1 km.

Open
14 April - 18 September.

At a glance
Welcome & Ambience	✓✓✓✓	Location	✓✓✓✓
Quality of Pitches	✓✓✓✓	Range of Facilities	✓✓✓

Directions
From Skibbereen town centre take R596 (signed Casteltownsend). Site is on the left after approx.1 km. GPS: N51:32.500 W09:15.605

Charges 2005
Per unit incl. 2 adults	€ 15,00 - € 16,00
hiker, cyclist or m/cyclist and tent per person	€ 7,00
extra adult	€ 5,00
extra child (under 16 yrs.)	€ 2,00
electricity	€ 2,00
No credit cards.

Reservations
Contact site. Tel: 028 33280.
Email: the_hideaway@oceanfree.net

IR9510 Eagle Point Caravan & Camping Park

Ballylickey, Bantry (Co. Cork)

Midway between the towns of Bantry and Glengarriff, the spectacular peninsula of Eagle Point juts into Bantry Bay. The first impression is of a spacious country park rather than a campsite. As far as the eye can see this 20 acre, landscaped, part-terraced park, with its vast manicured grass areas separated by mature trees, shrubs and hedges, runs parallel with the shoreline. Suitable for all ages, this is a well run park devoted to tourers, with campers pitched mostly towards the shore. It provides 125 pitches (60 caravans, 65 tents), and electric hook-ups, thus avoiding overcrowding during peak periods. For wet weather, a timbered building towards the water's edge houses a TV room – the brightly decorated interior is guaranteed to brighten the dullest of days. Eagle Point makes an excellent base for watersports enthusiasts – swimming is safe and there is a slipway for small craft.

Facilities
Three well maintained, well designed toilet blocks are above expected standards. Laundry and dishwashing. Motorcaravan services. Play area. Tennis courts. Football field to the far right, well away from the pitches. Fishing. Supermarket at park entrance. Dogs are not accepted. Off site: Bicycle hire 6 km. Riding 10 km. Golf 2 km.

Open
21 April - 30 September.

At a glance
Welcome & Ambience	✓✓✓✓	Location	✓✓✓✓
Quality of Pitches	✓✓✓✓✓	Range of Facilities	✓✓✓✓

Directions
Take N71 to Bandon, then R586 Bandon to Bantry. From Bantry take N71 to Glengarriif. 6.4 km. from Bantry; park entrance is opposite EMO petrol station. GPS: N51:43.207 W09:26.977

Charges 2006
Per unit incl. 2 persons	€ 21,00 - € 26,00
extra adult	€ 6,50
motorcyclist, hiker or cyclist (per person)	€ 9,00

Reservations
Bookings not essential. Tel: 027 50630.
Email: eaglepointcamping@eircom.net

303

IR9550 **Anchor Caravan Park**

Castlegregory (Co. Kerry)

Of County Kerry's three long, finger like peninsulas which jut into the sea, Dingle is the most northerly. Tralee is the main town and Anchor Caravan Park is 20 km. west of this famed town and under 4 km. south of Castlegregory on Tralee Bay. A secluded and mature, five acre park, it is enclosed by shrubs and trees, with a gateway leading to a beautiful, sandy beach which is safe for bathing, boating and shore fishing. There are 30 pitches, all with electric hook-ups and some also with drainage and water points. Although there are holiday homes for hire, these are well apart from the touring pitches. In this area of great beauty, miles of sand abounds and taking in the panorama of mountain scenery from the top of the Conor Pass is a wonderful experience.

Facilities

Toilet facilities (entry by key) are kept clean (three or four times daily in busy periods) providing showers on payment (€ 0,50), two private cabins, toilet with handrail, dishwashing and laundry facilities (incl. clothes lines). Motorcaravan services. Two play areas. Games/TV room. Night lighting. Off site: Beautiful sandy beach 2 minutes. Fishing 2 km. Riding or bicycle hire 3 km. Golf 4 km.

Open

Easter - 30 September.

At a glance

Welcome & Ambience	✓✓✓✓	Location	✓✓✓
Quality of Pitches	✓✓✓	Range of Facilities	✓✓✓

Directions

From Tralee follow the Dingle coast road for 19 km. Park is signed from Camp junction.
GPS: N52:14.646 W09:59.141

Charges 2005

Per unit incl. all persons	€ 17,00 - € 18,00
small tent incl. 1 or 2 persons	€ 12,00 - € 13,00
motorcyclist, hiker or cyclist incl. tent	€ 10,00 - € 11,00
electricity	€ 2,00
awning	€ 2,50

No credit cards.

Reservations

Contact site. Tel: 066 7139157.
Email: anchorcaravanpark@eircom.net

IR9580 **Beara Camping The Peacock**

Coornagillahagh, Tuosist, Post Killarney (Co. Kerry)

Five minutes from Kenmare Bay, The Peacock is a unique location for campers who would appreciate the natural surroundings of a campsite where disturbance to nature is kept to a minimum. This five-acre site offers simple, clean and imaginative camping facilities. Located on the Ring of Beara, bordering the counties of Cork and Kerry, visitors will be treated with hospitality by a Dutch couple, almost more Irish than the Irish, who have made Ireland their home and run the site with their family and Kleintje, the pot-bellied Vietnamese pig. Bert and Klaske are only too anxious to share with visitors the unspoiled natural terrain, the local wildlife, the opportunity of a cosy sheltered campfire and advice on the walking and hiking routes in the area aided by maps provided on loan. The variety of accommodation at Beara Camping includes the hostel, caravan holiday homes, secluded hardstanding pitches with electricity and level grass areas for tenting. In addition, there are cabins sleeping two or four people and hiker huts sleeping two, ideal to avoid a damp night or to dry out. The homely restaurant provides Bert an opportunity to exhibit his artistic talents, not only with his paintings on display, but with simple and wholesome salmon or fillet of steak and salads that are meals in themselves. Breakfast, lunch and dinner plus 'good' coffee are available, plus fresh bread each morning. All of this and the possibility of travelling the Ring of Beara to see stone-circles, the Healy Pass, Ardea Castle, Derreen Gardens and the fishing town of Castletownbere and much more. The well-known towns of Kenmare and Killarney are both havens for tourists.

Facilities

Three small blocks, plus facilities at the restaurant provide toilets, washbasins and free hot showers. Laundry service for a small fee. Campers' kitchens, dishwashing and sheltered eating area. Restaurant and takeaway (May - Oct). Small shop (May - Oct). Bicycle hire. Off site: Public transport from the gate during the summer months. Pub 900 m. Riding 6 km. Golf 12 km. Boating, fishing and sea angling 200 m. Beach (pebble) 500 m.

At a glance

Welcome & Ambience	✓✓✓✓✓	Location	✓✓✓✓
Quality of Pitches	✓✓✓	Range of Facilities	✓✓✓

Directions

From the A22, 17 km. east of Killarney, take the R569 south to Kenmare. In Kenmare take R571, Castletownbere road and site is 12 km.

Charges 2005

Per unit incl. 2 persons	€ 12,50 - € 17,50
extra person	€ 3,00
child (4-10 yrs)	€ 1,75
electricity	€ 2,00

Reservations

Contact site. Tel: 064 84287.
Email: campingthepeacock@eircom.net

Open

All year.

IR9570 Creveen Lodge Caravan & Camping Park

Healy Pass, Lauragh (Co. Kerry)

The address of this park is rather confusing, but Healy Pass is the well known scenic summit of the road (R574) crossing the Beara Peninsula, which lies between Kenmare Bay to the north and Bantry Bay to the south. Several kilometres inland from the north coast road (R571), the R574 starts to climb steeply southward towards the Healy Pass. Here, on the mountain foothills, is Creveen Lodge, a working hill farm with a quiet, homely atmosphere. Although not so famed as the Iveragh Peninsula, around which runs the Ring of Kerry, the northern Beara is a scenically striking area of County Kerry. Creveen Lodge, commanding views across Kenmare Bay, is divided among three gently sloping fields separated by trees. To allow easy access, the steep farm track is divided into a simple one-way system. There are 20 pitches, 16 for tents, 4 for caravans, with an area of hardstanding for motorcaravans, and electrical connections are available. The park is carefully tended with neat rubbish bins and rustic picnic tables informally placed. This is walking and climbing countryside or, of interest close by, is Derreen Gardens.

Facilities

Well appointed and immaculately maintained, the small toilet block provides showers on payment (€ 0.65), plus a communal room with a fridge, freezer, TV, ironing board, fireplace, tables and chairs. Reception is in the farmhouse. Play area. Off site: Water sports, riding, 'Seafare' cruises, shops and a restaurant nearby. Fishing 2 km, bicycle hire 9 km, boat launching 9 km.

Open

Easter - 31 October.

At a glance

Welcome & Ambience	✓✓✓✓✓	Location	✓✓✓✓
Quality of Pitches	✓✓✓	Range of Facilities	✓✓✓✓

Directions

Park is on the Healy Pass road (R574) 1.5 km. southeast of Lauragh. GPS: N51:45.312 W09:45.615

Charges 2006

Per person	€ 3,00
child	€ 1,00
pitch	€ 14,00
motorcyclist incl. tent	€ 7,00

No credit cards.

Reservations

Write to site with an S.A.E. Tel: 064 83131. Email: info@creveenlodge.com

IR9560 Wave Crest Caravan & Camping Park

Caherdaniel (Co. Kerry)

It would be difficult to imagine a more dramatic location than Wave Crest's on the Ring of Kerry coast. Huge boulders and rocky outcrops tumble from the park entrance on the N70 down to the seashore which forms the most southern promontory on the Ring of Kerry. There are spectacular southward views from the park across Kenmare Bay to the Beara peninsula. Sheltering on grass patches in small coves that nestle between the rocks and shrubbery, are 65 hardstanding pitches and 20 on grass offering seclusion. Electricity connections are available (13A). A unique feature is the TV room, an old stone farm building with a thatched roof. Its comfortable interior includes a stone fireplace heated by a converted cast iron marker buoy. Caherdaniel is known for its cheerful little pubs and distinguished restaurant. The Derrynane National Park Nature Reserve is only a few kilometres away, as is Derrynane Cove and Bay. This park would suit older people looking for a quiet, relaxed atmosphere.

Facilities

Two blocks house the sanitary facilities and include hot showers on payment (€ 1), toilet for disabled people and dishwashing sinks. Laundry service. Small shop and takeaway service (May - Sept). Play area. Fishing and boat launching. Off site: Riding 1 km, bicycle hire or golf 10 km. Small beach near and Derrynane Hotel with bar and restaurant.

Open

All year.

At a glance

Welcome & Ambience	✓✓✓✓	Location	✓✓✓✓
Quality of Pitches	✓✓✓✓	Range of Facilities	✓✓✓✓

Directions

On the N70 (Ring of Kerry), 1.5 km. east of Caherdaniel.

Charges 2005

Per person	€ 2,00
child	€ 1,00
pitch	€ 13,00
small tent	€ 12,00
awning	€ 4,00
electricity (13A)	€ 2,00

Reservations

Write for details. Tel: 066 947 5188. Email: wavecrest@eircom.net

IR9590 Fossa Caravan & Camping Park

F0550, Killarney (Co. Kerry)

This mature, well equipped park is in a scenic location, ten minutes drive from the town centre. Fossa Caravan Park is recognisable by its forecourt on which stands a distinctive building housing a roof top restaurant, reception area and shop. The well laid out park is divided in two - the touring area lies to the right, tucked behind the main building and to the left is an open grass area mainly for campers. Touring pitches, with electricity and drainage, have hardstanding and are angled between shrubs and trees in a tranquil, well cared for garden setting. To the rear at a higher level and discreetly placed are 30 caravan holiday homes. Sheltered by the thick foliage of the wooded slopes which climb high behind the park, these are unobtrusive. Not only is Fossa convenient for Killarney (5.5 km), it is also en-route for the famed 'Ring of Kerry', and makes an ideal base for walkers and golfers.

Facilities

Modern toilet facilities kept spotlessly clean include showers on payment. Laundry room, washing up area. Campers' kitchen. Shop (April - Sept). Restaurant (1 June - end Aug) and takeaway (July/Aug). TV lounge. Play area. Picnic area. Games room. Night lighting and security patrol.
Off site: Fishing and golf 2 km. Riding 3 km. Bicycle hire 5 km.

Open

1 April - 30 September.

At a glance

Welcome & Ambience	✓✓✓✓✓	Location	✓✓✓✓
Quality of Pitches	✓✓✓✓	Range of Facilities	✓✓✓✓

Directions

Approaching Killarney from all directions, follow signs for N72 Ring of Kerry/Killorglin. At last roundabout join R562/N72. Continue for 5.5 km. and Fossa is the second park to the right.
GPS: N52:04.246 W09:35.147

Charges 2005

Per adult	€ 4,50
child (under 14 yrs)	€ 1,50
pitch	€ 5,00 - € 6,50
awning	€ 3,00
electricity (10/15A)	€ 3,50
motorcycle and tent per person	€ 7,00 - € 7,75

Reservations

Advisable in high season and made for min. 3 nights with €20 deposit. Tel: 064 31497.
Email: fossaholidays@eircom.net

IR9620 Fleming's White Bridge Caravan Park

Ballycasheen Road, Killarney (Co. Kerry)

Once past the county border, the main road from Cork to Killarney (N22) runs down the valley of the Flesk river. On the final approach to Killarney off the N22 Cork road, the river veers away from the road to enter the Lower Lake. On this prime rural position, between the road and the river, and within comfortable walking distance of the town, is Fleming's White Bridge, a nine acre woodland park. The ground is flat, landscaped and generously adorned with flowers, shrubs and trees. There are now 92 pitches (46 caravans and 46 tents) that extend beyond a wooden bridge to an area surrounded by mature trees and where a new toilet block, one of three, is sited. This is obviously a park of which the owners are very proud, and the family personally supervise the reception and grounds, maintaining high standards of hygiene, cleanliness and tidiness. The park's location so close to Ireland's premier tourism centre makes this park an ideal base to explore Killarney and the southwest.

Facilities

Three toilet blocks are maintained to high standards. Dishwashing sinks. Motorcaravan service point. Campers' drying room and two laundries. Shop (1/6-1/9). Two TV rooms and a games room. Fishing (advice and permits provided). Canoeing (own canoes). Bicycle hire. Woodland walks. Off site: Riding 3 km. Golf 2 km.

Open

13 April - 15 October; 26 - 30 October.

Reservations

Advised for high season; write with € 5 non-refundable reservation fee. Tel: 064 31590.
Email: info@killarneycamping.com

At a glance

Welcome & Ambience	✓✓✓✓✓	Location	✓✓✓✓
Quality of Pitches	✓✓✓✓	Range of Facilities	✓✓✓✓

Directions

From Cork and Mallow: at N72/N22 junction continue towards Killarney and take first turn left (signed Ballycasheen Road). Proceed for 300 m. to archway entrance on left. From Limerick: follow N22 Cork road. After passing Super Valu and The Heights Hotel take first right (signed Ballycasheen Road) and continue as above. From Kenmare: On N71, pass Gleneagles Hotel and Flesk Bridge. Turn right at traffic lights into Woodlawn Road and Ballycasheen Road and continue 2 km. to archway.
GPS: N52:03.372 W09:28.463

Charges 2006

Per person	€ 7,00
child (under 14 yrs)	€ 2,50
pitch	€ 6,00 - € 8,00
hiker or cyclist incl. tent	€ 8,00 - € 8,50
electricity (10A)	€ 4,00
No credit cards.	

IR9600 Glenross Caravan & Camping Park

Glenbeigh (Co. Kerry)

Its situation on the spectacular Ring of Kerry and the Kerry Way gives Glenross an immediate advantage, and scenic grandeur around every bend of the road is guaranteed as Glenbeigh is approached. Quietly located before entering the village, the park commands a fine view of Rossbeigh Strand, which is within walking distance. On arrival, a good impression is created with the park well screened from the road and with new stone entrance and gates. There are 30 touring pitches all on hardstanding and with electricity and, although there are six caravan holiday homes, the park is attractively laid out. There is no on site catering but the Glenbeigh Hotel next door is popular and village shops are near. Not least is the Kerry Bog Village where you can go back in time in this reconstructed pre-famine village.

Facilities
Well maintained modern toilet block includes facilities for laundry and dishwashing. Motorcaravan service point. Games room. Bicycle hire. Shelter for campers. Sun lounge and barbecue patio. Off site: Watersports and tennis near. Riding and fishing 200 m. Golf 500 m.

Open

28 April - 26 September.

At a glance

Welcome & Ambience	✓✓✓✓	Location	✓✓✓✓
Quality of Pitches	✓✓✓✓	Range of Facilities	✓✓✓

Directions

Park is on the N70 Killorglin - Glenbeigh road, on the right just before entering the village. GPS: N52:03.524 W09:55.914

Charges 2006

Per person	€ 7,00
child (under 14 yrs)	€ 2,50
pitch	€ 6,00 - € 8,00
electricity (10A)	€ 4,00
awning	€ 3,00
motorcyclist and tent	€ 8,50 - € 9,00

No credit cards.

Reservations

Write to site for details Tel: 066 97 68451.
Email: glenross@eircom.net

A Nature Lovers Paradise

Winner of the Award of Excellence 2003. The best Park in Ireland - Overall. Best 3 Star Park in Ireland 2002 & 2004.

Mannix Point 00353 66 9472806 www.campinginkerry.com
email - mortimer@campinginkerry.com

IR9610 Mannix Point Camping & Caravan Park

Cahirciveen (Co. Kerry)

A quiet and peaceful, beautifully located seashore park, it is no exaggeration to describe Mannix Point as a nature lovers' paradise. Situated in one of the most spectacular parts of the Ring of Kerry, overlooking the Portmagee Channel towards Valentia Island, the park commands splendid views in all directions. It is flat and open being right on marshland which teems with wildlife (a two acre nature reserve) with direct access to the beach and seashore. The owner has planted around 500 plants and around 1,000 more trees and shrubs which have matured now. There are 42 pitches, 15 for tourers and 27 for tents, with electrical connections (13A) available. A charming old fisherman's cottage has been converted to provide reception, there is a cosy sitting room with turf fire, and an 'emergency' dormitory for campers is a feature. There is no television, but compensation comes in the form of a knowledgeable, hospitable owner who is a Bord Fáilte registered local tour guide. This park retains a wonderful air of Irish charm aided by occasional impromptu musical evenings. Watersports, bird watching, walking and photography can all be pursued. Local cruises to Skelligs Rock with free transport to and from the port for walkers and cyclists. This is also an ideal resting place for people walking the Kerry Way.

Facilities
Toilet facilities, now upgraded and immaculate, have well designed showers (on €0.80 payment). Modern campers' kitchen. Laundry facilities with washing machines and dryer. Motorcaravan service facilities. Dogs are not accepted in July and August. Off site: Bicycle hire 800 m. riding 3 km, golf 14 km. Pubs, restaurants and shops 15 minutes walk.

Open

15 March - 1 October.

At a glance

Welcome & Ambience	✓✓✓✓✓	Location	✓✓✓✓
Quality of Pitches	✓✓✓	Range of Facilities	✓✓✓

Directions

Park is 250 m. off the N70 Ring of Kerry road, 800 m. southwest of Cahirciveen (or Caharsiveen) on the road towards Waterville. GPS: N51:56.571 W10:14.607

Charges 2005

Per adult	€ 7,00
child (1 or 2 children)	€ 2,00
pitch	€ 5,00
electricity (13A)	€ 3,00

Book 7 nights, pay 6. Reductions for groups if pre-paid. No credit cards.

Reservations

Made with deposit of one night's fee. Tel: 066 9472806. Email: mortimer@campinginkerry.com

IR9630 Donoghues White Villa Farm Caravan & Camping Park

Cork Road (N22), Killarney (Co. Kerry)

This is a very pleasing small touring park in scenic surroundings on the N22 Killarney-Cork road. It is set on a 100 acre farm which stretches as far as the River Flesk, yet is only five minutes away from Killarney town. Trees and shrubs surround the park but dominant is a magnificent view of the MacGillicuddy's Reeks. There are 24 pitches for caravans and tents, 15 with hardstanding and a grass area for awnings, electricity (10A), water points and night lighting. An unusual novelty is old school desks placed around the site, plus an antique green telephone box. One can also enjoy walking through the oak wood, fishing on the Flesk or visiting the site's own National Farm Museum.

Facilities

The toilet block, a sandstone coloured building, is kept spotlessly clean and houses showers on payment, a good toilet/shower room for disabled visitors, laundry room and dishwashing sinks. Motorcaravan service area. Campers' kitchen with TV. Play area. Bicycle hire. Max. 2 dogs per pitch are accepted (not certain breeds). Daily coach tours from park.; Off site: Riding, golf and boat launching 3 km. Pub/restaurant 1 km. Killarney town 5 minutes, the National Park is 10 minutes away.

Open

1 April - 3 October.

At a glance

Welcome & Ambience	✓✓✓✓	Location	✓✓✓✓
Quality of Pitches	✓✓✓✓	Range of Facilities	✓✓✓

Directions

Park is 3 km. east from Killarney town on N22 Cork road. Park entrance is 500 m. east of N22/N72 junction. From Killarney follow N22 Cork road signs and 'White Villa Farm' finger signs from Park Road roundabout. From Kenmare take R569 via Kilgarvan to the N22, or N71 to Killarney, then the N22 Cork road. GPS: N52:02.837 W09:27.224

Charges 2006

Per person	€ 5,00
child	€ 2,00
pitch	€ 4,00 - € 5,00
hiker or cyclist incl. tent	€ 6,25 - € 6,50
electricity	€ 3,00

No credit cards.
Seven nights for the price of six.

Reservations

Made with deposit (€ 15 or UK £10). Tel: 064 20671. Email: killarneycamping@eircom.net

IR9640 The Killarney Flesk Caravan & Camping Park

Muckross Road, Killarney (Co. Kerry)

At the gateway to the National Park and Lakes, near Killarney town, this family run, seven acre park has undergone extensive development and offers high quality standards. Pitches are well spaced and have electricity (10A), water, and drainage connections; 21 also have hardstanding with a grass area for awnings. The grounds have been well cultivated with further shrubs, plants and an attractive barbecue and patio area. This is to the left of the sanitary block and is paved and sunk beneath the level roadway. Surrounded by a garden border, it has tables and chairs, making a pleasant communal meeting place commanding excellent views of Killarney's mountains.

Facilities

Modern, clean toilet blocks are well designed and equipped. Baby bath/changing room. Laundry room. Campers' kitchen with dishwashing sinks. Comfortable games room. Other on site facilities include petrol pumps, supermarket (all year), delicatessen and café (March - Oct) with extra seating on the sun terrace. Night lighting and night time security checks. Winter caravan storage. Off site: Fishing 300 m. Boat launching 2 km.

Open

17 April - 30 September.

At a glance

Welcome & Ambience	✓✓✓✓	Location	✓✓✓✓
Quality of Pitches	✓✓✓✓	Range of Facilities	✓✓✓✓

Directions

From Killarney town centre follow the N71 and signs for Killarney National Park. Site is 1.5 km. on the left beside the Gleneagle Hotel. GPS: N52:02.594 W09:29.921

Charges 2005

Per adult	€ 6,00
child (under 14 yrs)	€ 1,50
pitch	€ 6,50 - € 7,00
electricity (10A)	€ 4,00
awning	€ 2,50
hiker or cyclist incl. tent	€ 7,50 - € 8,00

Reservations

Advisable in peak periods, write to park.
Tel: 064 31704. Email: killarneylakes@eircom.net.

The best magazines, whatever your lifestyle

For buying information, top tips and technical help, **Caravan, Motor Caravan Magazine** and **Park Home & Holiday Caravan** are all you need — every month!

FISHING

We are pleased to include details of parks which provide facilities for fishing on the site. Many other parks, particularly in Scotland and Ireland, are in popular fishing areas and have facilities within easy reach. Where we have been given details, we have included this information in the site reports. It is always best to contact parks to check that they provide for your individual requirements.

England

UK0170	Trevella
UK0220	Trevornick
UK0250	Pentewan Sands
UK0270	Mena
UK0302	South Penquite
UK0315	White Acres
UK0380	Wooda Farm
UK0530	Trethiggey
UK0750	Minnows
UK0790	Harford Bridge
UK0810	Riverside
UK0950	River Dart
UK0970	Cofton
UK1020	Oakdown
UK1060	Yeatheridge
UK1075	Golden Coast
UK1090	Peppermint Park
UK1150	Ruda
UK1390	Old Oaks
UK1420	Southfork
UK1450	Bath Marina
UK1460	Newton Mill
UK1480	Home Farm
UK1520	Waterrow
UK1540	Batcombe Vale
UK1570	Northam Farm
UK1575	Unity
UK1580	Warren Farm
UK1590	Exe Valley
UK1630	Brokerswood
UK1640	Greenhill Farm
UK1740	Golden Cap
UK1760	Wood Farm
UK1780	Freshwater Beach
UK2130	Grove Farm
UK2150	Woolsbridge
UK2290	Sandy Balls
UK2360	Hill Cottage
UK2450	The Orchards
UK2510	Whitecliff Bay
UK2520	Thorness Bay
UK2610	Bo Peep
UK2690	Wellington
UK2700	Hurley
UK2810	Chertsey
UK2820	Horsley
UK2900	Horam Manor
UK2965	Brakes Coppice
UK3030	Tanner Farm
UK3210	Lee Valley
UK3290	Fen Farm
UK3300	Homestead Lake
UK3400	Old Brick Kilns
UK3430	Kelling Heath
UK3440	Gatton Waters
UK3455	Deer's Glade
UK3480	Little Lakeland
UK3520	Searles
UK3575	Stroud Hill
UK3750	Foreman's Bridge
UK3760	Tallington Lakes
UK3765	Woodland Waters
UK3940	Smeaton`s Lakes
UK3970	Glencote
UK4080	Riverside
UK4090	Island Meadow
UK4100	Hoburne Cotswold
UK4140	Winchcombe
UK4150	Croft Farm
UK4170	Tudor
UK4190	Kingsgreen
UK4200	The Boyce
UK4210	Lickhill Manor
UK4220	Riverside
UK4300	Poston Mill
UK4310	Luck`s All
UK4320	Broadmeadow
UK4330	The Millpond
UK4345	Townsend
UK4380	Fernwood
UK4390	Westbrook
UK4410	Beaconsfield
UK4440	The Green
UK4500	Burton Constable
UK4510	Thorpe Hall
UK4610	Moorside
UK4640	Goose Wood
UK4660	Woodhouse Farm
UK4715	Riverside
UK4720	Knight Stainforth
UK4790	Bronte
UK5280	Abbey Farm
UK5540	Fallbarrow
UK5600	Pennine View
UK5615	Hill of Oaks
UK5710	Doe Park

Wales

UK5880	Springwater
UK6040	Pencelli Castle
UK6245	Morben Isaf
UK6250	Dolswydd
UK6290	Glan-y-Mor
UK6305	Smithy Park
UK6345	Glanlynn
UK6590	Beddgelert
UK6600	Bryn Gloch
UK6670	The Plassey

Scotland

UK6890	Mossyard
UK6910	Hoddom Castle
UK6930	Brandedleys
UK6950	Brighouse Bay
UK7220	The Gart C P
UK7260	Ardgartan
UK7270	Auchterarder
UK7710	Ardmair Point
UK7720	Woodend
UK7740	Loch Greshornish
UK7790	Invercoe
UK7800	Resipole
UK7840	North Ledaig
UK7850	Linnhe Lochside
UK7860	Glendaruel

Northern Ireland

UK8330	Sixmilewater
UK8340	Drumaheglis
UK8405	Cranfield
UK8420	Tollymore
UK8510	Mullynascarthy
UK8550	Dungannon

Republic of Ireland

IR8770	Parkland
IR8815	Willowbrook
IR8825	Lough Key
IR8960	Lough Ree
IR8965	Lough Ennell
IR9230	Nore Valley
IR9380	Parsons Green
IR9510	Eagle Point
IR9560	Wave Crest
IR9620	Flemings
IR9630	White Villa

BICYCLE HIRE

We understand that the following parks have bicycles to hire on site or can arrange for bicycles to be delivered. However, we would recommend that you contact the park to check as the situation can change.

England

UK0150	Sea View
UK0220	Trevornick
UK0250	Pentewan Sands
UK0255	Sun Valley
UK0306	Ruthern Valley
UK0360	Lakefield
UK0450	Pennance
UK0690	Stowford Farm
UK0750	Minnows
UK1075	Golden Coast
UK1150	Ruda
UK1350	Quantock Orchard
UK1390	Old Oaks
UK1400	Avalon
UK1490	Greenacres
UK1550	Bucklegrove
UK1575	Unity
UK1590	Exe Valley
UK2100	Sandford
UK2270	Oakdene Forest
UK2290	Sandy Balls
UK2315	Riverside (Hamble)
UK2350	Red Shoot
UK2450	The Orchards
UK2500	Heathfield Farm
UK2580	Cotswold View
UK3325	The Oaks
UK3330	Moat Barn
UK3370	Kessingland
UK3390	Dower House
UK3430	Kelling Heath
UK3520	Searles
UK3660	Walesby Woodlands
UK3750	Foreman's Bridge
UK3904	Greendale Farm
UK4410	Beaconsfield
UK4560	Golden Square
UK4620	Upper Carr
UK4638	Alders
UK4660	Woodhouse Farm
UK5505	Stanwix Park
UK5520	Skelwith Fold
UK5590	Westmorland
UK5800	Ord House

Wales

UK5925	Cardiff
UK5980	Moreton Farm
UK6040	Pencelli Castle

Scotland

UK6950	Brighouse Bay
UK7000	Strathclyde Country Park
UK7230	Trossachs
UK7280	Nether Craig
UK7740	Loch Greshornish
UK7780	Faichem

Republic of Ireland

IR8740	Cong
IR8790	Carra
IR8810	Lough Lanagh
IR9080	Forest Farm
IR9130	Roundwood
IR9455	Adare
IR9580	Beara The Peacock
IR9600	Glenross
IR9620	Flemings
IR9630	White Villa
IR9640	Killarney Flesk

Channel Islands

UK9720	Beuvelande
UK9770	Vaugrat
UK9780	Fauxquets

GOLF

We understand that the following parks have facilities for playing golf on site. Where facilities are within easy reach and we have been given details, we have included this information in the individual site reports. However, we recommend that you contact the park to check that they meet your requirements.

UK0200	Newquay	UK2250	Hoburne Bashley	UK6670	The Plassey
UK0220	Trevornick	UK3230	Lee Valley	UK6910	Hoddom Castle
UK0380	Wooda Farm	UK3520	Searles	UK6950	Brighouse Bay
UK0690	Stowford Farm	UK3690	Bainland	UK7060	Tantallon
UK0720	Easewell Farm	UK4070	Somers Wood	UK7690	Torvean
UK1010	Lady`s Mile	UK4300	Poston Mill	UK8310	Carnfunnock
UK1020	Oakdown	UK4520	Flower of May	IR9150	River Valley
UK1070	Woolacombe Bay	UK4710	Rudding	IR9480	Blarney
UK1575	Unity	UK6330	Daisy Bank		

HORSE RIDING

We understand that the following parks have horse riding stables on site. Where facilities are within easy reach and we have been given details, we have included this information in the individual site reports. However, we recommend that you contact the park to check that they meet your requirements.

UK0360	Lakefield	UK1780	Freshwater Beach	UK2950	Washington
UK0690	Stowford Farm	UK2100	Sandford	UK5550	Limefitt
UK1060	Yeatheridge	UK2290	Sandy Balls	UK6950	Brighouse Bay
UK1370	Burrowhayes	UK2520	Thorness Bay	UK8510	Mullynascarthy
UK1575	Unity	UK2900	Horam Manor		

BOAT LAUNCHING

We understand that the following parks have boat slipways on site. Where facilities are within easy reach and we have been given details, we have included this information in the individual site reports. However, we recommend that you contact the park to check that they meet your requirements.

UK0250	Pentewan Sands	UK4210	Lickhill Manor	UK7850	Linnhe Lochside
UK0750	Minnows	UK4310	Luck`s All	UK8310	Carnfunnock
UK1450	Bath Marina	UK4500	Burton Constable	UK8330	Sixmilewater
UK1530	Slimeridge	UK5540	Fallbarrow	UK8340	Drumaheglis
UK1540	Batcombe Vale	UK5615	Hill of Oaks	UK8405	Cranfield
UK2510	Whitecliff Bay	UK6345	Glanlynn	IR8825	Lough Key
UK2520	Thorness Bay	UK6890	Mossyard	IR8960	Lough Ree
UK2690	Wellington	UK6950	Brighouse Bay	IR8965	Lough Ennell
UK2700	Hurley	UK7260	Ardgartan	IR9510	Eagle Point
UK3290	Fen Farm	UK7710	Ardmair Point	IR9560	Wave Crest
UK3760	Tallington Lakes	UK7740	Loch Greshornish	IR9610	Mannix Point
UK4080	Riverside	UK7800	Resipole		
UK4150	Croft Farm	UK7840	North Ledaig		

We list here the sites that have indicated to us that they do not accept children at any time during the year, at certain times, or in certain areas of their site.

The following parks have made the decision not to accept children:

UK0010	Chacewater	(30 yrs+)		UK3650	Cherry Tree	
UK0012	Killiwerris			UK3864	Firs Farm	
UK0820	Moor View			UK3980	Longnor Woods	(18 yrs+)
UK1390	Old Oaks	(18 yrs+)		UK4070	Somers Wood	
UK1510	Chew Valley			UK4410	Beaconsfield	(21 yrs+)
UK1520	Waterrow	(18 yrs+)		UK4580	Foxholme	
UK1640	Greenhill Farm	(18 yrs+)		UK4610	Moorside	(16 yrs+)
UK1770	Binghams Farm			UK4790	Bronte	
UK2620	Wysdom			UK5240	Lamb Cottage	
UK3420	Two Mills			UK5510	The Larches	
UK3440	Gatton Waters	(18 yrs+)		UK5650	The Ashes	(18 yrs+)
UK3450	Little Haven			UK6330	Daisy Bank	
UK3470	Breckland					
UK3575	Stroud Hill					

The following parks also do not accept children at certain times or in certain areas of their site:

UK0280	Powderham Castle		UK4400	Stanmore Hall
UK3800	Highfields		UK4430	Oxon Hall
UK4380	Fernwood			

The following parks are understood to accept caravanners and campers all year round, although the list also includes some parks that are open for at least ten months. These parks are marked with a star (*) – please refer to the park's individual entry for details. It is always wise to phone the park to check as the facilities available, for example, may be reduced.

England

UK0030	Ayr
UK0180	Carnon Downs
UK0310	Trekenning
UK0430	Padstow
UK0440	Dolbeare
UK0530	Trethiggey *
UK0710	Hidden Valley
UK0800	Higher Longford
UK0810	Riverside
UK0870	Beverley *
UK0910	Ross Park *
UK1075	Golden Coast *
UK1130	Hoburne Torbay *
UK1350	Quantock Orchard
UK1400	Isle of Avalon
UK1420	Southfork
UK1440	Baltic Wharf
UK1450	Bath Marina
UK1460	Newton Mill
UK1480	Home Farm *
UK1500	Long Hazel *
UK1510	Chew Valley
UK1520	Waterrow
UK1550	Bucklegrove *
UK1630	Brokerswood
UK1640	Greenhill Farm
UK1650	Coombe
UK1655	Church Farm
UK1670	Alderbury
UK1700	Devizes
UK1810	Newlands
UK2020	Ulwell Cottage *
UK2030	Wareham Forest
UK2080	Merley Court *
UK2100	Sandford *
UK2270	Oakdene Forest *
UK2280	Lytton Lawn *
UK2285	Forest Edge *
UK2290	Sandy Balls
UK2360	Hill Cottage *
UK2450	The Orchards *
UK2600	Barnstones
UK2620	Wysdom
UK2750	Highclere *
UK2810	Chertsey
UK2930	Sheepcote
UK2940	Honeybridge
UK2950	Washington
UK3030	Tanner Farm
UK3040	Broadhembury
UK3050	Pine Lodge
UK3070	Canterbury
UK3090	Black Horse
UK3230	Lee Valley *
UK3260	Abbey Wood
UK3270	Crystal Palace
UK3310	Low House

UK3330	Moat Barn *
UK3340	Polstead
UK3345	The Dell
UK3382	Rose Farm
UK3400	Old Brick Kilns *
UK3420	Two Mills *
UK3455	Deer's Glade
UK3470	Breckland *
UK3550	Old Manor
UK3575	Stroud Hill
UK3580	Ferry Meadows
UK3690	Bainland *
UK3730	Skegness Sands
UK3760	Tallington Lakes *
UK3765	Woodland Waters
UK3815	Lickpenny
UK3850	Rivendale *
UK3864	Firs Farm
UK3910	Shardaroba
UK3920	Riverside
UK3940	Smeaton's Lakes
UK4070	Somers Wood *
UK4075	Hollyfast
UK4130	Moreton-in-Marsh
UK4140	Winchcombe *
UK4150	Croft Farm *
UK4170	Tudor
UK4210	Lickhill Manor
UK4300	Poston Mill
UK4345	Townsend *
UK4400	Stanmore Hall
UK4410	Beaconsfield
UK4420	Severn Gorge
UK4430	Oxon Hall
UK4540	St Helens *
UK4550	Cayton Village *
UK4640	Goose Wood *
UK4710	Rudding *
UK4740	Jasmine Park *
UK5280	Abbey Farm
UK5350	Holgates *
UK5360	Willowbank *
UK5505	Stanwix Park
UK5560	Sykeside
UK5570	Wild Rose
UK5740	White Water
UK5755	South Meadows
UK5800	Ord House

Wales

UK5925	Cardiff
UK5927	Acorn *
UK5930	Cwmcarn Forest *
UK5994	Redlands *
UK6010	Cenarth Falls *
UK6040	Pencelli Castle *
UK6240	Cringoed *

UK6310	Bacheldre
UK6330	Daisy Bank
UK6355	Woodlands *
UK6370	Hendre Mynach *
UK6590	Beddgelert *
UK6600	Bryn Gloch *
UK6680	James'
UK6690	Bron-Y-Wendon

Scotland

UK6870	Glenearly
UK6930	Brandedleys
UK6950	Brighouse Bay
UK7020	Aird Donald
UK7030	Gibson Park
UK7050	Edinburgh
UK7240	Lomond Woods
UK7270	Auchterarder
UK7400	Lochlands
UK7680	Glenmore *
UK7735	Sango Sands
UK7790	Invercoe *

Northern Ireland

UK8420	Tollymore Forest

Republic of Ireland

IR8740	Cong
IR8750	Belleek *
IR8810	Lough Lanagh *
IR8815	Willowbrook
IR9080	Forest Farm
IR9100	Camac Valley
IR9380	Parsons Green
IR9560	Wave Crest
IR9580	The Peacock

Channel Islands

UK9870	Pomme de Chien

INSPECTED CAMPSITES & SELECTED

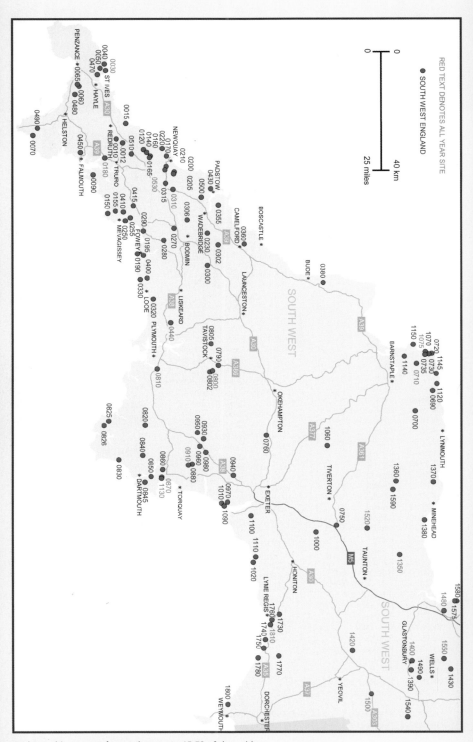

RED TEXT DENOTES ALL YEAR SITE

● SOUTH WEST ENGLAND

0
0

40 km

25 miles

PENZANCE ●
0040
0050
0470
0030
0065 ●
0060
0480

ST IVES *
HAYLE *

0490
0070

HELSTON *

0450
0090

FALMOUTH ●

0015

0510
0010
0012
0120
0140
0165
0160
0170
0220
0210

REDRUTH *
TRURO *
0180
0155
0150
0250
0255
0415
0410
0290
0195
0190
0400
0330

NEWQUAY *
0200
0205
0500
0430
0315
0310
0306
0270
0280
0300

MEVAGISSEY *
FOWEY *
LOOE *
0320
0440

PADSTOW *
WADEBRIDGE *
BODMIN *
0355
0230
0302
0360

CAMELFORD ●

BOSCASTLE *

LAUNCESTON *

LISKEARD *

PLYMOUTH *

0810

0805
0790
0800
0802

TAVISTOCK *

0825
0826

0830

0820

0840
0850
0860
0880
0910
0960
0870
1130

0930
0950
0980
0940
0970
1010
1090

0845
DARTMOUTH *
TORQUAY *

BUDE *
0380

SOUTH WEST

OKEHAMPTON *
0760

1060

TIVERTON *

1000

0750

EXETER *

1100
1110
1020

0700

BARNSTAPLE *
1150
1075
1070
1140
0720
1145
0730
1120
0735
0690
0710

* LYNMOUTH
1370
* MINEHEAD
1380

1360
1590

1520
1350

TAUNTON *

HONITON *

LYME REGIS *
1760
1730
1810
1740
1750
1780
1770

DORCHESTER *

1800

WEYMOUTH *

YEOVIL *
1500

1420

1540

GLASTONBURY *
1400
1490
1390

WELLS *
1550
1430

1580
1575
1480

1540

Parks on this map are featured on pages 15-78 of the guide.
Please refer to the numerical index (page 341) for exact campsite page references.

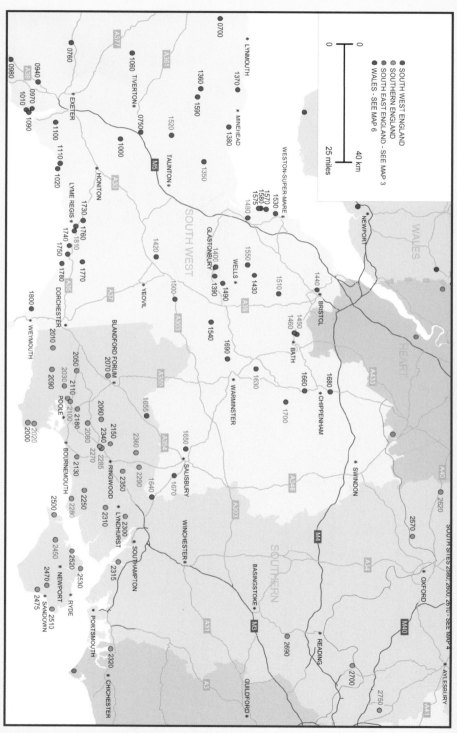

South West & Southern England – Map 2

SOUTH WEST ENGLAND
SOUTHERN ENGLAND
SOUTH EAST ENGLAND - SEE MAP 3
WALES - SEE MAP 6

0   0
25 miles   40 km

NEWPORT
WALES
HEART
SOUTHERN

SOUTH SITES 2380, 2600, 2610 - SEE MAP 4

* AYLESBURY
* OXFORD
2750
2700
2620
2570
2690
* READING
* GUILDFORD
2320
* CHICHESTER
* PORTSMOUTH
2475
2510
* SANDOWN
2470
* RYDE
2450
2520
2530
* NEWPORT
2315
2300
2280
2250
2310
* LYNDHURST
2350
* SOUTHAMPTON
* WINCHESTER
2290
2360
2500
1640
1570
1650
* SALISBURY
* RINGWOOD
2270
2285
2340
2150
2080
2060
2130
2100
2180
2090
2110
2030
2050
2070
BLANDFORD FORUM *
POOLE *
2010
BOURNEMOUTH
2020
2000
* WEYMOUTH
1800
DORCHESTER *
1780
1750
1740
1810
1770
1760
1730
LYME REGIS *
HONITON *
* EXETER
1020
1110
1100
1120
0980
1010
1090
0970
0940
0760
0700
* LYNMOUTH
1370
* MINEHEAD
1380
1060
TIVERTON *
0750
1000
1520
1590
1360
1350
TAUNTON *
1420
SOUTH WEST
* YEOVIL
1500
1540
1390
1490
1400
GLASTONBURY
WELLS *
1430
1550
1480
1575
1560
1570
1530
WESTON-SUPER-MARE *
1510
1690
1630
* WARMINSTER
1700
* CHIPPENHAM
1660
1680
BATH *
1460
1450
1440
BRISTOL *
1655
1550

Parks on this map are featured on pages 79-125 of the guide.
Please refer to the numerical index (page 341) for exact campsite page references.

331

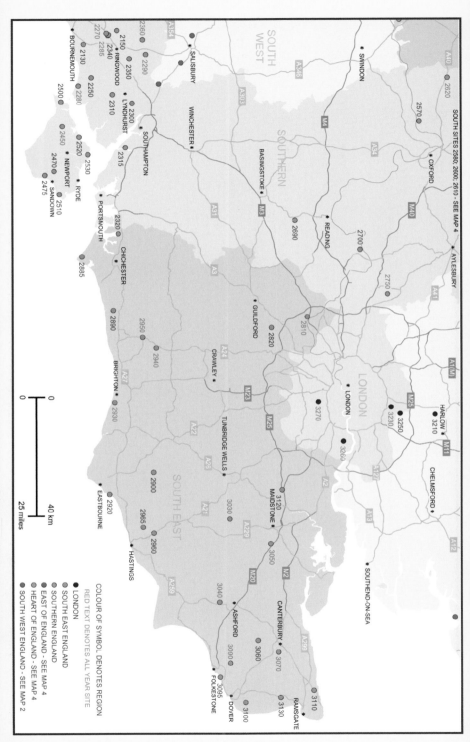

COLOUR OF SYMBOL DENOTES REGION

RED TEXT DENOTES ALL YEAR SITE

- LONDON
- SOUTH EAST ENGLAND
- SOUTHERN ENGLAND
- EAST OF ENGLAND - SEE MAP 4
- HEART OF ENGLAND - SEE MAP 4
- SOUTH WEST ENGLAND - SEE MAP 2

SOUTH SITES 2580, 2600, 2610 - SEE MAP 4

0   0

25 miles   40 Km

Parks on this map are featured on pages 127-141 of the guide.
Please refer to the numerical index (page 341) for exact campsite page references.

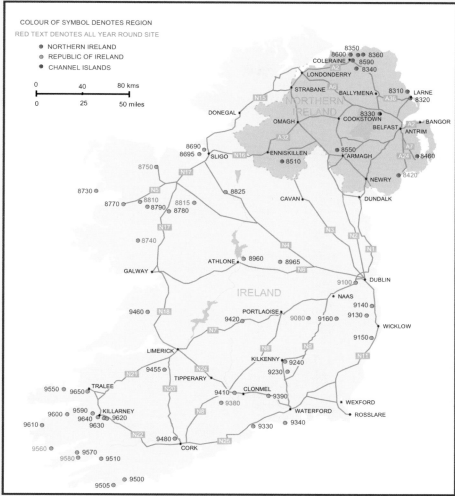

COLOUR OF SYMBOL DENOTES REGION
RED TEXT DENOTES ALL YEAR ROUND SITE

- NORTHERN IRELAND
- REPUBLIC OF IRELAND
- CHANNEL ISLANDS

Parks on this map are featured on pages 280-309 of the guide.
Please refer to the numerical index (page 341) for exact campsite page references.

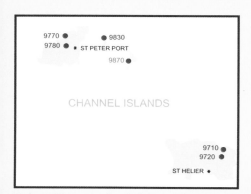

CHANNEL ISLANDS

Parks on this map are featured on pages 311-313 of the guide.
Please refer to the numerical index (page 341) for exact campsite page references.

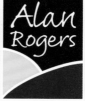

England

South West England

Cornwall

UK0030	Ayr Holiday Park	30
UK0480	Boscrege Caravan Park	27
UK0290	Carlyon Bay Caravan Park	20
UK0180	Carnon Downs Caravan Park	25
UK0010	Chacewater Park	32
UK0440	Dolbeare Caravan Park	15
UK0230	Glenmorris Park	45
UK0410	Heligan Woods Holiday Park	19
UK0210	Hendra Holiday Park	36
UK0330	Killigarth Manor Caravan Park	17
UK0012	Killiwerris Caravan Park	31
UK0360	Lakefield Caravan Park	46
UK0470	Little Trevarrack Tourist Park	29
UK0270	Mena Caravan Park	16
UK0165	Monkey Tree Holiday Park	34
UK0490	Mullion Holiday Park	26
UK0160	Newperran Holiday Park	33
UK0200	Newquay Holiday Park	34
UK0430	Padstow Touring Park	44
UK0195	Penmarlam Caravan Park	18
UK0450	Pennance Mill Farm	25
UK0140	Penrose Farm Touring Park	40
UK0250	Pentewan Sands Holiday Park	22
UK0320	Polborder House Caravan Park	17
UK0050	Polmanter Tourist Park	29
UK0190	Polruan Holidays	18
UK0280	Powderham Castle Tourist Park	15
UK0060	River Valley Country Park	28
UK0015	Rose Hill Touring Park	30
UK0306	Ruthern Valley Holidays	44
UK0355	Saint Minver Holiday Park	42
UK0150	Sea View International	23
UK0070	Silver Sands Holiday Park	26
UK0120	Silverbow Park	31
UK0302	South Penquite Farm	46
UK0510	Summer Valley Touring Park	32
UK0255	Sun Valley Holiday Park	19
UK0300	The Colliford Tavern Campsite	47
UK0155	Tregarton Park	21
UK0310	Trekenning Tourist Park	42
UK0400	Trelay Farmpark	16
UK0205	Treloy Touring Park	41
UK0415	Trencreek Farm Country Park	21
UK0090	Trethem Mill Touring Park	24
UK0530	Trethiggey Touring Park	37
UK0040	Trevalgan Holiday Farm	28
UK0170	Trevella Caravan Park	36
UK0220	Trevornick Holiday Park	37
UK0500	Trewince Farm Holiday Park	45
UK0065	Wayfarers Caravan Park	27
UK0315	White Acres Holiday Park	40
UK0380	Wooda Farm Park	47

Devon

UK0930	Ashburton Caravan Park	69
UK0760	Barley Meadow Caravan Park	58
UK0870	Beverley Park Holiday Centre	67
UK0970	Cofton Country Holidays	72
UK0880	Dornafield	68

UK0720	Easewell Farm Holiday Parc	50
UK1000	Forest Glade Holiday Park	78
UK0850	Galmpton Park	64
UK1075	Golden Coast Holiday Village	52
UK0700	Greenacres Touring Park	56
UK0790	Harford Bridge Park	59
UK1145	Hele Valley Holiday Park	56
UK0710	Hidden Valley Touring Park	55
UK0800	Higher Longford Caravan Park	60
UK0826	Higher Rew Caravan Park	62
UK0845	Hillhead Holiday Park	66
UK1130	Hoburne Torbay	66
UK0940	Holmans Wood Holiday Park	70
UK0825	Karrageen Caravan Park	62
UK1010	Lady's Mile Touring Park	73
UK0802	Langstone Manor Holiday Park	59
UK0980	Lemonford Caravan Park	70
UK1140	Lobb Fields Caravan Park	48
UK0750	Minnows Touring Caravan Park	58
UK0820	Moor View Touring Park	61
UK1120	Napps Touring Holiday Park	57
UK1020	Oakdown Touring Park	76
UK0960	Parkers Farm Holiday Park	69
UK1090	Peppermint Park	74
UK0950	River Dart Adventures	71
UK0810	Riverside Caravan Park	61
UK0910	Ross Park	68
UK1150	Ruda Holiday Park	48
UK1110	Salcombe Regis Caravan Park	75
UK0830	Slapton Sands C&C Club Site	64
UK0690	Stowford Farm Meadows	49
UK0730	Twitchen Parc	50
UK1100	Webbers Caravan Park	75
UK0860	Whitehill Country Park	65
UK0840	Woodlands Leisure Park	63
UK0805	Woodovis Park	60
UK1070	Woolacombe Bay Holiday Village	52
UK0735	Woolacombe Sands Holiday Park	54
UK1060	Yeatheridge Farm Caravan Park	57

Somerset

UK1440	Baltic Wharf Caravan Club Site	85
UK1540	Batcombe Vale Campsite	88
UK1510	Bath Chew Valley Caravan Park	85
UK1450	Bath Marina & Caravan Park	86
UK1550	Bucklegrove Caravan Park	87
UK1370	Burrowhayes Farm Caravan Site	80
UK1430	Cheddar C&C Club Site	86
UK1590	Exe Valley Caravan Site	79
UK1490	Greenacres Camping	87
UK1360	Halse Farm Touring Caravan Park	80
UK1380	Hoburne Blue Anchor	81
UK1575	Holiday Resort Unity	83
UK1480	Home Farm Holiday Park	82
UK1500	Long Hazel Park	90
UK1460	Newton Mill Camping Park	84
UK1570	Northam Farm Touring Park	82
UK1350	Quantock Orchard Caravan Park	81
UK1530	Slimeridge Farm Touring Park	84
UK1420	Southfork Caravan Park	89
UK1400	The Isle of Avalon Touring Park	89
UK1390	The Old Oaks Touring Park	88
UK1580	Warren Farm Touring Park	83
UK1520	Waterrow Touring Park	79

Wiltshire

UK1670	Alderbury Caravan Park	94
UK1630	Brokerswood Country Park	90
UK1655	Church Farm Caravan Park	94
UK1650	Coombe Touring Park	93
UK1700	Devizes C&C Club Site	92
UK1640	Greenhill Farm Caravan Park	93
UK1690	Longleat Caravan Club Site	91
UK1660	Piccadilly Caravan Park	91
UK1680	Plough Lane Caravan Site	92

West Dorset

UK1770	Binghams Farm Touring Park	98
UK1800	East Fleet Farm Touring Park	99
UK1780	Freshwater Beach Holiday Park	97
UK1740	Golden Cap Holiday Park	98
UK1750	Highlands End Holiday Park	99
UK1730	Monkton Wyld Caravan Park	96
UK1810	Newlands Caravan Park	95
UK1760	Wood Farm Caravan Park	96

Southern England

East Dorset

UK2180	Beacon Hill Touring Park	105
UK2130	Grove Farm Meadow	107
UK2080	Merley Court Touring Park	105
UK2110	Pear Tree Touring Park	106
UK2050	Rowlands Wait Touring Park	102
UK2100	Sandford Caravan Park	104
UK2010	Sandyholme Holiday Park	102
UK2000	Swanage Coastal Park	107
UK2070	The Inside Park	101
UK2020	Ulwell Cottage Caravan Park	109
UK2030	Wareham Forest Tourist Park	103
UK2090	Whitemead Caravan Park	101
UK2060	Wilksworth Farm Caravan Park	109
UK2150	Woolsbridge Manor Farm	108

Hampshire

UK2300	Ashurst Caravan Site	114
UK2320	Chichester C&C Club Site	116
UK2285	Forest Edge Touring Park	112
UK2360	Hill Cottage Farm Caravan Park	111
UK2250	Hoburne Bashley	114
UK2310	Hollands Wood Caravan Site	116
UK2280	Lytton Lawn Touring Park	112
UK2270	Oakdene Forest Park	110
UK2350	Red Shoot Camping Park	111
UK2315	Riverside Holidays	117
UK2290	Sandy Balls Holiday Centre	115
UK2340	Shamba Holidays	110

Isle of Wight

UK2500	Heathfield Farm Camping	118
UK2475	Lower Hyde Holiday Park	120
UK2470	Southland Camping Park	119
UK2450	The Orchards Holiday Park	119
UK2520	Thorness Bay Holiday Park	121
UK2530	Waverley Park Holiday Centre	120
UK2510	Whitecliff Bay Holiday Park	118

Oxfordshire

UK2600	Barnstones Caravan Park	123
UK2610	Bo Peep Caravan Park	123
UK2580	Cotswold View Caravan Park	122
UK2570	Lincoln Farm Park	122
UK2620	Wysdom Touring Park	124

Buckinghamshire

UK2750	Highclere Farm Country Park	125

Berkshire

UK2700	Hurley Riverside Park	125
UK2690	Wellington Country Park	124

South East England

West Sussex

UK2940	Honeybridge Park	127
UK2885	Warner Farm	127
UK2950	Washington Caravan Park	128
UK2890	White Rose Touring Park	128

East Sussex

UK2920	Bay View Park	130
UK2965	Brakes Coppice Park	130
UK2960	Crazy Lane Tourist Caravan Park	130
UK2900	Horam Manor Touring Park	129
UK2930	Sheepcote Valley Caravan Club	129

Kent

UK3090	Black Horse Farm Caravan Club	134
UK3040	Broadhembury Caravan Park	132
UK3070	Canterbury C&C Club Site	133
UK3120	Gate House Wood Touring Park	131
UK3100	Hawthorn Farm Caravan Site	135
UK3095	Little Satmar Holiday Park	135
UK3050	Pine Lodge Touring Park	132
UK3110	Quex Caravan Park	135
UK3130	Sandwich Leisure Park	133
UK3030	Tanner Farm Touring Park	131
UK3060	Yew Tree Park	134

Surrey

UK2810	Chertsey C&C Club Site	136
UK2820	Horsley C&C Club Site	136

London

UK3260	Abbey Wood Caravan Club Site	138
UK3270	Crystal Palace Caravan Club Site	138
UK3230	Lee Valley Caravanning Park	140
UK3250	Lee Valley Campsite	141
UK3210	Lee Valley Caravan Park	140

East of England

Essex

UK3290	Fen Farm Caravan Site	143
UK3300	Homestead Lake Park	143

Scotland

Lowlands

Heart of Scotland

Grampian

Highlands and Islands

Northern Ireland

Co. Antrim

Co. Down

Co. Tyrone

Co. Fermanagh

Co. Londonderry

Republic of Ireland

Co. Sligo

Co. Mayo

Co. Roscommon

Co. Westmeath

Co. Kildare

Co. Dublin

IMAGES We would like to thank the following Tourist Boards for supplying images for this guide:

Somerset Tourist Board
South West Tourist Board
Southern Tourist Board
Southeast Tourist Board
East of England Tourist Board
Heart of England Tourist Board
Yorkshire Tourist Board

North West Tourist Board
Cumbria Tourist Board
Northumbria Tourist Board
Wales Tourist Board
Scotland Tourist Board
Fáilte Ireland
Jersey Tourism

Tell Us About the Alan Rogers Guides!

We're keen to constantly improve our service to you and the key to this is information. If we don't know what makes our readers 'tick' then it's difficult to offer you more of what you want.

About the Alan Rogers Guides

1 **For how many years have you used the Alan Rogers Guides?**

Never	1-2 yrs	3-6 yrs	7-10 yrs	Over 10 yrs
❏	❏	❏	❏	❏

2 **How frequently do you refer to it?**

Never	Each year	Every 2 yrs	Every 3 yrs
❏	❏	❏	❏

3 **How frequently do you buy a new copy?**

Never	Each year	Every 2 yrs	Every 3 yrs
❏	❏	❏	❏

4 **If you lend it to friends, how many others might refer to it?**

1 ❏   2 ❏   3 ❏   4 ❏   Over 4 ❏

5 **Please rate the Alan Rogers Guides on a scale of 1–10 where 10 is excellent and 1 is extremely poor**

1 ❏   2 ❏   3 ❏   4 ❏   5 ❏   6 ❏   7 ❏   8 ❏   9 ❏   10 ❏

6 **Do you have any comments about the Alan Rogers Guides?**

....

....

7 **What do you consider to be the best thing about the guides?**

Independent reviews	Honest descriptions	Accurate information	Range of sites	Depth of information
❏	❏	❏	❏	❏

Other

8 **What do you consider to be the worst thing about the guides?**

....

9 **How many sites featured in the guides have you visited in the past?** *(best estimate)* ....

10 **Can you comment on any other campsite guides?**

Title .... Your opinion

About Your Holidays

11 **a) Do you own any of the following?**

Caravan ❏   Motorhome ❏   Trailer Tent ❏   Tent ❏

Other *(please specify)* ....

b) How many times a year do you use it?

1 ❏   2-3 ❏   4-6 ❏   7-10 ❏   More than 10 ❏

12 **When on holiday, do you participate in any of the following?**

Fishing	Golf	Cycling	Sailing/Boating	Walking	Bird Watching
❏	❏	❏	❏	❏	❏

Other *(please specify)* ....

13 **How many years have you been camping/caravanning?**

3 yrs or less	4 – 7 yrs	8 – 12 yrs	13 – 15 yrs	16 – 20 yrs	Over 20 yrs
❏	❏	❏	❏	❏	❏

About You

Mr/Mrs/Ms, etc.   Initial   Surname

Address

                       Post code

e-mail address   @   Telephone

(If you would like to receive monthly e-newsletter with offers and news).

14 **Your age**   30 and under ❑   31-50 ❑   51-65 ❑   Over 65 ❑

15 **Do you have children – if so, how old is the youngest?**

                6 and under ❑   7-12 ❑   Over 12 ❑

16 **Do you work (full or part time)?**   Yes ❑   No ❑

17 **Are you retired?**   Yes ❑   No ❑

About Your Leisure Time

18 **Are you a member of any caravan/motorhome clubs?**

The Caravan Club   The Camping & Caravanning Club   The Motor Caravanners Club
      ❑   ❑   ❑

Other *(please specify)*

19 **Are you a member of the following?**

National Trust	English Heritage	RSPB	CSMA	Ramblers
❑	❑	❑	❑	❑

20 **Which (if any) camping/caravanning magazines do you read regularly?**

MMM	Practical Motorhome	Practical Caravan	Caravan Life	Which Motorcaravan	Motor-caravan	Caravan
❑	❑	❑	❑	❑	❑	❑

21 **Which other magazines do you read regularly?**

22 **Which newspapers do you read regularly?**

Express	Mail	Telegraph	Times	Guardian	Observer	Sun
❑	❑	❑	❑	❑	❑	❑

Other (please specify)

23 **Do you enjoy any particular hobbies?** *(please specify)*

24 **Do you have regular access to the internet?**   Yes ❑   No ❑

    If yes, which camping/caravanning websites do you visit regularly?

And Finally

25 **Do you have any useful camping/caravanning tips?**

26 **If you could change one thing about camping/caravanning holidays what would it be?**

We may wish to publish your comments, please tick this box if you would prefer us not to. ❑

Might you be interested in becoming an Alan Rogers site inspector?
If so, please tick the box and we will send you further information ❑

Camping Cheque and Alan Rogers may use this data to send you information and Special Offers.
Please tick here if you do not wish to receive such information ❑

Thank you very much for your time and trouble in completing this questionnaire
Please return to: Alan Rogers Travel Service, FREEPOST NAT17734, Cranbrook, TN17 1BR